Standard
LESSON COMMENTARY®

2006–2007

International Sunday School Lessons

Edited by

Ronald L. Nickelson

Published by
STANDARD PUBLISHING

Jonathan Underwood,
Senior Editor, Adult Church Resources

Mark A. Taylor,
Director of Church Resources

Fifty-fourth Annual Volume

© 2006
STANDARD PUBLISHING
A division of STANDEX INTERNATIONAL Corporation
8121 Hamilton Avenue, Cincinnati, Ohio 45231
Printed in U. S. A.

In This Volume

Artist
TITLE PAGES: James E. Seward

Cover design by DesignTeam

Lessons based on International Sunday School Lessons © 2004 by the Lesson Committee.

CD-ROM AVAILABLE

The *Standard Lesson Commentary®* is available separately in an electronic format. This compact disk contains the full text of the King James *Standard Lesson Commentary®* and *The NIV Standard Lesson Commentary®*, a variety of preparation resources powered by the Libronix Digital Library System, and a collection of presentation helps that can be projected or reproduced as handouts. Order #06007.

System Requirements: Windows XP/2000/ME/98/95; Pentium 133 MHz processor (300MHz recommended), 64 Meg RAM (128 recommended); 60 Meg Available Hard Drive Space; 2x or better CD-ROM drive.

Index of Printed Texts, 2006–2007

The printed texts for 2006-2007 are arranged here in the order in which they appear in the Bible. Opposite each reference is the number of the page on which it appears in this volume.

Cumulative Index

A cumulative index for the Scripture passages used in the STANDARD LESSON COMMENTARY
for the years September, 2004—August, 2007, is provided below.

How to Say It

The following pages list some of the names and other hard-to-pronounce words used in the lessons of this edition of the *Standard Lesson Commentary*® along with a phonetic pronunciation guide for each. In each lesson is an abridged version of this list that includes only the words used in that lesson.

A

AARON. *Air*-un.
ABIATHAR. Ah-*bye*-uh-thar.
ABIMELECH. Uh-*bim*-eh-lek.
ABINOAM. Uh-*bin*-o-am.
ABRAHAM. *Ay*-bruh-ham.
ABRAM. *Ay*-brum.
ABSALOM. *Ab*-suh-lum.
AD HOMINEM. add *hah*-muh-nem.
ADONIJAH. Ad-o-*nye*-juh.
AHAB. *Ay*-hab.
AI. *Ay*-eye.
ALEXANDRIA. Al-iks-*an*-dree-uh.
ALPHA. *Al*-fa.
AMALEKITES. *Am*-uh-leh-kites or Uh-*mal*-ih-kites.
AMON. *Ay*-mun.
AMORITES. *Am*-uh-rites.
ANTIPAS. *An*-tih-pus.
APOCALYPSE. Ah-*pock*-uh-lips.
ARC DE TRIOMPHE. Ark du treh-*onf*.
ARIANISM. *Air*-ee-uh-nih-zim.
ARIMATHEA. *Air*-uh-muh-*thee*-uh (*th* as in *thin*; strong accent on *thee*).
ARTAXERXES. Are-tuh-*zerk*-seez.
ASHDOD. *Ash*-dod.
ASHERAH. Uh-*she*-ruh.
ASHKELON. *Ash*-ke-lon or *As*-ke-lon.
ASHTAROTH. *Ash*-tuh-rawth.
ASHTORETHS. *Ash*-toe-reths.
ASSYRIAN. Uh-*sear*-e-un.
ATHENS. *Ath*-unz.

B

BAAL. *Bay*-ul.
BAALIM. Bay-uh-*leem*.
BABEL. *Bay*-bul.
BABYLON. *Bab*-uh-lun.
BABYLONIA. Bab-ih-*low*-nee-uh.
BABYLONIAN. Bab-ih-*low*-nee-un.
BARAK. *Bair*-uk.
BARNABAS. *Bar*-nuh-bus.
BATHSHEBA. Bath-*she*-buh.
BEDOUIN. *Bed*-uh-wun.

BEERSHEBA. Beer-*she*-buh.
BERECHIAH. Bair-uh-*kye*-uh.
BETHANY. *Beth*-uh-nee.
BETH-AVEN. *Beth*-ay-ven (strong accent on *ay*).
BETHCAR. *Beth*-kar or Beth-*kar*.
BETHEL. *Beth*-ul.
BETHESDA. Buh-*thez*-duh.
BETHLEHEM. *Beth*-lih-hem.
BETHPHAGE. *Beth*-fuh-gee.
BOANERGES. *Bo*-uh-*nur*-geez (strong accent on *nur*).
BYZANTINE. *Bih*-zen-teen.

C

CAESAR AUGUSTUS. *See*-zer Aw-*gus*-tus.
CAIAPHAS. *Kay*-uh-fus or *Kye*-uh-fus.
CALEB. *Kay*-leb.
CANAAN. *Kay*-nun.
CANAANITES. *Kay*-nun-ites.
CAPERNAUM. Kuh-*per*-nay-um.
CAPHTOR. *Kaf*-tor.
CARCHEMISH. *Kar*-key-mish.
CARNELIAN. kar-*neel*-yun.
CHALDEANS. Kal-*dee*-unz.
CHALDEES. *Kal*-deez.
CHERITH. *Key*-rith.
CHIOS. *Ki*-as (*i* as in *eye*).
CICERO. *Sih*-suh-row.
COLOSSIANS. Kuh-*losh*-unz.
CONSTANTINOPLE. *Kahn*-stan-ten-oh-puhl.
CORNELIUS. Cor-*neel*-yus.
CYRUS. *Sigh*-russ.

D

DAGON. *Day*-gon.
DARIUS HYSTASPES. Duh-*rye*-us Hiss-*tas*-pus.
DEMAS. *Dee*-mus.
DIOGENES OF SINOPE. Die-*ah*-jin-eez of Suh-*no*-peh.
DOCETISM. Doe-*set*-iz-um.
DOMITIAN. Duh-*mish*-un.

E

EBAL. *Ee*-bull.
EBENEZER. *Eb*-en-ee-zer.
EGYPT. *Ee*-jipt.
EHUD. *Ee*-hud.
EKRON. *Ek*-run.
ELASAH. *El*-ah-sah.
ELIJAH. Ee-*lye*-juh.
EPAPHRODITUS. Ee-*paf*-ro-*dye*-tus (strong accent on *dye*).
EPHESUS. *Ef*-uh-sus.
EPHRAIM. *Ee*-fray-im.
ESAU. *Ee*-saw.
ESDRAELON. *Es*-druh-*ee*-lon (strong accent on *ee*).
EUPHRATES. You-*fray*-teez.

G

GALILEE. *Gal*-uh-lee.
GATH. Gath (a as in bath).
GAZA. *Gay*-zuh.
GEMARIAH. Gem-uh-*rye*-uh (G as in get).
GENTILE. *Jen*-tile.
GERIZIM. *Gair*-ih-zeem or Guh-*rye*-zim.
GIBEON. *Gib*-e-un (G as in *get*).
GILGAL. *Gil*-gal (G as in *get*).
GNOSTICISM. *nahss*-tih-*sizz*-um (strong accent on *nahss*).
GNOSTICS. *nahss*-ticks.
GOLIATH. Go-*lye*-uth.
GOMORRAH. Guh-*more*-uh.

H

HADES. *hay*-deez.
HAGAR. *Hay*-gar.
HAGGAI. *Hag*-eye or *Hag*-ay-eye.
HAGIA SOPHIA. *Hag*-ee-uh So-*fee*-uh.
HARAN. *Hair*-un.
HAROSHETH. Huh-*roe*-sheth.
HAZOR. *Hay*-zor.
HERESY. *hair*-uh-see.
HERNANDO DE SOTO. Er-*nan*-do da So-tow.

HEZEKIAH. Hez-ih-*kye*-uh.
HILKIAH. Hill-*kye*-uh.
HOREB. *Ho*-reb.
HULDAH. *Hul*-duh.

I

ISAAC. *Eye*-zuk.
ISHMAEL. *Ish*-may-el.
ISSACHAR. *Izz*-uh-kar.
ISTANBUL. *Is*-tun-bull.

J

JACOB. *Jay*-kub.
JAEL. *Jay*-ul.
JECONIAH. *Jek*-o-*nye*-uh (strong accent on *nye*).
JEDIDIAH. Jed-ih-*die*-uh.
JEHOAHAZ. Jeh-*ho*-uh-haz.
JEHOIACHIN. Jeh-*hoy*-uh-kin.
JEHOIAKIM. Jeh-*hoy*-uh-kim.
JEREMIAD. jair-uh-*my*-ud.
JERICHO. *Jair*-ih-co.
JEROBOAM. Jair-uh-*boe*-um.
JEZEBEL. *Jez*-uh-bel.
JOAB. *Jo*-ab.
JOCHEBED. *Jock*-eh-bed.
JOSHUA. *Josh*-yew-uh.
JOSIAH. Jo-*sigh*-uh.
JOTHAM. *Jo*-thum.
JUDAS ISCARIOT. *Joo*-dus Iss-*care*-ee-ut.

K

KEDESH-NAPHTALI. *Kee*-desh-*naf*-tuh-lye (strong accent on *naf*).
KETURAH. Keh-*too*-ruh.
KOINONIA (Greek). koy-no-*nee*-uh.
KRZYZEWSKI. Sha-*shef*-ski.

L

LABAN. *Lay*-bun.
LAODICEA. Lay-*odd*-uh-*see*-uh (strong accent on *see*).
LAPIDOTH. *Lap*-ih-doth.
LAZARUS. *Laz*-uh-rus.
LEVITES. *Lee*-vites.
LOGOS (Greek). *law*-goss.

M

MACCABEES. *Mack*-uh-bees.
MACEDONIA. Mass-eh-*doe*-nee-uh.
MACHIR. *May*-ker.

MAGDALENE. *Mag*-duh-leen or Mag-duh-*lee*-nee.
MANASSEH. Muh-*nass*-uh.
MARDI GRAS. *Mar*-dee Grah.
MARDUK. *Mar*-duke.
MESOPOTAMIA. *Mes*-uh-puh-*tay*-me-uh (strong accent on *tay*).
MICHAIAH (MICAIAH). My-*kay*-uh.
MIDIAN. *Mid*-ee-un.

N

NAPHTALI. *Naf*-tuh-lye.
NAPOLEON BONAPARTE. Nuh-*pole*-yun Bo-nuh-*part*.
NATHAN. *Nay*-thun (*th* as in *thin*).
NAVAJO. *Na*-vuh-ho.
NAZARENES. *Naz*-uh-reens.
NAZARETH. *Naz*-uh-reth.
NEBUCHADNEZZAR. *Neb*-yuh-kud-*nez*-er (strong accent on *nez*).
NICODEMUS. *Nick*-uh-*dee*-mus (strong accent on *dee*).
NINEVEH. *Nin*-uh-vuh.
NISAN. *Nye*-san.

O

OMEGA. O-*may*-guh.
OMNIPOTENT. ahm-*nih*-poh-tent.
OMNIPRESENCE. *ahm*-nih-*prez*-ence (strong accent on *prez*).
OMNISCIENCE. ahm-*nish*-ence.
ORIGEN. *Or*-uh-jen.

P

PADAN-ARAM. *Pay*-dan-*a*-ram.
PATMOS. *Pat*-muss.
PEDAIAH. Peh-*day*-yuh.
PENTATEUCH. *Pen*-ta-teuk.
PENTECOST. *Pent*-ih-kost.
PERSIA. *Per*-zhuh.
PHARAOH. *Fair*-o or *Fay*-roe.
PHARISEES. *Fair*-ih-seez.
PHILIPPI. Fih-*lip*-pie or *Fil*-ih-pie.
PHILISTINE. Fuh-*liss*-teen or *Fill*-us-teen.
PLATO. *Play*-tow.
PONTIUS PILATE. *Pon*-shus or *Pon*-ti-us *Pie*-lut.
PROLOGUE. *proh*-lahg.
PROPITIATION. pro-*pih*-she-*ay*-shun (strong accent on *ay*).
PUNIC. *Pyu*-nik.

R

RABBONI. Rab-*o*-nye.
REBEKAH. Reh-*bek*-uh.
REHOBOAM. Ree-huh-*boe*-um.
REPHIDIM. *Ref*-ih-dim.
RIBLAH. *Rib*-luh.

S

SABAOTH. *Sab*-a-oth.
SAMARIA. Suh-*mare*-ee-uh.
SAMARITANS. Suh-*mare*-uh-tunz.
SENIORITIS. seen-your-*eye*-tuss.
SEPTUAGINT. Sep-*too*-ih-jent.
SERAPH. *sair*-uhf.
SERAPHIM. *sair*-uh-fim.
SHALOM (Hebrew). shah-*lome*.
SHAPHAN. *Shay*-fan.
SHECHEM. *Shee*-kem or *Shek*-em.
SHEOL. *she*-ol.
SIDON. *Sigh*-dun.
SILOAM. Sigh-*lo*-um.
SINAI. *Sigh*-nye or *Sigh*-nay-eye.
SISERA. *Sis*-er-uh.
SODOM. *Sod*-um.
SOLOMON. *Sol*-o-mun.
SYNAGOGUE. *sin*-uh-gog.

T

TEKOA. Tih-*ko*-uh.
THEOPHANOS (Greek). Thee-*ah*-fun-us (*Th* as in *thin*).
TIMNATH-HERES. *Tim*-nath-*hee*-reez (strong accent on *hee*).
TSUNAMI. sue-*nah*-me.

U

URIAH. Yu-*rye*-uh.
UZZIAH. Uh-*zye*-uh.

W

WITTENBERG. *Wih*-ten-berg or *Vih*-ten-berk.

Z

ZACCHEUS. Zack-*key*-us.
ZADOK. *Zay*-dok.
ZAREPHATH. *Zair*-uh-fath.
ZEBUDAH. Ze-*bu*-duh.
ZEBULUN. *Zeb*-you-lun.
ZEDEKIAH. Zed-uh-*kye*-uh.
ZERUBBABEL. Zeh-*rub*-uh-bul.
ZIPPORAH. Zi-*po*-ruh.

Fall Quarter 2006

God's Living Covenant

Special Features

Lessons

Unit 1: God's Covenant with the Patriarchs

Unit 2: God's Covenant with Judges and Kings

Unit 3: Living Under God's Covenant

About These Lessons

Marriage vows. Mortgages. Credit card agreements. We don't use the word *covenant* much in everyday speech, but covenants are all around us nonetheless. They are part of the very fabric of our lives. Nowhere is this more important than in the spiritual sense. Learning about God's covenants makes us more attuned to His will. May we be more pleasing to Him as we do so.

Sep 3
Sep 10
Sep 17
Sep 24
Oct 1
Oct 8
Oct 15
Oct 22
Oct 29
Nov 5
Nov 12
Nov 19
Nov 26

Three Times Two!

IN THE 2004–2005 EDITION of the *Standard Lesson Commentary,* we noted that the six-year cycle of the past had become a three-year cycle. That change has now been enhanced: the six-year cycle is back, but it is divided into two three-year segments.

Each three-year segment features six themes. Those themes are *Creation, Call, Covenant, Christ, Community,* and *Commitment.* If you look carefully at the chart below, you can see those themes reflected in the quarter titles.

This new arrangement means that each of the six themes will be covered four times in the course of the six-year cycle. But each of the four treatments is distinctive. For example, consider the theme of *Call,* which presents itself in winter 2004–05, summer 2005–06, winter 2007–08, and summer 2008–09. Those studies draw on different texts, from both Old and New Testaments; each study stands on its own.

May these changes serve to lift our eyes ever upward to Jesus. To Him be the glory. —R. L. N.

International Sunday School Lesson Cycle
September 2004—August 2010

YEAR	FALL QUARTER (Sept., Oct., Nov.)	WINTER QUARTER (Dec., Jan., Feb.)	SPRING QUARTER (Mar., Apr., May)	SUMMER QUARTER (June, July, Aug.)
2004-2005	The God of Continuing Creation (Bible Survey)	Called to Be God's People (Bible Survey)	God's Project: Effective Christians (Romans, Galatians)	Jesus' Life, Ministry, and Teaching (Matthew, Mark, Luke)
2005-2006	"You Will Be My Witnesses" (Acts)	God's Commitment— Our Response (Isaiah, 1 & 2 Timothy)	Living in and as God's Creation (Psalms, Job, Ecclesiastes, Proverbs)	Called to Be a Christian Community (1 & 2 Corinthians)
2006-2007	God's Living Covenant (Old Testament Survey)	Jesus Christ: A Portrait of God (John, Philippians, Colossians, Hebrews, 1 John)	Our Community Now and in God's Future (1 John, Revelation)	Committed to Doing Right (Various Prophets, 2 Kings, 2 Chronicles)
2007-2008	Creation (Genesis)	God's Call to the Christian Community (Luke)	God, the People, and the Covenant (1 & 2 Chronicles, Daniel, Haggai, Nehemiah)	Images of Christ (Hebrews, Gospels)
2008-2009	The New Testament Community (New Testament Survey)	Human Commitment (Old Testament, Luke)	New Creation in Christ (Ezekiel, Luke, Acts, Ephesians)	Call Sealed with Promise (Exodus, Leviticus, Numbers, Deuteronomy)
2009-2010	Covenant Communities (Joshua, Judges, Ezra, Nehemiah, Mark, 1 & 2 Peter)	Christ the Fulfillment (Matthew)	Teachings on Community (Johannine, Ruth, New Testament)	Christian Commitment in Today's World (1 & 2 Thessalonians, Philippians)

"Creation"	"Call"	"Covenant"	"Christ"	"Community"	"Commitment"

A Living, Loving Covenant

by Douglas Redford

MANY ARE FAMILIAR with the concept of a "living will." This is a document in which a person can stipulate that no extraordinary measures are to be used to prolong his or her life in the event of a terminal illness. Given that the lessons for the upcoming quarter develop the theme of "God's Living Covenant," we can pause to consider how different the definition of God's living covenant is from that of a living will.

With His living covenant God chooses to take extraordinary measures in revealing His will to individuals. Instead of avoiding the prolonging of life as a living will potentially does, God's desire is that all humanity experience the fullness of life and blessing. The problem God seeks to address is the terminal spiritual illness that no human remedy can cope with: sin.

The lessons we will study this quarter provide a survey of the Old Testament. A primary focus is on how God used both individuals and groups in the unfolding of His covenant program.

Unit 1: God's Covenant with the Patriarchs

Lesson 1 and **Lesson 2** of this unit call attention to God's special relationship with two men: Noah and Abraham. Both were commanded by God to do something that seemed utterly absurd at the time. Noah was instructed to build an ark in preparation for a coming flood (in an area that was predominantly dry); Abraham was commanded to leave his homeland for a place with an address known only to God.

Both men obeyed the Lord. As a result, they received very special promises from God. To Noah God promised that He would never again destroy the earth by means of flood. Abraham was informed that he and his wife Sarah would become proud parents in spite of their advanced age. The experiences of Noah and Abraham illustrate a key principle: the blessings of a covenant relationship with God come only to those who are willing to obey Him, even when His directives appear to defy human logic.

Lesson 3 deals with a very special covenant of God. This one concerns not an individual but an entire nation: Old Testament Israel, which became His "peculiar treasure" (Exodus 19:5). What a sacred privilege and responsibility!

The people apparently understood God's expectations of them when they responded to Moses at Sinai, "All the words which the Lord hath said will we do" (Exodus 24:3). The people said much the same thing to Joshua during a time of covenant renewal (Joshua 24:24). That occasion of renewal at Shechem is the focus of **Lesson 4.**

Unit 2: God's Covenant with Judges and Kings

Sadly, the book of Judges portrays the abject failure of God's people to live up to the good intentions that they had voiced at the close of the book of Joshua. **Lesson 5** describes what might be termed the *sui-cycle* (playing on the word *suicide*) that characterized their behavior during this distressing segment of Old Testament history.

The cycle could be labeled in the following alliterative manner: *S*in, *S*lavery (to foreign peoples whom God raised up to oppress His people), *S*upplication (crying out to God to "supply" help), and *S*alvation (deliverance through judges such as Deborah, who is the subject of **Lesson 6**). The period of the judges illustrates a sobering truth: the greatest threat to the Israelites was not to be found in any outside threat. Rather, it was they who were their own worst enemies!

Lesson 7 highlights the ministry of Samuel. He served as a kind of transition figure as Israel moved from life under judges to life under kings.

Among Samuel's many roles was that of intercessor, praying for God's people in times of crisis (1 Samuel 12:23). Intercessory prayer remains one of the most meaningful privileges of God's people. Whenever someone says to us, "Pray for me," we may agree rather flippantly to do so without really intending to follow through on our promise. In reality we should consider such a request a sacred trust.

The theme of **Lesson 8** is God's covenant with David, as described in 2 Samuel 7. This chapter begins with David expressing his concern that the ark of the covenant be placed in more suitable surroundings; thus he desired to build an appropriate house for the ark.

God's response to David was, in effect, "No, David, let *me* build a house for *you.* I can build a much better house for you than you could ever build for me." God proceeded to give David this promise: "Thine house and thy kingdom shall be established for ever before thee" (2 Samuel 7:16). It is a stunning promise indeed, with messianic foreshadowings.

Lesson 9, the final lesson in this second unit, covers Solomon's request to God for wisdom. Solomon asked for this so that as king of Israel he might carry out the Lord's desires as faithfully as did David, his father. For Christians the passion for living by God's wisdom should lead us to further devotion to the one "greater than Solomon" (Matthew 12:42), "in whom are hid all the treasures of wisdom and knowledge" (Colossians 2:3). That wisdom is still "principal" (Proverbs 4:7). It can provide reliable counsel for anyone, whether king or commoner.

Unit 3: Living Under God's Covenant

This section of our study confronts us with the sobering reminder that living under God's covenant is not just a matter of receiving blessing after blessing. Rather, His covenant also makes certain requirements of those who receive these blessings. He calls these recipients to account if they fail to live up to those requirements.

Lesson 10 draws our attention to the contest on Mount Carmel between Elijah and the prophets of Baal. The Lord's victory there came at a time when Baal worship had made serious inroads into the northern kingdom of Israel, thanks mostly to the aggressive and ruthless efforts of Jezebel.

Elijah's construction of an altar made of 12 stones reflected his conviction that the covenant God—the God of all of Israel's 12 divided tribes—was still on His throne. This was true despite Jezebel's best efforts to remove Him.

Lesson 11 examines one of Judah's most godly kings, namely Josiah. This lesson calls special attention to Josiah's leadership in spearheading a ceremony of covenant renewal, climaxed by a celebration of the Passover.

How such leadership is needed in today's world, both in the church and in society! The presence of godly kings such as Josiah in Judah's history is a primary reason why Judah lasted approximately 130 years longer than did the northern kingdom, Israel. Those ten tribes had no kings who were considered godly.

Lesson 12 covers the tragic, bitter consequences of refusing to honor the Lord and keep His covenant. One of the printed texts for this lesson, Psalm 137:1-6, captures quite vividly the anguish of a people who longed to be back home in their beloved city of Jerusalem. Yet they had no one to blame for their plight of exile except themselves. God had tried time and time again to get their attention by means of His prophets, but they had stubbornly rejected these messengers' pleas (2 Chronicles 36:15, 16).

Nebuchadnezzar, king of the Babylonians, led the onslaught against God's city and temple. But the Scriptures make it quite clear that he did not act alone. God "brought upon them" the Babylonians or Chaldeans (2 Chronicles 36:17); Nebuchadnezzar was simply His tool.

Thankfully, our studies do not end with the somber message of Lesson 12. **Lesson 13** concludes the quarter with a study entitled, "God Offers Return and Restoration."

Just as God had used one foreign ruler to punish His people, He used another foreign ruler to issue the decree that allowed them to go back to Judah. The God of the living covenant has never been limited by any earthly ruler in fulfilling the promises of His covenants. In the New Testament, this is illustrated in the way God used the decree of Caesar Augustus to bring Joseph and Mary to Bethlehem so that Jesus could be born there in fulfillment of prophecy (Micah 5:2).

Our Faithful God

Throughout the course of this Old Testament survey, we see God as faithful and committed to keeping His side of the covenants. He is just as faithful to those who live under His new covenant today in Jesus Christ.

Yet the competition for our allegiance is fierce! We know all too well of the constant and intense pressures to listen to other voices beside the Lord's. Thus Joshua's challenge uttered at Shechem rings across the centuries to confront us in our time: "Choose you this day whom ye will serve; . . . but as for me and my house, we will serve the Lord" (Joshua 24:15).

Answers to Quarterly Quiz on page 8

Lesson 1—1. false. 2. rainbow. **Lesson 2**—1. Canaan. 2. circumcision. 3. Sarai. **Lesson 3**—1. third. 2. true. 3. false. **Lesson 4**—1. Shechem. 2. true. **Lesson 5**—1. judges. 2. false. **Lesson 6**—1. true. 2. nine. 3. sword. **Lesson 7**—1. water. 2. Philistines. **Lesson 8**—1. true. 2. Nathan. **Lesson 9**—1. Gibeon. 2. false. **Lesson 10**—1. 450. 2. three. 3. Abraham. **Lesson 11**—1. Hilkiah. 2. Hilkiah. 3. pillar. **Lesson 12**—1. Chaldees. 2. true. **Lesson 13**—1. true. 2. temple.

Mt. Carmel •

Harosheth •

Kishon River

Mt. Tabor •

Yarmuk River

Jordan River

Mt. Ararat •

Jerusalem •

• Babylon

SINAI

EGYPT

Jabbok River

• Shechem

Bethel •

Mizpeh •

• Ramah

Jerusalem •

Bethlehem •

DEAD SEA

OLD TESTAMENT WORLD

Judges of Israel

Judge	Major Oppressor	Years as Judge
Othniel (Judges 3:8-11)	Mesopotamia (Cushan-Rishathaim)	1373–1334 B.C.
Ehud (Judges 3:12-30)	Moabites (Eglon)	1319–1239 B.C.
Shamgar (Judges 3:31)	Philistines	1300 B.C.
Deborah (Judges 4, 5)	Canaanites (Jabin)	1239–1199 B.C.
Gideon (Judges 6–8)	Midianites	1192–1152 B.C.
Abimelech (Judges 9)	Period of Civil War	1152–1150 B.C.
Tola (Judges10:1, 2)	Ammonites	1149–1126 B.C.
Jair (Judges 10:3-5)	Ammonites	1126–1104 B.C.
Jephthah (Judges 10:6–12:7)	Ammonites	1086–1080 B.C.
Ibzan (Judges 12:8-10)	Philistines	1080–1075 B.C.
Elon (Judges 12:11, 12)	Philistines	1075–1065 B.C.
Abdon (Judges 12:13-15)	Philistines	1065–1058 B.C.
Samson (Judges 13–16)	Philistines	1075–1055 B.C.
Eli (1 Samuel 1–4)	Philistines	1107–1067 B.C.
Samuel (1 Samuel 7–9)	Philistines	1067–1043 B.C.

Leadership and the Bible

by Mark S. Krause

MAXWELL. COVEY. POSNER. WARREN. These are the authors that are read by many today in the quest to become better leaders. These writers speak powerfully to the contemporary situation in which we are called to do ministry.

The constant trend is to find fresh new principles for leadership that will work in our churches. Is it possible, though, that the Bible itself has value in teaching us how to be better leaders? Is there guidance beyond basic biblical principles such as prayer, service, and honesty? Let's look at examples of specific leadership actions in the Bible that help us find our way in today's world.

Gideon

The book of Judges tells of a God-ordained leader named Gideon. Gideon was a reluctant leader, but was also faithful to his calling. When asked to assemble a military force to expel foreign invaders, Gideon probably was dismayed when God kept shrinking his army (Judges 7:7).

Leaders often desire a vast army of followers. "The more workers, the more work done." "The bigger the church, the better the church." Yet that is not the lesson that Gideon's story teaches. Gideon's mighty army was quickly diminished by the Lord himself, for God directed Gideon to send many troops home.

The principle here is that sometimes a small group, chosen and focused, accomplishes great things. Those who work within smaller churches may take heart in this principle. Focusing on a small, select group of potential leaders may have a big payoff in the long run. Don't despair if God has not given you an army. Invest yourself in developing that squad of willing workers you have.

Paul

As an apostolic leader, Paul always functioned with a handicap because he was not one of the original twelve disciples of Jesus. This caused some early Christians to cast doubts on his authority.

Furthermore, many believe that there was a degree of rivalry between Paul and Peter in the first-century church. While many details are lacking, we are told of one of the flashpoints of this relationship from Paul's perspective in the book of Galatians: "But when Peter was come to Antioch, I withstood him to the face, because he was to be blamed" (Galatians 2:11).

When Paul found a peer in gross error, what was he to do? He tackled the problem head-on by confronting Peter personally. The principle for us today is that the best leaders do not avoid confrontation. That does not mean that church leaders are granted unlimited powers of criticism and control. We must choose battles wisely, realizing that the purpose of confrontation is not dominance but redemption. In the church we do not challenge in order to crush and win; we confront in order to correct and save.

Jesus

As a respected teacher during His earthly ministry, Jesus fielded many different kinds of requests from the people He encountered. Luke relates one such occasion: "And one of the company said unto him, Master, speak to my brother, that he divide the inheritance with me. And he said unto him, Man, who made me a judge or a divider over you?" (Luke 12:13, 14).

An ongoing frustration in leadership is being expected to solve problems created by others. It seems fair that a leader should have to fix only his or her own mistakes, for there are always plenty of those!

Yet the reality is that leaders are often called upon to clean up other people's messes. Just as a parent may frequently be called upon to end arguments or fights between children, so too church leaders often feel obligated to mediate personal disputes between members.

But it is important to notice the response of Jesus here: He declined to involve himself. To be *called upon* to referee a fight between others does not necessarily *require* such participation. The principle here is that good leaders encourage others to settle their own disputes. A leader who serves as judge may end up with two enemies.

You?

These are but a few examples of timeless leadership principles found in the Bible. You undoubtedly will see more in this year's studies. May God grant us wisdom to use them all as we continue in the ongoing task of serving as godly, biblical leaders for Christ's church.

Quarterly Quiz

The questions on this page may be used in several ways: as a pretest at the beginning of the quarter; as a review at the end of the quarter; or as a review after each lesson. The questions are based on the Scripture text of each lesson (King James Version). **The answers are on page 4.**

Lesson 1

1. After the flood Noah was forbidden to eat anything with a split hoof. T/F. *Genesis 9:3*

2. What is the sign that God will never again use a flood to destroy the earth? (rainbow, solar eclipse, lunar eclipse?) *Genesis 9:11-16*

Lesson 2

1. What land was to be given to Abraham? (Egypt, Midian, Canaan?) *Genesis 17:8*

2. The sign of God's covenant with Abraham was that every male was to undergo _____. *Genesis 17:10-14*

3. Sarah's original name was what? (Sheryl, Sarai, Abram?) *Genesis 17:15*

Lesson 3

1. In which month did the Israelites come to the desert of Sinai after leaving Egypt? (first, second, third?) *Exodus 19:1*

2. The Israelites were to be a kingdom of priests. T/F. *Exodus 19:6*

3. Moses built an altar at the top of Mount Sinai to represent the 12 tribes of Israel. T/F. *Exodus 24:4*

Lesson 4

1. Joshua assembled the tribes of Israel at which location? (Shechem, Jerusalem, Caesarea Philippi?) *Joshua 24:1*

2. Joshua affirmed that God is a jealous God. T/F. *Joshua 24:19*

Lesson 5

1. To deliver the Israelites from oppression after Joshua's death, the Lord raised up _____. *Judges 2:8, 16*

2. Before Joshua died he had driven out all the nations in the land of Canaan that could harm the Israelites. T/F. *Judges 2:21-23*

Lesson 6

1. Deborah was not only a judge but a prophetess as well. T/F. *Judges 4:4*

2. The Canaanite general Sisera had ____ hundred chariots. *Judges 4:13*

3. All of Sisera's army perished by what? (sword, famine, plague?) *Judges 4:16*

Lesson 7

1. _____ was poured out before the Lord at Mizpeh. *1 Samuel 7:5, 6*

2. Who attempted to attack the Israelites at Mizpeh? (Philistines, Egyptians, Midianites?) *1 Samuel 7:7*

Lesson 8

1. God's covenant with David included a promise of a great name. T/F. *2 Samuel 7:9*

2. The prophet who communicated the word of the Lord to David was whom? (Isaiah, Nathan, Jeremiah?) *2 Samuel 7:17*

Lesson 9

1. The Lord appeared to Solomon in a dream at what location? (Gibeon, Jerusalem, Ur of the Chaldees?) *1 Kings 3:5*

2. In addition to asking for wisdom, Solomon also requested wealth. T/F. *1 Kings 3:11*

Lesson 10

1. The prophets of Baal present on Mount Carmel numbered _____. *1 Kings 18:22*

2. Elijah ordered that water be poured on the altar _____ times. *1 Kings 18:34*

3. Elijah prayed to the God of _____, Isaac, and Israel. *1 Kings 18:36*

Lesson 11

1. The name of the high priest when Josiah was king was what? (Hilkiah, Shaphan, Ahaz?) *2 Kings 22:4*

2. Who found the book of the law? (Hilkiah, Shaphan, Ahaz?) *2 Kings 22:8*

3. King Josiah stood by a _____ when making a covenant before the Lord. *2 Kings 23:3*

Lesson 12

1. The king of the _____ carried the Jews into exile. *2 Chronicles 36:17*

2. While in exile in Babylon, the captives wept while sitting beside rivers. T/F. *Psalm 137:1*

Lesson 13

1. Cyrus was king of Persia. T/F. *Ezra 1:1*

2. Cyrus permitted the Jews to return and build what? (walls, roads, temple?) *Ezra 1:3*

God's Covenant with Noah

September 3
Lesson 1

DEVOTIONAL READING: Psalm 36:5-9.

BACKGROUND SCRIPTURE: Genesis 9:1-17.

PRINTED TEXT: Genesis 9:1-15.

Genesis 9:1-15

1 And God blessed Noah and his sons, and said unto them, Be fruitful, and multiply, and replenish the earth.

2 And the fear of you and the dread of you shall be upon every beast of the earth, and upon every fowl of the air, upon all that moveth upon the earth, and upon all the fishes of the sea; into your hand are they delivered.

3 Every moving thing that liveth shall be meat for you; even as the green herb have I given you all things.

4 But flesh with the life thereof, which is the blood thereof, shall ye not eat.

5 And surely your blood of your lives will I require: at the hand of every beast will I require it, and at the hand of man; at the hand of every man's brother will I require the life of man.

6 Whoso sheddeth man's blood, by man shall his blood be shed: for in the image of God made he man.

7 And you, be ye fruitful, and multiply; bring forth abundantly in the earth, and multiply therein.

8 And God spake unto Noah, and to his sons with him, saying,

9 And I, behold, I establish my covenant with you, and with your seed after you;

10 And with every living creature that is with you, of the fowl, of the cattle, and of every beast of the earth with you; from all that go out of the ark, to every beast of the earth.

11 And I will establish my covenant with you; neither shall all flesh be cut off any more by the waters of a flood; neither shall there any more be a flood to destroy the earth.

12 And God said, This is the token of the covenant which I make between me and you, and every living creature that is with you, for perpetual generations:

13 I do set my bow in the cloud, and it shall be for a token of a covenant between me and the earth.

14 And it shall come to pass, when I bring a cloud over the earth, that the bow shall be seen in the cloud:

15 And I will remember my covenant, which is between me and you and every living creature of all flesh; and the waters shall no more become a flood to destroy all flesh.

GOLDEN TEXT: I will establish my covenant with you; neither shall all flesh be cut off any more by the waters of a flood; neither shall there any more be a flood to destroy the earth.—Genesis 9:11.

God's Living Covenant
Unit 1: God's Covenant with the Patriarchs
(Lessons 1-4)

Lesson Aims

After participating in this lesson, each student will be able to:

1. Summarize the commands and promises that God gave to Noah immediately after the flood.

2. Explain the security that results from knowing God's expectations and promises.

3. Tell how he or she will use each observance of a rainbow as a reminder that God keeps His promises.

Lesson Outline

INTRODUCTION
   A. "The Good of the People"
   B. Lesson Background
 I. GOD'S COMMANDS (Genesis 9:1-7)
   A. Procreation Prescribed (v. 1)
   B. Protection Promised (v. 2)
   C. Provisions Concerning Food (vv. 3, 4)
   D. Punishment for Taking Life (vv. 5, 6)
     The Purpose of Pain
   E. Procreation Emphasized (v. 7)
II. GOD'S COVENANT (Genesis 9:8-15)
   A. Covenant's Parties (vv. 8-10)
   B. Covenant's Promise (v. 11)
   C. Covenant's Permanence (vv. 12-15)
     The End Will Come!
CONCLUSION
   A. Faithful or Faithless
   B. Prayer
   C. Thought to Remember

Introduction

A. "The Good of the People"

In about 360 BC the Greek philosopher Plato wrote, "Mankind must have laws and conform to them, or their life would be as bad as that of the most savage beast." This is simply another way of saying that laws are necessary for each person to know the mutual obligations that are expected in any social group.

Observing those expectations will ordinarily promote the general welfare of both the individual and the group. The Roman statesman and orator Cicero (106–43 BC) said, "The safety of the people shall be the highest law." The popular version of his statement is, "The good of the people is the highest law."

We humans seem to be in a constant state of give-and-take with our laws. The year 1957 saw the governor of the U.S. state of Arkansas defy a 1954 U.S. Supreme Court ruling concerning racial integration in schools. He used the Arkansas National Guard to prevent the ruling from taking effect in Little Rock, the state capital. President Eisenhower responded by federalizing the National Guard and sending a unit of the U.S. Army to Little Rock. The ruling of the court was enforced.

The fall of that same year saw the establishment of a new Bible college, and a social experiment was suggested. Would it be possible for the students in such an institution to function together with only the laws of the state and the Bible to guide them? The students expressed an eagerness to cooperate in such an endeavor. A plan to devise a complete set of rules by using student handbooks from other colleges thus was abandoned.

As time went on, however, rules were added as various liberties were abused. For example, a person could play a radio as loudly as desired, but that liberty would end where the ears of another were involved. This liberty had to be balanced with another person's right to quiet, especially if the hours for nighttime sleeping were involved! The list of rules slowly grew, and within a few years a handbook came into being.

People need to know what they should and should not do. Toddlers, for example, learn that parents have a favorite word: *No!* As children crawl, walk, or run, they must understand that there are boundaries and that there are consequences for bold adventures into prohibited areas. Children learn that the family's unwritten code of laws also increases. A child may have to tolerate the fact that older siblings have privileges that are not yet granted to those who are younger. Laws or rules—whether at the level of the government, Bible college, or family—are for the common good.

One frequent designation for the first five books of the Bible is "the Law." The main reason for this designation is that these books record the covenantal laws that the Lord put into place at various times. We have much to learn from God's Old Testament laws and covenants yet today.

B. Lesson Background

The flood that occurred the year Noah was 600 had just ended. Noah, his family, and the animals emerged from the ark after spending many months within it.

The account of the flood is always fascinating to read. It is interesting that over 200 similar accounts have been found in legends around the world. These sagas have common threads of a god or gods who were displeased with humanity and thus destroyed just about everything except for one individual and his family. Over two-thirds of the stories indicate that animals also were saved. Over half of the stories have the vessel of safety landing on a mountain. There are many differences among the accounts, so the conclusion for the Christian is that the straightforward presentation as found in Genesis is the only one that is authentic.

The New Testament contains several references to the events of the great flood. Matthew 24:38, 39; Hebrews 11:7; 1 Peter 3:20; and 2 Peter 2:5; 3:6 confirm that Jesus and the inspired writers of the New Testament were confident that the flood was a historical event.

As the family of Noah departed from the ark, they found themselves alone in a world that had been cleansed. We can only wonder how the raging waters of the flood affected continents and climates, topography and temperatures. In His wisdom God does not reveal those things to us.

Noah's first action upon leaving the ark was to offer sacrifices of the clean animals and birds (Genesis 8:20). As the aroma arose, the Lord spoke first to himself about the earth—its daily and annual cycles. He then spoke the words that are the printed text for today's lesson.

The word *covenant* is a very important word in God's expression of His will for humanity in every age. That word occurs nearly 300 times in the Bible. It is a vital part of today's lesson, "God's Covenant with Noah."

I. God's Commands
(Genesis 9:1-7)

Noah needs assurance about the things that the Lord desires for him, his three sons, and the wives of each man. Their experiences convince them that God keeps His word and that He punishes sin. But they also need to know of the blessings that await them.

A. Procreation Prescribed (v. 1)

1. And God blessed Noah and his sons, and said unto them, Be fruitful, and multiply, and replenish the earth.

The phrase *God blessed Noah and his sons* means that God is granting the abilities for them to enjoy prosperity in the areas of life that are important. They will be successful in their endeavors. This assurance provides a confidence that they need in their changed situations. God had made a similar pronouncement at the creation of humans (Genesis 1:28). In that case the ensuing prosperity led to humanity's detriment as people used God's blessings to focus on evil (Genesis 6:5).

God sets forth His plan with three terse imperatives: *be fruitful, multiply, replenish.* The last command adds that it is *the earth* that is to be restored. The ancients correctly viewed this command to fill the earth as God's authorization of marriage. That naturally involves a man and a woman.

Obeying the command to multiply is not considered an ideal in certain nations today. Children often are viewed as expensive (and they are!) and as interfering in the quest for life at its fullest. The gift of procreation with which God endowed humanity has deteriorated in many cases into a selfish, sensual sexuality. Many seek ever more perverse ways to find elusive fulfillment. But disobedience to God will result in emptiness. [See question #1, page 16.]

B. Protection Promised (v. 2)

2. And the fear of you and the dread of you shall be upon every beast of the earth, and upon every fowl of the air, upon all that moveth upon the earth, and upon all the fishes of the sea; into your hand are they delivered.

The statement that animals of all types will *fear* humans introduces a new concept. It produces speculation that the eight people in the ark originally experience fright as they watch the animals leave (perhaps from the size or appearance of some of the animals), but that fright is now on the part of the animals. All we can do is wonder whether this indicates a change from the past.

The promise by God that the animals will fear humans is a general principle. It is normally true

---

How to Say It

CICERO. *Sih*-suh-row.

DEUTERONOMY. Due-ter-*ahn*-uh-me.

FESTUS. *Fes*-tus.

GALATIANS. Guh-*lay*-shunz.

GENTILES. *Jen*-tiles.

HEBREWS. *Hee*-brews.

MOSES. *Mo*-zes or *Mo*-zez.

PLATO. *Play*-tow.

TSUNAMI. sue-*nah*-me.

that wild animals do whatever they can to avoid humans, but we all know about the exceptions. The exceptions ordinarily have to do with the self-preservation instincts that God placed within the animals. In normal circumstances most animals run from encounters with us. [See question #2, page 16.]

C. Provisions Concerning Food (vv. 3, 4)

3. Every moving thing that liveth shall be meat for you; even as the green herb have I given you all things.

Humanity receives permission to eat the flesh of animals. This becomes a new source of protein. Immediately after the initial creation, God said that He was giving plants and fruit as food for humanity and plants for the animals (Genesis 1:29, 30). We would like to know more about this situation in the years before the flood, but in His wisdom God does not reveal it to us.

The law of Moses, which is to be given at Mount Sinai, will modify the acceptability of food sources for the Israelites. They are to distinguish between clean and unclean animals that they can eat (see Leviticus 11).

That restriction, however, is for Old Testament Israel only. In the Christian age the distinction is removed entirely. A person may eat whatever he or she wishes (Mark 7:19; 1 Timothy 4:4). If, however, an individual chooses not to eat a specific type of food, he or she should not attempt to enforce that choice on others (Romans 14:2, 6). Also, our freedom to eat certain foods is restricted when the faith of others may be at stake (1 Corinthians 8).

4. But flesh with the life thereof, which is the blood thereof, shall ye not eat.

The eating of meat does have a restriction: *the blood* of the animal is not to be consumed. Moses will repeat this restriction for the nation of Israel (see Leviticus 17:12-14). The same limitation is found in Acts 15:20, 29 among the restrictions that Gentile Christians are encouraged to observe. Many scholars see parallels between Genesis 9 and Acts 15.

VISUALS FOR THESE LESSONS

The visual pictured in each lesson (example: page 13) is a small reproduction of a large, full-color poster included in the *Adult Resources* packet for the Fall Quarter. The packet is available from your supplier. Order No. 192.

D. Punishment for Taking Life (vv. 5, 6)

5, 6. And surely your blood of your lives will I require: at the hand of every beast will I require it, and at the hand of man; at the hand of every man's brother will I require the life of man. Whoso sheddeth man's blood, by man shall his blood be shed: for in the image of God made he man.

Clearly, God views the taking of human life to be a very serious thing. The sanctity of *blood* as the life principle puts it into God's domain to render such a judgment. It also becomes evident that the taking of human life is much different from taking the life of an animal; in the previous verses God approved the latter as means of obtaining food.

No one should interpret the dramatic loss of life in the great flood to mean that human life is cheap. God can choose to take human life in any manner He chooses, because He is the one who gives the breath of life to all in the first place. Anyone who deliberately and with malice aforethought takes the life of someone else must understand that there can and should be severe consequences from earthly tribunals. There also will be an accounting in the final judgment of God.

The reason for the equal retribution *Whoso sheddeth man's blood, by man shall his blood be shed* is very specific: *for in the image of God made he man.* Since each person is made in the image of God, no individual should endanger the lives of the innocent.

In verse 6 God authorizes governments and those who are in places of authority to exercise capital punishment for murder. Romans 13:4 states that the person in authority, "the minister of God," bears a sword "to execute wrath upon him that doeth evil." The individual who is authorized to use deadly force is sometimes called a peace officer, for he or she is to restore peace. When Paul stood before Festus, he recognized the authority of the court to impose the death penalty (Acts 25:11).

The Mosaic law demonstrates the mind of God in that He recognizes exceptions in applying the death penalty. While the Mosaic law is no longer binding (see Galatians 3:24, 25), it is helpful to use it to show that accidental death is duly recognized (Deuteronomy 19:4, 5). God gave the Israelites a method to protect the individual who took life accidentally (without hatred or malice). Further, those who serve as executioners are never assigned any penalty. Certain traditional teachings cite verse 6 as disallowing abortion. [See question #3, page 16.]

THE PURPOSE OF PAIN

Wouldn't it be wonderful if we didn't have any aches or pains? Parents wouldn't have to deal with a baby's cry because he or she could not tell Mom where it hurts. Middle-aged weekend athletes wouldn't wake up hurting on Monday because they had abused their aging muscles in Sunday afternoon church softball games. Aching, arthritic joints wouldn't plague senior citizens!

On second thought, maybe it wouldn't be so wonderful. Grade-school student Ashlyn Blocker is one of a very few people who suffers from congenital insensitivity to pain (CIPA) with anhidrosis (inability to sweat)—a rare genetic disorder. She can't tell if her food is too hot; if she falls on the playground and skins her knee, she won't know it until her teacher sees the blood; if she gets overheated, she won't perspire; if she gets too cold, she won't shiver. The way God has created us, pain is a blessing; it is a "wake-up call" to the fact that something is wrong with our bodies.

The nightly news is filled with tragic stories of murder and attempted murder. Do these reports alarm us, or have we become numb to them? Nations agonize over the issue of capital punishment. Yet nations that allow grievous crimes to go without sure and serious punishment will see their moral fabric disintegrate. The pain that a God-fearing nation feels when serious crime occurs is God's way of saying, "Look at the danger you are in!" May we heed His warning. —C. R. B.

E. Procreation Emphasized (v. 7)

7. And you, be ye fruitful, and multiply; bring forth abundantly in the earth, and multiply therein.

The imperatives of the first verse of the chapter are repeated and therefore emphasized. God seems not to be concerned about overpopulation.

II. God's Covenant
(Genesis 9:8-15)

The first use of the word *covenant* in the Bible occurs in Genesis 6:18. That occurrence was before the flood as God promised Noah that He would make a covenant with him when the flood-judgment was complete. Now we see God ready to fulfill His promise.

A. Covenant's Parties (vv. 8-10)

8, 9. And God spake unto Noah, and to his sons with him, saying, And I, behold, I establish my covenant with you, and with your seed after you.

Visual for Lesson 1

Do You Remember Your Covenant With God?

Pose this question to your class to open a discussion of our obligations under the new covenant.

A *covenant* often serves to establish a relationship, and that is the case here. It is God who is presenting the covenant. The recipients first named are *Noah* and *his sons with him.* But they are not the only recipients!

This particular covenant and its preceding promises are to extend to future generations, for it is to Noah and his *seed after* him. The proper response is to serve obediently the one who is offering such a covenant with its attendant blessings. [See question #4, page 16.]

10. And with every living creature that is with you, of the fowl, of the cattle, and of every beast of the earth with you; from all that go out of the ark, to every beast of the earth.

The covenant's scope also includes *every living creature* that goes out of the ark. It is universal in its reach and effect. During the creation week, God pronounced blessings on the animals and upon humanity (Genesis 1:22, 28). The establishment of this covenant relationship is now added to the blessings, and it includes both humanity and the animals.

B. Covenant's Promise (v. 11)

11. And I will establish my covenant with you; neither shall all flesh be cut off any more by the waters of a flood; neither shall there any more be a flood to destroy the earth.

The *covenant* affirms that never again will God destroy all life on the earth *by the waters of a flood.* The history of the earth demonstrates that God has been faithful to keep this promise. There have been local floods involving terrible loss of life. But there has not been another flood to destroy all life on earth.

C. Covenant's Permanence (vv. 12-15)

12, 13. And God said, This is the token of the covenant which I make between me and you, and every living creature that is with you, for perpetual generations: I do set my bow in the cloud, and it shall be for a token of a covenant between me and the earth.

The word *bow* translates a Hebrew word that may mean either the bow as a weapon or the rainbow. The context determines the meaning. In this case the bow is the rainbow, and it is the *perpetual* sign of the covenant being announced by God.

Isn't it marvelous to see a rainbow yet today? When conditions are just right, we can even see two rainbows. No need to search for the mythical pot of gold at the end of the rainbow. God's promise is better than gold!

14, 15. And it shall come to pass, when I bring a cloud over the earth, that the bow shall be seen in the cloud: and I will remember my covenant, which is between me and you and every living creature of all flesh; and the waters shall no more become a flood to destroy all flesh.

Some have conjectured that the appearance of a rainbow in the heavens was a new phenomenon. The conditions on *the earth* prior to the flood are not precisely understood, but it is very likely that the combination of light and moisture to form a spectrum was not new. God, however, gives it a new significance. He repeats that this is a perpetual reminder that He will never again *destroy all* living creatures on the face of the earth. [See question #5, page 16.]

THE END WILL COME!

On December 26, 2004, the world was shocked by news of the massive earthquake and tsunami in the Indian Ocean. We can still remember the mind-numbing reruns of the destruction captured on video that day. Within a week the death toll had passed 150,000 in a dozen nations. More would die from disease in the weeks that followed. No one will ever know for sure how many died in the event. But it was one of the greatest losses of life by flood in modern history.

There is no end to natural disasters. In a rather macabre acknowledgement of this fact, some newspapers carry a regular "Earth Watch" column listing the previous week's earthquakes, floods, cyclones, and unusual weather phenomena such as extreme cold or heat. So, does this mean that God has not kept His covenantal promise? Not at all! Even the most extensive floods of the past thousand years have not come close to equaling the devastation of Noah's day.

In that day God destroyed almost the entire human race by *super*natural disaster. God has promised that He will not do so again by means of floodwaters. Even so, "the end of all things is at hand" (1 Peter 4:7). The end of creation as we know it will come by fire (2 Peter 3:10). The time to prepare ourselves is now.   —C. R. B.

Conclusion

A. Faithful or Faithless

One lady stated that her first connection between the God of Scripture and the God of her own little world as a child came after being read this account of Noah and the flood in a Bible-story book and then being shown the rainbow after a particularly heavy rainstorm. Such an association is exactly what God intended. The beauty of the brilliant spectrum of light in the sky is to remind people of any age, in every age, that they have a connection to God. It is up to individuals to determine whether they will be faithful or faithless in their responses to the God who makes covenants with us.

B. Prayer

Lord, today I promise to be more alert to Your perpetual promise. Help me not to be so busy with things that I fail to keep my promise to live, so that everyone recognizes that Jesus is my Lord and Savior. In His name, amen.

C. Thought to Remember

Look for the rainbow.
Remember God's promise.

Home Daily Bible Readings

Monday, Aug. 28—God Is Gracious (Psalm 36:5-9)

Tuesday, Aug. 29—Noah Enters the Ark (Genesis 7:1-12)

Wednesday, Aug. 30—The Flood Rages (Genesis 7:13-24)

Thursday, Aug. 31—The Water Subsides (Genesis 8:1-12)

Friday, Sept. 1—God Makes a Promise (Genesis 8:13-22)

Saturday, Sept. 2—God Instructs Noah (Genesis 9:1-7)

Sunday, Sept. 3—God Covenants with Noah (Genesis 9:8-17)

Learning by Doing

This page contains an alternative lesson plan emphasizing learning activities.
Classes desiring such student involvement will find these suggestions helpful.

Learning Goals

After participating in this lesson, each student will be able to:

1. Summarize the commands and promises that God gave to Noah immediately after the flood.

2. Explain the security that results from knowing God's expectations and promises.

3. Tell how he or she will use each observance of a rainbow as a reminder that God keeps His promises.

Into the Lesson

Write THEGEYESRAOFCTHEELORD on the board so that students can see it as they arrive. Someone should quickly decipher it as "Finding *grace* in *the eyes of the Lord.*"

Into the Word

Right after the Into the Lesson puzzle is deciphered, have one of your good oral readers stand before the group and read Genesis 6:5, 7, 8, 13, 22; 7:1, 7-10, 21, 22; 8:1, 4, 15, 16, 20-22 consecutively. After the reading, ask the students to look for all the demonstrations of God's grace toward Noah as the study progresses.

Say to your class, "A covenant is a 'what-is' and 'what-is-not' document or statement. Such a statement—whether contract or license or will—says what is permitted and expected and what is not. Consider each of the following statements as you look at today's text in Genesis 9:1-15. Decide whether the statement is accurate and then what verse or verses reveals the *yes* or *no* involved."

Read the following statements in random order. Allow your class to respond, both with verse numbers and relevant comments. Verse numbers are given here, but do not mention them before students respond.

(1) God says *yes* to marriage and sexual activity *(v. 1).* (2) God says *no* to filling the earth with people *(v. 1).* (3) God says *yes* to domestication of animals *(v. 2).* (4) God says *yes* to our dominion over creatures of the sea *(v. 2).* (5) God says *no* to humans eating animals *(v. 3).* (6) God says *no* to humans consuming blood *(v. 4).* (7) God says *yes* to capital punishment *(vv. 5, 6).* (8) God says *yes* to humans being made in His image *(v. 6).* (9) God says *no* to making covenants with people *(v. 8).* (10) God says *yes* to making a covenant with animals *(v. 9).* (11) God says *no* to a second universal flood *(v. 11).* (12) God says *yes* to using a visual reminder of His will *(vv. 12, 13).* (13) God says *yes* to repeating His promises for emphasis *(vv. 14, 15).*

As students respond to each statement, take the opportunity to ask follow-up questions. Repeat Genesis 6:8 and comment, "We usually think of God showing grace to Noah in saving him from the death of the flood—and that is true —but God continued to show His grace in a variety of ways. Let's look at today's text to see the continuous outpouring of grace on Noah and his family."

Ask the class to look at Genesis 8:22–9:15 and identify examples of God's grace. Accept reasonable answers. If responses are slow in coming, ask a few questions, such as, "How does God's dietary expansion, such as in Genesis 9:3, represent His grace?" *(Humans have more variety in tastes and dietary opportunity.)* "How does God's imposition of capital punishment in Genesis 9:5, 6 indicate grace?" *(The existence of every moral principle is a sign of God's concern for our welfare in spite of sinful choices; this one offers protection from the inclination to assume that "might makes right.")* "How is the rainbow a sign of grace?" *(When rain is falling, thoughts might well hark back to the deluge of destruction. But at just such a time God says with His beautiful science of prismatic reflection, "Remember my grace!")*

Into Life

Prior to class collect eight-inch pieces of yarn or thread in a variety of colors from some of the crafters in your class. Let each learner select a piece in the color of his or her choice. Challenge students to complete this assignment sometime this week: "Have someone tie a simple bow around one of your fingers on a day in the week ahead. When someone asks about the significance of the bow, relate your confidence in the promises of God as studied in class today."

For those not quite so bold, suggest that they tie the bow somewhere they will see it often, perhaps near the bathroom mirror. This should serve as a reminder of today's study and of the assurance of God's many promises to those who find His grace.

Let's Talk It Over

The questions on this page are designed to promote discussion of the lesson by the class and to encourage application of the lesson Scriptures. The answers provided are only discussion starters. Let your class talk it over from there.

1. With blessings come responsibilities! What are some of the responsibilities that you and your church have received because of the blessings available in Christ? How well are you living up to these?

The responsibilities revolve around the same words given to Noah in verse 1. Christians should be fruitful, bearing the fruit of the Spirit in their lives. The world needs to see us living out love, joy, peace, etc. (Galatians 5:22, 23). It is also our task to multiply ourselves in Christ by reaching others with the message of the gospel (Matthew 28:19, 20). When we do, we replenish the kingdom of God on earth, ensuring that the church continues into the next generation.

2. "Into your hand" reflects the earlier part of Genesis, where God gave humanity dominion over the world. What are some ways this responsibility has been misused? How can we do better?

Dominion means that God has invited us into partnership in caring for the earth. Responsible treatment of God's creation is necessary in this regard. Abuse of animals for the sheer pleasure of it (example: cockfighting) is a misuse of responsibility. Hunting animals to extinction (example: the passenger pigeon) is a detriment to all. Overfishing of the seas is a known problem. Pollution is a festering issue in some areas.

God's invitation to exercise dominion still stands. Ask your class to brainstorm ways to do this in a God-honoring way.

3. How can Christians take the lead in promoting the sanctity of innocent life?

God values life and expects us, the crown of His creation, to do the same. Yet the horrors of the Nazi gas chambers, the genocide in Rwanda, and the taking of the lives of millions of the unborn demonstrate a failure to honor life.

There are many paths to a solution. Churches can become actively involved in local crisis pregnancy centers and other organizations that seek to provide help and counsel to those who are considering abortion. Supporting governmental efforts to stop tyrannical regimes is another avenue. Caring for senior citizens and helping them face the end of life are roles that the church and the individual Christian should embrace.

These are just a few ways to demonstrate our concern (and God's concern) for life. Expect a wide-ranging discussion.

4. God is a maker and keeper of covenants! What are some covenants we make that we often fail to honor? How can we do better? What will be the result if we don't?

God expects His people to keep their covenants, their agreements, and their promises (Matthew 23:16-22). When we make any pledge, vow, or promise, we are making a covenant. That means that when we sign a contract to purchase a house or car, we live up to that by making the payments in a timely way. When we take a job, we are making a contract with our employer to give an honest day's work for the pay we receive. The marriage covenant is also to be kept. The words "till death shall separate us" are words of commitment.

Unfortunately, Christians often are not all that different from non-Christians in keeping covenants. The divorce rate of Christians and non-Christians is about the same (www.barna.org). Yet breaking covenants by declaring bankruptcy, getting a divorce, etc., should not be embraced too quickly, if at all. Credit and marriage counseling are available. Your church can have ministries that honor God in both of these areas.

5. When we see the rainbow, we remember God's promise not to destroy the world again with water. Why not use the rainbow to remind us of God's other promises as well? The next time you look at a rainbow, what other promises of God will you remember?

God has promised in His Word that He will never leave nor forsake His people. He has promised that He will not allow any temptation to come upon us that will be too much for us to bear. God has promised that when we are faithful in our stewardship He will open up the floodgates of Heaven and pour out a blessing. The ultimate promise God has made is that if we are faithful to Him until death, He will give to us the crown of life.

God's Covenant with Abraham

September 10
Lesson 2

DEVOTIONAL READING: Hebrews 6:13-20.

BACKGROUND SCRIPTURE: Genesis 17.

PRINTED TEXT: Genesis 17:1-8, 15-22.

Genesis 17:1-8, 15-22

1 And when Abram was ninety years old and nine, the LORD appeared to Abram, and said unto him, I am the Almighty God; walk before me, and be thou perfect.

2 And I will make my covenant between me and thee, and will multiply thee exceedingly.

3 And Abram fell on his face: and God talked with him, saying,

4 As for me, behold, my covenant is with thee, and thou shalt be a father of many nations.

5 Neither shall thy name any more be called Abram, but thy name shall be Abraham; for a father of many nations have I made thee.

6 And I will make thee exceeding fruitful, and I will make nations of thee, and kings shall come out of thee.

7 And I will establish my covenant between me and thee and thy seed after thee in their generations, for an everlasting covenant, to be a God unto thee and to thy seed after thee.

8 And I will give unto thee, and to thy seed after thee, the land wherein thou art a stranger, all the land of Canaan, for an everlasting possession; and I will be their God.

. . . .

15 And God said unto Abraham, As for Sarai thy wife, thou shalt not call her name Sarai, but Sarah shall her name be.

16 And I will bless her, and give thee a son also of her: yea, I will bless her, and she shall be a mother of nations; kings of people shall be of her.

17 Then Abraham fell upon his face, and laughed, and said in his heart, Shall a child be born unto him that is a hundred years old? and shall Sarah, that is ninety years old, bear?

18 And Abraham said unto God, O that Ishmael might live before thee!

19 And God said, Sarah thy wife shall bear thee a son indeed; and thou shalt call his name Isaac: and I will establish my covenant with him for an everlasting covenant, and with his seed after him.

20 And as for Ishmael, I have heard thee: Behold, I have blessed him, and will make him fruitful, and will multiply him exceedingly; twelve princes shall he beget, and I will make him a great nation.

21 But my covenant will I establish with Isaac, which Sarah shall bear unto thee at this set time in the next year.

22 And he left off talking with him, and God went up from Abraham.

GOLDEN TEXT: I will establish my covenant between me and thee and thy seed after thee in their generations, for an everlasting covenant, to be a God unto thee and to thy seed after thee.—Genesis 17:7.

God's Living Covenant
Unit 1: God's Covenant with the Patriarchs
(Lessons 1-4)

Lesson Aims

After participating in this lesson, each student will be able to:

1. Retell the promises of God's covenant with Abraham.

2. Compare and contrast with his or her own life both the faith and the doubt expressed by Abraham.

3. Suggest a specific area in his or her life where applying a faith like Abraham's can make (or is making) a difference.

Lesson Outline

INTRODUCTION
  A. Singing, Exercise, and Doctrine
  B. Lesson Background
I. PROMISES TO ABRAHAM (Genesis 17:1-8, 15, 16)
  A. Name for God (vv. 1, 2)
    "What's in a Name?"
  B. Nations to Result (vv. 3, 4)
  C. New Name for Abram (v. 5a)
  D. Nations and the Kings (vv. 5b, 6)
  E. People of the Covenant (v. 7)
  F. Place Assigned (v. 8)
  G. Position for Sarai (vv. 15, 16)
II. PERPLEXITIES OF ABRAHAM (Genesis 17:17-22)
  A. Problems Stated (vv. 17, 18)
  B. Problems Solved (vv. 19-22)
    Unintentional Fraud
CONCLUSION
  A. If It Sounds Too Good . . .
  B. Prayer
  C. Thought to Remember

Introduction

A. Singing, Exercise, and Doctrine

We used to call them action choruses. Young people of varying ages were encouraged to use their arms and hands to simulate motions for the fountain that flowed deep and wide, the little light that shined, or the rains that threatened the houses of the wise and foolish builders. The choruses taught spiritual truths, helped the youngsters expend pent-up energy, and enabled youth workers to fill prolonged periods of time.

In recent years another such chorus was very popular with young people. The opening phrase affirms that Abraham had many sons. That is biblically true, for Paul says the same thing—that Abraham is the father of all who believe (Romans 4:11, 16; compare Galatians 3:7). As the lyrics reach the refrain, the words prompt several physical exercises that require agility, balance, and much energy. Most youngsters love to sing this exhilarating chorus, but it is doubtful that they realize the doctrinal implications of the opening words. That initial affirmation is a part of the lesson today.

Abraham is the great example of faith for all who believe in Christ. Abraham is the first person in the Bible of whom it is said that his belief was reckoned for righteousness (Genesis 15:6). He has more verses about him in the Faith Chapter (Hebrews 11) than any other Old Testament saint. His name appears more than 200 times in the New Testament. So the next time you hear young people singing the chorus about Abraham having many sons, remember that that really is a profound truth (with or without the suggested athletic movements!).

B. Lesson Background

The lesson last week was about the covenant that God made with Noah. Using the Genesis chronology, there are hundreds of years between Noah and Abraham. The Bible is silent about any direct communication from God to humankind during that period of time.

After the flood the sons of Noah and their descendants did well in obeying the command to fill the earth (Genesis 9:1, 7). The "table of nations" in Genesis 10 gives the names of individuals who were the founders of nations or tribal groups. The incident at the tower of Babel (Genesis 11:1-9) served to separate people by language, which God devised and assigned to the families of humankind. It is said that language, more than any other difference, serves to divide people yet today.

God's first message to Abraham occurred while he was still in Ur of the Chaldees. There are several sites named Ur, with the traditional site of Abraham being the one in southern Mesopotamia (Acts 7:2). It was a city with sanitary sewers, schools, and the worship of a moon god and goddess. This was a very modern city in the twenty-first century BC when Abraham left to become a sojourner.

Abraham's obedient response to leave with his family is a positive example of faith, for he did not know where God was leading him (Hebrews

11:8). The family traveled toward northwestern Mesopotamia, finally stopping in Haran (Genesis 11:31). [See question #1, page 24.]

It is interesting that both Ur and Haran are known as centers of worship for a moon god and goddess. Idolatry eventually was common after the flood, and it was even practiced by Abraham's father and brother (Joshua 24:2). Some, however, did maintain a genuine faith. (It is often assumed that Job lived during this time, and his faith is highly exemplary.)

When God selected Abraham, He chose a man without children, land, or reputation. To such a person God is ready to promise a son, a land, and greatness!

I. Promises to Abraham (Genesis 17:1-8, 15, 16)

Abraham, Isaac, and Jacob, patriarchs in the book of Genesis, receive promises by God on different occasions. God gives messages to Abraham several times in Genesis (12:1-3, 7; 13:14-17; 15:4, 5, 13-18; 17:1-22; 18:17-33; 22:15-18). Acts 7:2 indicates an earlier contact before the family leaves Ur.

Similar promises are given twice to Isaac (Genesis 26:4, 24) and Jacob (Genesis 28:14, 15; 35:9-12). As we open our lesson, we remember that Abraham's name originally was Abram (Genesis 17:5, below).

A. Name for God (vv. 1, 2)

1. And when Abram was ninety years old and nine, the LORD appeared to Abram, and said unto him, I am the Almighty God; walk before me, and be thou perfect.

How to Say It

ABRAHAM. *Ay*-bruh-ham.
ABRAM. *Ay*-brum.
BABEL. *Bay*-bul.
CANAAN. *Kay*-nun.
CHALDEES. *Kal*-deez.
ESAU. *Ee*-saw.
HAGAR. *Hay*-gar.
HARAN. *Hair*-un.
ISAAC. *Eye*-zuk.
ISHMAEL. *Ish*-may-el.
JACOB. *Jay*-kub.
KETURAH. Keh-*too*-ruh.
MESOPOTAMIA. *Mes*-uh-puh-*tay*-me-uh
   (strong accent on *tay*).
MESSIAH. Meh-*sigh*-uh.

The factor of Abram's age is of interest. He was 75 when he, Lot (his nephew), and others departed from Haran to go to the land of Canaan (Genesis 12:4, 5). When Abraham was 85, his wife suggested that perhaps she could have children through Hagar, her handmaid (16:2, 3). Abraham accepted the proposal, which was a contemporary practice for a wife who was barren. Ishmael was born when Abraham was 86 (16:16).

Such statistics interest some people, but the message underneath them is very important: God keeps His promises, but the time of waiting may be a testing of the patience and faith of those who are the recipients of the promises. In this case Abram and his wife Sarai were "running ahead" of God instead of waiting for His time. [See question #2, page 24.]

The Lord identifies himself with His first words to Abram. He is not just *God,* but He is *Almighty.* [See question #3, page 24.] This God is one who can accomplish things that are considered impossible. Over 1,400 years later Jeremiah will echo the same thought when he writes that nothing is too difficult for God (Jeremiah 32:17).

Two imperatives are used by the Lord to express His expectations. First, Abram is to *walk before* God. Second, his walk must be unblemished; Abram is to do his best in meeting his obligations to God.

"WHAT'S IN A NAME?"

In the early 1960s General Motors tried unsuccessfully to sell its new, economical compact model the *Nova* in Latin America. The problem, it seems, was that the name *Nova* means "no go" in Spanish. After GM changed the car's name to *Caribe,* sales took off—at least so the story goes. Actually, this is one of those urban legends we hear from time to time. For one thing, sales weren't really that bad, and the Caribe was sold by Volkswagen (www.snopes.com). However, this story has gained lots of "mileage" (pardon the pun) by being repeated many times in marketing textbooks and business seminars.

Let's try another one. When Coca-Cola entered the Chinese market, it had to find Mandarin characters that sounded like "Coca-Cola." The characters they chose could mean "to allow the mouth to be able to rejoice" but could also be translated "bite the wax tadpole." Hmmm.

Whether or not either story is true, in the final analysis their very existence points to the fact that names are important. So it was with the name by which God revealed himself to Abram. Abram's culture believed in many gods, but the God who spoke to Abram was the Almighty God!

He was significantly different from the fictitious gods that people worshiped. He was—and is— the God who has power and who makes covenants with those who believe Him.   —C. R. B.

2. And I will make my covenant between me and thee, and will multiply thee exceedingly.

This is the first of 13 uses of the word *covenant* in this chapter. It is used only once with Abram prior to this chapter, in Genesis 15:18. In that chapter God specifically promises that Abram will have a son and that his descendants will be as numerous as the stars (Genesis 15:5).

The words *will* or *shall* accompany many of God's blessings as given in this chapter. This construction shows that the fulfillments are in the future, but God will keep His promises.

B. Nations to Result (vv. 3, 4)

3, 4. And Abram fell on his face: and God talked with him, saying, As for me, behold, my covenant is with thee, and thou shalt be a father of many nations.

Abram's immediate response is to fall and assume a position of utmost respect. The implications of what the Lord has just said are racing through his mind, and he is overwhelmed! God's next words reinforce the thought that Abram is to have many descendants.

An excellent commentary on Abram's thoughts can be found in Romans 4:19, 20. In these verses Paul states that Abraham was not weak in faith, even as he considered his own body and his wife's womb to be dead. The God who created life in the beginning could do the same again for this elderly couple!

In verse 4 God states that the covenant being made is with Abram, and one outcome is that *many nations* will result. The factor of *nations* (plural) is a new concept. The singular form of the word is used in Genesis 12:2, so this adds a dimension to the promises that God is making.

Of course, living in the twenty-first century AD means that we are aware of the historical fulfillment of this prophecy. But it must be a staggering thought for Abram in the twenty-first century BC! Some of the descendants of Abram who will produce many sons include Ishmael and the six sons that Abraham had by his second wife, Keturah (Genesis 25:1, 2).

C. New Name for Abram (v. 5a)

5a. Neither shall thy name any more be called Abram, but thy name shall be Abraham.

A new name is given to *Abram*, and it is very meaningful as a part of this covenant. Whereas *Abram* means "exalted father," the name *Abraham* means "father of a multitude." This new name itself is a challenging part of this expanded covenant.

The exact nature of this exchange between God and Abraham is not given; it may have been a personal, private event. One can only wonder at the responses of others when Abraham tells them that his name is now "father of a multitude." Abraham has a private army (Genesis 14:14); when those men think of Abraham as a childless, elderly man, how can they use his new name without a snicker?

D. Nations and the Kings (vv. 5b, 6)

5b, 6. For a father of many nations have I made thee. And I will make thee exceeding fruitful, and I will make nations of thee, and kings shall come out of thee.

The thought that Abraham will be a *father of many nations* is repeated from verse 4. This time the concept is amplified: Abraham's descendants will be *exceeding fruitful.*

Abraham's offspring will also include kings. This is a new factor, not mentioned previously. Moses (the author of Genesis) will later record the names of several kings who are descendants of Abraham's grandson Esau (Genesis 36:31-39). Students of biblical history are aware of Saul, David, Solomon, and other kings who trace their lineage to Abraham (Matthew 1:2-11). God's promises do come to pass! [See question #4, page 24.]

E. People of the Covenant (v. 7)

7. And I will establish my covenant between me and thee and thy seed after thee in their generations, for an everlasting covenant, to be a God unto thee, and to thy seed after thee.

This special *covenant* relationship will continue into the future for the children of Abraham, for it is *an everlasting covenant.* It must first be noted that the applications of these phrases are restricted: in this same chapter the descendants of Ishmael are excluded, in spite of Abraham's expressed thought that the covenant could be fulfilled in him (vv. 18-21, below).

This verse also allows us to compare the use the word *seed* in the *King James Version* with the word *descendants* in the *New International Version.* The selection of the word *seed* seems to be better, for Paul uses the fact that it is singular to show that the ultimate fulfillment is a spiritual one in Christ, that He is the promised seed (Galatians 3:16; compare Acts 3:25).

The same word occurs again in Genesis 22:18. There the promise takes a phrase from Genesis

12:3 and states that it is through Abraham's seed that all the families of the earth will be blessed. The beauty of the apostles' argument is that all people now have access to the spiritual blessings that the redemptive work of the Messiah makes available.

F. Place Assigned (v. 8)

8. And I will give unto thee, and to thy seed after thee, the land wherein thou art a stranger, all the land of Canaan, for an everlasting possession; and I will be their God.

The land of Canaan had been promised to Abraham previously (Genesis 12:5, 7; 15:18). These words from God provide a further confirmation of that promise. There is a certain irony here: it has been 24 years since Abraham entered Canaan (compare Genesis 12:4, 5; 17:1), and so far Abraham does not possess any of it. God told Abraham previously that his descendants would be oppressed 400 years in another land, and in the fourth generation they would occupy Canaan when the iniquity of the inhabitants was full (Genesis 15:13, 16). [See question #5, page 24.]

G. Position for Sarai (vv. 15, 16)

15, 16. And God said unto Abraham, As for Sarai thy wife, thou shalt not call her name Sarai, but Sarah shall her name be. And I will bless her, and give thee a son also of her: yea, I will bless her, and she shall be a mother of nations; kings of people shall be of her.

The intervening verses record the establishment of circumcision as a sign of the covenant for Abraham's male descendants. Now the role of *Sarai* in the promises is expressed for the first time. God begins by changing *her name* for the role that she will have in redemptive history: to become the *mother of nations* and *kings*. This will have its beginning in her own *son*, Isaac.

The meanings of the names *Sarai* and *Sarah* seem to be the same, but there is the difference in spelling. Both names mean "princess."

II. Perplexities of Abraham (Genesis 17:17-22)

Abraham finally has an opportunity to express his reactions. Those reactions concern two people: Sarah and Ishmael.

A. Problems Stated (vv. 17, 18)

17. Then Abraham fell upon his face, and laughed, and said in his heart, Shall a child be born unto him that is a hundred years old? and shall Sarah, that is ninety years old, bear?

Visual for
Lessons 2 & 12

Keep this map posted throughout the quarter to help set the geographical context.

Abraham's emotional response is laughter. The fact that *Sarah* is to become a mother goes beyond what is humanly reasonable. If God is in it, however, then it becomes reasonable!

Abraham projects the promises a year into the future, the earliest time for a son to be born. Abraham will then be 100 and Sarah will be 90, and he inwardly wonders about what he has just heard. Could it possibly be true?

18. And Abraham said unto God, O that Ishmael might live before thee!

At this time *Ishmael* is 13 years old (compare Abraham's age in Genesis 16:16 and 17:1). Abraham loves this young teenager and states that he is willing to accept him as the child of promise. In his humility he does not demand that God go to any special trouble.

B. Problems Solved (vv. 19-22)

19. And God said, Sarah thy wife shall bear thee a son indeed; and thou shalt call his name Isaac: and I will establish my covenant with him for an everlasting covenant, and with his seed after him.

God speaks and assures Abraham that *Sarah* is the one who will bear the son who will fulfill the promise. In addition, God continues to provide names for the people involved, and He states that the son is to be called *Isaac*. The name *Isaac* means "laugh," and it will ever serve as a reminder of Abraham's reaction when he heard the prediction.

The *I will* statements of this section continue. God asserts that it is through Isaac that the everlasting covenant is to be established and that it will continue for generations *after him*.

20. And as for Ishmael, I have heard thee: Behold, I have blessed him, and will make him fruitful, and will multiply him exceedingly; twelve princes shall he beget, and I will make him a great nation.

God assures Abraham that his concerns for *Ishmael* have been *heard* and that blessings are included for *him*. They are similar in nature to the promises of the covenant. But limitations are set concerning the number of future leaders among his descendants *(twelve princes)*. The final promise is that Ishmael's descendants will become *a great nation.*

21. But my covenant will I establish with Isaac, which Sarah shall bear unto thee at this set time in the next year.

The closing words of God in this account restate the factors that are to have imminent fulfillments: that the *covenant* is to be continued through *Isaac,* that *Sarah* is to be the mother, and that these things will occur *the next year.* One can only wonder concerning Abraham's final reflections and actions: will they be outwardly exuberant and joyful, silent and profound contemplation, or overwhelming gratitude? It will take time for the reality of the promises to be grasped fully.

UNINTENTIONAL FRAUD

Alceo Dossena (1878–1937) was a stonemason from northern Italy. He became skilled at carving reproductions of sculptures from ancient times, and his work was so good that others began selling his carvings as genuine antiques. Despite Dossena's best efforts to spread the truth of the matter, dealers in antiquities continued the fraud since they were reaping handsome profits. So many pieces of his work were in circulation as genuine that it became impossible to trace them all. It is said that some of Dossena's copies are accepted as genuine antiquities yet today.

With the best of motives, Abraham and Sarah also perpetrated an unintentional fraud. They had received God's promise of a son as a sign of God's covenant with them. Time went by, and still there was no pregnancy. Their solution was for Abraham to have a son by Sarah's servant girl, Hagar.

The consequences of their decision were far-reaching. We see the effects today in strife in the Middle East, as some elements of religious extremism claim covenantal blessings through Ishmael. Although the child Ishmael would be blessed by God, he was not the "genuine article"—the son of the covenantal promise. We always get into trouble when we try to push God's timetable!
—C. R. B.

22. And he left off talking with him, and God went up from Abraham.

God departs from Abraham, and this brings to a conclusion this stage of Abraham's developing role in the covenant. There are more interactions to follow, but the new factors are overwhelming.

Conclusion

A. If It Sounds Too Good . . .

If it sounds too good to be true, it probably is—unless God is in it. The covenant that God made with Abraham offered promises that another human could not deliver. It is comforting to know that God did not hold the negative reactions of Abraham and Sarah against them. Their reservations did not thwart God's redemptive plan.

It is God's plan to provide Heaven for all the redeemed. That's something that sounds just too good to be true, but it is true. It sounds too good to be true that God forgives and forgets the sins of the redeemed, but God does that—even though we tend to burden ourselves with memories of our failures.

God offers Heaven to sinners who believe on His Son and follow His plan of salvation. That sounds too good to be true—but it is true!

B. Prayer

Thank You, Lord, for the trials of life that develop patience. Forgive my lack of trust in those times. In the name of Your Son, amen.

C. Thought to Remember

Trust God despite your doubts.

Home Daily Bible Readings

Monday, Sept. 4—God's Promise Is Sure (Hebrews 6:13-20)

Tuesday, Sept. 5—Abraham Had Heroic Faith (Hebrews 11:8-16)

Wednesday, Sept. 6—God's Promise to Abram (Genesis 15:1-6)

Thursday, Sept. 7—God Foretells Future Greatness (Genesis 15:12-21)

Friday, Sept. 8—God Blesses Hagar (Genesis 16:1-15)

Saturday, Sept. 9—God Covenants with Abraham (Genesis 17:1-8)

Sunday, Sept. 10—God Promises a Son (Genesis 17:15-22)

Learning by Doing

This page contains an alternative lesson plan emphasizing learning activities.
Classes desiring such student involvement will find these suggestions helpful.

Learning Goals

After participating in this lesson, each student will be able to:

1. Retell the promises of God's covenant with Abraham.

2. Compare and contrast with his or her own life both the faith and the doubt expressed by Abraham.

3. Suggest a specific area in his or her life where applying a faith like Abraham's can make (or is making) a difference.

Into the Lesson

Several years ago, a Christian singer made her song "El Shaddai" a top tune. The words recited many of the biblical names of God, and so the song has remained popular for devotional and worship occasions. Obtain a recording of that song (by any artist) and play it for the class as your study session begins.

Say, "When God comes to Abram in verse 1 of today's text in Genesis 17, *El Shaddai* is the way God identifies himself. 'Almighty God' or 'God Almighty' are the common ways that that name is translated into English." Highlight that concept by asking, "Why is this name that God chooses for himself especially appropriate on the occasion of Genesis 17?" (Use the commentary to enhance your students' responses.)

Into the Word

Say, "Abram's given name reflects the optimism of his parents and perhaps the work of the Holy Spirit. Abram's name means 'exalted father,' yet for more than 80 years he fathered no children at all. For such a childless one to become a father, indeed an 'exalted father,' shows the grace and power of God the Father."

Give a half sheet of paper and a pencil to each student. Ask students to write "Exalted Father" at the top of their papers. Then instruct students to make a list indicating how Abram became "Father of _____," using today's text or their own general knowledge of Abraham, his life, and his physical and spiritual heritage.

Give students one example: "Father of Isaac," from verse 17 of today's text. Indicate to the class that they can coin their own labels if they can explain their reasoning. Here are other such des-

ignations, from the text and elsewhere: "Father of the Century" (v. 1 and Abram's age); "Father of the Covenant" (v. 2); "Father of Many Nations" (v. 4); "Father of a Multitude" (per lesson writer's note on Abram's new God-given name); "Father of Kings" (v. 6); "Father of the Everlasting Covenant" (v. 7); "Father of the Land" (v. 8); "Father of Laughter" (v. 17 and Isaac's name); "Father of the Faithful" (traditional); "Father of Division" (based on later animosity of the descendants of the two sons); "Father of Twenty-First-Century Conflict" (based on tensions and hatreds between various religious factions today).

Give students eight to ten minutes to compile their lists, then compare and contrast lists. Be sure to get explanation for any that are unclear to you or appear to be unclear to others.

Into Life

Ask, "If you had a faith like Abraham's, what would you do for God?" Accept general answers, then give each student a printed sheet with these completion statements: (1) "By faith [student's name], when called to _____, obeyed and _____." (2) "By faith [student's name], when God tested him/her, offered _____." (3) "By faith [student's name], was looking forward to _____."

Read Hebrews 11:8-19 to the class and suggest that they use this passage as a pattern for their responses.

As an alternative activity, label Abraham's faith as a "countercultural faith." Read Hebrews 11:8-19 and ask, "What exactly did Abraham believe about God that is unlike the common belief system of the twenty-first century?" Accept reasonable responses, but insert the following answers if they are not identified by the group: (1) Abraham believed God was capable of giving life to a dead body; (2) Abraham believed that no matter where he was that God would provide for his needs; (3) Abraham believed God was capable of overcoming the laws of nature; (4) Abraham believed he did not have to understand fully everything about God and His will.

Finish the discussion by asking, "How is your belief system? Is it culturally biased, or is it culturally free?" (If your class uses the student books, consider the Abraham's Child activity as a concluding experience.)

Let's Talk It Over

The questions on this page are designed to promote discussion of the lesson by the class and to encourage application of the lesson Scriptures. The answers provided are only discussion starters. Let your class talk it over from there.

1. Just as God called Abraham to move out by faith, so He continues to desire that Christians walk by faith today. In what areas do you need to do a little more "faith-walking"? How do you know when you've crossed the line into foolishly walking by blind faith?

Walking by faith, not by sight, occurs when we put the will of God first in our lives. Walking by faith will show our trust that He really does exist and is in charge. In the way we use our money and time, for example, we demonstrate who really controls our lives.

Perhaps you know of someone who needs to hear the message of salvation through Christ. God may very well be calling you to be the agent through whom this person is taught. God may be calling you to give more time to a certain ministry in your church. The call of God upon our lives may be to deny ourselves something we desire so that the money spent on self can be used to help advance God's kingdom on earth. All this requires walking by faith.

The faith by which we walk is a faith based on evidence from the past: God has proven His existence and His trustworthiness. We foolishly begin to walk by blind faith when our actions are not grounded in these facts. Stepping out of a third-story window and expecting God to save us is an example. God is quite consistent in the way He allows the law of gravity to operate!

2. Our timing often is not God's timing, nor is God's timing ours. What was an occasion in your life when you tried to force your timing on God? How did things turn out?

We often want to tell God what we want and when we want it. God may be delaying the answer to test our patience or our ability to trust Him. Since God knows all things from beginning to end, He knows what is best for us in the long run. When we press forward trying to "answer" our own prayers in our time, we preempt God's plan for greater blessings. Failure to wait upon God and trust His timing is to fail to allow God's sufficient grace to have its work.

3. Five years ago tomorrow is a day etched in history. The September 11, 2001, terrorist attacks in New York City, Washington, DC, and Pennsylvania challenged the faith of many. How do you hold to the truth that God is the Almighty in the face of such atrocities?

We must understand that we live in a fallen world where God has granted us the choice to sin or not sin. Sinful atrocities do not find their source in God but rather in Satan.

Remembering God's promise that He will be faithful to us is imperative. Remembering also how God has demonstrated His power through history, beginning with creation and continuing through the resurrection of Christ, reminds us that God is indeed the all-powerful one. The words of the psalmist that the shepherd will be with us even in the valley of the shadow of death will help us to face the difficulties of life.

4. Covenants are based upon promises. These include promises of commitment on the part of both parties entering into the covenant. What promises of God, revealed in both His old and new covenants, help you to face life daily?

God has promised to give comfort (Isaiah 51:3) as well as hope (Hebrews 6:18, 19). God has promised that those who go forth with weeping for the master will return to Him with rejoicing (Psalm 126:6). In John 10:10 God has promised abundant life to His people. God has promised that those who seek first His kingdom will receive all things they need (Matthew 6:33). The list could go on!

5. We jokingly say, "God, give me patience and give it to me *now*!" When there is a delay in our receiving something, our faith and patience are put to the test. In what ways has your patience, and the patience of your church, been put to the test?

Answers are wide open! Sometimes we have financial hardships, personally or as a church. We want them to be taken care of now while God perhaps wants to test our patience and trust in Him. Sometimes it may be a prodigal child who causes our patience to be tested. Patience can be tested in a church when difficult people create tensions. But through all of these trials, God is not the one who will be unfaithful!

God's Covenant with Israel

DEVOTIONAL READING: **Psalm 119:33-40.**

BACKGROUND SCRIPTURE: **Exodus 19:1-6; 24:3-8.**

PRINTED TEXT: **Exodus 19:1-6; 24:3-8.**

Exodus 19:1-6

1 In the third month, when the children of Israel were gone forth out of the land of Egypt, the same day came they into the wilderness of Sinai.

2 For they were departed from Rephidim, and were come to the desert of Sinai, and had pitched in the wilderness; and there Israel camped before the mount.

3 And Moses went up unto God, and the LORD called unto him out of the mountain, saying, Thus shalt thou say to the house of Jacob, and tell the children of Israel;

4 Ye have seen what I did unto the Egyptians, and how I bare you on eagles' wings, and brought you unto myself.

5 Now therefore, if ye will obey my voice indeed, and keep my covenant, then ye shall be a peculiar treasure unto me above all people: for all the earth is mine:

6 And ye shall be unto me a kingdom of priests, and a holy nation. These are the words which thou shalt speak unto the children of Israel.

Exodus 24:3-8

3 And Moses came and told the people all the words of the LORD, and all the judgments: and all the people answered with one voice, and said, All the words which the LORD hath said will we do.

4 And Moses wrote all the words of the LORD, and rose up early in the morning, and builded an altar under the hill, and twelve pillars, according to the twelve tribes of Israel.

5 And he sent young men of the children of Israel, which offered burnt offerings, and sacrificed peace offerings of oxen unto the LORD.

6 And Moses took half of the blood, and put it in basins; and half of the blood he sprinkled on the altar.

7 And he took the book of the covenant, and read in the audience of the people: and they said, All that the LORD hath said will we do, and be obedient.

8 And Moses took the blood, and sprinkled it on the people, and said, Behold the blood of the covenant, which the LORD hath made with you concerning all these words.

GOLDEN TEXT: Ye shall be a peculiar treasure unto me above all people: for all the earth is mine: and ye shall be unto me a kingdom of priests, and a holy nation. These are the words which thou shalt speak unto the children of Israel.
—Exodus 19:5b, 6.

God's Living Covenant
Unit 1: God's Covenant with the Patriarchs
(Lessons 1-4)

Lesson Aims

After participating in this lesson, each student will be able to:

1. Describe the covenant relationship that God designed for Old Testament Israel.

2. Discuss the meaning and importance of God's covenant relationship with Old Testament Israel.

3. State one specific way he or she will demonstrate greater faithfulness to the new covenant.

Lesson Outline

INTRODUCTION
   A. Keeping Your Word
   B. Lesson Background
  I. ARRIVAL AT SINAI (Exodus 19:1, 2)
   A. Departure Remembered (v. 1)
   B. Destination Reached (v. 2)
 II. ANNOUNCEMENTS AT SINAI (Exodus 19:3-6)
   A. Ascent by Moses (v. 3)
   B. Assertions by the Lord (vv. 4-6)
     A Treasured Possession
III. ACCEPTING THE COVENANT (Exodus 24:3-8)
   A. Resolve of the People (v. 3)
     Promises, Promises
   B. Responses by Moses (vv. 4-7a)
   C. Ratification Completed (vv. 7b, 8)
CONCLUSION
   A. Setting Your Priorities
   B. Prayer
   C. Thought to Remember

Introduction

A. Keeping Your Word

Governor William Penn arrived in North America on October 27, 1682. One of his first actions was to confer with the leaders of nearby Indians. Penn and his men arrived unarmed, as did the Indians. Penn spoke through an interpreter and gave the principles that he intended to follow. Penn said that since they were all of one flesh and blood, and therefore brothers, they would settle any disputes in council, not with warfare. There would be openness and love. One account notes that the Indian chiefs said that as long as the rivers ran and the sun shone that they would live in peace with Penn's children.

For over 70 years there were no battle cries between the two groups. It is easy to conclude that the original participants kept the words that they had spoken as a treaty or covenant.

When an individual becomes a Christian, he or she becomes a part of the new covenant that is provided through Christ. It is evident that many people want the benefits of the covenant, but they do not desire to fulfill their covenantal obligations. To keep one's commitment to Christ seems to have an extremely low priority—unless there is a crisis, and then prayers and laments are expressed that implore God to hear and answer the prayers.

The conscientious person will always try to keep his or her word. Whether that word is simply spoken, involves a handshake, is a lengthy business contract, concerns marriage vows, or confesses Jesus as Lord: keep your word!

B. Lesson Background

The statistics given in Genesis and Exodus show that there are 621 years between the lesson of last week (Genesis 17, which states that Abraham was 99 years old) and the initial giving of the law through Moses at Mount Sinai. The first of the 621 years is the time between the promise of Isaac's birth and its fulfillment when Abraham was 100 years old.

Three references account for the other 620 years. Isaac's age is given as 60 when Jacob is born (Genesis 25:26). Jacob, upon the occasion of his family's entering Egypt, states that he is 130 years old (47:9). Finally, Exodus 12:40, 41 states that the Israelites spent 430 years in Egypt.

Many familiar events of biblical history are within that period of 620 years. With the help of his mother, Rebekah, Jacob deceived his father in order to receive the patriarchal blessing. Jacob was compelled to flee from the wrath of his brother, and he goes to Padan-aram to find a wife. (He never saw his mother again.) Jacob himself was deceived by his Uncle Laban: on Jacob's wedding night he received Leah as his wife instead of Rachel—the younger sister for whom he had worked seven years. After one week Rachel became his wife also. These two women plus their two handmaids became the mothers of the 12 sons of Jacob.

The providential work of God shows itself in the fascinating account of Joseph being sold into slavery by his brothers. Joseph rose to be second-in-command of Egypt. In a time of famine,

Joseph was able to provide for his father, his 11 brothers, and their families.

The Israelites entered Egypt as a family, but 430 years later they left as a nation. The military census of men over age 20 totaled 603,550, and that did not include the tribe of Levi (Numbers 1:46, 47).

Moses became the leader of that nation. The events of his birth, exile at age 40, and his initial call by God at age 80 are thrilling to read. The 10 plagues credentialed Moses' leadership for the nation. They demonstrated to the Egyptians that the God of Israel was the only God. As a result, the pharaoh finally allowed this "nation of slaves" to begin its journey back to the land that had been promised to Abraham.

In Exodus 12 several things of importance were noted. First, instructions were given so that the Israelites could be spared the death of their firstborn in the tenth plague. Second, the departure from Egypt gave rise to the Passover and the Feast of Unleavened Bread (Exodus 12:14, 15, 43-49; 13:3-10). Third, the Lord announced that the nation of Israel was to have its own calendar, beginning with the month that they left Egypt (Exodus 12:2). It was a lunar calendar, with each new moon marking the beginning of a month.

I. Arrival at Sinai
(Exodus 19:1, 2)

As our lesson opens, the year is about 1446 BC.

A. Departure Remembered (v. 1)

1. In the third month, when the children of Israel were gone forth out of the land of Egypt, the same day came they into the wilderness of Sinai.

How to Say It

AARON. *Air*-un.
ABRAHAM. *Ay*-bruh-ham.
AMALEKITES. *Am*-uh-leh-kites or Uh-*mal*-ih-kites.
ISAAC. *Eye*-zuk.
JACOB. *Jay*-kub.
LABAN. *Lay*-bun.
LEVI. *Lee*-vye.
LEVITICUS. Leh-*vit*-ih-kus.
MIDIAN. *Mid*-ee-un.
MOSES. *Mo*-zes or *Mo*-zez.
PADAN-ARAM. *Pay*-dan-*a*-ram.
REBEKAH. Reh-*bek*-uh.
REPHIDIM. *Ref*-ih-dim.

The experiences of the Israelites after leaving *Egypt* involved several miracles that should have developed trust in the Lord. These mighty works of God included the pillar of fire or cloud (Exodus 13:21; 40:36), the crossing of the Red Sea (Exodus 14), the making of bitter water into sweet water (15:25), the provisions of manna in the mornings and quail in the evenings (16:12), Moses' striking of a rock to produce water (17:6), and an unusual method of victory over enemies (17:11-13).

The Israelites reach the area *of Sinai* in the *third month*. The exact meaning of that phrase is uncertain. Does it mean the first day of the third month, or does it imply that it is exactly three months since leaving Egypt? The traditional view is that it is the first day of the third month.

B. Destination Reached (v. 2)

2. For they were departed from Rephidim, and were come to the desert of Sinai, and had pitched in the wilderness; and there Israel camped before the mount.

Three major events occur after the Israelites reach *Rephidim* (Exodus 17, 18). This is (1) where the Israelites receive water from a rock, (2) where they are victorious over the Amalekites, and (3) where Moses receives advice from his father-in-law on the importance of delegating leadership duties to others.

The arrival at *Sinai* fulfills the promise that was made to Moses. In this very place he had turned aside to see the burning bush (Exodus 3:2, 4). God had promised the sign that when Moses brought the people out of Egypt that he would serve God here.

The exact location of Mount Sinai is uncertain. About 15 different sites are suggested! Recently a theory has been proposed that a certain mountain in Saudi Arabia (ancient Midian) could be Mount Sinai, but access to it is denied for any thorough investigation.

The Israelite nation spends almost a year at Sinai. It is interesting that archaeologists are not able to find evidence of such an encampment at the traditional site. The important fact is that the events recorded did take place, even if archaeology cannot accurately determine the location.

II. Announcements at Sinai
(Exodus 19:3-6)

This new nation needs a constitution—a covenant to guide them in their daily living before God and with their fellow humans. Sinai is the place where it is to be given.

A. Ascent by Moses (v. 3)

3. And Moses went up unto God, and the LORD called unto him out of the mountain, saying, Thus shalt thou say to the house of Jacob, and tell the children of Israel.

What a privilege it is to be addressed personally by God himself! But with great privilege comes great responsibility. God isn't just making small talk with Moses. God has a vital message to deliver *to the house of Jacob, and . . . the children of Israel.* [See question #1, page 32.]

The expression *house of Jacob* is used only here in the writings of Moses. The phrase *the children of Israel* is probably just a parallel expression of the previous phrase. This is typical of Hebrew literature. If there is any significance in the difference, it may be a subtle reminder that to be able to change another person's name (as God changed Jacob's name to Israel in Genesis 32:28; 35:10) indicates that you are superior to that person. (See examples in 2 Kings 23:34; 24:17.) By using both terms, God may be asserting that He has the right to grant covenants. He is both God and Lord!

B. Assertions by the Lord (vv. 4-6)

4. Ye have seen what I did unto the Egyptians, and how I bare you on eagles' wings, and brought you unto myself.

The opening phrase *Ye have seen what I did unto the Egyptians* is a reminder that the Lord has the credentials to provide a covenant. The second assertion *how I bare you on eagles' wings* is a reminder of how God has provided for the Israelites' every need on the journey to Sinai (compare Deuteronomy 32:11). The implication

Visual for
Lesson 3

This timeline will remind your students of God's patient watchfulness through the centuries.

usually given is that an eagle may force its young out of the nest to compel flight, but the older eagle is ready to catch the fledgling bird if necessary. In a similar way the Lord has provided care for His people. [See question #2, page 32.]

5. Now therefore, if ye will obey my voice indeed, and keep my covenant, then ye shall be a peculiar treasure unto me above all people: for all the earth is mine.

The little word *if* indicates that the Lord is ready to announce the stipulations of the *covenant.* The requirement is that Israel is to *obey* the Lord and *keep* the covenant's terms. Accepting and entering into a covenantal relationship is often rather simple. It is the keeping of a covenant over an extended period of time that becomes difficult! [See question #3, page 32.]

The first stated blessing is that Israel will be elevated above other nations *(above all people).* God does not, however, surrender His control over the nations, for the final phrase is a reminder that God owns the entire *earth.*

The expression *peculiar treasure* may refer to a valuable possession owned by a king. The concept shows the special relationship that God's people have. In the New Testament the concept is applied to Christians (Ephesians 1:14; Titus 2:14; 1 Peter 2:9).

6. And ye shall be unto me a kingdom of priests, and a holy nation. These are the words which thou shalt speak unto the children of Israel.

The second blessing of the pending covenant is that *Israel* will be a *kingdom of priests.* A priest has access to God in prayer. This concept is also applied to Christians in 1 Peter 2:9 and Revelation 5:10. [See question #4, page 32.]

The final phrase that Moses delivers is a challenge for Israel to be *a holy nation.* God's holiness is foundational. Those who serve God are commanded to be holy as He is holy (Leviticus 11:44, 45; 1 Peter 1:16).

A TREASURED POSSESSION

If you ever stand in the check-out line at the grocery store, you know the name of Anna Nicole Smith from the tabloids. While working as an "exotic dancer" in 1991 at age 23, she met J. Howard Marshall II, age 86. They married in 1994; he died about a year later. Very quickly, the legal fight for the "treasured possession" of Marshall's $780 million estate began. Smith claimed her husband had promised her half of his estate.

After six years, a court awarded her $475 million. Another court subsequently ruled in favor of Marshall's son and left Smith with no money. Still another court later ruled in her favor and gave her $88.5 million. Then in 2004, that ruling was reversed and Smith was again without an inheritance. As they say at the end of some television programs, "To be continued"!

Israel was to become God's treasured possession, a concept that cannot be valued in monetary terms—not $88.5 million, not $475 million, not $780 million! But along with privilege came the responsibility to be a holy nation. Sadly, this was a duty that the people failed to perform. God's covenants contain both duty and privilege. Our covenant with God through Christ is no different from the others in this respect. "Be ye holy; for I am holy" (1 Peter 1:16).   —C. R. B.

III. Accepting the Covenant (Exodus 24:3-8)

The material between the two segments of today's lesson contains the covenant's fundamentals, including the Ten Commandments. The Israelites may be free from their slavery in Egypt, but this new freedom must be accompanied by virtuous living. Otherwise, chaos and anarchy will be the result.

A. Resolve of the People (v. 3)

3. And Moses came and told the people all the words of the LORD, and all the judgments: and all the people answered with one voice, and said, All the words which the LORD hath said will we do.

The first two verses of the chapter tell of yet another trip up the mountain by *Moses,* and this time he was accompanied by others. When Moses descends the mountain, his purpose is to tell *the people* all that God has prescribed. [See question #5, page 32.] The people pledge their obedience *with one voice.* This is the second such affirmation by the people (see Exodus 19:8 for the first one).

PROMISES, PROMISES

If you plan to lie to someone, make sure you aren't near an MRI machine! Magnetic Resonance Imaging can show a difference in brain activity between liars and truth tellers.

A 2004 study at Temple University School of Medicine showed that different parts of the brain are used for lying and truth telling. Seven areas of the brain were activated in subjects who lied and only four were used in the brains of those who told the truth. One conclusion drawn from the study was that it takes more work to lie than

to tell the truth. And that's not counting the work it takes telling more lies to cover up the first one!

We've all heard the phrase *promises, promises* spoken with sarcasm and disdain when someone has a history of not keeping his or her word. We don't know whether the Israelites were telling the truth when they gave multiple assurances to Moses that they would do whatever God commanded them to do. Probably they were sincere.

Yet we all know how easy it is to make promises under the influence of a moment's emotional pressure and then forsake the promise when the moment is gone or when other pressures are at work on us. God could well have responded, "Promises, promises!" Israel's example should be a caution to us about the need to speak the truth and then faithfully follow through with what we have vowed to do.   —C. R. B.

B. Responses by Moses (vv. 4-7a)

4. And Moses wrote all the words of the LORD, and rose up early in the morning, and builded an altar under the hill, and twelve pillars, according to the twelve tribes of Israel.

Three responses by Moses are given. First, he *wrote* what the Lord had communicated through him. In the past it was sometimes taught that Moses may have used picture writing because at this time in history alphabetic writing is not yet developed. Such a theory is now proven to be invalid because examples of alphabetic writing have been found from the era in which Moses lived and even before his time. In 1999 the earliest alphabetic writing discovered to date was found in Upper Egypt. It is dated to around 1900 or 1800 BC, hundreds of years before the exodus (see www.jhu.edu and www.archaeology.org).

Since Moses was trained in all the learning of Egypt (Acts 7:22), his writing with an alphabet is not a problem. If you had lived a century ago, you would have been hard pressed to answer the critics on this issue. One lesson from this is that it is essential to maintain your faith against such attacks. You may not have the answers personally; however, in the places where God's Word can be tested against the evidence of archaeology, the integrity of the Bible is validated.

After writing, Moses begins work *early* the next day to construct an *altar.* He also erects *twelve pillars* (or standing pillars), one for each of the *tribes of Israel.* These pillars not only represent the tribes, but they seem to become a part of the ratification of the new covenant (see v. 8, below).

5. And he sent young men of the children of Israel, which offered burnt offerings, and sacrificed peace offerings of oxen unto the LORD.

Aaron (Moses' brother) and his sons are not yet functioning as priests; that won't come until Exodus 28. So Moses commissions *young men of the children of Israel* to offer *burnt offerings* and *peace offerings*. Ordinarily, a burnt offering is completely burned (Leviticus 1). For the peace offering, however, only a portion is burned, and the remainder becomes something of a fellowship meal (Leviticus 3). This sharing is a part of the ceremony of commitment. The fact that blood is shed to confirm the covenant adds to the solemnity and seriousness of the event.

6. And Moses took half of the blood, and put it in basins; and half of the blood he sprinkled on the altar.

The reason for taking *half of the blood* and putting *it in basins* will be made clear in verse 8, below. For now, the other half of the blood is *sprinkled on the altar,* perhaps to sanctify it.

7a. And he took the book of the covenant, and read in the audience of the people.

The things that Moses had written are now read in the presence of *the people* (or at least before the leaders). The phrase *book of the covenant* is the designation for this early form of the covenant (compare 2 Kings 23:2).

C. Ratification Completed (vv. 7b, 8)

7b, 8. And they said, All that the LORD hath said will we do, and be obedient. And Moses took the blood, and sprinkled it on the people, and said, Behold the blood of the covenant, which the LORD hath made with you concerning all these words.

This marks the third declaration by *the people* that they will keep the *covenant* (see comments on 9:3, above). They test the Lord's patience before Sinai with their constant complaining, but for now they express a determination to do what *the Lord* has *said*.

Moses completes the ceremony by taking the other half of *the blood* that was collected and sprinkling it on the people. Many have assumed that the blood is actually sprinkled on the leaders who are near or that it is sprinkled on the 12 pillars as representing the people (see v. 4). For New Testament references to the sprinkling of blood, see Hebrews 9:13-22; 11:28.

The final part of the ratification process is Moses' declaration that this is the blood of the covenant for all the *words* that the Lord had spoken. The ratification of the new covenant is complete, and it is in effect for this new nation.

God's ultimate purpose for the nation is that the promised Messiah will be an Israelite and that He will be a member of the tribe of Judah. History records that these things are fulfilled just as God had promised. We have the blood of Jesus sprinkled on us (Hebrews 12:24; 1 Peter 1:2).

Conclusion

A. Setting Your Priorities

Almost 2000 years ago a young man in Galilee said something about seeking first the kingdom of God and the righteousness of God (Matthew 6:33). The current culture prefers not to be reminded of such claims by Jesus, so it has become preferred to avoid mentioning even His name.

That same young man also said something about the importance of confessing Him before men (Matthew 10:32). Only then will He acknowledge such persons to the Father in Heaven.

As each Christian goes through life, he or she will be making decisions that involve loyalties to the Christ who gave the new covenant. It is possible, but often difficult, to maintain the proper priorities when others have no respect for Jesus. The consequences of faithfulness are not always pleasant, but to do otherwise is a violation of covenant. It is a serious thing to be ashamed of Jesus.

B. Prayer

Almighty God, help us to make the right choices today in those areas that pertain to Your Son and His church. In the name of Your Son and our Savior, amen.

C. Thought to Remember

Live up to the meaning of the new covenant.

Home Daily Bible Readings

Monday, Sept. 11—Our Pledge to God (Psalm 119:33-40)

Tuesday, Sept. 12—Moses Chooses Judges (Exodus 18:13-27)

Wednesday, Sept. 13—Moses Goes Up to God (Exodus 19:1-9a)

Thursday, Sept. 14—Preparing for God's Covenant (Exodus 19:9b-15)

Friday, Sept. 15—God Gives the Commands (Exodus 20:1-17)

Saturday, Sept. 16—The People Vow Loyalty (Exodus 24:3-8)

Sunday, Sept. 17—Moses Enters God's Presence (Exodus 24:12-18)

Learning by Doing

This page contains an alternative lesson plan emphasizing learning activities.
Classes desiring such student involvement will find these suggestions helpful.

Learning Goals

After participating in this lesson, each student will be able to:

1. Describe the covenant relationship that God designed for Old Testament Israel.

2. Discuss the meaning and importance of God's covenant relationship with Old Testament Israel.

3. State one specific way he or she will demonstrate greater faithfulness to the new covenant.

Into the Lesson

Recruit three class members to play the game "Pin the Mountain on the Sinai." Display an outline map of the exodus area—either a simple hand drawn one or a commercial map. Tell your recruits you want them to close their eyes and let you turn them around once before they approach the map and put their token where they think the children of Israel encamped for a year.

Give each recruit a small (one-inch round) token with reusable adhesive applied to the back. Let each student adhere his or her "mountain" to the map. After all three are adhered, ask, "Which of these three tokens comes the closest to the real mountain where God gave the law to Moses?" As noted by the lesson writer (see notes on verse 2), the true location remains disputed, but the traditional site is well known. Review the exodus from Egypt to the mount to establish the setting for today's texts.

Into the Word

Prepare copies of the text below. Call this, "Today's text as copied by a nearsighted, careless scribe." Ask the class to make corrections to the error-filled text with their Bibles closed.

In the third day when the children of Moses were gone forth out of the land of England, the same day they came into the forests of Sinai. For they were delayed at Seraphim and were come to the desserts of Sinai and had pitched their tents in the wilderness, and there they camped before sunset.

And Moses went over unto God, and the Lord called him up the mountain, say-

ing, This shalt thou say to the house of Abraham, and tell the children of Aaron. Ye have seen what I did unto the Egyptian army, and how I bare you on angels' wings and brought you unto this place. Now, therefore, if you will hear my voice indeed and keep my laws, then ye shall get a special treatment from me above all people: for all the nations are mine. And ye shall be unto me a kind of priest and wholly a nation. These are the words which thou shalt present unto the children at Sinai.

And Moses came and told the people all the works of the Lord and all the requirements: and all the people answered with one sound and said, All the things the Lord hath said will we try to do. And Moses copied all the words of the Lord, and rose up early in mourning, and builded a hill under the altar and 12 pillows, according to the 12 tributes of Israel. And he sent young children of the men of Israel, which burned offerings and stacked rice piece offerings and oxen unto the Lord. And Moses took half of the blood and poured it in barrels, and half of the blood he spread over the alter. And he took the back of the covenant and repeated it in the ears of the people.

And they said, Part of all that the Lord hath said will we deny and be disobedient. And Moses took the blood and sprinkled it on the covenant, and said, Behold the covenant, which the Lord hath mandated to you concerning all these works.

This can be a small-group activity, if desired. After students identify errors, have them open their Bibles to verify their corrections. Share points from the commentary as appropriate.

Into Life

Have students turn to Hebrews 8, a passage affirming the superiority of the new covenant in Christ. Read that short chapter responsively—you reading the odd-numbered verses and the class reading the even-numbered. Ask students how they will live up to the holy status that they hold in covenant with God in the week ahead.

Let's Talk It Over

The questions on this page are designed to promote discussion of the lesson by the class and to encourage application of the lesson Scriptures. The answers provided are only discussion starters. Let your class talk it over from there.

1. Moses went up to God to hear a word from Him. In what ways do we expect to hear God but fail to do so when we neglect to "go up to Him"? How can we be more faithful at doing so?

We fail to go to God seeking His will and direction because often we feel as if we know what is best for our lives. Yet we still expect God's approval of what we've decided to do! Our feeling is often that we can handle things on our own, so why should we bother God with these things? As long as He isn't interfering in what we are doing, then that's the same as having His approval—so we think.

A regular period of quiet devotions and Bible reading is invaluable. During one of these daily quiet times, try this: *invite* God to put a halt to your plans if those plans don't fit His will. And don't be surprised when He honors your request!

2. History reveals that God is the provider, sustainer, and protector of His people. In what ways has God carried you and your church "on eagles' wings"?

God has been faithful at providing for His people all those things necessary for eternal life. God has sustained us through good and bad, in sickness and grief, as well as in joys and victories. God has protected us through storms, in travel, and many ways that we simply take for granted.

We also look at the way missionaries in difficult places are protected and provided for by God. Even when martyrdom occurs, the result is more growth of the church. The attacks of Satan and the ravages of war have not been enough to stop the church.

3. From Genesis 4:7 to Revelation 22:19, Scripture is filled with the conditional word *if*. In what ways do people sometimes bypass the *ifs* of God's Word? Why?

For some, there is a false understanding of grace. Paul spoke of this in Romans 6:1 when he asked, "Shall we continue in sin, that grace may abound?" At other times Christians want to justify their sin. There is the desire to be able to sin and not have to accept personal responsibility for it. It is imperative to remember the teaching of Scripture: "Not every one that saith unto me,

Lord, Lord, shall enter into the kingdom of heaven; but he that doeth the will of my Father which is in heaven" (Matthew 7:21).

The "surely God would not . . . " line of thinking is a very dangerous way of predicting how God will and won't react to our sin. This mode of thought often can be traced to ignoring (intentionally or unintentionally) the *ifs* of Scripture.

4. What are some ways that you fulfill your priestly role as God intends? What will interfere with your priestly service?

Priests are a select and special group. We are sacred, set apart for God. This means that as Christians we are a special people to God. First Peter 2:5 states that Christians are a holy priesthood. Our task is to live holy lives that reflect the holiness of God. Without holiness as a backdrop, our priesthood won't mean much. First Peter 2:9 states that we as Christians are a royal priesthood. As royalty we represent the spiritual kingdom in which we live. Our king, who grants us our royal position, expects holiness because He is holy (1 Peter 1:15, 16).

A job of priests is to offer sacrifices to God. These sacrifices include our time and our finances. We intercede with one another in prayer. As priests we recognize that we are to be living sacrifices, holy and acceptable unto God (Romans 12:1). We fulfill the role of priests when we recognize that we are not our own but that we belong to God.

5. Telling the truth, the whole truth, and nothing but the truth is not always appreciated. In what ways do preachers and teachers fail to tell "all the words of the Lord"? In what ways do people close their ears to these words of truth?

Those who preach the gospel may, at times, fail to teach the whole truth out of fear of losing a job. In Sunday school classes teachers may avoid touching sensitive or controversial issues for fear of creating dissension. On the other hand churches have been known to tie the hands of preachers and teachers by telling them to stay away from certain topics that "hit too close to home." Is our church guilty in any of these areas?

Covenant Renewed

DEVOTIONAL READING: Psalm 51:1-12.

BACKGROUND SCRIPTURE: Joshua 24.

PRINTED TEXT: Joshua 24:1, 14-24.

Joshua 24:1, 14-24

1 And Joshua gathered all the tribes of Israel to Shechem, and called for the elders of Israel, and for their heads, and for their judges, and for their officers; and they presented themselves before God.

· · · · · · · · · · · · ·

14 Now therefore fear the LORD, and serve him in sincerity and in truth; and put away the gods which your fathers served on the other side of the flood, and in Egypt; and serve ye the LORD.

15 And if it seem evil unto you to serve the LORD, choose you this day whom ye will serve; whether the gods which your fathers served that were on the other side of the flood, or the gods of the Amorites, in whose land ye dwell: but as for me and my house, we will serve the LORD.

16 And the people answered and said, God forbid that we should forsake the LORD, to serve other gods;

17 For the LORD our God, he it is that brought us up and our fathers out of the land of Egypt, from the house of bondage, and which did those great signs in our sight, and preserved us in all the way wherein we went, and among all the people through whom we passed:

18 And the LORD drave out from before us all the people, even the Amorites which dwelt in the land: therefore will we also serve the LORD; for he is our God.

19 And Joshua said unto the people, Ye cannot serve the LORD: for he is a holy God; he is a jealous God; he will not forgive your transgressions nor your sins.

20 If ye forsake the LORD, and serve strange gods, then he will turn and do you hurt, and consume you, after that he hath done you good.

21 And the people said unto Joshua, Nay; but we will serve the LORD.

22 And Joshua said unto the people, Ye are witnesses against yourselves that ye have chosen you the LORD, to serve him. And they said, We are witnesses.

23 Now therefore put away, said he, the strange gods which are among you, and incline your heart unto the LORD God of Israel.

24 And the people said unto Joshua, The LORD our God will we serve, and his voice will we obey.

GOLDEN TEXT: The people said unto Joshua, The LORD our God will we serve, and his voice will we obey.—Joshua 24:24.

God's Living Covenant
Unit 1: God's Covenant with the Patriarchs
(Lessons 1-4)

Lesson Aims

After participating in this lesson, each student will be able to:

1. Describe the renewal of the covenant by Israel in the last days of Joshua's life.

2. Evaluate the benefits that come from regular reviews of commitments to God.

3. Make a plan for periodic reaffirmations of faithfulness to God.

Lesson Outline

INTRODUCTION

    A. Seeing the Potential

    B. Lesson Background

  I. CONVOCATION (Joshua 24:1)

      The Necessity of Godly Leaders

  II. CHOICES (Joshua 24:14-18)

    A. Proposals by Joshua (vv. 14, 15)

    B. Preference of the People (vv. 16-18)

 III. CHALLENGE (Joshua 24:19-21)

    A. Presentation by Joshua (vv. 19, 20)

    B. Priority of the People (v. 21)

 IV. COMMITMENT (Joshua 24:22-24)

    A. Pronouncement by Joshua (v. 22a)

    B. Proclamation of the People (v. 22b)

    C. Distinctive Reminder (v. 23)

      Idolaters Anonymous?

    D. Definite Rejoinder (v. 24)

CONCLUSION

    A. Most Favored Nation Status

    B. Prayer

    C. Thought to Remember

Introduction

A. Seeing the Potential

A very ordinary, jagged piece of marble may seem as nothing in the eyes of the average person. It can, however, become an elaborate, detailed statue when shaped by the hands of an experienced sculptor. A rough-hewn block of wood may seem fit only to be burned. However, it can be carved into a thing of polished beauty by a master craftsman.

A conscientious teacher or youth worker cannot look at a group of students as immature and time-consuming. For there may be one or more in that group who, with careful teaching, can become great leaders for God and humankind. A slave people in a foreign land may appear to be nothing, but they may be chosen by the God of Heaven and earth to receive a special covenant. Despite their many failures in being faithful, in the fullness of time that nation can have the Son of God as one of its offspring—the long-awaited Messiah who offers salvation to all.

The potential within each person obviously is different. If, however, each person's resolve to fulfill his or her potential is combined with God's discipline and love, that potential can be realized.

B. Lesson Background

The biblical accounts are usually interpreted to show that the Israelites spent 11 months and 20 days at Sinai, from the first day of the third month (Exodus 19:1) to the twentieth day of the second month of the second year (Numbers 10:11). At that time the cloud lifted from the tabernacle, and the journey to Canaan continued.

While at Sinai, other details of the law were given. The Israelites were instructed how to build the tabernacle, and it was constructed according to the pattern given. The incident of the golden calf (Exodus 32) was a sobering event during Moses' 40 days on the mount. The intricacies of the sacrificial system and the priesthood are given in the book of Leviticus. Numbers 1:3 tells of a military census of all men who were age 20 and older. The total was 603,550 (2:32).

As the nation of Israel approached Canaan, 12 spies were sent into the land. Ten of the spies brought back a negative message of fear, and they prevailed over the minority report of Caleb and Joshua (Numbers 13). The punishment was announced by the Lord: the people were to spend a total of 40 years as shepherds in the desert (one year for each day the spies were gone; 14:33, 34); all the men of war except Caleb and Joshua were to perish in the wilderness (14:38). This means that 603,548 did not reach Canaan. That is an average of more than 40 deaths per day if we count only men age 20 and over!

The Israelites ultimately were successful in conquering the lands east of the Jordan. Two and one-half tribes were granted permission to settle on that side. Moses died at the age of 120, and the leadership fell to Joshua.

The miraculous crossing of the Jordan when it was in flood stage validated Joshua's role as the new leader (Joshua 3). The conquest of Jericho was offset in part by a temporary reversal at Ai (Joshua 7:3-5), the second city to be conquered. The victories continued in the central cities of Canaan (including the miracle of the long day as given in Joshua 10), southern Canaan, and then against the northern coalition. These primary battles consumed several years, ending in approximately 1400 BC. The land was divided among the remaining nine and one-half tribes. Cities were assigned for the Levites, with six of the cities designated as cities of refuge (Joshua 20).

Each of the last two chapters of the book of Joshua depicts national gatherings for covenant renewal. It is the second such event that is the background for today's lesson. There are no chronological references for these events. They are often assumed to be as early as 1390 BC but probably are later.

I. Convocation
(Joshua 24:1)

In one sense you cannot go back to where special events took place in the past and expect to find things as they were. Even so, there is value in returning—not to try to "live in the past," but just to reminisce and to walk among the monuments of memories. To visit again the place where a person was baptized or married, or other locations of special interest, can produce a nostalgia that is good for the soul.

The last major event in the book of Joshua takes place in a special location. It has special meaning to those assembled, for it produces memories of their spiritual heritage.

How to Say It

AI. *Ay*-eye.
AMORITES. *Am*-uh-rites.
BABYLONIAN. Bab-ih-*low*-nee-un.
CALEB. *Kay*-leb.
CANAAN. *Kay*-nun.
EBAL. *Ee*-bull.
EGYPT. *Ee*-jipt.
EUPHRATES. You-*fray*-teez.
GERIZIM. *Gair*-ih-zeem or Guh-*rye*-zim.
JERICHO. *Jair*-ih-co.
JOSHUA. *Josh*-yew-uh.
LEVITES. *Lee*-vites.
LEVITICUS. Leh-*vit*-ih-kus.
SHECHEM. *Shee*-kem or *Shek*-em.
SINAI. *Sigh*-nye or *Sigh*-nay-eye.
TIMNATH-HERES. *Tim*-nath-*hee*-reez (strong accent on *hee*).

---

1. And Joshua gathered all the tribes of Israel to Shechem, and called for the elders of Israel, and for their heads, and for their judges, and for their officers; and they presented themselves before God.

Two things prompt Joshua to gather the principal persons of *all the tribes of Israel.* First, as indicated in Joshua 23:1, his advanced age moves him to request that the nation again experience a formal covenant renewal. In this action he has the example set by Moses. Moses, just before his death, called the nation together to renew the covenant (Deuteronomy 29–34).

Second, Joshua is fully aware that this nation needs to be reminded again of its special relationship to *God.* Moses had commanded that the law be read to the nation every seven years (Deuteronomy 31:10-14). It is possible that this occasion is one of the fulfillments of Moses' command. A commitment on a national scope should be followed by continued and regular instruction in each community and home.

The first verse of the chapter specifies that *Shechem* is the location where Joshua chooses to have this ceremony. Since Joshua's hometown is Timnath-heres (same as Timnath-serah; Joshua 19:49, 50; Judges 2:9), his selection requires him to make a full day's journey to the northwest.

Shechem is an appropriate site for several reasons. First, it is the first place in Canaan where Abraham built an altar to the Lord. It is here that the promise of this land was made for Abraham's descendants (Genesis 12:6, 7). It may be assumed that since Joshua had been commanded by God to meditate on the law (Joshua 1:8), that Joshua was fully aware of this historical background.

Second, a part of the heritage of Israel is that Jacob also built an altar at Shechem upon his return to the land with his family (Genesis 33:18-20). When Jacob left Shechem, he led his family in a spiritual housecleaning. This rededication involved burying all the accumulated household gods (Genesis 35:2, 4).

Third, this is the place where Joseph's bones are buried (Joshua 24:32). Joshua is of the tribe of Ephraim (1 Chronicles 7:20-27), so Joseph (Ephraim's father) is an ancestor. Joseph's exemplary life could be cited for anyone who comes to Shechem.

Fourth, Joshua had assembled the entire nation in this vicinity immediately after conquering Jericho and Ai. Joshua 8:30-35 records that the nation divided itself into two groups in accord with the command that Moses had given toward the end of his life (Deuteronomy 27:12, 13). One group stood on Mount Ebal and responded with "Amen" when the curses of the covenant were read, and the other group stood on Mount Gerizim and answered in the same way when the blessings were read.

The town of Shechem is immediately to the west of the pass between the two mountains. To be at this site again undoubtedly brings back many memories to the older leaders. It is very probable that the plastered stones, with the law written on them, are still visible as reminders of that earlier occasion (Deuteronomy 27:2, 3; Joshua 8:30-32). The large altar of uncut stones that Joshua had erected on Mount Ebal was a part of the earlier covenant renewal ceremony. It may be assumed that it is still in place at the occasion before us. [See question #1, page 40.]

THE NECESSITY OF GODLY LEADERS

In the mid-nineteenth century, European Christians were awakening in their faith. The natural result was a desire to spread the gospel of Christ around the world. Dutch and German missionaries worked to gain access to the tribes of Indonesia. The first missionaries were rejected and many were killed. By the 1860s only 50 members of the Batak tribe had become Christians.

But then the missionaries, led by Ludwig Nommensen (1834–1918), turned their focus to reaching the tribal leaders in an attempt to create a church that was culturally Indonesian rather than European. The church mushroomed. By 1911 the number of converts had reached more than 100,000. Over the next half-century, ever-larger numbers of Western missionaries worked to create indigenous churches in Indonesia and other countries. The result is astounding: today there are more Christians in the developing nations than in the Western world.

When Joshua gave his final exhortation to Israel, he used this principle of focusing on the leaders. He challenged Israel's tribal leaders to be faithful to God. He knew that without godly leaders the nation would be lost. This principle would be proven true numerous times in Israel's history over the next few hundred years. The principle is still valid today. Seldom do people rise above their leaders.   —C. R. B.

II. Choices
(Joshua 24:14-18)

There is a dramatic change in the emphasis between the first part of the book of Joshua and these final chapters. The early chapters of the book stress the faithfulness of God in helping Is-

rael to conquer Canaan (Joshua 1:9; 3:10; 4:23, 24). In the last chapters the continued faithfulness of the people is emphasized (Joshua 23:6-8). To express faithfulness and thankfulness is one thing; to live it is much more demanding.

A. Proposals by Joshua (vv. 14, 15)

14. Now therefore fear the LORD, and serve him in sincerity and in truth; and put away the gods which your fathers served on the other side of the flood, and in Egypt; and serve ye the LORD.

The historical review like the one in Joshua 24:2-13 (not in today's text) is a standard part of the covenants of the second millennium BC. Following that review, Joshua now begins to assert the foundational requirements that the Lord expects to receive from His covenant nation: the people are to *fear* and to *serve* Him.

Jesus makes a similar statement in Matthew 10:28. It is more logical to worship the creator instead of what He created (compare Romans 1:25). That is why the Israelites are to *put away the gods which your fathers served on the other side of the flood, and in Egypt*.

That second part of Joshua's statement is intriguing. After experiencing all the mighty miracles of God, does this covenant nation still have idols in its midst? The text makes it very clear that they did—both in Egypt and also over the 700 years prior to that time when Abraham and his family crossed the Euphrates River (called *flood*, here and in vv. 2, 15). [See question #2, page 40.]

This command by Joshua to give up their idolatry is similar to Jacob's command in Genesis 35:2. The people of Israel seem to maintain a fascination for idolatry until after the Babylonian exile in 586 BC. It will take a 70-year captivity before they are more or less cured of this spiritual weakness.

15. And if it seem evil unto you to serve the LORD, choose you this day whom ye will serve; whether the gods which your fathers served that were on the other side of the flood, or the gods of the Amorites, in whose land ye dwell: but as for me and my house, we will serve the LORD.

This is considered one of the greatest verses in the entire book. It presents the choice in vivid language. The Israelites must choose whom they will serve: *the gods* that some of their ancestors worshiped before Abraham entered Canaan, or *the gods of the Amorites* where they now live, or *the Lord*!

Joshua boldly announces his own decision. As Joshua looks back over his life, this choice is the only one that makes sense. He is able to recall the many miracles that he has witnessed—from the plagues in Egypt to the battle of the long day. In Joshua 23:14 he states that not one promise of the Lord has failed. With these things in his mind, he can make what is now that famous declaration: *as for me and my house, we will serve the Lord.* Many Christian homes have this saying posted on a wall in the form of an embroidery, etc.

B. Preference of the People (vv. 16-18)

16. And the people answered and said, God forbid that we should forsake the LORD, to serve other gods.

Prompted by the power of Joshua's reason and example, the people are moved to make the same choice. At this moment it is preposterous to think of serving *other gods.*

17, 18. For the LORD our God, he it is that brought us up and our fathers out of the land of Egypt, from the house of bondage, and which did those great signs in our sight, and preserved us in all the way wherein we went, and among all the people through whom we passed: and the LORD drave out from before us all the people, even the Amorites which dwelt in the land: therefore will we also serve the LORD; for he is our God.

Sometimes the choices of the past are conveniently ignored when tough decisions are made. This time the vigorous, vibrant review of the nation's history (vv. 2-13) moves the Israelite leaders to express their own account of days gone by. They are compelled to remember where they had been (in *Egypt*), where they are now, and what it took to get there. Faced with this evidence, they affirm again that they will *serve the Lord.* [See question #3, page 40.]

III. Challenge
(Joshua 24:19-21)

Is the affirmation of verses 17, 18 enough for Joshua? Apparently not!

A. Presentation by Joshua (vv. 19, 20)

19, 20. And Joshua said unto the people, Ye cannot serve the LORD: for he is a holy God; he is a jealous God; he will not forgive your transgressions nor your sins. If ye forsake the LORD, and serve strange gods, then he will turn and do you hurt, and consume you, after that he hath done you good.

Joshua's reply seems to be out of place, for the affirmation by the people was certainly the desired result—or was it? Do his words *Ye cannot serve the Lord* simply reflect Joshua's previous

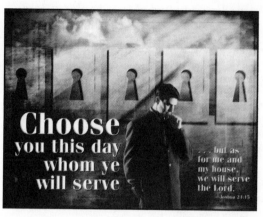

Visual for lesson 4. *Ask for a show of hands: Who among your students has this famous passage displayed somewhere in the house?*

experiences of this fickle nation? Does he discern a hollow mockery in their affirmation?

Joshua's charge that they are unable to serve the Lord in the long run is based on two reasons. First, the God of Israel is *a holy God,* and Joshua's experiences make him doubt that the Israelites are able to be faithful for an extended period of time. Second, the God of Israel *is a jealous God.* Such a jealousy demands absolute loyalty. There is to be no spiritual adultery, no going after other gods.

B. Priority of the People (v. 21)

21. And the people said unto Joshua, Nay; but we will serve the LORD.

This reaffirmation by the people produces the result that Joshua's challenge desires. It also makes their priority even stronger in that they can be reminded in the future of what they have said so emphatically. [See question #4, page 40.]

IV. Commitment
(Joshua 24:22-24)

Now we come to the climax. Things have reached a fever pitch!

A. Pronouncement by Joshua (v. 22a)

22a. And Joshua said unto the people, Ye are witnesses against yourselves that ye have chosen you the LORD, to serve him.

Joshua reminds *the people* that their commitment to *the Lord* is quite serious. What they have said cannot be taken lightly. They have become their own *witnesses* before God and people in their declaration.

B. Proclamation of the People (v. 22b)

22b. And they said, We are witnesses.

In short, pithy statements the dialogue goes back and forth. The people testify to their commitment for the third time.

C. Distinctive Reminder (v. 23)

23. Now therefore put away, said he, the strange gods which are among you, and incline your heart unto the LORD God of Israel.

Joshua says that the first test of the covenant's renewal by the Israelites is to discard *the strange gods,* which they still had. These gods could be items of value or located in special places of devotion. Sometimes it costs to serve the Lord, but it costs even more not to serve Him.

IDOLATERS ANONYMOUS?

Alcoholics Anonymous (A.A.) was founded in 1935 by a New York stockbroker and an Ohio surgeon. Both men admitted to having been hopeless drunks. Their goal was to stay sober themselves and help others to overcome their addiction to alcohol. Today there are over two million A.A. members in 150 countries.

The success of A.A. has led to the founding of other "anonymous" groups. These groups are for drug addicts, compulsive shoppers, overeaters, and even for those who cannot seem to control their use of profanity! The literature of these "anonymous" groups often recognizes that the source of the cure is a Higher Power. That may be a little vague for those of us who think the reference should be specifically to God, yet therein lies the genius of the whole "anonymous" movement.

It would not be far off the mark to state that Joshua was, in effect, trying to start an "Idolaters Anonymous" movement. He knew the power idolatry had over Israel; the people seemed incapable of helping themselves. He also knew that trust in God was the only source of a cure. The same can be said for any sin that besets us. Without the intervention of the cross of Christ, our sin problem can never be finally solved.   —C. R. B.

D. Definite Rejoinder (v. 24)

24. And the people said unto Joshua, The LORD our God will we serve, and his voice will we obey.

For the fourth time the people affirm their intention to *serve* and *obey* the Lord. [See question #5, page 40.] The entire scenario is almost a preview of Jesus' challenges to Peter after the resurrection (John 21:15-19). Joshua 24:25-27 is not part of the lesson text, but provides the close of the covenant's renewal.

Joshua is to be admired in calling this assembly as he tries to instill faith in the generation to follow. It is extremely important that this be done. If the second generation sees compromise in the first generation, then the second generation will deviate even more. And the third generation, with these examples, will essentially abandon the faith.

Conclusion

A. Most Favored Nation Status

Until 1998 the phrase *Most Favored Nation Status* was used to designate nations that received equal treatment by the U.S. in trading relations. The term was discontinued because most nations were in this category, and it seemed deceptive. The newer term is *Normal Trade Relations.* The nation of Israel, however, definitely was a nation with a "most favored" status before God. Yet, as has been expressed many times, *there is peril in privilege.*

The teaching of the New Testament is similar. The individual who becomes a member of the body of Christ enjoys the privileges of sins forgiven, the gift of the Holy Spirit, and the promise of Heaven. Yet Hebrews 6:4-6 warns about those who have enjoyed the privileges of the gospel and then fall away. *There is peril in privilege.*

B. Prayer

Our God in Heaven, we resolve to study Your Word in order to understand better our obligations to You and to others. In Jesus' name, amen.

C. Thought to Remember

To serve the Lord is costly.
Not to serve Him costs even more.

Home Daily Bible Readings

Monday, Sept. 18—Pray for Renewal (Psalm 51:1-12)

Tuesday, Sept. 19—Be Strong and Bold (Deuteronomy 31:14-23)

Wednesday, Sept. 20—God Commands Joshua (Joshua 1:1-9)

Thursday, Sept. 21—Recalling God's Mighty Acts (Joshua 24:1-7)

Friday, Sept. 22—God Gives a Land (Joshua 24:8-13)

Saturday, Sept. 23—Choose Whom You Will Serve (Joshua 24:14-18)

Sunday, Sept. 24—The People Renew Their Vows (Joshua 24:19-24)

Learning by Doing

This page contains an alternative lesson plan emphasizing learning activities.
Classes desiring such student involvement will find these suggestions helpful.

Learning Goals

After participating in this lesson, each student will be able to:

1. Describe the renewal of the covenant by Israel in the last days of Joshua's life.

2. Evaluate the benefits that come from regular reviews of commitments to God.

3. Make a plan for periodic reaffirmations of faithfulness to God.

Into the Lesson

As students arrive, offer each a choice: either a pencil or a penny. After all have made choices, say, "I'm going to show you both sides of six cards. Pick one letter of the two from each card and write it down. When we're finished, we'll see if anyone has a key word from today's study." Before class prepare six large cards with the following pairs of letters front and back: A, C (card 1); K, H (card 2); O, S (card 3); D, O (card 4); S, T (card 5); E, Y (card 6). Show the cards in the order given. Make certain all students see both sides.

After you have revealed all six cards and each student has chosen six letters, ask, "Does anyone have the six letters that—taken in sequence—spell the key word?" *(The word is CHOOSE.)* If no one has the word, ask, "Does anyone think he or she knows what the word is?" After the word has been revealed, comment on the choice each student had at the beginning: one choice was critical to success while the other was inconsequential.

Into the Word

Read aloud Joshua 8:30-35 to remind your class of the appropriate location for the assembly described in today's text from Joshua 24. Emphasize the division of the Israelite people into two "amen choruses." (See the commentary for verse 1.) Divide your class into two sides. (This can be done without anyone physically moving.) Recruit two of your good oral readers to share in a reading of today's text in the manner that follows, with pauses for "amen" responses from the half of the class assigned to each reader.

Reader One (R1): Now therefore fear the Lord and serve him in sincerity and truth.

Reader Two (R2): Put away the gods which your fathers served on the other side of the flood, and in Egypt.

R1 & R2: Serve ye the Lord.

R1: And if it seem evil unto you to serve the Lord, choose you this day whom ye will serve.

R2: Whether the gods which your fathers served that were on the other side of the flood, or the gods of the Amorites, in whose land ye dwell,

R1 & R2: but as for me and my house, we will serve the Lord.

R1: And the people answered and said, God forbid that we should forsake the Lord, to serve other gods.

R2: For the Lord our God, he it is that brought us up and our fathers out of the land of Egypt, from the house of bondage, and which did those great signs in our sight, and preserved us in all the way wherein we went, and among all the people through whom we passed.

R1: And the Lord drave out from before us all the people, even the Amorites which dwelt in the land.

R1 & R2: Therefore will we also serve the Lord; for he is our God.

R2: And Joshua said unto the people, Ye cannot serve the Lord: for he is a holy God; he is a jealous God; he will not forgive your transgressions nor your sins.

R1: If ye forsake the Lord, and serve strange gods, then he will turn and do you hurt, and consume you, after that he hath done you good.

R1 & R2: And the people said unto Joshua, Nay; but we will serve the Lord.

R2: And Joshua said unto the people, Ye are witnesses against yourselves that ye have chosen you the Lord, to serve him.

R1 & R2: And they said, We are witnesses.

R1: Now therefore put away, said he, the strange gods which are among you, and incline your heart unto the Lord God of Israel.

R1 & R2: And the people said unto Joshua, The Lord our God will we serve, and his voice will we obey.

Into Life

Prepare and distribute copies of the following statement, on business card stock if possible: "I will serve the Lord . . . TODAY!" Ask class members to carry or post the card where they will see it often. Suggest that they read it aloud at least once a day.

Let's Talk It Over

The questions on this page are designed to promote discussion of the lesson by the class and to encourage application of the lesson Scriptures. The answers provided are only discussion starters. Let your class talk it over from there.

1. If you were to go back to that "special place" to reaffirm your initial commitment to Christ, where would it be and why?

Those who live in mobile societies are often a long distance from the place where they first began a personal walk with God. For some that place could be at a Christian camp where a challenge for Christian commitment was made around a campfire. For others, it could be the old home church where they grew up. We make these commitments sometimes in a hospital emergency room or a surgical waiting room.

Just as we may want to go back to a home we grew up in and see what it looks like now, we also have special attachments to those "spiritual homes." They can be special, sacred places because of the significance of the event that happened there. It's worth the trip to go back!

2. The people of Israel had a hard time letting go of some of the false gods they had been introduced to. We can have the same problem. What are some of the gods we hold on to? Why is it so hard to put away these gods?

Idol-gods come in many shapes and sizes. These gods are anything that displaces the one true God and His desires.

Sometimes an idol-god may come in the form of material possessions; at other times it may be a certain relationship we have with another person. It may be a job or a position we hold in the community or the church. These are things we can "put our hands on," so to speak. Thus they are very real to us in our day-to-day lives. By contrast, the things that God considers important, such as a personal walk with Him and acting by faith, can seem rather mystical at times. The fear of losing control is a very real reason why we hold on to our "gods."

3. The Israelites made commitments to God in the context of remembering God's blessings. What blessings has God given your church that should lead to even deeper commitments to Him? How can we make sure we count and recount these blessings?

Often we take for granted many of the things that happen in our churches. The freedom we

have even to be a church is often taken for granted. In some places this freedom does not exist. Whereas we often glory in our property and buildings (and these are blessings for which we should give thanks to God), we also need to remember the people who have been saved out of their bondage of sin.

We can remember the prayers that God has answered. We are quick to mention our prayer requests in our programs and services. Are we as quick to keep a record of the answers, to proclaim and celebrate these?

4. Sometimes our actions belie our words. In what ways can the things that we do devalue our promise of allegiance to God? How can we do better?

We used to sing a hymn that said, "I'll put Jesus first in my life." This is a promise that our relationship with God is more important than anything else.

Then we allow recreational activities to take precedence over, say, a Bible study. When we are challenged to give to help support a missionary endeavor or to respond financially to a crisis situation, we focus instead on that new car or new gadget that advertisers have convinced us we just can't live without. Solutions will be individual to each person, but undoubtedly all solutions must begin with prayer.

5. In quick succession the people of God offered their allegiance to God four times. How can we follow their example in reaffirming our dedication to God?

We can first verbalize our commitment. In personal testimonies or small group settings, we can speak of ways we want to be more committed in our walk with God and ask for others to pray for us and hold us accountable.

We then back up our talk with actually serving others and obeying God. Keeping our eyes open to needs in our church and in our community where the love of Christ needs to be made known is important. Service in the name of Christ in a homeless shelter, a soup kitchen, or an organization to help children are ways we can respond in obedience.

God Sends Judges

DEVOTIONAL READING: Deuteronomy 6:4-9.

BACKGROUND SCRIPTURE: Judges 2:6-23.

PRINTED TEXT: Judges 2:11-14, 16-23.

Judges 2:11-14, 16-23

11 And the children of Israel did evil in the sight of the LORD, and served Baalim:

12 And they forsook the LORD God of their fathers, which brought them out of the land of Egypt, and followed other gods, of the gods of the people that were round about them, and bowed themselves unto them, and provoked the LORD to anger.

13 And they forsook the LORD, and served Baal and Ashtaroth.

14 And the anger of the LORD was hot against Israel, and he delivered them into the hands of spoilers that spoiled them, and he sold them into the hands of their enemies round about, so that they could not any longer stand before their enemies.

· · · · · · · · · · · ·

16 Nevertheless the LORD raised up judges, which delivered them out of the hand of those that spoiled them.

17 And yet they would not hearken unto their judges, but they went a whoring after other gods, and bowed themselves unto them: they turned quickly out of the way which their fathers walked in, obeying the commandments of the LORD; but they did not so.

18 And when the LORD raised them up judges, then the LORD was with the judge, and delivered them out of the hand of their enemies all the days of the judge: for it repented the LORD because of their groanings by reason of them that oppressed them and vexed them.

19 And it came to pass, when the judge was dead, that they returned, and corrupted themselves more than their fathers, in following other gods to serve them, and to bow down unto them; they ceased not from their own doings, nor from their stubborn way.

20 And the anger of the LORD was hot against Israel; and he said, Because that this people hath transgressed my covenant which I commanded their fathers, and have not hearkened unto my voice;

21 I also will not henceforth drive out any from before them of the nations which Joshua left when he died:

22 That through them I may prove Israel, whether they will keep the way of the LORD to walk therein, as their fathers did keep it, or not.

23 Therefore the LORD left those nations, without driving them out hastily; neither delivered he them into the hand of Joshua.

GOLDEN TEXT: The LORD raised up judges, which delivered them out of the hand of those that spoiled them.—Judges 2:16.

God's Living Covenant
Unit 2: God's Covenant with Judges and Kings
(Lessons 5-9)

Lesson Aims

After participating in this lesson, each student will be able to:

1. Describe the situation Israel repeatedly faced when the faith held by one generation was not passed on to the next.

2. Compare and contrast Israel's challenge of passing on its faith to the next generation with the twenty-first-century church's challenge to do the same.

3. Identify one way that he or she will help prepare the next generation of church leaders.

Lesson Outline

INTRODUCTION
  A. The Passing of Generations
  B. Lesson Background
I. GENERATION VEERS OFF COURSE (Judges 2:11-14)
  A. People's Betrayal (vv. 11-13)
    The Price of "Fun"
  B. Lord's Anger (v. 14)
II. STORY SADLY REPEATS (Judges 2:16-19)
  A. God Delivers (v. 16)
  B. People Turn Away (v. 17)
  C. God Still Delivers (v. 18)
  D. People Still Turn Away (v. 19)
    Some Call it Stubborn
III. COVENANT BROKEN (Judges 2:20-23)
  A. Delaying Promises (vv. 20, 21)
  B. Testing Each Generation (vv. 22, 23)
CONCLUSION
  A. Chasing Other Gods
  B. Generational Legacies
  C. Prayer
  D. Thought to Remember

Introduction

A. The Passing of Generations

In 2004 the Allies marked the sixtieth anniversary of the Normandy D-Day invasion. It was a reunion of the primary World War II partners: U.S., Canada, Russia, Britain, and France. The Germans were also invited for the first time, because there was some recognition that the German people suffered terribly in World War II.

Many noted that this was likely the last big hurrah for the World War II veterans. At the time the youngest of these veterans were in their late seventies. Quickly fading was what Tom Brokaw had labeled *The Greatest Generation.*

The World War II generation had dominated the national and international scene for 50 years, far beyond the normal cycle. Hard work, integrity, and a willingness to fight for freedom characterized that generation. What will the world be like when its influence becomes a legacy and then that legacy fades?

In the book of Judges, a surprisingly similar state of affairs is presented in the history of Israel. After the miraculous events of the exodus and the period of temporary residence in the wilderness, the people of Israel entered the promised land. There the armies of Israel fought many battles to liberate territory from the Canaanites. In this week's lesson Joshua and his warrior generation have died off. The next generation is in control, and its stories are told in the book of Judges.

B. Lesson Background

The book of Judges records the history of Israel from the time of Joshua's death until the time of Samuel, Israel's last judge (see 1 Samuel 7:15). This is roughly the time period 1400–1050 BC. During this time period, Israel had no king but was instead guided by judges. Judges were men and women who arose providentially in times of national crisis to deliver the nation. They seemed to be endowed with the Spirit of God in a special way (at least some of them). The judges were a colorful cast of characters, including the woman-warrior Deborah, the fleece-man Gideon, the left-handed assassin Ehud, and the ancient "superman" Samson.

The judges of Israel served several functions. At times they were judicial arbiters. More often they were national deliverers, frequently as military leaders. Judges were not like kings in that there was no hereditary succession. The one son of a judge who tried to succeed his father in this manner failed (Abimelech, son of Gideon; Judges 9).

Furthermore, the judges of Israel did not function like kings by imposing taxes or negotiating treaties with other nations—functions expected of kings. Israel's judges had no standing army but relied on the tribal leaders of Israel to provide men when military action was necessary. The judges did not have grand palaces or courtiers. They were seen as regular citizens with extraordinary responsibilities.

The period of the judges is in many ways the record of Israel's "Dark Ages." The Israelites had become a settled nation, living in cities and villages. They were farmers, not nomadic shepherds like the patriarchs. Yet this is a time of crisis between faith and culture, between covenant loyalty and the enticing sins of the Canaanites.

Chapter 2 gives a preview of the book and outlines a cycle that is repeated many times in the period before Israel has a king. The cycle is tragically repetitive: apostasy leads to crisis, which leads to repentance, which leads to deliverance, which drifts back to apostasy. The verdict of the book of Judges is that this was a time of moral chaos. "In those days there was no king in Israel: every man did that which was right in his own eyes" (Judges 21:25). [See question #1, page 48.]

I. Generation Veers Off Course (Judges 2:11-14)

A. People's Betrayal (vv. 11-13)

11, 12. And the children of Israel did evil in the sight of the LORD, and served Baalim: and they forsook the LORD God of their fathers, which brought them out of the land of Egypt, and followed other gods, of the gods of the people that were round about them, and bowed themselves unto them, and provoked the LORD to anger.

The previous generations of Israelites had experienced many mighty things. They had seen the parting of the Red Sea and the destruction of the Egyptian army (Exodus 14). They had been the beneficiaries of miraculous food and water in the wilderness (16:11-15; 17:6). They had witnessed the supernatural on the mountain of Sinai (19:16-20). They had beheld the mighty presence of God in the tabernacle (40:34, 35).

Now the descendants of the exodus generation have settled in the land of Canaan and become infatuated with Canaanite religion. They have violated God's covenant and embraced idolatry. They have become conformed to the darkness of

---

How to Say It

ABIMELECH. Uh-*bim*-eh-lek.
ASHTAROTH. *Ash*-tuh-rawth.
BAALIM. Bay-uh-*leem*.
CANAANITES. *Kay*-nun-ites.
EHUD. *Ee*-hud.
HOSEA. Ho-*zay*-uh.
LAODICEA. Lay-*odd*-uh-*see*-uh (strong accent on *see*).
PHILISTINES. Fuh-*liss*-teens or *Fill*-us-teens.
SINAI. *Sigh*-nye or *Sigh*-nay-eye.

---

the world. From our vantage point it is easy to understand why God becomes angry with them. [See question #2, page 48.] God has fulfilled every one of His promises to them, and they have rejected Him.

THE PRICE OF "FUN"

J. L. Hunter "Red" Rountree was the oldest known bank robber in America. He was 92 when he died in prison on October 12, 2004.

Red got a late start in his profession. In his late eighties he pulled off his first robbery at a Mississippi bank. He was given three years' probation, a fine, and was told to get out of the state. A year later, in 1999, he robbed a Florida bank and received a three-year sentence. He was released in 2002. In 2003 he robbed a Kansas bank and was sentenced to nearly 13 years in prison.

Red Rountree had turned bitter many years earlier because of something about a bank loan that didn't go well. The bitter spirit festered for years before he acted upon it. In a prison interview he said, "You want to know why I rob banks? It's fun. I feel good, awful good. I feel good for sometimes days, for sometimes hours." No family member claimed his body upon his death. Apparently his bitterness had made him a lonely old man.

Israel's time-and-again pursuit of fictitious gods shows some of that same futility. Like Red Rountree, Israel persisted in doing what was "fun." But sinful "fun" is fleeting. In the long run the cost of sinful "fun" is always very steep. Both the experiences of Red Rountree and Israel should teach us a lesson. Will we learn?—C. R. B.

13. And they forsook the LORD, and served Baal and Ashtaroth.

As we look at this from a vantage point of over 3,000 years after the event, it is puzzling as to why the people of Israel would abandon their God and turn to the Canaanite gods. What was so enticing there?

There are two deities mentioned as receiving worship from the Israelites. *Baal* is actually a title meaning "lord." *Baalim* (in Judges 2:11) is the plural form of Baal. The ancient Canaanites worship a chief male god whom they had given the title *lord*. He is seen as the weather god or storm god, and thus he is the god who controls the destiny of the people. If Baal withholds the rain, the crops do not grow and the people starve.

It also appears that the Canaanites believe that each field has a lesser god that controls its fertility. These gods are lords of the fields and have the power to give abundant or meager crops. Thus, the Canaanites serve the "big Baal" of the weather as well as the "little Baals" of each individual farm.

Ashtaroth is also a plural form and is feminine. In Canaanite religion she is the consort of Baal. She is a fertility deity who is thought to control the fertility of both women and of fields. See also Judges 10:6.

The agricultural society of the Canaanites venerates these gods by practices that included ritual prostitution (male and female), child sacrifice, and orgy-like worship. Some scholars believe that almost every woman living in a Canaanite village served a term as a temple prostitute before marriage. The Canaanite religions thus combine idolatry with forbidden sexuality. This is why it is common in the Old Testament to see the worship of false gods as "whoring" (see Deuteronomy 31:16; Judges 2:17). To make sexual immorality an act of devotion is strictly opposed to the holy morality of the law that the Israelites had received from God.

The Canaanites have gods with no morality, and this makes it easy to see why the men of Israel are attracted to this religion. Yet it is also clear why there can be no accommodation here for those who are supposed to live according to the holy covenant that their nation has with the holy God of Israel.

B. Lord's Anger (v. 14)

14. And the anger of the LORD was hot against Israel, and he delivered them into the hands of spoilers that spoiled them, and he sold them into the hands of their enemies round about, so that they could not any longer stand before their enemies.

Are we surprised that this outrageous behavior provokes the hot *anger* of God? The result is the lifting of God's providential protection for Israel. The nation is powerless to fight off the *spoilers* from surrounding peoples. A common strategy in those days is for an armed force to swoop down at harvesttime and steal the crops while killing all who resist. Thus, the tragedy of deaths and destruction is followed by grim times of famine and starvation.

II. Story Sadly Repeats
(Judges 2:16-19)

A. God Delivers (v. 16)

16. Nevertheless the LORD raised up judges, which delivered them out of the hand of those that spoiled them.

The author is clear that the people of Israel stand powerless before these foreign marauders.

Their deliverance comes only when God chooses and empowers leaders, called *judges*, to rescue them. This is a primary lesson found throughout the Bible. We can never hope to save ourselves. Salvation comes from God, who hears our cries, understands our helplessness, and comes to save us (see Isaiah 35:4).

B. People Turn Away (v. 17)

17. And yet they would not hearken unto their judges, but they went a whoring after other gods, and bowed themselves unto them: they turned quickly out of the way which their fathers walked in, obeying the commandments of the LORD; but they did not so.

We are drawn to share God's frustration in this cycle. The people suffer for their sin, so God delivers them. But then they sin again, bringing on another cycle of suffering. Why can't they figure out this pattern?

From a coolly analytical viewpoint, it is easy for us to see their folly. However, our life experiences are filled with similar cases. Sin leads to punishment and suffering (see Jeremiah 14:10). God notices our cries of suffering (see Exodus 3:7; Nehemiah 9:9). Repentance saves us from destruction (see Jonah 3:10), because God never stops loving us (see Psalm 89:32, 33, which applies these principles to the royal descendants of David).

The text draws a strong contrast to the faithfulness of "the Joshua generation" and the faithlessness of "the Judges generations." Their ancestors obeyed God's commandments, but *they did not so.* False worship and disobedience go hand in hand.

C. God Still Delivers (v. 18)

18. And when the LORD raised them up judges, then the LORD was with the judge, and delivered them out of the hand of their enemies all the days of the judge: for it repented the LORD because of their groanings by reason of them that oppressed them and vexed them.

God is involved repeatedly in the deliverance of His people. He provides a *judge* to deliver them, and He is *with the judge.* The book of Judges tells the stories of the judges with all their human failings. For example, Samson is presented as a slow-witted show-off who can be tempted easily by an attractive woman (Judges 14–16). Although Samson is humiliated due to disobedience, God is with him until the end, empowering him to destroy many of the enemy Philistines through his own death (Judges 16:28-30).

In the antique language of the *King James Version*, the phrase *it repented the Lord* should not be misunderstood. Today we think of repentance as a humble response to personal sin. But God does not repent in this way because God is without sin. The issue, rather, is that of the Lord's compassion as He relents from His anger. God's wrath has yielded to His mercy. God is never overwhelmed by anger (see Hosea 11:9). [See question #3, page 48.]

D. People Still Turn Away (v. 19)

19. And it came to pass, when the judge was dead, that they returned, and corrupted themselves more than their fathers, in following other gods to serve them, and to bow down unto them; they ceased not from their own doings, nor from their stubborn way.

There is a great sadness in this verse. It is not just that the people lapse into disobedience, but that they return to their sin so energetically! Depravity can quickly become a downward spiral of destruction.

The root cause of this pattern is given to us: human stubbornness. This is sometimes celebrated as a virtue, but it should not be. Stubbornness is not the same as faithfulness and an uncompromising stand for righteousness. Stubborn people are usually prideful and unwilling to admit error. Stubbornness is equated with an unrepentant heart in Scripture (see Romans 2:5). God will not abide this type of human defiance.

SOME CALL IT *STUBBORN*

"Bullheaded," "set in their ways," or some just call it being "stubborn." That's how we describe other people when they are being inflexible. Examples of this trait might be a crotchety old person who refuses to take medications or the proverbial husband who rejects his wife's pleading to stop the car and ask directions.

On the other hand, when it is we who are being inflexible, we see ourselves to be acting with "dogged persistence," having "steadfast fidelity to a cause," or exhibiting "plain ol' stick-to-it-ive-ness." Perhaps we see ourselves in the mold of a detective who single-mindedly pursues a "cold case" for years and finally brings a criminal to justice. Or as a Thomas Edison, who may work diligently for years, performing hundreds of experiments to perfect the light bulb. We all like to believe that we act with motives that are more noble than the motives of others, don't we?

There is an important difference between the virulent trait of stubbornness and the virtuous trait of fidelity. During the time of the judges, Israel made no pretense of holding to righteousness. Instead, the people stubbornly resisted

Judges of Israel

Judge	Major Oppressor	Years as Judge
Othniel (Judges 3:8-11)	Mesopotamia (Cushan-Rishathaim)	1373-1334 B.C.
Ehud (Judges 3:12-30)	Moabites (Eglon)	1319-1239 B.C.
Shamgar (Judges 3:31)	Philistines	1300 B.C.
Deborah (Judges 4, 5)	Canaanites (Jabin)	1239-1199 B.C.
Gideon (Judges 6-8)	Midianites	1192-1152 B.C.
Abimelech (Judges 9)	Period of Civil War	1152-1150 B.C.
Tola (Judges 10:1, 2)	Ammonites	1149-1126 B.C.
Jair (Judges 10:3-5)	Ammonites	1126-1104 B.C.
Jephthah (Judges 10:6-12:7)	Ammonites	1086-1080 B.C.
Ibzan (Judges 12:8-10)	Philistines	1080-1075 B.C.
Elon (Judges 12:11, 12)	Philistines	1075-1065 B.C.
Abdon (Judges 12:13-15)	Philistines	1065-1058 B.C.
Samson (Judges 13-16)	Philistines	1075-1055 B.C.
Eli (1 Samuel 1-4)	Philistines	1107-1067 B.C.
Samuel (1 Samuel 7-9)	Philistines	1067-1043 B.C.

Visual for Lesson 5. *You may wish to post this chart alongside the* Old Testament World *map visual or the* Timeline of Old Testament Events.

God's warnings and refused to see the plain evidence of what their sinfulness got them. What do you think: has human nature changed much since then?

—C. R. B.

III. Covenant Broken (Judges 2:20-23)

A. Delaying Promises (vv. 20, 21)

20, 21. And the anger of the LORD was hot against Israel; and he said, Because that this people hath transgressed my covenant which I commanded their fathers, and have not hearkened unto my voice; I also will not henceforth drive out any from before them of the nations which Joshua left when he died.

Before his death *Joshua* reminded the people of Israel that God had never failed to keep His promises to them (Joshua 23:14). God's promises are always true. The land of Canaan was referred to as the land promised to the fathers of Israel (see Exodus 13:11). But Joshua also warned the people that if they worshiped the false gods of the Canaanites, then God had promised to punish them and make the land an inhospitable and oppressive place (Joshua 23:12-16).

God's promises, then, are both absolute and contingent. God sets the terms of the covenant. God always upholds His end, absolutely keeping His promises. However, when the human participants fail to honor the covenant's terms, then God withholds the promised blessings. Instead, He delivers the curses or punishments also promised in the covenant. Thus the contingency element lies in God's promised response to human obedience or disobedience.

B. Testing Each Generation (vv. 22, 23)

22, 23. That through them I may prove Israel, whether they will keep the way of the LORD to walk therein, as their fathers did keep it, or not. Therefore the LORD left those nations, without driving them out hastily; neither delivered he them into the hand of Joshua.

I had the measles as a child and now have an immunity to this disease. My daughter is also immune to measles because she received a childhood immunization against them. She arrived at her immunity via a different path, but the result is the same. But if my daughter has a child, that baby will not be protected. Measles immunity cannot be inherited; it must be acquired by enduring either the disease or painful inoculations.

Each generation is tested. Because faith is a personal relationship, it cannot be inherited. Furthermore, the true nature of faith is unknown *until* it is tested. The tireless God knows that the faith of each generation of His people must be proved (see 1 Peter 1:7). [See question #4, page 48.]

Conclusion

A. Chasing Other Gods

The Bible is an account of God's pursuit of His lost children. It is also the story of humanity's flight from God and continual quest of other gods.

Our society embraces the worship of a surprising array of other gods. We see open worship of the gods of the occult and the pagan deities of nature. We see the worship of wealth and of power. We see the worship of sexuality and celebrity. We see the worship of sports and entertainment. We see the worship of technology and of materialism.

Home Daily Bible Readings

Monday, Sept. 25—Love the Lord (Deuteronomy 6:4-9)
Tuesday, Sept. 26—God and the Hebrew People (Psalm 78:1-8)
Wednesday, Sept. 27—Prayer for a Nation (Psalm 85:4-13)
Thursday, Sept. 28—Israel Disobeys God (Judges 2:1-5)
Friday, Sept. 29—A New Generation (Judges 2:6-10)
Saturday, Sept. 30—Israel Abandons God (Judges 2:11-15)
Sunday, Oct. 1—Call to Repentance (Judges 2:16-23)

Our generations are not pursuing a single false god but many!

The Bible labels such vain pursuit as idolatry. Today's lesson gives the inevitable results. First, we kindle the anger of God (Judges 2:12). Second, we suffer the withdrawal of God's blessings (2:14). Third, God begins to oppose us or may even fight against us (2:15). But, fourth, God sends a rescuer (2:16). [See question #5, page 48.] As Christians, we realize that this gets to the core of the gospel. We have strayed in sin, incurred the wrath of God, and experienced the withdrawal of His blessings. Our deliverer, Jesus Christ the Savior, rescues us from much more than national peril. He wants to save us, individually, from sin and the curse of eternal death.

B. Generational Legacies

There have been no world wars for over half a century, and we hope the twenty-first century will not see their return. The "greatest generation" with its many virtues and accomplishments has given way to its children and grandchildren. The transition has been difficult, and the church bears the scars of generational conflict. It is not easy to step aside when one has been in control for a long time. It is difficult to trust those who are younger, less experienced, and whom we have seen make serious mistakes growing up.

Yet we cannot stop the transition. It will take place whether we facilitate it or resist it. We must trust God to work patiently with the new crop of leaders, as he has for thousands of years.

So ask yourself: Have the leaders of my church allowed a place of influence for those younger, those in their twenties and thirties? Are the primary leaders of my church all 50 and older? What can I do to facilitate the transition? Do I have an attitude of encouragement or one of criticism for younger leaders? What can I do to support new and younger leaders in my church? Is there a particular young leader I can pray for this week?

C. Prayer

Mighty God, we marvel at Your eternal consistency. You always keep Your promises. May we be faithful and receive promised blessings rather than curses. If we are caught in the downward spiral of sin, please, dear God, intervene in our lives and rescue us as Your judges delivered Israel. We pray this in the name of Your mighty Son, Jesus, amen.

D. Thought to Remember

Those of each new generation must build a relationship of faith and obedience with God.

Learning by Doing

This page contains an alternative lesson plan emphasizing learning activities.
Classes desiring such student involvement will find these suggestions helpful.

Learning Goals

After participating in this lesson, each student will be able to:

1. Describe the situation Israel repeatedly faced when the faith held by one generation was not passed on to the next.

2. Compare and contrast Israel's challenge of passing on its faith to the next generation with the twenty-first-century church's challenge to do the same.

3. Identify one way that he or she will help prepare the next generation of church leaders.

Into the Lesson

Display the following four scrambled words as your class assembles: AAOPSSTY; CIIRSS; ACEEENNPRT; ACDEEEILNRV. Also display a poster board circle, 12" in diameter, that is centered and attached by a paper fastener to a poster board circle that is 20" in diameter. On the smaller circle have an arrow pointing from center to edge. Work the attached circle until it rotates easily.

As class members decipher the four scrambled words *(apostasy, crisis, repentance, deliverance)*, write each respectively at the 12 o'clock, 3 o'clock, 6 o'clock, and 9 o'clock positions on the larger circle. Make a short statement based on the lesson writer's comments on the cycle of destruction from the lesson Introduction.

Into the Word

As today's text pictures the foolish sinfulness of the people of Israel, it also reveals the grand characteristics of God. Display each of the short affirmatives about God below, but don't reveal the verses and thoughts that are in italics. (This can be done with simple paper strips, with an overhead transparency, or as a PowerPoint® presentation.) As each affirmation is revealed, ask your class, "How and in what verses is this attribute of God revealed in today's text?"

Sample verse numbers and explanations are given here, but accept other reasonable and insightful responses. (Though listed in a verse-by-verse sequence, the statements should be displayed randomly.) (1) "God is a moral God" *(vv. 11, 12 affirm that God sees evil and it angers Him)*; (2) "God is not bound by time or space" *(vv. 11, 12 affirm His relationship with previous generations and His presence in Egypt is a given)*; (3) "God can decide not to impose His will over human choice" *(v. 13 indicates that He can be ignored, at least temporarily)*; (4) "God will demonstrate His justice and wrath" *(v. 14 pictures His punishment of His wayward nation)*; (5) "God controls the destinies of all nations" *(v. 14 indicates God's use of pagan nations as His agents)*; (6) "God loves His people" *(v. 16 reveals that the judge-deliverers were God's loving idea)*; (7) "God expects His people to obey His commandments" *(v. 17)*; (8) "God will support individual leaders to fulfill His purposes" *(v. 18 states that God was with the judge He called forth to service)*; (9) "God stays the same; His expectations and His mercy do not vary" *(see v. 18)*; (10) "God deals with people individually, one generation at a time" *(v. 19 pictures the failure of succeeding generations and individuals to remain consistent to God's truth)*; (11) "There is a limit to God's patience with sinfulness" *(vv. 20, 21 describe God's decision about His sinful people)*; (12) "God will test the faith of His people" *(v. 22 indicates God's plan to prove His people by allowing sinful nations to continue alongside them)*; (13) "God can intervene on behalf of His people, or He can choose not to" *(v. 23 affirms God's decision not to intervene, not to overwhelm Israel's enemies)*.

A similar activity is included in the student book.

Into Life

As adults, your class members need to take an active role in the Christian education of their own children, grandchildren, and other children of your church and community. "Faithful unto death" should be each generation's goal. But all godly parents will look beyond their own generation to help the next generation to gain a faith that will last a lifetime.

Ask your class to make a list of the various ways that they can participate in the godly nurture of your church's children and teens. When the list is complete, indicate that you will make copies and distribute them next Sunday. Then each class member can choose one way to enlarge his or her presence in the lives of the next generation.

Let's Talk It Over

The questions on this page are designed to promote discussion of the lesson by the class and to encourage application of the lesson Scriptures. The answers provided are only discussion starters. Let your class talk it over from there.

1. The book of Judges shows all too clearly the cycle of apostasy, crisis, repentance, deliverance, and apostasy. Where do you think we are right now in this cycle? Or is it even appropriate to draw a parallel between then and now?

Obviously, there are no simple answers to these questions. For one thing Old Testament Israel was unique in being chosen by God for a specific task: to usher in the Messiah. No modern nation has been chosen by God in this way. Thus we should be careful in drawing parallels.

Second, a nation is a complexity of interrelated parts. There are so many different ideas, individuals, and structures to be considered! Think of all the national and local governmental powers, educational institutions, religious groups, businesses, charities, etc. It may be fair to say that we are experiencing each part of the cycle to some extent. Nonetheless, all cultures and generations have cycles that can be identified broadly. You may find it useful to bring up the latest hot topic on the national scene and which part of the cycle it speaks to.

2. What false gods do you find today's generation chasing after that make God angry? Is it fair to say that we are all idolaters at some level? Explain.

Certainly, contemporary culture has its fair share of seductive temptations: power, fame, sensuality, and entertainment are obvious candidates. But two other major culprits appear to be individualism and money. Rampant individualism has led us down a deceptive path to put faith in ourselves rather than in God. That attitude is dangerously close to the temptation presented to Adam and Eve in Genesis 3:5.

A lust for money and things (covetousness) is called idolatry by Paul (Colossians 3:5). This seems to have been the problem of the church of Laodicea (Revelation 3:14-22)—the only one of the seven churches in Revelation about which Jesus had nothing good to say. Bottom line: anything we place on the throne of our heart instead of God is an idol.

3. Repentance from sin begins with a change in heart and attitude. Following that, what spe-cific steps of repentance can individuals, churches, or even nations take to beseech God's mercy? How do these steps change from generation to generation—or do they change?

In prayer we can confess to God our sins and pledge to abandon our idols. Yet there must be more than penitent prayers. We must also confess our sins to one another (James 5:16). This is certainly required of individuals, but it can also be beneficial of groups.

We must also demolish our idols and things that lead us into sin. How we go about doing that in practical terms can make for interesting discussion! (Compare Acts 19:19.) Further, repentance can involve restitution where appropriate (Luke 19:8). Finally, we realize that methods of repentance may change from culture to culture. Daniel repented in sackcloth and ashes for the sins of his people (Daniel 9:3), a method that we do not use today.

4. In what ways can we help the next generation avoid the cycle of apostasy and repentance? What could happen to our church and nation if we neglect our duty in this regard?

Try to explore practical methods that could include immediate application. This can include parents praying with their children or encouraging them to memorize important Scriptures, grandparents sharing their testimony with the family on formal occasions, etc. Probe hard here. Push your students to see the seriousness of the consequences if they fail in this. The second question will help your students see how important their legacy is.

5. Share a time in your life when you went through this cycle of apostasy and repentance. What caused your downward spiral, and what or whom did God use to pull you out of it?

This is very personal, and not everyone will be comfortable with this question. But if two or three students could give a brief testimony (perhaps you could arrange this beforehand), it would make this lesson very real. By especially identifying who helped them out of the spiral and how they did so, you can give participants concrete ideas for application in their own lives.

God Leads Through Deborah

DEVOTIONAL READING: Psalm 91.

BACKGROUND SCRIPTURE: Judges 4.

PRINTED TEXT: Judges 4:4-10, 12-16.

Judges 4:4-10, 12-16

4 And Deborah, a prophetess, the wife of Lapidoth, she judged Israel at that time.

5 And she dwelt under the palm tree of Deborah, between Ramah and Beth-el in mount Ephraim: and the children of Israel came up to her for judgment.

6 And she sent and called Barak the son of Abinoam out of Kedesh-naphtali, and said unto him, Hath not the LORD God of Israel commanded, saying, Go and draw toward mount Tabor, and take with thee ten thousand men of the children of Naphtali and of the children of Zebulun?

7 And I will draw unto thee, to the river Kishon, Sisera the captain of Jabin's army, with his chariots and his multitude; and I will deliver him into thine hand.

8 And Barak said unto her, If thou wilt go with me, then I will go: but if thou wilt not go with me, then I will not go.

9 And she said, I will surely go with thee: notwithstanding the journey that thou takest shall not be for thine honor; for the LORD

shall sell Sisera into the hand of a woman. And Deborah arose, and went with Barak to Kedesh.

10 And Barak called Zebulun and Naphtali to Kedesh; and he went up with ten thousand men at his feet: and Deborah went up with him.

. . . .

12 And they showed Sisera that Barak the son of Abinoam was gone up to mount Tabor.

13 And Sisera gathered together all his chariots, even nine hundred chariots of iron, and all the people that were with him, from Harosheth of the Gentiles unto the river of Kishon.

14 And Deborah said unto Barak, Up; for this is the day in which the LORD hath delivered Sisera into thine hand: is not the LORD gone out before thee? So Barak went down from mount Tabor, and ten thousand men after him.

15 And the LORD discomfited Sisera, and all his chariots, and all his host, with the edge of the sword before Barak; so that Sisera lighted down off his chariot, and fled away on his feet.

16 But Barak pursued after the chariots, and after the host, unto Harosheth of the Gentiles: and all the host of Sisera fell upon the edge of the sword; and there was not a man left.

GOLDEN TEXT: Deborah, a prophetess, the wife of Lapidoth, . . . judged Israel at that time.
—Judges 4:4.

Lesson Aims

After participating in this lesson, each student will be able to:

1. Retell the story of Deborah, noting the qualities that made her a model leader.

2. Point out how leadership qualities like Deborah's can help the church.

3. Create a personal prayer plan for his or her church's leadership.

Lesson Outline

INTRODUCTION
　A. Women in the Old Testament
　B. Lesson Background
　I. DEBORAH THE JUDGE (Judges 4:4-5)
　　A. Prophetess and Wife (v. 4)
　　B. Judge of Israel (v. 5)
　　　Honest and Dishonest Judges
　II. DEBORAH THE ORGANIZER (Judges 4:6-10)
　　A. Recruiting General Barak (v. 6a)
　　B. Planning a Strategy (vv. 6b, 7)
　　C. Traveling with the Troops (vv. 8-10)
　III. DEBORAH THE WARRIOR (Judges 4:12-16)
　　A. Powerful Enemy (vv. 12, 13)
　　B. Confidence in God's Presence (v. 14)
　　　Thoughts into Action
　　C. Victory with God's Power (vv. 15, 16)
CONCLUSION
　A. Faithful Women Today
　B. Overcoming Leadership Conflicts
　C. Prayer
　D. Thought to Remember

Introduction

A. Women in the Old Testament

The Old Testament is treated by some as little more than a book of fantastic children's stories. To do this is to miss the rich treasury of insights into the lives of men and women who struggled in their relationships with God. Sometimes they are heroically successful, and we learn how they are pleasing to God. At other times they are colossal failures, and we can observe the patience and redemptive nature of God in dealing with them.

The Old Testament is dominated by the lives and exploits of men. Because of this, it is common to overlook the crucial and inspirational roles played by women in the history of Israel. Rarely are women presented as recognized community or national leaders. More often we find them in supporting roles as mothers, sisters, and wives of important men.

Consider Moses, the great man, whose life was influenced by women who functioned in all three of these supporting roles. The name of Moses' mother was Jochebed (Numbers 26:59). Exodus 2 relates the story of her daring actions to save baby Moses from a death edict. She stood against Egyptian tyranny, and God providentially rewarded her by allowing her to keep her baby and nurse him before turning him over to the Egyptian princess.

Also involved in this incident was Moses' sister, Miriam. This brave little girl, maybe just five or six years old, hid near her baby brother in the Nile and had the presence of mind to suggest to the princess her mother as a nurse. Later, Miriam played a key leadership role in the exodus. After the destruction of Pharaoh's army in the Red Sea, she led the women of Israel in a celebration of singing and dancing (Exodus 15:20, 21). In this passage she is referred to as a prophetess, although we have no record of her prophetic activities. Centuries later, the prophet Micah remembered the leaders of the exodus as three: Moses, Aaron, and Miriam (Micah 6:4).

An often-overlooked woman in the life of Moses is his wife, Zipporah. Exodus 4:24-26 tells a sobering story of a time when God sought to kill Moses. Zipporah saved Moses' life. She moved to guard her family in a time of crisis. Had she failed to understand the perplexing threat and act decisively, the history of Israel would have been very different.

Many other women can be identified as examples of faith in action in the Old Testament. Today's lesson is about one of the most famous of them all: the prophetess, judge, and warrior named Deborah. [See question #1, page 56.]

B. Lesson Background

Last week's lesson presented the destructive cycle of Israel that is found repeatedly in Judges: apostasy, crisis, repentance, and then deliverance by a judge raised up by God. After the death of the judge, this cycle began again and grew worse with each repetition (Judges 2:19). This week's lesson examines the story of the judge Deborah.

Many enemies threaten Israel in the book of Judges. The people who pose a threat to the Israel of Deborah's day are called simply the Canaanites. Genesis presents them as descendants of Canaan, the grandson of Noah. This Canaan was cursed because of an unfortunate incident related in Genesis 9:20-27.

The primary city of this particular group of Canaanites was Hazor, a large city located about 10 miles north of the Sea of Galilee. The site of Hazor has been excavated extensively. It is the largest biblical-era site in Israel, covering approximately 200 acres. Archaeologists estimate that ancient Hazor was a city with a population of more than 20,000—very substantial for the time.

The story of Deborah is told twice in Judges. In chapter 4 it is presented in prose form, as if from the hand of a recording historian. In chapter 5 the story is told as a song or in poetic fashion. This is likely the earlier version, for ancient peoples were great storytellers. Their stories were composed in a poetic manner so that they could be more easily learned and remembered.

The triumphal ode of chapter 5 is ascribed to Deborah herself (Judges 5:1). Scholars recognize the Song of Deborah as one of the oldest texts in the Old Testament.

I. Deborah the Judge
(Judges 4:4, 5)

A. Prophetess and Wife (v. 4)

4. And Deborah, a prophetess, the wife of Lapidoth, she judged Israel at that time.

How to Say It

ABINOAM. Uh-*bin*-o-am.
BARAK. *Bair*-uk.
EPHRAIM. *Ee*-fray-im.
ESDRAELON. *Es*-druh-*ee*-lon (strong accent on *ee*).
HAROSHETH. Huh-*roe*-sheth.
HAZOR. *Hay*-zor.
HULDAH. *Hul*-duh.
ISSACHAR. *Izz*-uh-kar.
JAEL. *Jay*-ul.
JOCHEBED. *Jock*-eh-bed.
KEDESH-NAPHTALI. *Kee*-desh-*naf*-tuh-lye (strong accent on *naf*).
LAPIDOTH. *Lap*-ih-doth.
MACHIR. *May*-ker.
MANASSEH. Muh-*nass*-uh.
NAPHTALI. *Naf*-tuh-lye.
SISERA. *Sis*-er-uh.
ZEBULUN. *Zeb*-you-lun.
ZIPPORAH. Zi-*po*-ruh.

The author introduces Deborah as a *wife, prophetess*, and judge. With all of these jobs, she must have been as "busy as a bee" and indeed her name means "bee" in Hebrew.

The Old Testament gives the title *prophetess*, in a godly sense, only to Miriam (Exodus 15:20), Huldah (2 Kings 22:14), Deborah, and the unnamed wife of Isaiah (Isaiah 8:3). This title is the feminine equivalent of *prophet*, with no real difference aside from gender.

We usually think of a prophet as one who has divine insight into future events, but this is only part of a prophet's function. Old Testament prophets are God's mouthpieces. As such, they are inspired by God to keep Israel on track in religious and moral matters. Deborah, then, is presented as more than a wise judge. She is an inspired judge, used by God to guide the development of the young nation.

Deborah is also presented as a wife. Her husband's name, *Lapidoth,* means "torches" or "wicks." One tradition outside the Bible holds that Lapidoth was responsible for providing the wicks for the sacred lamps of the sanctuary in Shiloh. There is no record that Deborah and Lapidoth had any children.

B. Judge of Israel (v. 5)

5. And she dwelt under the palm tree of Deborah, between Ramah and Bethel in mount Ephraim: and the children of Israel came up to her for judgment.

Deborah and Lapidoth live in a rural area less than a dozen miles north of Jerusalem. This is in the tribal territory of *Ephraim.* It is a semi-mountainous region. Deborah uses an outdoor courtroom under a famous *palm tree* also called *Deborah.*

The fact that people come *to her for judgment* indicates that Deborah's judging is akin to what we would call binding arbitration. It is doubtful that she is dealing with criminal cases. Those would have been quickly resolved in the various communities of Israel, usually at the city gate (see Deuteronomy 17:5; 21:19).

More likely, Deborah is an agreed-upon judge for difficult private disputes (more like our civil litigation). The two disputing parties would agree to abide by her decision before it was given, perhaps having been sent by the elders of a village or city. Deborah likely receives a fee for each judgment.

Such a system would have no strict legal basis, because there is no king or government to appoint and validate Deborah's authority. This makes her judgeship all the more remarkable.

Deborah must have a widespread reputation for fairness and wisdom. She would be fulfilling the qualities stated to Moses by his father-in-law, Jethro, for a judge: capable, God-fearing, truthful, and not open to bribery (Exodus 18:21).

She judges the thorniest matters, a role filled by Moses during an earlier period (see Exodus 18:14, 15, 25, 26). The people appreciate this just and impartial judge, because government officials in the ancient world are known for corruption (see Isaiah 1:23). [See question #2, page 56.]

HONEST AND DISHONEST JUDGES

A little-known lawyer was sworn in as a U.S. Supreme Court Justice on December 19, 1975. How he got there is an intriguing story.

In 1958 a man by the name of Sherman Skolnick sued a Chicago brokerage firm for allegedly mishandling his life savings. Skolnick lost his case. He also lost his appeal to the Illinois Supreme Court. The experience embittered him against the justice system and he began a judicial watchdog organization. In 1969 Skolnick accused two state supreme court justices of accepting thousands of dollars' worth of bank stock in return for deciding a case in favor of a powerful Chicago lawyer.

Media pressure forced the state supreme court to appoint a special commission to investigate. John Paul Stevens became the chief counsel. The meticulous care with which he built his case, combined with his courtroom strategy, brought down two previously respected but now-tainted justices. (Ironically, both had ruled against Skolnick in his case years earlier.) Stevens was exactly the kind of person President Gerald Ford was looking for to restore respect for the federal government after the Watergate scandal of 1974.

Deborah was such a judge: careful and honest in her judgments. The common people of every nation are blessed when people of impeccable reputation, practical wisdom, and honest judgment control the judicial system. —C. R. B.

II. Deborah the Organizer
(Judges 4:6-10)

A. Recruiting General Barak (v. 6a)

6a. And she sent and called Barak the son of Abinoam out of Kedesh-naphtali.

As a leader of the people, Deborah's role extends beyond maintaining an outdoor courtroom. She recognizes a crisis among her people and summons a man who can do what she cannot: lead an army into battle. This man is *Barak*, from the city of *Kedesh* (meaning "sanctuary").

Kedesh is located about 5 miles north of Hazor or about 15 miles north of the Sea of Galilee. Although in the tribal territory of *Naphtali*, Kedesh is one of the six cities of refuge controlled by the Levites (Numbers 35; see Joshua 20:7).

The crisis is a state of Canaanite banditry. That had caused trade caravans to disappear and farming villages to be abandoned (Judges 5:6, 7).

B. Planning a Strategy (vv. 6b, 7)

6b, 7. And said unto him, Hath not the LORD God of Israel commanded, saying, Go and draw toward mount Tabor, and take with thee ten thousand men of the children of Naphtali and of the children of Zebulun? And I will draw unto thee, to the river Kishon, Sisera the captain of Jabin's army, with his chariots and his multitude; and I will deliver him into thine hand.

Barak is instructed to gather an army of 10,000 men to *mount Tabor*, a solitary dome that rises about 1,500 feet above the surrounding countryside. It is located in the northeast end of Israel's central Plain of Esdraelon. The army is primarily drawn from the northern tribes of *Naphtali* and *Zebulun*; Judges 5:14, 15 tells us that there are also present men from Benjamin, Issachar, and Machir (or Makir, a subtribe of Manasseh).

The enemy *army* has gathered under the leadership of *Sisera*, the military expert of King Jabin. Jabin rules from Hazor in the northern Galilean area. Hazor is reckoned as the great city of the Canaanites (compare Joshua 11:10). Although Joshua had defeated and burned the city, it was not conquered. By the time of Deborah, the Canaanites had rebuilt it. Deborah determines the strategy of the coming battle, choosing to engage Sisera on the banks of *the river Kishon*, to the east of Mount Tabor.

C. Traveling with the Troops (vv. 8-10)

8-10. And Barak said unto her, If thou wilt go with me, then I will go: but if thou wilt not go with me, then I will not go. And she said, I will surely go with thee: notwithstanding the journey that thou takest shall not be for thine honor; for the LORD shall sell Sisera into the hand of a woman. And Deborah arose, and went with Barak to Kedesh. And Barak called Zebulun and Naphtali to Kedesh; and he went up with ten thousand men at his feet: and Deborah went up with him.

Barak may be the most able military leader in Israel, but he recognizes the value of having *Deborah* accompany him. [See question #3, page. 56.] Deborah warns him that this will divert the glory of victory from himself to her.

The result will be that the mighty chariot army of *Sisera* suffers defeat at *the hand of a woman*. The biggest disgrace in being defeated by a woman is the fact that women are not participants in the armies of the ancient world. Thus Sisera will lose to a nonmilitary adversary. This will also diminish the recognition of Barak's victory.

III. Deborah the Warrior
(Judges 4:12-16)

A. Powerful Enemy (vv. 12, 13)

12, 13. And they showed Sisera that Barak the son of Abinoam was gone up to mount Tabor. And Sisera gathered together all his chariots, even nine hundred chariots of iron, and all the people that were with him, from Harosheth of the Gentiles unto the river of Kishon.

We now begin to understand the daunting challenge, for Sisera's army is known to have *nine hundred* armored *chariots*. These are the most fearsome battle machines of the ancient world (see Judges 4:3). The author paints an imposing picture: the Canaanite forces are spread for several miles across the broad Plain of Esdraelon. Sisera's army is vulnerable, however, because of its dependence upon this chariot force.

B. Confidence in God's Presence (v. 14)

14. And Deborah said unto Barak, Up; for this is the day in which the LORD hath delivered Sisera into thine hand: is not the LORD gone out before thee? So Barak went down from mount Tabor, and ten thousand men after him.

The faith and determination of *Deborah* shine brightly here. She announces that *this is the day*— the day of victory! Deborah understands that God is willing to fight on the side of Israel, and, therefore, "safety is of the Lord" (Proverbs 21:31). With this great blessing of assurance, Barak and his men rush *down from mount Tabor* to meet the Canaanites in battle. [See question #4, page 56.]

THOUGHTS INTO ACTION

Matthew Nagle is a quadriplegic. He made history in June 2004 when surgeons implanted a silicon wafer into his brain. The wafer, known as BrainGate, is one-sixth of an inch square and has 100 electrodes that extend one-sixteenth of an inch into Nagle's brain. When he thinks about moving his arm, the brain signals are sent to another device on the outside of his head. From there an electronic message is sent to a computer that translates it into code that enables a machine to do things such as change the TV channel or perform simple tasks on Nagle's computer.

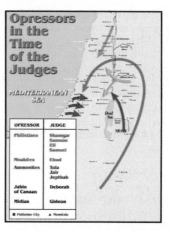

Visual for Lesson 6

You may wish to post this chart alongside one of the other charts for the quarter.

The device is far from perfect. Scientists had to figure out the signals Nagle's brain sends before the computer could be programmed. Because brain patterns are always changing, the device has to be "retuned" every time Nagle uses it. Still, the technology enables him to turn his thoughts into action and gives him some control over his life that he has been missing.

Deborah's role in Israel's victory started with her being in touch with the will of God, hearing the message God gave her for Israel's good, and using her wisdom and strength of character to turn God's thoughts into human action. Not all of us have Deborah's gifts, and, like Nagle's machine, we don't respond perfectly to "divine input." But when we are "properly tuned," we each have the ability to use what God has given us to turn His thoughts into action. —C. R. B.

C. Victory with God's Power (vv. 15, 16)

15, 16. And the LORD discomfited Sisera, and all his chariots, and all his host, with the edge of the sword before Barak; so that Sisera lighted down off his chariot, and fled away on his feet. But Barak pursued after the chariots, and after the host, unto Harosheth of the Gentiles: and all the host of Sisera fell upon the edge of the sword; and there was not a man left.

Despite Sisera's superior technology, Barak's army is able to rout the enemy. There is both an earthly and a heavenly reason. First, the mighty *chariots* become bogged down in the sandy soil in and around the river Kishon, rendering them ineffective (Judges 5:21). Judges 5:20 may indicate that this was made worse by a providential downpour of rain.

Second, the superior forces of *Sisera* were *discomfited.* This is a panic sent from God himself. The deep fear that follows causes Sisera's troops to flee chaotically. God is fighting on Israel's behalf. This is the opposite of the periods in Judges where God withdrew His blessing and fought against Israel (Judges 2:15).

The victory is complete, for there is *not a man left.* Sisera himself is reduced to fleeing on foot. He dies at the hand of another woman, Jael, the wife of Heber (Judges 4:21).

Conclusion

A. Faithful Women Today

Are there lessons for the church in this Old Testament story? Is Deborah a model for women today? These are good questions, and there are thorny problems of interpretation regarding the the role of women in church leadership (see 1 Timothy 2:12). Perhaps, however, this story can give us at least partial insight into how God views these issues.

First, we see that God is not opposed to using women to help His people. Deborah enjoyed God's blessings in her work as a righteous judge, in her voice as a prophetess, and in her planning as a military strategist. The judges of Israel are overwhelmingly male but not exclusively.

Second, we see that capable women can earn the respect of the people of God. It would be fascinating to learn exactly how Deborah developed her reputation as a judge, but we meet her after this had been accomplished. Undoubtedly, this did not happen overnight. It probably took many years of consistent excellence as a judge for Deborah to achieve her position of authority.

Home Daily Bible Readings

Monday, Oct. 2—The God in Whom I Trust (Psalm 91)

Tuesday, Oct. 3—No Need to Fear (Psalm 27:1-6)

Wednesday, Oct. 4—Othniel Judges Israel (Judges 3:7-11)

Thursday, Oct. 5—Courageous Leaders (Hebrews 11:1, 2, 32-34)

Friday, Oct. 6—Deborah Leads the People (Judges 4:1-10)

Saturday, Oct. 7—Success Assured (Judges 4:12-16)

Sunday, Oct. 8—Deborah's Song of Praise (Judges 5:1-12)

Third, we should understand that it is unnecessary for men to deny women credit for effective service. Barak was warned that his need for Deborah's presence would result in her receiving the people's acclaim for the great victory over the Canaanites. Barak didn't seem to have a problem with this. The wisest players are those who sometimes step aside to let someone else carry the ball and hear the roar of the crowd.

B. Overcoming Leadership Conflicts

Why are some churches in constant turmoil? Why is growth sporadic or absent altogether? These are complex issues, and there is no single answer that fits every situation. However, many churches fail to grow and thrive because of conflicts among the leaders. Here are three lessons from the story of Deborah that can help us.

First, egos need to be checked at the church door. Judges 4 and 5 paint a beautiful picture of two cooperating leaders, each recognizing the abilities of the other. Churches that are controlled by isolated, inflexible leaders will have problems. Congregations led by win-at-all-costs personalities will suffer. Some qualities that make a person successful in the business world may become destructive in church leadership.

Second, good leadership decisions have the welfare of the people sharply in focus. Neither Deborah nor Barak are presented as bloodthirsty warriors itching for glory. They pursue the terrible option of war because the people must be freed from oppression. When making leadership decisions, we should ask ourselves, "Why am I doing this? Am I choosing this course because it is most comfortable for me? Am I making a choice that is best for the long-term health of the church?"

Third, leadership success ultimately is determined by God. Deborah knew that the battle would be won because God was fighting for Israel. All church leaders should be accountable to God and open to His leading. The church is not a private little empire for any leader. Whatever leadership roles we are given, we should approach our ministries with the desire to serve people and to serve God. [See question #5, page 56.]

C. Prayer

Holy God, we are in Your hands. We pray that You will provide our church with leaders who are brave and strong, yet humble and obedient. Give those called to leadership the wisdom to trust You fully. We pray in Jesus' name, amen.

D. Thought to Remember

Tough times require strong leaders.

Learning by Doing

This page contains an alternative lesson plan emphasizing learning activities.
Classes desiring such student involvement will find these suggestions helpful.

Learning Goals

After participating in this lesson, each student will be able to:

1. Retell the story of Deborah, noting the qualities that made her a model leader.

2. Point out how leadership qualities like Deborah's can help the church.

3. Create a personal prayer plan for his or her church's leadership.

Into the Lesson

Display an outline of a person (on roll paper or poster board) as your class assembles. Have the following heading over the drawing: "The Ideal Leader." As students arrive, hand them a marker and say, "Go up to the drawing and write in a characteristic you think is important in the ideal leader." (Make sure the marker won't bleed through the paper and damage the wall.)

As class begins, point to the list and ask, "Are there other qualities you want to add, now that you have had more time to think?" Then introduce Deborah as a judge of Old Testament Israel.

Into the Word

Before class recruit a volunteer to be interviewed as the Israelite judge Deborah. Encourage your volunteer to be well studied on the time period of the judges generally and on the life and work of Deborah specifically. Provide your volunteer a copy of the lesson writer's commentary and the questions that you (or a class member) are going to ask. Be sure to allow some spontaneity from your class and from your interviewee.

Interview questions are provided here, but you may choose to write your own questions to match your class's level of biblical maturity. Of course some answers may be speculative; be sure your students understand that. You should discuss the reasonableness of answers that are not directly revealed in Scripture. Related verse numbers from today's text in Judges 4 are given after each question.

(1) "Deborah, what did your husband think about your work on behalf of God's people?" *(v. 4)*; (2) "What was the nature of your prophesying? How did you receive the Spirit's Word?" *(v. 4)*; (3) "Why was your work done under a tree by the side of the road?" *(v. 5)*; (4) "What sort of cases did you handle?" *(v. 5)*; (5) "How did you know of Barak, who lived so far away?" *(v. 6)*; (6) "What would Barak have known of the Canaanite oppressors?" *(v. 6)*; (7) "How could Barak raise an army of 10,000 men from only two tribal groups?" *(v. 7)*; (8) "Where exactly is this Kishon River, and why would God want the battle to take place there?" *(v. 7)*; (9) "Why do you think Barak refused to go to war without you?" *(vv. 8-10)*; (10) "Why did you caution Barak that the honor of victory would come to a woman and not to him?" *(vv. 8-10)*; (11) What is significant about the fact that your army was to face 900 iron chariots? Didn't your 10,000 men seem to be the stronger army?" *(vv. 12, 13)*; (12) When you assumed command of Barak's army and gave the command to charge, how did Barak respond?" *(v. 14)*; (13) "From Mount Tabor you had a good view of the battle. Exactly what happened?" *(vv. 15, 16 and Judges 5:18-22)*; (14) "Your poem of victory that we have recorded in Judges 5 is a beautiful expression. How do you account for such a response to the defeat of God's enemies?"

As your "Deborah" responds, stop to discuss key elements of the text. Allow students to interact with her assumptions and conclusions.

Into Life

Give each student an index card. Display a list of the primary leaders of your congregation: ministers, elders, deacons, and others. Pair up each student with a leader's name. If your class is not large enough to cover pairing up all the names, ask for volunteers to take two or more names. If there are more class members than leaders, have more than one student responsible for each leader.

Have students make the following commitment: on one side of their cards, write out a plan for how they will offer prayer support for their chosen leader. On the other side of their cards, write a commitment to visiting with their chosen leader. This visitation may be at the leader's home, by going out for coffee, etc. By participating in this activity, students will have an opportunity to express appreciation for their leaders and enjoy being in their presence. This will reflect Barak's appreciation and reliance on Deborah's leadership.

Let's Talk It Over

*The questions on this page are designed to promote discussion of the lesson
by the class and to encourage application of the lesson Scriptures. The answers
provided are only discussion starters. Let your class talk it over from there.*

1. What can we learn about the character of godly women through the portions of Scripture that record their words?

Three lengthy sections are Judges 5 (song of Deborah), 1 Samuel 2:1-10 (Hannah's prayer), and Luke 1:46-55 (song of Mary). A shorter section is Exodus 15:21 (song of Miriam). Interestingly, all four have military/political elements. Take a moment to read them (perhaps one group per poem). Report on the major themes, how much Scripture these women knew, and any insights into God, leadership, and faith that they demonstrate.

2. What do you think made Deborah such a good judge? Why do you think God used a woman in a role traditionally filled by a man?

Scripture doesn't explicitly say why Deborah was a good judge. But using our "sanctified imaginations," we can suppose that she had the same qualities that would make any man a good judge: a sense of justice, knowledge of the law, compassion, courage, zeal, honesty, etc.

Also, the Scripture doesn't say why God honored her in this role rather than having a man do it. Thus any answer we give would be speculative. We can note that it is somewhat rare for God to use women in leadership roles in the Bible. For instance, the Bible uses the masculine words *prophet* and *prophets* about 480 times, but the feminine word *prophetess* only 8 times (with no plural forms).

Yet the presence of women in certain leadership roles is not unknown. We can take note of the prophetess Anna, who stepped forward to praise God at the presentation of the baby Jesus (Luke 2:36-38). Lydia hosted Paul (and probably a church) in her home (Acts 16:11-15, 40). Priscilla, with her husband, taught Apollos privately (Acts 18:24-26). The apostle Paul notes some role restrictions in 1 Timothy 2:12.

3. How is a partnership like the one Deborah and Barak had a model for us today?

Judges 4:8-10 makes it clear that Barak would forfeit the honor of the battle if he demanded Deborah's partnership. But Barak apparently was not a "glory hog." He recognized that her presence would give him confidence. Not only did he trust her judgment for civil affairs, he apparently relied on her for military strategy, mutual prayer, and accountability.

Since Deborah was a prophetess, we can assume that God somehow spoke through her. This would be a great comfort to Barak. Thus the moral, godly strength of one person assisted another through a difficult time. Encouraging Christians to draw upon the moral strength of one another is still a good practice to emulate.

4. How are Deborah and Barak models for Christian faith? How do their stories mirror ours?

Here we want to assist students in making connections between this Old Testament story and New Testament living. Remind them that Barak is among the heroes of the faith in Hebrews 11:32.

Some students probably will make odd or unrestrained connections. Try to steer the discussion to things like the kind of enemies we face that make it seem like we're fighting overwhelming odds; the importance of relying on the promises and faithfulness of God; the hope of a great victory, even if is brought about in surprising ways. The discussion can reveal the spiritual alertness of the class. You may also succeed in helping students read the Scriptures with a view toward practical application.

5. What problems are the leaders of our church facing right now? How can we support them in the battles they face and the service they provide to God's people?

Leaders are under constant attack from Satan and often from church members as well. Make sure that your discussion affirms these leaders—both those who serve in official capacities and those who lead unofficially by character and reputation.

Make a list of things that will affirm your leaders: prayers, notes of encouragement, public recognition, etc. Encourage students to commit to doing one of these within the next seven days. At the close of the lesson, pray for any church leaders in attendance. (You may wish to tell them in advance that you will be doing this.)

God Answers Samuel's Prayer

October 15
Lesson 7

DEVOTIONAL READING: Psalm 31:14-24.

BACKGROUND SCRIPTURE: 1 Samuel 7:3-13.

PRINTED TEXT: 1 Samuel 7:3-13.

1 Samuel 7:3-13

3 And Samuel spake unto all the house of Israel, saying, If ye do return unto the LORD with all your hearts, then put away the strange gods and Ashtaroth from among you, and prepare your hearts unto the LORD, and serve him only: and he will deliver you out of the hand of the Philistines.

4 Then the children of Israel did put away Baalim and Ashtaroth, and served the LORD only.

5 And Samuel said, Gather all Israel to Mizpeh, and I will pray for you unto the LORD.

6 And they gathered together to Mizpeh, and drew water, and poured it out before the LORD, and fasted on that day, and said there, We have sinned against the LORD. And Samuel judged the children of Israel in Mizpeh.

7 And when the Philistines heard that the children of Israel were gathered together to Mizpeh, the lords of the Philistines went up against Israel. And when the children of Israel heard it, they were afraid of the Philistines.

8 And the children of Israel said to Samuel, Cease not to cry unto the LORD our God for us, that he will save us out of the hand of the Philistines.

9 And Samuel took a sucking lamb, and offered it for a burnt offering wholly unto the LORD: and Samuel cried unto the LORD for Israel; and the LORD heard him.

10 And as Samuel was offering up the burnt offering, the Philistines drew near to battle against Israel: but the LORD thundered with a great thunder on that day upon the Philistines, and discomfited them; and they were smitten before Israel.

11 And the men of Israel went out of Mizpeh, and pursued the Philistines, and smote them, until they came under Beth-car.

12 Then Samuel took a stone, and set it between Mizpeh and Shen, and called the name of it Ebenezer, saying, Hitherto hath the LORD helped us.

13 So the Philistines were subdued, and they came no more into the coast of Israel: and the hand of the LORD was against the Philistines all the days of Samuel.

GOLDEN TEXT: Samuel cried unto the LORD for Israel; and the LORD heard him.
—1 Samuel 7:9.

Lesson Aims

After participating in this lesson, each student will be able to:

1. Tell how repentance and prayer were important to the deliverance of the Israelites from the Philistines.

2. Describe how repentance and prayer are important today.

3. Write an intercessory prayer for someone who is plagued by some trouble.

Lesson Outline

Introduction

A. National Repentance

"O Israel, return unto the Lord thy God; for thou hast fallen by thine iniquity" (Hosea 14:1). This type of call to national repentance is found repeatedly throughout Scripture. It was a constant message of the Old Testament prophets (example: "Say unto the house of Israel, . . . repent," Ezekiel 14:6). Jonah was sent to Nineveh, a non-Israelite city, to call that city to repentance; Jesus used that example in His call for a generation to repent (Matthew 12:41).

We often view calls for repentance from an individualistic perspective. That is, we assume that a call for repentance is a call to each person to get right with God. While individual repentance is vital, the Bible also issues calls of repentance to communities and nations. God will not bless a society that encourages sin. History is littered with stories of communities and nations that descended into depravity and eventually were blotted out by God. A striking example is the city of Sodom (Genesis 19:24; Isaiah 3:9).

Today's lesson relates the story of a period of repentance for the nation of Israel. Israel was called by Samuel, God's prophet and judge, to give up its pagan idolatry and return to God. The resulting repentance brought deliverance from a national threat. It brought a period of revival and spiritual blessing.

We should take encouragement from this story, for such calls to national repentance are not just relics of the biblical world. We need godly voices in modern nations to resist evil and to call for repentance, even in the face of ridicule and disbelief. We cannot predict the success or failure of such appeals, but we can be sure of God's blessings if such calls are heeded.

B. Lesson Background

Samuel is one of the most multitalented characters in the Bible. His amazing story starts even before his birth. His mother, Hannah, prayed fervently for God to remove her inability to bear a child. She vowed that if a son were given to her, he would be dedicated to the service of the Lord (1 Samuel 1:11). When God answered her prayer, she named her son Samuel, meaning, "his name is God" or perhaps "heard of God." This name is an acknowledgment of the one true God.

Samuel grew up in the tabernacle at Shiloh under the tutelage of Eli the priest. There, as a young boy, Samuel received a message directly from God (1 Samuel 3:1-14). The message concerned God's displeasure with the household of Eli, but its reception confirmed the extraordinary ministry that awaited Samuel.

Beyond that of child prodigy, consider some of the other roles played by Samuel in the Bible. He was a prophet, meaning that he was God's spokesman (1 Samuel 3:20). He was a seer, meaning that he received supernatural visions from God (1 Samuel 9:19, 20). He "judged Israel all the days of his life" and was the last of the judges (1 Samuel 7:15; Acts 13:20); that fact makes him a transitional figure to the era of the prophets

(Acts 3:24; 13:20). Finally, he was a kingmaker, the one who anointed both Saul (1 Samuel 10:1; 15:1) and David (1 Samuel 16:13) as kings of Israel. [See question #1, page 64.]

Today's lesson is the aftermath of a horrifying incident in the history of Israel in which the ark of the covenant was used as a tool for war (1 Samuel 4:3, 4). This ill-conceived plan resulted in the defeat of Israel and the capture of the ark by the Philistines (4:10, 11). The Philistines are often seen as the traditional enemy of the people of God in the Old Testament. They occupied the seacoast area of Gaza in southwest Israel, south of Joppa. They had five strong cities in this area: Gaza, Ashkelon, Ashdod, Gath, and Ekron.

The Bible and other sources tell us that the Philistines were originally foreign invaders from the land of Caphtor (see Amos 9:7), which some scholars identify as the island of Crete. At the time of the exodus, the Philistines were already well established in their territory (see Exodus 13:17). They appear prominently in Judges and 1 Samuel and are finally conquered by David.

After Solomon, however, the Philistines seem to have a small revival of independence and resume their role as the bane of Israel. Although now gone, they left their name on the region, for *Palestine* is derived from *Philistine*. In matters of religion the Philistines are often pictured as polar opposites to the Israelites. There seems to be no more degrading title than to be called an "uncircumcised Philistine" (see 1 Samuel 17:26).

The recovery of the precious ark is the occasion for Samuel's call for national repentance.

How to Say It

ASHDOD. *Ash*-dod.
ASHKELON. *Ash*-ke-lon or *As*-ke-lon.
ASHTAROTH. *Ash*-tuh-rawth.
ASHTORETHS. *Ash*-toe-reths.
BAAL. *Bay*-ul.
BAALIM. Bay-uh-*leem*.
BETHCAR. *Beth*-kar or Beth-*kar*.
CAPHTOR. *Kaf*-tor.
CRETE. Creet.
DAGON. *Day*-gon.
EBENEZER. *Eb*-en-*ee*-zer.
EKRON. *Ek*-run.
GATH. Gath (a as in bath).
GAZA. *Gay*-zuh.
GILGAL. *Gil*-gal (G as in *get*).
JONAH. *Jo*-nuh.
NINEVEH. *Nin*-uh-vuh.
PHILISTINES. Fuh-*liss*-teens or *Fill*-us-teens.

I. Call and Repentance
(1 Samuel 7:3, 4)

A. Abandoning False Gods (v. 3)

3. And Samuel spake unto all the house of Israel, saying, If ye do return unto the LORD with all your hearts, then put away the strange gods and Ashtaroth from among you, and prepare your hearts unto the LORD, and serve him only: and he will deliver you out of the hand of the Philistines.

Repentance is described here as a *return* to God. Sin is when we wander away from God, disregard His will, and become alienated from Him. Samuel was saying in effect, "If you're serious about getting right with God, here is what you must do."

Samuel then outlines a four-part process of national repentance for Israel. First, they are to do this wholeheartedly, not holding anything back. Partial repentance is false repentance. Second, they are to stop all worship of other, pagan *gods*. God does not allow for multiple allegiances in matters of worship. Third, they are to *prepare* their *hearts*. Repentance requires determination to change. Fourth, they are to pledge themselves to serve God exclusively. Repentance is more than the passive elimination of sinful practices. It is turning to active obedience to God and His will. [See question #2, page 64.]

B. Serving the Lord Only (v. 4)

4. Then the children of Israel did put away Baalim and Ashtaroth, and served the LORD only.

Since entering the land of Canaan, the Israelites had struggled with rejecting pagan gods. These gods are summarized here as the *Baalim* (Baals, or male deities), and the *Ashtaroth* (Ashtoreths, or female deities). The chief Philistine god was called Dagon (see 1 Samuel 5:1-5).

The author is pleased to tell us that *the children of Israel* heard Samuel's message. They abandoned their false gods in order to serve and worship *the Lord* God exclusively.

WHEN CHANGE IS NEEDED

Maya Angelou is a well-known professor, poet, and actress. She tells a story that helps to explain her success. Her grandmother was a storekeeper in rural Arkansas. When a person with a reputation for complaining would come into the store, the child Maya would be called inside to listen to the litany of complaints about weather, work, etc.

As an adult, Angelou remembers her grandmother's words to her after the complainer had left: "Sister, there are people who went to sleep last night, poor and rich and white and black, but they will never wake again. And those dead folks would give anything at all for just five minutes of this weather or ten minutes of plowing. So you watch yourself about complaining. What you're supposed to do when you don't like a thing is change it. If you can't change it, change the way you think about it."

The wise old woman's words summarize Israel's actions in today's text. Samuel had told the nation what it should do; the people recognized the change that needed to be made, and they made it! Sometimes the call for change comes from a messenger of God such as Samuel; sometimes it comes directly from the Bible; sometimes it comes from the circumstances of life. In any of these cases, wise people change their ways. They repent. That's when they find that God has blessings waiting for them.   —C. R. B.

II. Crisis and Victory
(1 Samuel 7:5-11)

A. Prayer of National Repentance (vv. 5, 6)

5, 6. And Samuel said, Gather all Israel to Mizpeh, and I will pray for you unto the LORD. And they gathered together to Mizpeh, and drew water, and poured it out before the LORD, and fasted on that day, and said there, We have sinned against the LORD. And Samuel judged the children of Israel in Mizpeh.

Mizpeh (also spelled *Mizpah*) is a location of special significance in ancient Israel. The city is one of three in central Israel that Samuel uses as locations for his circuit-court judging (the others being Gilgal and Bethel; 1 Samuel 7:16). It was also a site for national assembly (Judges 10:17; 20:1; 1 Samuel 10:17).

Samuel leads Israel in a powerful symbolic act before their admission of sin: he has them pour water on the ground. This probably is to represent emptying their hearts, purging them of sin. The accompanying call for fasting, a traditional sign of repentance, reinforces this interpretation. After these acts of preparation, the people confess their sin aloud. This is also an important component in the process of repenting. [See question #3, page 64.]

B. Treachery of the Philistines (v. 7)

7. And when the Philistines heard that the children of Israel were gathered together to Mizpeh, the lords of the Philistines went up against Israel. And when the children of Israel heard it, they were afraid of the Philistines.

How do *the Philistines* hear about this gathering *of Israel*? The Philistine leadership probably maintains a spy network within Israel. At any rate, the Philistines decide to take advantage of a peaceful national prayer meeting as an opportunity to massacre their enemies. Not surprisingly, the people of Israel are *afraid* when they become aware of this Philistine threat.

C. Prayer for Deliverance (vv. 8, 9)

8, 9. And the children of Israel said to Samuel, Cease not to cry unto the LORD our God for us, that he will save us out of the hand of the Philistines. And Samuel took a sucking lamb, and offered it for a burnt offering wholly unto the LORD: and Samuel cried unto the LORD for Israel; and the LORD heard him.

Having repented, the Israelites turn to Samuel for deliverance. This continues the pattern of judges-as-deliverers that we saw repeatedly in the book of Judges. Samuel now agrees and cries out in a great prayer of intercession for *the children of Israel*.

Doctrinally, we should not understand this as God rewarding Israel's repentance with deliverance. This mistaken notion is what leads people to "make deals with God" when they are in a desperate situation. "God, get me out of this and I'll give up drinking." Or, "Lord, help me survive this terrible mistake and I'll give money to the church." But it doesn't work this way. God always seeks our repentance.

When we are in proper fellowship with God, we have His favor. When we are at odds with Him, He may use adverse circumstances to bring us to repentance.

D. Defeat of the Philistines (vv. 10, 11)

10, 11. And as Samuel was offering up the burnt offering, the Philistines drew near to battle against Israel: but the LORD thundered with a great thunder on that day upon the Philistines, and discomfited them; and they were smitten before Israel. And the men of Israel went out of Mizpeh, and pursued the Philistines, and smote them, until they came under Bethcar.

God's choice for Israel's deliverance is both powerful and dramatic: a supernatural roar of *thunder*. We should also understand that while this terrifies the Philistines, *the men of Israel* are not afraid. Because their hearts are right with repentance, they know that God is fighting for them. This allows them to rally quickly and rout the enemy. When we are right with God, we are able to remain calm and confident in the most frightening situations.

III. Proclamation and Ebenezer (1 Samuel 7:12, 13)

A. Lord's Help (v. 12)

12. Then Samuel took a stone, and set it between Mizpeh and Shen, and called the name of it Ebenezer, saying, Hitherto hath the LORD helped us.

When the battle is over, *Samuel* proclaims victory by erecting a memorial. This memorial is in the form of a large stone, which Samuel calls *Ebenezer.* In Hebrew this means "stone of help." (What an irony that Ebenezer Scrooge, the miser character in *A Christmas Carol,* has that name!)

Samuel's actions are significant for three reasons. First, he clearly gives credit for the victory to God, not the men of Israel. Second, he names the stone to emphasize Israel's dependence upon God. Third, he establishes a tradition of remembering, calling Israel to understand all the events that led to its repentance and subsequent deliverance. [See question #4, page 64.]

REMEMBERING

Many monuments erected around the world memorialize wars and their victims. America has monuments dedicated to the soldiers who fought in her wars. Napoleon intended the Arc de Triomphe in Paris to memorialize his greatness, but it has since become a French memorial to those who died in World War I. Canada has its National War Memorial in Ottawa.

There are other kinds of memorials. The Statue of Liberty was a birthday gift to America to remind the world of the victory of independence that America had achieved. The Lincoln, Washington, and Jefferson Memorials in Washington, DC remind people of the character and contributions of those men. Many people will never visit such memorials, but it is now possible to view "virtual" memorials on the Internet.

When Samuel raised his Ebenezer, he was creating a reminder for Israel that God had acted to save them from their enemy. A far simpler—but much more profound—memorial than any we have mentioned is the one we Christians have: the Lord's Supper. When we partake of its rudimentary elements, we remember the victory of Christ over sin. And we need not go to Ottawa, Paris, or Washington to appreciate it.　　—C. R. B.

B. Lord's Protection (v. 13)

13. So the Philistines were subdued, and they came no more into the coast of Israel: and the hand of the LORD was against the Philistines all the days of Samuel.

Visual for Lesson 7. *This picture illustrates one way that the Lord helps us. Point to it as you ask your students to list some other ways.*

This summary statement reflects Israel's continued reliance on God and God's continued protection *of Israel.* With God as Israel's shield, the strong rival, *the Philistines,* no longer trouble them. The text leaves us with a small sense of foreshadowing, however: this situation continued *all the days of Samuel.* Repentance is not a one-time thing. It must continue and go beyond generational boundaries through the years. When relationship with God falls into neglect and sin, disaster looms.

Conclusion

A. Raising Ebenezers

Robert Robinson (1735–1790) was an English preacher. In 1758 he wrote the hymn, "Come, Thou Fount" when he was only 23 years old. Stanza 2 of this famous hymn says, "Here I raise mine Ebenezer; Hither by Thy help I'm come." For Robinson this was a reference to the salvation he had found after a youth of horrible sin. His early years of evil had been so destructive that he nearly lost his life. After conversion, however, Robinson drifted away. He fell back into a life of sin and abandoned the Bible.

Many years later, Robinson was riding in a coach. Seated across from him was a woman deeply engrossed in a hymnbook she had just acquired. She was humming one of her favorites, the tune of "Come, Thou Fount." Having no idea whom she was talking to, she innocently asked Robinson if he knew that hymn.

Robinson burst into tears and replied, "Madam, I am the poor unhappy man who wrote that hymn many years ago, and I would give a thousand worlds, if I had them, to enjoy the feelings I had then." Robinson had accidentally stumbled back upon that Ebenezer of his. Sitting there beside his own hymn, he realized how far he had wandered and how awful was his journey and destination.

In today's lesson Samuel built a monument to help Israel remember God's providential deliverance from the Philistines. Building a monument is an attempt to ensure that a person or event will be remembered by succeeding generations. The Bible teaches that "the memory of the just is blessed" (Proverbs 10:7). Monuments can be powerful tools for interpreting and remembering our history. Do you have monuments in your spiritual history? Are there people and places that stand out as turning points for you, where you were rescued from self-destruction or where you made commitments that shaped your future? Take some time to remember.

B. The Ministry of Intercessory Prayer

An acquaintance of mine named Paul shared an amazing story with me in church one Sunday. Paul was an older gentleman and not in very good health (a leukemia survivor). He had a heart for missions and frequently traveled to an Asian country to encourage churches and to transport Bibles and materials for a mission agency.

On a recent trip Paul's health problems caught up with him. He returned with an infection that led to pneumonia and a high fever. He was taken to a hospital directly from the airport in San Francisco. After a stay of 11 days, he was finally allowed to go home. But he ended up in the hospital again. The fever would not go away. After a few days Paul was released, but the fever persisted and he got even worse. He was unable to go to work.

On Saturday afternoon he lay down to take a nap, the fever raging. He awoke rather suddenly a few hours later and realized that the fever was completely gone. He was very weak but well.

Why is this amazing? Don't people recover from pneumonia all the time, every day, in every city? My friend Paul didn't understand it either until he began to do some time-zone calculations. One of the churches he had visited in the Asian country had a small intercessory prayer group that had met every Sunday for many years. They had learned of his illness that week. When Paul calculated the time differential, he realized his fever had left him at the precise time they were praying for him.

There are many reasons to pray. We pray as an act of worship. We pray as an act of repentance. We pray in times of personal trial to seek God's help and mercy. But one of the greatest ways to use the marvelous gift of prayer is as an act of intercession: praying for other people.

Any church is stronger if believers know the great needs of fellow believers and take time to petition God on their behalf. That's what Samuel did. This type of praying allows us to move beyond self-centered prayers. Too often our prayers are like a Christmas list to Santa Claus, packed with our own wants and needs. When we pray sincerely for the needs and pains of others, we begin to think more like God, who cares for all. My friend Paul's story (along with many Bible examples) is a witness to the effectiveness and power of intercessory prayer (compare Romans 15:30-32; Ephesians 6:19, 20).

If you have never prayed for other people, start today—it is not difficult. Share some real needs among fellow class members; then agree to pray for those people during the week. Begin by committing to doing it once; then do it. Keep sharing and praying; you may be surprised at how rewarding the ministry of intercessory prayer can be. [See question #5, page 64.]

C. Prayer

O Lord, our help and protector, give us a heart to pray for others. Help us repent of the sins that foul our relationship with You. Please be merciful to us as You were to the people of Israel. Continue to deliver Your people in their times of need. In Jesus' name, amen.

D. Thought to Remember

Intercessory prayer develops the church into a community of repentance and remembrance.

Home Daily Bible Readings

Monday, Oct. 9—Call to Prayer (Colossians 4:2-6)

Tuesday, Oct. 10—The Psalmist Prays (Psalm 31:14-24)

Wednesday, Oct. 11—Hannah Pays Her Vows (1 Samuel 1:21-28)

Thursday, Oct. 12—Hannah Prays (1 Samuel 2:1-10)

Friday, Oct. 13—The Lord Calls Samuel (1 Samuel 3:1-10)

Saturday, Oct. 14—Israel Returns to God (1 Samuel 7:2-6)

Sunday, Oct. 15—The Lord Helps the Hebrew People (1 Samuel 7:7-13)

Learning by Doing

This page contains an alternative lesson plan emphasizing learning activities. Classes desiring such student involvement will find these suggestions helpful.

Learning Goals

After participating in this lesson, each student will be able to:

1. Tell how repentance and prayer were important to the deliverance of the Israelites from the Philistines.

2. Describe how repentance and prayer are important today.

3. Write an intercessory prayer for someone who is plagued by some trouble.

Into the Lesson

Carry into the classroom a rock that is as large as practical. Write EBENEZER conspicuously on the rock. Cover the rock with a cloth, and then display the rock as class begins.

Lead the class (or have someone else lead) in singing the old hymn, "Come, Thou Fount." Make sure to include the stanza that begins, "Here I raise mine Ebenezer." Point out that today's text includes the Bible verse (v. 12) on which hymn writer Robert Robinson based his poem. Also, plan to use the hymn at the end of class. You may want to include the lesson writer's story of Robinson's writing and re-experiencing the truth of his song.

Into the Word

Establish brainstorming pairs. Give each pair one of the letters of the word *REPENTANCE*. (Repeat the *E* and the *N* if you have an adequate number of students; if you have more than 20 students, repeat the letters *R, P,* and *C*.)

Direct the pairs to look at today's text and any other biblical texts on repentance, if they choose. They are to make a list of components or actions involved in repentance that begin with their assigned letter. Give pairs six to eight minutes to work, and then call for responses.

Though you will get some surprises, expect such responses as the following: *R*—returning, regretting, restoring, realizing; *E*—ending, eliminating, embarrassment, examining; *P*—peace, pain, past, pleading; *N*—need, necessity, nearness (to God), neglect, newness; *T*—talking, tears, tenderheartedness, tenacity, thinking, truth; *A*—abandonment, anguish, accountability, action, admitting, atonement; *C*—commitment, change, character, choice, cleanness, conscience.

After the pairs have deliberated, ask them to connect their ideas to specific verses in today's text. When they report their decisions, you should hear such connections as these: *returning* is the call of verse 3; *eliminating* relates to the call to put away idolatry in verse 3; *commitment* is shown in verse 4 as the Israelites obeyed God and destroyed their enemies as God had long commanded; etc.

Ask each pair to present its list and its connections to the text. Have the word *REPENTANCE* displayed in large letters. Point letter by letter, asking for students' comments.

As a visual reminder of the components of repentance, recruit pantomime players to stand in a row and do the following: the first player squints his eyes as he puts a finger to the side of his nose, cradling his chin in his other fingers while slowly nodding his head pensively *(to represent thinking)*; a second player rubs her eyes vigorously with her clenched hands and silently sobs *(to represent sorrow/remorse)*; a third player assumes the classic prayer pose with hands palm-to-palm and head bowed *(to represent sharing his decision with God in prayer)*; a fourth player walks across the room and abruptly turns to retrace his steps *(to represent the turning aspect of repentance)*; a fifth player pulls play money from her purse and starts giving it to the other players *(to represent a sacrificial offering aspect of repentance.)*

Give your players the freedom to represent their ideas in other ways. As class members identify each component of repentance, write it clearly into a list for display. Come back together once again to ask, "Where do you see these components of repentance in today's text?"

Into Life

Distribute to each class member a small round stone with an *E* written on it. Tell students that this stone is their "Ebenezer." Ask students to use their stones throughout the coming week as a reminder of this study and as a stimulus to pray for someone they know who needs to repent and receive Christ's forgiveness.

Finally, lead the class in singing again "Come, Thou Fount," or at least the stanza beginning, "Here I raise mine Ebenezer."

Let's Talk It Over

The questions on this page are designed to promote discussion of the lesson by the class and to encourage application of the lesson Scriptures. The answers provided are only discussion starters. Let your class talk it over from there.

1. What experiences in Samuel's life equipped him to pray effectively? What personal experiences have taught you how to pray?

Samuel grew up in the temple surrounded by the leaders of God's people. He had a mother who modeled a life of fervent prayer. He was called by God as a prophet and served as a judge of God's people. Sometimes the very experience of being thrown into leadership causes a person to pray more fervently.

As a general rule, most of us pray more out of need than from self-discipline. Thus when we step out into ministries that are larger than our abilities, we pursue prayer as the only available means to fulfill our tasks for God! To move from praying primarily out of need to praying out of self-discipline is a mark of spiritual maturity.

2. What should biblical repentance look like today? Does Samuel's four-part process still apply? Why, or why not?

We often think of repentance as feeling sorry for our personal sins. But biblical repentance also requires a change of our will. That is, we change our allegiance from the world (or self) to God.

But there is more. Biblical repentance includes recompense (Exodus 22:1-15; Numbers 5:5-8; Luke 19:8). That is, we make restitution to the one wronged whenever possible. Furthermore, the concept of *repentance* in the Bible often has a plural subject. Thus it is not merely something an individual does (as important as that is), it is also a group activity. National repentance, especially one accompanied by a fast, is very biblical.

3. If God called you to be a Samuel in the twenty-first century, how would you lead your nation to repentance? What activities would you call people to participate in?

We must be careful here not to allow this to become a political debate. However, there are some things in the Bible that are beyond question. For example, idolatry is the main thing that Samuel called his own people to repent of. But we should not restrict our thinking of idols as being merely blocks of wood and stone. Idols of the heart are most displeasing to God (Ezekiel 14:4, 7; Ephesians 5:5; Colossians 3:5, 6). Unfor-

tunately, the casual use of the word *idol*, as in the TV show *American Idol*, has desensitized many to the sobering nature of the word.

Certainly, sexual immorality is a blight that calls for repentance; it is listed alongside idolatry in 1 Corinthians 5:10, 11. The ease with which we abort babies must make God sad. Our list could include violence, neglect of the poor, abuse of women, and abandonment of children. As always, repentance begins in our own hearts. We may not pour out water on the ground as did Samuel; we may write letters to sponsors of lurid TV programs instead.

4. What kind of an Ebenezer could we raise today? In other words what kinds of memorials could we establish that would remind us to pray for our nation and repent of our sins?

Every year the ancient Israelites were to observe a Day of Atonement (Leviticus 23:26-32). It was a time of national repentance. Some Christian groups have similar observances surrounding Easter or (in America) the anniversary of the court decision *Roe* v. *Wade,* which legalized abortion. Could we participate in such traditions? Could we combine a national day of prayer with a fast for forgiveness? Could we use the Lord's Supper as an Ebenezer that would remind us to repent as a church? Try to create a realistic list of Ebenezer events you could practice.

5. What are the various kinds of prayers and petitions that we could lift up to God? Which kind do you pray most often? Why?

Obviously, there are different kinds of prayers. Help your students think through the following: *praise* (honoring God for who He is and what He has done), *confession of sins* (both individual and corporate), *thanksgiving* (recognizing and appreciating God's provisions), *requests* (presenting our needs before God for healing, provision, comfort, guidance, and strength), *imprecation* (praying against some person, thing, idea or behavior that stands in the way of God's church), *intercession* (asking God to help someone else, whether an individual or a nation). This last kind of prayer is the focus of this lesson. Perhaps you could end by putting this one into practice.

God Makes a Covenant with David

DEVOTIONAL READING: **Psalm 5.**

BACKGROUND SCRIPTURE: **2 Samuel 7.**

PRINTED TEXT: **2 Samuel 7:8-17.**

2 Samuel 7:8-17

8 Now therefore so shalt thou say unto my servant David, Thus saith the LORD of hosts, I took thee from the sheepcote, from following the sheep, to be ruler over my people, over Israel:

9 And I was with thee whithersoever thou wentest, and have cut off all thine enemies out of thy sight, and have made thee a great name, like unto the name of the great men that are in the earth.

10 Moreover I will appoint a place for my people Israel, and will plant them, that they may dwell in a place of their own, and move no more; neither shall the children of wickedness afflict them any more, as beforetime,

11 And as since the time that I commanded judges to be over my people Israel, and have caused thee to rest from all thine enemies.

Also the LORD telleth thee that he will make thee a house.

12 And when thy days be fulfilled, and thou shalt sleep with thy fathers, I will set up thy seed after thee, which shall proceed out of thy bowels, and I will establish his kingdom.

13 He shall build a house for my name, and I will stablish the throne of his kingdom for ever.

14 I will be his father, and he shall be my son. If he commit iniquity, I will chasten him with the rod of men, and with the stripes of the children of men:

15 But my mercy shall not depart away from him, as I took it from Saul, whom I put away before thee.

16 And thine house and thy kingdom shall be established for ever before thee: thy throne shall be established for ever.

17 According to all these words, and according to all this vision, so did Nathan speak unto David.

GOLDEN TEXT: Thine house and thy kingdom shall be established for ever before thee: thy throne shall be established for ever.—2 Samuel 7:16.

God's Living Covenant
Unit 2: God's Covenant with Judges and Kings
(Lessons 5-9)

Lesson Aims

After participating in this lesson, each student will be able to:

1. List the major features of God's covenant with David.

2. Explain the importance of God's covenant with David for the New Testament era.

3. State a specific area of personal weakness in which he or she will trust God's promises more fully.

Lesson Outline

INTRODUCTION
  A. Keeping Promises
  B. Lesson Background
I. DAVID IS CHOSEN (2 Samuel 7:8-11a)
  A. God's Preparation of David (vv. 8, 9a)
  B. God's Plans for David (vv. 9b-11a)
      From the Bottom to the Top
II. DAVID'S HOUSE IS CHOSEN (2 Samuel 7:11b-17)
  A. Covenant Will Continue (vv. 11b, 12)
  B. Temple Will Be Built (v. 13)
      To the Glory of God
  C. Relationship Will Stay Firm (vv. 14, 15)
  D. Throne Will Be Eternal (vv. 16, 17)
CONCLUSION
  A. Jesus and David
  B. The Eternal Kingdom
  C. Prayer
  D. Thought to Remember

Introduction

A. Keeping Promises

The word *promise* is capable of many shades of meaning. A coach might evaluate a young player by saying, "He shows lots of promise." This implies that the player has potential, in the opinion of the coach. Yet sports fans are well aware that many players who show promise never deliver.

Another form of this word may be seen when a person takes out a loan and signs a promissory note. This indicates an agreement to pay off the loan. If the person defaults on the loan, he or she will still be held accountable and may be forced to pay the money back. This type of promise speaks of obligation, and such obligation may be involuntarily enforced.

Many parents have encountered a third variation on this word when they fail to meet the anticipation of a demanding child. The parent may be confronted with the guilt-inducing complaint, "But you promised!" In this case the word *promise* takes on the idea of "expectation." A hazard of parenting is the failure to live up to the expectations of one's children!

Potential, obligation, and expectation are three components in the range of meaning for the word *promise*. But none of these is adequate to describe the biblical concept of *promise* when applied to God. God always keeps His promises. God's promises are more than potential; they are assurances. God's promises are not simply obligations; they are vows of commitment. God's promises are far beyond expectations; they are declarations of intention. This week's lesson teaches us that God's promise to one man, David, not only blessed David and his descendants but all who find salvation in Jesus Christ. That includes you and me.

B. Lesson Background

During the time of Samuel, a major shift occurred in the history of Israel. Since the death of Joshua in about 1365 BC, judges had "run the show" in Israel. These were God-ordained leaders who often acted as military leaders or coordinators in times of national crisis. But there was no central government for the people of Israel. The nation of Israel was actually a confederation of the 12 tribes. Participation in national events was dependent upon the cooperation of tribal leaders.

The people of Israel finally rejected this style of government and asked Samuel to give them a king. This turning point was a sad day, for God saw this as a rebuff of Him and His rule over the nation (1 Samuel 8:7). Tragically, the people of Israel demanded this so that they could be "like all the nations" (1 Samuel 8:5). The heartbreak was that Israel became like the nations in more than just its choice of rule by a king; Israel also followed its neighbors in sin. Thus the history of the kingdom of Israel was an ongoing battle against idolatry and failure to be the holy people of God.

This was further compounded by the performance of Israel's first king, Saul. Although chosen by God and anointed by Samuel, Saul did not live up to the heavy responsibilities of making Israel into a godly kingdom. God saw Saul's disobedience as a rejection of His Word, which resulted in God's rejection of Saul as king (1 Samuel 15:26; 1 Chronicles 10:13, 14). Even while Saul was still reigning, God directed Samuel to anoint Saul's successor, a new king who was not Saul's son (1 Samuel 16:1). The dynasty of Saul's house lasted only one generation, approximately 40 years (see Acts 13:21).

David had no royal qualifications to be king. Yet he had personal qualities that added up to the extraordinary credentials that God desired. His bravery was a hallmark (1 Samuel 17). David became a victorious military leader in the service of Saul, so successful that Saul became jealous (18:6-9). David was also a talented musician (see 16:23), the author of many psalms.

Most importantly, though, was the fact that God saw in David "a man after his own heart" (1 Samuel 13:14). Paul explained this phrase to mean that God was confident that David would "fulfil all my will" (Acts 13:22). Although David, like King Saul, failed and committed sin, his response was unlike Saul's response. Saul responded to sin with arrogance, stubbornness, and rationalizing. David, however, came to God in humility and repentance.

After the hideous episode of adultery and murder caused by David's lust for Bathsheba, David wrote, "Create in me a clean heart, O God; and renew a right spirit within me" (Psalm 51:10). David was spiritually submissive to God. In fact, David's career was characterized by the strong presence of God's Holy Spirit in his life (1 Samuel 16:13). This week's lesson will help us understand why God's love for David has implications for us today. [See question #1, page 72.]

I. David Is Chosen
(2 Samuel 7:8-11a)

A. God's Preparation of David (vv. 8, 9a)

8, 9a. Now therefore so shalt thou say unto my servant David, Thus saith the LORD of hosts, I took thee from the sheepcote, from following the sheep, to be ruler over my people, over Israel: and I was with thee whithersoever thou wentest, and have cut off all thine enemies out of thy sight.

The message of David's covenant with God is being delivered by Nathan the prophet (2 Samuel 7:4). Nathan plays several important roles in the reign of David. He is the one who risks David's wrath by confronting the king and revealing David's sin with Bathsheba and the murder of Uriah (2 Samuel 12). He also anoints Solomon as David's successor (1 Kings 1:34).

Nathan reminds David that God has been looking out for him since his days in *the sheepcote*. God raised David from the humblest of occupations, shepherd, to the pinnacle of success, king of God's chosen nation. In all situations the Lord protects David from danger and treachery. [See question #2, page 72.]

B. God's Plans for David (vv. 9b-11a)

9b. And have made thee a great name, like unto the name of the great men that are in the earth.

God promises that David will have *a great name*. This is a promise of legitimate fame and respect that will be widespread in Israel and in other nations.

This kind of fame is nothing like the modern "cult of celebrity," where men and women become famous for outrageous behavior or their ability to garner publicity. In the ancient world, fame and respect are built on accomplishment. David is a great man because he is powerful, talented, successful, and just. Yet he is also humble, for he always rules in the fear of the Lord (see 2 Samuel 23:3). [See question #3, page 72.]

10, 11a. Moreover I will appoint a place for my people Israel, and will plant them, that they may dwell in a place of their own, and move no more; neither shall the children of wickedness afflict them any more, as beforetime, and as since the time that I commanded judges to be over my people Israel, and have caused thee to rest from all thine enemies.

God ties the fortunes of David's house to the fate of the nation of Israel. The strength provided by the Davidic monarchy will allow Israel to achieve a much higher degree of stability in the promised land. This land will become a permanent home and a place of safety, for the nation will finally gain relief from its pagan *enemies*.

How to Say It

ABSALOM. *Ab*-suh-lum.
ADONIJAH. Ad-o-*nye*-juh.
BATHSHEBA. Bath-*she*-buh.
JEROBOAM. Jair-uh-*boe*-um.
JERUSALEM. Juh-*roo*-suh-lem.
MANASSEH. Muh-*nass*-uh.
MESSIAH. Meh-*sigh*-uh.
NATHAN. *Nay*-thun (*th* as in *thin*).
REHOBOAM. Ree-huh-*boe*-um.
URIAH. Yu-*rye*-uh.
ZECHARIAH. *Zek*-uh-*rye*-uh (strong accent on *rye*).

FROM THE BOTTOM TO THE TOP

Andrew Carnegie (1835–1919) is among the most famous of American philanthropists. His father lost his job when steam-powered looms changed Scotland's textile industry. The family moved to America in 1848, where Andrew got his first job, working in a textile mill for $1.20 per week.

From that point his life became the proverbial "rags to riches" story. His diligence and ability to solve problems creatively soon put him on the road to success. He took a job with the Pennsylvania Railroad, where his innovative style led to further advancement. By the time he was 24, he had become the western superintendent of the railroad. His investments and involvement in the oil, steel, and telegraph industries soon made him rich.

In 1889 Carnegie published his essay "Gospel of Wealth," which argued the moral obligation of the wealthy to serve as society's stewards (see www.pbs.org). He lived up to his credo: by the time of his death in 1919, he had given away 90 percent of his fortune after having become the wealthiest man in the world.

David's humble beginning as a shepherd would not have made anyone predict his rise to the height of power. But godly character and willingness to serve others were traits that served him well, both at the bottom and the top of the social hierarchy. Every society needs people who see their gifts as a trust from God to be used for others.   —C. R. B.

II. David's House Is Chosen (2 Samuel 7:11b-17)

A. Covenant Will Continue (vv. 11b, 12)

11b. Also the LORD telleth thee that he will make thee a house.

To be made *a house* does not indicate David is becoming a three-bedroom ranch with attached garage! It indicates God's plan to establish a royal dynasty beginning with David.

12. And when thy days be fulfilled, and thou shalt sleep with thy fathers, I will set up thy seed after thee, which shall proceed out of thy bowels, and I will establish his kingdom.

The kings of Israel reigning in Jerusalem will have David's royal blood flowing in their veins. Future kings will be David's son, grandson, great grandson, and so on.

After the death of King Solomon, David's son, the nation unfortunately will split in two. The northern kingdom (usually called Israel) ends up being ruled by Jeroboam. The southern kingdom (usually called Judah) comes to be ruled by David's grandson Rehoboam. The history of Judah's kings shows both good and bad rulers, but all were heirs of David. This stands in contrast to the northern kingdom, where dynasties were short-lived, and coups by military strongmen were common.

B. Temple Will Be Built (v. 13)

13. He shall build a house for my name, and I will stablish the throne of his kingdom for ever.

The Lord lays out a twofold promise: the privilege of building the temple in Jerusalem and the permanence of the Davidic dynasty. These promises are not made to David directly—as if David would never die—but to his son. At this point in David's life, it is unclear which one of his many sons will be his heir. At one point it seemed that David's third son, Absalom, would succeed David by overthrowing his father (2 Samuel 15). When David became old, his fourth son, Adonijah, tried to become king (1 Kings 1:5). Despite his advanced age, David orchestrated the events to make Solomon the next king (1 Kings 1:28-37).

David was prohibited from building the temple because he was "a man of war" and had blood on his hands (1 Chronicles 28:3). There is no haste in God's plans. He is infinitely patient, willing to wait until the right king is in place to build the temple.

TO THE GLORY OF GOD

St. Paul's Cathedral in London is one of the great church buildings of the world. Its architect was Sir Christopher Wren (1632–1723). Wren was trained in anatomy and astronomy and was teaching at Oxford when his architectural career began.

At age 31 he was requested to draw the plans for a chapel in Cambridge. So impressive was his work that more soon followed. After the Great London Fire of 1666, Wren proposed a visionary master plan for rebuilding the city. The plan included the dome of St. Paul's cathedral, which ended up being Wren's most famous work. Over the next half-century he designed more than 50 church buildings in London. He has come to be regarded as Great Britain's greatest architect.

God promised David that his son (whom we know to be Solomon) would build a house for God. And what a house it was! It is said to have been the most magnificent building of ancient times. It reflected the glory of God and the greatness of the kingdom over which Solomon reigned. But that now-gone structure of stone and wood does not compare with God's greatest building project: the church. What part are you playing in its construction?   —C. R. B.

C. Relationship Will Stay Firm (vv. 14, 15)

14, 15. I will be his father, and he shall be my son. If he commit iniquity, I will chasten him with the rod of men, and with the stripes of the children of men: but my mercy shall not depart away from him, as I took it from Saul, whom I put away before thee.

Here we see that the relationship between the king of Israel and God has a unique element: the king is considered to be a *son.* This type of situation has parallels and differences with other ancient cultures. The kings of Egypt (the pharaohs) are considered to be gods, direct descendants of the Egyptian deities. Yet there is no hint of that here. For David or Solomon to be God's son does not mean that these men are some type of demigods themselves.

These verses explain the relationship in some detail. God is the king's *father* in that God intends to take a special, personal interest in such men. As their father He will discipline them and show mercy to them, the qualities all fathers should show to their children.

The most sobering expression of this relationship will come with the reign of King Manasseh, one of David's descendants. That king will stray far from God's will into the evils of bloodshed and idolatry—so much so that he comes to be named as the cause for the destruction of Jerusalem in 586 BC and the deportation of the nation for exile in Babylon (2 Kings 24:2-4). God's discipline will be harsh indeed.

Love includes discipline. It is popular today to refer to this as "tough love." Good parents are sometimes hard on their children, not allowing them to fall into sinful patterns and sloth. But this hardness must be tempered with mercy. Discipline should never be a matter of revenge. This is the painful task of a parent who seeks to keep his or her child on the right path.

D. Throne Will Be Eternal (vv. 16, 17)

16, 17. And thine house and thy kingdom shall be established for ever before thee: thy throne shall be established for ever. According to all these words, and according to all this vision, so did Nathan speak unto David.

This final section of the words of *Nathan* lays out the three primary elements of God's covenant with *David.* David is to have an eternal *house,* an eternal *kingdom,* and an eternal *throne.* The eternal house means that the line of David will never

die out. There will always be a king with David's royal blood. The eternal kingdom indicates that this king will have subjects and a territory. The eternal throne means that the sons of David will inherit extraordinary authority to carry out the will of God.

All three concepts are reinforced in Psalm 89, the parallel text. There David is promised to have a "throne to all generations" (v. 4). There is a pledge to preserve the kingdom by crushing all "his foes" (v. 23). And the exceptional authority of the Davidic king is strengthened by the mighty "hand" and "arm" of God (v. 21).

The records show that none of David's descendants (except Christ) really lived up to the implications of these promises. God always kept His side of the covenant, but even wise Solomon fell into the sin of false worship due to foreign wives (see 1 Kings 11:4). The three-fold promise of an eternal house, kingdom, and throne is completely fulfilled only in David's descendant Jesus. He is the eternal one who conquered death to ascend to Heaven and take His throne at the right hand of God (see Romans 8:34; Ephesians 1:20; Hebrews 1:3). [See question #4, page 72.]

Conclusion

A. Jesus and David

God's covenant with David is a major theme in the Old Testament. Not only did the Davidic line of kings continue to reign in Jerusalem without interruption for almost 400 years, but the prophets of Israel began to reveal that a future king would come from David's line to be the redeemer of Israel (compare Luke 24:21).

Thine house and thy kingdom shall be established for ever . . . thy throne shall be established for ever (2 Samuel 7:16).

Visual for Lesson 8. *Point to this picture and say, "Some things will endure even longer than mountains. Can you name some of those things?"*

This future redeemer was referred to in several ways including "my servant David" (Ezekiel 34:23, 24), and the "Branch" of David (Isaiah 11:1; Jeremiah 23:5). This branch image represents the idea of a reborn line of David—new growth from the stump of the tree.

The prophets wrote of future blessings on the "house of David" (Zechariah 12:10). But the most significant of these predictions are the ones that see a coming Messiah (Psalm 132:17; Daniel 9:25). This person has been specially chosen or appointed by God.

The New Testament shows many connections between Jesus and David. Jesus is called the "Son of David" (Matthew 1:1; Mark 10:47, 48), the "King of Israel" (John 1:49; 12:13; compare Matthew 27:42; Zechariah 9:9). The most common link is the reference to Jesus as the Messiah or Christ. We have heard the two-word designation *Jesus Christ* so often that we forget that this includes a title: "Jesus the Christ." To claim that Jesus is the Christ is to claim that He is the Davidic king, the promised heir to David's throne.

A central conviction of the New Testament authors is that Jesus meets all the qualifications to be the heir of David. Jesus' earthly father, Joseph, is from the house of David (Luke 2:4). Paul is often found arguing with his fellow Jews that Jesus is the Messiah (see Acts 9:22; 28:23). Peter decisively concludes his Pentecost sermon by declaring that Jesus' resurrection confirms that God had made Him Christ (Acts 2:36).

The significance of this is enormous. Our salvation is not an accident of history. Jesus is more than an ordinary man who accomplished extraordinary things. The church is much more than the work of creative geniuses like Paul. God's covenant with David teaches us that God planned the church, that He sent His Son, Jesus, and that our salvation was His intentional design. As believers we should find assurance in God's loving provision for us.

B. The Eternal Kingdom

The old spiritual sang, "Ride on, king Jesus!" The New Testament frequently speaks of Jesus as a king. The first book tells of the wise men who came looking for the newborn "King of the Jews" (Matthew 2:2). The last book reveals Jesus as the "King of Kings" (Revelation 19:16).

What kind of king was Jesus, though? Jesus told Pilate, "My kingdom is not of this world" (John 18:36). If not of this world, what kind of kingdom does Jesus rule?

God promised David that He would establish "the throne of his kingdom for ever" (2 Samuel 7:13). Yet Jesus had no interest in being the reigning king of Jerusalem. When His followers tried to make Him king, He refused (see John 6:15). His disciples continually failed to understand that He was not going to claim a throne in Jerusalem (see Acts 1:6). [See question #5, page 72.]

The author of Hebrews shows a strong appreciation for the eternal throne of Jesus (Hebrews 1:8). Jesus reigns in righteousness and truth. His kingdom is far more than a time-bound, earthly kingdom. Jesus is king of the universe in a timeless, cosmic way. For us the eternal nature of Jesus' throne means that a man who walked the earth 2,000 years ago is still alive, still in power, still reigning from Heaven.

His reign is not fully realized on earth, where sinful rebels still operate outside His will. But Christians take comfort in the promise that a day will come in which every creature will acknowledge and submit to King Jesus by bowing before Him (Philippians 2:9-11). On that day we will see that "The kingdoms of this world are become the kingdoms of our Lord, and of his Christ; and he shall reign for ever and ever" (Revelation 11:15). This is the ultimate vision of the covenant with David (see Revelation 22:16).

C. Prayer

Great God, the Father of David and the Father of Jesus Christ, we bow before You and thank You for not forgetting us despite the many sins of humanity. As You remembered David, You have remembered each one of us as Your sons and daughters. To You alone we look for salvation. In Jesus' mighty name we pray, amen.

Home Daily Bible Readings

Monday, Oct. 16—Samuel Anoints Young David (1 Samuel 16:1-13)

Tuesday, Oct. 17—David's Lyre Soothes Saul (1 Samuel 16:14-23)

Wednesday, Oct. 18—David Protects the Sheep (1 Samuel 17:32-37)

Thursday, Oct. 19—A Cry for Help (Psalm 5)

Friday, Oct. 20—Judah Anoints David King (2 Samuel 2:1-7)

Saturday, Oct. 21—God's Promises to David (2 Samuel 7:8-17)

Sunday, Oct. 22—David Speaks to God (2 Samuel 7:18-29)

D. Thought to Remember

God's covenant with David is fulfilled in Jesus.

Learning by Doing

This page contains an alternative lesson plan emphasizing learning activities.
Classes desiring such student involvement will find these suggestions helpful.

Learning Goals

After this lesson, each student will be able to:

1. List the major features of God's covenant with David.

2. Explain the importance of God's covenant with David for the New Testament era.

3. State a specific area of personal weakness in which he or she will trust God's promises more fully.

Into the Lesson

From a craft shop, toy store, or parents in your congregation, obtain children's alphabet blocks for the following letters: *A, D, D, E, F, H, I, O, O, S, U, V.* Have the blocks stacked as a pyramid, with the letters showing toward your class. As class begins, ask for acrostic responses to the question, "What are the components—let us say 'building blocks'—of the house of David, as God promises to build it?"

Have the class look at 2 Samuel 7:8-17 as an initial source, but also suggest they use their general knowledge of the kingdom of David. Accept reasonable answers; a sample of responses may include *A*=announced; *D*=disciplined; *D*=directed (by God); *E*=everlasting; *F*=famous; *H*=heavenly; *I*=independent; *O*=otherworldly; *O*=optimistic; *S*=spiritual; *U*=universal; *V*=victorious. At the end rearrange the blocks to show *HOUSE OF DAVID* toward the class.

Into the Word

Prepare the following monologue of David, as if he were revealing today's text to us personally, rather than as a prophet revealing it to David. Some of the phrasing from the lesson Scripture text (in bold below) is used.

Monologue: "The prophet's announcement to me—of course, I knew it came from **the Lord**—was startling but joyful. I was fully aware that it was God who called me from tending **sheep** to become **ruler over** His **people, Israel**. I always sensed His presence and care; **all** my **enemies** were as good as **out of my sight**.

"God has **made** me **a name** among **the great men in the earth**. I thank Him! And His **people** have been planted **in a place** all **their** own. They will **move no more.** He has caused us to **rest from all** our **enemies**.

"Even more, **the Lord** has said, 'I **will make** you into a royal **house**, a dynasty.' He has promised that once I die and **sleep with** my **fathers**, my own son will see God establish his house. That son's great pride will be that he **shall build a house for** God's **name**, a blessing I will not do or see.

"God assures me that He **will be father** to my **son,** as He has been for me. Oh, yes, **if** my son should **commit iniquity**, God **will chasten him with the rod,** just as I would as his earthly father. He will have **the stripes of** loving discipline. But he will never be forsaken as **Saul** was, **put away** out of God's sight. God's **mercy** will **not depart away from him.**

"The royal **house** he grants to me will **be established for ever**. Praise His name! The **throne** that I sit on, likewise, will seat a king **for ever.** Who shall that king be?"

At the end, give to each learner a copy of the monologue *without any text being marked in bold.* Say, "Compare the monologue you have just heard with the printed text and mark all the words and phrases that are identical." (This can be a small-group activity.) Allow time to discuss discoveries.

Into Life

Give to each student a "blueprint," as it were, for a simple house. Areas that should be identified are family room, bedroom, living room, laundry room, kitchen, dining room, closets, computer room, etc. Tell the class, "If you have your own little room in David's house, which is it? Why do you say so?"

Direct them to take the sketch and decide where they best fit in David's house, the kingdom of God. Give them an example: "I see myself in the computer room, because I want to communicate the good news to people all around the world." Another possibility is "I see myself in the bedroom, because I am so looking forward to that heavenly rest."

Suggest that students keep their "blueprints" handy in the coming week. After having a day or two to think about it, they may be able to think of better ways to see their places in *all* the rooms of David's house: service, rest, hospitality, evangelism, and others.

Let's Talk It Over

*The questions on this page are designed to promote discussion of the lesson
by the class and to encourage application of the lesson Scriptures. The answers
provided are only discussion starters. Let your class talk it over from there.*

1. What characteristics that made David a good king (humanly speaking) do we still look for in political leaders today? Which of these characteristics are good and which are bad from a spiritual perspective? Defend your answer.

David had many characteristics of a typical human king. These included an appetite for war and a tendency to use his power to get women. (Sound familiar?) But David also was strategic in his planning, loved his nation, and worked with wisdom, energy, and integrity.

The fact that David's early life was that of a shepherd rather than royalty may intrigue us. Aren't we still drawn toward leaders with humble origins? David's accomplishments as poet and musician may catch us by surprise. Also, we don't expect modern politicians to dance with abandon, weep publicly, or show personal weakness before God and his subjects as did David. Nonetheless, these characteristics came together to make David a man after God's own heart.

2. How were David's early years as a shepherd a preparation for him to be king? What was a time when hindsight revealed that God was preparing you for a future task?

Working on the family farm undoubtedly instilled an important work ethic in David. Life in the fields resulted in a skill that enabled him to slay Goliath. There is much about David's earliest life that we would like to know but don't!

Many folks get their start toward adulthood by working in low-paying jobs as teenagers. Often this involves work in a fast food restaurant. Yet skills learned here—teamwork, customer service, scheduling, cleanliness, etc.—can last a lifetime. These lessons can carry over into volunteer and vocational work in the church. God expects our faithfulness no matter what our life situation. What He is preparing us for in the future through our work today may come as quite a surprise!

3. What are some dangers of a man becoming king? What can we learn from the example of David that will help us curb these dangers in leaders today?

It is trite but true: power tends to corrupt. David, unfortunately, succumbed to the power of

his position by committing adultery, murder, and taking a census of his troops (2 Samuel 11:1-24; 24:1). At the same time, however, David had the prophet Nathan to hold him accountable when he crossed the line.

This can lead us to ask about the accountability systems we have in place today. Are there certain people in your congregation who know they can speak frankly to the church's leaders about the appropriateness of the leaders' actions?

4. Which of God's promises to David are we able to claim for the church? Which are we not able to claim? How will we get into trouble if we don't sort this out properly?

David was promised that his lineage would be the royal lineage of Israel. He was promised that there would always be one of his descendants on the throne. God assured him that his son Solomon would build a temple.

After the destruction and exile of 586 BC, it may look as though God made good on none of the promises. But look to Jesus! He is David's descendant (Matthew 1:1-16). By divine power He rebuilt the temple of His crucified body (John 2:19). He is the enduring King of kings (Revelation 19:16). God does not fail, even when people do.

5. Following question #4, what difference does it make in your day-to-day life to know that Jesus is the fulfillment of ancient promises made to David?

To know that God keeps His promises after hundreds and hundreds of years should be a marvelous source of daily comfort! Jesus is the Messiah, the permanent King of kings. Jesus fulfilled God's prophecies about David's house better than David himself did or could have. The God who brought His Son through crucifixion to resurrection is able to meet all our needs. Jesus is the ultimate man after God's own heart.

Sin is what separates us from God; Jesus is the one who closes the gap. As a result, God is not far from any of us (compare Acts 17:27). God's record of promises kept helps us to look forward with confidence that we are always under His watchful and caring eye. We are His most important project!

God Grants Wisdom to Solomon

October 29
Lesson 9

DEVOTIONAL READING: Psalm 119:97-104.

BACKGROUND SCRIPTURE: 1 Kings 3.

PRINTED TEXT: 1 Kings 3:3-14.

1 Kings 3:3-14

3 And Solomon loved the LORD, walking in the statutes of David his father: only he sacrificed and burnt incense in high places.

4 And the king went to Gibeon to sacrifice there; for that was the great high place: a thousand burnt offerings did Solomon offer upon that altar.

5 In Gibeon the LORD appeared to Solomon in a dream by night: and God said, Ask what I shall give thee.

6 And Solomon said, Thou hast showed unto thy servant David my father great mercy, according as he walked before thee in truth, and in righteousness, and in uprightness of heart with thee; and thou hast kept for him this great kindness, that thou hast given him a son to sit on his throne, as it is this day.

7 And now, O LORD my God, thou hast made thy servant king instead of David my father: and I am but a little child: I know not how to go out or come in.

8 And thy servant is in the midst of thy people which thou hast chosen, a great peo-ple, that cannot be numbered nor counted for multitude.

9 Give therefore thy servant an under-standing heart to judge thy people, that I may discern between good and bad: for who is able to judge this thy so great a people?

10 And the speech pleased the LORD, that Solomon had asked this thing.

11 And God said unto him, Because thou hast asked this thing, and hast not asked for thyself long life; neither hast asked riches for thyself, nor hast asked the life of thine ene-mies; but hast asked for thyself understand-ing to discern judgment;

12 Behold, I have done according to thy word: lo, I have given thee a wise and an understanding heart; so that there was none like thee before thee, neither after thee shall any arise like unto thee.

13 And I have also given thee that which thou hast not asked, both riches, and honor: so that there shall not be any among the kings like unto thee all thy days.

14 And if thou wilt walk in my ways, to keep my statutes and my commandments, as thy father David did walk, then I will length-en thy days.

Oct
29

GOLDEN TEXT: Behold, I have done according to thy word: lo, I have given thee a wise and an understanding heart; so that there was none like thee before thee, neither after thee shall any arise like unto thee.—1 Kings 3:12.

God's Living Covenant
Unit 2: God's Covenant with Judges and Kings
(Lessons 5-9)

Lesson Aims

After participating in this lesson, each student will be able to:

1. Retell the account of Solomon's prayer for wisdom and God's response.

2. Cite other examples, biblical and modern, of God's answering prayer.

3. Suggest one specific improvement he or she will implement in his or her personal prayer life.

Lesson Outline

INTRODUCTION
  A. The Explosion of Knowledge
  B. Lesson Background
  I. GOD'S APPEARING (1 Kings 3:3-5)
    A. Abundance of Sacrifices (vv. 3, 4)
    B. Offer to Solomon (v. 5)
      The Meaning of Dreams
  II. SOLOMON'S REQUEST (1 Kings 3:6-9)
    A. Solomon as David's Successor (vv. 6-8)
    B. Solomon Seeks Wisdom (v. 9)
  III. GOD'S PROMISES (1 Kings 3:10-14)
    A. Solomon's Request Pleases God (v. 10)
    B. Solomon's Request Granted (vv. 11, 12)
    C. Solomon's Request Exceeded (vv. 13, 14)
      Sudden Wealth Syndrome
CONCLUSION
  A. The Search for Wisdom
  B. Prayer
  C. Thought to Remember

Introduction

A. The Explosion of Knowledge

Near the end of his life, King Solomon wrote, "of making many books there is no end; and much study is a weariness of the flesh" (Ecclesiastes 12:12). The modern world has realized both parts of this observation, perhaps far beyond Solomon's wildest expectations. It is estimated that as many as 2,000 new books are published every week worldwide. Add to this the enormous output of newspapers, journals, magazines, Web pages, and other media. The total is far beyond the capacity of any one individual to keep track of, let alone to read and digest.

This ever-increasing rate of publication has been labeled the information explosion. Its close cousin is called the knowledge explosion: the constantly growing store of facts and theories. These twin phenomena have many implications. One of these is the short shelf life of any education or training. For example, someone who earned a college degree in computer science 20 years ago would be woefully lacking in expertise about today's computers unless he or she had been updating constantly. Every field of study requires constant study to stay current. At times this may feel like "weariness of the flesh"!

Yet it is important to ask whether or not this avalanche of knowledge has made us any wiser. Has society's increased stock of information solved the basic problems of wars, poverty, or disease? Has more knowledge eliminated the age-old vices of greed, pride, anger, or lust? If anything, we seem to be in a world that is greedier, prouder, angrier, and more sexually oriented than ever before. Remember: the most destructive wars of the twentieth century were fought between the most "educated" countries on earth!

There is a lot of overlap in meaning among the concepts of knowledge, understanding, and wisdom. But one key idea that sets wisdom apart is that wisdom is a godly use of knowledge and understanding. This week's lesson is about a man who requested wisdom from God and was rewarded with godly wisdom and much, much more. [See question #1, page 80.]

B. Lesson Background

The third king of Israel was David's son Solomon. Solomon reigned as king in Jerusalem from about 970 to 930 BC. His name is derived from the Hebrew word *shalom* ("peace"), thus *Solomon* means "peaceful one." Nathan the prophet also gave him the name *Jedidiah*, meaning "beloved of Yahweh" (2 Samuel 12:25). Solomon's mother was Bathsheba, David's partner in adultery. Bathsheba's first child, the product of their sin, died in his first week. David and Bathsheba's second child was Solomon.

Solomon was the first king of Israel to inherit the throne from his father. After David's death, Solomon acted quickly to remove any threats to his throne by executing Adonijah, his scheming half-brother (1 Kings 2:24) and Joab, a traitorous army general (2:33, 34). He also exiled the high priest, Abiathar, and replaced him with the loyal Zadok (2:35).

During the reign of Solomon the kingdom of Israel expanded its boundaries to its greatest extent, from the Euphrates River to the border of

Egypt (1 Kings 4:21). The kings in some of these territories paid annual tribute to Solomon, providing him with vast wealth.

The riches of Solomon have been the subject of theories and speculation, but the Bible itself has a great deal of information on this subject. His yearly tribute income was 666 talents of gold (1 Kings 10:14). The modern equivalent of this amount is difficult to estimate, but this may have been eight to ten tons of gold every year—and this was only part of his income. His hoard was so plentiful that Solomon made hundreds of ceremonial shields out of gold to adorn his palace (1 Kings 10:17).

Solomon is also famous for his building projects. His greatest accomplishment in this area was the construction of a house for the Lord, the Jerusalem temple. The primary purpose of the temple was to provide suitable and permanent housing for the holy ark of the covenant (see 1 Chronicles 28:2).

The detailed description of this structure is found in 1 Kings 5–7 and 2 Chronicles 2–4. The construction took seven years and required more than 150,000 laborers (1 Kings 5:15). When finished, this edifice was undoubtedly one of the most splendid buildings of the ancient world.

The Bible also tells us "King Solomon loved many strange women" (1 Kings 11:1). It is recorded that he had 700 official wives and 300 concubines (secondary wives). Unfortunately, we are also told that these wives led him away from the Lord in his old age (1 Kings 11:3, 4). We do believe, however, that the elderly Solomon sorted through all these things and returned to

---

How to Say It

ABIATHAR. Ah-*bye*-uh-thar.
ADONIJAH. Ad-o-*nye*-yuh.
BATHSHEBA. Bath-*she*-buh.
ECCLESIASTES. Ik-*leez*-ee-*as*-teez (strong accent on *as*).
EUPHRATES. You-*fray*-teez.
GIBEON. *Gib*-e-un (G as in *get*).
JEDIDIAH. Jed-ih-*die*-uh.
JOAB. *Jo*-ab.
JUDEAN. Joo-*dee*-un.
NEBUCHADNEZZAR. *Neb*-yuh-kud-*nez*-er (strong accent on *nez*).
PHARAOH. *Fair*-o or *Fay*-roe.
PILATE. *Pie*-lut.
SHALOM (Hebrew). shah-*lome*.
SOLOMON. *Sol*-o-mun.
ZADOK. *Zay*-dok.

God before his death. This seems to be the lesson of the book of Ecclesiastes—a book thought to have been written by Solomon near the end of his life. He finishes this book by admonishing his readers that our primary duties are to love God and to keep His commandments (Ecclesiastes 12:13).

Today's lesson presents a young Solomon who finds himself in a powerful position that exceeds his capabilities. When the weight of his responsibilities is combined with his inadequacy, he does not despair. He trusts God.

I. God's Appearing (1 Kings 3:3-5)

A. Abundance of Sacrifices (vv. 3, 4)

3, 4. And Solomon loved the LORD, walking in the statutes of David his father: only he sacrificed and burnt incense in high places. And the king went to Gibeon to sacrifice there; for that was the great high place: a thousand burnt offerings did Solomon offer upon that altar.

To sacrifice *in high places* is not necessarily an act of paganism or idolatry (compare 2 Chronicles 33:17). The high place at Gibeon is the semi-permanent site of "the tabernacle of the Lord" (see 1 Chronicles 16:39). Gibeon is located in the Judean hill country, about seven miles northwest of Jerusalem.

The text does not tell us exactly what the burnt offerings are, but likely they are animals, probably young bulls. In this type of offering the entire animal is burned to ashes, giving it all to God. For Solomon to do this with a thousand bulls is a large, impressive display of his wealth, his devotion, and the seriousness of the occasion.

B. Offer to Solomon (v. 5)

5. In Gibeon the LORD appeared to Solomon in a dream by night: and God said, Ask what I shall give thee.

The offerings likely take more than one day. Because of the length of the time involved, Solomon stays in Gibeon overnight. During one of these nights he is visited by God in a dream. This type of communication from God is not unknown, but it is rare. There are fewer than 20 people in the Bible who are said to have received dreams from God, and not all of these are believers (examples: Pharaoh, Nebuchadnezzar, Pilate's wife). Nevertheless, dreams have long been recognized as a powerful way by which God has spoken to humans on rare occasions.

God does not confront Solomon with a call for action or obedience. Instead, God presents

Solomon with a blank check: *Ask what I shall give thee.* There are no limits or guidelines given by God. Already, the wisdom of Solomon is being tested. Will he choose wisely or selfishly?

THE MEANING OF DREAMS

An old story tells of a woman who awoke in the morning and told her husband of her dream. "Last night I dreamed that you gave me a diamond necklace and earrings for our anniversary," she said. "Do you have any idea what my dream means?" His cryptic answer was, "Tonight you will know."

After work that evening, he presented her with a small package. Eagerly opening it, she found a book titled, *The Meaning of Dreams.* We can imagine what happened next! Seriously, though, you could spend a small fortune on all the books written about how to interpret your dreams.

Solomon's dream was not about diamond jewelry, although we should consider a vision of God in a dream to be of inestimable value! Just as the fictional woman's dream came in the context of her relationship with her husband, it is likewise significant that Solomon's dream came in the context of his relationship with God.

The day before his dream, Solomon had made an exceedingly large number of offerings to God. That night God came to him in the dream. We shouldn't make the mistake of assuming that we can "buy" God's presence with devotion or sacrifice. However, Solomon's sacrifices were a tangible indication of his love for God. At the very least, we can see that God responds positively to those who seek to please Him.   —C. R. B.

II. Solomon's Request
(1 Kings 3:6-9)

A. Solomon as David's Successor (vv. 6-8)

6. And Solomon said, Thou hast showed unto thy servant David my father great mercy, according as he walked before thee in truth, and in righteousness, and in uprightness of heart with thee; and thou hast kept for him this great kindness, that thou hast given him a son to sit on his throne, as it is this day.

Solomon does not blurt out a request, like "Gimme a new Cadillac!" Instead, he evaluates his needs by talking them through with God. (Isn't this what prayer should be?) In this process he rehearses the marvelous relationship his father, *David,* had had with the Lord. Being king gives Solomon occasion to remember how God had kept His promise to David by allowing his son to succeed him as king.

7. And now, O LORD my God, thou hast made thy servant king instead of David my father: and I am but a little child: I know not how to go out or come in.

Solomon has come to a strong conviction that he is inadequate for the task he has been given. Who could possibly fill the shoes of the great and famous *David?*

8. And thy servant is in the midst of thy people which thou hast chosen, a great people, that cannot be numbered nor counted for multitude.

Solomon is aware that Israel is the chosen nation of God and that it has grown to be a very populous people. These factors combine to make him feel like *a little child,* unequal to his responsibilities. We may experience something similar when we observe the children of capable and powerful leaders. Sometimes a child is expected to live up to the legacy left by the father but cannot possibly fulfill these expectations. Following a famous father is not an easy path.

B. Solomon Seeks Wisdom (v. 9)

9. Give therefore thy servant an understanding heart to judge thy people, that I may discern between good and bad: for who is able to judge this thy so great a people?

David had left Solomon with the charge, "He that ruleth over men must be just, ruling in the fear of God" (2 Samuel 23:3). Solomon understands that a major component of being a successful king is related to his judgment. Therefore he asks for divine understanding in dealing with his people. He cannot do it by himself. Solomon asks, rhetorically, *Who is able to judge this thy so great a people?* The answer is that only the Lord himself can do this. Solomon desperately needs God's help. [See question #2, page 80.]

In this request Solomon submits his heart to God. Any cry to God for help is a cry of faith. He is following the advice of his father, to rule "in the fear of God." He understands that even the greatest leaders are answerable to a higher authority and need God's assistance to rule justly. We don't have many kings left in our world, but any nation with a leader who depends on God will receive blessings because of this relationship.

III. God's Promises
(1 Kings 3:10-14)

A. Solomon's Request Pleases God (v. 10)

10. And the speech pleased the LORD, that Solomon had asked this thing.

Oh, to please *the Lord*! All too often we find ourselves in need of humility and repentance because we have displeased God. That Solomon is able to set aside petty, personal, selfish desires and pinpoint what he will need to serve God effectively is a display of wisdom at a young age. He has already learned the lesson he later teaches to others: "The fear of the Lord is the beginning of wisdom" (Proverbs 9:10).

B. Solomon's Request Granted (vv. 11, 12)

11, 12. And God said unto him, Because thou hast asked this thing, and hast not asked for thyself long life; neither hast asked riches for thyself, nor hast asked the life of thine enemies; but hast asked for thyself understanding to discern judgment; behold, I have done according to thy word: lo, I have given thee a wise and an understanding heart; so that there was none like thee before thee, neither after thee shall any arise like unto thee.

God well knows that Solomon could have asked for personal favors: longevity, wealth, or victories. [See question #3, page 80.] God promises to make Solomon a unique individual in history: the wisest man who ever lived.

There are related yet distinct qualities that are promised here. When we see that Solomon is granted a *wise . . . heart,* we should realize that wisdom goes beyond the ability to discern good from evil. The wise person recognizes the difference and chooses to do the good. The one who understands but chooses evil is a fool (see Proverbs 14:16; Romans 16:19). Solomon's gift is more than just the ability to know righteousness. He is enabled to choose righteousness.

Solomon's heart is also to be one of *understanding.* This has the sense of clear perception of a situation and insight into its implications. This means that Solomon will be able *to discern.* This is actually based on the Hebrew word for "to hear." It has the implication of one who listens judiciously, evaluating all factors carefully.

These three qualities are repeated in Proverbs 1:5: "A wise man will hear [discern], and will increase learning; and a man of understanding shall attain unto wise counsels" (see also 1 Kings 4:29). Wisdom builds on wisdom. Wise choices lead to more wise choices. Deeper understanding results from listening to wise teachers.

C. Solomon's Request Exceeded (vv. 13, 14)

13. And I have also given thee that which thou hast not asked, both riches, and honor: so that there shall not be any among the kings like unto thee all thy days.

There are those who attain great wealth but are despised. There are others who gain great

Visual for
Lesson 9

Use this picture to open a discussion about prayer requests that do and do not please the Lord.

honor and dignity yet die penniless. And, of course, there are many who perish being neither rich nor honorable. But few are recognized as persons with both riches and honor. Such ones are doubly blessed by God. Here God makes a promise to Solomon: he will be a person of vast wealth and someone respected very highly. [See question #4, page 80.]

As mentioned above, Solomon's wealth becomes legendary. God's gift of wisdom, however, causes Solomon's reputation to spread far and wide. His wisdom is unlimited (1 Kings 4:29-31). He is the author of 3,000 wise sayings (proverbs) and over 1,000 songs (1 Kings 4:32). Some of these are preserved in our Bible books of Proverbs, Ecclesiastes, and the Song of Solomon (see also Psalm 72).

SUDDEN WEALTH SYNDROME

"In a lot of ways, I was happier living a simpler life." Those are the words of a multimillionaire who had made an amazing amount of money in the high-tech stock market boom of the 1990s. His household was one of some 275,000 in America with assets of over $10 million at the end of that decade—a group that was five times larger than it had been just 15 years earlier.

Psychologists say people who become very rich very quickly complain about becoming isolated from their former friends; they even feel alienated from their sense of who they are (www.webmd.com). One man who sold his company for tens of millions of dollars said he felt a "gnawing anxiety that his money could disappear as quickly as it had come." He found it hard to talk to his old friends about things they had easily conversed about before he was struck with sudden wealth. Many poorer people would be willing to change places with the rich, but they obviously aren't aware of the psychological and relationship costs of having lots of money!

God's promised gift to Solomon could have been an unparalleled blessing. But it turned out to be a responsibility that Solomon was not fully prepared to exercise. He did not always "walk in my ways," as God had said he must if he were to enjoy the blessings fully. Solomon's experience proves once again that who you are—your character, etc.—is far more important than how much you have. —C. R. B.

14. And if thou wilt walk in my ways, to keep my statutes and my commandments, as thy father David did walk, then I will lengthen thy days.

While the promises of wisdom and honor are unconditional, God does place conditions on the gift of a long life. This promise is contingent upon Solomon's obedience to God's laws, an obedience that God had seen in Solomon's father, David. God had not seen in David a perfect record of obedience, of course. But God had indeed seen a general life pattern of obedience, described as to *walk in my ways.*

Unfortunately, Solomon will not match his father David. Solomon's disobedience causes God to be very angry. God then modifies His earlier promise to David of a continuing king in Jerusalem from David's family: much of Solomon's kingdom will be taken away from his son Rehoboam (1 Kings 11:9-13). This promise is made good after the death of Solomon, and the kingdom is split into Judah and Israel.

Home Daily Bible Readings

Monday, Oct. 23—The Value of Wisdom (Proverbs 1:1-7)
Tuesday, Oct. 24—Where Is Wisdom Found? (Job 28:12-28)
Wednesday, Oct. 25—Add to Wisdom Understanding (Psalm 119:97-104)
Thursday, Oct. 26—Solomon Chosen to Be King (1 Kings 1:28-40)
Friday, Oct. 27—Solomon Requests Wisdom (1 Kings 3:3-9)
Saturday, Oct. 28—God Answers Solomon's Request (1 Kings 3:10-15)
Sunday, Oct. 29—Solomon Was Wise (1 Kings 4:29-34)

Conclusion

A. The Search for Wisdom

Solomon apparently was not content with God's gift of wisdom. Ecclesiastes is a record of his wretched search for the meaning of life in many different areas. He confessed that he denied himself nothing (Ecclesiastes 2:10) and concluded that he hated life (2:17). "All is vanity," he said (1:2); life is meaningless. How can wise people sometimes be so stupid?

Fortunately Solomon overcame the cynicism of his foolish quest and regained some of the wisdom he displayed at a younger age. Solomon was able to reaffirm that our purpose is to be found in our fear of God and in our obedience to Him (Ecclesiastes 12:13).

In modern society we find people seeking wisdom from curious sources. The media bombards us with the opinions of celebrities, as if being famous automatically brings wisdom. Why do we think the ability to hit home runs or make music videos gives a person understanding and discernment? Conversely, people who live wisely, fearing God and striving to keep His commandments, are rarely seen as those who should be honored and followed. Solomon knew that sinners were fools and fools were sinners.

So how do we seek and find wisdom? An obvious treasure, yet one we often ignore, is to study God's Word. We are promised that Scripture is able to make us "wise unto salvation" (2 Timothy 3:15). The people of God should be people of His Word. [See question #5, page 80.]

We should also seek to be taught by those whose lives display God's wisdom. Solomon's story teaches us that great wisdom will attract disciples. Great understanding and discernment is not often found in the very young, so we should listen to those whose faith has been tested, "tried with fire" (1 Peter 1:7). Not all old people are wise. But we are more likely to strike the rich vein of wisdom among our elders than among the young.

B. Prayer

O Lord, we can never be wise without Your presence. Give us hearts that seek wisdom, even when the wise choices are the hard choices. Give us peace in knowing that Your ways transcend the ways of the world, the paths of foolishness. We pray in the name of Your Son, Jesus, amen.

C. Thought to Remember

Recognition and development of true wisdom is tied directly to our relationship with God.

Learning by Doing

This page contains an alternative lesson plan emphasizing learning activities.
Classes desiring such student involvement will find these suggestions helpful.

Learning Goals

After participating in this lesson, each student will be able to:

1. Retell the account of Solomon's prayer for wisdom and God's response.

2. Cite other examples, biblical and modern, of God's answering prayer.

3. Suggest one specific improvement he or she will implement in his or her personal prayer life.

Into the Lesson

Display an image or a video clip of a genie rising from a magic lamp. Ask the class, "Given three wishes, what would most people name?" Give time for responses, noting the egocentric, materialistic nature of most. Then say, "Given a much greater opportunity to satisfy personal needs and wants, Solomon made an altogether different request."

Make a transition by saying in a manner similar to PBS's *Sesame Street*, "Today's lesson is brought to you by the number 3 and the letter I." Display large images of both 3 and I.

Into the Word

Direct the class to read silently today's text in 1 Kings 3:3-14, noting elements that appear in threes. After a time of reading and pondering, ask the following questions, either in the order of the verses (as given here) or in some random order. Suggested answers are in italics.

(1) "What three attributes of Solomon indicate his relationship with God?" *(loved the Lord, walked in the statutes of his father David, and offered sacrifices—vv. 3, 4)*; (2) "What three attributes of God are indicated to Solomon at Gibeon?" *(God appeared, God spoke, God offered a gift—v. 5)*; (3) "What three characteristics of David are noted in verse 6?" *(walked in truth, righteous, upright—v. 6)*; (4) "What three expressions of humility and inadequacy does Solomon make in response to God?" *(too young, not smart enough, overwhelmed by the number of people—vv. 7, 8)*; (5) "What three end results does Solomon want when he asks God for an understanding heart?" *(for governing wisdom, for ability to distinguish good and evil, and for strength to deal with so many people—v. 9)*; (6) "What three things does God commend Solomon for not asking?" *(long*

life, riches, and victories over enemies—v. 11); (7) "What three 'extra' things did God grant Solomon?" *(riches, honor, and long life—vv. 13, 14)*.

First Kings 4 ends with a summary statement of the nature and extent of the wisdom God granted to Solomon. Arrange with a student before class to do the following: After surveying the lesson text (having used the preceding activity), turn to your prearranged helper and ask, "[Student's name], did God grant Solomon's request for wisdom?" Tell your helper to answer enthusiastically and emphatically with words such as, "Did He? Why . . ." and then have the helper read 1 Kings 4:29-34. Once the helper finishes, affirm, "God does answer prayer—especially when it is not self-centered and when it is for the welfare of His people."

Now ask the class to explain how "this class is brought to you by the letter I." Accept reasonable answers. These will certainly include the ideas that Solomon's request refused to focus on "I" (himself) and that God's "I" statements clearly revealed His personal intentions of what He would do for Solomon.

Into Life

Note to your class again the unselfish nature of Solomon's request and the abundant grace God showered as a result. After a brief discussion of the things people typically pray for, ask, "What are some of the nonmaterial things the Scriptures admonish us to pray for?" When someone suggests wisdom (based on James 1:5), stop and ask, "Yes, but what kind of wisdom?" Have someone read James 3:13-18. List the characteristics of earthly wisdom: envy, strife, confusion, every evil work. Ask, "How do these things keep one from praying for the right things?" *(Example: envy certainly keeps one from praying for others, for it is others who are being envied.)*

Continue with a list of the wisdom that is "from above." Once that list is made (from James 3:17, 18), ask the class, "And how do these attributes give impetus to praying for the right things? *(Example: "full of mercy" gives direction to prayers of compassion for the needy and the distressed.)* Recommend that your learners keep this passage open during their times of prayer this week, as a guideline for how to pray in wisdom.

Let's Talk It Over

*The questions on this page are designed to promote discussion of the lesson
by the class and to encourage application of the lesson Scriptures. The answers
provided are only discussion starters. Let your class talk it over from there.*

**1. Share a time in your life when you received
either really good or really bad advice. What lesson did this teach you about wisdom?**

This question will get the class thinking in
practical terms about the importance of wisdom
and where that wisdom often comes from. Try to
get one or two people to share life stories about
words of wisdom that spared them from negative
consequences. Likewise, the class may profit
from some negative stories (perhaps starting with
the teacher!) of bad advice they received, perhaps
from friends during the teenage years.

**2. What are some ways that the world defines
wisdom? Which of these are compatible with
Christianity and which are not? Why?**

Worldly wisdom presents itself in many ways:
IQ scores, college degrees, street smarts, common
sense, etc. These may be valuable to the Christian in varying degrees, provided that they are
undergirded with a desire to honor God.

Solomon proclaims that, "The fear of the Lord
is the beginning of knowledge: but fools despise
wisdom and instruction" (Proverbs 1:7). Every
quest for knowledge, wisdom, and instruction
must stand on this foundation. Wisdom must include leading people to know and worship the
one true God, embracing His priorities.

**3. First Kings 3:11 lists some things that Solomon could have asked for. Why is wisdom so far
superior to anything else, both then and now?**

It's been said that what will be our undoing in
any endeavor or project are the things that "we
don't know that we don't know." Say that I am
building a house. I realize that electrical codes
exist, but I don't know what those codes are
specifically. Since that's something that "I know
that I don't know," I can solve the problem with a
bit of research. That's quite different from being
totally ignorant to the idea that electrical codes
even exist. That would be a case of something
that "I don't know that I don't know." What a
dangerous situation!

It's wisdom that will keep us out of the "don't
know what we don't know" situations. It would
be natural for an ancient king to request military
power or to pray for protection from jealous

brothers who might like to have him assassinated. Wisdom is better because it provided
Solomon a sense of discernment concerning the
real need or threat in such areas.

Solomon's request for wisdom also demonstrated a humility that all leaders should have
before God. The request also showed that Solomon had the people's needs in mind above his
own. Each of these is a superior quality in a
leader, especially one on David's throne.

**4. God gave Solomon more than he asked for.
Do you think that those who seek and practice
the wisdom of God are also blessed with earthly
rewards? Why, or why not?**

We can agree that this is true, while acknowledging obvious exceptions. When Israel kept the
law, they experienced better health, more productive economies, and ethical, safe communities and families. In Ephesians 6:2 Paul quotes
the Fifth Commandment: "Honor thy father and
mother; which is the first commandment with
promise; that it may be well with thee, and thou
mayest live long on the earth." When we live according to God's plans and priorities, we can experience many earthly benefits in health,
security, honor, etc., even though those things
are not our main focus.

**5. Why do you think wisdom is so hard to
attain? What are the obstacles to acquiring it in
our world today?**

One obvious problem is that we are too busy
to read our Bibles. It is in His Word that God
gives us wisdom, but we simply do not take time
to fill our minds with His thoughts. Instead, we
succumb to the many other sources of information that bombard us with falsehood and distractions. It's been said that we are living in the
Information Age, but from a godly perspective
we could call it the Disinformation Age.

Could it also be that we are seeking the very
things Solomon didn't seek but received anyway? When we seek wealth, security, vengeance,
and recognition, we disable ourselves from receiving wisdom. When we seek God's wisdom,
all that we truly need tends to come to us in due
time.

Elijah Triumphs with God

DEVOTIONAL READING: Psalm 86:8-13.

BACKGROUND SCRIPTURE: 1 Kings 18:20-39.

PRINTED TEXT: 1 Kings 18:20-24, 30-35, 38, 39.

1 Kings 18:20-24, 30-35, 38, 39

20 So Ahab sent unto all the children of Israel, and gathered the prophets together unto mount Carmel.

21 And Elijah came unto all the people, and said, How long halt ye between two opinions? if the LORD be God, follow him: but if Baal, then follow him. And the people answered him not a word.

22 Then said Elijah unto the people, I, even I only, remain a prophet of the LORD; but Baal's prophets are four hundred and fifty men.

23 Let them therefore give us two bullocks; and let them choose one bullock for themselves, and cut it in pieces, and lay it on wood, and put no fire under: and I will dress the other bullock, and lay it on wood, and put no fire under:

24 And call ye on the name of your gods, and I will call on the name of the LORD: and the God that answereth by fire, let him be God. And all the people answered and said, It is well spoken.

. . . .

30 And Elijah said unto all the people, Come near unto me. And all the people came near unto him. And he repaired the altar of the LORD that was broken down.

31 And Elijah took twelve stones, according to the number of the tribes of the sons of Jacob, unto whom the word of the LORD came, saying, Israel shall be thy name:

32 And with the stones he built an altar in the name of the LORD: and he made a trench about the altar, as great as would contain two measures of seed.

33 And he put the wood in order, and cut the bullock in pieces, and laid him on the wood, and said, Fill four barrels with water, and pour it on the burnt sacrifice, and on the wood.

34 And he said, Do it the second time. And they did it the second time. And he said, Do it the third time. And they did it the third time.

35 And the water ran round about the altar; and he filled the trench also with water.

. . . .

38 Then the fire of the LORD fell, and consumed the burnt sacrifice, and the wood, and the stones, and the dust, and licked up the water that was in the trench.

39 And when all the people saw it, they fell on their faces: and they said, The LORD, he is the God; the LORD, he is the God.

Nov 5

GOLDEN TEXT: When all the people saw [the fire of the LORD], they fell on their faces: and they said, The LORD, he is the God; the LORD, he is the God.—1 Kings 18:39.

God's Living Covenant
Unit 3: Living Under God's Covenant
(Lessons 10-13)

Lesson Aims

After participating in this lesson, each student will be able to:

1. Give the significant details of the account of Elijah's contest with the prophets of Baal on Mount Carmel.

2. Tell why this confrontation was such a crucial event in the history of God's people.

3. Write a prayer that commits him or her to take a stand for God's truth in a situation where doing so will go against an ungodly viewpoint.

Lesson Outline

INTRODUCTION
  A. The Power of One
  B. What Profit Were the Prophets?
  C. Lesson Background
 I. PEOPLE ADDRESSED (1 Kings 18:20-24)
  A. The Place (v. 20)
  B. The Plea (v. 21)
  C. The Plan (vv. 22-24)
 II. PREPARATION ACCOMPLISHED (1 Kings 18:30-35)
  A. Setting Up the Altar (vv. 30-32)
    Symbolic Stones
  B. Soaking the Sacrifice (vv. 33-35)
III. PRAYER ANSWERED (1 Kings 18:38, 39)
  A. The Lord's Response (v. 38)
  B. The People's Reaction (v. 39)
    "Don't Try This at Home"
CONCLUSION
  A. Demonstrating Power Today
  B. Prayer
  C. Thought to Remember

Introduction

A. The Power of One

During the summer of 2004, Mike Krzyzewski, head coach of the men's basketball team at Duke University, was approached about becoming head coach of the National Basketball Association's Los Angeles Lakers. "Coach K," as he is known, had gained a reputation as one of the premier coaches in college basketball. The high salary and prestige that accompanied coaching a team like the Lakers were tempting.

In the midst of his deliberations, Krzyzewski received an e-mail that proved to be the pivotal influence in his decision. Andrew Humphries, a junior at Duke, sent an impassioned message for Coach K to stay. The e-mail brought tears to the eyes of Krzyzewski; he rejected the Lakers' offer and chose to remain at Duke.

Andrew Humphries was just one person—yet he had the power to persuade! The prophet Elijah also was just one man. His voice seemed like a whisper in Israel when compared with the powerful, government-backed influence of Baal worship. Yet when just one person chooses to stand firm on behalf of the one true God, the results can be one of a kind! Coach K could well have made a different decision even after Humphries' e-mail. Would the people on Mount Carmel dared to have chosen Baal after seeing the power of God before their eyes?

B. What Profit Were the Prophets?

Many associate the word *prophet* with someone who has the ability to predict the future. The role of the Old Testament prophets, however, went much further than this. Every prophet conveyed a significant message and was raised up by the Lord during a particularly critical time in the history of God's people.

Prophets were raised up by the Lord during periods when paganism became an especially serious threat to God's people. This is one of the reasons that the prophet Elijah's ministry was pivotal. Ahab and Jezebel (particularly Jezebel) were intent on promoting the worship of pagan gods throughout Israel. Baal was considered a god of storms and fertility, meaning that he was believed to be in charge of providing life—to crops, animals, and human beings.

God used Elijah to counter this false and repulsive system of worship. Elijah demonstrated that the God who had called Israel to be His people was still in control.

C. Lesson Background

By the time Elijah's ministry began, the nation of Israel had been divided for approximately half a century. (*Israel* is often used to designate the ten tribes that constituted the northern kingdom with *Judah* referring to the two tribes of the southern kingdom.) Elijah himself appears in the biblical record quite suddenly. Nothing is said about his parents, his childhood, or even his call to be a prophet.

The first time he is mentioned is in 1 Kings 17:1, where he announces a period of drought in the land of Israel. This challenge was a slap in the face of the god Baal and of those who worshiped him, since Baal was believed to be the provider of storms that would bring rain.

Elijah was then guided through a series of circumstances that served to prepare him further for his ministry and assure him of God's presence. First, he was told to go to the Cherith brook, where ravens brought him food twice a day (1 Kings 17:5, 6). When the brook dried up because of the drought, the Lord told Elijah to travel northward to Zarephath of Sidon. There the Lord used a widow to provide Elijah with food in a miraculous manner. Later when the widow's only son became ill and died, Elijah prayed to the Lord and the boy was brought back to life (vv. 7-24).

Notice that the miracles had something to do with providing food in life-areas where Baal was believed to be in control. Sidon was Jezebel's homeland (1 Kings 16:31). Elijah thus saw God's clear superiority to the pagan gods!

In the third year of the drought, the Lord told Elijah to "Go, show thyself unto Ahab; and I will send rain upon the earth" (1 Kings 18:1). Elijah sent a message to Ahab through Obadiah, an official of Ahab's who was also a devout follower of the Lord.

When prophet and king met, Elijah issued a challenge to Ahab to summon all Israel to assemble at Mount Carmel. Ahab was also to gather the 450 prophets of Baal "and the prophets of the groves four hundred" (1 Kings 18:19). The term *groves* refers to the images of the goddess Asherah, who was believed to be Baal's consort. Because these images were often made of wood, the term *groves* (describing groups of such wood) is used.

At this point, Elijah did not specify what he planned to do at Mount Carmel. Our printed text begins by describing Ahab's compliance with Elijah's challenge.

I. People Addressed
(1 Kings 18:20-24)

A. The Place (v. 20)

20. So Ahab sent unto all the children of Israel, and gathered the prophets together unto mount Carmel.

Ahab does as Elijah says, sending word throughout all Israel and gathering *the prophets* on Mount Carmel. Later Elijah observes that the 450 prophets of Baal are present (v. 22), but he says nothing about the 400 prophets of Asherah. For some unknown reason, Jezebel apparently forbids her prophets to come to Mount Carmel.

Probably her failure to comply with Elijah's challenge is simply an act of defiance. Maybe Ahab is willing to do what Elijah says, but Jezebel is not about to!

One may ask why Mount Carmel serves as the place for this assembly. Mount Carmel is actually a mountain ridge some 12 miles in length. Near the summit of the ridge is a plateau where a contest such as this one can take place. A spring of water is close at hand. It flows even during extremely dry seasons. This is why Elijah can have 12 containers of water poured on his sacrifice (vv. 33, 34, below) even though this incident occurs during drought conditions.

B. The Plea (v. 21)

21. And Elijah came unto all the people, and said, How long halt ye between two opinions? if the LORD be God, follow him: but if Baal, then follow him. And the people answered him not a word.

Elijah begins his address to the Israelites with a question: *How long halt ye between two opinions?* In the antique language of the *King James Version*, the word *halt* in this passage does not mean "stop." The term (translated from Hebrew to Greek) can also convey the idea of limping or lameness (Luke 14:21; John 5:3). In certain cases in the Gospels it describes those who could not walk whom Jesus healed.

Elijah thus is describing the spiritual unsteadiness of the people in the crowd that day. The alternative to such hobbling will be a confident, steady walk with the Lord, which they do not possess. [See question #1, page 88.]

The issue facing the people on this occasion is remarkably simple. Two options confront them: the way of *the Lord* and the way of *Baal*. In today's pluralistic religious climate, Elijah's statement is still timely. We may choose a narrow road to salvation or a wide road to destruction (Matthew 7:13, 14).

How to Say It

AHAB. *Ay*-hab.
ASHERAH. Uh-*she*-ruh.
CHERITH. *Key*-rith.
ELIJAH. Ee-*lye*-juh.
JEZEBEL. *Jez*-uh-bel.
KRZYZEWSKI. Sha-*shef*-ski.
MICHAIAH (MICAIAH). My-*kay*-uh.
OBADIAH. O-buh-*dye*-uh.
SIDON. *Sigh*-dun.
ZAREPHATH. *Zair*-uh-fath.

Observe the audience's passive, apathetic response: *the people answered him not a word.* Perhaps they are cowering in fear, knowing that to answer in favor of Baal will displease Elijah, while answering in favor of the Lord will ignite the rage of Jezebel. Perhaps their silence reflects their lack of passion for or interest in anything having to do with spiritual matters. It is also possible that Elijah's uncompromising words make all too clear their failure to obey the Lord; thus their silence may indicate a sense of shame or embarrassment. In any case, the safe response (from a worldly point of view) is to keep quiet.

C. The Plan (vv. 22-24)

22. Then said Elijah unto the people, I, even I only, remain a prophet of the LORD; but Baal's prophets are four hundred and fifty men.

Elijah observes that he is the only one of the Lord's prophets left. Yet we know from an earlier statement in 1 Kings 18:4 that Obadiah, one of Ahab's officials, has hidden 100 prophets of the Lord from Jezebel's murderous fury. In addition there are prophets such as Micaiah (22:8) and various unnamed men who are part of the group known as the "sons of the prophets" (20:35). Elijah probably means that he is the only one of the Lord's prophets who is present for this confrontation.

Elijah's emphasis on the contrast between 1 and 450 highlights a key principle: truth is not determined by the numbers who embrace a certain position. Truth is truth, no matter how many or how few hold to it at any given time. [See question #2, page 88.]

23, 24. Let them therefore give us two bullocks; and let them choose one bullock for themselves, and cut it in pieces, and lay it on wood, and put no fire under: and I will dress the other bullock, and lay it on wood, and put no fire under: and call ye on the name of your gods, and I will call on the name of the LORD: and the God that answereth by fire, let him be God. And all the people answered and said, It is well spoken.

The rules of the contest are simple. Each side is to prepare a bull in the same manner: *cut it in pieces, and lay it on wood.* Then each side is to call on the name of its deity. *The God* who responds *by fire* will prove himself to be the true *God.*

The fire may refer to lightning. Remember that the issue is which deity is in control of the rains. Lightning would serve as a signal of the coming of the drought-ending rains and would demonstrate to those gathered on Mount Carmel which God is in control of the forces of nature.

Perhaps the prophets of Baal relish the opportunity to go first. Should Baal respond to their cries, the contest essentially will be over. However, their going first only sets the stage for what Elijah will do, because it will highlight how powerless Baal really is.

Verses 25-29 (not in our printed text) record the futile efforts of the followers of Baal. The threefold emphasis at the conclusion of verse 29 provides a solemn closure to the failure of Baal's prophets: "there was neither voice, nor any to answer, nor any that regarded." The stage is now set for a dramatic display of divine power.

II. Preparation Accomplished (1 Kings 18:30-35)

A. Setting Up the Altar (vv. 30-32)

30. And Elijah said unto all the people, Come near unto me. And all the people came near unto him. And he repaired the altar of the LORD that was broken down.

While nothing is said specifically about the altar used by the prophets of Baal, it is noted that Elijah repaired *the altar of the Lord,* which was *broken down.* No doubt this altar had been a victim of the apathy and neglect of the people toward the worship of the true God.

31. And Elijah took twelve stones, according to the number of the tribes of the sons of Jacob, unto whom the word of the LORD came, saying, Israel shall be thy name.

The use of *twelve stones* by Elijah is noteworthy in light of the fact the nation of Israel has been divided for several decades by this time. Yet Elijah recognizes through this action that God's original intention is that the Israelites be 12 tribes—yet one nation—under Him.

SYMBOLIC STONES

In the sixteenth century English royal power increasingly asserted itself over Ireland. That pressure set off some four centuries of political and religious struggle. The Anglo-Irish war of 1919–1921 resulted in two separate countries. Mostly Catholic southern Ireland became independent. Northern Ireland was mostly Protestant and aligned with Britain.

Throughout much of the twentieth century, dissidents hoped for political reunification of Ireland. These dissidents used terrorist methods to try to force the British out of Northern Ireland. One could have hoped that since each side of the Protestant-Catholic divide claimed to be Christian, they could all act as if they were and quit killing each other.

The century-long division of the Irish peoples is somewhat similar to that of God's people of old. Israel and Judah were divided politically and religiously. Israel in the north had turned mostly to Baalism; Judah in the south had remained somewhat faithful to Yahweh (although it had dabbled in idolatry also). By building his altar out of 12 stones, Elijah hoped that the symbolic number would speak to all the tribes of divided Israel. Perhaps they would remember their common heritage before the one true God.

Faithfulness to God is without doubt the best way for any nation to find internal peace. That fact should not be lost on the people of any democracy when they go to the polls to elect their leaders.
—C. R. B.

32. And with the stones he built an altar in the name of the LORD: and he made a trench about the altar, as great as would contain two measures of seed.

The act described earlier in verse 30 as repairing the altar of the Lord is now described in another way: Elijah *built an altar in the name of the Lord.* Elijah is building an altar under the authority of and in reverence for the true God. God's name has lost none of its power, in spite of Ahab and Jezebel's attempts to stamp it out. [See question #3, page 88.]

This verse also notes that Elijah makes *a trench about the altar, as great as would contain two measures of seed.* This computes to about 13 quarts. If such an act seems odd to the onlookers, it does not compare with what Elijah does next.

B. Soaking the Sacrifice (vv. 33-35)

33, 34. And he put the wood in order, and cut the bullock in pieces, and laid him on the wood, and said, Fill four barrels with water, and pour it on the burnt sacrifice, and on the wood. And he said, Do it the second time. And they did it the second time. And he said, Do it the third time. And they did it the third time.

Elijah proceeds to prepare the sacrifice according to the rules established earlier. But then he does something else quite unexpected: he commands that *four barrels* of *water* be poured on the offering three times. As noted earlier, water may be available from the streams that flow at higher elevations, such as that of Mount Carmel, despite the severe drought that is now in its fourth year (Luke 4:25; James 5:17).

35. And the water ran round about the altar; and he filled the trench also with water.

By soaking completely the sacrifice and *the altar,* Elijah sets the stage for an even more im-

pressive demonstration of the power of the true God. At the same time, Elijah is also putting his own reputation as the Lord's prophet on the line. He will look utterly foolish if God fails to answer.

Elijah's actions also indicate to the audience that he is not engaging in any kind of trickery to ignite his sacrifice. If the sacrifice is ignited, the only possible explanation will be that God has done it.

The prayer of Elijah, recorded in verses 36 and 37, is not part of our printed text. His simple, earnest plea to the Lord contrasts markedly with the frenzied madness of the prophets of Baal. And whereas there was no response of any kind to the prophets of Baal, such is not the case now.

III. Prayer Answered
(1 Kings 18:38, 39)

A. The Lord's Response (v. 38)

38. Then the fire of the LORD fell, and consumed the burnt sacrifice, and the wood, and the stones, and the dust, and licked up the water that was in the trench.

In a spectacular display of unmistakably divine power, the fire of the Lord consumes everything that is part of the preparation for the sacrifice. Even the *water* in *the trench* is *licked up* by the fire. [See question #4, page 88.]

B. The People's Reaction (v. 39)

39. And when all the people saw it, they fell on their faces: and they said, The LORD, he is the God; The LORD, he is the God.

All the people, who were silent earlier when confronted by Elijah (v. 21), do not hesitate to

Visual for Lesson 10. *Point to this artwork as an illustration of someone standing alone for God. Use it to introduce question #4 on page 88.*

express their reaction after what they witness. What else could they conclude? *The Lord, he is the God.*

The aftermath of the contest on Mount Carmel includes the slaughter of the prophets of Baal. That is in accordance with the Law of Moses concerning false prophets (Deuteronomy 18:20). Also come the long-awaited rains. The drought has ended, and—more importantly—the Lord, His prophet, and His Word have been vindicated.

"DON'T TRY THIS AT HOME"

We've all heard of fire-breathing preachers of the gospel. Colin Davis, a Church of England vicar in Devon, England, is a fire-*eating* preacher! While he was in college training for the ministry, he saw a fire performer and thought he would be able to use the trick to attract attention to the message of Christ. Neither his former work as a banker nor his current work as a preacher would seem to predict this particular avocation!

Davis says he uses the trick for its attention-grabbing impact, comparing the feat to Jesus' use of parables. Only occasionally does his performance take place in church; more often he does it in school assemblies. On those occasions he makes students vow before the demonstration that they will not try it.

In one sense, Elijah's use of fire was like Colin Davis's use of fire: it certainly captured the attention of his audience! On the other hand, there is a striking difference: Davis's performance is just that—a trick that has no physical effect. But Elijah's fire was sent by God from Heaven to consume everything in its path. We can respond, "Don't try this at home" to both. Seeing the con-

stant shower of God's blessings in our everyday lives should be all we need to evoke the same reaction as that of Elijah's audience: "The Lord, He is the God!" This bears repeating.   —C. R. B.

Conclusion

A. Demonstrating Power Today

Perhaps after reading an account such as that of Elijah we may wonder, "Why don't we see demonstrations of God's power such as this today? If we could offer the kind of evidence that Elijah did on Mount Carmel, think of the impact it would have on our culture! Does God no longer provide these demonstrations, or do we as His people lack faith?"

We should remember that as Christians we bear witness to the greatest of all demonstrations of God's power: the resurrection of Jesus His Son from the dead. That always has been the essence of the gospel message (1 Corinthians 15:1-4).

Interestingly, when the New Testament instructs Christians on how to live in light of that event, it points to the quiet, often inconspicuous deeds of service done in the name of Christ. The metaphors of salt and light (Matthew 5:13-16) are hardly noisy or flamboyant in how they function. But no one can question their effectiveness or their necessity.

Elijah's surroundings demanded the kind of highly visible, dramatic manifestation of power that God wrought at Mount Carmel. We see similar demonstrations during other critical periods in biblical history (the plagues in Egypt and the miracles of Jesus, for example). But a primary challenge issued to New Testament believers today is that of a consistently holy lifestyle. Peter challenged the Christians of his time to live holy lives among unbelievers that "whereas they speak against you as evildoers, they may by your good works, which they shall behold, glorify God" (1 Peter 2:12). [See question #5, page 88.]

B. Prayer

Father, may we have the courage to stand for You in our time as Elijah did in his. When we feel intimidated by the strength or loudness of the opposition, help us to be unmoved. Help us to remain faithful and consistent in our testimony. May we thereby give no one cause to question our devotion to Your Son, Jesus. In His name, amen.

C. Thought to Remember

God will give us the courage we need for any opposition we face.

Home Daily Bible Readings

Monday, Oct. 30—God Is Great (Psalm 145:1-7)

Tuesday, Oct. 31—None Is Like God (Psalm 86:8-13)

Wednesday, Nov. 1—God's Majesty and Might (Psalm 93)

Thursday, Nov. 2—Contest on Mount Carmel (1 Kings 18:17-24)

Friday, Nov. 3—Elijah Taunts the Baal Worshipers (1 Kings 18:25-29)

Saturday, Nov. 4—Elijah Builds an Altar to God (1 Kings 18:30-35)

Sunday, Nov. 5—Elijah Prays, God Acts (1 Kings 18:36-39)

Learning by Doing

This page contains an alternative lesson plan emphasizing learning activities.
Classes desiring such student involvement will find these suggestions helpful.

Learning Goals

After participating in this lesson, each student will be able to:

1. Give the significant details of the account of Elijah's contest with the prophets of Baal on Mount Carmel.

2. Tell why this confrontation was such a crucial event in the history of God's people.

3. Write a prayer that commits him or her to take a stand for God's truth in a situation where doing so will go against an ungodly viewpoint.

Into the Lesson

Display a sign saying *Impact—The Power of One!* Tell the class that one person can make a difference in the world, a culture, a church, or in a life. Ask the class members to think of one person who made such an impact.

While the class members are thinking about this challenge, tell the story of Andrew Humphries found in the Introduction. Then allow class members to share the name and events of one person who made an impact.

Make the transition to Bible study by telling the class that the prophet Elijah is a wonderful example of just one man making a huge impact on culture. Say, "But Elijah's influence was backed by a miracle of God. That ancient miracle still serves as an encouragement to us."

Into the Word

Give a very brief lecture based on the Lesson Background. Emphasize the division of the tribes, the drought, Elijah's history, and the nature of Baal. As you lecture, write the following words on the board while speaking on each topic: Israel, Drought, Elijah, and Baal.

Prepare a handout as follows (also printed in the student book). The students will need Bibles, since some of the information is found in verses not included in the printed text. Students can complete the handout individually, in pairs, or in small groups as you think best.

Heading: *A Contest of Gods*
Contestants
　　The bad guys (v. 22):
　　The good guy (v. 22):
　　The contest location (v. 20):

The challenge for the teams (vv. 23, 24):
The team strategies
　　The bad guys (vv. 26-29):
　　The good guy (vv. 30-37):
The victor (vv. 38, 39):
The fate of the defeated (v. 40):
The fate of the drought (vv. 41-45):

For follow-up discussion, use these questions: (1) Why do you think Elijah selected 12 stones for his altar (vv. 31, 32)? (2) Why do you suppose Elijah chose to pour water on the sacrifice before offering his prayer (vv. 33, 34)? (3) What lessons about prayer do we learn as we contrast the pleas of Baal's prophets and Elijah's prayer? (4) Why do you think this contest was a crucial event in the history of Israel? (Write answers on the board and discuss as appropriate.)

Into Life

Make the transition to application by telling the class that God still calls people to take a stand in cultures that value pluralistic religious views. Despite the common view of varied "paths to God," we are taught that Jesus is the only way to the Father. Like Israel, God calls us to take a stand for the one true God. However, does our stand need always to be confrontational? Why or why not? (Allow for discussion.)

Tell the students that underneath three chairs are taped Scripture references that have clues that may be helpful in determining how to live an influential life. Have the students find and read the following Scriptures, then ask the attendant questions:

Matthew 5:13-16. Do these metaphors of salt and light suggest an alternative to noisy and flamboyant confrontation? Is there a way to make an impact through quiet and less conspicuous means? How?

1 Peter 2:12. What does this Scripture offer or imply about influencing lives or society? What is the wisdom of this verse and its appeal?

1 Peter 3:1-4. What clues do we find in this passage about a way to influence the unsaved?

Conclude by asking each student to write a prayer that commits him or her to take a stand for God's truth in a situation where doing so will go against the majority, ungodly viewpoint.

Let's Talk It Over

The questions on this page are designed to promote discussion of the lesson by the class and to encourage application of the lesson Scriptures. The answers provided are only discussion starters. Let your class talk it over from there.

1. In what ways does our culture waver between a multitude of opinions? How do we respond?

Pluralism and postmodernism reign supreme in certain Western democracies. Under these concepts, a multiplicity of contradictory viewpoints is celebrated. Normally, the concept of *waver* (or *halt* in the *King James Version*) brings with it the idea of "Maybe idea A is right or maybe idea B is right—we're not sure." However, postmodernism says, "Idea A can be right for me while Idea B is right for you—to each his own." Demonstrating and refuting such inconsistencies requires a great deal of alertness.

Other parts of the world have their problems too. Alternatives to worship of the living God abound. These include animistic faiths in tribal areas, the Hindu deities that dominate India, or "Allah" that Muslims worship. The task of confronting these can seem overwhelming at times. A good start for forming a response is to become more informed in the area of Christian apologetics. This field of study deals with defense of the faith (see, for example, www.rzim.org).

2. In what ways is Elijah's confrontation with 450 ungodly opponents an example for Christians today? In what ways is it *not* an example?

We should be careful to get these two questions right! Elijah received specific, personal instructions to go to King Ahab (1 Kings 18:1). We, on the other hand, have general instructions to go into all the world (Matthew 28:19, 20). If a Christian were to go to Mount Carmel today and attempt to reproduce Elijah's confrontation, the possibility is very real that God would not participate in such an endeavor!

Further, we have no approval from God to kill His enemies as Elijah apparently had (compare Luke 6:27-36; 9:54, 55). Our challenge is to realize that God is in control no matter how people react to our witness.

3. Elijah built an altar to God in the presence of all of the people, including the prophets of Baal. When is public expression of Christian faith especially appropriate today? When can such expressions be counterproductive?

Public expressions of the Christian faith take many forms on many occasions. Tying such expressions to familiar calendar events may have the most impact (Christmas, Easter, anniversary of *Roe* v. *Wade*, etc.).

Public expressions of faith that involve confrontation with those who advocate abortion, homosexuality, etc., should be handled with great care. Such expressions and confrontations may be more productive if they are characterized by grief and sorrow than by anger.

4. What was a time in your life when you stood alone (or nearly alone) for something you believed was right? What was the result for the cause you supported? How did taking this stand affect you personally?

Taking a stand can be very difficult. Standing all alone is even more difficult—it's emotionally exhausting and faith can waver. Yet history abounds with examples of people who honored God by acting alone in the face of established, entrenched opposition. No doubt there are examples in your class of those who have walked in the footsteps of Elijah in a figurative way.

We gain strength when we remember that when we stand for God, He stands with us. We are not really standing alone. Elijah felt very alone at times, but God was with him all the way. Elijah's protégé Elisha knew this as well (see 2 Kings 6:15-17). Whenever we stand together with God against opposition, we will find ourselves changed. One cannot stand that close to God without experiencing the effects!

5. When was a time that you stepped out so far on faith that you could have been successful only if God intervened?

Let's face it: God's intervention in the form of fire from Heaven is a rare thing! Much more likely for us is God's intervention in the form of opened and closed doors of opportunity. Stories will be personal, of course, but try to steer the discussion along that line. As students share their stories, ask, "What opened or closed doors of opportunity led you to believe that God rather than humans or random chance was opening and closing those doors?"

Josiah Brings Reform

DEVOTIONAL READING: Psalm 103:1-18.

BACKGROUND SCRIPTURE: 2 Kings 22, 23.

PRINTED TEXT: 2 Kings 22:8-10; 23:1-3, 21-23.

2 Kings 22:8-10

8 And Hilkiah the high priest said unto Shaphan the scribe, I have found the book of the law in the house of the LORD. And Hilkiah gave the book to Shaphan, and he read it.

9 And Shaphan the scribe came to the king, and brought the king word again, and said, Thy servants have gathered the money that was found in the house, and have delivered it into the hand of them that do the work, that have the oversight of the house of the LORD.

10 And Shaphan the scribe showed the king, saying, Hilkiah the priest hath delivered me a book. And Shaphan read it before the king.

2 Kings 23:1-3, 21-23

1 And the king sent, and they gathered unto him all the elders of Judah and of Jerusalem.

2 And the king went up into the house of the LORD, and all the men of Judah and all the inhabitants of Jerusalem with him, and the priests, and the prophets, and all the people, both small and great: and he read in their ears all the words of the book of the covenant which was found in the house of the LORD.

3 And the king stood by a pillar, and made a covenant before the LORD, to walk after the LORD, and to keep his commandments and his testimonies and his statutes with all their heart and all their soul, to perform the words of this covenant that were written in this book. And all the people stood to the covenant.

. . . .

21 And the king commanded all the people, saying, Keep the passover unto the LORD your God, as it is written in the book of this covenant.

22 Surely there was not holden such a passover from the days of the judges that judged Israel, nor in all the days of the kings of Israel, nor of the kings of Judah;

23 But in the eighteenth year of king Josiah, wherein this passover was holden to the LORD in Jerusalem.

Nov
12

GOLDEN TEXT: The king stood by a pillar, and made a covenant before the LORD, to walk after the LORD, and to keep his commandments and his testimonies and his statutes with all their heart and all their soul, to perform the words of this covenant that were written in this book. And all the people stood to the covenant.
—2 Kings 23:3.

God's Living Covenant
Unit 3: Living Under God's Covenant
(Lessons 10-13)

Lesson Aims

After participating in this lesson, each student will be able to:

1. List the causes and outcomes of Josiah's reform movement.

2. Predict the conditions that would have to be present for a similar reform movement to occur in the church today.

3. Choose one area in his or her personal life in which to make a "Josiah reform."

Lesson Outline

INTRODUCTION
  A. "Accidental" Discoveries
  B. Lesson Background
 I. DISCOVERING A BOOK (2 Kings 22:8-10)
  A. Hilkiah Informs Shaphan (v. 8)
    "Losing" the Bible
  B. Shaphan Informs Josiah (vv. 9, 10)
 II. DEDICATING A PEOPLE (2 Kings 23:1-3)
  A. Rallying the People (vv. 1, 2a)
  B. Reading the Book (v. 2b)
  C. Renewing the Covenant (v. 3)
III. DECLARING A PASSOVER (2 Kings 23:21-23)
  A. Command (v. 21)
  B. Comparison (vv. 22, 23)
    A One-of-a-Kind Celebration
CONCLUSION
  A. The Need for "Re-Bible"
  B. Prayer
  C. Thought to Remember

Introduction

A. "Accidental" Discoveries

One day in 1947 a young Bedouin goatherd left his companions in order to find a stray goat. Eventually, he came upon a cave with a small opening at its top. Suspecting that the goat may have fallen inside, he threw some stones into the opening. Instead of hearing the sound of a startled goat, he heard the sound of broken pottery.

The goatherd lowered himself into the cave and found some ancient clay jars containing various leather scrolls. He had discovered what came to be called the Dead Sea Scrolls—one of the foremost archaeological discoveries of the twentieth century. These scrolls have since shed significant light on life during the time between the testaments and on the history (and reliability) of the Old Testament text. It is an oddity that often the most important archaeological finds in the field of biblical studies have occurred quite unexpectedly.

Today's Scripture text records another "accidental" discovery that was of enormous significance in the history of God's people. The priest Hilkiah was assisting with the renovation of the temple when he came across a book. What he discovered was not just any book; it was the Book of the Law, which was then read to King Josiah.

Josiah was so moved by the book's contents and by the nation's failure to comply with the laws written therein that he intensified his efforts to turn Judah back to the Lord. Sometimes in God's providence what appears to be a chance occurrence is actually a divine appointment.

B. Lesson Background

The incident covered in last week's lesson (the contest on Mount Carmel) took place around 850 or 860 BC. Today's lesson moves us forward roughly 200 years. By this time the northern kingdom of Israel (over which the wicked duo Ahab and Jezebel had ruled) already had fallen to the Assyrians; that happened in 722 BC. Judah likely would have suffered the same treatment from Assyria in 701 BC had it not been for the reign of godly King Hezekiah. It was his cries to the Lord that resulted in a miraculous deliverance (2 Kings 19:35, 36).

The first half of the seventh century BC was a spiritual nightmare for Judah. Most of those years were part of the reign of Manasseh, the son of Hezekiah. He ruled from about 698 to 644 BC, and he was as wicked as his father was righteous. Judah and Jerusalem's eventual downfall is traced to the sinfulness of Manasseh (2 Kings 21:10-15; 24:1-4). There was, however, one last glimmer of hope for Judah—one Hezekiah-like king who sought to call the nation back to its spiritual roots. If he were successful, perhaps his country could avoid a tragedy such as that which befell the ten tribes of the northern kingdom. That king was Josiah, who reigned from 640 to 609 BC.

Today's lesson puts us into the eighteenth year of Josiah's reign. The lesson will focus on a period of revival in Judah that was given additional impetus by the discovery of the Book of the Law. We say *additional impetus* because it is clear that some spiritual renewal had occurred in Judah prior to this book's discovery (2 Chronicles 34:3-7).

I. Discovering a Book
(2 Kings 22:8-10)

Second Kings 22 begins with the account of King Josiah's reign. Unlike the Chronicles account, the Kings account does not record the efforts of Josiah to promote righteousness in Judah prior to the discovery of the Book of the Law. It opens by mentioning Josiah's age at becoming king (eight!) and provides a general analysis of his reign: "He did that which was right in the sight of the Lord, and walked in all the way of David his father, and turned not aside to the right hand or to the left" (2 Kings 22:2).

The account in Kings then notes how Josiah, in the eighteenth year of his reign, had initiated a program to renovate the temple in Jerusalem. (Most likely the temple had suffered from neglect during the reigns of Manasseh and his wicked son Amon, who was Josiah's father.) The high priest Hilkiah had been instructed by Josiah, through the king's secretary Shaphan, to make certain that the workers involved in the project were paid correctly. They were to be provided with the funds to purchase any materials necessary for the rebuilding.

Apparently, after Shaphan had conveyed these instructions to Hilkiah, the high priest informed Shaphan of a surprising discovery.

A. Hilkiah Informs Shaphan (v. 8)

8. And Hilkiah the high priest said unto Shaphan the scribe, I have found the book of the law in the house of the LORD. And Hilkiah gave the book to Shaphan, and he read it.

As a *scribe*, Shaphan would be quite interested in the discovery we read about here. Just what constitutes *the book of the law* has been the subject of much discussion. Some believe it comprises all of Genesis through Deuteronomy (the Pentateuch). Others suggest that it was made up of a smaller portion of those five, specifically the book of Deuteronomy. The phrase *book of the law* is used in Deuteronomy 31:24-26 to refer to the contents of that particular book.

A third possibility is suggested by 2 Kings 23:2, which states that Josiah read in the people's hearing "all the words of the book of the covenant." The term *book of the covenant* is used in Exodus 24:7 to describe (most likely) the material included in Exodus 20–23.

The contents of Deuteronomy certainly would be enough to generate the kind of intense re-

sponse that Josiah later spearheaded. For example the references to the "wrath of the Lord" (2 Kings 22:13) and to promises to bring correction (vv. 16, 20) would fit with the list of curses pronounced in Deuteronomy 28:15-68 as a punishment for disobeying God's law.

Deuteronomy 31:26 says that a copy of the Book of the Law originally had been placed in the ark of the covenant. Deuteronomy 17:18 stipulates that a king, upon beginning his reign, should "write [for himself] a copy of this law in a book out of that which is before the priests the Levites." Perhaps it is a copy of this law produced under these circumstances that was ignored by kings such as Manasseh and Amon. Now, by the providence of God, it has been discovered. Its discovery comes during the reign of a king who will take its message seriously. [See question #1, page 96.]

"LOSING" THE BIBLE

In 1985 a church building in Braham, Minnesota, burned to the ground. The church's brass bell, weighing 1,400 pounds, was sold to a scrap metal company as a result. Church members thought they had seen the last of the bell, and most of them forgot about it.

About 15 years later an employee at the scrap metal company discovered the bell hanging on the company's property. The employee saw the inscription on the bell and recognized it for what it was. Communications between the church and the scrap company were interrupted when both went through reorganizations.

Thus the bell was forgotten about again. Everyone assumed it had been melted down for

Visual for Lesson 11. *Ask, "How does this picture illustrate how the Bible can be 'lost' today? What can we do to guard against this?"*

scrap. In 2004 the bell was "re-rediscovered" and returned to the church, nearly 20 years after it had first been "lost."

Doesn't it seem strange that something as significant as a church bell could be overlooked for so long? And doesn't it strike us as unbelievable that a much more significant treasure—the Book of the Law—could get lost in ancient Judah? But here is something else that is amazing: churches and individuals who have abundant copies of the Bible, yet still disregard what it says when it comes to some of the moral issues of our time!

In effect these churches and individuals have "lost" the Bible. How do you think such a thing can happen?   —C. R. B.

B. Shaphan Informs Josiah (vv. 9, 10)

9. And Shaphan the scribe came to the king, and brought the king word again, and said, Thy servants have gathered the money that was found in the house, and have delivered it into the hand of them that do the work, that have the oversight of the house of the LORD.

After reading the contents of the book (v. 8), *Shaphan* then returns to King Josiah and reports on his conversation with Hilkiah. Shaphan first mentions the matter that Josiah had instructed him to address concerning *the money* that was in the temple. This is to make sure that the workers and supervisors receive proper compensation for their labors. [See question #2, page 96.]

10. And Shaphan the scribe showed the king, saying, Hilkiah the priest hath delivered me a book. And Shaphan read it before the king.

Though not included in our printed text, it is important to observe King Josiah's reaction upon hearing the Lord's Word: "he rent his clothes" (2 Kings 22:11). This is worth noting because Josiah's son, Jehoiakim, will exhibit a brazen contempt for the Lord's message that comes through Jeremiah by cutting it up, casting it into the fire, and refusing to tear his robes (Jeremiah 36:22-24).

How to Say It

AMON. *Ay*-mun.
BEDOUIN. *Bed*-uh-wun.
HEZEKIAH. Hez-ih-*kye*-uh.
HILKIAH. Hill-*kye*-uh.
HULDAH. *Hul*-duh.
JOSIAH. Jo-*sigh*-uh.
MANASSEH. Muh-*nass*-uh.
PENTATEUCH. *Pen*-ta-teuk.
SHAPHAN. *Shay*-fan.

II. Dedicating a People
(2 Kings 23:1-3)

Following his anguished response to the law of the Lord, King Josiah tells some of his officials, including Hilkiah and Shaphan, to inquire of the Lord. Huldah the prophetess confirms the message of judgment found within the book. But she also promises that King Josiah will be spared from seeing all of this because of his desire to obey God and His law (2 Kings 22:14-20).

A. Rallying the People (vv. 1, 2a)

1. And the king sent, and they gathered unto him all the elders of Judah and of Jerusalem.

How easy it would be for King Josiah simply to allow the nation to continue on its downward path toward judgment, secure in the knowledge that at least he himself is going to escape the wrath of God! But Josiah is not one to rest on his laurels by focusing on himself. He determines, rather, that the entire nation needs to hear the same solemn message that he has heard.

So *the king* calls together *all the elders of Judah and Jerusalem*. Jerusalem is singled out because of its status as the capital city of Judah. The elders are probably local leaders of towns or villages. Josiah knows that the support of these men is crucial. The king by himself cannot generate any renewal of interest in God's law that will have a lasting impact. [See question #3, page 96.]

2a. And the king went up into the house of the LORD, and all the men of Judah and all the inhabitants of Jerusalem with him, and the priests, and the prophets, and all the people, both small and great.

Various groups take part in this ceremony of rededication. The reference to *the men of Judah* may highlight the vital part that godly men must play in any effort to promote national spiritual renewal. The presence of *the priests, and the prophets* at such a public ceremony testifies of their desire to obey God's law.

Later, however, the prophet Jeremiah (who lives during the reign of Josiah) will lament over how corrupt the priests and the prophets had become throughout Judah (Jeremiah 5:30, 31; 6:13; 23:11). When the leaders are unstable spiritually, there is little hope that the general populace will be any better.

At this point, however, *all the people* from the *small* to the *great* are in attendance. Distinctions based on social class or income are meaningless on an occasion such as this. Everyone needs to hear what the law of the Lord says! [See question #4, page 96.]

B. Reading the Book (v. 2b)

2b. And he read in their ears all the words of the book of the covenant which was found in the house of the LORD.

The book that had been found earlier by Hilkiah now is being "found" by the general populace through Josiah's public reading of it. Since many people in the ancient world are illiterate, the public reading of documents is quite important for communicating vital information.

C. Renewing the Covenant (v. 3)

3. And the king stood by a pillar, and made a covenant before the LORD, to walk after the LORD, and to keep his commandments and his testimonies and his statutes with all their heart and all their soul, to perform the words of this covenant that were written in this book. And all the people stood to the covenant.

The fact that the king stands *by a pillar* indicates a specific place to stand (compare 2 Kings 11:14; 2 Chronicles 23:13). The term *pillar* could refer to one of the two pillars that Solomon erected at the main entrance of the temple (1 Kings 7:15-22). Or, it may be a special pillar built for special occasions associated with royalty. Whatever the specific location is, from that place Josiah leads God's people in a special ceremony of dedication. It is there that Josiah renews the *covenant* in the presence of the Lord.

The word *stood* in the *King James Version* here is literal to the Hebrew. Perhaps at this time the crowd gathered before Josiah actually stands up before the Lord to voice a desire to honor and obey God. Here is the kind of leadership that God's people so desperately need!

III. Declaring a Passover (2 Kings 23:21-23)

The passage between verse 3 and verse 21 (not in today's text) gives an account of the various steps taken by Josiah in obedience to the law of the Lord. Pagan shrines of worship are destroyed. Pagan priests are removed from office. Josiah's efforts include the fulfillment of a prophecy given some 300 years earlier by an anonymous man of God from Judah (2 Kings 23:15-18; compare 1 Kings 13:2). That man of God had even mentioned Josiah by name!

A. Command (v. 21)

21. And the king commanded all the people, saying, Keep the passover unto the LORD your God, as it is written in the book of this covenant.

Another important phase of Josiah's rededication of all the people involves the observance of *the passover.* Instructions may be found in Exodus 12:1-20, 43-49 and Deuteronomy 16:1-8. The Exodus passage deals with how families are to observe this feast, while the Deuteronomy passage deals more with observing the Passover on a national level. The latter of these two circumstances fits the occasion described in the passage before us. This may support the view that the book discovered in the temple was Deuteronomy. [See question #5, page 96.]

B. Comparison (vv. 22, 23)

22. Surely there was not holden such a passover from the days of the judges that judged Israel, nor in all the days of the kings of Israel, nor of the kings of Judah; but in the eighteenth year of king Josiah, wherein this passover was holden to the LORD in Jerusalem.

These verses provide an assessment of the significance of this *passover* observance under Josiah's leadership. Josiah's celebration surpasses any that has taken place since the days of the judges or during the time of the divided monarchy.

Why is this so? What is so special about the way Josiah observes the Passover? Second Chronicles 35:1-19 provides additional details about Josiah's celebration and includes an evaluation similar to that found in 2 Kings: "And there was no passover like to that kept in Israel from the days of Samuel the prophet; neither did all the kings of Israel keep such a passover as Josiah kept, and the priests, and the Levites, and all Judah and Israel that were present, and the inhabitants of Jerusalem" (v. 18). Josiah's compliance with the law's requirements is especially noted; for example, the Chronicles account records that all the Passover lambs are slaughtered exclusively by the Levites, as the law stipulates (2 Chronicles 35:3, 5, 6).

Josiah's devotion to the Law of Moses is also emphasized in 2 Kings 23:25. That passage provides this evaluation of one of Judah's most godly kings: "And like unto him was there no king before him, that turned to the Lord with all his heart, and with all his soul, and with all his might, according to all the law of Moses; neither after him arose there any like him."

Such a one-of-a-kind tribute may appear to contradict what is said of Hezekiah, who receives similar praise in 2 Kings 18:3-5. Hezekiah, however, is specifically commended for his trust in the Lord, while Josiah's scrupulous observance of the law of Moses is stressed. Each king is exemplary in a different area of devotion to the Lord. Such kings are a primary reason why Judah lasts approximately 130 years longer than the northern kingdom, Israel.

A ONE-OF-A-KIND CELEBRATION

Lakshmi Mittal, an Indian magnate in the steel industry, is listed by *Forbes* magazine as one of the richest people in the world. As such, he was able to offer his daughter a one-of-a-kind celebration when he spent $60 million on her wedding just a couple of years ago.

The wedding took place in the environs of Paris and lasted for six days. There were 1,500 invited guests. One night a banquet and theatrical performance was held in the rented Tuileries (*twee*-luh-reez) Garden in Paris. Another venue for the celebration was a made-for-the-occasion castle that the proud father had erected in a Paris suburb. One dinner was held at the palace at Versailles (Ver-*sigh*) and another at the Vaux-le-Vicomte (Voh-luh-Vee-*kohnt*), considered by some to be one of the finest chateaus and gardens in all of France.

Mittal probably said to himself, "Now that's the way to celebrate a wedding!" Perhaps it is, if one has unlimited wealth. But most of us would shy away from such an ostentatious display (even if we could afford it!).

Josiah's elaborate celebration of the Passover was also a one-of-a-kind event. The difference was that its purpose was not to display one's wealth, but to help a whole nation recommit itself to God. The world has a twisted sense of what makes a celebration! How should those who belong to the family of God demonstrate that they have a different set of priorities?　　—C. R. B.

Home Daily Bible Readings

Monday, Nov. 6—God Restores Us (Psalm 103:1-12)

Tuesday, Nov. 7—Renewal in the Lord (Psalm 32)

Wednesday, Nov. 8—Return to the Lord (Joel 2:12-17)

Thursday, Nov. 9—Josiah Made King of Judah (2 Kings 22:1-7)

Friday, Nov. 10—A Lost Book Is Found (2 Kings 22:8-13)

Saturday, Nov. 11—The People Renew Their Covenant (2 Kings 23:1-25)

Sunday, Nov. 12—The Passover Is Celebrated (2 Kings 23:21-25)

---

23. But in the eighteenth year of king Josiah, wherein this passover was holden to the LORD in Jerusalem.

This verse notes the time that *this passover* celebration occurs: it is *in the eighteenth year of King Josiah.* Mentioning the timeframe at this point serves to call attention to the urgency of Josiah's efforts at spiritual renewal in Judah since that was the same year that the Book of the Law was found (2 Kings 22:3, 8).

The discovery of the Book of the Law in that same eighteenth year, along with Josiah's whole-hearted commitment to its contents, gives Judah a reprieve from the judgment of God. Sadly, it is only a reprieve, for Josiah is the last of Judah's godly kings.

Conclusion

A. The Need for "Re-Bible"

Someone has wisely observed that the Bible has been given to us not merely for information but for transformation. The example of Josiah in today's lesson provides a powerful illustration of that principle.

Transformation involves allowing the words of the Bible to come across in the language and conduct of our daily lives. It is one thing to know what the Bible says about its people, places, and events. It is quite another to know what the Bible says to me about the people, places, and events that are a part of my life today.

A little boy heard an announcement concerning the upcoming revival services at his church. Later he told one of his friends in the neighborhood, "We're going to have a 're-Bible' at our church!"

Although it's clear that the young fellow hadn't heard the original statement quite correctly, his unintended revision wasn't bad! Let's take a close look at our lives and ask whether we need to be "re-Bibled." The need is urgent; the time is now.

B. Prayer

Father, thank You for Your holy Word and its truth. Like King Josiah, may we be so convicted by what it says that we will do all we can to apply its truth to our lives and share its message with others. This is the best way to treat Your Word with the respect that it deserves. In Jesus' name, amen.

C. Thought to Remember

Reform happens
when God's Word transforms us.

Learning by Doing

This page contains an alternative lesson plan emphasizing learning activities. Classes desiring such student involvement will find these suggestions helpful.

Learning Goals

After participating in this lesson, each student will be able to:

1. List the causes and outcomes of Josiah's reform movement.

2. Predict the conditions that would have to be present for a similar reform movement to occur in the church today.

3. Choose one area in his or her personal life in which to make a "Josiah reform."

Into the Lesson

Option #1. Write "New" on the board. Ask, "What are sights, sounds, smells, or symbols that remind you of newness?" (Some ideas include new car smell, butterflies, eggs, fresh paint.)

Option #2. Write "Old Car/New Car" on the board. Ask, "What are some of the steps needed to refurbish or restore an old car back to its original newness?" Interact with responses.

Make the transition to Bible study by saying that God tells us that newness, or restoration, can be brought to people's lives, churches, or even nations. This restoration, of course, happens through God's wonderful grace. The truest restoration of people or of churches is grounded in a renewed commitment to God's Word. We'll discover that principle as we read of an adventure in the life of God's chosen people.

Into the Word

Provide the following resources to three study groups: to Group #1, a photocopy of the lesson background, Bible dictionary, a marker, and poster board; to Group #2, string, letter-sized paper (punch holes in two corners of the paper), and a photocopy of the lesson commentary; to Group #3, a marker, poster board, and a Bible dictionary. Distribute the instructions below to the groups. (If you have a large class, you may create extra groups to divide up activities for #1 and #3, but only one group should do #2.)

Group #1: Deliver a brief background of today's Scripture to the rest of the class. Study the lesson commentary and outline your remarks about the timing of the event, the impact of some of the kings, the spiritual condition of Judah, and a snapshot of Josiah's influence. A Bible dictionary is available, if needed.

Group #2: Prepare a dramatization of 2 Kings 22:8-11; 23:1-3, 21-23. String and paper is provided for name tags to hang around the character's necks. Feel free to insert dialogue that gives clues to why or how things may have happened. But be sure to tell the story clearly enough so the class understands what happened.

Group #3: Deliver a report about how Josiah worked to change Judah's worship focus. You will read a portion of Scripture that is not included in today's printed text, namely 2 Kings 23:4-19. Be sure to include a brief definition of Baal and Asherah. A Bible dictionary is available as a resource.

Allow each group to share its discoveries.

Into Life

Make the transition to application by writing "Re-Bible" on the board. Tell the story included in the lesson commentary of the little boy saying to his friends they were going to have a "Re-Bible" (revival) at his church. Explain the irony of his statement. The Bible is at the core of spiritual revivals, including Josiah's. It is also the basis of personal spiritual renewal and of a church's renewal.

Ask the groups that worked together earlier to choose one of the following two tasks. (If you are short on time, you may choose simply to do choice #1 as an entire class.)

Choice #1: Develop a worship program for your church that emphasizes renewed commitment to the Lord and His Word. What special feature would you include? What are a few appropriate songs? What would be an appropriate sermon theme or text? How would you issue a call to commitment?

Choice #2: Suppose you have a friend who has drifted away from the Lord. This friend still attends church occasionally but has not been growing spiritually. He or she seems to be focusing energies on work and family. Your task is to develop a plan to encourage this person to renew a commitment to the Lord. What are some steps you might take to help bring this about?

Conclude by reminding class members that spiritual renewal is important in each person. Ask each person to identify two or three steps to take to refresh his or her relationship with the Lord.

Let's Talk It Over

The questions on this page are designed to promote discussion of the lesson by the class and to encourage application of the lesson Scriptures. The answers provided are only discussion starters. Let your class talk it over from there.

1. In Western cultures there is no shortage of Bibles. Yet widespread biblical illiteracy means that the Bible often is effectively "lost." What would you suggest to address the problem?

Biblical illiteracy is caused by people not reading the Bible. Therefore, the solution to the problem is for people to read their Bibles! We recognize, however, that although that answer is right, it may not be helpful in and of itself in solving the problem.

A more productive start is to consider *why* people fail to read their Bibles. Perhaps they don't recognize the value or importance of Scripture, or they have trouble understanding the Bible (and thus give up too soon), or they aren't readers of anything—period. A contributing factor may be a cultural dismissal of Scripture as being irrelevant. Each problem calls for a different approach. We can start by examining our own worship services: How often is there a public reading of Scripture on Sunday morning?

2. What advantages are there to having a godly person in a position of political power? What are the disadvantages or potential pitfalls?

When Christians are in positions of influence and power, we can hope that their decisions and leadership are guided by their faith and by prayer. Ideally, they should have a strong sensitivity to issues and matters of God. That person's leadership style should also reflect those values; leadership should be strong, yet compassionate and just.

Challenges for these leaders include navigating the different expectations of fellow Christians. For some, issues of morality are the most important. For others, issues of social justice are paramount. There is, at least potentially, the danger of Christians confusing political success with spiritual progress. The church's mission and purpose remain unchanged, regardless of the direction that the political winds are blowing.

3. How should a leader go about gaining consensus for change in today's church? Or is it better just to proceed with a majority, since building a consensus is often time consuming or even impossible?

It is worth noting that Josiah began with a personal commitment. Only then was he able to generate momentum among other leaders in order to present a unified leadership and a clear direction to the people.

Josiah also made a point of gathering leaders from across the spectrum of society. As we work through the lesson, we will see Josiah present the facts, allow the people to assimilate the data, and then call for one specific action. Achieving consensus (or reaching a "tipping point") was perhaps easier here because Josiah was merely reimplementing something that should never have been allowed to fall into disuse in the first place.

4. Josiah met with "all the people, both small and great." What elements of society tend to be overlooked by churches? How can we make sure that we are communicating the gospel to everyone?

Individual churches tend to reach out to relatively narrow slices of their communities through "targeted demographics." As a result, many churches miss certain segments of the population completely. Plans to address the deficiencies can also be put into place at the level of the individual church. One church may offer English as a Second Language classes for outreach, while another may start a contemporary (or traditional) worship service. Perhaps the best strategies for outreach and evangelism have yet to be devised.

5. What circumstances would make a command to corporate worship effective? Why do we seldom hear these kinds of commands from political or spiritual leaders today?

Today many believe that worship must be an internal and personal event. Worship in Josiah's time was much more a communal function, held at a central place.

Western societies that have a tradition of separation of church and state may find it hard to imagine a political leader commanding people to worship. However, in times of crisis leaders have been known to ask their country to pray. An example is Abraham Lincoln's "Proclamation Appointing a National Fast Day" of March 30, 1863, available on the Internet.

The People Go into Exile

DEVOTIONAL READING: Proverbs 1:20-33.

BACKGROUND SCRIPTURE: 2 Chronicles 36:15-21; Psalm 137.

PRINTED TEXT: 2 Chronicles 36:15-21; Psalm 137:1-6.

2 Chronicles 36:15-21

15 And the LORD God of their fathers sent to them by his messengers, rising up betimes, and sending; because he had compassion on his people, and on his dwelling place:

16 But they mocked the messengers of God, and despised his words, and misused his prophets, until the wrath of the LORD arose against his people, till there was no remedy.

17 Therefore he brought upon them the king of the Chaldees, who slew their young men with the sword in the house of their sanctuary, and had no compassion upon young man or maiden, old man, or him that stooped for age: he gave them all into his hand.

18 And all the vessels of the house of God, great and small, and the treasures of the house of the LORD, and the treasures of the king, and of his princes; all these he brought to Babylon.

19 And they burnt the house of God, and brake down the wall of Jerusalem, and burnt all the palaces thereof with fire, and destroyed all the goodly vessels thereof.

20 And them that had escaped from the sword carried he away to Babylon; where they were servants to him and his sons until the reign of the kingdom of Persia:

21 To fulfil the word of the LORD by the mouth of Jeremiah, until the land had enjoyed her sabbaths: for as long as she lay desolate she kept sabbath, to fulfil threescore and ten years.

Psalm 137:1-6

1 By the rivers of Babylon, there we sat down, yea, we wept, when we remembered Zion.

2 We hanged our harps upon the willows in the midst thereof.

3 For there they that carried us away captive required of us a song; and they that wasted us required of us mirth, saying, Sing us one of the songs of Zion.

4 How shall we sing the LORD's song in a strange land?

5 If I forget thee, O Jerusalem, let my right hand forget her cunning.

6 If I do not remember thee, let my tongue cleave to the roof of my mouth; if I prefer not Jerusalem above my chief joy.

GOLDEN TEXT: By the rivers of Babylon, there we sat down, yea, we wept, when we remembered Zion.—Psalm 137:1.

God's Living Covenant
Unit 3: Living Under God's Covenant
(Lessons 10-13)

Lesson Aims

After participating in this lesson, each student will be able to:

1. Retell the events leading up to and following the destruction of Jerusalem.

2. Review how God continues to warn humanity of the consequences of sin.

3. Write a personal "psalm" confessing one specific area of spiritual need.

Lesson Outline

INTRODUCTION
  A. One Unforgettable Day
  B. Lesson Background
I. PLEAS OF THE PROPHETS (2 Chronicles 36:15, 16)
  A. God's Mercy (v. 15)
  B. People's Mocking (v. 16)
II. POWER OF BABYLON (2 Chronicles 36:17-21)
  A. Lives Lost (v. 17)
  B. Treasures Taken (v. 18)
  C. Buildings Burned (v. 19)
    Burning Treasures
  D. Remnant Removed (v. 20)
  E. Rest Remembered (v. 21)
III. PASSION OF GOD'S PEOPLE (Psalm 137:1-6)
  A. Bitter Memories (v. 1)
  B. Brutal Masters (vv. 2, 3)
  C. Better Memories (vv. 4-6)
    Longings, Worthwhile and Otherwise
CONCLUSION
  A. The Enemy Is Us!
  B. Look in the Mirror
  C. Prayer
  D. Thought to Remember

Introduction

A. One Unforgettable Day

Some older Americans will remember where they were and what they were doing on December 7, 1941—the day Pearl Harbor was attacked. The memory of the events of such a tragic day is impossible to erase. A more current example of an unforgettable day would certainly be September 11, 2001. Who can forget what he or she was doing or the emptiness that was felt upon hearing and seeing the Twin Towers in New York City being attacked?

Whatever you feel inside when such events occur, it may be quite similar to how the people of Jerusalem felt as they witnessed the Babylonians ravaging their holy city and setting Solomon's magnificent temple on fire. We should not miss what the religious implications of this action were at the time it took place. The Babylonians' destruction of the temple of the God of Judah implied that their pagan gods were mightier than Judah's God. After all, so the thinking went, if the Lord were stronger, wouldn't He have intervened to protect His sacred dwelling place? If He failed to do so, then it must be because the Babylonian gods were superior. [See question #1, page 104.]

Of course, that was not at all the case. Prophets such as Jeremiah repeatedly emphasized that the Babylonians were not conquering Jerusalem through their own might; the Lord was giving Jerusalem into their hands as punishment for the sins of His people (Jeremiah 27:5-7; 34:2). Even some Babylonians (Chaldeans) recognized this truth (see Jeremiah 40:2, 3).

The destruction of Jerusalem and the captivity of God's people did not signal the absence of the Lord; on the contrary, these events provided evidence of His control. The events validated His prophets as authoritative messengers who conveyed His truth.

B. Lesson Background

Conditions in Judah deteriorated rapidly following the death of Josiah in about 609 BC, the last godly king in that country. Here is a summary of the reigns of Judah's last four kings:

Jehoahaz, also called Shallum, was a son of Josiah. He reigned over Judah only three months. He was taken captive to Egypt, where he died (2 Kings 23:31-34; Jeremiah 22:11, 12).

Jehoiakim was put on the throne by the Egyptians after they had removed Jehoahaz from power. This was another son of Josiah. He ruled for 11 years (609–598 BC). He was a striking contrast to his father. Jehoiakim lived in personal extravagance (Jeremiah 22:13-15), pursued dishonest gain, and set his eyes and his heart "to shed innocent blood, and for oppression, and for violence" (22:17). As noted in last week's lesson, Jehoiakim cut up into pieces a scroll from Jeremiah and cast the pieces into a fire (36:22-24).

During Jehoiakim's reign, King Nebuchadnezzar came to power in Babylon as Egypt declined in influence. Jehoiakim switched his loyalty to Babylon in an attempt to keep up with the times, but rebelled after three years (2 Kings 24:1). The Scriptures do not indicate how Jehoiakim died; possibly he was assassinated.

Jehoiachin, Jehoiakim's son, ruled for only three months. He was taken captive to Babylon by Nebuchadnezzar in 597 BC. His later release from prison and elevation to a position of honor in Babylon is mentioned in 2 Kings 25:27-30 and Jeremiah 52:31-34.

Zedekiah, the last king of Judah, was another son of Josiah. Zedekiah reigned for 11 years until Jerusalem fell in 586 BC. Weak and unstable, he refused to heed the counsel of Jeremiah to surrender to the Babylonians (Jeremiah 27:12-15; 38:17, 18). When the Babylonians finally overtook Jerusalem, Zedekiah watched as they slaughtered his own sons. The Babylonians then put out his eyes and took him to Babylon (Jeremiah 39:5-7), where he most likely was at the time of his death.

The two printed texts for today examine the fall of Jerusalem from two perspectives. The first, from 2 Chronicles, summarizes why this tragedy occurred. It also provides a somber description of the Babylonians' destruction of the city and the exile of its residents.

The second passage is taken from Psalm 137. Though the author of this psalm is not named, the contents clearly reflect the perspective of someone experiencing the anguish of living as a captive in a foreign land. However, the psalm also conveys the dogged determination not to forget the beloved city of Jerusalem. Jerusalem may have been out of sight, but it was certainly not out of mind.

I. Pleas of the Prophets (2 Chronicles 36:15, 16)

The verses immediately preceding the section covered in our printed text recount what took place during the reign of Zedekiah, the last king of Judah. In particular, it is noted, "all the chief of the priests, and the people, transgressed very much after all the abominations of the heathen; and polluted the house of the Lord which he had hallowed in Jerusalem" (2 Chronicles 36:14).

A. God's Mercy (v. 15)

15. And the LORD God of their fathers sent to them by his messengers, rising up betimes, and sending; because he had compassion on his people, and on his dwelling place.

The Lord has responded by giving *his people* fair and frequent warning of the judgment they face if they continue in their sinful practices.

God is described as *rising up betimes,* or repeatedly, and sending these faithful *messengers.* As noted earlier, these messengers include prophets such as Jeremiah. Others who serve at this time include Habakkuk and Zephaniah.

Notice that God's *compassion* extends not only to His people, but also to *his dwelling place.* God had promised to put His name in Jerusalem after the temple had been completed (1 Kings 9:3; 2 Kings 21:4). In addition the identity of the people is so closely bound to the temple in Jerusalem that God knows that its destruction will be an especially devastating burden for them to bear.

Yet, as 2 Chronicles 36:14 tells us, the people have defiled the temple through their introduction of pagan practices. The time has come when God's judgment can no longer be avoided. [See question #2, page 104.]

B. People's Mocking (v. 16)

16. But they mocked the messengers of God, and despised his words, and misused his prophets, until the wrath of the LORD arose against his people, till there was no remedy.

Here is how God's efforts to reach out in pity to His people have been received: *they mocked the messengers of God, and despised his words, and misused his prophets.* When the Son of God comes in compassion to save mankind from sin, a similar response is noted in John 1:11. See also Stephen's description in Acts 7:52.

What patience God has! [See question #3, page 104.] Yet eventually such callous treatment of the Lord's messengers results in God's wrath. He is aroused against His people and there is *no remedy.* No remedy is available, not because God cannot supply one, but because the people's sinfulness has reached the stage where they are not willing to accept any remedy. Their spiritual

---

How to Say It

ASSYRIANS. Uh-*sear*-e-unz.
BABYLONIANS. Bab-ih-*low*-nee-unz.
CARCHEMISH. *Kar*-key-mish.
CHALDEANS. Kal-*dee*-unz.
CHALDEES. *Kal*-deez.
HABAKKUK. Huh-*back*-kuk.
JEHOAHAZ. Jeh-*ho*-uh-haz.
JEHOIACHIN. Jeh-*hoy*-uh-kin.
JEHOIAKIM. Jeh-*hoy*-uh-kim.
NEBUCHADNEZZAR. *Neb*-yuh-kud-*nez*-er (strong accent on *nez*).
ZEDEKIAH. Zed-uh-*kye*-uh.
ZEPHANIAH. Zef-uh-*nye*-uh.

condition may be likened to those whom Paul describes as becoming so ensnared in sin that God "gave them up" to the consequences of their actions (Romans 1:24, 26, 28).

II. Power of Babylon
(2 Chronicles 36:17-21)

The Babylonians (also known as Chaldeans or Chaldees) defeated the Egyptians at the Battle of Carchemish in 605 BC (see 2 Chronicles 35:20; Jeremiah 46:2). This epic battle changed the balance of power in the ancient world. After defeating the Egyptians, the Babylonians turn their attention to Judah.

A. Lives Lost (v. 17)

17. Therefore he brought upon them the king of the Chaldees, who slew their young men with the sword in the house of their sanctuary, and had no compassion upon young man or maiden, old man, or him that stooped for age: he gave them all into his hand.

Both the beginning and the conclusion of this verse highlight a pivotal truth: it is the Lord who brings up against His people *the king of the Chaldees*, and God hands His people over to Nebuchadnezzar. A secular historian may explain the Chaldean (Babylonian) triumph over Jerusalem as the exercise of sheer political and military supremacy. The Bible reveals the primary cause to be the Lord's deliverance of His people to be judged. [See question #4, page 104.]

B. Treasures Taken (v. 18)

18. And all the vessels of the house of God, great and small, and the treasures of the house of the LORD, and the treasures of the king, and of his princes; all these he brought to Babylon.

Suppose you pulled into the driveway of your home one day only to see someone dousing your home with gasoline and preparing to strike a match and set it on fire. What would you do? The answer is obvious: you would do all you could to stop him! As noted earlier, the mind-set of the time would ask why Israel's God does not come to the rescue of His *house*—His temple and its *treasures*. The answer has nothing to do with the weakness of the Lord. He allows these tragedies to occur in fulfilling His promises of judgment.

C. Buildings Burned (v. 19)

19. And they burnt the house of God, and brake down the wall of Jerusalem, and burnt all the palaces thereof with fire, and destroyed all the goodly vessels thereof.

The two main structures of many cities of the time are the temple (a spiritual landmark) and *the wall* (the primary source of defense). The Babylonians destroy both. In addition, *the palaces*—symbolic of status and wealth—suffer the same tragic end.

BURNING TREASURES

It was February 13, 1945, and it seemed as if the sky itself was on fire. By the end of the two-day bombing raid, 650,000 incendiary bombs had fallen on Dresden, Germany. Dresden's cultural treasure had been epitomized in the *Frauenkirche* (*frau*-in-kur-kuh), the "Church of Our Lady," built in 1743. It had been called one of the most remarkable buildings in the world. Now it was a burning treasure, lying in ruin.

The morality of the Dresden attack is still debated. At best, the bombing of Dresden can be said to be an example of the consequences of warfare. The nation of Judah felt similar consequences when Babylon's forces sacked Jerusalem. Those forces burned its greatest treasure, the temple, and either destroyed or pillaged everything of value in the temple and in the city.

There is a similarity of cause in the burning of the treasures of these two cities: the cause, somewhere along the line, was sin. None of us can say whether a calamity such as the burning of Dresden was an act of God. But Scripture is clear that Jerusalem was destroyed because it had forgotten God. We should heed the warning.   —C. R. B.

D. Remnant Removed (v. 20)

20. And them that had escaped from the sword carried he away to Babylon; where they were servants to him and his sons until the reign of the kingdom of Persia.

Not only does Nebuchadnezzar carry *away* various objects, he also carries into exile the remnant: *those who escaped from the sword*. In faraway Babylon they become servants to him.

"The doctrine of the remnant" is one of the most important in Old Testament prophecy. In spite of God's judgment, He does not completely destroy His people. Just as He speaks words of warning through His prophets (see v. 15), so also He speaks words of hope and promise through these same messengers. In time a remnant will return (Isaiah 10:21; Jeremiah 23:3; Ezekiel 6:8; Micah 2:12). That remnant eventually will be the source from which the Messiah comes to offer deliverance to all peoples from the captivity of sin.

This verse reveals another important truth: the Babylonians' days on the center stage of world history will reach their limit—just as the Assyrians reached theirs before being overthrown by Babylon. Eventually, the Persians will take control of the Babylonian empire. Under the Persian ruler Cyrus the Great (next week's lesson), the remnant will be granted the opportunity to return to their homeland and start anew.

E. Rest Remembered (v. 21)

21. To fulfil the word of the LORD by the mouth of Jeremiah, until the land had enjoyed her sabbaths: for as long as she lay desolate she kept sabbath, to fulfil threescore and ten years.

The Law of Moses prescribed a Sabbath year for the promised land—a time (every seventh year) during which *the land* was to be given a rest. It was not to be cultivated or harvested (Leviticus 25:1-7). The people were instead to eat what grew in the Sabbath year (vv. 6, 7). Such a procedure gave the land the opportunity to be replenished for further use. This law also reminded the people of Israel that they were caretakers who cared for the land according to the giver's stipulations.

However, like many of the laws God gave to His people, this one had been ignored. In a sense the land cried out for God's judgment to be administered, for it had not been treated according to the giver's directives. The punishment for violating this law is found in Leviticus 26:34, 35, the language of which is very similar to the wording found here in 2 Chronicles.

III. Passion of God's People (Psalm 137:1-6)

This psalm captures the bitter sentiments of one who is enduring captivity in a foreign land.

A. Bitter Memories (v. 1)

1. By the rivers of Babylon, there we sat down, yea, we wept, when we remembered Zion.

Memory can be a wonderful gift, but it can also be a source of unbearable heartache. Tragedy often causes one to look back and long for happier days. Emotions run high whenever the captives in pagan *Babylon* remember the sacred site of *Zion*. Zion gained significance because of David, who brought the ark of the covenant there (2 Samuel 6:12). Eventually the term *Zion* comes to mean the entire city of Jerusalem (2 Kings 19:21).

It should be noted that Jeremiah, known as the weeping prophet, had shed countless tears while warning God's people of the coming judgment (Jeremiah 13:17; 14:17). Now, because they had refused to heed the prophet's tears, they are the ones weeping.

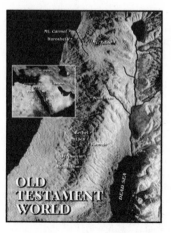

Visual for
Lessons 2 & 12

Keep this map posted throughout the quarter to help set the geographical context.

B. Brutal Masters (vv. 2, 3)

2, 3. We hanged our harps upon the willows in the midst thereof. For there they that carried us away captive required of us a song; and they that wasted us required of us mirth, saying, Sing us one of the songs of Zion.

The people's despair in their captivity is multiplied by the way their captors are making light of their sorrow. *Sing us one of the songs of Zion,* they say mockingly. But this is hardly a time for songs of joy, whether vocal or instrumental.

C. Better Memories (vv. 4-6)

4. How shall we sing the LORD's song in a strange land?

Some music is just not appropriate in certain settings. Songs of the Lord do not seem right when sung on foreign soil or sung simply to comply with the sarcastic requests of one's oppressors.

5, 6. If I forget thee, O Jerusalem, let my right hand forget her cunning. If I do not remember thee, let my tongue cleave to the roof of my mouth; if I prefer not Jerusalem above my chief joy.

In verse 1 the memory of Zion had brought tears to the captives. But that memory is also the source of hope to them. Here the writer expresses his fierce loyalty to Jerusalem in an oath, pronouncing a kind of curse on his *right hand* and on his *tongue* if he should forget Jerusalem. Having earlier mentioned the harps (v. 2) and the songs of Zion (v. 3), the writer says, in effect, "May I lose the ability to play the harp and sing if I allow the circumstances of captivity to affect my devotion to the beloved city of God—*Jerusalem!*" [See question #5, page 104.]

LONGINGS, WORTHWHILE AND OTHERWISE

Between 1830 and 1850, the total mileage of railroad track in the United States went from 23 to 9,000. At the same time steamboats were providing a new form of transportation. In 1844 the first telegraph message was sent. It was about the year 1850 that former New York City mayor Philip Hone, age 69, bemoaned, "The world is going too fast!" He longed for the good ol' days when horse-drawn coaches sped along at the rate of six miles an hour (*Newsweek*, November 29, 2004).

The nineteenth-century Industrial Revolution was just the beginning. The rate of change has been accelerating ever since. Some of us lament the increasing complexity of technology. The classic example is the inability of some of us to program our VCRs. We might as well give up: DVDs are now the state of the art. Yet even they will likely be outmoded soon by another technology.

"Even nostalgia ain't what it used to be!" That comic's quip says a lot about our longing for a more peaceful past, or a healthier past, or an [add your own longing here] past. We catch some of that spirit in Psalm 137. But it contains more than a longing for days past, lost in the "daze" of imperfect memory. There is a recognition that some values of the past are worth keeping. When we think wistfully about the past, is it to long for something important—something that is "of God"—or is it for something trivial?   —C. R. B.

Conclusion

A. The Enemy Is Us!

From the comic strip "Pogo" by Walt Kelly comes an often-quoted line: "We have met the enemy and he is us." That statement could be applied to a variety of situations, including the history of God's people in the Old Testament.

From the beginning of its existence as God's holy nation, Israel was warned repeatedly of the need to remain faithful and obedient to the Lord. The people's worst enemy would not be any of the peoples cited in Deuteronomy 7:1—the various names ending in "ites," whom they were commanded to destroy. The "ites" who became their worst enemy were the Israelites themselves! Today's text from 2 Chronicles highlighted this tragic truth: God's people had no one to blame for their captivity but themselves.

To what extent is this principle applicable to the church? While it is true that our world has grown increasingly hostile to the Christian faith, is it not also true that at times Christians have brought some hostility upon themselves? Think of our arrogance toward others, our infighting, our general lack of love (John 13:35). These have caused many to treat the Christian faith as if it were a disease instead of the hope of the world.

B. Look in the Mirror

The story is told of a minister who began serving a church in a small town. After he arrived, he spent a few days visiting the homes of the members and urging them to attend his first service that coming Sunday. But only a few people came.

After several Sundays like this, the minister placed a notice in the newspaper announcing that the congregation appeared to be dead, thus it was his duty to give it a decent burial. The funeral was to be held the following Sunday afternoon.

The next Sunday the building was filled nearly to capacity. (Many had come simply out of curiosity.) In front of the pulpit was an open casket. The minister read an obituary and delivered a eulogy. He then invited those present to step forward and pay their respects to the deceased.

Each mourner who filed by peered into the casket and then turned away with a sheepish look. In the casket, tilted at just the correct angle, was a mirror. Each person saw himself or herself as the reason for the death of the congregation.

C. Prayer

Father, help us to see that we are not immune to the problems that led to Judah's downfall. Let us realize that judgment must begin with the house of God. May each of us do whatever "housecleaning" needs to be done. In Jesus' name, amen.

D. Thought to Remember

Let God's judgment sound a warning yet today.

Home Daily Bible Readings

Monday, Nov. 13—Embrace Wisdom (Proverbs 1:20-33)

Tuesday, Nov. 14—Key to the Good Life (Proverbs 8:32-36)

Wednesday, Nov. 15—Jeremiah Prophesies Judgment (Jeremiah 1:11-19)

Thursday, Nov. 16—Jeremiah Predicts Jerusalem's Fall (Jeremiah 25:1-11)

Friday, Nov. 17—Zedekiah Rebels Against God (2 Chronicles 36:11-14)

Saturday, Nov. 18—Jerusalem Falls (2 Chronicles 36:15-21)

Sunday, Nov. 19—Psalm of Remorse (Psalm 137)

Learning by Doing

This page contains an alternative lesson plan emphasizing learning activities.
Classes desiring such student involvement will find these suggestions helpful.

Learning Goals

After participating in this lesson, each student will be able to:

1. Retell the events leading up to and following the destruction of Jerusalem.

2. Review how God continues to warn humanity of the consequences of sin.

3. Write a personal "psalm" confessing one specific area of spiritual need.

Into the Lesson

Begin the lesson by reminding the class that losing someone or something precious to you is a very traumatic moment. Then ask class members to form small groups of four or five and share a time they lost someone or something dear to them. They may also share how God helped them get through this difficult time. Keep this portion of the lesson brief.

After this time of sharing, expand the discussion by saying, "Times of loss are traumatic to individuals . . . and to nations." Ask about traumas that are specific to your country (examples: Pearl Harbor, December 7, 1941; terrorist attacks, September 11, 2001). Make a transition to Bible study by saying, "Our feelings about these events help us understand the emotional impact on God's people when they lost their beloved Jerusalem."

Into the Word

Form five or more groups to do the following tasks and report conclusions to the class as a whole. Give each group written instructions, a marker, poster board, and the materials mentioned. Before the groups begin their work, read the printed text to the class and include a brief explanation of the background for this text. The notes in the Lesson Background will be helpful.

Group #1. Read the printed text and answer the following questions: Why did Jerusalem fall? Who were the major players in this drama, and what were their roles? Who ultimately was responsible for Jerusalem's destruction? You will find it helpful also to read 2 Chronicles 36:1-14 and Jeremiah 27:5-7; 32:28; 34:2.

Group #2. (Provide for this group a photocopy of the lesson commentary for 2 Chronicles 36:17 and a Bible dictionary.) Tell the class about the Chaldeans, also called Babylonians. Use the Bible dictionary and lesson commentary to prepare your summary about this powerful nation.

Group #3. (Give this group a photocopy of the lesson commentary for 2 Chronicles 36:20 and a Bible dictionary that includes an article on "the remnant.") Do research and tell the class about the group known as "the remnant." What was the experience and significance of this group in Israel's history?

Group #4. (Give this group a Bible dictionary and a copy of the lesson commentary for 2 Chronicles 36:21. Mark the article or section of the article that talks about the land having a Sabbath rest.) Focus on the comments about the Sabbath in 2 Chronicles 36:21. Read about Sabbath rests in the Bible dictionary and lesson commentary. Describe this topic for the class and tell why you think this was specifically mentioned in today's text.

Group #5. (Give this group a copy of the lesson commentary on Psalm 137:1-6.) Read Psalm 137:1-6 and explain the significance of this passage that speaks of singing about Zion. If time permits, you can also explain a few of the colorful word pictures used in this psalm.

Allow time for group presentations. With five groups, you will need to keep things moving along briskly.

Into Life

Activity #1: Keeping in the groups established earlier, have each group discuss and address the following: God's chosen people brought this sorrow and captivity upon themselves. Apply the lessons learned to today's church. What actions or inaction of today's believers have brought negative consequences to the church in general?

Activity #2: Give each person a piece of paper and ask students to write a personal psalm that expresses a need, sorrow, or regret. Encourage students to use the colorful language of Psalm 137:1-6 as a model. The psalm should include a need or regret in his or her personal life, the life of the church, or the nation (v. 1); a place to express the sorrow or need (vv. 1. 2); a creative expression of the need or sorrow (vv. 3, 4); a statement of commitment or determination (vv. 5, 6).

Allow each person to share his or her "psalm" with members of the group.

Let's Talk It Over

*The questions on this page are designed to promote discussion of the lesson
by the class and to encourage application of the lesson Scriptures. The answers
provided are only discussion starters. Let your class talk it over from there.*

**1. What is your most vivid personal memory
of a national tragedy? How did this tragedy
affect you spiritually, if at all?**

Most people will have some memory of September 11, 2001. Within the United States, other
memories may include the shootings of Presidents Reagan and Kennedy, the two space shuttle
disasters, the attack on Pearl Harbor, or the assassination of Martin Luther King, Jr. Many will
think also of natural disasters, such as the tsunami of 2004.

Traumatic events have a way of searing images
into our memories. The result is vivid memories
not only of the event itself, but also our recollections of where we were and what we were doing
when we learned of the event. Such events either
result in people being closer to God or more distant from Him. It's probably quite rare that a person's relationship with God is totally unaffected in
such instances. The church should be poised to
help people see God more clearly in trying times.

**2. What sins do you think could bring God's
judgment upon our country today? How would
we be able to tell the difference between the
judgment of God and what may be called "natural consequences"?**

The first question will reveal different opinions
among believers. Some believers will think that
God is most concerned about sins related to sexuality. Others will focus on human life issues such
as abortion and euthanasia (on the political right)
and capital punishment (on the political left).
Some Christians will stress issues of social justice, racial inequalities, environmental abuse, etc.

These different opinions may provide part of
the answer to the second question: sincere believers are unlikely to reach consensus on what
sins would be "bad enough" to call forth God's
judgment. We are certain, however, that God's
patience is for our benefit (2 Peter 3:9, 15). See
the next question.

**3. In what ways have you benefited from
God's patience?**

This question can call forth some very emotional stories. Certainly the fact that our world
still exists despite our sinfulness is a sign that

God is patient! Beyond that, 2 Peter 3:9 reminds
us that God is patient because He wants everyone to come to salvation.

**4. In reaction to a national tragedy, someone
says, "I guess this is God's punishment." How
do you respond?**

The book of Job shows us that there are other
reasons for tragedy. In that case Satan was the
cause of the devastation that affected Job and his
family. Other tragedies may be the consequences
of otherwise positive events: the storm that ends
your drought may cause my flood. In an interconnected world, many blessings have accompanying challenges. This may be more the general
result of living after the fall than of direct punishment from God.

Since God does use natural and human means
to effect His punishments, we often cannot tell
which is specifically divine and which is merely
natural. The best response is to turn to God in repentance and seek restoration in any circumstance. (Jesus addressed this very issue in Luke
13:1-5.) We can use tragedy as a reminder to seek
His face and turn from our wicked ways.

**5. When is it appropriate to hold on to and
nurture a bitter memory, and when is it better
to try to let go and move on with our lives? How
could our decision be different if the memory is
of a shared community event rather than of a
more individual, personal tragedy?**

Some memories must stay alive, even if they
are very painful. The fact that God chose to retain in Scripture the horror of the fall of Jerusalem is proof of this. Were the exiles to forget
Jerusalem, they would have no hope of returning
and restoring the city. To some degree community events are better kept in our collective memories because they allow us to grieve and heal
together. Such memories allow us to come up
with a shared strategy for recovery.

Individual hurts, for their part, have more of a
tendency to foster bitterness when they are kept
"bottled up inside." When that happens, the bitterness of individual tragedy breeds isolation. Allowing others to help us work through our grief
is a key.

God Offers Return and Restoration

November 26
Lesson 13

DEVOTIONAL READING: Jeremiah 29:10-14.

BACKGROUND SCRIPTURE: 2 Chronicles 36:22, 23; Ezra 1:5-7.

PRINTED TEXT: 2 Chronicles 36:22, 23; Ezra 1:5-7.

2 Chronicles 36:22, 23

22 Now in the first year of Cyrus king of Persia, that the word of the LORD spoken by the mouth of Jeremiah might be accomplished, the LORD stirred up the spirit of Cyrus king of Persia, that he made a proclamation throughout all his kingdom, and put it also in writing, saying,

23 Thus saith Cyrus king of Persia, All the kingdoms of the earth hath the LORD God of heaven given me; and he hath charged me to build him a house in Jerusalem, which is in Judah. Who is there among you of all his people? The LORD his God be with him, and let him go up.

Ezra 1:5-7

5 Then rose up the chief of the fathers of Judah and Benjamin, and the priests, and the Levites, with all them whose spirit God had raised, to go up to build the house of the LORD which is in Jerusalem.

6 And all they that were about them strengthened their hands with vessels of silver, with gold, with goods, and with beasts, and with precious things, besides all that was willingly offered.

7 Also Cyrus the king brought forth the vessels of the house of the LORD, which Nebuchadnezzar had brought forth out of Jerusalem, and had put them in the house of his gods.

GOLDEN TEXT: Thus saith Cyrus king of Persia, All the kingdoms of the earth hath the LORD God of heaven given me; and he hath charged me to build him a house in Jerusalem, which is in Judah. Who is there among you of all his people? The LORD his God be with him, and let him go up.—2 Chronicles 36:23.

God's Living Covenant
Unit 3: Living Under God's Covenant
(Lessons 10-13)

Lesson Aims

After participating in this lesson, each student will be able to:

1. List the divine and human factors in the return of God's people from captivity.

2. Explain why the terms *return* and *restoration* are appropriate to describe people's response to the gospel message today.

3. Prepare a testimony of how God has restored his or her life through Jesus, and share that testimony with an unsaved person.

Lesson Outline

INTRODUCTION
  A. The God Who Rebuilds
  B. The Chronicles Factor
  C. Lesson Background
I. DECREE ORDAINED (2 Chronicles 36:22, 23)
  A. God's Working (v. 22)
  B. Cyrus's Words (v. 23)
II. DECREE OBEYED (Ezra 1:5-7)
  A. God's Action (v. 5)
  B. Neighbors' Assistance (v. 6)
    Skipping Christmas
  C. Cyrus's Assistance (v. 7)
    Rebooting
CONCLUSION
  A. "It's in There!"
  B. Prayer
  C. Thought to Remember

Introduction

A. The God Who Rebuilds

Most of us have watched a small child play with building blocks. He or she takes great delight in stacking a certain number, and then with one gleeful swipe scatters the blocks everywhere. Then the child gathers the blocks together and does it again—each time squealing with delight until boredom sets in. Then it becomes time to move on to some other form of entertainment.

Rebuilding scattered building blocks is one thing; rebuilding a place of worship is quite another matter. Solomon's temple had been constructed with great care and much effort. First

Kings 6:38 records that this magnificent structure took seven years to build. Yet once the Babylonian army had entered Jerusalem (following a siege of about 18 months), it required far less time to demolish what had been so carefully erected and so prayerfully dedicated (1 Kings 8:22-61). Tearing down always takes much less time than building.

But God had other plans for the temple; destruction would not be the final word. The same prophets who spoke so passionately of God's coming judgment on His people and His temple were just as passionate about the promise that a remnant would return and rebuild.

On one occasion, Jesus used the language of destroying and rebuilding to describe what would eventually happen to Him: "Destroy this temple, and in three days I will raise it up" (John 2:19). The text later notes, "But he spake of the temple of his body" (v. 21). The same language can be applied to what God can do with our broken, sin-ravaged lives. What we have ruined He can rebuild, restore, and renew. Paul writes of our bodies as a temple in which God's Spirit dwells (1 Corinthians 3:16; 6:19). We are not our own; we are under new management.

Whether the damage has been done to sacred structures or to sin-marred souls, God is in the business of rebuilding and restoring.

B. The Chronicles Factor

At first glance the books of 1 and 2 Chronicles may seem to be unnecessary additions to the Old Testament. After all, don't they cover the same period of history covered by much of 1 and 2 Samuel and 1 and 2 Kings? And why the extensive genealogies that take up the first nine chapters of 1 Chronicles? (Those aren't exactly the most thrilling portions of the Bible to read!)

Most students of the Bible believe that the books of Chronicles were written after the Babylonian captivity and after God's people had returned home to rebuild their temple in Jerusalem. (Their return is the topic of today's lesson.) It is worth noting that the final two verses of 2 Chronicles and the first three verses of the book of Ezra are virtually the same. Because of this, some have proposed that Ezra may have been the author of the books of Chronicles as well as the book that bears his name. Certainly Ezra was well qualified for such a task (see Ezra 7:6, 10).

Why would Ezra (assuming him to be the author) compose such a record as that found in the books of Chronicles? Consider the following hypothetical situation: A congregation experiences an especially trying set of circumstances, such as a fire that destroys its sanctuary, a split of some kind, or a crisis within the leadership. The result would likely be a keen sense of loss of purpose and direction within the congregation. Questions would surface, such as, "Where do we go from here?" and "What is God's will for us now?" How would a church in such a situation get the people back on track and restore a sense of direction and purpose?

One answer might be to call attention to the history of the congregation and review God's faithfulness over the years in preserving the people through other difficult times. By considering such examples from the congregation's history, the people may be encouraged to continue to "fight the good fight." They would do what was necessary to see themselves through the current series of events.

A similar scenario confronted God's people following the crisis of the Babylonian captivity and the return to their homeland. They too must have wondered, "Where do we go from here? Does God still have a purpose for us?" For God's covenant people, there were other burning issues as well: "Is God's covenant still intact? Are the promises made to Abraham and David still binding?"

The material found in 1 and 2 Chronicles seems especially intended (through the guidance of the Holy Spirit) to address these and other crucial issues in the minds of those who were part of the rebuilding effort in Judah. The genealogies in 1 Chronicles 1–9 would not have been dull or boring to the original readers; they would have given the postexilic generation a sense of identity with their past. They would have been encouraged by realizing that the link with the individuals and tribes mentioned in these chapters had not been severed by the captivity and exile.

There is a special emphasis in 1 and 2 Chronicles on the reigns of David and Solomon and all their achievements. This let the postexilic community know that this was still a part of their history and their identity. God was not finished with them yet!

C. Lesson Background

The conclusion of 2 Chronicles, from which our text for today is taken, is a key part of the previously mentioned encouragement to the postexilic community. As we learned from last week's text, God's people had repeatedly spurned the appeals of His prophets to turn from their sins. Eventually, His judgment fell. God used the Babylonians to destroy the temple—believed by some

in Jerusalem and Judah to be indestructible. That belief was based on a theory that God would never allow His people to be overtaken by pagans (compare Jeremiah 7:4).

I. Decree Ordained
(2 Chronicles 36:22, 23)

Did the destruction of the temple mean that God had turned His back completely on His chosen people? The end of 2 Chronicles provides the answer, and it is a resounding *no!* That the temple will be rebuilt indicates that God still has a purpose for His people. [See question #1, page 112.]

A. God's Working (v. 22)

22. Now in the first year of Cyrus king of Persia, that the word of the LORD spoken by the mouth of Jeremiah might be accomplished, the LORD stirred up the spirit of Cyrus king of Persia, that he made a proclamation throughout all his kingdom, and to put it also in writing, saying.

Cyrus king of Persia is the human instrument whom God uses to keep His promise to bring His people home. Second Chronicles 36:20 records that Nebuchadnezzar exiled the remnant of God's people to Babylon "where they were servants to him and his sons until the reign of the kingdom of Persia." Persia came to power in 539 BC through the series of events described in Daniel 5.

King Cyrus possesses a discernment and fair-mindedness that many rulers in the ancient world lack. He understands that it will enhance his reputation and get his reign started on a positive note if he provides some measure of relief from the cruel tactics of the Babylonians.

Thus Cyrus demonstrates an attitude of diplomacy and tolerance in his dealings with conquered peoples. He gives these peoples a wide latitude in allowing them to practice their religions. Thus it should be noted that what the Scriptures describe Cyrus as doing for the Jews, he does also for other peoples: permitting them to return to their respective homelands. There they may reestablish themselves and be free to practice their religious beliefs.

Secular historians may view Cyrus's actions as simply the exercise of capable and discerning leadership. The Scripture, however, is clear in emphasizing that the Lord uses this policy of Cyrus to accomplish His own purpose. This is all part of His plan as announced by *the word of the LORD spoken by the mouth of Jeremiah*. That Word, mentioned in the previous verse (v. 21, not in today's text), describes the captivity as lasting 70 years (also Jeremiah 29:10). Cyrus is not acting alone; the Lord, the heavenly king, has moved the heart of the earthly king to implement a program of restoration for the Lord's people.

It is noteworthy that another prophet gave Spirit-inspired insight into the Lord's master plan some 100 years before Jeremiah uttered his prophecy. Isaiah prophesied not only before Persia became a dominant force, but also he prophesied even before Babylon gained such a stature! Yet Isaiah gave a message from the Lord that specifically named Cyrus (Isaiah 44:28; 45:1). Thus, some 160 years before Cyrus conquered Babylon and issued his decree, Isaiah's prophetic perspective named that ruler as the man whom God would use to fulfill His own plan.

B. Cyrus's Words (v. 23)

23. Thus saith Cyrus king of Persia, All the kingdoms of the earth hath the LORD God of heaven given me; and he hath charged me to build him a house in Jerusalem, which is in Judah. Who is there among you of all his people? The LORD his God be with him, and let him go up.

As noted previously, Cyrus allows other captive peoples to return to their homelands—not just the Jews. Thus the acknowledgment of *the Lord* as the *God of heaven,* etc., should not be considered as a sign of any kind of conversion to the God of Israel on Cyrus's part. That ruler uses equally grand language of other deities. For example, on the famous Cyrus Cylinder, unearthed by archaeologists, are inscribed these words: "Marduk, king of the gods [the leading deity of

Build Up the House of the Lord

Visual for Lesson 13. *Point to this picture and ask, "How does this illustrate one way we build the Lord's house today? What are some other ways?"*

the Babylonian gods] . . . designated me to rule over all the lands." [See question #2, page 112.]

Nevertheless, it is clear that Cyrus is indeed God's instrument to carry out His purpose. This is also true of Caesar Augustus, a later ruler whom God will use to issue a decree that results in Joseph and Mary's journey to Bethlehem. There Jesus will be born in fulfillment of prophecy (Micah 5:2; Matthew 2:6).

Following the claim to be authorized by the Lord, Cyrus's decree continues by granting permission to any of the Lord's people to *go up* to *Jerusalem.* There they can participate in the rebuilding effort. The Hebrew word translated as *go up* occurs elsewhere in the Old Testament in the context of another significant movement of God's people: the exodus from bondage in Egypt (see Exodus 3:8, 17; 33:1).

To *go up* thus has a special meaning for God's people and gives them a sense of kinship with the exodus event that established them as a "holy nation" (Exodus 19:5, 6). In a sense they can consider themselves reborn as a nation, for they are coming out of bondage in Babylon much as they had come out of Egypt under Moses. The promise of God's presence *(the Lord his God be with him)* was also a key source of encouragement during the exodus and subsequent events (Exodus 3:11, 12; 33:14-17; Numbers 14:9).

II. Decree Obeyed
(Ezra 1:5-7)

The remainder of our printed text describes the compliance of God's people with the decree of Cyrus.

A. God's Action (v. 5)

5. Then rose up the chief of the fathers of Judah and Benjamin, and the priests, and Levites, with all them whose spirit God had raised, to go up to build the house of the LORD which is in Jerusalem.

This verse lists those who prepare to go up and *build the house of the Lord* in *Jerusalem* (just as the decree had stated). *The chief of the fathers* are probably the leaders of the various tribal clans, or extended families, within the tribes of *Judah and Benjamin.* These two tribes provide the primary makeup of the southern kingdom of Judah, which the Babylonians had conquered and taken captive.

Included in those who return are the *priests* and *Levites.* Their spiritual leadership will be necessary in guiding and mentoring those who choose to return. Sadly, some of these priests and Levites eventually commit sin by marrying women from outside the covenant people. This causes great distress to Ezra and others among those who return (Ezra 9:1-4).

In this verse it is also important to note the guidance of the Lord's hand in this series of events. Those who choose to return include everyone *whose spirit God had raised*. The same God who has "stirred up the spirit" of a pagan king (Ezra 1:1) now moves among His people to stir them to action. This also means that the same God who had brought the king of Babylon *against* His people (2 Chronicles 36:17) is now working *for* His people. He is fulfilling His promise to bring them home.

B. Neighbors' Assistance (v. 6)

6. And all they that were about them strengthened their hands with vessels of silver, with gold, with goods, and with beasts, and with precious things, besides all that was willingly offered.

Here one sees another parallel to the events surrounding the exodus of some 900 years before. Exodus 11:2 records these instructions given by the Lord to Moses: "Speak now in the ears of the people, and let every man borrow of his neighbor, and every woman of her neighbor, jewels of silver, and jewels of gold." And now, as a kind of "second exodus" unfolds for God's people, all their neighbors assist them with numerous contributions and offerings. The *beasts* that are provided most likely include animals that can be used for the various sacrifices required by the law of Moses. [See question #3, page 112.]

SKIPPING CHRISTMAS

Crossroads Christian Church in Lexington, Kentucky, recently took a different approach to Christmas: they encouraged skipping it (the bad parts, that is). What triggered the new thinking was that the church staff was hearing people say such things as "I wish we didn't spend so much on gifts" or "I feel like I have to buy gifts for some people even though I don't want to." So they took a page from John Grisham's recent book, *Skipping Christmas*. (The book was made into the 2004 movie *Christmas with the Kranks*.)

Crossroads's response to the laments was *not* to tell people that they shouldn't give gifts or put up Christmas trees. Instead, the church leadership decided that what it really needed to do was to help people change their focus. The fivefold emphasis was skip excess, find simplicity; skip obligations, find joy; skip rush, find rest; skip loneliness, find belonging; skip Christmas, find

How to Say It

BABYLONIANS. Bab-ih-*low*-nee-unz.
BETHLEHEM. *Beth*-lih-hem.
CAESAR AUGUSTUS. *See*-zer Aw-*gus*-tus.
CYRUS. *Sigh*-russ.
EZRA. *Ez*-ruh.
JERUSALEM. Juh-*roo*-suh-lem.
JUDAH. *Joo*-duh.
LEVITES. *Lee*-vites.
MARDUK. *Mar*-duke.
NEBUCHADNEZZAR. *Neb*-yuh-kud-*nez*-er (strong accent on *nez*).
PERSIA. *Per*-zhuh.

Christ. The foundational idea was to bring back the joy that should be in a season that celebrates giving (www.skipchristmas.net).

When the leaders of Judah and Benjamin began the task of rebuilding the temple, all whose hearts were moved by God's gift of freedom caught the spirit of the occasion and freely gave to the cause. They had found the true focus of giving: gratitude for what God had done. We detect no sense of "Aw, do I have to?"

Christmas is right around the corner. How many of us have that same mind-set?   —C. R. B.

C. Cyrus's Assistance (v. 7)

7. Also Cyrus the king brought forth the vessels of the house of the LORD, which Nebuchadnezzar had brought forth out of Jerusalem, and had put them in the house of his gods.

Furthermore, *Cyrus* brings out the articles that rightfully belong to the temple of the Lord. This shows his personal support for the return home. [See question #4, page 112.] Second Chronicles 36:18, part of last week's printed text, describes how Nebuchadnezzar carried these items to Babylon. That king's successor had used some of those *vessels* in a most unholy way (Daniel 5:1-4).

Now these actions are reversed, as the temple articles are removed from Babylon and taken to their original, rightful home in *Jerusalem*. This will give the returning captives some sense of continuity with the past when they are in a position to place the items in the new temple.

The removal of articles from a conquered people's place of worship is a significant religious statement in the ancient world. It is interpreted as a sign of the superiority of the conqueror's *gods*. In this case the Lord God of Israel, who had allowed the Babylonians to remove the articles from His temple, now allows the Persians to send them back! [See question #5, page 112.]

REBOOTING

One of the most famous lines in English literature was uttered in *Macbeth,* which is one of Shakespeare's darker works. Evil piles upon evil throughout the play. At one point Lady Macbeth pushes her husband to kill King Duncan of Scotland so that Macbeth might be king. With Duncan dead Lady Macbeth goes back to the scene of the assassination and smears blood on guards (who had been drugged). This implicates them in the crime.

But then her conscience begins to work. She starts sleepwalking, rubbing her hands as if trying to wash away the blood that remains. In this state she admits her part in the murder and utters the famous words, "Out, [foul] spot! out, I say!" Guilt over the murder is driving her insane as her fevered mind tells her that there is no atoning for the evil she has done. In computer terminology her mind is desperately trying to "reboot," to no avail.

Many atrocities had been committed against the people of Judah by the Babylonians. Now, many decades later, Cyrus performs an act of atonement for what his predecessor had done. Does he feel a sense of shared guilt? We don't know. For whatever reason seems best to him personally, Cyrus is trying to "reboot" the situation as he gives back the sacred vessels that had been looted.

Perhaps we may be tempted to say "Not my fault" or "Not my problem" when confronted with the need to clean up someone else's mess. When that happens, stop to consider if God needs to "reboot" your thinking!   —C. R. B.

Conclusion

A. "It's in There!"

A few years ago, a certain brand of spaghetti sauce advertised its product by making the claim, "Homemade taste—it's in there!" The same can be said of the idea of *grace* in the Old Testament. Most Christians associate that concept with the New Testament. And while the doctrine of grace is most clearly expressed through the coming of Jesus, grace is not absent from the Old Testament. It is most definitely "in there." A powerful example comes from today's lesson.

As noted earlier, the books of 1 and 2 Chronicles were most likely written to encourage the returning exiles that God still had a purpose for them and that the captivity did not spell "the end." Both the conclusion of 2 Chronicles and the beginning of Ezra highlight the fact that God took the initiative in fulfilling His promise. He did that by moving the heart of Cyrus and then moving His people to take the necessary steps to return to Judah and rebuild. If ever there were doubts in the minds of those who returned from captivity concerning God's intentions, they needed only to look back and remember God's grace in using the right man at the right time to achieve His holy purpose.

Christians have a similar perspective, based on what Jesus Christ has done for us through His death and resurrection. Sometimes circumstances we encounter may cause us to doubt the validity of our faith. In those situations we can remind ourselves, as Paul did the Roman Christians, that nothing "shall be able to separate us from the love of God, which is in Christ Jesus our Lord" (Romans 8:39).

That love—and that grace—were also revealed during the Old Testament era. It was revealed from the time of Adam and Eve receiving the promise of what the woman's seed would accomplish (Genesis 3:15). Is grace found within the pages of the Old Testament? Make no mistake—it's in there!

B. Prayer

Father, where would we be without Your grace? We would be hopelessly lost. May we never forget the difference that Your grace through Jesus Christ has made in our lives. It is a difference for eternity. Remind us of our responsibility to share that grace with others. In Jesus' name, amen.

C. Thought to Remember

God is still in the business of rebuilding and restoring.

Home Daily Bible Readings

Learning by Doing

This page contains an alternative lesson plan emphasizing learning activities.
Classes desiring such student involvement will find these suggestions helpful.

Learning Goals

After participating in this lesson, each student will be able to:

1. List the divine and human factors in the return of God's people from captivity.

2. Explain why the terms *return* and *restoration* are appropriate to describe people's response to the gospel message today.

3. Prepare a testimony of how God has restored his or her life through Jesus, and share that testimony with an unsaved person.

Into the Lesson

Have the following question displayed before students arrive: "Can God use non-Christian or ungodly people to accomplish His purpose? Give examples." Have small groups of three to five discuss the question. Then ask groups to share their conclusions and illustrations with the whole class.

Next, make the transition to Bible study by saying, "Yes, God can use ungodly people to accomplish His purpose. We'll find another example of God's sovereignty in this regard in today's lesson from Israel's history."

Into the Word

Begin with a brief lecture titled "The Chronicles Factor," using the Lesson Background. Have on display a picture of Solomon's temple while you speak.

Next, use three or more groups of four to five people each to do the following tasks.

Group #1: Decree Ordained: God's Working—2 Chronicles 36:22. Read today's printed text and focus on your assigned verse. Prepare and deliver to the class a brief lecture with outline. A possible outline is

  I. Babylon and Persia
  II. Cyrus's Attitude
  III. The Lord's Will
  IV. Isaiah's Prophecy

Group #2: Decree Ordained: Cyrus's Words—2 Chronicles 36:23. Read today's printed text and focus on your assigned verse. Prepare and deliver to the class a brief lecture with outline. A possible outline is

  I. Cyrus: Instrument of God
  II. "Go Up"

Group #3: Decree Obeyed—Ezra 1:5-7. Read today's printed text and focus on your assigned verses. Prepare and deliver to the class a brief lecture with outline. A possible outline is

  I. Those Who Went
  II. Neighbors Who Helped
  III. Cyrus, Who Helped

In addition to the written assignments above, give each group the following materials: a poster board with the group headings (but not the possible outlines) already written, a marker, and a photocopy of the lesson commentary on the verses assigned. Explain that their combined efforts will provide a comprehensive outline and study of today's text.

Each group will select two people to make the presentation to the class. One will deliver a brief lecture on the assigned passage and another person will write the outline for all to see as the report is being delivered.

Into Life

After each group reports, offer the following for discussion: (1) The doctrine of God's grace is often thought of as a New Testament doctrine. However, God's grace is often demonstrated in the Old Testament too. How do you see God's grace powerfully at work in this piece of history? (You may need also to ask for a definition of *grace*.) (2) The terms *return* and *restoration* are key concepts in this Old Testament picture of God's grace. How are these terms appropriate for describing people's response to the gospel message today?

After discussion, say, "We can personalize the concepts of return and restoration in our own testimonies." Give each student an index card and ask him or her to write "My Journey" at the top. Ask each student to jot notes about his or her life's spiritual journey, including them in a personal testimony.

Testimonies should include the concepts of return and restoration. Students who have accepted Jesus as Savior should include that in the testimony. Those who haven't can still make notes about their heart's movement toward or away from Him. Ask two volunteers to share their testimonies. Then ask the class as a whole, "How will you share your testimony this week?"

Let's Talk It Over

The questions on this page are designed to promote discussion of the lesson by the class and to encourage application of the lesson Scriptures. The answers provided are only discussion starters. Let your class talk it over from there.

1. What are some things that can be rebuilt only by the power of God? How are humans sometimes arrogant in thinking that such power belongs to them?

Given the power of our technology, it is tempting to assume that nothing is beyond building or repairing—eventually. Think of all the wonder medications we have today! They hold out the tantalizing promise of repairing human emotions and bodies. Some people have their bodies cryogenically frozen at death, hoping for the day when ultramodern science will resurrect them. But human arrogance is nothing new—see Daniel 4:28-33; Acts 12:21-23. Only God can reclaim sinners and save them for eternity.

2. Cyrus said that God had given him a mission to rebuild the temple, but other decrees from Cyrus gave equal credence to other deities. Is this an early form of "political correctness"? Why, or why not?

Unfortunately, political leaders will refer occasionally to God in more of a manipulative or pandering fashion rather than as an expression of genuine, personal faith. The goal of gaining political support from religious people sometimes is more important than the goal of attaining God's support. In such cases God may be referred to in a bland, generic way in order to include as many religions as possible and to offend as few as possible. This is sometimes called *ceremonial theism.*

For a politician to attune his or her policies to God's will and fight the prevailing political winds is a big challenge. But God can ensure that even a politician who isn't particularly interested in Him will carry out God's will regardless. There may be no obvious way to know when that is happening at the time—it may take hindsight to tell.

3. Material support for this "second exodus" came from the gifts of fellow Jews. Support for the original exodus came from non-Jews (Exodus 12:36). When should a church rely on support from the world to accomplish a ministry, if ever?

Some churches feel very strongly that ministries must be supported only from the offerings of the members. We need to acknowledge, though, that outside support is essential for some ministries to happen. Church building projects require support from zoning boards and neighbors. After-school programs may require at least tacit support from teachers and school officials.

Your church's reputation within the town can influence how effective it is for ministry in areas like these. But expecting the community to support the church by participating in church fundraisers involving pancake breakfasts, the sale of Christmas trees, etc., may be going too far. The apostle John notes that "because that for his name's sake they went forth, taking nothing of the Gentiles" (3 John 7).

4. In what ways can a non-Christian ruler become an agent for God?

Ideally, of course, we would love to see every non-Christian ruler come to Christ. Yet God can use even the most unholy ruler to be His unwilling agent. Pharaoh from the book of Exodus may be the most obvious example.

Even outside the testimony of Scripture, we can see examples of rulers who seem to be acting as agents for God in at least one area of their leadership. (To avoid politicizing these observations, we won't suggest names here!) This may be done actively, with a politician promoting pro-Christian policies intentionally—though perhaps from less-than-holy motives. Other times it can be done unintentionally, through policies enacted for reasons that God uses to achieve His purposes.

5. What special items from your church's past are worth holding on to because of their legacy value? What things are best discarded as pointless relics of a bygone era? How do you decide which is which?

Symbolically, the temple objects connected the Jews to both the lost glory of Solomon's temple and God's favor that allowed that temple to be built in the first place (1 Kings 5:5). The articles reminded the Jews that the God of Solomon was the same God leading them back to the promised land. Objects from your church's past that serve as reminders of the unchanging God in the midst of an ever-changing world may well be worth keeping.

Winter Quarter 2006–2007

Jesus Christ: A Portrait of God

Special Features

Lessons

Unit 1: Christ, the Image of God

Unit 2: Christ Sustains and Supports

Unit 3: Christ Guides and Protects

About These Lessons

When a fashion from the past comes back into style, we call it a "retro look." We may also use the term "throwback." Jesus lived 2,000 years ago, but those terms do not apply to Him. The simple fact is that His message never goes out of style. The texts about Jesus this quarter are ever new!

Dec 3

Dec 10

Dec 17

Dec 24

Dec 31

Jan 7

Jan 14

Jan 21

Jan 28

Feb 4

Feb 11

Feb 18

Feb 25

Quarterly Quiz

The questions on this page may be used in several ways: as a pretest at the beginning of the quarter; as a review at the end of the quarter; or as a review after each lesson. The questions are based on the Scripture text of each lesson (King James Version). **The answers are on page 116.**

Lesson 1

1. Jesus is the image of the invisible _____. *Colossians 1:15*

2. Jesus made peace through the _____ of His cross. *Colossians 1:20*

Lesson 2

1. In these last days God has spoken by His Son. T/F. *Hebrews 1:2*

2. A _____ of righteousness is the _____ of Jesus' kingdom. (Hint: the same word goes in each blank.) *Hebrews 1:8*

Lesson 3

1. John wrote so that his readers' joy might be made what? (perfect, visible, full?) *1 John 1:4*

2. If we confess our sins, He is faithful and just to forgive us. T/F. *1 John 1:9*

3. Our advocate with the Father is who? (Gabriel, Abraham, Jesus?) *1 John 2:1*

Lesson 4

1. In the beginning was the what? (universe, Word, tree of life?) *John 1:1*

2. Jesus came unto His own, and His own received Him. T/F. *John 1:11*

3. Grace and _____ came by Jesus Christ. *John 1:17*

Lesson 5

1. Christ took the form of a what? (angel, emperor, servant?) *Philippians 2:7*

2. Christ was obedient unto _____. *Philippians 2:8*

Lesson 6

1. Jesus said that we would be made free by what? (law, truth, prayer?) *John 8:32*

2. Jesus opponents accused Him of being a what? (Gentile, Roman, Samaritan?) *John 8:48*

3. After Jesus said "I am," the Jews tried to do what to Him? (stone Him, worship Him, laugh at Him?) *John 8:58, 59*

Lesson 7

1. The Father judgeth no man. T/F. *John 5:22*

2. There is such a thing as a "resurrection of damnation." T/F. *John 5:29*

Lesson 8

1. Jesus is the what of life? (bread, spice, milk?) *John 6:35*

2. Those who have everlasting life will be raised up on the next-to-last day. T/F. *John 6:40*

Lesson 9

1. Jesus is the light of the world. T/F. *John 8:12*

2. The Pharisees reluctantly admitted that Jesus' testimony about himself was true. T/F. *John 8:13*

3. Whoever believes in Jesus does not abide in what? (confusion, Rome, darkness?) *John 12:46*

Lesson 10

1. Whoever enters the sheepfold by a way other than the door is a thief and a what? (porter, robber, hireling?) *John 10:1*

2. John the Baptist is the door of the sheep. T/F. *John 10:7*

3. Although there are to be two folds, there is only one shepherd. T/F. *John 10:16*

Lesson 11

1. Lazarus, Mary, and Martha were of what town? (Bethlehem, Nazareth, Bethany?) *John 11:1*

2. Jesus delayed ___ days when He heard that Lazarus was sick. *John 11:6*

3. When Jesus approached their house, Mary and Martha ran together to meet Him. T/F. *John 11:20*

Lesson 12

1. Jesus said, "Let not your thinking be troubled." T/F. *John 14:1*

2. Which of the disciples asked Jesus to show them the Father? (Peter, Judas, Philip?) *John 14:8*

3. Jesus said that He was in the Father and the Father was in Him. T/F. *John 14:11*

Lesson 13

1. The Father is the vine and Jesus and the disciples are the branches. T/F. *John 15:5*

2. What happens to branches that are cut off? (nothing, burned, buried?) *John 15:6*

3. Jesus wants us to bear much what? (fruit, vegetables, foliage?) *John 15:8*

Jesus This Christmas

by Tom Thatcher

One of my favorite things about Christmastime as a child was the holiday TV specials. I can hardly think of Christmas without recalling the Grinch, Rudolph and Yukon Cornelius, and Frosty the Snowman. My favorite holiday program yet today is Charles Schulz's *A Charlie Brown Christmas*.

As is so often the case, Charlie Brown has the blues. This time it's because he "just doesn't know what Christmas is all about." Lucy tells him it's about getting presents; his sister, Sally, says it's about Santa Claus; Snoopy thinks it's about winning the neighborhood lights and display contest. Even the Christmas pageant turns into a dance-a-thon, with all the kids complaining about their parts.

One proposal is that Christmas must have something to do with a Christmas tree, a big artificial tree. But all this celebration only leaves Charlie Brown more miserable. Eventually he cries out in despair, "Isn't there anyone who knows what Christmas is all about?"

When we look around and see what Christmas means in our culture, we're often forced to ask the same question. Even in Japan, a country where there never have been many Christians, Christmas is celebrated with decorations and parties and presents as a commercial holiday. In many ways it's hard to see how things are any different where we live. Did Jesus come so that we could celebrate His birthday with expensive cards and presents and parties? And, honestly, do we really need Jesus to have Christmas, or would it be just as much fun without Him?

At the end of the show, Linus steps into the spotlight with an answer. In a bold move that barely got by the censors when the program was first aired in 1965, Schulz insisted that his TV special end with a summary of the true meaning of Christmas. "And there were in the same country shepherds abiding in the field," Linus begins. Then, after quoting the rest of Luke 2:8-14, he says, "That's what Christmas is all about, Charlie Brown. 'For unto you is born this day in the city of David a Saviour, which is Christ the Lord.'" What better summary could there be of the meaning of Christmas and, indeed, of the meaning of Jesus?

This quarter's lessons explore the identity of this remarkable person whose birth we celebrate every December 25. Who was Jesus? What was His mission? What did He say about himself? What blessings come to those who accept Him?

Unit 1: December
Christ, the Image of God

Lesson 1 focuses on Colossians 1 to establish Jesus' complete equality with God the Father. We will see Paul stress that Christ is the perfect image of God, and that He shares all of God's power and authority. Jesus was not just a great rabbi while He walked the earth; He is, in fact, the one who created the universe and who now sustains everything we see by His unmatched power.

Lesson 2, from Hebrews, explores Jesus' role as the ultimate revelation of God on earth. In Old Testament times God revealed himself through the words of prophets. Sometimes He even sent messages through angels, special agents of God who move between Heaven and earth. In Christ, however, God revealed himself to the world in a unique way.

Lesson 3 focuses on a popular text from 1 John that tells us several things about Christ. Although Jesus is fully God, He was also fully human during His time on earth. People saw, heard, and touched Him. As a man He died on a cross; as God He rose and returned to Heaven. Knowing that He did all this for us should lead us to confess our sinfulness and attempt to walk as He walked.

Lesson 4, our Christmas Eve lesson, will examine the prologue to the Gospel of John (1:1-18). John's Gospel does not include a Christmas story but instead opens by showing the role that Christ has filled from the beginning of time. Drawing on Old Testament imagery, John reminds us that Jesus was involved in the creation of the world.

Lesson 5, our New Year's Eve lesson, allows us to explore the mind and attitude of Christ through Paul's great letter to the Philippians. What better way to bring the year 2006 to a grand close than to learn to think as Jesus thought!

Unit 2: January
Christ Sustains and Supports

Lesson 6 discusses Jesus' claim, in the Gospel of John, to be the ultimate revelation of God's truth. Often we know in our hearts that we should behave a certain way, yet we constantly fall prey to temptations and the influences of the world around us. Jesus' teaching helps us here. His words are true, and in them we find clarity and freedom from sin.

Lesson 7 touches on a familiar theme from the Gospel of John: Jesus' spiritual authority. While on earth, He didn't just make up new doctrines and force them on people. Instead, as God's Son, He spoke directly on God's behalf. For this reason we can be sure that His words will either save us or condemn us on judgment day.

Lesson 8 examines two of the best known images of Christ from the Gospel of John: "Bread of Life" and "Living Water." Just as our bodies require food and water to live, our spirits require nourishment from Christ. Even though none of us has had a chance to meet Jesus face-to-face, we continue to experience His presence and power in our lives through the Holy Spirit.

Lesson 9 closes this unit on Christ's provision by looking at His role as "Light of the World." The Bible often describes the world as a dark place in the sense that it's hard for us to know the right thing to do. Where is God in all the evil and chaos that surround us? How do we know what God has called us to do? In John 8 and 12 Jesus promises to light our path if we look to Him. His teaching and example show us the way to the Father.

Unit 3: February
Christ Guides and Protects

Lesson 10 looks at Jesus' role as the good shepherd from the Gospel of John. He is the one who loved His sheep so much that He gave His life for them (us). Some religious leaders seek to "fleece the flock." They claim to speak for God when they really only want to increase their own power and influence. Others have good intentions but act like part-time, hired babysitters. They abandon the job when things get tough.

Jesus, though, is a "good" shepherd. He is forever loyal to His sheep, proving His love by dying for them (us). We can therefore always trust Him to give us guidance and protection.

Lesson 11 looks at the Gospel of John to explore Jesus' ability to meet our ultimate need. What happens to us when we die? Is this the end, or can we hope for something beyond the grave?

Before Jesus proved His power over death by calling Lazarus from the tomb, Martha found her faith tested by the death of her brother. The pain and hardship of this world will test our faith as well. Will we remain confident that Christ will make it all worthwhile in the end?

Lesson 12 takes us to the upper room. There Jesus and the disciples gather for their final meeting the night before His death. After washing their feet and urging them to love one another, Jesus assures His followers that He is "the way, the truth, and the life." He is the only route to the Father. No other person in history can make and prove such a claim. For this reason we find salvation in Christ alone. Jesus shows us how to live lives pleasing to God, lives founded on the truth of His message.

Lesson 13 closes our series with a familiar passage from John 15. Here Jesus compares himself to a grapevine and His disciples to the branches that bear clusters of grapes. As the branches draw life from the vine, believers draw strength from Jesus to serve God.

If we fail, it is not because Christ has abandoned us. Rather, it is because we have separated ourselves from Him. Also in this passage Jesus shows His care for the disciples by saying that He no longer calls them *servants* but *friends*. What an awe-inspiring privilege! This should reflect the way that we work with Christ to bring glory to God.

One True Way

We live in a world where many voices call us to follow their lead. Our jobs, friends, hobbies, habits, and family members all demand our loyalties. In the process it's easy to get confused and off track. Even at Christmastime, when we should be focusing on the coming of Christ, the demands of the season make it hard to remember who Jesus is and what He is all about. The lessons in this series should serve as a reminder that the son of Mary was also the only-begotten Son of God.

Answers to Quarterly Quiz
on page 114

Lesson 1—1. God. 2. blood. **Lesson 2**—1. true. 2. sceptre. **Lesson 3**—1. full. 2. true. 3. Jesus. **Lesson 4**—1. Word. 2. false. 3. truth. **Lesson 5**—1. servant 2. death. **Lesson 6**—1. truth. 2. Samaritan. 3. stone Him. **Lesson 7**—1. true. 2. true. **Lesson 8**—1. bread. 2. false. **Lesson 9**—1. true. 2. false. 3. darkness. **Lesson 10**—1. robber. 2. false. 3. false. **Lesson 11**—1. Bethany. 2. two. 3. false. **Lesson 12**—1. false. 2. Philip. 3. true. **Lesson 13**—1. false. 2. burned. 3. fruit.

Rome
Philippi
ASIA MINOR
Ephesus
Colossae
Mediterranean Sea

Capernaum
Sea of Galilee

GALILEE

Mediterranean
Sea

Jordan River

Jerusalem
Bethany
Bethlehem

JUDEA

Dead Sea

The Holy Land in the Time of Christ

I Am . . . the true vine. —John 15:1

the bread of life. —John 6:35

the good shepherd. —John 10:11, 14

the resurrection, and the life. —John 11:25

Alpha and Omega. —Revelation 1:8; 21:6; 22:13

the way, the truth, and the life. —John 14:6

the living bread. —John 6:51

the light of the world. —John 8:12; 9:5

"Well, What Do You Know?"

The Importance of Content

by Ronald G. Davis

EDUCATORS ARE SOMETIMES ACCUSED of being more concerned about content than about life. That accusation, perhaps occasionally justified, often overlooks one basic truth: life decisions are made from a cognitive foundation. What one knows (and doesn't know) strongly affects his or her behavioral decisions. Even a child makes choices relative to perceived consequences, that is, what he or she "knows" to expect.

Poor choices—even sinful choices—often come as a result of either inadequate knowledge or erroneous "knowledge." Perhaps one doesn't know enough of God's truth. Or maybe he or she has believed a lie and mistaken it for the truth.

Teacher preparation for a lesson session must include two questions at some early point: (1) "What do my learners know about the content at hand?" and (2) "What do they need to know to make better life decisions?"

Adult teachers, especially of long-running study groups, may proceed with the (wrong) assumption that the students already know the content of the typical Bible lesson. (If they do, then they need to be studying something else, something deeper!) But sincere Bible students want to know more and more about the character and the plan of God, the history of His people, and the application of godliness to daily life.

In this light the teacher's first goal is to establish a firm cognitive base for the students. This will allow them to develop godly attitudes and behaviors. Ten of this quarter's studies are from the pen of John the apostle, who said of his record of the gospel, "These are written, that ye might believe that Jesus is the Christ, the Son of God; and that believing ye might have life through his name" (John 20:31).

Truths to be known, resulting in faith to be affirmed, leading to right living to be blessed—that is why we all teach. No teacher need apologize for emphasizing knowledge of the Bible and Bible backgrounds.

The Background

Historical and geographical settings characterize truth. Myth and folklore are set in "once upon a time" and "countries far away." The Bible is set in real times and real places. Fiction cre-ates people (and lesser creatures) to do the whims of the author. Truth records the deeds of real people. Understanding the culture of the biblical story helps one understand the Bible texts and the Bible people. Seeing how individuals lived their daily lives—through their hopes, fears, and aspirations—and how they responded to the good news of Christ helps the contemporary person make right decisions.

Introducing your students to some typical residents of Jesus' first-century Galilee and Judea and the wider Roman world is important. To do this, consider using an occasional dramatic monologue. Possibilities include a Christian living in Colosse when Paul's letter arrives (**Lesson 1**), a Roman centurion stationed in Palestine, a Judean shepherd (**Lesson 10**), a believing Jew (**Lesson 6**), a Galilean peasant present at the feeding of the thousands (background of **Lesson 8**), and a vine grower (**Lesson 13**).

Perhaps a member of your class or congregation who enjoys drama would like to write his or her own monologue. This requires a diligent study of texts and commentary sources. About 300 to 400 words is needed for a three-minute presentation. Here is a sample for a shepherd, a "bad" shepherd:

Yeah, I'm one of those "bad" shepherds you hear about in the big city of Jerusalem. If we shepherds do our jobs well, no one notices. When our sheep are sold for sacrifice, the buyer is looking forward not backward. When our sheep become someone's tasty meal, thoughts of our work are "swallowed" along with the meat.

But I've heard all the snide remarks: "Wouldn't trust him as far as I could throw the temple." Our reputation precedes us from field to field. Sure, they trust us with their sheep, but step out of the field and we're suspected of everything: thievery, drunkenness, profanity, irreverence. We end up dirty, smelly, tired, and hungry.

So perhaps our manners don't quite match the standards of the Pharisees. We don't rightly care a fig. And maybe we don't get to the synagogue as often as we should.

But those sheep don't protect themselves, don't water themselves, don't find new grass for themselves—even on the Sabbath.

Perhaps a Pharisee could come out and watch the sheep while we go to the synagogue? Ha! I'll see that the day the Messiah comes, greets me by name, and says, 'Say, friend, I'm a shepherd too. Let me watch the sheep while you rest for a while!'

Obviously geography is a part of every lesson as well. From the towns and villages around the Sea of Galilee to the "big city" of Jerusalem, Jesus lived and served in real places. Maps of those areas around the sea and the city will significantly support your learners' understanding of the context of His teaching. John is very careful to indicate Jesus' location, which varies from Galilee to Jerusalem and back to Galilee. Two basic learning principle for maps are "the bigger the better" and "the more interactive the more instructional."

Because the Sea of Galilee is only about 12 miles from north to south and about 6 miles at its widest, a wall of your room can become a "one foot = two miles" map, or six feet by three feet, very easily. The sea on your map should approximate the shape of an upside down pear.

Use stick-on labels to designate places of Jesus' teaching. For example the site of the Feeding of the 5,000 on the northeast shore is a background for **Lesson 8**. This geographical context will help students see the way Jesus and His disciples sailed across the sea before the people ran around the shore to meet Him on "the other side" near Capernaum. Let students guess and measure the distances, given the simple scale.

You can use a scanner to capture a drawing of Jerusalem to create an overhead transparency or a computer-projected image. This will promote a clearer concept of Jesus' movements around the city at various times. Your discussion can include His birth in Bethlehem, only a few miles to the south (larger context of **Lessons 2 and 4**). You can also point out the temple (for **Lessons 6 and 9**) and nearby Bethany (**Lesson 11**). Students may not realize that the Jerusalem of Jesus' day was little more than one mile square; overlaying that with your local street grid can be insightful.

Any pictorial material of Israel, in any format, that you use to decorate your room will help students confirm the reality of Jesus' places.

The Word

With every lesson the Scripture text is a starting point. Seeing it, reading it, and hearing it should be "givens" for the students. The old-fashioned strategy of letting students read one verse at a time in sequence around the group may be a novel idea in contemporary classrooms. But your class probably has some who are excellent oral readers; you will want to use those God-given talents as well. Also consider letting students hear the text read professionally from a prerecorded format. These are available in Christian stores and from Bible societies.

In a lesson series that emphasizes one writer as this one does (John), seeing the repeated use of key words and terms will have a cumulative effect that is nothing but positive. You might like to keep a running tally of the times certain key words are used from lesson to lesson. Put up a large sheet of paper with the heading "John's Frequent Words." List several, such as *light, darkness, life, know, word, God, Father, world, truth*. Mark the times the words are found week to week. Your learners will be surprised how emphatically repetitious John is!

Rather than doing all this yourself, you may want to have learners perform the tally on a week-to-week basis. Even if individuals differ on their tallies, all will see the way that John writes. For example have the class make an initial quick tally of the times "sheep" (or a derivative) is used in **Lesson 10**. The tally will surprise everyone!

Because John uses the same words repeatedly, your class may enjoy and appreciate an introduction to some of the Greek language words that stand behind those frequent uses. For example when Jesus calls himself "the light of the world," the Greek for "light" is *phos* (pronounced *fos* with a long *o*) while the Greek for "world" is *cosmos*. These two Greek words form the basis of some common English words. "Photograph" and "cosmic" are just two examples. If you don't have skills in Greek personally, a Bible dictionary will help.

Never Too Much

Your students can never know too much Scripture nor too much about Scripture. God's Word is deep and wide. Scholars have plumbed those depths and widths for centuries. Ordinary Bible students have delighted in its riches from the time Moses began writing it down by God's Spirit.

As Paul insists, "All Scripture is given by inspiration of God, and is profitable for doctrine, for reproof, for correction, for instruction in righteousness: that the man of God may be perfect, thoroughly furnished unto all good works" (2 Timothy 3:16, 17). The diligent teacher of adults will never stop asking the students, "Well, what do you know?"

Who Is Jesus Christ?

December 3
Lesson 1

DEVOTIONAL READING: Isaiah 9:2-7.

BACKGROUND SCRIPTURE: Colossians 1.

PRINTED TEXT: Colossians 1:15-23.

Colossians 1:15-23

15 Who is the image of the invisible God, the firstborn of every creature:

16 For by him were all things created, that are in heaven, and that are in earth, visible and invisible, whether they be thrones, or dominions, or principalities, or powers: all things were created by him, and for him:

17 And he is before all things, and by him all things consist:

18 And he is the head of the body, the church: who is the beginning, the firstborn from the dead; that in all things he might have the preeminence.

19 For it pleased the Father that in him should all fulness dwell;

20 And, having made peace through the blood of his cross, by him to reconcile all things unto himself; by him, I say, whether they be things in earth, or things in heaven.

21 And you, that were sometime alienated and enemies in your mind by wicked works, yet now hath he reconciled

22 In the body of his flesh through death, to present you holy and unblamable and unreprovable in his sight:

23 If ye continue in the faith grounded and settled, and be not moved away from the hope of the gospel, which ye have heard, and which was preached to every creature which is under heaven; whereof I Paul am made a minister.

GOLDEN TEXT: Who is the image of the invisible God, the firstborn of every creature: for by him were all things created, that are in heaven, and that are in earth, visible and invisible, whether they be thrones, or dominions, or principalities, or powers: all things were created by him, and for him.—Colossians 1:15, 16.

Jesus Christ: A Portrait of God
Unit 1: Christ, the Image of God
(Lessons 1-5)

Lesson Aims

After participating in this lesson, each student will be able to:

1. Tell how the creation is dependent on the creator.

2. Explain why Paul emphasized the doctrine of Christ in his battle against heresy in the church.

3. Write a prayer that expresses worship for Jesus in His role as creator.

Lesson Outline

INTRODUCTION
  A. The Path to Heresy
  B. Lesson Background
I. DIVINE CHRIST FOR CREATION (Colossians 1: 15-20)
  A. Jesus: Image of God (v. 15)
    The Invisible God
  B. Jesus: Creator and Sustainer (vv. 16, 17)
  C. Jesus: Preeminent One (v. 18)
  D. Jesus: Dwelling of Deity (v. 19)
  E. Jesus: Peace Offering (v. 20)
II. HUMAN SAVIOR FOR HUMANITY (Colossians 1: 21-23)
  A. Jesus: Justifier and Sanctifier (vv. 21, 22)
    Alienated . . . Reconciled
  B. Jesus: Core of the Gospel (v. 23)
CONCLUSION
  A. The Ageless Jesus
  B. The Christ of Christmas
  C. Prayer
  D. Thought to Remember

Introduction

Jesus. Although secular society continually attempts to exclude Him, He still seems to be everywhere. We see Him as a plastic dashboard statue in a passing car. We watch Him portrayed in Hollywood productions. We observe Him in many variations as the manger baby for Christmas. In spite of all of this attention, we sometimes neglect to ask the most crucial question: "Who is Jesus Christ?" The lessons for this quarter will explore this vital question.

A. The Path to Heresy

Perhaps you have heard the word *heresy* at some time in your life. Merriam-Webster says that heresy is "an opinion, doctrine, or practice contrary to the truth." Heresy is dangerous false teaching that negates or denies the central truths of the Christian faith (see 2 Peter 2:1).

Many heresies that have arisen in the history of the church are centered on Jesus Christ himself. The first major heresy about Jesus came from a collection of false teachings we call *gnosticism*. While there were several false doctrines within gnosticism, the most dangerous was the belief that Jesus was not really human—He just seemed or appeared to be human. Gnostics had no problem with the divinity of Jesus; they denied His humanity. But, as Hebrews 2:14 teaches, if Jesus had not been a man, He could not die. Thus, acceptance of gnostic beliefs would deny the basic doctrine that Jesus died on the cross to pay the price for our sins, the doctrine of the atonement.

A second major heresy that was centered specifically on Jesus was a fourth-century teaching we call *Arianism*. Arians taught that while Jesus was indeed a powerful, supernatural being, He had not always existed. He was a created being. This was recognized as a heresy because it ultimately denied the divinity of Christ. If He were a creature, then He could not be the creator—He could not really be God. If this were true, then Jesus' claims about himself were delusions or lies, and He should be rejected as a false teacher.

Both of these heresies can be found in the church today. There are those who do not like to think of Jesus as a man, thus falling into a modern gnosticism. For example, this viewpoint has trouble thinking about the baby Jesus of Christmastime without also thinking that He never cried or while assuming that He was spouting words of wisdom while in the cradle.

There are others today who see Jesus as the ultimate man but not as God, thus agreeing with the Arians. These modern Arians admire Jesus as an advocate for the downtrodden, a wise teacher, or even as a revolutionary leader. This line of thought stops short of seeing Jesus as God in flesh.

Biblical Christians are called to affirm that Jesus was fully human and fully divine. To do anything less sets one on the path of heresy and departure from the Christian faith.

B. Lesson Background

Paul's letter to the Colossian church was sent primarily to combat a growing threat of heresy within that group of believers. Paul never says exactly what the heresy is, but we can see that he refers to it as a type of "philosophy" (Colossians 2:8); it seems to have been an early form of gnosticism, perhaps combined with a type of Judaizing. Judaizing was the belief that Christians were obligated to keep every aspect of the Old Testament law, including circumcision. Paul wrote to correct the problem and call the church to a return to the simple faith in Christ (2:6, 7).

Today's lesson text comes on the heels of Paul's opening prayer for the needs of the Colossian church. Paul has asked God that the Colossian believers would be spiritually wise (1:9), live upright lives (1:10), be strong in the face of persecution (1:11), and be thankful for their glorious salvation through Jesus Christ (1:12-14). Having ended his prayer on this high note, he then proceeds to discuss the true nature of Christ and what this means to his readers.

I. Divine Christ for Creation (Colossians 1:15-20)

The six verses in this subsection (1:15-20) have been labeled the "Christ Hymn" or the "Hymn to Christ."

A. Jesus: Image of God (v. 15)

15. Who is the image of the invisible God, the firstborn of every creature.

This extraordinary verse is one of the most profound doctrinal statements of the entire New Testament. Yet it is susceptible to misunderstanding in at least two ways.

First, when Paul says Jesus is the *image of . . . God,* he does not mean that Jesus is some type of "copy" of God. We know from our experience with copy machines that the copying process always causes degradation, and each copy is less perfect than the original. Such experiences do not apply here. Paul means that Jesus is "imaging" or revealing the unseen God, the creator who does not normally allow human eyes to see Him (compare John 1:18). Jesus is the visible expression of God. See also John 14:9.

Second, when Paul describes Jesus as *the firstborn of every creature,* he is not saying that Jesus himself is a created being. Rather, this is his way of saying that Jesus is the ruler over all creation. In the ancient world the firstborn son has authority over the father's household that is essentially equal to that of the father himself. The only one who can overrule the firstborn son is the father. Since there is complete unity of purpose between Jesus and His Father, the authority of the Son over creation is equal to that of the Father.

The word translated *firstborn* here is translated "first-begotten" in Hebrews 1:6. There it is even clearer that Jesus enters the world of humans from the outside as an uncreated being.

Thus Paul begins the Christ Hymn with a robust statement of the divinity of Christ. He does this by affirming two mighty characteristics of Jesus: His role in revealing the true God and His authority over creation.

THE INVISIBLE GOD

Most religions in the ancient world worship gods represented by idols. Yet the God of the Bible refuses to be represented by an idol of any kind; He commanded that His people not make "any graven image" (Exodus 20:4). When the Romans first occupied Palestine, some officers entered the Holy of Holies in the temple and were dismayed that there was no image there. Because there was no idol present, they concluded that these Jews did not worship any God at all and thus were atheists.

Today many people doubt God's existence because they cannot see Him. Yet in other areas of life we readily accept what we cannot see. We cannot see carbon monoxide, but we know that this gas can be lethal. We cannot see love, but we feel its presence and power. We cannot see radio waves, but that does not stop us from tuning in our favorite stations. Even though all these things are invisible, we still order our lives around them because we know they are real.

God too is real. And Jesus is the image of God. That means that what we see in Jesus is a picture of what God is like. The apostle John tells us that no one has even seen God, except as God's Son has revealed Him (John 1:18). What a privilege to see Jesus in the pages of Scripture!   —J. B. N.

B. Jesus: Creator and Sustainer (vv. 16, 17)

16. For by him were all things created, that are in heaven, and that are in earth, visible and invisible, whether they be thrones, or dominions, or principalities, or powers: all things were created by him, and for him.

VISUALS FOR THESE LESSONS

The visual pictured in each lesson (example: page 125) is a small reproduction of a large, full-color poster included in the *Adult Resources* packet for the Winter Quarter. The packet is available from your supplier. Order No. 292.

Paul expands upon Jesus' role as creator by giving an inclusive statement with important implications. First, *all things* were *created* by Him. Paul makes sure that his readers do not exclude anything from this broad statement. There are no exceptions. Paul wants the Colossians to know that this includes both the physical realm *(in earth)* and the spiritual realm *(in heaven)*.

Paul also insists that all things were created *for him*. This, of course, further excludes Jesus from the realm of created beings and things. While the full purpose of creation is not laid out here, we know from elsewhere in Scripture that creation was undertaken by God for His glory. Paul includes Jesus in this goal; there is no separation of purpose.

17. And he is before all things, and by him all things consist.

Paul's mighty statements about Christ continue at an intense pace. In this verse he asserts the preexistence of Christ. The affirmation that Jesus is *before all things* tells us that the divinity of Christ is not limited by time or space. This statement is similar to Jesus' own claim that "before Abraham was, I am" (John 8:58).

Paul goes on to declare that Jesus is not only the creator but is also the sustainer of all things. The word translated *consist* has the sense of "continue to exist." The Bible never sees God-the-creator as some kind of divine clockmaker who makes the clock, winds it up, and then abandons it. Christ continues to be involved in the ongoing affairs of the created order. Without this involvement the world would quickly cease to exist.

C. Jesus: Preeminent One (v. 18)

18. And he is the head of the body, the church: who is the beginning, the firstborn from the dead; that in all things he might have the preeminence.

How to Say It

ARIANISM. *Air*-ee-uh-nih-zim.
BETHLEHEM. *Beth*-lih-hem.
COLOSSIANS. Kuh-*losh*-unz.
CORINTHIANS. Ko-*rin*-thee-unz (*th* as in *thin*).
EPHESIANS. Ee-*fee*-zhunz.
GNOSTICISM. *nahss*-tih-*sizz*-um (strong accent on *nahss*).
GNOSTICS. *nahss*-ticks.
HERESY. *hair*-uh-see.
NAZARETH. *Naz*-uh-reth.
SHALOM (Hebrew). shah-*lome*.

Having established that Christ is the creator and ruler of the world, Paul now narrows the focus of the Christ Hymn to Jesus' role in *the church*. As elsewhere, the church is seen as *the body* of Christ (see Romans 12:5, 1 Corinthians 12:27), a beautiful metaphor. Compare Ephesians 1:22, 23; 4:15; 5:23. [See question #1, page 128.]

In regard to Christ's relationship to the church, Paul lifts up three important concepts. First, Christ is *the beginning* or originator of the church. He founded the church (Matthew 16:18) and purchased it with His own blood (Acts 20:28).

Second, Jesus' resurrection is the crucial doctrine of the church. Without the resurrection of Jesus, the faith of Christian believers is futile and useless (1 Corinthians 15:14), and the church is based on fraud. The doctrine of the resurrection emphasizes the flesh-and-blood side of Jesus. As a man Jesus died, but God raised Him *from the dead*. As *the firstborn* of the resurrection, He will lead all believers to victory over death.

Third, Paul states that all of these things work to establish Christ's *preeminence*. This word means first place or highest rank. There is no authority in the church that exceeds the authority of Christ in any matter. It is His church, not ours. We must remind ourselves that we exist as the church for His service and for His glory.

D. Jesus: Dwelling of Deity (v. 19)

19. For it pleased the Father that in him should all fulness dwell.

This verse lifts up the doctrine of the incarnation. Although we may not be able to understand this teaching completely, it is a foundational doctrine for the Christian faith. This is the belief that the deity of God was present in the person of a man, Jesus of Nazareth.

Paul adds more detail to this statement in Colossians 2:9: "For in him dwelleth *all* the *fulness* of the Godhead bodily." Understanding the term *Godhead* allows us some insights into Paul's thought on this matter. This word is an abstract form of the word for God, thus meaning deity or divinity. This may be a less than satisfactory explanation except for Paul's important qualification that in Christ we find full deity. Jesus did not merely have a "spark of the divine," or "a more intense relationship with God." Christ was and is God. As the apostle John wrote, "the Word [Christ] was God" (John 1:1), and this Word "was made flesh and dwelt among us" (John 1:14).

E. Jesus: Peace Offering (v. 20)

20. And, having made peace through the blood of his cross, by him to reconcile all things

unto himself; by him, I say, whether they be things in earth, or things in heaven.

From the doctrine of the incarnation, Paul continues the Christ Hymn with the equally foundational doctrine of the atonement. Briefly stated Paul teaches that Jesus' death on the *cross* was an act that paid the price for human sins; it thereby returned all creation back to God. [See question #2, page 128.]

There are many aspects to the doctrine of the atonement, and Paul draws on three of them here. First, the cross of Christ served as a type of peace offering to God. The biblical concept of *peace* can mean more than lack of hostilities. In the Old Testament peace (Hebrew *shalom*) could be used in the sense of "satisfaction of a debt." For example, a landowner who failed to cover a pit, thus allowing his neighbor's ox to fall to its death, was obligated to give the neighbor a new ox. To do so was to make peace with the neighbor (see Exodus 21:34, where the idea of payment is represented by the Hebrew *shalom*). Elsewhere, Paul teaches that Christ is our peace, having breached the wall of separation between Jews and Gentiles and between God and humanity (Ephesians 2:11-22).

Second, Paul uses the concept of Jesus' death as a *blood* offering for sins. The Bible teaches that without the shedding of blood there is no forgiveness of sins (Hebrews 9:22). This is the essence of Paul's "preaching of the cross" (1 Corinthians 1:18), that the blood of Jesus serves as an ultimate, once-for-all sin offering (see Hebrews 10:10).

Third, this verse speaks of the atonement in terms of reconciliation. Two parties who were once on good terms but who have been alienated from one another need to be reconciled. They are reconciled when the cause for alienation is removed. We were alienated from God because of sin but reconciled when Jesus' death covered our sin (see Romans 5:10). What is even more remarkable is that Jesus' death does more than *reconcile* humankind with God; it also reconciles all of creation—*all things . . . whether they be things in earth, or things in heaven*—with its creator.

II. Human Savior for Humanity (Colossians 1:21-23)

Verse 20 marks the end of the Christ Hymn. Paul now turns to its direct implications for his readers.

A. Jesus: Justifier and Sanctifier (vv. 21, 22)

21, 22. And you, that were sometime alienated and enemies in your mind by wicked works,

Visual for
Lesson 1

Use this map to help your students gain a geographical perspective of this quarter's lessons.

yet now hath he reconciled in the body of his flesh through death, to present you holy and unblamable and unreprovable in his sight.

Paul reminds his readers of our side of the problem: we are the ones who caused the alienation by our sin *(wicked works)*. Our movement away from God brings to mind the story of the wife who was riding with her husband in their big old car with the old-fashioned bench seats. She asked, "Honey, why don't we sit next to each other like we did on our honeymoon?" Her husband, who was driving, answered, "Dear, I haven't moved." Alienation from God is not due to any failing or moving away on His part. The moving away has been entirely our work.

When we are *reconciled* to God through the blood of Jesus, He is able to present us completely restored before the throne of God. We are *holy* (cleansed of sin), *unblamable* (without fault), and *unreprovable* (not accused of any wrongdoing). [See question #3, page 128.]

ALIENATED . . . RECONCILED

Our family likes to watch old movies. One fond memory is the 1968 comedy *With Six You Get Egg Roll*, starring Doris Day and Brian Keith. Day is a widow with three boys; Keith is a widower with one daughter. Day and Keith meet and the chemistry begins to flow. At one point Keith breaks a date with her in order to go to a birthday party. But when Day sees him at a restaurant with a much younger woman, she is furious—not knowing that the young woman is his daughter and her birthday party is at the restaurant.

After that is cleared up, Day and Keith get married. When Keith discovers that his daughter has to spend much of her day doing housework while Day's son plays basketball, the fireworks begin anew! He moves out of the house, and their relationship is on the rocks again. Eventually the misunderstandings are straightened out, and they live happily ever after.

Alienated, and then reconciled. Unfortunately, our alienation from God was more than a simple misunderstanding. We sinned, and this created a great gulf between us and God. But God pursued us. It took the sacrifice of His Son to unite us once again with God. It was that great sacrifice that makes it possible for us to live happily—and eternally—ever after.   —J. B. N.

B. Jesus: Core of the Gospel (v. 23)

23. If ye continue in the faith grounded and settled, and be not moved away from the hope of the gospel, which ye have heard, and which was preached to every creature which is under heaven; whereof I Paul am made a minister.

Here Paul speaks of *the faith* as the body of doctrine that is to be believed by Christians (see Jude 3). If we depart from the central doctrines of Jesus Christ as contained in the Christ Hymn, then we abandon the faith (see 1 Timothy 4:1). The danger that is in view here is not that we will quit believing altogether, but that our beliefs will become false as we drift into heresy. [See question #4, page 128.]

While Paul's books may have different emphases, they are consistent concerning these central doctrines, as is all of the New Testament. This is why we are able to use verses from one part of Scripture to help us understand a verse in another book. This is known as the "analogy of faith," since Scripture never fights with itself. It speaks with one voice in teaching us about the implications of Jesus' life, death, and resurrection. These teachings are both secure and timeless, serving with equal value every generation of Christian believers. [See question #5, page 128.]

Conclusion

A. The Ageless Jesus

"Jesus Christ the same yesterday, and today, and for ever" (Hebrews 13:8). Some things about the church must change as culture and society changes. For example, no churches in the first century AD had Web sites or parking lots. However, the church has no need for new, updated doctrines about Jesus. Those doctrines as taught in the New Testament were adequate for Paul's churches and they remain sufficient for ours.

Church history tells sad stories of teachers who wanted to redefine what the church taught about Jesus. Gnosticism and Arianism were only two of several threats that the church battled to retain "the faith": the true doctrines concerning Christ. Until Jesus returns there will be false Christs (Mark 13:22). These may be flesh-and-blood impostors. They may be teachers presenting warped views of the nature of Christ and His work of salvation. Church leaders should always be on guard against the infiltration of such false teachings into the congregation (see Titus 1:9).

B. The Christ of Christmas

Paul never tells the Christmas story of baby Jesus, either in his letters or in his recorded preaching in the book of Acts. (The closest he comes is in Galatians 4:4.) Yet Paul would agree that the basic story of a baby born in Bethlehem is essential to our understanding of who Jesus is.

Jesus did not appear on the scene as a full-grown man, like gods of Greek mythology. The story of Jesus is an account both of human frailty and of divine, awe-inspiring power. He was born on the road and cradled in a feed trough. Yet He was worshiped by wise kings, and His birth was heralded by an angel choir. Even at His birth He was truly God and truly human.

C. Prayer

Father God we stand in awe of the mystery of the true nature of Your Son, Jesus Christ. May we rest assured in the knowledge that Jesus' blood has purchased our salvation. We pray this in the name of Jesus, amen.

D. Thought to Remember

Jesus was both fully human and fully divine.

Home Daily Bible Readings

Monday, Nov. 27—An Angel Promises (Luke 1:5-20)

Tuesday, Nov. 28—Elisabeth Is with Child (Luke 1:21-25)

Wednesday, Nov. 29—Zechariah Praises God (Luke 1:67-80)

Thursday, Nov. 30—John Prepares the Way (Matthew 3:1-6)

Friday, Dec. 1—A Son Is Promised (Isaiah 9:2-7)

Saturday, Dec. 2—Into the Kingdom of His Son (Colossians 1:9-14)

Sunday, Dec. 3—Who Jesus Is (Colossians 1:15-23)

Learning by Doing

This page contains an alternative lesson plan emphasizing learning activities. Classes desiring such student involvement will find these suggestions helpful.

Learning Goals

After participating in this lesson, each student will be able to:

1. Tell how the creation is dependent on the creator.

2. Explain why Paul emphasized the doctrine of Christ in his battle against heresy in the church.

3. Write a prayer that expresses worship for Jesus in His role as creator.

Into the Lesson

Before class begins display a large wall sign titled, "The Path to Heresy." Begin the lesson by asking for a definition of *heresy*. After the discussion summarize and write on the sign the definition(s) that your class comes up with. Compare it (or them) with the dictionary definition given in the lesson Introduction. Then ask for examples of heresy within modern Christianity.

Make a transition by reminding the class that there were heresies in the church of the New Testament that still persist today. Deliver a brief lecture to include discussion of gnosticism and Arianism, based on the lesson Introduction.

Into the Word

This activity is an opportunity to develop leadership in your class. Assign the following phrases to eight class members during the week before class. Ask each to be ready to give a brief definition or explanation of his or her assigned phrase. Give each of these students a copy of appropriate part of the lesson commentary. Encourage them to read the lesson Introduction to help them understand the significance of their assigned phrases.

The eight phrases to assign are *The image of the invisible God* (v. 15); *The firstborn* (v. 15); *By him all things were created* (v. 16); *He is before all things* (v. 17); *The preeminence* (v. 18); *In him should all fulness dwell* (v. 19); *Made peace through blood* (v. 20); *Reconcile all things unto himself* (v. 20). (If your class is small, you may wish to double up on verses 16, 17 and/or verses 19, 20.)

Before asking the assigned students to share their findings, distribute to all class members a copy of the printed text with each of the phrases mentioned above underlined. Have a wide margin available for students to write notes. Read Colossians 1:15-20 together and ask the assigned class members to help clarify the phrases mentioned above.

Next tell the class that in verses 21-23 Paul explains the implications for this wonderful snapshot of Jesus. Read these verses and ask the following discussion questions:

1. How would you describe *reconciliation* in everyday language to an unbeliever?

2. How is this a "before and after" story?

3. What are the differences among, and implications of, the three words concerning how Christ presents us to God as "holy," "unblamable," and "unreprovable"?

4. What does the word *if* imply in verse 23?

Into Life

Allow class members to form small groups of no more than five people each. Each group will choose to do either *Activity #1* or *Activity #2* below. Because you may not know how many groups will choose to do each activity, it will be necessary to have several sheets of each of the following instructions available. You will also need several hymnals and chorus books for Activity #1.

Activity #1. Your task is to select hymns or choruses for a worship service that will focus on the supremacy of Jesus Christ. Today's printed text will be the text for the sermon in this service. Find several hymns and choruses that speak of some of the qualities or characteristics of Jesus that are mentioned in today's study. Be ready to share with the rest of the class the reasons you chose these songs based on the specific lines or words in the songs that reflect today's text.

Activity #2. Your task is to write a prayer of worship based on the concepts of today's printed text. The prayer of worship will be incorporated into the worship service that those doing Activity #1 are working on. It will become the prayer that many class members will pray throughout the week; for this, have someone from your group go to the church office and make a photocopy of the prayer for each member of the class.

Allow time for discussion. Make sure to give each group equal time.

Let's Talk It Over

The questions on this page are designed to promote discussion of the lesson by the class and to encourage application of the lesson Scriptures. The answers provided are only discussion starters. Let your class talk it over from there.

1. One power struggle within a church is one too many! This may be one reason why Paul reinforced the preeminence of Christ in verse 18. How would you compare and contrast Christ's role within the church with the roles that church leaders are to fill? How well do your church's leaders recognize what their roles should be? How can you support them?

This is an issue that needs to tug persistently at the hearts of those who have leadership responsibilities in the local church. Christ's role is unique in that He alone provides the means by which individuals can come to know God. No church leader can bring an individual into God's presence directly without Christ's intervention. That is why Christians are called upon to be servant-leaders of the church rather than Chief Executive Officers of God's corporation.

2. Colossians 1:20 identifies the cross as the means through which peace entered the world. How do you explain this to an unbeliever? What roadblocks might you expect?

In 1 Corinthians 1:23 Paul identifies the crucifixion as a stumbling block to Jews and foolishness to Greeks. That skepticism and confusion still exists. As He has done on other occasions, God used a very unusual procedure to accomplish His purposes.

Possible roadblocks are almost too numerous to mention. Many will not see the relevance of much of anything that happened 2,000 years ago. Whatever the resistance we need to help the non-Christian to see that it was only the shedding of Christ's blood that allows us to come back into a proper relationship with God. This is so because Jesus' death paid the penalty for sin that God had decreed. No matter what illustrations or analogies we use in our discussion, this core idea must be present.

3. In our new relationship with Christ, we are to be "holy and unblamable and unreprovable." What are some difficulties that these standards have caused for you? How did you (or how will you) overcome these problems?

This new walk with Christ is certain to be misunderstood by friends and those who do not understand the calling we have received. Folks are going to be watching to see how quickly we will fall from the standards we have accepted. They will be quick to note what they see as hypocrisy. They may resent our holy choices or exclude us from their activities. They may accuse us of being "holier than thou."

We may also kick ourselves when we stray from doing what we know is right. However, we should notice that the passage refers to being blameless in God's sight. As much as we want to create a good witness, it is God's approval that is most important.

4. Verse 23 begins with a conditional "if-statement." What things are most likely to cause you to stray from the faith? How do you guard against these?

This is a very personal question. What sways one person may not be a factor at all in the life of another. Some of the differences may lie in our personal heritage or the environment in which we currently live or work. The challenge is the same to all: we must be faithful in our calling because it is our eternal hope!

5. How do you embrace as your own Paul's calling as a "minister" to preach "to every creature which is under heaven"? Or do you see this calling to be relegated to a select few rather than being a general call to all Christians? Explain.

There is no doubt that Jesus called Paul to a unique apostolic ministry. Some things that Jesus required Paul to do were for Paul and Paul alone.

Yet Jesus issues general calls to all Christians today through the pages of Scripture (Matthew 28:19, 20). There undoubtedly are specific calls that God lays on the hearts of some Christians to serve in unique ministry roles. God's call for a fellow Christian to serve as a long-term missionary in a far-off land is not necessarily God's call for you to do the same. (God may be calling you to support that missionary financially.) We can discern God's call to us in a general way through His Word. Discerning a specific call to a particular ministry takes much prayer and an awareness of open and closed doors of opportunity.

What God Says About Jesus

December 10
Lesson 2

DEVOTIONAL READING: Luke 1:46-55.

BACKGROUND SCRIPTURE: Hebrews 1.

PRINTED TEXT: Hebrews 1:1-9.

Hebrews 1:1-9

1 God, who at sundry times and in divers manners spake in time past unto the fathers by the prophets,

2 Hath in these last days spoken unto us by his Son, whom he hath appointed heir of all things, by whom also he made the worlds;

3 Who being the brightness of his glory, and the express image of his person, and upholding all things by the word of his power, when he had by himself purged our sins, sat down on the right hand of the Majesty on high;

4 Being made so much better than the angels, as he hath by inheritance obtained a more excellent name than they.

5 For unto which of the angels said he at any time, Thou art my Son, this day have I begotten thee? And again, I will be to him a Father, and he shall be to me a Son?

6 And again, when he bringeth in the first-begotten into the world, he saith, And let all the angels of God worship him.

7 And of the angels he saith, Who maketh his angels spirits, and his ministers a flame of fire.

8 But unto the Son he saith, Thy throne, O God, is for ever and ever: a sceptre of righteousness is the sceptre of thy kingdom.

9 Thou hast loved righteousness, and hated iniquity; therefore God, even thy God, hath anointed thee with the oil of gladness above thy fellows.

GOLDEN TEXT: God, who at sundry times and in divers manners spake in time past
unto the fathers by the prophets, hath in these last days spoken unto us
by his Son, whom he hath appointed heir of all things,
by whom also he made the worlds.—Hebrews 1:1, 2.

Jesus Christ: A Portrait of God
Unit 1: Christ, the Image of God
(Lessons 1-5)

Lesson Aims

After participating in this lesson, each student will be able to:

1. List ways that Jesus is superior to angels.

2. Predict how the church could be damaged if the natures of Jesus and angels are misunderstood.

3. Write a testimony that articulates how his or her faith in Christ is stronger because of today's lesson.

Lesson Outline

INTRODUCTION

  A. The Self-Revealing God

  B. Lesson Background

 I. JESUS: GOD'S SELF-EXPRESSION (Hebrews 1:1-3)

  A. Revelation Before Jesus (v. 1)

  B. Revelation in Jesus (v. 2a)

  C. Revelation Through Jesus (vv. 2b, 3)

    On the Right Hand

II. JESUS: SUPERIOR TO CREATED BEINGS (Hebrews 1:4-9)

  A. Name Above Angels' (vv. 4, 5)

  B. Worthy of Worship (v. 6)

  C. Rules in Heaven (vv. 7-9)

    What Do You Love?

CONCLUSION

  A. Personal Revelations

  B. Prayer

  C. Thought to Remember

Introduction

A. The Self-Revealing God

Have you ever been part of a "secret sisters" program (or the men's counterpart)? In this type of program, each participating member is assigned secretly the name of another woman. The secret sister then sends notes and gifts to her counterpart during a set period of time. When time is up a party is held in which the secret sisters are revealed. It can be a fun way to get to know another person and to practice spiritual disciplines such as generosity and encouragement.

Revelation is based on the idea that something hidden has been uncovered and can now be known. In the case of God, we should remember that we know nothing about Him except that which He has chosen to reveal to us. God is sovereign even with regard to our knowledge about Him. There is much about God that we do not know but might like to know. We can speculate on such things, but we know with certainty only what God has graciously chosen to reveal to us.

Reliable knowledge about God is not discovered by accident or chance. It has come to humanity through the process of revelation. We know about God because He is the God who reveals himself. Our knowledge of God is not due to our brilliance or our worthiness.

In this sense human knowledge about God is *progressive*. This means that God reveals himself in stages. There are some striking examples of this in the Old Testament. In his experience with the near-sacrifice of his son, Abraham learned that God is both demanding of faithful obedience and ultimately merciful (Genesis 22). At the burning bush God revealed to Moses that His name is I Am. This places God outside human existence controlled by time (Exodus 3). In his vision of God on His throne in Heaven, Isaiah learned that God seeks those who will speak for Him, delivering even difficult messages (Isaiah 6). In his sufferings Job learned that God is great and that he (Job) had no right to challenge God's actions (Job 38). Through his experience of adultery and the death of a son, David learned that only God can truly cleanse a person's heart and renew the human spirit (Psalm 51).

To speak of revelation as *progressive* or *ongoing* has certain dangers, however. Christians who are faithful to the Bible need not look to modern "prophets" to reveal more and more about God. Historically the church has believed that the Old Testament serves to prepare for God's ultimate revelation in Jesus. The New Testament is the testimony of this revelation in Christ.

Today's Scripture text teaches us that God has revealed himself in His Son, Jesus Christ. In other words, God has told us everything about himself that we need to know for our earthly existence. We can assume that we will understand God even more fully when we join Him in Heaven. But for now we have no need to know more than that which has been revealed in the Old and New Testaments.

B. Lesson Background

While there is some early tradition that concludes that the book of Hebrews was written by the apostle Paul, many scholars today do not accept this conclusion. The book does not begin with Paul's personal name, as all his other letters do. Furthermore, the author of the book seems to place himself in the second generation of Christian believers, not as an apostle (see Hebrews 2:3). It is doubtful that Paul would do this, since elsewhere he defends his apostleship vigorously. For these reasons and others, the great scholar Origen (AD 185–254) concluded, "Who wrote Hebrews, only God knows."

The anonymous nature of this book in no way lessens its importance or authority as a major source for our understanding of Christ. The author appears to have been writing to a community of Jewish Christians who were in danger of abandoning their faith in Jesus in order to return to the community of the Jewish synagogue. The author addresses this potential apostasy by carefully laying out the roles of Jesus in relationship to the Old Testament Scriptures. Hebrews is a uniquely significant New Testament book, for it delves into explanations about Jesus that are not found anywhere else in the Bible.

Hebrews has two primary functions overall. First, it defends the church's teachings about Jesus from outside attacks. Hebrews in particular shows that Jesus is superior to the older system of the Jews.

Second, Hebrews shows that Jesus and the Old Testament system are not in conflict with each other. Rather, the Christian system grows out of and is a fulfillment of the Jewish system. Hebrews does this by using many Old Testament texts and allusions to show that Christians should understand themselves as heirs to a faith that began long before the first century AD.

I. Jesus: God's Self-Expression (Hebrews 1:1-3)

Hebrews begins with no preliminary material. Instead it plunges immediately into its main topic: a doctrinal presentation of the nature and role of Christ in relationship to previous revelations of God.

A. Revelation Before Jesus (v. 1)

1. God, who at sundry times and in divers manners spake in time past unto the fathers by the prophets.

The author begins by describing the partial nature of revelation before Christ. Two rare and unusual Greek adverbs, translated *at sundry times* and *in divers manners*, present themselves. Literally, the author is saying that God spoke "in many parts" and "in many ways." Before Jesus, God's revelation of himself came in bits and pieces, delivered sporadically over a long period of time.

These revelations of God were delivered to *the fathers* of Israel's history. The messages came via God's spokesmen, *the prophets.* The author of Hebrews does not minimize the importance of this prophetic voice. Rather, the author wants the readers to realize that there is incompleteness if we stop with the Old Testament. The Old Testament tells of many people who were commended for their faithfulness, yet "received not the promise" (Hebrews 11:39). Thus they were at a certain disadvantage compared with Christians.

B. Revelation in Jesus (v. 2a)

2a. Hath in these last days spoken unto us by his Son.

By *last days* the author is not intending a reference to the final few days or weeks just before the second coming of Jesus. Rather, *last days* refers to the final period of human history, the era of Christ. This period is characterized by a new age of revelation. No longer do we receive our knowledge of God in bits and pieces. God now speaks through *his Son.*

There are two major implications to this statement. First, the ministry of Jesus was strategically chosen by God as a way to reveal himself. As John wrote, by experiencing Jesus, "We beheld his glory, the glory as of the only begotten of the Father" (John 1:14). Later in this same Gospel, Jesus declared, "He that hath seen me hath seen the Father" (14:9).

The second implication is that Jesus is the perfect and complete revelation of the Father. The Old Testament prophets, for all their virtues, were able to give only a fragmentary picture of who God is. God has revealed himself fully by sending His Son; we neither need nor should expect further revelation about God while we're still in our earthly existence. Therefore Jesus is the culmination of God's revelation about himself in this, the final period of human history.

C. Revelation Through Jesus (vv. 2b, 3)

2b. Whom he hath appointed heir of all things, by whom also he made the worlds.

Understanding the exact relationship between Jesus and God is difficult. One of the best ways to understand it is the frequent biblical description of the Father-Son relationship. This passage matches this description in two ways. First, as *heir of all things*, Jesus is the unique Son of God. He shares this level of sonship with no one else. We are able to become sons and daughters of God through faith (John 1:12; Galatians 3:26), but not in the way that Jesus is God's Son. [See question #1, page 136.]

This unique relationship is further explained by the second description: Jesus as co-creator with the Father. In the ancient world a son commonly worked with his father in the family business. The Son has worked with the Father, even in creating the universe. This serves as a further confirmation of Jesus' sonship and also affirms His preexistence. The Son is not a created being but rather the creator himself.

3. Who being the brightness of his glory, and the express image of his person, and upholding all things by the word of his power, when he had by himself purged our sins, sat down on the right hand of the Majesty on high.

To define and explain the true nature of the Christ completely is impossible because of the limitations of human language and understanding. However, the author gives four powerful images to help us.

First, the Son is the *brightness* of the Father's *glory*. This could be translated as the "reflection of God's glory." In this the author emphasizes that Jesus was a visible revelation of God. The glory of God in Jesus was partially uncovered at the transfiguration for the disciples to see (Mark 9:2, 3). The miracles of Jesus also were partial revelations of God's glory (John 2:11).

Second, the Son is the *express image of* the Father's *person*. The original, Greek word used is the one from which we get our English word *character*. In the ancient world it was used to describe an exact imprint of a coin, a complete and faithful reproduction stamped from the original, engraved coin die. The author is saying that Jesus is a full and faithful representation of the Father, without flaw or defect. [See question #2, page 136.]

Third, the description *upholding all things by the word of his power* expands upon Jesus' role as creator. This includes the power to *sustain* His creation (see Colossians 1:17, last week's lesson).

How to Say It

DEUTERONOMY. Due-ter-*ahn*-uh-me.
GALATIANS. Guh-*lay*-shunz.
HEBREWS. *Hee*-brews.
MESSIAH. Meh-*sigh*-uh.
MOSES. *Mo*-zes or *Mo*-zez.
ORIGEN. *Or*-uh-jen.
PHARAOH. *Fair*-o or *Fay*-roe.
SEPTUAGINT. Sep-*too*-ih-jent.
SOLOMON. *Sol*-o-mun.
SYNAGOGUE. *sin*-uh-gog.
THEOPHANOS (Greek). The-*ah*-fan-us.

In some religions the creator and the sustainer are different gods. The fully revealed truth is that the Son shares in both functions.

Fourth, the author reminds his readers that after Jesus' death and resurrection, He ascended to Heaven to be seated at *the right hand* of the throne of God. This presents the Son as a ruler and judge equal to the Father. It also shifts the focus to the realm of Heaven, where the position of Jesus is far superior to that of any angel. This is the next topic of discussion.

ON THE RIGHT HAND

In the English language the phrase *right hand* is rich in symbolism. It can mean the hand that is normally stronger (than the left). The *Oxford English Dictionary* cites a source from the year 1000 with this connotation. Another meaning is to symbolize friendship or alliance. This connotation is cited as early as 1591. We normally shake hands with the right hand.

A third meaning is to indicate a person of usefulness or importance, an indispensable or efficient helper. We use the phrase *right-hand man,* a usage that goes back to 1537. In 1863 General Thomas J. "Stonewall" Jackson's left arm was amputated after a wound (which eventually proved fatal); to this General Robert E. Lee exclaimed, "You have lost your left arm, but I have lost my right!"

A similar meaning is that the right hand is the position of honor. This is probably the meaning intended in Hebrews 1:3. After He had fulfilled His task on earth, Jesus ascended and was seated at the right hand of the Father. Jesus represents the right hand of God in all ways—in strength, in alliance, and in honor. Do we hold Jesus in as much honor as the Father does?   —J. B. N.

II. Jesus: Superior to Created Beings (Hebrews 1:4-9)

Recently we have experienced a renewed fascination with angels. Television programs, movies, and novels are filled with fanciful accounts of divine visitations. Cards, pictures, and artwork have used angels as a decorative motif.

The Bible has comparatively little information about angels. We know that they are a class of beings with supernatural powers. They serve at the pleasure of God. We even know the names of a couple of them: Gabriel (Luke 1:19) and Michael (Revelation 12:7).

While our knowledge of angels is limited, some things about them are very clear in the Bible. First, they are not to be worshiped. Worship is for God alone (see Revelation 19:10). Second, Jesus Christ is not some type of glorified angel. He is the divine Son and far superior to any angel. Apparently the author of Hebrews is aware of misunderstandings related to both of these things. He seeks to correct them in the following verses.

A. Name Above Angels' (vv. 4, 5)

4. Being made so much better than the angels, as he hath by inheritance obtained a more excellent name than they.

What does your *name* mean? I recently learned that the name "Tiffany" does not mean "expensive jewelry." It comes from the Greek word *Theophanos,* meaning "presence of the divine." What a powerful name for a baby girl!

The author's first point in showing that Jesus is superior to *angels* has to do with His name. We treat names casually in the modern world. We use nicknames, shortened names, informal names, and other variations. In the biblical world, however, names were highly significant. They were chosen carefully and usually had a clear meaning. For example, Pharaoh's daughter named her adopted baby "Moses" (meaning *drawn*) because she "drew" him out of the water (Exodus 2:10). The *more excellent name* in mind here is not "Jesus" or "Christ" but "Son," as will be explained in the following verses.

5. For unto which of the angels said he at any time, Thou art my Son, this day have I begotten thee? And again, I will be to him a Father, and he shall be to me a Son?

The author draws upon two well-known Old Testament passages to make his point: 2 Samuel 7:14 and Psalm 2:7. Jesus is designated *Son* by God himself. This is a name and (more importantly) a title that Jesus shares with no one else, not even angels. [See question #3, page 136.] Although these verses probably applied to Kings David and Solomon in their original context, Jesus had discussed this question during His ministry (see Matthew 22:42-45). In so doing He had shown himself to be the ultimate Son of God, superior to David (compare Acts 2:25-32).

B. Worthy of Worship (v. 6)

6. And again, when he bringeth in the first-begotten into the world, he saith, And let all the angels of God worship him.

The author uses another Old Testament quotation to show the readers what it means to be the Son of the Father in Heaven: He is worthy of worship. See Revelation 5:13, where worship includes both God and the Lamb (Jesus).

Visual for
Lesson 2

As a background sketch point to this poster and ask for names of prophets who came before Christ.

The source of this quotation is probably the Greek (Septuagint) version of Deuteronomy 32:43. In that version heavenly beings are commanded to *worship* God. No creature, including *angels,* is exempt from the obligation of worshiping God and worshiping His Son.

C. Rules in Heaven (vv. 7-9)

7. And of the angels he saith, Who maketh his angels spirits, and his ministers a flame of fire.

The author now quotes Psalm 104:4 to define the glorious function of *angels.* They are powerful spiritual beings who are servants of God. To describe them as *a flame of fire* reminds us of passages such as Genesis 3:24 and Exodus 3:2.

8, 9. But unto the Son he saith, Thy throne, O God, is for ever and ever: a sceptre of righteousness is the sceptre of thy kingdom. Thou hast loved righteousness, and hated iniquity; therefore God, even thy God, hath anointed thee with the oil of gladness above thy fellows.

The author now uses his most formidable quotation: Psalm 45:6, 7. David and Solomon had been promised an eternal throne or dynasty (see Psalm 89:4, 29, 36). But neither of these esteemed kings was ever promised he would be a god. Thus their promise of an eternal *throne* is fulfilled only in Jesus. [See question #4, page 136.]

There is another important detail in this quotation that should not be missed. When God the Father anoints God the Son, He literally makes Him Christ. The term *Christ* (or its Old Testament counterpart, *Messiah*) means "Anointed One." Jesus is not a self-anointed messiah. He is anointed by God for a special ministry, the most important ministry in the history of the world.

Jesus himself proclaimed, "The Spirit of the Lord . . . hath anointed me to preach the gospel" (Luke 4:18).

The sweeping claims about Jesus Christ in this beautiful text still serve today as guideposts in our quest to know Him more fully. He is the unique Son of God, the ultimate revelation of God the Father, the co-creator and sustainer of our world. [See question #5, page 136.]

WHAT DO YOU LOVE?

When I was a youngster, I used to love going to my grandfather's farm. There were fascinating animals, and the wooded area at the rear of the farm was an exciting place to a suburban kid. When I got older, I used to love riding my bike and exploring residential and factory areas several miles away. I loved eating banana splits. I also loved playing baseball; the kids on our block often would play several hours every day, all summer, straight through the heat and humidity of July and August.

In my adult years my tastes have changed. Now I love to sit in a comfortable chair with a tall, cold glass of caffeine-free diet cola and a big bowl of popcorn, and read a book. Other people love to go to NASCAR races. I have a friend who loves to participate in Civil War reenactments. Some people love watching sunsets. Others love taking walks along the beach or in the woods.

What do you love? Jesus loved righteousness. That's a much more lofty value, isn't it? We tend to love things. Jesus loved virtues. He loved doing God's will. He loved doing what was right in God's sight. When He was baptized, He said it was to fulfill all righteousness. He did not live just to fulfill His own selfish desires or seek His own pleasures; He wanted to fulfill God's will in all things. He loved righteousness. Do we?

—J. B. N.

Conclusion

A. Personal Revelations

A recent newspaper story claimed that a majority of people have hidden aspects to their lives that would embarrass them if revealed. The classic example of this is the traveling salesman who has two wives and families residing in different cities. He may operate for years by spending part of each week at the different locations. When such arrangements are made public, the result is tragic, with strong feelings of betrayal.

Many people, however, have "dirty little secrets" on a smaller scale. The ability to remain anonymous in our electronic age has led many into online pornography, affairs, and other secret yet sinful behavior. An overemphasis on the "right to privacy" has proved to be a stumbling block to some Christians, even Christian leaders. The secular press delights in uncovering these transgressions and revealing the hypocritical lifestyles of guilty believers. There is nothing more comical to the critics of the church than the preacher who rails against adultery on Sunday morning and visits his mistress Sunday night.

There are some things about God that remain hidden to us. There are, however, no foul details that are hidden. God is pure and holy and righteous consistently, without any deviation at any time.

We can learn much about God from studying the Old Testament, but even more by looking at Jesus. The life of Jesus shows us that God is loving and compassionate. God loved us enough to send His only Son to redeem the world as an offering for human sin (see John 3:16, 17; Romans 5:8). God's self-revelation in Jesus Christ is the sure foundation of all Christian faith and hope. This stands as a great assurance and comfort to all believers.

B. Prayer

Holy Father, thank You for sending Your Son to help us understand You better. Because of His death, we need never doubt Your love for us. He has revealed Your heart to us, and we rejoice in that revelation. We pray in His name, the name far above any angel's, amen.

C. Thought to Remember

Jesus is God's ultimate revelation and is far superior to the angels.

Home Daily Bible Readings

Monday, Dec. 4—Jesus, the Promised One (Matthew 12:15-21)

Tuesday, Dec. 5—You Will Name Him Jesus (Luke 1:26-33)

Wednesday, Dec. 6—Jesus, Son of God (Luke 1:34-38)

Thursday, Dec. 7—Mary Sings Her Joy (Luke 1:46-55)

Friday, Dec. 8—Listen to Him! (Matthew 17:1-5)

Saturday, Dec. 9—God's Anointed Son (Hebrews 1:1-9)

Sunday, Dec. 10—More Than the Angels (Hebrews 1:10-14)

Learning by Doing

This page contains an alternative lesson plan emphasizing learning activities.
Classes desiring such student involvement will find these suggestions helpful.

Learning Goals

After participating in this lesson, each student will be able to:

1. List ways that Jesus is superior to angels.

2. Predict how the church could be damaged if the natures of Jesus and angels are misunderstood.

3. Write a testimony that articulates how his or her faith in Christ is stronger because of today's lesson.

Into the Lesson

Fill the classroom with as many pictures, images, and knickknacks of angels that you can find. Also attach two posters to the wall with the following headings: "What We Know About Angels" and "Angels at Work in the Bible."

As class begins, appoint two "scribes" to be ready to write on these posters as class members brainstorm answers. Ask students to share what they know about the nature of angels and to cite appearances of angels in the Bible. After the exercise ask students what songs they know that include references to angels (examples: "Angels from the Realms of Glory," "Angels We Have Heard on High"). Ask, "What do those songs teach us about angels, if anything?"

Make the transition to Bible study by saying, "While the world has a special fascination with angels, we really don't know a lot about them. But the existence of angels becomes part of a great revelation about the nature of Jesus. That revelation about Jesus, as it speaks of His distinction from angels, is found in today's text."

Into the Word

Give to four study groups copies of their respective instructions below and copies of their assigned passages from the lesson commentary. Also give Groups #2 and #3 poster board and markers. Ask each group to appoint a spokesperson to report the group's conclusions. Larger classes may have more than one group working on each task. Keep group sizes to five people or fewer.

Group #1. Your task is to give a report on how God revealed himself progressively before the arrival of Jesus (Hebrews 1:1). You will find the lesson commentary on verse 1 and the Introduction to the commentary to be helpful. Also discuss the dangers of believing in progressive (ongoing) revelation after Christ.

Group #2. Your task is to focus on verse 2a of our printed text as you describe how God has revealed himself in Jesus. Write on the board the two major implications of this verse for our understanding of Christ; be ready to explain these to the class. Illustrate on the poster board each implication, if possible. The attached lesson commentary will be helpful.

Group #3. Your task is to report how God has revealed himself through Jesus' many roles and attributes (vv. 2b, 3). The lesson commentary on these verses will be helpful. Write the four images of Christ from verse 3 on the poster board and be ready to explain them to the class.

Group #4. Your group will discuss the significance of angels as the writer of Hebrews uses them to illustrate the superiority of Jesus. The attached lesson commentary will be helpful. Be sure to include remarks about the significance of Jesus' name (v. 4), the significance of Jesus' being called God's Son (v. 5), the issue of who is worshiped (v. 6), and the heavenly roles of Jesus and angels (vv. 7-9).

Allow each group to share its conclusions with the class.

Into Life

Use the following discussion questions to help make this lesson personal. Say, "The focus of today's lesson is on Jesus rather than on angels. Nevertheless, we learn some things about angels and their relationship with Jesus. What have you learned about angels in this study? Why do you think it is important that today's church understands the relationship of Jesus and angels? Why would God include this significant teaching in His everlasting Word? Look at verses 2-4. Of all the qualities and notations about Jesus mentioned in these three verses, which grabs your attention today? Why?"

Give each student an index card. Remind the class that several issues have been discussed that are important to their faith. Ask class members to jot down key words they could use in a testimony about how their faith is stronger because of this study. Allow volunteers to share their thoughts.

Let's Talk It Over

The questions on this page are designed to promote discussion of the lesson by the class and to encourage application of the lesson Scriptures. The answers provided are only discussion starters. Let your class talk it over from there.

1. How does the concept of Jesus as an heir help you understand more about Him and draw closer to Him? How do we bring this imagery from the first century into the twenty-first?

Today's concept of an heir is more limited than it was in the first century. In ancient societies fathers and sons often worked side by side to develop the family business. Even though the ownership technically belonged to the father, a son knew that his efforts would be rewarded eventually by what he would inherit.

Today those who receive an inheritance often have not been part of developing the resources that are being passed on. Consequently they may not feel the same obligation for preserving the family's assets. The Bible establishes that we are "joint-heirs with Christ" (Romans 8:17). He invites us to help build His kingdom, and He empowers us to do so. We will inherit this kingdom (Matthew 25:34). We should stress both points when we try to explain the heir-imagery today.

2. Which parts of God's revelation of himself through Jesus Christ help you gain a better understanding of who He is?

The appearance of Jesus Christ corrected many of the misconceptions that had formed about God. He was neither distant nor uncaring. He was so devoted to His creation that He was willing to have His Son die to redeem it. Furthermore, those who saw Him in person began to understand how real holiness was to be enacted.

A distinguishing mark between a great and a mediocre piece of art is often whether the artist was able to capture the real essence of what is depicted. In Jesus we have the greatest picture of God we could possibly have! Sadly many who refused to let go of their misconceptions came to view Jesus as a mediocre piece of art, or worse.

3. Why do you think that there is such a modern interest in angels? How can we use this infatuation to point people to Jesus instead?

Modern portrayals often treat angels as if they were superheros—intervening at just the right moment to avert a tragic mistake. Some people fantasize about having someone or something that can keep them from hurting themselves.

They long for a supernatural being to avenge a wrong on their behalf. This mentality seems to be an upgraded fantasy of "Superman," who intervened to help the oppressed.

Jesus offers a far greater hope because those who follow Him are saved for eternity, not from just momentary blunders. His is the perfect and eternal protection plan! When angels speak in the Bible, they point to God and not to themselves (Revelation 19:10).

4. One who holds a sceptre (or scepter) is a king on a throne. Yet we who live in democratic societies may balk at the idea of having a king. If you live in a democratic society, what challenge does this pose for you?

Those of us who live in Western democracies have grown used to "having a say" through the ballot box. Yet any earthly ruler—whether a king or an elected representative—can disappoint us. Their power and ability to make right decisions often is limited by political concerns and incomplete ethical structures.

Jesus has no limit in either of these areas. He has the ability and intention to keep every "campaign promise." When He does He will bring us into a perfect eternity. Democracy is limited by the character strengths of the participants. Jesus' kingdom rests on His divine authority and flawless virtues.

5. Today's text directs the readers to Jesus as the true object for worship. How well is your church doing at pointing people toward Jesus? How will you help it do better?

Church growth is important, but *church health* is vital! Unfortunately, church growth is often depicted in terms of numbers alone. In an attempt to make those numbers grow, churches may shrink their focus on Jesus in favor of a well-planned, but spiritually unhealthy, sales pitch. Recently, a minister of a large church took a lengthy vacation and visited many other churches in the process. He was startled to realize how rare it was even to hear the name *Jesus* mentioned during their worship services! How can we reaffirm the central message of Jesus if we don't even mention His name?

Light That Conquers

December 17
Lesson 3

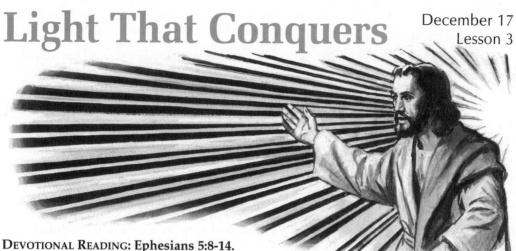

DEVOTIONAL READING: Ephesians 5:8-14.

BACKGROUND SCRIPTURE: 1 John 1:1–2:6.

PRINTED TEXT: 1 John 1:1–2:6.

1 John 1:1-10

1 That which was from the beginning, which we have heard, which we have seen with our eyes, which we have looked upon, and our hands have handled, of the Word of life;

2 (For the life was manifested, and we have seen it, and bear witness, and show unto you that eternal life, which was with the Father, and was manifested unto us;)

3 That which we have seen and heard declare we unto you, that ye also may have fellowship with us: and truly our fellowship is with the Father, and with his Son Jesus Christ.

4 And these things write we unto you, that your joy may be full.

5 This then is the message which we have heard of him, and declare unto you, that God is light, and in him is no darkness at all.

6 If we say that we have fellowship with him, and walk in darkness, we lie, and do not the truth:

7 But if we walk in the light, as he is in the light, we have fellowship one with another, and the blood of Jesus Christ his Son cleanseth us from all sin.

8 If we say that we have no sin, we deceive ourselves, and the truth is not in us.

9 If we confess our sins, he is faithful and just to forgive us our sins, and to cleanse us from all unrighteousness.

10 If we say that we have not sinned, we make him a liar, and his word is not in us.

1 John 2:1-6

1 My little children, these things write I unto you, that ye sin not. And if any man sin, we have an advocate with the Father, Jesus Christ the righteous:

2 And he is the propitiation for our sins: and not for ours only, but also for the sins of the whole world.

3 And hereby we do know that we know him, if we keep his commandments.

4 He that saith, I know him, and keepeth not his commandments, is a liar, and the truth is not in him.

5 But whoso keepeth his word, in him verily is the love of God perfected: hereby know we that we are in him.

6 He that saith he abideth in him ought himself also so to walk, even as he walked.

GOLDEN TEXT: This then is the message which we have heard of him, and declare unto you, that God is light, and in him is no darkness at all.—1 John 1:5.

Jesus Christ: A Portrait of God
Unit 1: Christ, the Image of God
(Lessons 1-5)

Lesson Aims

After participating in this lesson, each student will be able to:

1. Quote 1 John 1:8, 9 from memory.

2. Discuss the personal implications of what it means to walk as Jesus did.

3. Describe one way that he or she will walk as Jesus did.

Lesson Outline

INTRODUCTION
  A. Unresolved Guilt
  B. Lesson Background
 I. THE WALK OF FELLOWSHIP (1 John 1:1-4)
  A. Experiencing the Word of Life (vv. 1, 2)
  B. Experiencing Fellowship (v. 3)
  C. Experiencing Joy (v. 4)
 II. THE WALK IN THE LIGHT (1 John 1:5-10)
  A. Full Cleansing (vv. 5-7)
  B. Full Confession (vv. 8-10)
III. THE WALK OF LOVE (1 John 2:1-6)
  A. Jesus Our Advocate (v. 1)
    An Advocate
  B. Jesus Our Propitiation (v. 2)
  C. Jesus Our Standard (vv. 3-5)
    Keeping Commandments
  D. Jesus Our Trailblazer (v. 6)
CONCLUSION
  A. What Would Jesus Do?
  B. Prayer
  C. Thought to Remember

Introduction

A. Unresolved Guilt

She sat on the tailgate of a pickup in the parking lot, her body shuddering with silent sobs. In the nearby park the rest of the church was enjoying the annual picnic, but she didn't participate. She just sat there, hugging herself tightly, staring into nothing.

The preacher sat down next to her and asked, "What's wrong, dear? Can I help?" She gained control for a minute and blurted, "I take shower after shower, but I still feel dirty." Her problem? She had recently committed adultery with her best friend's husband. Her sin made her feel guilty and unclean, and she felt there was no way to get over it.

Counseling professionals say that unresolved guilt is one of the great problems facing troubled adults. The church knows the cause of unresolved guilt: sin. Some secular counseling theories deal with sin problems by saying, "That's who you are. Just accept yourself and be happy." They believe that clients want a therapist who will say that their sin is OK. Actually, no one needs to spend money to hear this. All you have to do is find a bunch of drinking buddies to party with, and they will tell you this for nothing!

God, who made us, knows that sin cannot be ignored or explained away. It must be confronted and overcome. Ignoring sin is a sin itself and is ultimately destructive. The apostle John has a strategy for dealing with sin that we will see today. This week's lesson uses bold symbolic language to guide us into a fellowship with God. This fellowship moves beyond paralyzing guilt to a joyous walk with the Lord.

B. Lesson Background

The apostle John was one of Jesus' closest associates. Jesus trusted him enough to task him with the care of His own mother, Mary, at the cross (see John 19:26, 27). Church tradition says that John later moved to the great city of Ephesus, taking Mary with him. There he ministered for many years, dying sometime between AD 95 and 100. His exile to Patmos is also well known (Revelation 1:9).

There are five books in the Bible written by the apostle John: the Gospel of John; 1, 2, 3 John; and Revelation. We are not sure who the intended audience was for 1 John, but apparently they were confronted with many threats to their faith. Some may have been Jewish believers who had denied Jesus in order to return to the synagogue (see 1 John 2:22). Others may have been former pagans who were being lured back into the worship of idols (see 1 John 5:21).

Still others were being tempted by an early form of the attractive heresy we call *gnosticism* (see discussion of this in the first lesson of this quarter). For this reason John emphasized his personal contact with the human Jesus, including seeing and touching (1 John 1:1).

First John deals with both extremes on the issue of sin: legalism and license. On the one hand, John confronts a legalism that refuses to recognize the sufficiency of Jesus to deal with sin. On the other hand, John will not stand for those who think that they have a license to sin because they believe that personal righteousness and life-style are unimportant (compare Romans 6:1, 2).

John's solution to both extremes is to combine forgiveness with godly living. If we try to live righteously but do not feel forgiven for those times we have failed, we will be miserable. If we glory in our forgiveness but disdain God's stan-dards of personal purity and integrity, then we have given up the possibility of a close relation-ship with God. We too will ultimately be miser-able. These issues of John's day are amazingly current for us today. The message of 1 John still has a place in the church and should be heard.

I. The Walk of Fellowship (1 John 1:1-4)

John begins his letter by outlining a dual pur-pose. First, he writes to bring about true fellow-ship among his readers. This is fellowship not only with one another but also with God (1 John 1:3). Second, he wants his readers to have hearts full of joy from hearing his words (1 John 1:4). John has no joy in knowing that some of his readers lack true, intimate fellowship. He wants to break down the barriers that destroy fellow-ship and cause joy to be stifled.

A. Experiencing the Word of Life (vv. 1, 2)

1. That which was from the beginning, which we have heard, which we have seen with our eyes, which we have looked upon, and our hands have handled, of the Word of life.

This verse contains strong echoes of the first verses of the Gospel of John. In both places the apostle opens with an affirmation of the preexis-tence of Christ: He *was from the beginning.* When the universe was created and time began, He was already there. John identifies the Christ as the *Word of life,* combining his descriptions of *Word* (John 1:1) and *life* (John 1:4). These are strong statements of Jesus' deity. [See question #1, page 144.]

How to Say It

EPHESUS. *Ef*-uh-sus.

GALATIANS. Guh-*lay*-shunz.

GNOSTICISM. *nahss*-tih-*sizz*-um (strong accent on *nahss*).

KOINONIA (Greek). koy-no-*nee*-uh.

PATMOS. *Pat*-muss.

PROPITIATION. pro-*pih*-she-*ay*-shun (strong accent on *ay*).

SYNAGOGUE. *sin*-uh-gog.

Also important are John's eyewitness reports of the humanity of Jesus. Jesus was not a divine being who merely seemed to be human. John employs three of the five senses to confirm how humanly real Jesus was: John *heard* Him, *saw* Him, and even touched Him. These things are burned into John's memory, and he shares them freely with his readers.

2. (For the life was manifested, and we have seen it, and bear witness, and show unto you that eternal life, which was with the Father, and was manifested unto us;).

John now explains further what he means when he calls Jesus the "Word of life" from verse 1. First, he describes Him as *eternal life.* In Jesus we both find and receive eternal life. Jesus is life (John 11:25), and Jesus grants life to His believ-ers (see John 10:28).

Second, true life cannot be found apart from a relationship with God the Father. One of the great promises of the Bible is that, in the end, we will be given renewed access to the tree of life that is in the presence of God (see Revelation 2:7). Believers, though, don't need to wait until Heaven to experience life. John wrote to assure us that Jesus brings us life in the here and now (John 20:31). By walking with Jesus, trusting and following Him, we will experience LIFE in all capital letters!

B. Experiencing Fellowship (v. 3)

3. That which we have seen and heard declare we unto you, that ye also may have fel-lowship with us: and truly our fellowship is with the Father, and with his Son Jesus Christ.

Fellowship is the Greek word *koinonia.* This word has the sense of "mutual sharing." Fellow-ship is not a matter of being part of an audience. How much fellowship can you have with strangers while watching a movie in the theater? *Koinonia* fellowship involves closeness and car-ing. A church with this type of fellowship will have members who care about one another far beyond the casual, "How are you doing?" on Sunday morning.

John teaches us that fellowship in the church must exist on two levels. First, we must have fel-lowship with God. God has already initiated this. He has revealed himself through His prophets and, finally, through His Son (Hebrews 1:1, 2, last week's lesson). We can know the very heart of God if we study the Scriptures.

Second, we will begin to have fellowship that is more authentic with fellow believers when we allow our relationship with God to flourish. We have much stronger mutual ties and learn to care for each other as God does. Christian fellowship, then, is experienced on both the vertical level (with God) and the horizontal level (with other believers). [See question #2, page 144.]

C. Experiencing Joy (v. 4)

4. And these things write we unto you, that your joy may be full.

John has no ulterior motives, no hidden agendas, in writing to his friends. He is seeking neither personal gain nor personal vindication over his critics. He simply wants his readers to experience the *joy* that comes from having a secure relationship with God. That result should control their relationship with others. This is the walk of fellowship. It is the abundant, joyous life (see John 10:10).

II. The Walk in the Light
(1 John 1:5-10)

Another powerful theme that 1 John shares with the Gospel of John is the image of Jesus as the light (see John 1:4; 8:12). Walking in His light implies two things for believers. First, it means that we walk without hiddenness, without private sin. We live with integrity, with no fear of public exposure of even the most intimate details of our lives. Darkness for John is equated with sin and ignorance. Walking in the light means we walk in truth and holiness.

Second, walking in the light means walking with God. God allows no darkness in His presence. The great barrier to walking with God, then, is sin. John outlines a two-part process to deal with sin: cleansing and confessing.

WHAT MESSAGE DO YOU SEND?

Visual for Lesson 3. *Point to the nativity scene that is "buried" behind the secular glitz. Ask your students if their Christmas is like this.*

A. Full Cleansing (vv. 5-7)

5. This then is the message which we have heard of him, and declare unto you, that God is light, and in him is no darkness at all.

We begin to understand personal spiritual cleansing by remembering that the cleanser (God) is without any taint of sin. John's image *God is light* means that God is pure and holy in every possible way. We should not understand this as an exclusive, absolute statement that conflicts with John's other basic declarations about God. For example, John can say "God is light" here and "God is love" later (1 John 4:8), and both statements are completely true.

6. If we say that we have fellowship with him, and walk in darkness, we lie, and do not the truth.

The church always has had false believers among its members. These are the ones who claim to be God's children but engage in behaviors that God abhors. We, from our human perspective, cannot always tell who is a true believer and who is a false believer. Sometimes the person with many chronic and visible sin problems is struggling sincerely to change his or her life every day.

In other cases a person who presents the appearance of great righteousness and piety may be living a secret life of evil and disdain for God. For John this is the person walking *in darkness.* His or her relationship with God is a sham as life is lived only for self. Jesus labeled such people hypocrites and reserved His strongest condemnation for them (see Mark 7:6). Elsewhere Jesus indicated that such evil persons may coexist with believers now, but they will be condemned at the time of judgment (Matthew 13:30).

7. But if we walk in the light, as he is in the light, we have fellowship one with another, and the blood of Jesus Christ his Son cleanseth us from all sin.

John follows the discussion of the hypocrite with a message of hope for the one struggling with sin (and this includes every believer). This is not addressed to the nonbeliever.

How does the Christian deal with sin? First, we maintain a strong relationship with God, walking *in the light.* [See question #3, page 144.] But, furthermore, we never lose sight of the fact that our sins have been paid for by *the blood of Jesus,* shed for us (see Revelation 1:5). [See question #4, page 144.]

B. Full Confession (vv. 8-10)

8. If we say that we have no sin, we deceive ourselves, and the truth is not in us.

It is unlikely that John is dealing with a hypothetical situation here. There apparently are false teachers trying to convince the church that they have *no sin* at all. We know this is not true, both from our experience and from God's Word. Even the strongest, most mature believers can stumble. Remember that Paul had to confront Peter over a matter of hypocrisy (Galatians 2:11-14).

9. If we confess our sins, he is faithful and just to forgive us our sins, and to cleanse us from all unrighteousness.

John offers another key to how Christians can overcome sin problems. We must *confess our sins*. To confess means to acknowledge our sin before God. It means we are not comfortable with it, nor do we ignore it. We come to God and say, "O wretched man that I am! Who shall deliver me from the body of this death?" (Romans 7:24).

We acknowledge our sinfulness and our helplessness. God cleanses us, meaning He forgives us. We who are unrighteous are reckoned by God as righteous because of His cleansing power.

10. If we say that we have not sinned, we make him a liar, and his word is not in us.

John now presents the most awful consequences of falsehood: if we deny our sinfulness, we are calling God *a liar*. We are saying that we don't need a Savior and that God didn't need to send Jesus to die for our sins. This is the complete, polar opposite of confessing our sins.

III. The Walk of Love
(1 John 2:1-6)

Our lives as believers are to be controlled and characterized by love (John 13:35). When we truly understand what God has provided for us in Jesus, our lives will radiate His love to others.

A. Jesus Our Advocate (v. 1)

1. My little children, these things write I unto you, that ye sin not. And if any man sin, we have an advocate with the Father, Jesus Christ the righteous.

In *Christ* we have another advantage when it comes to sin. In the heavenly court of judgment, we have the finest defense attorney available: *Jesus* our *advocate*. The Greek word for this can also be translated "comforter," as it is in John 14:26. There this word is used of the Holy Spirit by Jesus.

AN ADVOCATE

It was a common practice in my neighborhood when I was a youngster. If you wanted to do something with some of the other kids and you believed Mom might not approve, you brought in one of the other kids to ask her, "We're going to ride our bikes over to the park. Can Johnny come with us?" You could ask her yourself, of course, but you knew you had a better chance of getting her approval if one of the other kids asked. We wanted someone to stand alongside us and speak our request to Mom.

The word *advocate* suggests a lawyer who represents someone in court. Such a one stands alongside, speaks to the judge, and argues the case. The picture that emerges out of all this is that Jesus is our defense attorney, so to speak.

Jesus pleads our case. As He does He stresses that we can go free with no penalty, because He has paid sin's price on the cross. He knows our desire to live right, but He also knows how poorly we have been able to do it. Yet in all this He faithfully represents our best interests. What an advocate we have!   —J. B. N.

B. Jesus Our Propitiation (v. 2)

2. And he is the propitiation for our sins: and not for ours only, but also for the sins of the whole world.

John uses doctrinally heavy language to state a basic truth: Jesus is our *propitiation*, meaning our sacrifice for *sins*. This is the doctrine of the atonement; God's penalty for our sins is paid by the sacrificial death of Jesus on the cross. The statement here is remarkably similar to the declaration of John the Baptist about Jesus: "Behold the Lamb of God, which taketh away the sin of the world" (John 1:29). See also 1 John 4:10.

C. Jesus Our Standard (vv. 3-5)

3. And hereby we do know that we know him, if we keep his commandments.

A confused brother or sister may wonder, "Am I really a believer? Sometimes I doubt my own faith." John says the time for self-delusion is over. You *know* whether you are a believer by looking at your own life. Jesus said, "Ye shall know them by their fruits" (Matthew 7:16). John says that you can know yourself by your actions as you *keep his commandments*.

KEEPING COMMANDMENTS

Some years ago a friend of mine mentioned an incident that had occurred in his family. His children had various chores they were to do around the house. His youngest son, Jimmy, was to take the garbage each evening and put it in the garbage can at the back of their yard. His mother usually wrapped it in a newspaper and placed it on the corner of the kitchen cabinet.

One night Jimmy went out to play, and my friend asked his daughter, "Did Jimmy pick up the garbage?" She looked into the kitchen and noticed the garbage was still on the kitchen counter. My friend said, "Tell Jimmy to come back and get the garbage." She went to the back door and yelled out, "Jimmy, come back and get the garbage." Jimmy yelled back, "Who says so?" She replied, "Dad says so." Only at that point did Jimmy came back and pick up the garbage!

Jimmy had heard his sister's command, but there was no obedience because he did not respect her authority. When he understood whose authority lay behind the command, he obeyed readily. John says that if we know Jesus, we will keep His commands. Do we?   —J. B. N.

4, 5. He that saith, I know him, and keepeth not his commandments, is a liar, and the truth is not in him. But whoso keepeth his word, in him verily is the love of God perfected: hereby know we that we are in him.

Why do we keep God's *commandments*? Out of fear? To earn heavenly merit badges? No, there is only one valid reason: We follow God's will because we love Him. Some children obey their parents primarily out of the fear of punishment. Other children obey primarily because they love their parents and do not want to disappoint them or hurt them.

To obey out of love is a godly motivation, for God loves us consistently at all times. When we truly appreciate God's great love, the enjoyment of sin grows less and less enticing. We are moving toward what John sees as perfect *love*. When we achieve this type of relationship with God, we no longer fear Him (1 John 4:18).

Home Daily Bible Readings

Monday, Dec. 11—An Angel Speaks to Joseph (Matthew 1:18-25)

Tuesday, Dec. 12—Eyewitnesses of God's Majesty (2 Peter 1:16-21)

Wednesday, Dec. 13—We Preach Jesus Christ (2 Corinthians 4:1-6)

Thursday, Dec. 14—Live as Children of Light (Ephesians 5:8-14)

Friday, Dec. 15—Jesus Is the Word of Life (1 John 1:1-4)

Saturday, Dec. 16—Walk in the Light (1 John 1:5-10)

Sunday, Dec. 17—Following Jesus (1 John 2:1-6)

D. Jesus Our Trailblazer (v. 6)

6. He that saith he abideth in him ought himself also so to walk, even as he walked.

The section concludes by looking to the example of Jesus. When we don't know what to do, we should look at the pattern of Jesus' life. In this He is the "author and finisher of our faith" (Hebrews 12:2). He has walked before us and shown us how to live. [See question #5, page 144.]

Conclusion

A. What Would Jesus Do?

Over a century ago Charles Sheldon penned the classic Christian novel *In His Steps*. The main character, a minister named Henry Maxwell, is confronted by an angry poor man who asks, "But what would Jesus do? Is that what you mean by following His steps?"

This challenge sets off a series of events that transforms a town because the people begin to ask themselves, "What would Jesus do in this situation?" They allow the answer to determine their decisions.

The "What Would Jesus Do?" fad passed through many churches a few years ago, accompanied by *WWJD?* wristbands and other paraphernalia. The question *WWJD?* doesn't always work because Jesus did some miraculous things that we cannot; Jesus even died on a cross to pay sin's price—something we cannot and need not do. But by and large the *WWJD?* phenomenon was a good thing. Even if it is now out of fashion, the question still is worth asking.

Are you willing to do what Jesus would do, to live as Jesus lived, to walk as Jesus walked? Are you willing to act in a manner that acknowledges Christ's presence in your life and let Him be the controlling influence for your actions? This is the message of this lesson. When we do this, we are not automatically perfect. But we have yielded to God's conquering light in our lives, and we are truly walking with Him.

B. Prayer

Gracious and merciful God, thank You for loving us in spite of our sin. Thank You for being willing to allow us into Your close fellowship despite our weaknesses. And thank You for cleansing us despite our spiritual filthiness. We pray in the powerful name of Jesus, Your Son and our advocate in Heaven, amen.

C. Thought to Remember

Walking with Jesus means living with His presence in our lives.

Learning by Doing

This page contains an alternative lesson plan emphasizing learning activities.
Classes desiring such student involvement will find these suggestions helpful.

Learning Goals

After participating in this lesson, each student will be able to:

1. Quote 1 John 1:8, 9 from memory.
2. Discuss the personal implications of what it means to walk as Jesus did.
3. Describe one way that he or she will walk as Jesus did.

Into the Lesson

As class members enter the room, blindfold each of them and tell them not to remove their blindfolds until asked to do so. Say that this experience is a part of today's lesson. Tell class members to find a place to sit (have a helper ready to assist with this) and to feel free to visit with the people around them.

While the students remain blindfolded, tell them that both darkness and blindness bring special challenges and dangers. Ask, "What has your experience of being blindfolded been like? Tell us what has happened to you." Also ask, "What are some of the dangers of not being able to see?"

Have students remove their blindfolds. Make the transition to Bible study saying, "The contrast between darkness and light is not only something that relates to seeing. In the Bible darkness and light are often metaphors for sin and righteousness. The phrase 'walking in the light' has its roots in Scripture and is the core of today's study."

Into the Word

Before class begins hang four signs from the ceiling. Each sign will have one of the following headings: Appreciating Jesus; Rich Fellowship; Light and Darkness; Walking Like Jesus.

Begin the Bible study by reading the printed text. Tell the class that this text will be explored by looking at key phrases (these key phrases are also included in the student book). Ask class members to divide into study groups by standing underneath one of the signs hanging from the ceiling. Give each study group one set of the following printed instructions:

Group #1: Appreciating Jesus. Your task is to look at the following phrases from our text and to explain the significance of each. Be sure to read the entire text to glean information that will be helpful. Be prepared to share your conclusions with the class. The phrases are *That which was from the beginning* (1 John 1:1) and *The Word of life* (1 John 1:1, 2).

Group #2: Rich Fellowship. Your task is to look at the following phrases from our text and to explain the significance of each. Be sure to read the entire text to glean information that will be helpful. Be prepared to share your conclusions with the class. The phrases are *Fellowship with us . . . with the Father . . . with his Son* (1 John 1:3) and *Your joy may be full* (1 John 1:4).

Group #3: Light and Darkness. Your task is to look at the following phrases from our text and to explain the significance of each. Be sure to read the entire text to glean information that will be helpful. Be prepared to share your conclusions with the class. The phrases are *God is light, and in him is no darkness* (1 John 1:5) and *Walk in the light* (1 John 1:7).

Group #4: Walking Like Jesus. Your task is to look at the following phrases from our text and to explain the significance of each. Be sure to read the entire text to glean information that will be helpful. Be prepared to share your conclusions with the class. The phrases are *Propitiation for our sins* (1 John 2:1, 2) and *Ought himself also so to walk* (1 John 2:3-6).

Alternative activity. Prepare eight posters, each featuring one of the eight key phrases from the above group assignments. Affix the signs to the wall before you lead a discussion of each phrase in turn.

Into Life

Prepare cloth ribbons to be used as wristbands. Use adhesive-backed hook-and-loop dots for fastening the wristbands. Also have numerous cloth markers available. Tell the class that today's text reminds us of the *WWJD?* ("What Would Jesus Do?") phenomenon. Have class members assemble their wristbands and write on them: "WWJD? Walk in the light!" Ask class members to wear their wristbands for the week as reminders to walk faithfully and enjoy the light that God brings to life. (If you think your class members will resist wearing wristbands, make bookmarks instead.)

Let's Talk It Over

The questions on this page are designed to promote discussion of the lesson by the class and to encourage application of the lesson Scriptures. The answers provided are only discussion starters. Let your class talk it over from there.

1. Since Christ is the "Word of life," what life changes have you experienced after coming into a relationship with Him? What changes do you yet expect?

Obviously the promised inheritance of eternal life is the ultimate change for the Christian! We gain assurance of this eternal state when we first accept Jesus according to the biblical plan of salvation. That acceptance sets in motion (or should set in motion) a series of life changes that begin in the here and now. Being part of a "called out" community without the heavy taxation that sin brings helps us to live life with a different perspective and purpose.

If your students have trouble verbalizing changes, you can jump-start their thinking by mentioning the fruit of the Spirit from Galatians 5:22-26. The changes implied in that list should be discussed and celebrated.

2. How has your relationship with God affected your relationship with other Christians thus far? Have you discovered that your relationship with others serves as a barometer of your relationship with God? Or is it more the other way around? Explain.

When we become Christians, the way in which we measure our relationships changes. Too often secular friendships are based upon what each individual can *receive from* the shared experience. In forgiven, Christ-sanctified relationships, we discover our responsibilities for *contributing to* the spiritual well-being of others.

If we expect a strong relationship with God, then we must learn to live with His other sons and daughters. Be sure to read 1 John 4:20 on this point.

3. Think of some ways that light is used today that were not part of the daily life of John's contemporaries. How would you use these to illustrate how Jesus' light guides us today?

This can lead to a wide-open discussion, with many possible illustrations. Lasers certainly were not available in John's day. These are very common now, being used in things like "laser levels" to provide construction crews perfectly aligned reference points. Runway lights guide aircraft to safe landings. Dashboard lights allow us to see our car's fuel level, speed, etc. Even the light switches in our homes are themselves illuminated so we can find them easily in the dark. When the lights go out during a storm, our lives are disrupted. Without the light of Jesus, we would not see the way to God.

4. Verse 7 tells us that the blood of Christ cleanses us from all sin. In later verses, however, we are once again reminded that we are sinful creatures. How do these two facts affect your relationship with God and with others?

These two facts should help us avoid the extremes of pride and feelings of worthlessness. The recognition that we are still sinners eliminates the first of these two; the fact that we are sinners saved by grace eliminates the second.

Our relationships with God and with others improve when we keep in mind that sinful imperfections come from unholy patterns that we have learned. What was learned can be unlearned! When we stumble back into unholiness, we admit it (to God and, possibly, to others) and repent. Hopefully people will be gracious to us. We must certainly be gracious to others (Matthew 18:21-35). God wants us to keep working our way toward the sinless example of Jesus.

5. Sometimes Christians talk about how they hope they are doing what Jesus wants them to do. John suggests our relationship with Christ should be built on *knowledge* rather than just *hope*. What are some steps you need to take to increase both your knowledge of Christ and your hope in Him?

A good starting point is to begin to get to know His commandments (1 John 2:3). But the Christian walk will also demand that we get to know the person of Christ through His Word.

We also should build accountability relationships with other Christians who are struggling with the same concerns. An even better plan is to partner with those who have successfully conquered weaknesses similar to those with which we are struggling. The assurance of God's plan is always there. Learning to trust in His promises is a launching point.

The Word Became Flesh

DEVOTIONAL READING: **Isaiah 53:1-6.**

BACKGROUND SCRIPTURE: **John 1:1-34.**

PRINTED TEXT: **John 1:1-18.**

John 1:1-18

1 In the beginning was the Word, and the Word was with God, and the Word was God.

2 The same was in the beginning with God.

3 All things were made by him; and without him was not any thing made that was made.

4 In him was life; and the life was the light of men.

5 And the light shineth in darkness; and the darkness comprehended it not.

6 There was a man sent from God, whose name was John.

7 The same came for a witness, to bear witness of the Light, that all men through him might believe.

8 He was not that Light, but was sent to bear witness of that Light.

9 That was the true Light, which lighteth every man that cometh into the world.

10 He was in the world, and the world was made by him, and the world knew him not.

11 He came unto his own, and his own received him not.

12 But as many as received him, to them gave he power to become the sons of God, even to them that believe on his name:

13 Which were born, not of blood, nor of the will of the flesh, nor of the will of man, but of God.

14 And the Word was made flesh, and dwelt among us, (and we beheld his glory, the glory as of the only begotten of the Father,) full of grace and truth.

15 John bare witness of him, and cried, saying, This was he of whom I spake, He that cometh after me is preferred before me; for he was before me.

16 And of his fulness have all we received, and grace for grace.

17 For the law was given by Moses, but grace and truth came by Jesus Christ.

18 No man hath seen God at any time; the only begotten Son, which is in the bosom of the Father, he hath declared him.

GOLDEN TEXT: And the Word was made flesh, and dwelt among us, (and we beheld his glory, the glory as of the only begotten of the Father,) full of grace and truth.—John 1:14.

Jesus Christ: A Portrait of God
Unit 1: Christ, the Image of God
(Lessons 1-5)

Lesson Aims

After participating in this lesson, each student will be able to:

1. List three of John's titles for Jesus.

2. Paraphrase John's explanation of Jesus' preexistence and incarnation.

3. Choose one personal behavior to transform from darkness to light.

Lesson Outline

INTRODUCTION
  A. Rejection
  B. John's Titles for Jesus
  C. Lesson Background
 I. THE WORD BEGINNING THE WORLD (John 1:1-3)
  A. The Word from Eternity Past (vv. 1, 2)
    In the Beginning
  B. The Word at Creation (v. 3)
II. THE WORD BRINGING LIGHT (John 1:4-13)
  A. Shining Light (vv. 4, 5)
    Light in Darkness
  B. Witness to the Light (vv. 6-8)
  C. Light in the World (vv. 9-11)
  D. Faithful Response to the Light (vv. 12, 13)
III. THE WORD BECOMING FLESH (John 1:14-18)
  A. Incarnation of the Word (v. 14)
  B. Revelation of Grace and Truth (vv. 15-17)
  C. Declaration of the Father (v. 18)
CONCLUSION
  A. Grace in John
  B. Prayer
  C. Thought to Remember

Introduction

A. Rejection

I once arrived in a distant city very late for a convention. After the usual hassle of departing the airport, I finally arrived at my assigned hotel near midnight. I had been up since before dawn and was dead tired. I gave the hotel clerk my name and waited as she clicked away on her computer. My heart sank, though, when she said, "I'm sorry, sir. I have no record of your reservation." This was not the reception I was hoping for or expecting!

The Bible teaches that God had a plan for redemption when the first human couple sinned and was expelled from the garden. God planned for this by preparing the nation of Israel to be the people who would receive His redeemer, His Son Jesus. Yet in one of the terrible ironies of human history, this chosen people did not recognize their own promised Messiah. His reception was instead a rejection.

The apostle John begins his Gospel by putting the person and mission of Jesus into the perspective of a panoramic review of human history. This week's lesson looks at the first 18 verses of this great book. There John introduces his themes about Jesus from the broadest possible historical viewpoint.

B. John's Titles for Jesus

The Gospel of John is a treasure trove for Christians who want to understand Jesus Christ more fully. One of the ways John's Gospel can be appreciated is to look at the many titles or descriptions that John uses in explaining Jesus. A brief survey of some of these could start with the designation of Jesus as *the Word*. This emphasizes the communication element in the nature of the Christ (John 1:1, 14; compare Revelation 19:13).

Second, John often describes Jesus as the *Son*, emphasizing His relationship with God. This takes several forms. He may be the *only begotten* Son (John 3:16; compare 1 John 4:9), the *Son of God* (John 1:34, 49; compare 1 John 4:15), or the *Son of man* (John 1:51; 12:23; compare Revelation 1:13). Third, John depicts Jesus as the Jewish Messiah. This may be simply as *the Christ* (John 1:41) or as the *King of Israel* (John 1:49; 12:13).

Fourth, we find Jesus as the *Lamb of God* (John 1:29, 36; compare Revelation 5:6), highlighting Jesus' role as the sacrifice for human sins. Fifth, the most dramatic title of Jesus is *Lord and . . . God* (John 20:28; compare Revelation 19:16), emphasizing His deity and sovereignty.

This is not an exhaustive list. You may want to study John's titles further by reading through the Gospel of John, looking only for the various ways the author portrays Jesus.

C. Lesson Background

We have four Gospels in the New Testament that tell the story of Jesus. The first three Gospels (Matthew, Mark, and Luke) are very similar in their general structure. The fourth Gospel, John, is quite different from the other three. John wrote 30 or so years after those other three, and he was well acquainted with their material. For this reason he seems to avoid repeating most of their content. Instead, he chooses to give new information from his wealth of eyewitness recollections (see John 21:24, 25). About 90 percent of John's material is not found in the other three Gospels.

A significant difference among the four Gospels is the way the writers choose to begin their accounts. Mark begins with the ministry of John the Baptist, without any reference to the birth or childhood of Jesus. Luke begins with the birth of John the Baptist and includes the nativity story of Jesus. Matthew begins with Jesus' genealogy, thus pushing the story of Jesus back into the Old Testament.

John, for his part, pushes the story back to the very beginning of the Old Testament. Thus John's Gospel is an inclusive account of the entire sweep of human history, beginning before creation itself. Most of this is accomplished in John 1:1-18, often referred to as the prologue of John. Today's lesson explores the issues of the doctrine of the incarnation. We will try to understand how God could assume a human form.

I. The Word Beginning the World (John 1:1-3)

A. The Word from Eternity Past (vv. 1, 2)

1, 2. In the beginning was the Word, and the Word was with God, and the Word was God. The same was in the beginning with God.

John's opening statements are a retelling of the Genesis account of creation with an important addition: John includes the preexistent Christ. There are hints of the threefold nature of God in Genesis 1:26: "Let us make man in our image." But the relationship between God the Father and God the Son is not explored there.

In order to tell his story of Jesus more fully, this is where John must start. Genesis 1:1 begins, *"In the beginning* God." To this John adds three clarifications: (1) *the Word* was at the beginning,

(2) this Word was in fellowship *with God,* and (3) the Word, in some way, *was God.* These three in combination give us enormous truths about Jesus.

We may begin by asking what exactly it means for John to describe the preexisting Christ as *the Word.* The Greek term behind this is *logos.* This was a well-known term in Greek philosophy, where it means something like "the ordering principle of the universe." The Greeks saw *logos* as that which caused the universe to hold together and make sense. It is from *logos* that we get our term *logic.* [See question #1, page 152.]

While these ideas may touch some of John's Greek readers, this is probably not what he has in mind by using *logos.* For John *logos* is the creative Word of God. In Genesis God speaks the universe into existence (compare Psalm 33:6). God's Word is powerful and creative.

Also, there is no beginning for the Word. The preexistent Christ *is* the beginning (see Revelation 22:13). Just as Genesis begins creation with God already in place, so John starts his telling of the beginning with the Word already present.

John can say further that *the Word was God* while making a careful distinction between the Word and God. From a logical point of view, this seems curious: How can the Word be *distinct from* God, yet *be* God at the same time? Perhaps the best we can do is to say that there are three centers of consciousness in the Godhead (Father, Son, and Holy Spirit) and that these three share a single essence.

In any case, John expects us to believe that *the Word was God.* For John no other way of describing this will do. We must accept the truth of this relationship, even if it seems to strain our understanding. Remember: John walked side by side with Jesus. John knows what he is talking about!

In the Beginning

A friend once asked me, "Did you know that baseball is mentioned in the Bible?" I was rather dubious, so I asked him where. He replied, "The Bible says, 'In the big inning.'" Poor humor aside, the first phrase in both the Gospel of John and Genesis is significant: *In the beginning.* The beginning—what an appropriate place to start! It's far better than the fairy tale introduction, "Once upon a time." A story that begins "once upon a time" actually means that it has no historical framework. There is no attempt to place it in context with other events.

The ancient world normally dated things by the year of the ruler (compare 1 Kings 6:1; Isaiah 6:1; Luke 3:1; etc.). Yet how would one refer to events before there were any rulers or when there

---

How to Say It

ALEXANDRIA. Al-iks-*an*-dree-uh.

ATHENS. *Ath*-unz.

JERUSALEM. Juh-*roo*-suh-lem.

LOGOS (Greek). *law*-goss.

MESSIAH. Meh-*sigh*-uh.

NAZARENES. *Naz*-uh-reens.

NAZARETH. *Naz*-uh-reth.

NICODEMUS. *Nick*-uh-*dee*-mus (strong accent on *dee*).

PROLOGUE. *proh*-lahg.

SYNAGOGUE. *sin*-uh-gog.

was as yet no means of measuring time? In talking about the absolute beginning of things, the Bible writers do it very simply—*in the beginning.*

This is an acknowledgment that not only was God active in creation, He also preexisted before there was the concept of time, as did Christ. The Arian controversy in the fourth century AD wanted to make Christ less than God and so argued "there was when He was not." The other side responded with a double negative: "there was not when He was not." John puts it very simply—"In the beginning . . . the Word was with God." This is truth.   —J. B. N.

B. The Word at Creation (v. 3)

3. All things were made by him; and without him was not any thing made that was made.

John explicitly defines the Word's (Christ's) role in creation. The Word is uncreated and is fully involved in creation. There is no created *thing* that exists apart from the Word's creative power. [See question #2, page 152.] Paul wrote that creation is both a testimony to God (Romans 1:20) and waits for God's redemption (Romans 8:22). [See question #3, page 152.]

II. The Word Bringing Light (John 1:4-13)

A. Shining Light (vv. 4, 5)

4, 5. In him was life; and the life was the light of men. And the light shineth in darkness; and the darkness comprehended it not.

The Word does not become inactive when creation is completed. So John moves to the function of the Word as communication and enlightenment for humanity.

God's initial act of creation was to make *light* (Genesis 1:3). In so doing God separated light from *darkness.* Here light is the life-giving presence of God. Light is goodness, righteousness, and truth (see John 3:21). Darkness symbolizes evil, unrighteousness, and ungodliness (John 3:19).

The word *comprehended* is a good translation, but other possible translations are "conquered" or "overcame." Jesus' mission among men and women was to rescue them from spiritual darkness (John 12:46).

LIGHT IN DARKNESS

Thomas Kinkade has become known as The Painter of Light. His paintings have become so popular that his name has become virtually a household word. Other than prints of the pictures themselves, his paintings adorn Christmas cards, greeting cards, book covers, and various other items. His web site claims that he is "America's most collected living artist."

Part of his attraction is his unabashedly Christian and family orientation. He credits Christ for the inspiration of many of his subjects as well as his talent to depict them. Nostalgic views of faith, hope, and familial warmth shine forth from his canvases. He pays tribute to his wife, Nanette, by hiding the letter *N* in many of his scenes. The names of his four daughters also show up in his work. He has donated his efforts to numerous charitable and religious organizations and has helped raise millions of dollars for their projects.

Central in all his paintings is some feature of light—be it old-fashioned streetlights, lighted windows, sunlight, or reflected light. One finds few darkened windows, brooding clouds, stormy landscapes, or tempestuous waves of emotion. Instead, the central features are calm, serene, restful, and heartwarming. While Norman Rockwell painted humorous and inspiring personality sketches, Kinkade specializes in idyllic scenes of town and country living—all delivered through an imaginative use of light. His works of art display the point that the apostle John makes: light will overcome the darkness.   —J. B. N.

B. Witness to the Light (vv. 6-8)

6. There was a man sent from God, whose name was John.

This is *John* is John the Baptist, not John the apostle who writes this Gospel. We are told that John the Baptist was commissioned by *God;* he was not self-appointed. This puts him in the tradition of the great prophets of Israel (see Matthew 11:7-15; Luke 7:28).

7, 8. The same came for a witness, to bear witness of the Light, that all men through him might believe. He was not that Light, but was sent to bear witness of that Light.

Elsewhere Jesus describes John the Baptist as "a burning and a shining light" (John 5:35). But he was not *the Light,* the ultimate manifestation of God that was Jesus. John had a specific function: *to bear witness.* This means that he was to testify about Jesus, to be a reliable witness of His identity. When John the Baptist pointed out Jesus, some of John's own disciples followed Him (John 1:35-37).

C. Light in the World (vv. 9-11)

9. That was the true Light, which lighteth every man that cometh into the world.

John combines two of his most important concepts in this verse: truth and light. This helps us understand what the light imagery is all about.

God is a God of light and truth, and He brings these into the created world to help men and women be "enlightened." This means He has not abandoned us to darkness. Instead He continues to create light to banish our dark world of sin. God's enlightened truth is our way out, our guide to how we should live (see John 8:12).

10, 11. He was in the world, and the world was made by him, and the world knew him not. He came unto his own, and his own received him not.

In terse words these verses depict the greatest irony of history: when visited by its creator, *the world* did not recognize Him. It rejected Him instead. The phrase *his own* refers to the nation of Israel, the people chosen by God to be the receiving nation for His Messiah.

Undoubtedly, Jesus did not meet many people's expectation of Messiah. He was not born in a king's palace, but in a stable. His parents were not rich and powerful, but young and poor. His early education was not at the great centers of learning such as Alexandria, Athens, or Jerusalem, but at the local synagogue. The real reason for the rejection, however, was not Jesus' humble human origins but spiritual blindness (Romans 11:25). [See question #4, page 152.]

D. Faithful Response to the Light (vv. 12, 13)

12. But as many as received him, to them gave he power to become the sons of God, even to them that believe on his name.

Jesus' rejection was not universal, however. Even though the vast majority of Jews did not receive their Messiah, there were believers. The opposite of "received him not" in verse 11 is to *believe on his name.* In the ancient world the name of a person is symbolic of the full identity of that person. To trust a person fully, one might even adopt that person's name. This is seen when the early believers in Antioch take up the name *Christians* (Acts 11:26), meaning "one loyal to Christ." Other early believers were known as *Nazarenes* (Acts 24:5), meaning "loyal to the one from Nazareth."

The result of receiving and believing in Jesus is to be adopted by God. We *become* His children. We are reunited and reconciled with our creator. We become joint heirs with Jesus (Romans 8:17).

13. Which were born, not of blood, nor of the will of the flesh, nor of the will of man, but of God.

John introduces the concept of new birth at this point. Spiritually we become God's children by a rebirth. This is not any type of physical birth related to the conception of a child through normal means. This birth comes from God.

The idea of *new birth* comes up later in Jesus' conversation with Nicodemus. There Jesus says that without this new birth one "cannot see the kingdom of God" (John 3:3).

III. The Word Becoming Flesh (John 1:14-18)

A. Incarnation of the Word (v. 14)

14. And the Word was made flesh, and dwelt among us, (and we beheld his glory, the glory as of the only begotten of the Father,) full of grace and truth.

This verse is John's way of expressing what we call "the incarnation." It is the divine putting on *flesh*, God taking human form. This is a very difficult concept to understand, but it is vital for the Christian faith. It is only by becoming human that the Son of God could die for the sins of the world (Hebrews 2:14).

John and companions were witnesses to the *glory* of God in this regard. Jesus, the Son, reveals *the Father* in a way that allows Jesus to say that seeing Him means seeing the Father (John 14:9). This is a vision of grace and truth, which is explained in the next verses.

B. Revelation of Grace and Truth (vv. 15-17)

15. John bare witness of him, and cried, saying, This was he of whom I spake, He that cometh after me is preferred before me; for he was before me.

John the Baptist's testimony is recorded here. What is important for this passage is John the

"The Word was made flesh." —John 1:14

Visual for Lesson 4

Point to this passage as you ask, "Why is John 1:14 important to the twenty-first century A.D.?"

Baptist's knowledge of Jesus' true identity. Jesus *was before* John the Baptist, meaning that He existed before His incarnation. Therefore, John the Baptist knew well that Jesus deserved precedence over him in all things.

16. And of his fulness have all we received, and grace for grace.

John now expands upon one of the central concepts of the New Testament: *grace* (introduced in 1:14). *Grace for grace* could be translated "grace upon grace," with the image of gifts being piled upon one another endlessly. The grace that came through Jesus was not something we earned. It was given freely by the Father.

17. For the law was given by Moses, but grace and truth came by Jesus Christ.

The *law* in mind here is the Jewish law, the various commandments *given by Moses.* Laws can result in doing the right thing with no relationship with the lawgiver. Thus, while the law is not bad, it does not do what *Jesus* does. Jesus allows us to become true children of God through faith, far beyond any attempts to earn God's favor by keeping His rules. Jesus is the true light of the world. [See question #5, page 152.]

C. Declaration of the Father (v. 18)

18. No man hath seen God at any time; the only begotten Son, which is in the bosom of the Father, he hath declared him.

This final verse of John's prologue sums up everything he has said so far. God exists far above any possibility of human perception and experience. There are a few Old Testament descriptions of people seeing a kind of manifestation of God (Genesis 32:30; Exodus 24:11). But *no man hath seen God at any time* because

---

Home Daily Bible Readings

"Thou canst not see my face: for there shall no man see me, and live" (Exodus 33:20).

Even so, God has revealed himself in a way that we can understand and believe. He has done this by Jesus, God in flesh, God's only *Son.* Jesus reveals God in a way that no other human ever could. Through Jesus we have access to God.

Conclusion

A. Grace in John

What is the amazing thing we call *grace*? While that word is common in Paul's writings, it is used only a few times in the Gospel of John (1:14-17). This word gets tossed around in many ways in the church. Some people seem to equate grace with the Holy Spirit, as supernatural power ("I was overcome by grace"). Others see it as the same as God's presence ("God's grace is in this place"). Still others associate it with a mealtime prayer ("Bow your heads while I say grace").

An old acronym for grace is helpful: **G**od's **R**iches **A**t **C**hrist's **E**xpense. But this only gives a partial sense of this rich concept. There are two essential components to a biblical concept of grace. First, it always denotes an element of "gift." It is never something we earn or deserve. Second, grace involves both attitude and action. God's grace means that God determined to do something beneficial; then He did it.

I have another acronym for grace (which, unfortunately, doesn't make a real word): *BUA.* This is **B**eautiful **U**ndeserved **A**ction. John tells us that everything about God's self-revelation in Jesus is gracious. We didn't deserve Him. He is beautiful in ways we cannot even appreciate. The incarnation is a decisive act of enormous significance.

How much did it really cost God to sacrifice His Son? We cannot possibly know. But we can understand that this is not the way things normally work. Fathers don't usually sacrifice their sons for others. If anything, a father will sacrifice *for* his son. Yet God sent His Son to become a man and die on a cross to pay the price for sin. That is BUA grace!

B. Prayer

God of Heaven and earth, we thank You for seeing us lost in sin and sending Your only Son, Jesus Christ, to be our Savior. May we be blessed by Your grace and guided by Your truth in all things. In Jesus' name we pray, amen.

C. Thought to Remember

The gracious truth of God is the promise of eternal life as revealed through Jesus Christ.

Learning by Doing

This page contains an alternative lesson plan emphasizing learning activities.
Classes desiring such student involvement will find these suggestions helpful.

Learning Goals

After participating in this lesson, each student will be able to:

1. List three of John's titles for Jesus.

2. Paraphrase John's explanation of Jesus' pre-existence and incarnation.

3. Choose one personal behavior to transform from darkness to light.

Into the Lesson

Display three posters of multiple-choice questions. A religious Christmas card attached to each poster will help students connect the season with the activity. Give each student three colored, self-adhesive dots when entering the classroom. Ask students to stick a dot on each poster near or on the best answer for each question.

Poster #1. The word *Messiah* is the Hebrew form of (a) *Christ,* meaning "creator-God"; (b) *Christ,* meaning "anointed one"; (c) *Christ,* meaning "redeemer"; (d) a song written by a man named Handel.

Poster #2. The word *incarnation* refers to (a) God becoming a man; (b) the virginity of Mary when giving birth to Jesus; (c) another name for *communion;* (d) a nation with lots of cars.

Poster #3. The word *Immanuel* means (a) "redeemer"; (b) "anointed one"; (c) "God with us"; (d) "God against us."

After the class members have made their choices by placing stickers on the posters, review each question. Give the correct answer and comment on the significance of each.

The answer to question #1 is *b.* Ask, "What does the title *Messiah* tell us about Jesus—His nature and mission?" The answer to question #2 is *a.* Say, "The incarnation is a difficult concept. Today's text, however, enthusiastically explains this key to understanding Jesus' identity and origin." The answer to question #3 is *c.* Say, "The title *Immanuel* was introduced in Isaiah 7:14, teaching us even more about the nature of Jesus."

Transition to Bible study by stating that these and other titles given to Jesus in the Gospel of John help us know our God and Savior better.

Into the Word

Begin this section of study with a brief lecture on some titles given to Jesus in the Gospel of John. Also touch on the purpose of John's Gospel. On the board or overhead write "Titles for Jesus." As you speak, write some titles as found in the lesson Introduction. Give a brief explanation of each.

Next read today's printed text. Then ask the discussion questions that follow. You may wish to announce the focus of each group of questions. (These questions are also in the student book; this can be a small-group activity, one group per Focus.)

Focus: Jesus as the Word (John 1:1-5): (1) Why do you think John chose to call Jesus "the Word"? (2) What truths do verses 1-5 teach us about the nature of Jesus? (3) Why do you think John chose this way to introduce Jesus rather than beginning with Jesus' birth?

Focus: Jesus as the Light (John 1:6-13): (1) Why do you think John chose to insert John the Baptist into these verses? (2) What do verses 10-13 teach us about how people respond to Jesus? What comfort or challenge does this bring to your life?

Focus: Jesus in the Flesh (John 1:14-18): (1) What are some of the earthshaking implications of the incarnation—of God becoming a man? (2) What do you think is the main point of this passage of Scripture? (3) Why is the story of the incarnation precious to Christians at this time of year?

Into Life

Point to the three posters used at the beginning of class as you remind students that they have discovered a new and rich appreciation for words such as *Immanuel, incarnation, Messiah.* Say, "What happened was nothing less than God becoming flesh. This is our time to use that fact to help us walk more closely with Him."

Ask the class to work in teams of two or three to write an acrostic. This acrostic will provide some steps that will help change personal behavior from darkness to light, based on the word *Messiah.*

Give each team a poster board and marker with the letters to the word *Messiah* written vertically. Examples for the first three letters could be *M*aintain personal holiness, *E*xpect God's blessings, and *S*pend time in prayer.

Let's Talk It Over

The questions on this page are designed to promote discussion of the lesson by the class and to encourage application of the lesson Scriptures. The answers provided are only discussion starters. Let your class talk it over from there.

1. John called Jesus the Word, or *logos,* from which we get our word *logic*. Yet there are many who would say that belief in Jesus is anything but logical. Why do they say this? How do you respond?

People hold what we may call "sets of pre-understandings" (or presuppositions). Whatever doesn't fit those pre-understandings is rejected. That was the problem of the Jewish leaders in Jesus' day. They thought that they knew what the Messiah "should" be like. When Jesus didn't meet those expectations, they crucified Him.

We may make progress with a skeptic by gently probing his or her pre-understandings. We may discover, for example, that a person has a presupposition that miracles are impossible, thus the claims about Jesus are "illogical." This may require that we explore the idea that the God who set up the laws of nature to begin with is the one who has the authority and power to supersede those laws via miracles when He chooses.

2. John pointed to the creative ability of Jesus as a reason that we should believe in Him. What's the difference between human creativity and that of Jesus? How is this distinction important to your personal faith walk?

We see television shows about people who know how to take something that is in one form and transform it into something that is better. We admire them for their "creativity" as a result. Jesus is able to create without using preexisting materials—He creates, literally, from nothing.

His creative partnership with the Father in this regard demonstrates not only His power but also His absolute ownership. An atheist who believes in evolution does what he or she pleases, having no sense of being accountable to God. The Christian knows, however, that he or she has not only been created but has been "bought with a price" (1 Corinthians 6:20; 7:23). The Christian lives to please God as a result.

3. The apostle John, in writing his Gospel, chose to approach the study of Christ in a certain way. How and why should we adjust John's approach for today? Or should we leave well enough alone? Explain.

The facts of history are what they are. They cannot be revised. Jesus' role in creation, the lessons He taught, the type of life He modeled, His crucifixion, and His resurrection are unchanging historical facts.

However, the apostle John also described Jesus as one "which we have heard, which we have seen with our eyes, which we have looked upon, and our hands have handled" (1 John 1:1). John himself could use this approach because he was an eyewitness. Our approach is to pass along his testimony as reliable and credible. Remember to pray when talking about Christ to an unbeliever! To focus on finding a perfect witnessing approach or technique runs the risk of leaving the power of the Holy Spirit out of the picture.

4. John 3:19 says that "men loved darkness rather than light, because their deeds were evil." What was a time when you resisted Christ's light? What helped you change to prefer His light?

A primary reason that many prefer darkness undoubtedly is an unwillingness to see beyond the pleasures of the next five minutes to the consequences of eternity. This can be an ongoing internal battle, even for mature Christians. A desire not to be accountable to anyone but oneself is usually a major factor why people prefer spiritual darkness.

5. Jesus came with both grace and truth. Has there ever been a time in your life when you had to balance one of these ideas against the other? Explain.

Think about a man who gets an ugly tie for Christmas. Instead of being brutally truthful and saying "It's ugly," he is gracious and says, "Thanks for thinking of me!" There was a time when Peter was confronted with the potential need to pay a certain tax or tribute. Jesus responded that He was exempt from that tax. But this truth was not vital enough to "push" and thus risk causing offense. So He graciously made provision to pay (Matthew 17:24-27). At other times sharp truth was the most important thing (Matthew 23:1-36). To work through this balance on a daily basis requires spiritual maturity.

Humiliation and Exaltation

DEVOTIONAL READING: 1 Peter 3:8-12.

**BACKGROUND SCRIPTURE: Philippians 2:
1-11.**

PRINTED TEXT: Philippians 2:1-11.

Philippians 2:1-11

1 If there be therefore any consolation in Christ, if any comfort of love, if any fellowship of the Spirit, if any bowels and mercies,

2 Fulfil ye my joy, that ye be likeminded, having the same love, being of one accord, of one mind.

3 Let nothing be done through strife or vainglory; but in lowliness of mind let each esteem other better than themselves.

4 Look not every man on his own things, but every man also on the things of others.

5 Let this mind be in you, which was also in Christ Jesus:

6 Who, being in the form of God, thought it not robbery to be equal with God:

7 But made himself of no reputation, and took upon him the form of a servant, and was made in the likeness of men:

8 And being found in fashion as a man, he humbled himself, and became obedient unto death, even the death of the cross.

9 Wherefore God also hath highly exalted him, and given him a name which is above every name:

10 That at the name of Jesus every knee should bow, of things in heaven, and things in earth, and things under the earth;

11 And that every tongue should confess that Jesus Christ is Lord, to the glory of God the Father.

GOLDEN TEXT: Let nothing be done through strife or vainglory; but in lowliness of mind let each esteem other better than themselves.—Philippians 2:3.

Jesus Christ: A Portrait of God
Unit 1: Christ, the Image of God
(Lessons 1-5)

Lesson Aims

After participating in this lesson, each student will be able to:

1. Tell of ways that Christ humbled himself.

2. Discuss how Christ's humility gave way to His exaltation.

3. Identify one specific area in which he or she will adopt an attitude of service to others.

Lesson Outline

INTRODUCTION
  A. Servant Leadership
  B. Lesson Background
I. THE MIND OF CHRIST (Philippians 2:1-5)
  A. Attitude of Unity (vv. 1, 2)
  B. Attitude of Servanthood (vv. 3, 4)
    Esteeming Others
  C. Attitude of Christ (v. 5)
II. THE HYMN TO CHRIST (Philippians 2:6-11)
  A. Christ's Preexistence (v. 6)
  B. Christ's Incarnation (vv. 7, 8)
  C. Christ's Exaltation (vv. 9-11)
    Highly Exalted
CONCLUSION
  A. Thinking as Jesus Thought
  B. Prayer
  C. Thought to Remember

Introduction

A. Servant Leadership

I was recently shopping in a "big box" retail store for an electronics item. I briefly overheard three young employees of the establishment discussing an employee meeting that had been held that morning. They were making fun of the concept of "servant leadership," which apparently had been stressed at this meeting. As one put it, "If they think I'm here to serve customers, they're crazy. I'm just here for a paycheck until I can find something better." This got a good laugh of agreement from the other two.

Some retail establishments have found that a way to thrive is by offering fabulous customer service. A large department store chain where I live has been practicing this policy for years and is legendary for its customer service. It does not have the best prices, but loyal customers flock to this store because they are always treated with courtesy and respect. There is no hassle for a return or a special order, and salespeople go out of their way to please customers.

While most people enjoy *being* served, to *be* a servant is another matter! Modern society has demeaned the role of servant. Young people rarely aspire to be career servants. They all want to be boss. Even in the church we have allowed a "serve me" culture to dominate in many congregations. The paid church staff is under enormous pressure to provide many types of services for the members. Worship services sometimes degenerate into entertainment, with an audience that must be pleased. If a church is providing inadequate services, members may go elsewhere or cut down on their giving.

Yet the church, as a whole and individually, is tasked with cultivating a "mind of Christ." This is an attitude of service, of valuing others more than self. Today's lesson seeks to understand how Jesus can be Lord of all yet servant of all.

B. Lesson Background

Philippians is an unusual letter for Paul. Unlike most of his other writings, he was not writing to defend himself from attacks or to combat major doctrinal errors. Instead, it has been called "Paul's joy letter" because of his frequent use of the terms *joy* and *rejoice*. This peaks when Paul commands his readers to "Rejoice in the Lord always: and again I say, Rejoice" (Philippians 4:4), one of the best-loved verses of all Scripture.

The historical circumstances behind the letter help us to understand Paul's upbeat spirit. Paul had founded the Philippian church on his second missionary journey (Acts 16:11-40). Philippi was an important Roman city in the province of Macedonia.

Unlike most large Roman cities, Philippi had a very tiny Jewish population. The Bible doesn't say that Paul was able to locate a synagogue in Philippi when he visited that city. This leads us to presume that no synagogue existed there. Instead, he found a group of faithful Jewish women that included a prominent merchant named Lydia. We believe that Lydia became a close ally of Paul, and that the Philippian church met in her home. Acts also tells the dramatic story of Paul and Silas being thrown into the Philippian jail and gaining release through God's miraculous intervention.

The result was the conversion and befriending of the Gentile warden of the Philippian jail. Paul was asked to leave the city by the Philippian authorities, but he left behind a strong group of friends and fellow believers. His relationship with this congregation was in no way strained, so much so that he could begin the letter by saying, "I thank my God upon every remembrance of you" (Philippians 1:3).

Paul wrote Philippians while he was imprisoned. The Philippian congregation became aware of Paul's circumstances and sent one of its trusted young men, Epaphroditus, to assist the apostle personally. This young man fell ill and nearly died (Philippians 2:25-30).

Paul sent Epaphroditus back to the Philippian church with a letter that expressed deep thanks for their long-time support of his ministry (Philippians 4:15, 16). Paul was unable to bless them financially but instead gave them a marvelous letter full of wonderful statements of faith. As a result, the verses from Philippians are among the most popular for Scripture memorization (examples: 1:6, 21; 2:5; 3:7, 10, 14; 4:4, 7, 13).

One of the gems of this book is known as the Philippian Hymn (Philippians 2:6-11). As with the Christ Hymn in Colossians 1:15-20 (see the first lesson of this quarter), we can imagine Paul teaching this song to the new Christians at Philippi nearly a decade earlier. This hymn is full of beautiful and profound information concerning our Lord Jesus Christ.

I. The Mind of Christ (Philippians 2:1-5)

A. Attitude of Unity (vv. 1, 2)

1. If there be therefore any consolation in Christ, if any comfort of love, if any fellowship of the Spirit, if any bowels and mercies.

Paul begins this section with four rhetorical *if*-statements. These are rhetorical in the sense that Paul does not question whether these things are true but wants his readers to ponder them for a moment. Can we find *consolation* (or encourage-

ment) in knowing Christ? Yes. Can we find *comfort* in living a life of love? Yes. Can we find sweet *fellowship* through the Holy Spirit with God and other believers? Yes. And are we blessed recipients of the *bowels and mercies* of God? Yes. [See question #1, page 160.]

This last expression is confusing for modern readers. Both *bowels* and *mercies* refer literally to physical organs in the human abdomen. Such body parts are often used metaphorically to express emotions. For example, we might say, "it was a gut feeling," or "she touched my heart," and not be thinking about literal body parts at all. Ancient people do the same thing. They understand bowels to be the seat of compassion because a physical sensation inside the body can accompany great emotion.

Strong feelings are not just a brain process. They involve the entire person. When the Bible says that Jesus was "moved with compassion" (Matthew 14:14), similar language is used. Literally this verse says that Jesus felt a stirring in His bowels. The context tells us that this was not an upset stomach, but Jesus' body reflecting His deep love for the multitude.

2. Fulfil ye my joy, that ye be likeminded, having the same love, being of one accord, of one mind.

Paul is hundreds of miles away from his beloved Philippian brothers and sisters. But there is still something they can do to bring him great joy: they can be united in their thinking and controlled by a spirit of love. Paul is leading up to the great uniting factor: everyone trying to be like Christ. Unity is not achieved when we try to copy each other. In that case the strongest example will prevail temporarily but may change quickly and create ongoing disunity. True, lasting unity comes when all copies are made from an ultimate, unchanging pattern. For the church this pattern is Christ. [See question #2, page 160.]

B. Attitude of Servanthood (vv. 3, 4)

3. Let nothing be done through strife or vainglory; but in lowliness of mind let each esteem other better than themselves.

Why do we do the things we do? Almost any action has an underlying motivation. Why do we mow our lawns? One man does it because he loves things to be neat and tidy. Another man does it because he is afraid his neighbors will speak negatively of him if his home looks unkempt. A third man does it because that's the way his dad taught him, and he still wants to do things to please his father.

How to Say It

CORINTHIANS. Ko-*rin*-thee-unz (*th* as in *thin*).
EPAPHRODITUS. Ee-*paf*-ro-*dye*-tus (strong accent on *dye).*
GENTILE. *Jen*-tile.
LYDIA. *Lid*-ee-uh.
MACEDONIA. Mass-eh-*doe*-nee-uh.
PHILIPPI. Fih-*lip*-pie or *Fil*-ih-pie.
PHILIPPIANS. Fih-*lip*-ee-unz.
SYNAGOGUE. *sin*-uh-gog.

Paul uses the words *strife* and *vainglory* to describe improper motives. The meanings of these two words overlap to a great degree. The combined idea is to avoid doing things out of motivation of selfish recognition. Self-aggrandizement is just that! The Bible has a lot to say about the dangers of pride (examples: Proverbs 8:13; 11:2; 13:10; 14:3; 16:18; 29:23). Conceit brought down some high and mighty rulers in the Bible (Daniel 4:28-33; Acts 12:21-23). Church leaders must resist those who push personal agendas at the expense of the long-term health of the body of Christ.

Then Paul gives a single motivation for correct actions: we should do things out of our *esteem* for others, placing their interests above our own. I was once talking to an older Christian man about changes in worship style. I sensed that he was not happy about the direction his church had taken. I asked him, provocatively, "What do you think about having drums in worship?"

For a moment his countenance was angry, and he admitted, "I hate the drums." Then his face softened; he smiled and said, "But if that's what we need to reach young people for Jesus, I'll put up with drums." He was esteeming others more than himself. [See question #3, page 160.]

ESTEEMING OTHERS

Charles Dickens's classic *A Tale of Two Cities* centers on the figure of Sydney Carton, a drunken, listless attorney who helps acquit Charles Darnay of a mistaken charge of treason. Both wind up in love with Lucie Manette. But Carton steps aside when he realizes that he has nothing to offer her, and that she loves Darnay anyway.

At the height of the French Revolution, they are all in Paris. There Darnay is arrested because of crimes committed by his father and uncle. Convicted by the revolutionary court, he is sentenced to death by guillotine. Carton, who bears an uncanny resemblance to Darnay, trades places with him in prison so that Darnay, Lucie, and their family can escape. Carton then goes to the guillotine and dies in the place of Darnay.

The story is filled with the themes of unjust retribution as well as the redemption of the self-deprecating Carton. In essence he esteemed others better than he esteemed himself. Paul encourages the same attitude in the Philippians. Indeed, the fictional Carton's self-sacrifice bears a resemblance to what Jesus did. Dickens had a make-believe character gave up his life to save the earthly life of a friend; God sent His only Son to give up His life to save us for eternity. Do you live each day with that fact in view?   —J. B. N.

4. Look not every man on his own things, but every man also on the things of others.

Our motivations must extend beyond the desire to avoid offending *others*. We must truly look out for the interests of others, even though they may be at odds with our own interests. In the church this can be difficult. Should we spend our limited funds to hire a youth minister or a senior citizens minister? Should we be funding our church's own food pantry or the local food bank? Paul gives his answer in the next verse.

C. Attitude of Christ (v. 5)

5. Let this mind be in you, which was also in Christ Jesus.

All of our attitudes should be patterned after the attitudes of *Jesus*. This is why it is important to study His life; that is the only way to understand what He did.

This is a consistent message in Paul's writings. Earlier Paul warned the Christians in Rome to avoid being "conformed" to the selfish ways of the world. Instead, they were to be "transformed" by having new minds, minds that were in line with the mind of Christ (Romans 12:2). He told the Corinthian church that even though Christ in Heaven was rich beyond all measure, He became poor for our sakes (2 Corinthians 8:9).

II. The Hymn to Christ (Philippians 2:6-11)

A. Christ's Preexistence (v. 6)

6. Who, being in the form of God, thought it not robbery to be equal with God.

Many newer translations format this section as poetry, attempting to give the sense of how it may have been used in worship. The hymn begins with an affirmation of Jesus' divine status before He came to earth as a man. He was like *God* in both *form* and equality.

The seeming paradox of the nature of the Godhead is present here: Jesus is both distinct from God and at the same time *equal* to God. This verse is not talking about two equally powerful gods who are united only in purpose, a thought that might be at home in Greek philosophy. There is equality between the Father and the Son.

B. Christ's Incarnation (vv. 7, 8)

7. But made himself of no reputation, and took upon him the form of a servant, and was made in the likeness of men.

The hymn now gives us one of the most profound explanations of the incarnation in all of Scripture. *Made himself of no reputation* is literally "emptied himself." Christ debased himself. Why? The answer has been given already: He esteemed others (us) more important than himself.

Another insight into the significance of the incarnation is that Jesus ministered to others as *a servant*—literally, a slave. A slave is someone with no rights and is considered to be property of the master. Jesus, the King of kings, did not come as a conqueror. Instead He taught that the way to be great in the kingdom of God was to be the servant of all (Mark 10:44).

This was a prophesied role for the Messiah. Isaiah said that Jesus would be "despised, and we esteemed him not" (Isaiah 53:3). This reflects the ancient attitude towards slaves. They were looked down upon as the lowest rung of the ladder of humanity. We see the servant attitude of Jesus in His final meal with His disciples. At this dinner Jesus himself took on the role of a household slave and washed the feet of all present, a demeaning and odious task (John 13:14).

8. And being found in fashion as a man, he humbled himself, and became obedient unto death, even the death of the cross.

The hymn moves to Jesus' *death* on *the cross*, the ultimate act of servanthood and self-sacrifice. Jesus died an innocent man, guilty of no crime. His crucifixion was not an act of triumph or strength in a human sense. It was an act of self-humiliation and weakness (see 2 Corinthians 13:4). Even on the cross, Jesus could have rescued himself by summoning legions of angel warriors (see Matthew 26:53). Instead, He chose not to assert His equality with God but died for our sins (1 Corinthians 15:3). [See question #4, page 160.]

C. Christ's Exaltation (vv. 9-11)

9. Wherefore God also hath highly exalted him, and given him a name which is above every name.

The crucifixion was therefore necessary, and it required that Christ become human and submit obediently to this horrible, unjust death. That was not the end of the story, however. God honored Jesus, first by raising Him from the dead (Acts 2:32) and then by exalting Him to God's right hand, a position of honor and authority (Acts 2:33). He has a position unchallenged and unequaled by any other: King of kings and Lord of lords (1 Timothy 6:15; Revelation 19:16). [See question #5, page 160.]

HIGHLY EXALTED

Mark Twain's novel *The Prince and the Pauper* tells the story of Tom Canty and Edward Tudor. Tom was born into poverty; Edward was born

"Be like-minded, having the same love, being of one accord, of one mind."
—Philippians 2:2

Visual for Lesson 5

Point to this visual as you ask, "How can acts of service demonstrate that we are 'of one mind'"?

into the royal family, the son of King Henry VIII, and was the heir to the kingdom. Becoming acquainted in a chance meeting, the boys traded clothes, and circumstances soon traded their experiences. Edward, dressed in Tom's rags, was thrust from the palace; Tom, dressed in Edward's finery, dwelt in luxury.

Edward soon experienced the deprivation of the impoverished. Beaten, starved, and humiliated, he learned what it was like to become part of the urban poor. Through various experiences he discovered how the other side of England lived. When Henry VIII died, Edward was able to make himself known and was placed on the throne as king. From barely existing in the lowest levels of poverty, he was exalted to the highest station in the kingdom.

Although Jesus was in quite different circumstances, the change in His position also was startling. He gave up His position in Heaven to live in economic poverty on earth. He became poor (2 Corinthians 8:9). Living as a man among men, He came to know firsthand our struggles and failures. He was beaten, humiliated, and even crucified. Yet God took Jesus from that lowly position, raised Him from the dead, highly exalted Him, and restored Him to His rightful place in Heaven. This is the one we serve.   —J. B. N.

10, 11. That at the name of Jesus every knee should bow, of things in heaven, and things in earth, and things under the earth; and that every tongue should confess that Jesus Christ is Lord, to the glory of God the Father.

The implications of Jesus' exaltation are now given. First, every created being, whether in the physical realm or the spiritual realm, will *bow* before *Jesus*. We should understand this bowing as more than a mere act of respect or courtesy. It is an act of worship (see Revelation 5:14). The Bible teaches that worship is for God and God alone (see Revelation 22:9). For the hymn to envision universal worship of Jesus is a strong affirmation of His deity.

Second, the worshiping will be accompanied by a confession. This word *confession* is sometimes misunderstood. This is not a confession of our sins or crimes. It is confession in the sense of acknowledgment, a statement of strong and passionate belief. All creatures, including all men and women, thus will acknowledge that Jesus is indeed the *Lord*. The saved will do so gladly, eagerly. The unsaved will have no choice; resistance will be futile. The truth that they rejected in their earthly lives will be all too clear, to their eternal disgrace.

Conclusion

A. Thinking as Jesus Thought

Have you ever heard a tune that stuck in your head for days? Every time I visit a certain famous theme park and ride a particular ride, I am haunted by a song about a "small world" for days. But I still do it because I enjoy the ride.

What makes us think the way we do? How do certain thoughts (or tunes) get stuck in our minds? Why do we think some things to be trivial and other things to be important? What causes us to care about some things and ignore other things? To push this even further, why do we sometimes have thoughts we don't want to have (or, at least, that we regret later)?

Home Daily Bible Readings

Monday, Dec. 25—The Magi Give Honor (Matthew 2:1-11)
Tuesday, Dec. 26—Jesus Is Presented (Luke 2:22-38)
Wednesday, Dec. 27—Jesus, Our Brother (Hebrews 2:5-13)
Thursday, Dec. 28—Christ, Our Great High Priest (Hebrews 2:14-18)
Friday, Dec. 29—Unity of Spirit (1 Peter 3:8-12)
Saturday, Dec. 30—Be Like Christ (Philippians 2:1-5)
Sunday, Dec. 31—Jesus Emptied Himself (Philippians 2:6-11)

"The unwanted thought" seems to be part of the human condition. We get angry and think terrible things about an irritating coworker. Later, though, we may be ashamed at what we thought. We see an attractive person and our minds flash inappropriately. Later we are ashamed for thinking that way. We lose patience with our spouse and blame him or her for our inadequacies. Later, when we reflect, we are ashamed of such thoughts and appreciate this person deeply.

Paul speaks elsewhere about bringing every thought captive to our obedience to Christ (2 Corinthians 10:5). What he means is that we must make Jesus the Lord of our thought life. Our minds are not fortresses of solitude where Jesus is not welcome. If He is truly our Lord, then our minds must be open to His presence without shame or fear.

How can we accomplish this on a practical level? The Philippian Hymn outlines a very clear strategy: we begin to think like Jesus. This does not mean we try to imagine what we would do if we were the King of kings as He is. It means we look for ways to serve others. We think of how we can help others, not just help ourselves.

Jesus declared that He came to serve, not to be served (Matthew 20:28). When we adopt this attitude, we have made a giant leap toward adopting the mind of Christ. Paul described this attitude as the difference between being "carnally minded" and being "spiritually minded" (Romans 8:6). Those thoughts that cause us to be ashamed will not be welcome in the mind that is set on Christ and acknowledging His presence.

How can you improve your thought life in the new year ahead? Are there things you need to avoid, things that pull you from having your mind open to Jesus? Specifically is there an area in your church or family life where you have been selfish? Take a minute to think of a concrete example; then be resolved to eliminate this unchristlike attitude by fixing your mind on Jesus and adopting the desire to serve others rather than to be served.

B. Prayer

Loving God, help us to begin the new year with a deeper desire to serve You by serving others. May Your Spirit always be working within us to remake our minds to be like the mind of our Lord Jesus Christ. We pray this in His name, the name above all names, amen.

C. Thought to Remember

Submitting to the lordship of Jesus means we are willing to humble ourselves and serve others.

Learning by Doing

This page contains an alternative lesson plan emphasizing learning activities.
Classes desiring such student involvement will find these suggestions helpful.

Learning Goals

After participating in this lesson, each student will be able to:

1. Tell of ways that Christ humbled himself.

2. Discuss how Christ's humility gave way to His exaltation.

3. Identify one specific area in which he or she will adopt an attitude of service to others.

Into the Lesson

Before class begins, cluster the classroom chairs into groupings of two to five chairs. Prepare one slip of paper for each group with the phrase, *Why We Do the Things We Do*. Also write one of the following categories on each slip: mow the lawn; paint the house; get a college degree; clean and wax the car; buy new clothes; take a family trip. (Feel free to shrink or expand the list based on class size.)

Tape one slip of paper underneath a chair in each group. Write *Why We Do the Things We Do* on the board or overhead.

At the beginning of class, ask each group to pick a "scribe" to take notes for their group and to be ready to report. At your signal each group will find the slip of paper taped under one of its chairs. They then will have only two minutes to create a list of the reasons or motivations for accomplishing the task written on their paper. After two minutes only the group with the longest list will be allowed to share its list with the class.

Make the transition to Bible study by saying, "The kind of motivation and the strength of motivation we have for a task often determines what we do and how well we do it. God calls us to a task that is often difficult to accept or understand in a world that encourages us to be self-serving. God calls us to be *servants* as well as to be *leaders*. To accomplish that commission of being servant-leaders, we need to understand motivation: why Christians do (or should do) the things we do."

Into the Word

The class will continue to work in their groups. Have one of your good readers read the entire text aloud; then give each team one of the following group assignments.

Team #1: Attitude of Unity (Philippians 2:1, 2). Paul begins this passage on servant-leadership with four "if-statements." While the statements are rhetorical in nature, we know that Paul wants us to think about these truths. Examine verses 1 and 2; summarize your interpretation and application for the rest of the class.

Team #2: Attitude of Servanthood and of Christ (Philippians 2:3-5). Your group will address the theme "why we do the things we do." Paul lists reasons why *not* to do things in church while also telling us what to do. Discover what Paul teaches about motivation for servant-leadership and give examples of why these actions/attitudes are or are not important.

Team #3: Christ's Preexistence (Philippians 2:6). Your task is to examine one portion of this hymn and interpret its significance for the rest of the class. Keep in mind the hymn's theme of servant-leadership.

Team #4: Christ's Incarnation (Philippians 2:7, 8). Your task is to examine one portion of this hymn and interpret its significance for the rest of the class. Keep in mind the hymn's theme of servant-leadership.

Team #5: Christ's Exaltation (Philippians 2:9-11). Your task is to examine one portion of this hymn and interpret its significance for the rest of the class. Keep in mind the hymn's theme of servant-leadership.

Allow time for each group to report its conclusions. With five groups you will need to keep the reports somewhat brief. If you have a small class, double up some assignments.

Into Life

Ask and discuss the following questions with the entire class:

1. Why and how is the concept of servant-leadership of value in the business world?

2. What do those "business world values" teach us about why servant-leadership is good for the church and for Christians—or is the teaching the other way around? Explain.

3. What project or class activity could we do together that demonstrate servant-leadership?

Following discussion of the last question, select an activity and assign a planning team; then make that activity happen in the near future.

Let's Talk It Over

The questions on this page are designed to promote discussion of the lesson by the class and to encourage application of the lesson Scriptures. The answers provided are only discussion starters. Let your class talk it over from there.

1. Paul uses four rhetorical "if-statements." to depict an attitude of unity. Which of the four do you find most helpful personally? Why? What other phrases would you use to describe your relationship to the Lord?

Answers will be personal and wide-ranging. If starting a phrase with "if" seems awkward for the last question, use the word *because*. For example, "Because Christ held nothing back when He came to serve, we should be willing to share our deepest concerns for one another."

2. Wouldn't it be great if those in the church were always of one mind! What are some things that cause dissonance within the church? What actions can we take to keep dissonance and disunity from gaining a foothold?

Many examples could be cited—differences in musical tastes, different expectations on mission funding, and different preferences on how staff members should spend their time are just three. Worship, evangelism, nurture, and benevolence are core tasks of the church. Yet too often it is the peripheral activities are the ones that cause difficulties. For instance few churches seem to make it through a building program without hurt feelings.

Secular leadership philosophy may be able to offer the church some help by means of its theories on "change management." But the examples and teachings of Christ, Paul, Peter, etc. will undoubtedly be of the greater help. If your church is thinking about making a major change in some area, an advance Bible study on how characters of the Bible handled (or should have handled) change will be invaluable.

3. Well-intentioned counselors often equate good psychological health with certain assertive behaviors. How does verse 3 help you respond to this kind of philosophy?

While an entire study could be devoted to this topic, it is safe to generalize that self-assertiveness training often is not centered in the lifestyle that Paul is advocating. Yet we should not go to the extreme of thinking that Paul is teaching complete self-deprivation.

We see in Paul the stance that a very controlled, spiritually mature attitude is needed in

order to relinquish an opinion that can cause division. The same is needed in order to allow someone else to have the praise when it could be ours instead.

4. The ultimate test of Jesus' humility came as He submitted to the atrocities leading to the cross. How will you use Jesus' humility as a model in your own life?

An amazing thing about Jesus' humility was that He underwent such brutality when He had the power to put a stop to it at any time (Matthew 26:53). Often we speak of someone in a certain situation as being "brave" or "courageous." But if we examine that situation carefully, we may discover that the "brave" choice the person made was his or her only real option. This is quite different from the situation of Jesus. His humility best serves as an example for us when we have alternative paths from which to choose.

The discussion can help your class understand the amount of control that Jesus had to show as He yielded himself to the mocking crowds and taunting soldiers. We can note that the types of humiliation and sacrifices we make pale by comparison.

5. Before Jesus' exaltation to the right hand of the Father, He led an earthly life of humility. What are one or two specific things you will do this week to model that humility?

A smart aleck once said that he was trying to develop a sense of humility that he could be proud of. Hmmm! Joking aside, we realize that a life of humility probably won't yield many rewards in an earthly sense. We embrace this lifestyle because this is what Jesus desires (John 13:1-17). We embrace this lifestyle even though it runs counter to the me-first mentality that characterizes our world.

To fail to live a life of humility is very displeasing to God. James and John got themselves into a bit of trouble when they talked to Jesus about the exalted positions that they wanted (see Mark 10:35-45). Rather than spending too much time thinking how high we can rise, we are undoubtedly better off meditating on and practicing a lifestyle of humble service.

"I Am from Above"

DEVOTIONAL READING: John 14:23-31.

BACKGROUND SCRIPTURE: John 8:31-59.

PRINTED TEXT: John 8:31-38, 48-56, 58, 59.

John 8:31-38, 48-56, 58, 59

31 Then said Jesus to those Jews which believed on him, If ye continue in my word, then are ye my disciples indeed;

32 And ye shall know the truth, and the truth shall make you free.

33 They answered him, We be Abraham's seed, and were never in bondage to any man: how sayest thou, Ye shall be made free?

34 Jesus answered them, Verily, verily, I say unto you, Whosoever committeth sin is the servant of sin.

35 And the servant abideth not in the house for ever: but the Son abideth ever.

36 If the Son therefore shall make you free, ye shall be free indeed.

37 I know that ye are Abraham's seed; but ye seek to kill me, because my word hath no place in you.

38 I speak that which I have seen with my Father: and ye do that which ye have seen with your father.

. . . .

48 Then answered the Jews, and said unto him, Say we not well that thou art a Samaritan, and hast a devil?

49 Jesus answered, I have not a devil; but I honor my Father, and ye do dishonor me.

50 And I seek not mine own glory: there is one that seeketh and judgeth.

51 Verily, verily, I say unto you, If a man keep my saying, he shall never see death.

52 Then said the Jews unto him, Now we know that thou hast a devil. Abraham is

dead, and the prophets; and thou sayest, If a man keep my saying, he shall never taste of death.

53 Art thou greater than our father Abraham, which is dead? and the prophets are dead: whom makest thou thyself?

54 Jesus answered, If I honor myself, my honor is nothing: it is my Father that honoreth me; of whom ye say, that he is your God:

55 Yet ye have not known him; but I know him: and if I should say, I know him not, I shall be a liar like unto you: but I know him, and keep his saying.

56 Your father Abraham rejoiced to see my day: and he saw it, and was glad.

. . . .

58 Jesus said unto them, Verily, verily, I say unto you, Before Abraham was, I am.

59 Then took they up stones to cast at him: but Jesus hid himself, and went out of the temple, going through the midst of them, and so passed by.

GOLDEN TEXT: Then said Jesus to those Jews which believed on him, If ye continue in my word, then are ye my disciples indeed; and ye shall know the truth, and the truth shall make you free.—John 8:31, 32.

Jesus Christ: A Portrait of God
Unit 2: Christ Sustains and Supports
(Lessons 6-9)

Lesson Aims

After participating in this lesson, each student will be able to:

1. List some reasons people rejected Jesus.

2. Explain the concepts of spiritual slavery and freedom.

3. Move from slavery to freedom through Jesus in one area of thought or habit.

Lesson Outline

INTRODUCTION
  A. Slaves to Sin
  B. Lesson Background
 I. ABOUT THE JEWS' STATUS (John 8:31-38)
  A. Discipleship and Truth (vv. 31, 32)
  B. Servants and Sons (vv. 33-36)
  C. Attitude and Testimony (vv. 37, 38)
 II. ABOUT JESUS HIMSELF (John 8:48-56, 58, 59)
  A. First Accusation (v. 48)
    You Are a Samaritan
  B. First Response (vv. 49-51)
  C. Second Accusation (vv. 52, 53)
  D. Second Response (vv. 54-56, 58)
    Knowing God
  E. Actions (v. 59)
CONCLUSION
  A. The Freedom Center
  B. Prayer
  C. Thought to Remember

Introduction

A. Slaves to Sin

Ron is a longtime Christian who worked for many years as an information technology director for a large company. His boss and coworkers admired his dedication, honesty, and integrity. One day, however, Ron was called to his supervisor's office to be told that he was being fired for violating the company's "fair use" policy: a colleague had discovered a huge number of pornographic images stored in Ron's computer.

Ron confessed that he had become addicted to Internet porn. His technical expertise had enabled him able to hide the files for some time. Ironically Ron had become aware of Internet porn while investigating other employees, several of whom had been fired for similar violations. Ron lost his job but saved his marriage and family by confessing his sin and seeking counseling. He told his counselor that he was glad he had been caught because he had felt for a long time that the porn had taken control of him.

Ron's situation illustrates the irony of addiction to sinful habits: we fear the loss of short-term gratification if we quit, but at the same time we fear the long-term consequences if we don't. This is true not only of "high profile" sins such as pornography and drug abuse, but also of more common sins like anger, gossip, and lying. Once we develop a habit of doing the wrong thing, it becomes very difficult to change on our own. In our lesson today Christ offers us freedom from the power of sin and the fear of death.

B. Lesson Background

The events and teachings recorded in John 7 and 8 occurred during one of Jesus' visits to the Feast of Tabernacles in Jerusalem (see John 7:1, 2, 37; 8:20). God instituted this festival for two reasons. First, it was a time of thanksgiving during the season of the olive and fruit harvests (the September–October time frame). Second, it was as a time to remember deliverance from slavery in Egypt (see Leviticus 23:33-44).

As something of an object lesson, many who celebrated this festival would live in tents ("tabernacles") outside the city to reenact the 40 years that the Israelites had lived in tents while wandering in the wilderness. It is against this backdrop of deliverance from physical bondage that Jesus proceeds to demonstrate the way to deliverance from spiritual bondage.

I. About the Jews' Status
(John 8:31-38)

A. Discipleship and Truth (vv. 31, 32)

31. Then said Jesus to those Jews which believed on him, If ye continue in my word, then are ye my disciples indeed.

The word *Jews* seems somewhat out of place here because both Jesus and John (the author of this Gospel) are Jews by race, culture, and religion. Why would a Jewish person refer to other Jewish people as "Jews," as though they were somehow different from himself?

Scholars generally see this unusual terminology as evidence that John had been persecuted by Jewish people by the time he writes, just as Jesus had predicted (John 16:1-4). The story of the blind man in chapter 9 reveals that this sort of persecution already had begun during Jesus' ministry (see especially John 9:22).

Here at John 8:31 we see that some Jewish people have gone against the grain and have taken a positive view of Jesus. These are the ones *which believed on him* (see also v. 30). Jesus proceeds to test their faith by stressing that they must accept His teachings if they wish to be *disciples.* The verses to follow will reveal that they are not quite ready for that level of commitment.

32. And ye shall know the truth, and the truth shall make you free.

Truth refers back to Jesus' "word" in verse 31, which He now says will give freedom to believers. The context reveals that John is not referring to Jesus' ethical commands about lifestyle issues (the Gospel of John actually includes very little of that sort of teaching). In John 8:12-29 Jesus has been speaking about His identity as the light of the world, the one who reveals God in a special way. Believers *know the truth* in the sense that they accept what Jesus claims about himself; they recognize Him as the unique Son of God.

This is the truth that gives us freedom. Our acceptance of Christ through His plan of salvation allows us to become children of God. This liberates us from the power and consequences of sin and death (see John 1:12).

B. Servants and Sons (vv. 33-36)

33. They answered him, We be Abraham's seed, and were never in bondage to any man: how sayest thou, Ye shall be made free?

At first glance, the Jews seem to be very forgetful. Their people, in fact, had been *in bondage* many times over the years: slaves in Egypt; oppressed by foreign powers many times during the judges period; taken in exile to Babylon; dominated by Rome even as they spoke. The reference to Abraham suggests, however, that they are thinking of their spiritual status with God.

How to Say It

ABRAHAM. *Ay*-bruh-ham.
AD HOMINEM. add *hah*-muh-nem.
BABYLON. *Bab*-uh-lun.
EGYPT. *Ee*-jipt.
EZRA. *Ez*-ruh.
GENTILE. *Jen*-tile.
GERIZIM. *Gair*-ih-zeem or Guh-*rye*-zim.
JUDEA. Joo-*dee*-uh.
NEHEMIAH. *Nee*-huh-*my*-uh (strong accent on *my*).
SAMARITANS. Suh-*mare*-uh-tunz.

Ancient Jews believe that having God's favor comes from being born as descendants of Abraham, the person to whom God had made covenant promises (Genesis 12:1-3). Jesus, however, seems to say that their descent from that great man is not enough. So they want to know how He can make such a preposterous claim.

34. Jesus answered them, Verily, verily, I say unto you, Whosoever committeth sin is the servant of sin.

Jesus challenges the Jews' claim to spiritual freedom by stating the obvious: everyone *committeth sin.* That fact should eliminate any prideful belief that a person can somehow get to God through ancestral connections.

Even if the Jews do think of themselves as "born into God's family," every subsequent sin should have underlined how far away from God's will they had gone. Sin alienates us from God and enslaves us to carnal desires. [See question #1, page 168.] This is a problem that our parents cannot solve for us.

35, 36. And the servant abideth not in the house for ever: but the Son abideth ever. If the Son therefore shall make you free, ye shall be free indeed.

Jesus' words refer to legal relationships in ancient households. A son and a *servant* may live in the same house, and both serve the same person (the father, who is also the master). But the servant is, ultimately, not a permanent part of the family. He or she has no legal rights. The fact that the Jews are servants of sin shows that they do not enjoy full status as God's heirs.

A son, however, is heir to everything the father has. A son carries the family name from generation to generation. The son's status in a household is thus permanent *(abideth forever)* because he is a true member of the family. The genuine *Son* in view here is Jesus himself.

Jesus as this Son has the power to grant full membership in the family. Abraham, himself a sinner and a servant, cannot grant true spiritual freedom. The phrase *free indeed* brings with it the sense, "I am the one who can set you free from sin and its power forever."

C. Attitude and Testimony (vv. 37, 38)

37. I know that ye are Abraham's seed; but ye seek to kill me, because my word hath no place in you.

The word *but* highlights the irony of the situation. As the Jews well know, Abraham was famous for his faith (compare Genesis 12:1-4; 22:1-3). The Jews are not doing a very good job of following their famous forefather's example.

When they hear God's message through Jesus they respond not with belief but by trying to silence him (compare John 5:18; 7:19, 25, 32, 44).

38. I speak that which I have seen with my Father: and ye do that which ye have seen with your father.

Jesus stresses again and again that He speaks and acts in complete harmony with the *Father* (see John 4:34; 7:16; 10:38; 12:44; 14:9-11). Jesus' power both to do great works and to offer freedom from sin finds its source in this unity.

Similarly, the Jews' refusal to accept Him reveals the true source of their thinking. They claim to be Abraham's descendants. But their lack of faith in the one whom God sent reveals that they actually are children of the devil (John 8:43, 44, not in today's text). The Jews will remain under Satan's power as long as they reject Jesus' words. [See question #2, page 168.]

II. About Jesus Himself
(John 8:48-56, 58, 59)

A. First Accusation (v. 48)

48. Then answered the Jews, and said unto him, Say we not well that thou art a Samaritan, and hast a devil?

Just before this verse, Jesus had stressed again that His words come from God. Thus He condemns *the Jews* for their disbelief. He can only interpret their stubbornness as evidence that "ye are not of God" (v. 47).

This claim is extremely offensive to the Jews, but they do not know how to refute it. Jesus invited them to prove Him guilty of sin, but instead they resort to name-calling. The Samaritans are a people of mixed Jewish and Gentile descent who live just north of Judea and worship at Mount Gerizim. The hostility between Jews and Samaritans is well documented both in the Bible (Ezra 4:1-5; Nehemiah 4:1-8; John 4:9) and in other literature.

Jews and Samaritans each claim to be God's elect people. The accusation that Jesus is *a Samaritan* follows from His statement that the Jews are not acting as true children of Abraham. The accusation that Jesus is demon-possessed is an attempt to contradict Jesus' statement in verse 38. The Jews think that Jesus' words do not come from God but rather from the *devil*, because surely neither God nor a true prophet would call them "slaves to sin"!

YOU ARE A SAMARITAN

The *ad hominem* argument is one of the oldest fallacies in the history of logic. The name of this argument literally means that it is an argument against the person, rather than against the logic of the person's argument. It is an easy and convenient way of scoring points off an opponent.

Sometimes it can be used in a humorous way. As children we could end an argument by stating, "Your grandmother wears combat boots!" Modern politicians can dismiss certain issues by claiming their opponents are "left wing" or "right wing." Valid points can be ridiculed by commenting, "You're only a truck driver; what do you know about international diplomacy?" By giving people labels with negative overtones, we can dismiss their observations unfairly.

Jesus' opponents found it hard to respond to His discussion on the proper behavior of the children of Abraham—with the implication that the Jews were not acting as true children of Abraham should. So they simply dismissed His comments by saying that He was a Samaritan. In their minds that ended the discussion. Ethnic Samaritans could not be expected to contribute intelligently to a discussion on Judaism, so Jesus' comments could be ignored.

Yet *ad hominem* arguments don't prove anything. They are a fallacy and therefore irrelevant to the discussion. The observations that Jesus makes are still valid. His critique cannot be overlooked simply by name-calling. Neither can modern society dismiss Him by thinking of Him as a mere first-century carpenter.   —J. B. N.

B. First Response (vv. 49-51)

49, 50. Jesus answered, I have not a devil; but I honor my Father, and ye do dishonor me. And I seek not mine own glory: there is one that seeketh and judgeth.

Jesus, unlike the Jews, does not reject the word of the *Father* but rather obeys. Further, while the Jews are seeking affirmation of their own spirituality, Jesus is seeking only to do God's will. God, however, is seeking to glorify Jesus. God knows that what Jesus says is true. The Jews will therefore be in a dangerous situation unless they repent. [See question #3, page 168.]

51. Verily, verily, I say unto you, If a man keep my saying, he shall never see death.

Obviously Jesus is using the word *death* in a way other than in a physical sense, since everyone dies. Death here refers to the lost state of those who do not accept Christ (compare 1 John 3:14). That condition will become irreversible once we leave this world. Only those who believe Jesus' claims about himself will escape this fate and enjoy eternal life (John 6:63, 68).

The verse before us follows logically from Jesus' earlier remarks in verse 34 about slavery to sin. As Paul notes in 1 Corinthians 15:56, "the sting of death is sin." Those who accept Jesus need not fear judgment. Their belief in Him frees them from sin's power and makes them God's children. [See question #4, page 168.]

The phrase *verily, verily* appears often in the Gospel of John to draw attention to particularly important sayings by Jesus. As is the case here (and at v. 34), comments followed by this formula often relate to Jesus' divine identity or the need to accept Him in order to receive salvation (see John 1:51; 3:3, 5, 11; 5:19, 24, 25; 6:47; 12:24; 13:20).

C. Second Accusation (vv. 52, 53)

52, 53. Then said the Jews unto him, Now we know that thou hast a devil. Abraham is dead, and the prophets; and thou sayest, If a man keep my saying, he shall never taste of death. Art thou greater than our father Abraham, which is dead? and the prophets are dead: whom makest thou thyself?

Taking Jesus' discussion of *death* in a physical sense, the Jews mock His claim. Even their great heroes of the faith, *Abraham* and *the prophets*, could not grant life; in fact these people died themselves. The Jews' comment suggests that it would be impossible for any human being to do what Jesus claims He can do.

Apparently the Jews' earlier "faith" that we saw in John 8:31 was based on the idea that Jesus was some sort of prophet or holy man (compare John 7:40). Now, however, they suspect that He may be claiming something more.

D. Second Response (vv. 54-56, 58)

54. Jesus answered, If I honor myself, my honor is nothing: it is my Father that honoreth me; of whom ye say, that he is your God.

Jesus responds by pointing out that *God,* working through Him, is making Jesus' true identity plain to the world. Many people may refer to God as *Father* because they recognize Him to be the creator of the universe, yet Jesus is God's Son in a unique way. Thus the Jews (and others) reject God's offer of freedom and life when they refuse to believe Jesus. God honors Jesus both by empowering His miraculous works and, ultimately, by raising Him from the dead and restoring His divine glory in Heaven (John 17:5).

55. Yet ye have not known him; but I know him: and if I should say, I know him not, I shall be a liar like unto you: but I know him, and keep his saying.

Jesus now exposes the real reason that the Jews cannot accept Him: their misunderstanding of Jesus reflects a deeper misunderstanding of

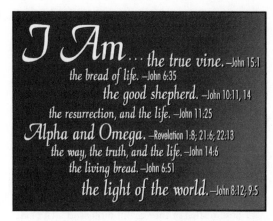

Visual for Lesson 6. *Point to this visual as you ask, "Which of these 'I am' statements do you find most meaningful personally? Why?"*

God. Everything that Jesus does and says reveals the Father in a dark world, so that one can see God in Jesus (John 14:7-10). Those who reject Jesus, then, actually are rejecting the God who sent Him. John raises this point at the very beginning of his gospel by noting that Jesus' "own [the Jews] received him not" (John 1:11). They refuse to recognize God's power at work in Him. [See question #5, page 168.]

KNOWING GOD

I know that World War II happened. I have read books about it, seen pictures taken during it, listened to recordings of speeches by Roosevelt and Churchill. Yet if my father were to say, "I know World War II happened," he could speak with more authority than I could. In 1943 he was drafted into the army and saw service in New Guinea and the Philippines. I know about the war, but he knew it firsthand.

The verb *to know* has two meanings, both in English and in Greek. On the one hand it can mean to know something intellectually, or to have what we often call "head knowledge." This applies to facts, information, etc. Another meaning of *to know* is to have experience of something. This goes beyond mere head knowledge. This has to do with life experience and awareness.

The Jews had knowledge of God. They had learned the Old Testament; they had studied the law. They performed the ritual cleansings; they practiced tithing. The Jews knew factual data and information *about* God. But had they really experienced God in their hearts?

Jesus could claim, "I know Him," because He had firsthand experience with God. Jesus invites us to go beyond mere knowledge about Him and experience Him in our hearts.   —J. B. N.

56, 58. Your father Abraham rejoiced to see my day: and he saw it, and was glad. . . . Jesus said unto them, Verily, verily, I say unto you, Before Abraham was, I am.

Jesus confirms the Jews' suspicions by noting two ways in which He is superior to Abraham. First, *Abraham rejoiced to see* Jesus' *day.* Some ancient rabbis believed that God had revealed the secrets of the messianic age to Abraham in a vision (compare Genesis 15:17-21). A better idea may be that Jesus is referring to the joy that Abraham experienced when told by God that "in thee shall all families of the earth be blessed" (Genesis 12:3). The Jews of Christ's day have the opportunity to see that promise fulfilled in the coming of Abraham's descendant Jesus. Abraham, then, was looking forward to what Christ would do.

Second, and much more substantially, Jesus existed before Abraham. Such a statement would be absurd if Jesus were a normal human being (compare John 8:57, not in today's text). But it is obvious that Jesus is claiming something more. *I am* is drawn from Exodus 3:13, 14, where God refers to himself as Yahweh, meaning "the one who exists."

The ancient Jews came to treat that "I am" phrase as God's sacred name. Many times in the Gospel of John, Jesus describes himself with a statement that begins with *I am*—"I am the light of the world," "I am the good shepherd," etc. But when *I am* is used in the absolute sense—alone and with no other words following—Jesus is applying God's sacred name directly to himself.

This highlights Jesus' own divine nature. Jesus can offer freedom from sin and eternal life because He is, in fact, completely one with the God who existed before Abraham. It is therefore pointless for the Jews to appeal to Abraham as their spiritual forefather; Jesus is much greater than he is anyway.

E. Actions (v. 59)

59. Then took they up stones to cast at him: but Jesus hid himself, and went out of the temple, going through the midst of them, and so passed by.

The Jews' actions reveal that they finally have come to understand the implication of Jesus' words. Stoning was prescribed in the law for blasphemy (Leviticus 24:16). Clearly they realize that Jesus is claiming to be God; sadly they reject that claim and the eternal life that He offers.

Conclusion

A. The Freedom Center

Recently a new museum opened in Cincinnati, Ohio, called *The Freedom Center.* This museum celebrates the men and women who led the Underground Railroad before America's Civil War. Those heroes helped escaping slaves secretly make their way northward to freedom. The Ohio River—a natural boundary marker between North and South—symbolized a new life of liberty. Many pre–Civil War houses and buildings in northern Kentucky and southwestern Ohio still include secret rooms, trap doors, and concealed crawlspaces for hiding. The Underground Railroad provided a means of escape from a world of harsh servitude.

How much more profound is the eternal freedom that Jesus offers! He, and only He, is our "eternal underground railroad." To reject His route to freedom is both sad and amazing. Yet that's just what we see people doing in today's lesson. It is a pattern that continues today.

B. Prayer

Lord, we live in a world full of doubts and temptations. Very often we don't understand why we do the things we do. We want to do what's right, but we fall back into our old, bad habits and patterns.

Please give us both the power to believe Your Word and the faith to follow it at all costs. Then we can experience the freedom that Christ promised us. In Jesus' name, amen.

C. Thought to Remember

When facing temptation, ask: Did Jesus come to earth so I could do this or be free not to do it?

Home Daily Bible Readings

Monday, Jan. 1—A Voice in the Wilderness (John 1:19-28)

Tuesday, Jan. 2—Jesus Is the Lamb of God (John 1:29-34)

Wednesday, Jan. 3—Promises Fulfilled (Matthew 13:10-17)

Thursday, Jan. 4—Jesus Gives Peace (John 14:23-31)

Friday, Jan. 5—Jesus Is the Christ (Matthew 11:2-6)

Saturday, Jan. 6—Jesus Promises Freedom (John 8:31-38)

Sunday, Jan. 7—Jesus Speaks of Eternal Life (John 8:48-59)

Learning by Doing

This page contains an alternative lesson plan emphasizing learning activities.
Classes desiring such student involvement will find these suggestions helpful.

Learning Goals

After participating in this lesson, each student will be able to:

1. List some reasons people rejected Jesus.

2. Explain the concepts of spiritual slavery and freedom.

3. Move from slavery to freedom through Jesus in one area of thought or habit.

Into the Lesson

Display the word *FREEDOM* in letters large enough to be read across your assembly area. Use a separate sheet of paper for each letter. Next write the following letters on seven separate sheets of paper: *A, E, L, R, S, V, Y.* As class begins, show these seven letters one at a time in the order given.

As you show each letter, ask, "What is a common sin that begins with this letter?" Accept group answers. (Answers could include the following: swearing and stinginess for *S*; lying and lasciviousness for *L*; adultery and avarice for *A*; violence and vengeance for *V*; envy and exclusion for *E*; ritualism and rebellion for *R*.)

As sins are identified write them on the sheet bearing the letter under discussion. Then stick each sheet over the letters in *FREEDOM* as follows: *A* over the first *E*; *E* over *D*; *L* over *R*; *R* over *O*; *S* over *F*; *V* over the second *E*. When you show *Y,* say, "Do you see 'Y' we're doing this? The simple answer is 'Sin takes away our freedom and makes us slaves to evil.' That's the theme of today's study and Jesus' words in John 8:32-34."

Into the Word

Now display a large copy of the word *IF,* either written to fill a poster board or cut out from two poster boards. As you display it, say, "Now here is a BIG word!" Then say, "And today's text is filled with the word *if.*"

Assign a verse from the text to each learner. Then say, "Look at your verse and write an 'If-statement' based on your verse's idea; then personalize it." Give this example, based on verse 31: "If I stand fast in Jesus' Word, then I truly am His disciple." Allow a few minutes for consideration. Ask for responses in verse order.

Though responses for most verses are probably obvious, expect such things as the following:

Verse 32: "If I know the truth, then I will be truly free."

Verse 34: "If I commit sin, then sin becomes my master."

Verse 36: "If I am made free from sin by the Son of God, then I can't be any freer."

Verse 48: "If I think Jesus to be less than the Son of God, then why would I listen to Him or follow Him?"

Verse 50: "If I seek my own spiritual glory, then I am substituting self for God."

Verse 52: "If there is no life after death, then I have believed a lie."

Verse 53: "If Jesus can give me life after death, then He obviously is greater than Abraham or any of the prophets."

Verse 54: "If I honor myself, then I am not acting as Jesus did."

Verse 55: "If I know something and then deny its truth, then I have made myself a liar."

Verse 56: "If I want to be like Abraham, then I will rejoice in God's plan as He reveals it!"

Verse 58: "If Jesus is indeed the great 'I Am,' then I must accept Him as God."

Into Life

Call attention back to the Into the Lesson activity, which used the words *freedom* and *slavery.* Give each student a sheet of paper and ask him or her to draw seven squares. On the front of the paper students are to write the letters of the word *SLAVERY,* one letter per square. On the back of the paper, students are to write the word *FREEDOM.* Say, "Place the letters of each word in order back to back: *F* on the back of *S, R* on the back of *L,* etc."

Then suggest to your students that they use this paper for repentance and prayer times in the week ahead. They can use one block on each of the seven days of the upcoming week.

Give the following instructions: "On Monday tear off the block that has *S* on one side and *F* on the other. Consider a personal sin that begins with *S* (such as stinginess), and then flip the square over and use the letter *F* to ask God for forgiveness. Follow the same pattern each day as a reminder of *freedom* that we have in God's grace and forgiveness." Close with a prayer that includes those two ideas.

Let's Talk It Over

The questions on this page are designed to promote discussion of the lesson by the class and to encourage application of the lesson Scriptures. The answers provided are only discussion starters. Let your class talk it over from there.

1. How can admitting that sin is slavery help us in our battle against temptation?

One of Satan's most successful strategies involves convincing God's people that sinful practices are liberating. This was a significant part of his approach to Eve (Genesis 3).

One of the most crucial and successful techniques to resist Satan in this regard involves the willingness to call sin what Scripture calls it: bondage (compare Hebrews 2:15). No one in his or her right mind would find the thought of slavery appealing. Yet many do not acknowledge the enslaving power of particular sins until they experience it firsthand. By classifying sin accurately at the outset, we allow the Holy Spirit to guard us against temptation. There is a very real sense in which "forewarned is forearmed."

2. What are some ways that we, like the ancient Jews, might be tempted to allow ancestry and tradition to produce an inaccurate view of our spiritual status before God? How do we guard against this?

Those who come from devoutly Christian families might be lulled into assuming that that "godly aura" guarantees a right relationship with God. Due to the impact of their upbringing, people who come from a particular Christian heritage or denomination can at times find it difficult to let the Bible speak on its own terms.

Practices such as the singing of familiar songs, gathering with familiar people, and worshiping in a familiar place can provide great security. Such spiritual rhythms can become dangerous, however, if they become ends in themselves rather than as means to authentic relationship with God.

3. What are some practical lessons the example of Jesus can teach us regarding how to present the exclusive claims of the gospel?

We can never compromise the gospel message by communicating that salvation can be found in any way apart from an acknowledgment and acceptance of Jesus' person and work. We must also strive to make sure that if people take offense at the gospel message it is due to the message itself and not to our presentation of it. If we

suffer rejection for the sake of the gospel, we need to examine if that rejection is a reaction to the gospel message or is a reaction to our own obnoxious or abrasive attitude (1 Peter 3:15, 16).

The example of Jesus shows that strong and dramatic language sometimes may be necessary to help people see their spiritual condition. We caution ourselves with the realization that Jesus could see into people's hearts, but we cannot.

4. How should you as a Christian witness to someone who fears death? How would your witness to a Christian and a non-Christian differ, or would it?

Examining your own view of death is an important first step. Our view should be that death is an enemy, but it is a defeated enemy (1 Corinthians 15:26). Next, finding out why a person fears death is important. Some fear death because it is a great unknown. Some fear death because they dread the painful and difficult ways that people sometimes die. The list goes on.

Christians are not exempt from the pain of death. Yet we know that Jesus has emerged victorious by God's power—that's our hope. The fear that each Christian or non-Christian goes through is unique to him or her, so a canned approach will be counterproductive. Pray!

5. In what ways can Jesus' example help us in efforts to share the gospel with Jewish people today? What are some cautions?

We must be careful not to make blanket comparisons between modern Judaism and the Judaism of Jesus' opponents in the text. Modern Judaism manifests itself in various streams of belief (Orthodox, Conservative, and Reformed) that are not precisely parallel to the Judaism of Jesus' day.

Even so, Jesus is still the way, the truth, and the life. To the modern Jew we can demonstrate that Jesus is the Messiah anticipated in the Scriptures. One thing we dare *not* do is give the idea that a person can reject Christ, stay within Judaism, and still be saved. The missionary work and teaching of the apostle Paul dispels any such possibility (Acts 13:44-46; etc.). Doing all from love is crucial.

Jesus Is Authority and Judge

January 14
Lesson 7

DEVOTIONAL READING: 2 Timothy 4:1-5.

BACKGROUND SCRIPTURE: John 5:19-29.

PRINTED TEXT: John 5:19-29.

John 5:19-29

19 Then answered Jesus and said unto them, Verily, verily, I say unto you, The Son can do nothing of himself, but what he seeth the Father do: for what things soever he doeth, these also doeth the Son likewise.

20 For the Father loveth the Son, and showeth him all things that himself doeth: and he will show him greater works than these, that ye may marvel.

21 For as the Father raiseth up the dead, and quickeneth them; even so the Son quickeneth whom he will.

22 For the Father judgeth no man, but hath committed all judgment unto the Son:

23 That all men should honor the Son, even as they honor the Father. He that honoreth not the Son honoreth not the Father which hath sent him.

24 Verily, verily, I say unto you, He that heareth my word, and believeth on him that sent me, hath everlasting life, and shall not come into condemnation; but is passed from death unto life.

25 Verily, verily, I say unto you, The hour is coming, and now is, when the dead shall hear the voice of the Son of God: and they that hear shall live.

26 For as the Father hath life in himself; so hath he given to the Son to have life in himself;

27 And hath given him authority to execute judgment also, because he is the Son of man.

28 Marvel not at this: for the hour is coming, in the which all that are in the graves shall hear his voice,

29 And shall come forth; they that have done good, unto the resurrection of life; and they that have done evil, unto the resurrection of damnation.

GOLDEN TEXT: Verily, verily, I say unto you, He that heareth my word, and believeth on him that sent me, hath everlasting life, and shall not come into condemnation; but is passed from death unto life.—John 5:24.

Jesus Christ: A Portrait of God
Unit 2: Christ Sustains and Supports
(Lessons 6-9)

Lesson Aims

After participating in this lesson, each student will be able to:

1. Describe the authority that Jesus has.

2. Discuss how Jesus expects us to live in this world in anticipation of eternity.

3. Write a plan to honor Jesus' authority in one specific way.

Lesson Outline

INTRODUCTION
    A. Like Father, Like Son
    B. Lesson Background
I. FATHER AND SON (John 5:19-23)
    A. Unity (vv. 19-21)
        From the Same Timber
        The Apprentice
    B. Trust (v. 22)
    C. Honor (v. 23)
II. DEATH AND LIFE (John 5:24-29)
    A. Importance of Belief (vv. 24, 25)
        Hearing and Living
    B. Son of Man (vv. 26, 27)
    C. His Voice (v. 28)
    D. Our Status (v. 29)
CONCLUSION
    A. Don't Argue with the Judge
    B. Prayer
    C. Thought to Remember

Introduction

A. Like Father, Like Son

People who know my father often say that I bear a very strong resemblance to him. We look very much alike, and people can match us up as parent and child in a crowd.

I also resemble my father in other very notable ways that have nothing to do with our appearance. For example, I inherited my father's energy and work ethic, and people are often surprised at how much I will take on. I also share some of his tastes and interests: we both like auto racing, and both of us eat way too much candy.

In many respects a person who knows me well will also come to know many things about my fa-

ther, as his traits are reflected in my life. We often say that someone is a "chip off the old block" when a child is very much like a parent. In such cases we can learn a lot about someone just by looking at his or her children. This fact is evident to teachers and youth workers, who often see kids do and say things that they could have learned only at home.

Jesus frequently appeals to this principle in the Gospel of John to discuss His "sonship"—His unique identity as God's only-begotten Son. While we often think of Jesus' "sonship" in terms of His virginal conception, etc., Jesus usually mentions the sonship issue to highlight His complete unity with, and obedience to, the Father. As such we learn what God is like by looking at Jesus.

B. Lesson Background

Our text today follows the story of the healing at Bethesda (John 5:1-9). While in Jerusalem for a feast (v. 1), Jesus visited a pool where many sick people gathered for medical care. There He met a man who had been lame for 38 years. To the great surprise of the crowd—and especially to the surprise of the man himself—Jesus commanded him to rise, take his cot, and walk.

The miracle generated controversy, however, because it took place on the Sabbath. That was the weekly day of rest, when Jews were not permitted to work (v. 9). Some Jewish authorities who believed that carrying cots and healing were works prohibited on the Sabbath confronted the man and learned what Jesus had done.

When those authorities challenged Jesus, He justified His actions by noting God's power at work (v. 17). If God chooses to work on the Sabbath, who can object? The Jews considered this blasphemous. So they conspired to kill Jesus for "making himself equal with God" (v. 18). Jesus' comments in our printed text are a response to this persecution.

I. Father and Son
(John 5:19-23)

A. Unity (vv. 19-21)

19. Then answered Jesus and said unto them, Verily, verily, I say unto you, The Son can do nothing of himself, but what he seeth the Father do: for what things soever he doeth, these also doeth the Son likewise.

Jesus begins His defense by noting that He and *the Father* work together in complete harmony. Verse 19 describes something that Jesus does to reveal this unity, while verse 20 (below) highlights something that God does. While Jesus is equal to the Father in nature, He is completely obedient to Him in service. An implication of this fact is that any complaint about Jesus' words or actions is ultimately a complaint against God the Father.

Jesus portrays himself, in a way, as God's apprentice. In Jesus' day sons normally follow the family trade. Such trades include farming, fishing, and carpentry. Often a boy is apprenticed to his father, who teaches him the skills of the job. Jesus, as the faithful *Son*, follows His Father's every step. The result is that Jesus perfectly implements the Father's will. "I do nothing of myself; but as my Father hath taught me, I speak these things" (John 8:28).

FROM THE SAME TIMBER

"He's cut from the same timber" is a familiar old saying. A variation of this is "He's cut from the same piece of cloth." These are usually said of blood relatives who have the same characteristics. It could be two brothers or a father and son. The mannerisms, virtues, and qualities of one individual show up equally as well in the other.

My wife and I have two daughters. In many ways the older daughter resembles me (fortunately she's prettier than I am!); the younger daughter resembles my wife. It is sometimes uncanny how my older daughter has many of the same characteristics that I do. Obviously there are some things that she has copied from my own behavior. But some things have gone beyond mere copied behavior. I remember how amazed I was when she was a preschooler, and I saw her do some things that I know she had never seen me do. Some things have simply been genetically programmed into her that she probably has little control over.

If such things are true between an earthly father and his children, we should not be surprised that Jesus says that the same is true between himself and God the Father. The divine Son of God does the same things as His Father. John relays to us that whatever the Father does, these are the same things the Son does. "Like fa-

ther, like son" is just as true in the spiritual sense as it is in the human world. Thus when we obey the Son, we also obey the Father.   —J. B. N.

20. For the Father loveth the Son, and showeth him all things that himself doeth: and he will show him greater works than these, that ye may marvel.

Jesus shows His unity with *the Father* through faithful service, and the Father shows that unity by revealing *all things* to Jesus. If Jesus is, in a sense, the apprentice, then God is the caring mentor who teaches Jesus everything He knows (compare Luke 2:52).

The word *for* at the beginning of this verse has the sense of "because" as an explanation of what Jesus has just said in verse 19: He is able to do the Father's works because God loves Him and shows Him everything. In the immediate context this would refer to the healing of the man at Bethesda (John 5:1-9); the *greater works* would then refer to the surpassing miracles yet to come. These include the raising of Lazarus (John 11:39-44) and, ultimately, Jesus' own resurrection. The greater works must also include the granting of eternal life, as we see in verse 21, next.

THE APPRENTICE

As I write this in early 2005, the television show *The Apprentice* is all the rage. The formula is unique and clever; there has never been a television show quite like it.

A handful of contestants compete with one another for the sole privilege of becoming Donald Trump's apprentice. The competition also involves cooperation since the participants must work in teams. Their tasks include everything from selling lemonade to designing lines of clothing to fixing up old motels—whatever the writers of the show can dream up.

The team that loses each week must then present itself before Trump in the dreaded "boardroom." It is a dark and somber place. It is the place where the losing team must answer for its failure. It is a place where one person each week will hear Trump say the words that no one wants to hear: *You're fired!*

Trump picks his apprentice through a process of elimination. In effect his apprentice is the one who has failed the least. How different it is with Jesus! He never failed at a single task; He proved himself to be God through His own resurrection. Jesus, as the Father's "apprentice" (if it's appropriate to use that term for Him), has the Father's complete confidence. That's where our confidence should be as well.   —R. L. N.

How to Say It

BETHESDA. Buh-*thez*-duh.
EZEKIEL. Ee-*zeek*-ee-ul or Ee-*zeek*-yul.
JERUSALEM. Juh-*roo*-suh-lem.
LAZARUS. *Laz*-uh-rus.
PHARISEES. *Fair*-ih-seez.

21. For as the Father raiseth up the dead, and quickeneth them; even so the Son quickeneth whom he will.

The ability to raise the dead belongs to God alone. It is He who controls the final destiny of every human being (compare 2 Kings 5:7).

Jesus obviously is claiming this divine power for himself. Yet the exact meaning of the phrase *the Son quickeneth whom he will* needs to be examined. In a physical sense the phrase could refer to the upcoming resurrection of Lazarus. Some suggest that Jesus is referring to the healing power that He has just demonstrated at Bethesda—although the man who was lame was not physically dead, his life was restored to wholeness in a remarkable way.

In view of the discussion to follow, it seems that Jesus is most likely claiming that He even shares God's power to grant eternal life, not just physical healing. This being the case, it is hardly relevant to accuse Him of breaking the Sabbath (John 5:16). If He has ultimate authority over eternal judgment, He certainly can heal someone whenever He wants!

B. Trust (v. 22)

22. For the Father judgeth no man, but hath committed all judgment unto the Son.

The Jewish authorities have taken it upon themselves to judge Jesus a sinner and a blasphemer. They reach this judgment because He does not meet their expectations. But God has not called them to judge the world; rather, God has given the power of *judgment unto the Son*.

Following verse 21 the judgment in question clearly refers to the final judgment at the Last Day. That is when God will assign eternal rewards and punishments. For this reason Christians treat Jesus' teachings as the ultimate authority.

At first glance this verse would seem to conflict with John 3:17. There Jesus says that He did not come to judge the world, but rather to save the world. The tension is resolved easily when we note the difference between Jesus' purpose and His role. In terms of purpose, John 3:16 tells us that Jesus came to earth to proclaim and provide salvation. Two verses later, however, John clarifies that "he that believeth not is condemned already" (3:18). This means that those who do not accept Jesus' teaching have no other hope of salvation.

Consistent with this emphasis John 5:22 stresses Jesus' role as judge. Although Jesus wants everyone to be saved—so much so that He died for the world—He eventually will sit in judgment to condemn those who reject Him. [See question #1, page 176.]

C. Honor (v. 23)

23. That all men should honor the Son, even as they honor the Father. He that honoreth not the Son honoreth not the Father which hath sent him.

This verse is a warning to those who deny Jesus' claims or who criticize His actions. Common sense tells us that only a fool would show disrespect to a judge who is about to pass sentence. The opponents of Jesus should therefore carefully consider what they are saying about Him.

Any disrespect these opponents show to Jesus automatically dishonors God. This is so because Jesus is God's designated agent who speaks on the Father's behalf. Ironically the Jews have been trying to protect God's honor by persecuting Jesus. In fact that very persecution shows disrespect for God's authority.

II. Death and Life
(John 5:24-29)

A. Importance of Belief (vv. 24, 25)

24. Verily, verily, I say unto you, He that heareth my word, and believeth on him that sent me, hath everlasting life, and shall not come into condemnation; but is passed from death unto life.

Eternal, *everlasting life* is something that begins in this world. When we accept Jesus according to the biblical plan of salvation, we pass *from death unto life*. The word *death* as used here refers to separation from God, while *life* refers to the relationship with God that comes through Christ. "Verily, verily, I say unto you, If a man keep my saying, he shall never see death" (John 8:51; compare Colossians 1:13).

Physical death will not change this relationship, although it will finalize our decision. Those who accept Christ have everlasting life that begins now. They begin to enjoy the benefits of salvation and will continue to enjoy God's love eternally in the age to come. [See question #2, page 176.]

25. Verily, verily, I say unto you, The hour is coming, and now is, when the dead shall hear the voice of the Son of God: and they that hear shall live.

Following the teaching of the Pharisees, most ancient Jews believe that God will one day judge the world. When He does He will resurrect all good Jews for eternal life in a renewed world (compare Acts 23:6-8). Jesus affirms this belief but revises the doctrine at key points. The hour of judgment, when the *dead* will *hear* God's *voice*, is right now. [See question #3, page 176.] Those who are spiritually dead but choose to listen to Jesus' words are granted eternal life. Those who are (or were) spiritually dead include people like the Jews, the man at Bethesda, and Jesus' disciples. It also includes all other, later readers of John's gospel (us!) who must make a decision about Jesus.

The Pharisees naturally attribute the power of resurrection to God alone. Yet Jesus establishes His own role and authority in the judgment. It is *the Son* who proclaims the arrival of *the hour* of judgment and salvation.

HEARING AND LIVING

A couple of years ago, there was a series of television commercials featuring cell phones and phone service. In numerous variations a man talking on a cell phone would move to different locations and ask, "Can you hear me now?"

The commercials thus depicted the technician trying to discover locations where the cell-phone transmission wouldn't reach. The point of the commercials was that that particular phone service was superior to that provided by other companies having inadequate technology or equipment. That *Can you hear me now?* phrase became a cultural staple for a brief time.

"To hear," however, means more than merely listening. When a parent is laying down the law to a child, the parent may say, "Do you hear what I'm saying?" This is not a question of just hearing. It means, "Do you recognize the significance of what I am saying, and is it going to change your behavior?"

The old message from the herald, "Hear ye, hear ye," meant more than just mere listening. The herald was providing information that should result in action. The U.S. Army uses the phrase *HUA* (pronounced *who-ah*). This stands for *H*eard, *U*nderstood, *A*cknowledged. "To hear" properly leads to obedience.

That is the impact of what Jesus is saying: "They that hear shall live." Merely listening is not sufficient. If we properly hear the words of Jesus, we will incorporate them into our thinking and modify our behavior accordingly. Those that hear appropriately shall then live because their actions will be in tune with God's will. —J. B. N.

B. Son of Man (vv. 26, 27)

26, 27. For as the Father hath life in himself; so hath he given to the Son to have life in him-

Visual for Lessons 7 & 11

Use this visual to ask students to list things that "expire." Then ask how life in Christ is different.

self; and hath given him authority to execute judgment also, because he is the Son of man.

Some have suggested that the phrase *Son of man* is used here in the general sense of "a human being." That is the way that God uses this term to refer to the prophet Ezekiel numerous times (example: Ezekiel 2:1). This approach would suggest that Jesus is given power to judge human beings because He, as a man, can sympathize with our experiences and temptations (see Hebrews 4:15).

While this may be the case as far as it goes, it seems likely that John has a more specific idea in mind. Following Daniel 7:13, 14, many ancient Jews believe that God will send a special agent to judge the world at the end of time. This agent is to be called the Son of man.

We see this title used in the Gospel of John to highlight Jesus' divinity and *authority* (see John 1:51; 3:13, 14; 6:27, 53; 8:28; 13:31). By calling himself *Son of man* in a unique sense, Jesus is claiming to be the one whom God has appointed to judge the world at the end of time. [See question #4, page 176.]

C. His Voice (v. 28)

28. Marvel not at this: for the hour is coming, in the which all that are in the graves shall hear his voice.

As noted earlier, eternal life is a present reality; it is something that those who accept Jesus can begin to experience in the here and now. Jesus clarifies, however, that His authority to grant life goes beyond this world and into eternity. Whereas "the dead" in verse 25 referred to those who are spiritually dead, Jesus now speaks of the situation of those who have physically died—those who are *in the graves.*

Even in the face of death, we can be confident in Christ's power to save. We know that we will one day *hear his voice* and rise to eternal life (see the next verse). Jesus thus has authority over both our present and our future. Hallelujah—what a Savior!

D. Our Status (v. 29)

29. And shall come forth; they that have done good, unto the resurrection of life; and they that have done evil, unto the resurrection of damnation.

Those who respond positively to Jesus and His call in the current life will be glad to hear His call in the next world. "And this is the will of him that sent me, that every one which seeth the Son, and believeth on him, may have everlasting life: and I will raise him up at the last day" (John 6:40; compare 6:54).

The same hope does not belong to those who reject Him. Their *resurrection* will be one *of damnation.* Indeed they have been condemned already. "And this is the condemnation, that light is come into the world, and men loved darkness rather than light, because their deeds were evil" (John 3:19).

We must stress that the phrase *done good* is not referring to a system of salvation by works. In this context the phrase *done good* is defined by verse 24: "He that heareth my word, and believeth on him that sent me, hath everlasting life." See also Jesus' declaration in John 6:29: "This is the work of God, that ye believe on him whom he hath sent."

By contrast, those who challenge Jesus' claims and refuse to accept Him will suffer eternal judgment. Jesus regrets this situation, but it cannot be otherwise in view of God's justice. The choice is ours. [See question #5, page 176.]

Conclusion

A. Don't Argue with the Judge

A good friend of ours is a police captain. I once asked him what we should do if a policeman came to our house or we were stopped for a traffic violation. He said, "In one word, 'cooperate.' You're not going to argue with a cop, so don't." My wife very recently profited from this advice when she parked momentarily in a fire lane to pick up a large item in a store. A police officer came in looking for her, and she avoided an expensive fine by listening quietly and following his orders.

Jesus offers similar advice in our passage today. God is the boss, and He has given Jesus all authority to judge us. We're not in a position to argue with Him or to question what He says. If we want to stay out of trouble, our only hope is simply to follow His instructions. Make no mistake: there won't be any arguing about the situation on Judgment Day!

But people foolishly try to argue with God, don't they? Such arguments can take several forms. The most serious way we argue with God is through sin itself. God, the judge and lawgiver, has defined what sin is. He has commanded us to avoid it. When we go ahead and commit sin anyway, we are saying, in effect, "I know better than You do, God." Thus our sin becomes our argument against Him and His will.

Such sin is obvious when we break one of the "Thou shalt not" commandments. A less obvious way to argue with God is in resisting His will for us after we become Christians. Jonah knew God's direction for his life but chose to do something different (Jonah 1:3). Is God calling you into a particular ministry or service? Don't argue—go!

B. Prayer

Lord, please help us to live lives that will honor Christ the way that Christ honored You. In times of temptation and stress, help us remember that eternal life is a gift we already have in this world. Keep us mindful at every moment that the things we do now have eternal consequences. In Jesus' name, amen.

C. Thought to Remember

We experience the blessings of resurrection life in every moment that we honor Christ.

Home Daily Bible Readings

Monday, Jan. 8—Jesus Heals a Lame Man (John 5:1-9)

Tuesday, Jan. 9—Whom God Has Sent (John 3:31-36)

Wednesday, Jan. 10—I Am the Christ (John 4:19-26)

Thursday, Jan. 11—Jesus Taught with Authority (Matthew 7:24-29)

Friday, Jan. 12—Christ Will Judge (2 Timothy 4:1-5)

Saturday, Jan. 13—Honor the Son (John 5:19-23)

Sunday, Jan. 14—Jesus Speaks of Judgment (John 5:24-30)

Learning by Doing

This page contains an alternative lesson plan emphasizing learning activities.
Classes desiring such student involvement will find these suggestions helpful.

Learning Goals

After participating in this lesson, each student will be able to:

1. Describe the authority that Jesus has.

2. Discuss how Jesus expects us to live in this world in anticipation of eternity.

3. Write a plan to honor Jesus' authority in one specific way.

Into the Lesson

Procure a small dart board and pair of darts. Over the board's bulls-eye, place a picture of a beloved member of your congregation (be sure to get the person's permission). Display the board. As class begins, ask a person who you know will refuse to do so to throw darts at the board.

When you sense the hesitancy and reluctance, say, "I thought it would be difficult for anyone to throw darts at our beloved [name]. Imagine those in Jesus' day attacking Him and His good deeds." Note that that is what happens in today's text, as the religious leaders attack Jesus for healing on the Sabbath. They also attack him for making himself equal with God, which in fact, He is (see John 5:18).

As an alternate beginning, ask the class to describe the ideal father/son relationship, using only adjectives or abstract nouns. Expect such responses as *respectful* and *submissive*.

Into the Word

Prepare a copy of the following table for each student. (The table is included in the student book.)

John 5	Father	Son	Jewish Leaders/Us
19			
20			
21			
22			
23			
24			
25			
26, 27			
28, 29			

Ask students to fill in the chart, briefly noting what each person at the top will do or not do according to each verse. Note that most verses will not use all three columns. For example, for verse 22: the *Father* does not judge; it is the *Son* who judges.

To continue the examination of the text, read aloud the following expressions in random order, one at a time. Ask the class to identify a related verse from today's text. (Do not read aloud the verse numbers provided in parentheses after each expression.)

"Escape with a pass key" *(v. 24)*. "Like Father, like Son" *(v. 19)*. "Dead men's ears—what shall they hear?" *(v. 28)*. "Love shows" *(v. 20)*. "Life and death; Father and Son" *(v. 21)*. "Who gets to judge? The judge!" *(v. 22)*. "Honor one, honor the other" *(v. 23)*. "Listen up; come alive!" *(v. 25)*. "Full of life; full of life" *(v. 26)*. "See good; do good" *(v. 19)*. "Just because" *(v. 27)*. "Risen up, risen down" *(v. 29)*. "Hear . . . believe . . . live!" *(v. 24)*. As the class identifies verse numbers, discuss the meaning of each.

Display the phrase *The Second Coming of Christ.* Ask the group to quote from the Bible some facts about that grand event. Make a quick list. Then say, "OK, this is a good list, but do we have everything Jesus reveals in today's text?" Have students look especially at verses 24-29. Add any important ideas to the earlier listing.

(Decide in advance which of the above three activities you will allow the most time for, depending on what content you wish to stress.)

Into Life

Put the following fill-in expression on display: *"I Res____t Jesus' Authority!"* (A similar activity is found in the student book.) Ask for letter combinations to fill in the blank (such as *is, en, pec,* and *tric*). Discuss how people's lives demonstrate how they would fill in the missing letters.

Next, give each student a slip of paper with the same phrase and have each fill in letters appropriate to his or her own attitude toward Jesus' authority. Then have each add an affirmation, "so I (will) _____." Each should complete the idea either with a description of how his or her life is being lived or how he or she will commit to begin living it.

Let's Talk It Over

The questions on this page are designed to promote discussion of the lesson by the class and to encourage application of the lesson Scriptures. The answers provided are only discussion starters. Let your class talk it over from there.

1. Think about the lesson's comparison between John 3:17 and John 5:22. How does this comparison help you approach texts that seem to conflict?

The Bible has been around for many centuries. During that time the critics have been busy pointing out all the seeming contradictions that they can possibly imagine. If someone points out to you something in the Bible that seems to be a contradiction, don't worry—chances are almost 100 percent that it's been seen before. It's nothing new. Talk to someone who is spiritually mature to resolve the apparent difficulty. It is appropriate to approach the Bible with the presumption that God can be trusted!

2. How does recognizing that *eternal life* begins in this world make a practical difference in your life right now?

Believers are sometimes tempted to view this life as a time frame in which non-Christians get the best end of the deal. They may view themselves as giving up lots of fun over the short haul for the sake of eventual, eternal blessings. At times some Christians even appear to begrudge the lifestyle of non-Christians, wishing they could live that way but afraid of eternal consequences.

This passage shows that God's way is the best way to live life right now. As the author and provider of abundant life, He is able to provide both earthly and eternal joy and fulfillment. This awareness helps us live contentedly and confidently in the present as we await the culmination of our hope.

3. How should recognizing that *judgment* occurs now make a practical difference in your life?

Christians should not fear God's final judgment as being some kind of "moment of decision" on God's part. The moment of decision is now! For those saved through Christ, Jesus' teaching provides a great sense of security and comfort. This should undergird all our daily actions.

For those who are outside of a saving relationship with God through Christ, this lesson serves as motivation to make an immediate response.

One cannot hope that the Judge will have a sudden change of heart on the Last Day; the decision already will have been reached as a result of one's choice for or against Jesus. This verse demonstrates that our eternal standing before God is determined while we are on earth.

4. How does John's portrait of Jesus as judge provide encouragement to you?

Verses 25-29 serve as a reminder that God gets the ultimate and final word in each and every circumstance, with each and every person. When we become frustrated with the imperfect justice meted out by human judicial authorities, these verses are a comfort. When we become discouraged with our limited awareness of situations and, therefore, with our difficulty in handling situations and people fairly, these verses provide peace.

This section also helps us keep spiritually balanced when non-Christians attack the character of God and the truthfulness of the Scriptures. Though God is patient, His justice will be satisfied and His character vindicated.

5. How can we avoid making mistakes similar to those Jesus' opponents, who thought they were protecting God's truth yet actually were violating it?

Let's face it: we can never be *completely* certain that our understanding of *every* Scripture or doctrine is correct. Even so we can put in place certain guard rails that help us avoid deluding ourselves into disobedience.

First, we can regularly engage in the spiritual disciplines of prayer, Bible study, worship, and service. These help keep our hearts soft toward God. Some errors find their source in hard hearts; excusing disobedience isn't far behind when that happens.

Second, we can maintain a teachable attitude. Assuming that we have all the right answers can lead to the wrong ones. We may be confident that if the evidence pointed to a certain conclusion the first time, then it will do so the next time. But if information that we hadn't considered before surfaces, then we should be willing to rethink and reexamine.

Jesus Is the Bread of Life and Living Water

DEVOTIONAL READING: Ephesians 3:14-21.

BACKGROUND SCRIPTURE: John 6:25-59; 7:37-39.

PRINTED TEXT: John 6:34-40; 7:37-39.

John 6:34-40

34 Then said they unto him, Lord, evermore give us this bread.

35 And Jesus said unto them, I am the bread of life: he that cometh to me shall never hunger; and he that believeth on me shall never thirst.

36 But I said unto you, That ye also have seen me, and believe not.

37 All that the Father giveth me shall come to me; and him that cometh to me I will in no wise cast out.

38 For I came down from heaven, not to do mine own will, but the will of him that sent me.

39 And this is the Father's will which hath sent me, that of all which he hath given me I should lose nothing, but should raise it up again at the last day.

40 And this is the will of him that sent me, that every one which seeth the Son, and believeth on him, may have everlasting life: and I will raise him up at the last day.

John 7:37-39

37 In the last day, that great day of the feast, Jesus stood and cried, saying, If any man thirst, let him come unto me, and drink.

38 He that believeth on me, as the Scripture hath said, out of his belly shall flow rivers of living water.

39 (But this spake he of the Spirit, which they that believe on him should receive: for the Holy Ghost was not yet given; because that Jesus was not yet glorified.)

Jan 21

GOLDEN TEXT: Jesus said unto them, I am the bread of life: he that cometh to me shall never hunger; and he that believeth on me shall never thirst.—John 6:35.

Jesus Christ: A Portrait of God
Unit 2: Christ Sustains and Supports
(Lessons 6-9)

Lesson Aims

After participating in this lesson, each student will be able to:

1. Identify the hunger and thirst that Jesus meets.

2. Discuss how the Holy Spirit is a "river of living water" in our lives.

3. Interview a spiritually mature Christian to discover how Christ meets that person's spiritual and emotional needs.

Lesson Outline

INTRODUCTION
   A. The God Who Is
   B. Lesson Background
 I. FEASTING ON THE BREAD (John 6:34-40)
   A. Who Jesus Is (vv. 34, 35a)
      Bread
   B. What Jesus Offers (v. 35b)
   C. What People Decide (vv. 36, 37)
   D. What the Father Wants (vv. 38-40)
      Lose Nothing
II. DRINKING FROM THE RIVER (John 7:37-39)
   A. Come and Drink (vv. 37, 38)
      Thirst
   B. Promise of the Spirit (v. 39)
CONCLUSION
   A. Bread and Water
   B. Prayer
   C. Thought to Remember

Introduction

A. The God Who Is

Exodus 3 records Moses' encounter with God at the burning bush. Before this event Moses had sacrificed his privileged position in the Egyptian government in order to protect one of his Hebrew kinsmen. As a result Moses fled the country (Exodus 2:11-15). He became a shepherd. One day while tending the sheep on Mount Horeb, he suddenly heard God's voice speaking from a flaming bush.

God had good news: He would rescue His people after years of suffering and slavery. Moses would have the special privilege of leading the people out of Egypt to the promised land. This would be the fulfillment of God's ancient covenant with Abraham (Genesis 15:18-20).

One can easily understand why Moses was shocked by this information (especially from a bush!). He questioned his own ability to fulfill the task. He pointed out that his name carried no weight with Pharaoh or the Jews. He was certain that he lacked the skills needed for the job. God assured him that He would empower him.

Moses also raised another significant problem. The Hebrews had lived in Egypt for centuries, and the Egyptians worshiped many gods. Over the course of time, the Hebrews had been exposed to this corrupt practice. They would therefore want to know which "god" Moses was talking about.

God replied "Thus shalt thou say unto the children of Israel, I Am hath sent me unto you" (Exodus 3:14). In other words: "Tell them that the one God who actually exists—the one 'who is'—sent you to deliver them."

This one-and-only God delivered the Hebrews from Egypt. He continues to work through His people to reveal himself to the world.

B. Lesson Background

In the Gospel of John, we notice Jesus making frequent statements about himself that involve God's sacred name, I Am. For the sake of convenience, we can call these "the 'I am' sayings."

These sayings form an important distinctive in John among the four Gospels. For those interested in statistics, Greek "I am" is used 5 times in Matthew, 3 times in Mark, 4 times in Luke, but 30 times in John. If we take off the "am" part and just consider how often Jesus refers to himself as "I" in an authoritative way, then the occurrences are 29 times in Matthew, 17 times in Mark, 23 times in Luke, but 134 times in John!

These sayings take two forms. We will explore both forms in our lessons over the next several weeks. The first form occurs when Jesus simply applies God's divine name, I Am, directly to himself. He does this to stress His complete union with the Father (John 8:24, 28, 58; 13:19). For those interested in technical things, this is known as the *absolute use* of *I am*.

The second form occurs in instances where Jesus uses this phrase to start a sentence in which He compares himself to something else. Some examples are "I am the vine" and "I am the good shepherd." Technically speaking these *I am* statements are said to have *explicit predicates*.

Jesus' *I am* remarks in our passage today follow John's account of the miraculous feeding of the 5,000 (John 6:1-13). Impressed with His power, the people sought to make Jesus king. Perhaps they hoped that He would lead them in a revolution against the Romans. To avoid this Jesus first withdrew to a mountain (v. 15), then to Capernaum (vv. 16-25).

But the crowds found Him anyway. When they did Jesus advised them not to focus on the bread that they had eaten but rather on food that is eternal (vv. 26, 27).

I. Feasting on the Bread
(John 6:34-40)

A. Who Jesus Is (vv. 34, 35a)

34, 35a. Then said they unto him, Lord, evermore give us this bread. And Jesus said unto them, I am the bread of life.

The manna in Moses' day was food for the body (see John 6:31, 32). Rather than focusing on this kind of nourishment, Jesus' hearers need to receive "the bread of God" that "cometh down from heaven, and giveth [eternal] life" (John 6:33). Of course Jesus' hearers want to eat *this bread*. So they ask Jesus to *give* it to them. [See question #1, page 184.]

Clearly, however, Jesus' audience does not understand fully that Jesus himself is the source of eternal life. Jesus uses an *I am* saying to show that He is superior to the old covenant. While Moses fed people bread in the wilderness, and while this was an incredible miracle of God, none of the people who ate that physical bread lived forever as a result of ingesting it. Jesus, by contrast, is *the bread of life*. The phrase *of life* has important implications, as we see next.

BREAD

We often refer to bread as "the staff of life." In our current culture with all the concern about carbohydrates, perhaps that is not as true as it once was.

How to Say It

ABRAHAM. *Ay*-bruh-ham.
CAPERNAUM. Kuh-*per*-nay-um.
EGYPT. *Ee*-jipt.
HOREB. *Ho*-reb.
JERUSALEM. Juh-*roo*-suh-lem.
JUDAS ISCARIOT. *Joo*-dus Iss-*care*-ee-ut.
LEVITICUS. Leh-*vit*-ih-kus.
MOSES. *Mo*-zes or *Mo*-zez.
PHARAOH. *Fair*-o or *Fay*-roe.
SILOAM. Sigh-*lo*-um.

But in first-century Palestine, bread was a crucial ingredient in the daily diet. The average family had meat only three times a month—it simply was too expensive. People subsisted on milk, cheese, vegetables, and bread. Of these, bread was probably the most important. Wheat flour for making bread was expensive. So most people ate bread made from barley (notice that in John 6:9 Jesus fed the 5,000 from barley loaves).

The Egyptians were the first to discover the effect of yeast spores in raising the dough. The result was a softer, lighter bread that most people considered a major improvement over the previously flat, unleavened loaves. The Egyptians were also the first to build ovens for baking bread; this was an improvement over baking in the open air and covering the dough with hot ashes. The importance of bread throughout history is demonstrated by how much attention has been paid trying to improve it!

Comparison to bread is thus a natural way for Jesus to illustrate truth. Throughout the Scriptures *bread* stands for food in general. "Breaking bread" stands for the entire meal. "Give us this day our daily bread" refers to more than merely loaves. When Jesus says He is the bread of life, He is making a major statement to the people of His time and ours. Our souls hunger for spiritual nourishment, and Jesus promises that He is that food. He is the "required daily allowance" in our spiritual diet.   —J. B. N.

B. What Jesus Offers (v. 35b)

35b. He that cometh to me shall never hunger; and he that believeth on me shall never thirst.

The bread to which Jesus refers is "living bread" (John 6:51). It's alive and standing right in front of them. (The two uses of *me* makes this emphatic.) This kind of bread is most unlike the inanimate manna that God provided through Moses! This bread gives life to those who accept it—to those who believe in Jesus.

Because the bread (Jesus) is eternal, the life that He provides is also eternal. Anyone who believes in Him will never be hungry or thirsty again in a spiritual sense because Jesus will satisfy his or her desire for God forever. This too is quite different from the manna that Moses provided, which quickly spoiled (Exodus 16:20).

C. What People Decide (vv. 36, 37)

36. But I said unto you, That ye also have seen me, and believe not.

At first glance it seems odd that Jesus would say this to people who have just tried to make

Him king because of the miraculous feeding in John 6:14, 15. The crowd clearly is impressed with Jesus, yet Jesus clarifies that their faith thus far is inadequate. It is not enough simply to believe that Jesus is a prophet or a great teacher; rather, one must accept that His miracles are signs that He is God's unique Son.

Those standing before Jesus believe that He can feed them with miraculous bread. But they have not yet come to understand His true identity as the one sent from Heaven. They do not grasp that Jesus is so much greater than Moses (compare Hebrews 3:3).

37. All that the Father giveth me shall come to me; and him that cometh to me I will in no wise cast out.

This verse can be perplexing. Jesus seems first to imply that only certain people receive a special, mandatory calling from God to believe in Him; then immediately Jesus insists that He will not reject anyone who chooses to believe.

We can reach a reasonable solution by first recognizing that God knows the future. Through His foreknowledge God is aware of who will and who won't accept Jesus by their freewill choice. Those whom the Father knows will accept Jesus are the ones whom *the Father giveth me.*

Jesus' words thus provide assurance to those who believe—to those who recognize that the one who does miracles is actually God in the flesh. Jesus will never relinquish His love for them (us!). As Paul says, nothing can separate us from His love (Romans 8:37-39). [See question #2, page 184.]

D. What the Father Wants (vv. 38-40)

38. For I came down from heaven, not to do mine own will, but the will of him that sent me.

Jesus now returns to a theme that we have seen several times in this series: He does not come to do His *own will,* but God's *will.* In this context doing God's will relates very specifically to His mission of providing eternal life to all who accept Him. This mission is explained in more detail in the next two verses. [See question #3, page 184.]

39. And this is the Father's will which hath sent me, that of all which he hath given me I should lose nothing, but should raise it up again at the last day.

The idea of "losing" refers to the separation of a believer from Christ and, consequently, from the eternal life that Jesus provides. In Jesus' great prayer in chapter 17, He will stress that He has protected His disciples so that none of them was "lost" except Judas, who betrayed Him. But even

that case wasn't really an exception (in the sense of Jesus failing at His task) since Judas Iscariot was a "son of perdition" by his own choice (John 17:12; compare 6:70, 71).

Jesus' assurance will be of great comfort as churches are persecuted for their Christian faith (John 16:1-4). Such persecutions can create fear and discouragement. But Jesus reminds us that these experiences do not affect His love for us or our ultimate safety in Him.

Raise it up again refers back to theme of John 5:25-29 (see last week's lesson). There Jesus assured believers that He would reward their perseverance with eternal life on *the last day.* Jesus is able to provide!

LOSE NOTHING

A friend of mine who went through medical school told me that many of his classes were like getting a drink from a fire hydrant without being able to spill a drop. I realize that's a bit of an exaggeration, but it points out how much he was required to learn—and lose nothing in the process. I have known only one person in my life who claimed to have a photographic memory. I'm not sure he remembered absolutely everything he had ever read but his memory was awesome, particularly for trivia.

I heard once that when Mozart was only about eight years old, he attended a concert and was fascinated by a ten-minute piece he had heard. Having heard it only once, he then went home and proceeded to write it out—every note for every instrument. He went back the next day to hear the piece again just to be sure he had transcribed it accurately. He had—every note for every instrument. How incredible to remember everything after just one hearing, and not lose a single note!

Jesus said that out of everything the Father had given to Him, He would lose nothing. If humans can mentally remember vast amounts of information and lose nothing in the process, it should not be surprising that Jesus is able to do much the same thing with all the responsibilities the Father has given to Him. We can be sure that our lives and our souls are safe in His hands.

—J. B. N.

40. And this is the will of him that sent me, that every one which seeth the Son, and believeth on him, may have everlasting life: and I will raise him up at the last day.

While many people do not accept Christ, this does not reflect on God's *will* for them. John 3:16, 17 stresses that God loved the world and sent His

Son to save the world. This is clear evidence of His desire for all people to *have everlasting life.*

Regrettably, however, many people reject this gift and refuse to accept Jesus' offer. Jesus thus challenges His audience to see past the miracle of the bread itself and realize what the miracle points to: He is God's only Son.

II. Drinking from the River (John 7:37-39)

A. Come and Drink (vv. 37, 38)

37, 38. In the last day, that great day of the feast, Jesus stood and cried, saying, If any man thirst, let him come unto me, and drink. He that believeth on me, as the Scripture hath said, out of his belly shall flow rivers of living water.

The feast here is the Feast of Tabernacles in Jerusalem, where Jesus has been impressing the crowds with His teaching. On each day of this celebration, a group of priests carries buckets of water from the pool of Siloam to the temple. They pour the water on the altar as an offering while reciting Isaiah 12:3, "Therefore with joy shall ye draw water out of the wells of salvation."

Jesus uses this ceremony as a symbol of the new life that is available to those who believe in Him. This feast lasts seven days, with a closing assembly on the eighth day (Leviticus 23:33-36). The phrase *In the last day, that great day of the feast* could refer to either the seventh or the eighth day—we're not certain.

Another uncertainty is the possibility of interpreting these verses in two different ways. Jesus begins with an invitation for those who thirst for God to come to Him and be filled. The way our English text is punctuated suggests that the person who drinks from Jesus (that is, the one who believes in Him) will then become a source of *living water.* This rendering appeals to verse 39, making Jesus' words a promise of the indwelling Spirit: every believer will have the Holy Spirit as an inner spring of life.

Some say, however, that the period in verse 37 should not come after *and drink* but after *come unto me.* Without getting too technical about English and Greek sentence structure, this view promotes Jesus to be the source of the water; it emphasizes His unique authority to give the Spirit to those who accept Him. Stated a little differently this interpretation takes *his belly* in verse 38 to be Jesus' belly: Jesus as the source of the Spirit that gives life to those who believe.

We should not be too concerned with the differences in these two possibilities. In either case

Visual for Lesson 8. *Point to this refreshing waterfall imagery as you introduce question #5 on page 184.*

Jesus emphasizes the fact that the spiritual water that He provides is *living.* The Spirit that Jesus gives is active in the life of the believer.

The Scripture that Jesus has in mind could be Isaiah 58:11: "And the Lord shall guide thee continually, and satisfy thy soul in drought, and make fat thy bones: and thou shalt be like a watered garden, and like a spring of water, whose waters fail not."

THIRST

Most of us live in areas where water is abundant. When I was a youngster, our neighborhood did not have city water; each house had its own shallow well that supplied all its water needs. The water had a high iron content that soon stained drinking glasses orange—but at least we had water.

Not everyone is so fortunate. Areas of California face water shortages. Much of the Central Valley of California was unable to sustain agriculture until canals brought water from the snow packs in the Sierras. When I lived in California a number of years ago, we often had to endure water rationing.

An abundance of water does not guarantee a lack of thirst, however. Those stranded at sea know this all too well. As *The Rime of the Ancient Mariner* has it, "Water, water, everywhere, Nor any drop to drink." Trying to drink seawater is a big mistake. The high salt content of seawater will leach water out of a person's internal organs. Then the thirst gets worse rather than better.

Desert areas are also dangerous. People who live in the Near East are familiar with the acute need for water. Witness the fame of an "oasis." Therefore when Jesus said that He could relieve the thirst of anyone who needed a drink, they understood the significance of the imagery.

Yet Jesus was talking about a spiritual thirst rather than a physical one. People might misunderstand what He really was talking about, as did the woman at the well in John 4. Is our comprehension any better than those who originally heard Jesus' words?   —J. B. N.

B. Promise of the Spirit (v. 39)

39. (But this spake he of the Spirit, which they that believe on him should receive: for the Holy Ghost was not yet given; because that Jesus was not yet glorified.)

Jesus' glorification refers to His forthcoming death and resurrection. In John 14:15-19 Jesus promises the disciples that *the Spirit* will come to take His place as their Comforter after His death.

The Spirit will act as the ongoing source of power and authority for the church. He will bring to mind Jesus' promises so that His followers may enjoy peace in the face of trial (John 14:25-27). In this way Jesus continues to provide for our needs long after He leaves this world. We enjoy this comfort until His return! [See question #4, page 184.]

Conclusion

A. Bread and Water

In times past, and in many countries yet today, bread and water was the food of criminals. Prisoners and captives in wartime were kept barely alive on a sustenance diet of minimal amounts of these two. This fact reflects, however, the essential role that bread and water play in human life: they are things that we must have to survive. Human beings can live a long, long time on only air, bread, and water.

In our passages for today, Jesus uses bread and water figuratively to stress that He provides everything essential for our spiritual lives. When we need to know God's will, we look to the one who "came down from heaven"; when we seek strength and guidance, His Spirit refreshes us with "living water." And unlike physical bread and water, we never grow tired of the heavenly food that Jesus gives us. It tastes new and exciting every day.

But how do we communicate these facts to an unbelieving world? Bread is viewed with disdain by the low-carbohydrate diet plans. Bread is hardly a centerpiece of meals in the industrialized West. Many people let the bread sit untouched in a basket off to the side of the table when they go to a restaurant. We may even caution ourselves "don't fill up on bread" before the main course arrives. The bread that most of us ingest these days seems to come in the form of pizza crusts.

Water imagery also causes problems. On the one hand pure, bottled water is all the rage in some quarters. This value enhances the image of Jesus as living water. On the other hand, we also see television commercials by companies selling sports drinks that attack the adequacy of water. They say we should buy their products instead, so we don't miss out on electrolytes, etc. Soft drinks also attract our attention from every vending machine we see. Water did not have this kind of competition back in the first century AD!

Jesus spoke with images that were vital to the people of His day. It is not our prerogative to change that imagery (as in "I am the pizza crust of life"). Our task, rather, is to explain that imagery carefully. The Scripture will come alive when we do! This honors God. [See question #5, page 184.]

B. Prayer

Lord, help us never forget that You already have met all of our spiritual needs through Christ. Give us strength as we feed on the bread and water that You have provided. We ask for Your forgiveness for those times when we have not been satisfied with what Christ provides. In Jesus' name, amen.

C. Thought to Remember

Christ is the source of everything that we should long for.

Home Daily Bible Readings

Monday, Jan. 15—May Christ Dwell Within (Ephesians 3:14-21)

Tuesday, Jan. 16—Do Not Be Afraid (John 6:16-21)

Wednesday, Jan. 17—Jesus, the Heavenly Bread (John 6:25-34)

Thursday, Jan. 18—I Am the Bread of Life (John 6:35-40)

Friday, Jan. 19—Sustained by Living Bread (John 6:41-51)

Saturday, Jan. 20—Sing for Joy (Isaiah 49:7-13)

Sunday, Jan. 21—Living Water (John 7:37-41)

Learning by Doing

This page contains an alternative lesson plan emphasizing learning activities.
Classes desiring such student involvement will find these suggestions helpful.

Learning Goals

After this lesson, each student will be able to:

1. Identify the hunger and thirst that Jesus meets.

2. Discuss how the Holy Spirit is a "river of living water" in our lives.

3. Interview a spiritually mature Christian to discover how Christ meets that person's spiritual and emotional needs.

Into the Lesson

Give each student a sheet of lined paper with the heading *Survival List.* Say, "You are stranded on an isolated isle. You know that you will not be rescued for at least seven days. What do you want included in the survival kit you have fortunately brought with you?"

Give the students a few minutes to list the items that they consider to be essential. Then let them share their lists, along with any explanation considered necessary. Expect such items as food, water, and matches.

After all have shared, say, "Certain things are essential for earthly existence, but certain things are also essential for heavenly preparation. In today's study Jesus makes it clear: He himself is the bread and water that we need!"

Into the Word

Read aloud John 6:28-33, the verses preceding today's text. In those verses the context for today's teaching about bread are given.

Then have two of your better oral readers read Exodus 16:11-31 and Exodus 17:5-7. These passages relate to the bread and water God provided for the Israelites during the wilderness wandering. Have one volunteer read the words spoken by God, Moses, and the people; the other volunteer will read the narrative. After looking at today's text, you may wish to return to these texts for a comparison and contrast between the desert bread and water and the bread and water that is Christ himself. (For example, both were sent by God for the welfare of His people; both came while the people were in sin—see Exodus 16:1 and 1 Timothy 1:15.)

Establish "Bread" and "Water" groups of five people per group. Give each group a stack of five cards, bearing either B-R-E-A-D or W-A-T-E-R, one letter per card. Give the cards to one person in each group with the direction to shuffle the cards and distribute one to each group member.

Announce, "The goal of your group is to develop an acrostic for your word, *bread* or *water.* Each word or phrase of the acrostic must be related to today's text (John 6:34-40; 7:37-39) or to the nature of Jesus. Each group member is responsible to create the word or phrase for the letter on his or her card. OK, those with the *B* or the *W*, get started!"

Give the groups five minutes. Then ask the person who holds the last letter of either word (*D* or *R*) to report the group's acrostic to the whole class, with any explanation deemed necessary.

Though you will accept the creations of each group, here is a sample for each: *B* equals "broken," as the body of Christ will be; *R* equals "requested," as in 6:34; *E* equals "eternal," also from 6:34; *A* equals "all," for He is all we need; and *D* equals "delightful," for tasting Jesus always is; *W* equals "wonderful," because it differs from the water we drink each day; *A* equals "anticipated," because 7:39 reveals "living water" as a reference to the Spirit to be given after Jesus' glorification; *T* equals "thirst-quenching," from 7:37; *E* equals "enough," for the bread and water that is Christ himself is totally sufficient; *R* equals "required" for eternal life.

Into Life

Before today's session collect empty personal water bottles so that you have one for each student. Also have on hand some blank peel-and-stick labels (at least 2 inches by 3 inches), two per student. After you distribute bottles and labels, direct students to prepare a name label reflecting the truths of John 6:35b and/or John 7:37, 38. If they need an example or two, suggest "Thirst Quencher" (from 6:35) and "Never Dry" (from 7:38). After students finish and attach their labels to their bottles, have several class members read the names they have chosen.

For the second label ask students to write, "What's in it?" Suggest that for the next several days each student should look at his or her bottle and add to the label one attribute of Jesus that "fills his or her bottle of living water." Examples are "divine vitamins," "pure grace," or "100 percent daily requirements."

Let's Talk It Over

The questions on this page are designed to promote discussion of the lesson by the class and to encourage application of the lesson Scriptures. The answers provided are only discussion starters. Let your class talk it over from there.

1. How can the example of Jesus help Christians deal with the temptations that accompany popularity and power?

Popularity and power are things that many of us won't have to worry about personally! Even so, we all are painfully aware of "high visibility" Christian leaders who have fallen with a loud crash. Popularity and power can be useful in advancing the kingdom, yet each has the potential to produce harmful effects. Jesus' example reminds us that the eternal, spiritual reality takes precedence over the temporary, physical reality. Despite Jesus' popularity, He made sure that everything in His life was aligned with God's agenda.

Jesus' example also reminds us of the need for regular reflection. Between John 6:14 and 6:16 Jesus separated himself from the clamoring crowds (compare also Luke 5:16). Given our tendency to misuse both popularity and power, meditation on the example of Jesus is vital.

2. The phrase *I will in no wise cast out* provides great comfort! But what are potential dangers to this assurance? Explain.

When we experience difficulties, especially persecution for our faith, it is tempting to question either God's goodness or the reality of our salvation. In effect we begin to ask, "If that promise is really true, then why did such and such happen to me?" We also should be wary that the phrase *I will in no wise cast out* may become an excuse for disobedience (see Romans 6).

3. What are some ways that the example and teaching of Christ can help you assess the will of God for your life?

There are clear differences between the will of God for Jesus' earthly life and His will for ours. Jesus' life is a reminder, however, that God's will for all people is a right relationship with Him.

In wrestling with the details of God's will for our lives, we remember that God has revealed in Scripture that which is central regarding his intentions for all Christians: the Great Commission of Matthew 28:19, 20. God wants us to be involved in helping reconcile people to Him. He wants us to help others learn to love and serve Him.

God also wants us to reflect His character in our lives. Personal holiness is a must (1 Peter 1:15, 16). While Christians sometimes disagree on the extent to which God has a specific will for each person's life, Scripture makes these primary concerns most clear.

4. In what ways have you found the Holy Spirit's indwelling presence to be an encouragement in living the Christian life?

The Holy Spirit is God's presence with and within us. Knowing of His presence is (or should be) a great source of strength, especially in places or life situations in which we are not surrounded by strong Christians.

The Spirit's ministry as described by Jesus also reminds us that the Christian life is not a matter of "trying harder" to employ our own meager resources. God's power is at work to transform our lives and fuel our service. Since the Holy Spirit indwells all believers, He also works through the community of faith. He encourages us through the Word and through the timely insights and input of others. This provides spiritual comfort or challenge according to our needs.

5. How do you intend to use the images of hunger and thirst to communicate the gospel in the twenty-first century?

The creative teaching style that Jesus demonstrates is still worth emulating. First, the images of hunger and thirst are relevant to all people of all times. Second, the images involve the whole person—thus they are memorable and powerful. Third, nothing is more fundamental than hunger and thirst (except perhaps the need for air). Fourth, these images are grounded in the rhythms of everyday life.

A big hurdle that we face is in transferring images of physical hunger and thirst into the spiritual realm. Spiritual hunger and thirst cannot be felt in quite the same way that physical hunger and thirst are sensed. Many people have suppressed their spiritual needs for so long that they barely are aware of them. In those cases the Holy Spirit can create the feelings of spiritual longings that we can then address.

"I Am the Light of the World"

January 28
Lesson 9

DEVOTIONAL READING: Isaiah 35:3-10.

BACKGROUND SCRIPTURE: John 8:12-20; 12:44-46.

PRINTED TEXT: John 8:12-20; 12:44-46.

John 8:12-20

12 Then spake Jesus again unto them, saying, I am the light of the world: he that followeth me shall not walk in darkness, but shall have the light of life.

13 The Pharisees therefore said unto him, Thou bearest record of thyself; thy record is not true.

14 Jesus answered and said unto them, Though I bear record of myself, yet my record is true: for I know whence I came, and whither I go; but ye cannot tell whence I come, and whither I go.

15 Ye judge after the flesh; I judge no man.

16 And yet if I judge, my judgment is true: for I am not alone, but I and the Father that sent me.

17 It is also written in your law, that the testimony of two men is true.

18 I am one that bear witness of myself, and the Father that sent me beareth witness of me.

19 Then said they unto him, Where is thy Father? Jesus answered, Ye neither know me, nor my Father: if ye had known me, ye should have known my Father also.

20 These words spake Jesus in the treasury, as he taught in the temple: and no man laid hands on him; for his hour was not yet come.

John 12:44-46

44 Jesus cried and said, He that believeth on me, believeth not on me, but on him that sent me.

45 And he that seeth me seeth him that sent me.

46 I am come a light into the world, that whosoever believeth on me should not abide in darkness.

Jan
28

GOLDEN TEXT: I am the light of the world: he that followeth me shall not walk in darkness, but shall have the light of life.—John 8:12.

Jesus Christ: A Portrait of God
Unit 2: Christ Sustains and Supports
(Lessons 6-9)

Lesson Aims

After participating in this lesson, each student will be able to:

1. List ways in which Jesus was and is a source of light in our dark world.

2. Explain Jesus' use of the "light" metaphor as proof of His unique authority.

3. Change one habit to better reflect Jesus' light.

Lesson Outline

INTRODUCTION
  A. The Power of a Match
  B. Lesson Background
  I. LIGHT OF THE WORLD (John 8:12)
    A. Jesus' Identity (v. 12a)
    B. Our Response (v. 12b)
      Follow the Light
 II. TESTIMONY OF THE FATHER (John 8:13-20)
    A. Pharisees Challenge Jesus (v. 13)
    B. Jesus Refutes Pharisees (vv. 14-18)
      Bearing Witness
    C. Know Me, Know My Father (vv. 19, 20)
III. ESCAPE FROM DARKNESS (John 12:44-46)
    A. God's Special Agent (vv. 44, 45)
      He Who Sent Me
    B. Leaving the Darkness (v. 46)
CONCLUSION
  A. Piercing the Deepest Darkness
  B. Avoiding Counterfeit Light
  C. Prayer
  D. Thought to Remember

Introduction

A. The Power of a Match

Kentucky's Mammoth Cave is one of the largest complexes of underground passages in the world. Many of the cave's farthest recesses have yet to be explored, but the largest known entrance is home to a national park. On one of the guided tours, rangers lead guests to a cavern deep below the surface and ask them to remain silent while they turn off the lights.

The resulting darkness is overwhelming. It is impossible to see anything at any distance. The ranger then illustrates the power of light by striking a single match. I have been on this tour several times, and on each occasion I find that it is impossible to look away from this tiny spark of light. Human beings were not made to live in utter darkness. We readily grasp for anything to light our way.

Darkness is a powerful figure of speech. At least part of the reason is because we fear the dark and what may be lurking there. The Bible often uses the imagery of darkness to describe the spiritual state of those whose lives are not directed by God. A few such passages are Acts 26:18; Colossians 1:13; 1 Thessalonians 5:4, 5; and 1 John 2:11. In today's lesson Jesus discusses His role as the light of the world.

In that role, He is the one who brings hope by revealing God to us. "In him was life; and the life was the light of men" (John 1:4). "This then is the message which we have heard of him, and declare unto you, that God is light, and in him is no darkness at all" (1 John 1:5).

B. Lesson Background

John 8 seems to follow directly on Jesus' teaching at the Feast of Tabernacles. There He promised the gift of "living water" (the Spirit) to those who believe in Him (last week's lesson).

Up to that point the crowds were divided on His message. Some had concluded that Jesus was the "Prophet" (Deuteronomy 18:15-18; John 7:40). Others thought Him to be the Messiah or Christ (John 7:41). The chief priests sent the temple guards to arrest Him, but they returned empty-handed after being overwhelmed by His authoritative teaching (John 7:45, 46).

Some of the leading Pharisees, including Nicodemus (compare John 3:1-10), debated among themselves about Jesus' identity (7:50-52). Jesus then explicitly identified himself as the one sent to reveal God in the midst of a dark world.

I. Light of the World
(John 8:12)

A. Jesus' Identity (v. 12a)

12a. Then spake Jesus again unto them, saying, I am the light of the world.

Jesus' illustration here, one of John's great *I am* sayings, is likely drawn from the celebrations during the Feast of Tabernacles. During this feast four huge lamps are lit in the temple courts. People then dance through the night with burning torches, singing songs of praise, accompanied by the music of the temple orchestra.

The glow from these festivities can be seen all over the city of Jerusalem. It is against this backdrop that Jesus proclaims himself to be the true *light of the world.*

B. Our Response (v. 12b)

12b. He that followeth me shall not walk in darkness, but shall have the light of life.

Jesus' claims probably reflect two aspects of His ministry. First, He brings *light* by revealing God and His nature in a fallen world. This revelation is vastly superior to the Old Testament system, for Jesus comes as the unique Son of God rather than as a mere prophet or priest. He thus shows people the way to eternal life through faith in Him. "The Lord shall be unto thee an everlasting light, and thy God thy glory" (Isaiah 60:19).

Second, Jesus' teaching and example provide moral guidance, showing believers how to live in a way that pleases God. Ancient Israelites should be very familiar with such imagery. They undoubtedly know Isaiah 42:16: "I will make darkness light before them, and crooked things straight. These things will I do unto them, and not forsake them."

FOLLOW THE LIGHT

When the children of Israel left Egypt, they were led by God in a pillar of cloud by day and a pillar of fire by night to give them light (Exodus 13:21). The cloud and the fire were important, for they were the evidence of God's leading.

Equally important, however, was the fact that the people had to follow. They could have stayed in one place and enjoyed the phenomenon of the cloud and fire. No one had ever seen such a thing before. Perhaps they could have built a

---

How to Say It

COLOSSIANS. Kuh-*losh*-unz.
DEUTERONOMY. Due-ter-*ahn*-uh-me.
GALILEE. *Gal*-uh-lee.
ISAIAH. Eye-*zay*-uh.
JERUSALEM. Juh-*roo*-suh-lem.
JUDAISM. *Joo*-duh-izz-um or *Joo*-day-izz-um.
LAZARUS. *Laz*-uh-rus.
MESSIAH. Meh-*sigh*-uh.
NICODEMUS. *Nick*-uh-*dee*-mus (strong accent on *dee*).
PHARISEES. *Fair*-ih-seez.
RABBINIC. ruh-*bin*-ik.
THESSALONIANS. *Thess*-uh-*lo*-nee-unz (strong accent on *lo*; *th* as in thin).

---

viewing stand and sold tickets. They could have advertised far and wide for people to come see this strange event—a pillar that changed from cloud by day into a fire by night! What a marvelous thing it would be!

All that would have been pointless, of course. The pillar was not there to fascinate them or become another one of the seven wonders of the ancient world. The purpose of the pillar was to lead them out of Egypt into the promised land. But by the same token, the pillar was not a magic carpet. It would not instantly transport them from Egypt into Canaan. In order to get from Egypt to Canaan, they would have to travel—on foot, every step of the way.

All that should be obvious. The pillar would lead them; but they must follow. Jesus is the light of the world. But we too must follow where He leads.   —J. B. N.

II. Testimony of the Father
(John 8:13-20)

A. Pharisees Challenge Jesus (v. 13)

13. The Pharisees therefore said unto him, Thou bearest record of thyself; thy record is not true.

Not true means that Jesus has not, in the opinion of *the Pharisees,* sufficiently substantiated His claims about himself. Rabbinic law assumes that such testimony will be biased. The Law of Moses requires that testimony and truth claims in criminal proceedings can be accepted only on the testimony of multiple witnesses (Deuteronomy 19:15). The Pharisees therefore plead that they, and everyone else, are allowed to dismiss Jesus' claims about himself. [See question #1, page 192.]

B. Jesus Refutes Pharisees (vv. 14-18)

14. Jesus answered and said unto them, Though I bear record of myself, yet my record is true: for I know whence I came, and whither I go; but ye cannot tell whence I come, and whither I go.

Jesus begins His defense by arguing that His case is unique, simply because no other human being is in a position to testify on His behalf. This verse looks ahead to John 13:3. That passage specifies that Jesus had come from God and was in the process of returning to God through death and resurrection.

Obviously, no one has ever seen God (John 1:18). It would therefore be impossible for anyone to verify or challenge Jesus' claims in the sense of being "witness" to His preexistence. For this reason Jesus does not depend even on the testimony of John the Baptist (John 5:31-36). This is so despite the fact that John was a prophet who pointed to Jesus as the Lamb of God (John 1:29-36).

Instead it is Jesus' unique origin and destiny that establish His credibility. His origin *(whence I came)* is from the Father (John 5:36, 37; 16:28); His destiny *(whither I go)* is to go back to the Father (John 13:1; 16:28; 17:5). Those hostile to Jesus know nothing about either. They are spiritually blind.

15, 16. Ye judge after the flesh; I judge no man. And yet if I judge, my judgment is true: for I am not alone, but I and the Father that sent me.

In Jesus' view, the Pharisees' objections simply reveal that they are unable to perceive spiritual matters. Instead they are stuck in judging *after the flesh.* When the Pharisees look at Jesus, they see a man from Galilee who has remarkable abilities but unorthodox teaching. He doesn't fit their understanding of a prophet or the Christ. They are therefore unable to recognize the source of His power (John 7:52; 9:29). [See question #2, page 192.]

As a result Jesus disqualifies the Pharisees from passing judgment on Him. He appeals instead to God as the ultimate witness to His identity. Jesus judges *no man* in the way that the Pharisees do.

17, 18. It is also written in your law, that the testimony of two men is true. I am one that bear witness of myself, and the Father that sent me beareth witness of me.

Jesus reminds His accusers that Moses had taught that *two* witnesses are sufficient to establish guilt or innocence (Deuteronomy 17:6; 19:15). On the topic of His identity, Jesus has testified on His own behalf, and He now calls *the Father* to the stand in His defense. The Father's *witness* (or *testimony*) here most likely refers to the works that Jesus does by God's power (John 5:36). The Gospels use Jesus' miracles as signs of His identity; the signs establish His credibility (John 2:11; etc.).

In the "purpose statement" of this Gospel (John 20:30, 31), the apostle makes clear the reason for the signs. When people watch Jesus turn water into wine or raise Lazarus from the dead, they should see the evidence for His claims about himself.

BEARING WITNESS

Several times I have been a witness in court cases. Once was for a traffic accident that I saw. I was asked to describe what I had seen, and it was used as evidence in the case. Another time I appeared on behalf of one of the parties to a suit because of my academic studies in a particular area. I was asked to give my assessment of the issue because I was considered an "expert" in the field. (I enjoyed that label, but my wife was not particularly impressed.)

A witness is a person who gives testimony in court proceedings. I appeared either because I had personally seen the incident or because I had special experience with the nuances of the situation. The task of witnesses is to relate to the judge and/or jury the facts that they know. The judge and jurors were not present at the incident, and they need to know exactly what happened. Or there may be some technical depth to the case, with the judge and jury needing an impartial, objective "expert" to interpret the situation and give an opinion on it.

Jesus relates that He can be a witness to himself, and even God the Father can be a witness on His behalf. The Pharisees of verse 13 were not willing to accept His testimony, not knowing that He did indeed have first-person experience of the situation. Jesus knew some technicalities of the situation that they did not. He was an excellent expert witness, even though they failed to recognize that fact. Do we recognize it?

—J. B. N.

C. Know Me, Know My Father (vv. 19, 20)

19. Then said they unto him, Where is thy Father? Jesus answered, Ye neither know me, nor my Father: if ye had known me, ye should have known my Father also.

The Gospel of John often follows the "theme of misunderstanding": frequently, no one, not even the disciples, can figure out what Jesus is talking about. No matter how obvious His remarks seem to be (to us!), usually people "just don't get it."

If John is following this theme here, then the Pharisees have missed the point of Jesus' remarks entirely. Thus they ask Him where they can find His father, meaning Joseph, so that they may question him about Jesus (compare John 6:42). They are still thinking "after the flesh" (John 8:15, above).

Jesus' answer implies what the reader already knows to be true: the *Father* of whom Jesus speaks is God, not Joseph. The fact that the Pharisees either cannot understand or will not accept Jesus does not discount His role as the light of the world. People may choose to close their eyes, but their decision to do so does not say anything about Jesus. It reveals, rather, that they do not *know* the God whom Jesus came to reveal more fully.

20. These words spake Jesus in the treasury, as he taught in the temple: and no man laid hands on him; for his hour was not yet come.

The implication of *no man laid hands on him; for His hour was not yet come* is that hostility is building but has not yet reached the boiling point. Jesus' *hour* in the Gospel of John refers to the time of His arrest and crucifixion. That is when He fulfills His task of dying on the cross (John 7:30; 12:23, 27; 17:1).

Jesus has complete control over His destiny (John 10:15-18). Jesus' enemies can do no harm because He still has much more to do. [See question #3, page 192.]

III. Escape from Darkness (John 12:44-46)

A. God's Special Agent (vv. 44, 45)

44, 45. Jesus cried and said, He that believeth on me, believeth not on me, but on him that sent me. And he that seeth me seeth him that sent me.

John 12:37-50 is sometimes referred to as a "saddle" or "bridge" in the outline of this Gospel. The reason for this designation is because it is here that John summarizes Jesus' public ministry before moving on to the private teachings to the disciples in the upper room (chapters 13–17). [See question #4, page 192.] In John 12:35, 36, Jesus urges the Jews one last time to believe in the light. This exhortation leads John to express disbelief at the Jews' inability to understand who Jesus really is (John 12:37-43).

As a closing refrain to His public teaching ministry, Jesus warns the Jews once again. His warning is that it is impossible to believe in God *(him that sent me)* while rejecting the Son. There are many different religious systems that claim to reveal God in a variety of ways, yet John insists that none of these, not even Judaism, can really lead us to a true vision of God's love and power. God's true nature is perfectly revealed in Jesus alone, making it essential that people accept Him.

HE WHO SENT ME

Major General George G. Meade was commanding officer, Army of the Potomac, as it faced the Confederate army under Robert E. Lee at Gettysburg. On Meade's staff was Brigadier General Gouverneur K. Warren, Chief of Engineers.

Acting on his authority as chief engineering officer, Warren was scouting the front lines on the afternoon of July 2, 1863. He came to the southern end of the Union line on a rocky hill called Little Round Top, where he saw that it was undefended. He also saw a large segment of the Confederate army moving toward the same hill. He knew that if the Confederates seized the height they could roll up the entire Union line, bringing disaster to the entire army.

Warren sent couriers down the hill and they soon met the brigade of Colonel Strong Vincent. Warren ordered him to go up, defend the hill, and prepare to repel the Confederates. Vincent instantly obeyed, and the defense of Little Round Top became famous. Yet it was a near thing. The Union forces beat the Confederates to the top by only fifteen minutes.

What if Vincent had argued with Warren? He could have said, "You are not my immediate commanding officer; why should I obey you?" Vincent knew that Warren represented the authority of General Meade, and that was sufficient for him. Jesus said that if we believe Him, we are really acknowledging the authority of God. To refuse to accept the words of Jesus is to refuse that authority.
—J. B. N.

B. Leaving the Darkness (v. 46)

46. I am come a light into the world, that whosoever believeth on me should not abide in darkness.

The world is spiritually dark in two senses. First, most people do not adequately understand the nature of God himself. As a consequence they do not really understand who they are as people created in God's image. Of course, the Jews of Jesus' day claim that they are God's elect

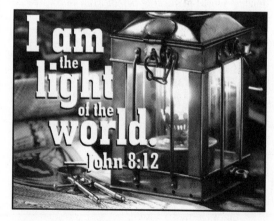

Visual for Lesson 9. *Point to this imagery of a light-producing apparatus as you introduce either question #2 or #5 on page 192.*

people, blessed with a special revelation of His true nature. Even they, however, are walking in darkness because only through faith in Christ can they truly know God's nature (compare John 12:35, 36).

Second, the world is dark in the sense that people do not live lives that please God. Instead they stumble blindly in pursuit of worldly pleasures that ultimately leave them longing for fulfillment (compare Romans 1:18-32). Like a thirsty man who is given saltwater instead of refreshing water, this pursuit only increases the thirst. Jesus came to rescue us from this ignorance and despair—for eternity. [See question #5, page 192.]

Conclusion

A. Piercing the Deepest Darkness

The image of Jesus as light is a powerful theme in the Gospel of John. Physical light has some marvelous characteristics that allow this image to function beautifully as a description of Christ. Consider this example: you can go into an utterly dark room and light a tiny birthday candle, and all the darkness of that room cannot stop the little light from shining. The smallest candle can dispel the deepest, blackest darkness.

On the other hand, you cannot go into a brightly lighted room with a box of darkness, open the box, and expect the darkness to dim the brightness. Darkness cannot overcome light (John 1:5). This is the case because darkness is, by definition, the absence of something—the absence of light.

When we speak figuratively of the dark world in which we live, we are highlighting the fact that the world is missing or ignoring God. Just as

light always overcomes darkness, God's purposes will always overcome evil in this world. Of course, some people choose to close their eyes. But those who open their eyes will find a way through the darkness to eternal life and peace.

B. Avoiding Counterfeit Light

The issue of "light vs. darkness" is well defined. Spiritually mature Christians clearly recognize the choice. But another issue we face is what we may call "true light vs. counterfeit light." We face this problem since "Satan himself is transformed into an angel of light" (2 Corinthians 11:14).

Many sincere Christians are determined to avoid the darkness of sin, and Satan knows this well. So instead of offering those Christians something that is obviously in the category of *dark*, he offers something that seems, at first glance, to fit within God's light.

This deception can take many forms, and Satan is very crafty. For example a harmless hobby that provides needed rest and relaxation can become an obsession and an addiction, wrecking the family budget. Eating that extra piece of pie at the restaurant buffet can be rationalized as "good stewardship" since "I'm getting my money's worth." Remember, when Satan offered certain temptations to Jesus, he even backed up his ideas with Scripture! (See Matthew 4:1-11.)

So how do we recognize and avoid counterfeit light? The first line of defense is to know the Scriptures thoroughly. Jesus is our example here, since that was how He refuted Satan during the temptation in the wilderness. "Thy word is a lamp unto my feet, and a light unto my path" (Psalm 119:105).

The second line of defense is prayer. Jesus saw this as an important part of avoiding temptation (Mark 14:38). A third line of defense is mutual accountability. Invite a fellow Christian to point out your spiritual blind spots. Then consider his or her counsel very carefully!

C. Prayer

Lord, we live in a dark and confused world. Sometimes it is hard even to know what we should do, much less to do it. Please light our way as we seek to serve You, and please also help us shine the light of Christ on others. In Jesus' name, amen.

D. Thought to Remember

The light of Jesus can—and does—pierce the deepest spiritual darkness.

Home Daily Bible Readings

Monday, Jan. 22—Promises for God's People (Isaiah 35:3-10)

Tuesday, Jan. 23—Jesus Brings Light (Matthew 4:12-17)

Wednesday, Jan. 24—Jesus Heals a Blind Man (John 9:1-11)

Thursday, Jan. 25—Who Is Jesus? (John 9:35-41)

Friday, Jan. 26—Knowing God's Will (Ephesians 5:15-21)

Saturday, Jan. 27—Jesus Is the World's Light (John 8:12-20)

Sunday, Jan. 28—I Have Come as Light (John 12:44-50)

Learning by Doing

This page contains an alternative lesson plan emphasizing learning activities.
Classes desiring such student involvement will find these suggestions helpful.

Learning Goals

After this lesson, each student will be able to:

1. List ways in which Jesus was and is a source of light in our dark world.

2. Explain Jesus' use of the "light" metaphor as proof of His unique authority.

3. Change one habit to better reflect Jesus' light.

Into the Lesson

Have two sides of your assembly area clearly marked, "This Side" and "That Side." As class begins, ask everyone to stand. Give these directions: "I want all the ____ on "This Side" and all the _____ on "That Side." Fill in an appropriate dichotomy, such as men/women, right-handed/left-handed, local sports team fans/fans of teams from other cities. If you like, you may perform this division two or three times rapidly, using different criteria each time. Then have students sit.

Say, "Many things divide us. But one matter must never divide us: who we consider Jesus to be." Have a student read John 6:40-43. Note, "Today's texts in John chapters 8 and 12 continue Jesus' answer regarding questions of who He is." Remind the class of this quarter's theme, "Jesus Christ: A Portrait of God" and remind them of Lesson 1, "Who Is Jesus Christ?"

Continue with an emphasis on the "I Am" theme of the Gospel of John. Say, "'I Am' is an affirmation of power and position." Ask students to affirm a position or role that each holds. Give them one personal example, such as, "I am the head of the class." Encourage metaphors, to be decoded by other members of the class.

Into the Word

Prepare in advance half sheets of paper with eight blocks drawn vertically down the left side. Each block should feature one of the letters of the word *darkness*. On the right side of the paper make eight numbered lines with a "T/F" by each line. Give each student eight yellow peel-and-stick dots (to resemble small suns), each large enough to cover a letter on the paper. (Such dots are available inexpensively at office supply stores.)

Say, "Read the text silently and then close your Bibles and books. We are going to have a true-false quiz on elements of today's lesson. Your goal is to 'dispel darkness' with the Word of light. For each answer you get correct, you may cover one letter with a 'sunlight' dot."

Read aloud each of the following statements. Allow time for students to mark their answers, and then give the answer and any explanation necessary. (1) Jesus calls himself the light of the world *[True; 8:12]*. (2) This is the first time in the Gospel of John that Jesus has been called "the light" *[False; 1:5, 7-9]*. (3) In the Pharisees' legal system, a person could not testify on his own behalf *[True; 8:13]*. (4) Jesus affirms that the Pharisees had no idea where He came from *[True; 8:14]*. (5) Jewish law required four witnesses to testify to confirm a truth *[False; 8:17]*. (6) The Jewish leaders asked Jesus to bring in his mother as witness *[False; 8:19]*. (7) No one was able to lay a hand on Jesus *[True; 8:20]*. (8) Seeing Jesus is the same as seeing God *[True; 12:45]*. (9) Jesus' discussion with the Jewish leaders in John 8 took place in the temple *[True; 8:20]*. (10) Believing in God requires believing in Jesus, and vice versa *[True; 12:44]*.

Into Life

Introduce the assignment below using this book summary. Say, "In Ursula LeGuin's fantasy *The Tombs of Atuan,* the hero, named Ged, rescues the princess, Arha, who has learned to love the darkness of the catacombs. There she has been made priestess of the dark powers. As Ged delivers her from the tombs, he assures her that she was not made for darkness but for light."

Explain that Arha was taken as a young child to replace a dying princess, but as most children are, she was afraid of the dark. As she grew comfortable entering the dark world of tombs she became fascinated. She gained a sense of power over the darkness, even as it gained power over her. Arha's name means "the eaten one."

Comment on how darkness first scares, then fascinates, then "eats alive." Liken this same sequence to most people in our world who get swallowed up in darkness and need a light bearer to rescue them.

Close with a time of sharing. Ask students how they plan to change one habit in the week ahead to better reflect Jesus' light.

Let's Talk It Over

The questions on this page are designed to promote discussion of the lesson by the class and to encourage application of the lesson Scriptures. The answers provided are only discussion starters. Let your class talk it over from there.

1. In what ways do people still say *not true* when it comes to Jesus? Why do they do this?

Some people are inclined to make decisions on the basis of what seems rational to them. While God gave us minds and expects us to love Him with those minds (compare Matthew 22:37), we need His revelation through Scripture to make accurate spiritual decisions (2 Timothy 3:16, 17).

Others are inclined to trust their feelings and subjective impulses. While God sometimes confirms our decisions through such subjective means (Acts 2:37), these urges cannot be trusted in and of themselves.

The popularity of a decision or the number of people making the same choice also is an untrustworthy means of assessment. The majority is not always right (though the minority is not always right either).

2. What causes people to reject Jesus as their source of spiritual guidance in favor of something or someone else? How do you protect yourself from making this kind of mistake?

In some cultures many people reject Jesus because of His absolute and exclusive claims. If He claimed to be *a* way to God rather than *the* way to God, they would find Him less offensive. If He offered ethical suggestions rather than commands, He would be more acceptable.

Pride deludes others into thinking that they have no need for spiritual guidance at all. These people prefer to live life without accountability. Believers, who claim Jesus as their source of spiritual guidance, guard themselves against falling into this error through prayer. Prayer by its very nature recognizes that God exists and that we are answerable to Him.

3. How does God's protection of Jesus provide spiritual encouragement to you? What are some dangers of directly applying this example to our own lives?

We can derive great spiritual strength and contentment from knowing that God's ultimate purposes are never thwarted. Nothing and no one could stand in the way of Jesus' mission of reconciliation! It is comforting to be reminded of God's authority and power (Isaiah 55:11).

The uniqueness of Jesus' person and work must also be noted, however. God undoubtedly protects and sustains His people as an expression of His concern for us and for His global mission. There are no passages in the Bible that guarantee that God will preserve our earthly lives. Through Christ, however, He does provide significance to our earthly lives and an eternal hope beyond them.

4. The lesson describes John 12:37-50 as bridging Jesus' public and private ministry. How does His example help us balance concern for the crowd with concern for the individual?

Jesus' example demonstrates that all people need the gospel; therefore, it is appropriate and necessary to present the message to anyone and everyone. While Jesus taught the masses, He also focused on pouring His life into a few. Jesus' relationship with the 12 disciples reflected this dynamic. Limited quantities of time, energy, and resources limit our ability to minister equally to each and every individual we encounter. Even so, a few people may warrant our most intense efforts as God leads.

5. How can we get people to accept the idea that there is such a thing as "spiritual darkness"? How important is this in getting them to see their need for Jesus?

If a person doesn't believe that he or she is "lost," you probably won't be successful in giving him or her directions! Helping others to see their condition as spiritual darkness may require powerful images to be effective. One thing that may make this a bit easier is that the word *dark* is already used metaphorically in modern culture (example: "I was in the dark on this").

Dark can relate to *fear* because places of complete darkness often create that emotion. Both physical and spiritual darkness are places of great danger. Realizing the seriousness of one's spiritual condition can motivate people to seek the gospel. Complete darkness brings with it a sense of helplessness. This, in turn, creates a greater sense of longing for light and the security it brings. People won't see the need for security in Christ unless they first realize their helpless condition.

"I Am the Good Shepherd"

DEVOTIONAL READING: Isaiah 40:10-14.

BACKGROUND SCRIPTURE: John 10:1-18.

PRINTED TEXT: John 10:1-18.

John 10:1-18

1 Verily, verily, I say unto you, He that entereth not by the door into the sheepfold, but climbeth up some other way, the same is a thief and a robber.

2 But he that entereth in by the door is the shepherd of the sheep.

3 To him the porter openeth; and the sheep hear his voice: and he calleth his own sheep by name, and leadeth them out.

4 And when he putteth forth his own sheep, he goeth before them, and the sheep follow him: for they know his voice.

5 And a stranger will they not follow, but will flee from him; for they know not the voice of strangers.

6 This parable spake Jesus unto them; but they understood not what things they were which he spake unto them.

7 Then said Jesus unto them again, Verily, verily, I say unto you, I am the door of the sheep.

8 All that ever came before me are thieves and robbers: but the sheep did not hear them.

9 I am the door: by me if any man enter in, he shall be saved, and shall go in and out, and find pasture.

10 The thief cometh not, but for to steal, and to kill, and to destroy: I am come that they might have life, and that they might have it more abundantly.

11 I am the good shepherd: the good shepherd giveth his life for the sheep.

12 But he that is a hireling, and not the shepherd, whose own the sheep are not, seeth the wolf coming, and leaveth the sheep, and fleeth; and the wolf catcheth them, and scattereth the sheep.

13 The hireling fleeth, because he is a hireling, and careth not for the sheep.

14 I am the good shepherd, and know my sheep, and am known of mine.

15 As the Father knoweth me, even so know I the Father: and I lay down my life for the sheep.

16 And other sheep I have, which are not of this fold: them also I must bring, and they shall hear my voice; and there shall be one fold, and one shepherd.

17 Therefore doth my Father love me, because I lay down my life, that I might take it again.

18 No man taketh it from me, but I lay it down of myself. I have power to lay it down, and I have power to take it again. This commandment have I received of my Father.

GOLDEN TEXT: I am the good shepherd: the good shepherd giveth his life for the sheep.—John 10:11.

Lesson Aims

After participating in this lesson, each student will be able to:

1. Recite reasons Jesus is the good shepherd.
2. Contrast Jesus as a spiritual shepherd with other religious leaders of His day.
3. Suggest one specific way to participate in the shepherding ministry of his or her church.

Lesson Outline

INTRODUCTION
    A. Knowing Your Own
    B. Lesson Background
  I. SHEPHERD AND THIEF (John 10:1-6)
    A. Reaction to the Shepherd (vv. 1-4)
      Known by Our Names
    B. Reaction to Strangers (v. 5)
    C. Reaction of the Listeners (v. 6)
 II. INDIVIDUALS AND MOTIVES (John 10:7-10)
    A. Now *vs.* Then (vv. 7, 8)
    B. Salvation *vs.* Destruction (vv. 9, 10)
III. SHEPHERD AND HIRED HAND (John 10:11-18)
    A. Shepherd's Actions, Part 1 (v. 11)
      Laying Down One's Life
    B. Hired Hand's Actions (vv. 12, 13)
    C. Shepherd's Actions, Part 2 (vv. 14-18)
CONCLUSION
    A. One of the Crowd
    B. Prayer
    C. Thought to Remember

Introduction

A. Knowing Your Own

For many years we had a large dog named Sassy. I could always identify Sassy's bark from several blocks away, even though there were dozens of dogs in our neighborhood; Sassy, in turn, could identify my call and would come to me in a crowd of people.

In a similar way my wife and I can identify our young daughter's cry in a room full of toddlers. My son's first-grade class at church, where I volunteer as a youth sponsor, includes a pair of twins who define the word *identical*. Their teachers are constantly in a quandary trying to

tell them apart. The teachers insist that the two must never wear matching clothes. Yet the parents of these boys can immediately tell one from the other.

Knowledge of this kind—the ability to pick out a voice or a face in a crowd—is a sign of intimacy: we know those we love and they know us, through constant interaction. In our lesson today Jesus will apply this principle to His loving relationship with His disciples.

B. Lesson Background

Most scholars today view John 9, just preceding today's lesson text, as a critical passage for understanding the background of John 10. In John 9 Jesus met a man who had been blind from birth and healed him. The healing came about when Jesus covered the man's eyes with mud and sent him to wash at the Pool of Siloam. The cure was effective, but it was impossible for the man to recognize Jesus or know much about Him. (Jesus was gone before the man had a chance to see Him.)

The Pharisees later interrogated the man who had been healed because Jesus, in their view, had violated the Law of Moses by healing on the Sabbath. The man refused to condemn Jesus and ultimately criticized the Pharisees for ignoring the obvious evidence of His divine power. As a result they excommunicated him (John 9:1-34).

Jesus later found the man and led him to faith, while the Pharisees continued to question Jesus' authority (John 9:35-41). Jesus' teaching in chapter 10 about His role as the good shepherd is a commentary on this situation. It includes several promises that Jesus will protect and save those who believe in Him.

This teaching undoubtedly was extremely meaningful to the apostle John. He, along with the other apostles, also experienced persecution and excommunication for faith in Christ (see John 16:1-4).

I. Shepherd and Thief
(John 10:1-6)

A. Reaction to the Shepherd (vv. 1-4)

1, 2. Verily, verily, I say unto you, He that entereth not by the door into the sheepfold, but climbeth up some other way, the same is a thief and a robber. But he that entereth in by the door is the shepherd of the sheep.

The opening phrase *verily, verily, I say unto you* leads us to ask a question: to whom is Jesus speaking? The context of John 9:40, 41 seems to indicate that Jesus is still talking to the Pharisees. On the other hand the phrase "they understood not" in John 10:6 (below) may indicate that a different audience is in view.

In either case Jesus' parable about *the sheep-fold* here in verses 1-6 is a sharp condemnation of the Jewish religious leaders. Jesus compares God's people to *sheep* in a pen; in the immediate context, the specific "sheep" in question is most likely the man whom Jesus has just healed of blindness in chapter 9.

The *shepherd* in this analogy is Jesus himself, while the thieves are the Pharisees and other Jewish leaders who are attempting to prevent people from believing in Him (compare John 9:40). Jesus' legitimate spiritual authority is evidenced by the fact that He enters *by the door*. He displays God's care and love, and people recognize Him as the one whom God has sent (compare John 9:30-34).

God's true sheep, however, refuse to accept the false teachings of the Pharisees. These sheep recognize that those teachings do not reflect a correct understanding of Christ in light of Jesus' miracles. Many Pharisees are thieves and robbers, bent on self-preservation at the sheep's expense (compare Ezekiel 34; Jude 12). [See question #1, page 200.]

3. To him the porter openeth; and the sheep hear his voice: and he calleth his own sheep by name, and leadeth them out.

Middle Eastern shepherds lead their flocks by voice commands. Consequently the *sheep* know the *voice* of their shepherd. Even when many different flocks graze together, a shepherd can gather his own simply by calling to them. In a similar way those who sincerely seek God's will recognize Jesus' voice and willingly follow Him. [See question #2, page 200.]

The porter is the person who guards the gate of the sheep pen. In the context of Jesus' illustration, this character probably does not refer to any specific person. Rather, the reference is to the general fact that Jesus has a legitimate claim to call God's people.

KNOWN BY OUR NAMES

For several years we had a professor on our college faculty who had an amazing gift. He would look at the pictures of all incoming freshmen that the admissions department provided. He would also notice the hometown of each. At freshmen orientation he would then have all new students stand up—usually over two hundred people whom he had never met.

Starting at one end of the group, he would begin to call out names and hometowns. Each student named would then sit down. By the time he got to the other end of the room, only one or two students would be standing—and often they were recent applicants for whom the admissions office did not have a picture!

In addition that man often taught at a particular "high school week" at a nearby Christian service camp. He would have all students who were there the previous year stand up. He had not seen these students in a year, but he called off their names without any mistakes.

In the 1996 movie *Fly Away Home,* Amy Alden raises a flock of orphaned Canada geese. She gives them all names and leads them into winter quarters in the southern United States. To most of us one goose looks just like another.

If a human being can have an ability to know names, hometowns, and individual geese, how much more is Jesus able to know us! He is the good shepherd, and He knows the names of His sheep. That's a comfort that will follow us into eternity. —J. B. N.

4. And when he putteth forth his own sheep, he goeth before them, and the sheep follow him: for they know his voice.

To heed the call of Christ is vital! Ancient shepherds walk ahead of their flocks to lead them from the pen to safe pasture, and Jesus uses this analogy to describe His leadership of God's people. The twofold emphasis is on knowing *his voice* and on following *him.* The first of these two speaks to the ability to recognize Jesus as the one who has come to reveal God to the world. The second speaks to being obedient to His teaching in all circumstances.

B. Reaction to Strangers (v. 5)

5. And a stranger will they not follow, but will flee from him; for they know not the voice of strangers.

In John 9 the man healed of blindness stubbornly refused to yield to the Pharisees. He would not condemn Jesus despite pressure. His reaction contrasted sharply with that of his parents, who tried to straddle the fence when called to testify (John 9:18-23).

How to Say It

CORNELIUS. Cor-*neel*-yus.
EZEKIEL. Ee-*zeek*-ee-ul or Ee-*zeek*-yul.
MESSIAH. Meh-*sigh*-uh.
PHARISEES. *Fair*-ih-seez.
SILOAM. Sigh-*lo*-um.

The attitude of the man healed of blindness parallels the way that sheep will scatter when *strangers* attempt to lure them away. God's people will listen to Jesus' voice and no other.

C. Reaction of the Listeners (v. 6)

6. This parable spake Jesus unto them; but they understood not what things they were which He spake unto them.

Although the meaning of Jesus' analogy seems obvious to us now, it is misunderstood by the original hearers. This confusion may suggest that Jesus is now speaking to a different audience: not to the Pharisees of John 9:40, 41 but to a larger group of Jews of John 10:19.

This view could be supported by the reaction of the chief priests and scribes in Luke 20:19. There we see that those religious leaders are able to understand all too well that Jesus uses a figure of speech against them. Here, however, the audience *understood not what things they were which He spake unto them.*

So perhaps this is a larger audience (again, John 10:19) that is not aware of Jesus' earlier discussion with the man whom He had cured of blindness. In either case Jesus proceeds to expand the illustration in order to explain its relevance to all people who are considering whether or not to follow Him (next verse). [See question #3, page 200.]

II. Individuals and Motives (John 10:7-10)

A. Now *vs.* Then (vv. 7, 8)

7. Then said Jesus unto them again, Verily, verily, I say unto you, I am the door of the sheep.

In ancient times *sheep* often are kept in caves or in pens made of rock walls in open fields. The shepherd brings his flock back to the pen at the end of the day. There he counts and inspects them.

These pens may have no physical doors or gates. For that reason the shepherd himself would stand or lie across the opening to prevent sheep from wandering out and wolves from entering. Thus the shepherd himself becomes *the door* or gate of the sheep pen. This is the imagery Jesus uses to describe how He watches over His sheep and guards them from harm.

8. All that ever came before me are thieves and robbers: but the sheep did not hear them.

The *thieves* here may refer again to the Jewish religious leaders as depicted in Jeremiah 23:1, 2; Ezekiel 34:2, 3. The term may also refer to the various false messiahs who led anti-Roman revolutionary movements after the death of Herod the Great in 4 BC (compare Acts 5:36, 37). In either case God's people are waiting for the true shepherd, Jesus. Thus *the sheep* do not heed the imposters who *came before* Jesus.

B. Salvation *vs.* Destruction (vv. 9, 10)

9. I am the door: by me if any man enter in, he shall be saved, and shall go in and out, and find pasture.

This verse pictures the sheepfold as the dwelling place of God's redeemed people. *Go in and out* does not suggest that one falls in and out of salvation. Rather, the reference is to the way that Jesus continually provides for His people by leading them to safe *pasture*—by providing for their spiritual needs. The sheep depend on the shepherd to lead them out of the pen for food and water. In the same way we depend on Christ to provide for us.

The imagery thus emphasizes the shepherd's ongoing, daily care for the flock. Jesus' concern for His people is constant.

10. The thief cometh not, but for to steal, and to kill, and to destroy: I am come that they might have life, and that they might have it more abundantly.

The false messiahs attempt to "call" God's sheep, but they do so for selfish reasons. They want to increase their own power and prestige in service of their own agendas. Jesus, here as elsewhere, stresses that His motives are entirely pure. He does not wish to promote himself at the expense of others. He seeks only to protect the lives and well being of His flock. In fact He is willing to sacrifice His own life to save them (v. 11, next). [See question #4, page 200.]

III. Shepherd and Hired Hand (John 10:11-18)

A. Shepherd's Actions, Part 1 (v. 11)

11. I am the good shepherd: the good shepherd giveth his life for the sheep.

Shepherds give their lives for their *sheep* in at least two ways. First, sheep need constant care and attention, with many long days and nights in the field. The job is all-consuming.

Second, and more specifically here, shepherds are called upon to protect the flock from dangerous predators. In these cases the *shepherd* risks *his life* by placing himself between the sheep and the wolves. Ancient Jews can well relate to this sort of imagery because so many of them work with livestock.

The Old Testament frequently refers to God as the shepherd of His people. Often the emphasis is on protection and provision. Perhaps the most famous of these passages is Psalm 23. Jesus calls himself *the good shepherd* against this backdrop to emphasize His loving care for His people. This is in contrast to the religious leaders of His day. It is Jesus alone who literally will give *his life* on the cross *for the sheep* (compare Hebrews 13:20).

LAYING DOWN ONE'S LIFE

On January 23, 1943, more than 900 men sailed from New York on the USAT *Dorchester*, a former luxury liner, now a troop ship bound for Greenland. Most of the travelers were young Army enlistees, plus some officers and Merchant Marine sailors. There were also four chaplains: George L. Fox, a Methodist minister; Clark V. Poling, a Dutch Reformed minister; John P. Washington, a Roman Catholic priest; and Alexander D. Goode, a Jewish rabbi.

About 150 miles from Greenland, at about 1:00 AM on February 3, German submarine U-223 torpedoed the aging transport. The attack killed about 100 men immediately. The rest groped for the openings in the darkness that would lead to the deck. The four chaplains helped where they could, lending some sense of calm to the fear-crazed young men. Lifeboats were readied, and the chaplains went to the lockers to hand out life jackets.

Unfortunately, there were not enough jackets for everyone. The four chaplains had theirs on, but all four removed their jackets and handed them to young men and directed them to the boats. The *Dorchester* sank in less than 30 minutes. As it went down the survivors noticed the four chaplains standing at the railing, arms linked together, singing and praying, giving strength to others.

About 75 percent of the men aboard perished in the sinking, including the four chaplains. Those four had laid down their lives for the men of their "flock." We marvel at their sacrifice, even after more than 60 years. Do we marvel as much about Jesus? He also laid down His life, but in a much more profound way. His sacrifice made it possible for us to live eternally. That's something that even the selfless sacrifice of the four chaplains could not accomplish. —J. B. N.

B. Hired Hand's Actions (vv. 12, 13)

12, 13. But he that is a hireling, and not the shepherd, whose own the sheep are not, seeth the wolf coming, and leaveth the sheep, and

Visual for Lesson 10. *Point to this visual as you ask, "In what ways do you allow Jesus to be your shepherd? In what ways do you resist?"*

fleeth; and the wolf catcheth them, and scattereth the sheep. The hireling fleeth, because he is a hireling, and careth not for the sheep.

While the thieves and robbers of verse 8 likely allude to the Pharisees who had persecuted the healed man in John 9, we're not really sure who the *hireling* represents. Whoever this is, such a person works among the flock (God's people) but without genuine concern.

Jesus, by contrast, knows His people and loves them as His own. The next several verses describe the ways that He expresses this love. [See question #5, page 200.]

C. Shepherd's Actions, Part 2 (vv. 14-18)

14, 15. I am the good shepherd, and know my sheep, and am known of mine. As the Father knoweth me, even so know I the Father: and I lay down my life for the sheep.

The verb *know* here refers to more than merely "know about." Of course Jesus knows His *sheep* in the sense that He knows who we are. But the hireling of verse 13 can also claim that he knows the sheep in this way—how many sheep there are, what they look like, which ones walk slower, etc.

Jesus therefore proceeds to outline two ways in which His ministry is unique. First, He emphasizes the special relationship that He has with His people through comparison with His own relationship to God. Jesus and *the Father* are completely united, and Jesus and His people are united as well (see Matthew 11:27). Second, Jesus restates His willingness to *lay down* His *life,* sacrificing everything for the well-being of His flock.

16. And other sheep I have, which are not of this fold: them also I must bring, and they shall hear my voice; and there shall be one fold, and one shepherd.

Who are the *other sheep* of whom Jesus speaks? Most commentators conclude that these are Gentiles (that is, non-Jewish people) who have not yet heard about Jesus and His message. Consider the prediction in Isaiah 42:6: "I the Lord have called thee in righteousness, and will hold thine hand, and will keep thee, and give thee for a covenant of the people, for a light of the Gentiles."

Jesus is thus making a prediction about the mission to the Gentiles that will follow the conversion of Cornelius in Acts 10. That mission ultimately will find its fullest expression in Paul's ministry.

Notice also the emphasis on the unity of the flock. The phrase *one fold* speaks to the unity of Jew and Gentile in Christ, *one shepherd*. Jesus' words are especially meaningful to John's churches in the late first century AD. These churches likely include believers from both Jewish and Gentile backgrounds. Christ cares for all of His people equally.

17. Therefore doth my Father love me, because I lay down my life, that I might take it again.

Take it again refers to Jesus' resurrection. Jesus enjoys the Father's love because He, unlike the Pharisees and false Messiahs, proves His love for God's people.

The ultimate proof comes when He lays down His *life* to pay the price for sin. After the resurrection Jesus is exalted once again to His heavenly position beside the *Father*.

Home Daily Bible Readings

Monday, Jan. 29—God Tends His Flock (Isaiah 40:10-14)

Tuesday, Jan. 30—A Warning to False Shepherds (Ezekiel 34:1-6)

Wednesday, Jan. 31—I Will Shepherd My Sheep (Ezekiel 34:11-16)

Thursday, Feb. 1—You Are My Sheep (Ezekiel 34:25-31)

Friday, Feb. 2—The Sheep Know Their Shepherd (John 10:1-5)

Saturday, Feb. 3—I Am the Good Shepherd (John 10:7-11)

Sunday, Feb. 4—The Shepherd Suffers for the Sheep (John 10:12-18)

18. No man taketh it from me, but I lay it down of myself. I have power to lay it down, and I have power to take it again. This commandment have I received of my Father.

John stresses throughout his Gospel that Jesus' death was not an accident of circumstance. Despite the fact that He died in a gruesome and humiliating way, Jesus was at every moment completely in control of everything that happened to Him. This makes His death so much more meaningful as an expression of His care for the flock.

Many shepherds may have to risk their lives to protect the sheep at a moment's notice; Jesus consciously chooses when and how He will die, confident that He has the power to live again. No one else could make such a claim.

Conclusion

A. One of the Crowd

Very often we are told (especially in advertisements) that it's bad to be "just one of the crowd." We are supposed to let our individuality stand out. We like to think of ourselves as independent individuals who don't need to rely on anyone else.

At the same time, however, it is very comforting to be a member of a group in which we can feel safe and at home. The hit television show *Cheers* (which ran from 1982 to 1993) portrayed a group of close friends at a small bar in Boston. That bar was a place "where everybody knows your name." That was an important part of the show's appeal: it illustrated the type of place that many of us long to find. A place to be "one of the gang." A place to be accepted for who one is.

The sad thing about that television program is that so many people seek these types of relationships in bars rather than in churches. While we are all individuals, together we make up Jesus' flock as we follow His voice. He knows each of our names, and we each have a special place in His family. In Him we find an eternal peace and comfort that the world cannot provide.

B. Prayer

Lord, we know that You call to us in every situation; help us to hear Your voice. We live in a world with many false ideas and self-serving teachers. Sometimes it's hard to know what's right. Keep us focused on the one who gave His life for us. In Jesus' name, amen.

C. Thought to Remember

Jesus still shepherds us today.

Learning by Doing

This page contains an alternative lesson plan emphasizing learning activities.
Classes desiring such student involvement will find these suggestions helpful.

Learning Goals

After participating in this lesson, each student will be able to:

1. Recite reasons Jesus is the good shepherd.

2. Contrast Jesus as a spiritual shepherd with other religious leaders of His day.

3. Suggest one specific way to participate in the shepherding ministry of his or her church.

Into the Lesson

As students arrive give each a piece of blank paper (or have students turn to "What Do You Think?" in the student books if you're using those). Write the following open-ended statements on the board:

To be a good shepherd, a person must . . .

Jesus was the good shepherd because . . .

Ask your students to write down as many responses to each statement as they can generate in a minute or two. Then call on volunteers to share their answers with the class.

After discussion say, "Today's lesson will stress Jesus' role as the good shepherd. We will also learn something about our responsibility to shepherd members of our congregation."

Into the Word

This *Yes or No* exercise will help students note contrasts among the shepherd, the thief, and the hireling. Hand out copies of this exercise (or direct students to their student books, where this exercise is also found). Each student should study John 10:1-18 and then answer *yes* or *no* to each question. Correct answers are in parentheses; do not hand the answers out.

1. Does he access the sheep by the door? Shepherd *(Y)*; Thief *(N)*; Hireling *(Y)*. 2. Do the sheep recognize his voice? Shepherd *(Y)*; Thief *(N)*; Hireling *(Y)*. 3. Do the sheep follow him? Shepherd *(Y)*; Thief *(N)*; Hireling *(Y)*. 4. Does he take care of the sheep? Shepherd *(Y)*; Thief *(N)*; Hireling *(Y, to a degree)*. 5. Does he care about other sheep besides those in his immediate fold? Shepherd *(Y)*; Thief *(N)*; Hireling *(N)*. 6. Will he give his life for the sheep? Shepherd *(Y)*; Thief *(N)*; Hireling *(N)*.

Review the correct answers, and then say, "Jesus made it clear that this figure of speech was about Him. What do we know about Jesus, from this text and from other passages of Scripture, that proves Him to be the good shepherd?" Discuss any passages the students mention. Then discuss the following questions:

1. How does Jesus "enter by the door"? (See John 9:35-41.)

2. How do the sheep recognize His voice? (See Mark 1:21-27.)

3. In what way is Jesus the "door" of the sheep? (See Acts 4:12; 2 Timothy 2:8-13.)

4. Who were the thieves and robbers?

5. Who were the hirelings?

6. Who were the "other sheep"?

7. How did Jesus have the power to lay His life down for the sheep? (See Matthew 26:53, 54; Hebrews 5:7-9.)

You can follow up on each question by asking, "Why is this important to know?" The above could be a small-group activity.

Into Life

Students will be completing two exercises. Both parts are found in the student book.

Exercise A: What Do Shepherds Do? Ask students to consider what is involved in shepherding a church today. Each student should list as many essential functions as he or she can think of. For example, they might list teaching, counseling, and praying for the sick. Direct students to Acts 20:28-31; 1 Timothy 5:17; James 5:14; and 1 Peter 5:1-3 for more ideas.

When your students are finished, have them share their answers. Write their ideas on the board. Then ask your students to complete the next exercise.

Exercise B: How Can We Shepherd Our Flock? For each of the shepherding functions listed in *Exercise A*, instruct each student to jot down at least one possible ministry that your congregation can do to fulfill it. For example, a hospital calling program would carry out the function of praying for the sick.

When your students are finished, list their answers as you did before. Ask students which programs your congregation currently performs. Brainstorm ways to begin new ministries that are not currently part of your church's program. Challenge your students to participate actively in a least one such ministry.

Let's Talk It Over

*The questions on this page are designed to promote discussion of the lesson
by the class and to encourage application of the lesson Scriptures. The answers
provided are only discussion starters. Let your class talk it over from there.*

1. The people of Jesus' day had to deal with Pharisees as thieves and robbers. Do the "thieves and robbers" that challenge your own spiritual vitality tend to be specific people or are they more likely to be various temptations? How do you counteract them?

All Christians have unseen treasures worth protecting. These treasures include our reputations, our friendships, and, ultimately, our spiritual destination. People and temptations can destroy these treasures, if we allow them to.

We all know people who "drain our batteries" in a spiritual or an emotional sense. They're exhausting to be around! A certain balance is needed: our task is to try to help them without becoming spiritually contaminated in the process (Jude 23). Falling into temptation is more likely when fatigue levels are high.

2. Caller ID is a helpful invention! But perhaps you ignored important messages by not responding to the ones marked "caller unknown." What was a time when you were confused about whether or not it was God who was trying to speak to you through a circumstance or situation? How did you sort things out?

Getting to know God's voice is a matter of staying connected to Him. God definitely speaks through the pages of Scripture (2 Timothy 3:16, 17); we stay connected by reading His Word (Psalm 119:105).

We also recognize God's ability to channel our activities through open and closed doors of opportunity. Recognizing which is which takes spiritual discernment. Having a godly conscience is important (Hebrews 13:18), but an untrained conscience is dangerous (1 Corinthians 8:7).

3. The people listening to Jesus were confused by His figures of speech. What subjects in the Bible still cause you confusion? How do you go about getting help to clarify those issues?

We sometimes say we look forward to being in Heaven where Jesus can explain all things to us. Until then we need to be able to sort through the traditions, the cunning speakers with personal agendas, and the mistaken interpretations to determine what Jesus is truly expecting us to know.

This requires personal discipline in studying, cross-referencing interpretations with other related teachings in the Scriptures, and prayer for understanding. Listening to respected speakers and reading commentaries can help. But these will not excuse us from the personal responsibility we have for building our own understanding of God's Word. The old saying is important: "Read all the books upon the shelf, but do all your thinking for yourself."

4. Christians often fill their lives to the brim with activities and duties. Churches may be partially responsible for this hyperactivity. How is this different from what Jesus meant by having an abundant life? What corrections do you need to make?

Some would suggest that our abundant life comes after we die, in eternity. But it should start when we give ourselves to the Lord. Cutting back on activities in order to have time to read the Bible, pray, etc., can be difficult. In some churches it seems that the only way to give up certain long-held jobs is either to move or die!

Feelings of guilt at the prospect of cutting back on activities can be a hindrance. Receiving counsel from a spiritually mature Christian may help.

5. Jesus distinguished between shepherds and hired hands. How do we use this distinction to help us discern between those who have good and bad motivations for being in leadership roles in the church?

Examining the motives of others is tricky. Jesus cautions us about passing judgment (Matthew 7:1), but He also challenges us to discern good teachers from bad through examining the fruit of their labors (Matthew 7:15-20). We have all known of those who donate many hours to the Lord and His church. They willingly put their own comfort or plans second. That's good fruit!

Such people become an embodiment of what Christ was trying to teach. Perhaps they don't even wish to see themselves as "shepherds," but their example serves this purpose. They probably will be the last to want attention, but they need to be commended for their efforts.

"I Am the Resurrection and the Life"

DEVOTIONAL READING: Jude 17-23.

BACKGROUND SCRIPTURE: John 11:1-44.

PRINTED TEXT: John 11:1-7, 17-27.

John 11:1-7, 17-27

1 Now a certain man was sick, named Lazarus, of Bethany, the town of Mary and her sister Martha.

2 (It was that Mary which anointed the Lord with ointment, and wiped his feet with her hair, whose brother Lazarus was sick.)

3 Therefore his sisters sent unto him, saying, Lord, behold, he whom thou lovest is sick.

4 When Jesus heard that, he said, This sickness is not unto death, but for the glory of God, that the Son of God might be glorified thereby.

5 Now Jesus loved Martha, and her sister, and Lazarus.

6 When he had heard therefore that he was sick, he abode two days still in the same place where he was.

7 Then after that saith he to his disciples, Let us go into Judaea again.

. . . .

17 Then when Jesus came, he found that he had lain in the grave four days already.

18 Now Bethany was nigh unto Jerusalem, about fifteen furlongs off:

19 And many of the Jews came to Martha and Mary, to comfort them concerning their brother.

20 Then Martha, as soon as she heard that Jesus was coming, went and met him: but Mary sat still in the house.

21 Then said Martha unto Jesus, Lord, if thou hadst been here, my brother had not died.

22 But I know, that even now, whatsoever thou wilt ask of God, God will give it thee.

23 Jesus saith unto her, Thy brother shall rise again.

24 Martha saith unto him, I know that he shall rise again in the resurrection at the last day.

25 Jesus said unto her, I am the resurrection, and the life: he that believeth in me, though he were dead, yet shall he live:

26 And whosoever liveth and believeth in me shall never die. Believest thou this?

27 She saith unto him, Yea, Lord: I believe that thou art the Christ, the Son of God, which should come into the world.

GOLDEN TEXT: I am the resurrection, and the life: he that believeth in me, though he were dead, yet shall he live.—John 11:25.

Lesson Aims

After participating in this lesson, each student will be able to:

1. Describe the mind-sets of Jesus, the disciples, Mary, and Martha just before the resurrection of Lazarus.

2. Explain how Martha is a model of faith in Jesus, as well as how her faith fell short.

3. Show how he or she can use Jesus' teaching to comfort someone in grief.

Lesson Outline

INTRODUCTION
   A. "The One You Love is Sick"
   B. Lesson Background
 I. SOBERING NEWS (John 11:1-7)
   A. Sickness (vv. 1-4)
     House of Affliction
   B. Delay (vv. 5-7)
II. COURAGEOUS BELIEF (John 11:17-27)
   A. Already Dead (vv. 17-20)
   B. Steady Faith (vv. 21-27)
     What If . . . ?
CONCLUSION
   A. The Final Breath
   B. Prayer
   C. Thought to Remember

Introduction

A. "The One You Love Is Sick"

My family originally came from western Kentucky. Not so long ago it was common for women there to marry at a young age. My grandmother was married at 14 and had three children by age 17. I was born when my mother was 19, and as a result I enjoyed the blessing of young grandparents.

My grandmother was a second mother to me. She figures large in almost every one of my childhood memories. She loved all of us dearly, and I cannot count the number of wonderful hours I spent in her home. Even now her house symbolizes peace and comfort and love to me.

I recently had the privilege of holding her hand while she died, someone who loved me unconditionally. As we stood by the hospital bed in her final days, I often wondered what Jesus would have done about her situation. I wondered why God had not healed her.

Since then I have come to see that such feelings reflected my own grief and selfish desires more than a real concern for my grandmother. In death she has now found a true life in God that I cannot yet comprehend. Do we maintain our trust in Jesus when death hits so close to home?

B. Lesson Background

John 1:19–12:50 has been called The Book of Signs within that great Gospel. The raising of Lazarus is one of the signs in the Gospel of John through which Jesus revealed himself to be the Son of God (compare John 2:11; 4:54). What we may call the "purpose statement" of John's Gospel stresses the importance of the signs: "And many other signs truly did Jesus in the presence of his disciples, which are not written in this book: but these are written, that ye might believe that Jesus is the Christ, the Son of God; and that believing ye might have life through his name" (John 20:30, 31).

While the earlier signs demonstrated Jesus' divine power, the resurrection of Lazarus revealed Jesus' authority over the grave. One can scarcely ignore a deed of this magnitude. The account is significant to the larger flow of John's Gospel in that it leads the chief priests and Pharisees to plot Jesus' death (11:45-53). Today's lesson is not about Lazarus's resurrection itself, but rather it is about the facts and attitudes that preceded it.

I. Sobering News
(John 11:1-7)

A. Sickness (vv. 1-4)

1, 2. Now a certain man was sick, named Lazarus, of Bethany, the town of Mary and her sister Martha. (It was that Mary which anointed the Lord with ointment, and wiped his feet with her hair, whose brother Lazarus was sick.)

Back in John 1:28 the apostle identified "Bethany beyond Jordan" as the place where John the Baptist had preached and baptized. At the end of John 10, Jesus left Jerusalem for a preaching tour in that same area after the Jews attempted to arrest Him for blasphemy (10:39-42). *Mary* and *Martha*, however, live in a different village named *Bethany*. This town is less than two miles from Jerusalem, east of the Mount of Olives.

Mary, Martha, and *Lazarus* (sisters and brother) seem to be close friends of Jesus. Perhaps He stays in their home whenever He attends a feast in Jerusalem. On one of these visits, Martha had criticized Jesus for not making Mary help her prepare a meal. In reply He reminded her that food is less important than devotion to His teaching (Luke 10:38-42). The mention here of the anointing by Mary looks forward to John 12:1-3.

HOUSE OF AFFLICTION

I am often fascinated by biblical place names. The name *Bethlehem* means "house of bread." Isn't that an interesting name for the place where Jesus was born—the one who proclaimed himself as the bread of life? *Jerusalem* means "city of peace"—the capital city of the land where the prince of peace walked. *Bethsaida*, on the shore of the Sea of Galilee, means "house of fishing." That is certainly an apt name for a fishing port.

The meaning of *Bethany*, for its part, is a bit uncertain. It could mean "house of dates or figs." Other possible meanings are "house of poverty," "house of the poor," or even "house of the afflicted ones."

There is no indication that Mary, Martha, and Lazarus were poor, but we can assume safely that the town of Bethany at least had its normal share of death, disease, disappointment, marital discord, family squabbles, and other perennial setbacks to human prosperity. Leprosy was a devastating disease, and in Bethany lived Simon the leper (Matthew 26:6). And then there was Lazarus. With his death there were two grief-stricken sisters plus a whole crowd of others weeping with them. Bethany was definitely a house of affliction at that time.

If you stop to think about it, each of us lives in a "house of affliction" of some kind—discord, strife, pain, delusion, fatigue, abandonment, despair. But it is Jesus, and only Jesus, who can move us into a permanent "house of joy." The change that Jesus brought about at Bethany with Lazarus's resurrection was temporary, since Lazarus obviously died again later. The change that Jesus is able bring to us because of His own

resurrection can be permanent and eternal, if we will allow it.
—J. B. N.

3. Therefore his sisters sent unto him, saying, Lord, behold, he whom thou lovest is sick.

The exact nature of Lazarus's illness is not specified and is probably not relevant to the story. Clearly, however, the *sisters* believe that his condition is critical—they would not bother Jesus over a minor case of the flu.

Mary and Martha naturally assume that Jesus will be concerned about His friend's condition. They probably expect Him to rush back to town for a healing (see comments on John 11:22, below). [See question #1, page 208.]

In addition to John's overall emphasis on Christ's divine power, we will see this story provide insight into Jesus' humanity. John depicts Jesus as experiencing the ups and downs of human feelings and relationships. Lazarus is His friend, and the sisters know that it will be natural for Jesus to be concerned about him.

4. When Jesus heard that, he said, This sickness is not unto death, but for the glory of God, that the Son of God might be glorified thereby.

When the message reaches *Jesus*, He immediately replies with what would seem to be very good news: *This sickness is not unto death*. When that statement is added to the remainder of the verse—*that the Son of God might be glorified thereby*—those who are listening probably infer that Jesus will honor the request to go and heal Lazarus. As on so many other occasions, Jesus' power will indeed be revealed. Lazarus's circumstance ultimately will bring greater glory to God—but not in a way that anyone is expecting!

We should pause to stress that this verse should not be taken to mean that God causes all sickness. Of course God is *glorified* by the confidence that believers can display in the face of illness or death. But here Jesus is simply saying that He plans to bring good from a bad situation.

B. Delay (vv. 5-7)

5. Now Jesus loved Martha, and her sister, and Lazarus.

John now confirms the sisters' claim in verse 3 ("he whom thou lovest") by noting that Jesus really does care deeply for *Lazarus* and his family. This verse leads the reader to expect that Jesus will leave for Bethany immediately, just as the sisters suppose.

6, 7. When he had heard therefore that he was sick, he abode two days still in the same place where he was. Then after that saith he to his disciples, Let us go into Judea again.

How to Say It
BETHANY. *Beth*-uh-nee.
JERUSALEM. Juh-*roo*-suh-lem.
JORDAN. *Jor*-dun.
JUDEA. Joo-*dee*-uh.
LAZARUS. *Laz*-uh-rus.
MESSIAH. Meh-*sigh*-uh.

These verses are stunning in light of what has preceded. Jesus loves Lazarus and seems to have just indicated in verse 4 that He would go to heal him. But after telling everyone, in effect, "Don't worry," Jesus chooses to wait *two days* before doing anything.

The disciples may interpret this delay as a sign of caution, for the Jewish authorities in Jerusalem apparently have put out a warrant for Jesus' arrest (John 10:39; 11:8). But in John 11:14, 15 (not in today's text) Jesus makes it clear that He is "glad" for the delay.

While Jesus' actions (and inactions!) may seem harsh or confusing, they are clearly calculated to glorify God to the fullest possible extent. In the first place this incident illustrates Jesus' claims throughout the Gospel of John that He does not act according to His human desires and interests. Instead He does everything to please God. "My meat is to do the will of him that sent me, and to finish his work" (John 4:34; compare 5:30; 7:17, 18). Everything must proceed on God's plan and God's timing, even if this is painful for Jesus and His friends.

Second, the event as it unfolds will show clearly that Jesus wants this to be more than a healing. He will demonstrate, rather, that His power reaches even beyond the grave. [See question #2, page 208.]

II. Courageous Belief
(John 11:17-27)

A. Already Dead (vv. 17-20)

17. Then when Jesus came, he found that he had lain in the grave four days already.

Jesus' intentional delay ensures that Lazarus has already *lain in the grave four days*. Jesus has the ability to heal from a distance, if He so desires (Luke 7:1-10). But that is not the plan here. [See question #3, page 208.]

By the time Jesus arrives, the tone has changed from hopeful expectation to that of grief and mourning. The reference to *four days* is significant. Some ancient Jews believe that the soul of a departed person hovers around the body for three days. On the fourth day, when signs of decomposition are clearly evident (such as the stench that Martha will mention in verse 39), the person's spirit supposedly departs for good. To be dead for four days would thus mean something like "really, really dead."

Whether or not this four-day theory is true, no one can doubt that Lazarus is actually dead. There is no reasonable way to suggest that Jesus simply resuscitates Lazarus or brings him out of a coma. The situation calls for a resurrection rather than a healing.

18, 19. Now Bethany was nigh unto Jerusalem, about fifteen furlongs off: And many of the Jews came to Martha and Mary, to comfort them concerning their brother.

The Jews place high value on the ethical need *to comfort* the bereaved. Funerals may last for a week. Lazarus's funeral seems to be especially remarkable in this regard. The fact that *many of the Jews* had come from *Jerusalem* to the little town of *Bethany* to mourn for him suggests that the family is well known and perhaps wealthy. Clearly Jesus is not the only person who loved Lazarus. [See question #4, page 208.]

John may also wish to emphasize the size of the crowd in order to stress that a large number of people will witness Lazarus's resurrection (11:45). *Fifteen furlongs* is about one and three-quarter miles.

20. Then Martha, as soon as she heard that Jesus was coming, went and met him: but Mary sat still in the house.

The fact that *Mary* stays *in the house* does not necessarily mean that she feels angry toward *Jesus.* She is not indifferent about His arrival, as verses 31-33 will reveal.

Perhaps the reason that Mary stays in the house can be explained this way. The house seems to be packed with mourners; a messenger arrives, finds *Martha,* and tells her that Jesus is on His way. In her excitement Martha perhaps goes straight to Jesus without pausing even to tell her sister. Note that Mary does not seem to be aware of Jesus' arrival until verse 28, after Martha goes back to the house.

We may also speculate that Martha does not want to draw too much attention to Jesus right away: when she finally does tell Mary that He has come, she pulls her aside so that the crowd can't hear (again, v. 28). Martha seems to see the need for Mary to have a private moment to share her grief with Jesus.

B. Steady Faith (vv. 21-27)

21. Then said Martha unto Jesus, Lord, if thou hadst been here, my brother had not died.

At first glance Martha's comment *Lord, if thou hadst been here, my brother had not died* may sound like criticism. But in view of the statements to follow, it appears that Martha wishes to reassure *Jesus* that she does not hold Lazarus's death against Him. Martha's mind is clouded with grief at the moment. We may guess that she assumes that Jesus had very legitimate reasons for His delay. One reason could include the obvious danger of visiting a town so close to Jerusalem.

WHAT IF . . . ?

History is filled with "what if" situations. What if General Robert E. Lee had remained in the Union Army as the American Civil War broke out? What if the apple had not fallen on Isaac Newton's head? What if Martin Luther had not been frightened by a lightning bolt in a thunderstorm? What if Christopher Columbus had believed that the earth was flat? What if U.S. President John F. Kennedy had not gone to Dallas in November 1963? What if U.S. President Franklin Delano Roosevelt had died of polio in the 1920s before his election? We can speculate endlessly about such situations, but it doesn't change anything now.

Martha told Jesus that if He had been there, then her brother would not have died. But Jesus had intentionally stayed away. In Jesus' wisdom He saw there was more ultimate benefit to Lazarus and his family (and, indeed, for the entire world) for Him not to be there.

Since God controls the present as well as the future, He can see things and place them in a perspective that we don't have. As Christians we believe that God is still ultimately in charge of the universe, and everything happens according to His plan. If we had our way, we would want things to work out for our immediate benefit, and we probably would miss out on some of the ultimately better benefits that God has in store for us.

We do well to remember that God is holding out for the grander good that we can't perceive. It's a good thing we can't control all the "what ifs" of history. Instead we can trust that God is in control and managing the world quite nicely in His own way. —J. B. N.

22. But I know, that even now, whatsoever thou wilt ask of God, God will give it thee.

This verse is clearly a statement of Martha's continuing faith in Jesus. Even so, commentators are divided on the exact meaning of her words. Lazarus needs more than a healing now, so perhaps by saying *whatsoever thou wilt ask of God, God will give it thee*, Martha thinks that God will empower Jesus to raise Lazarus from the dead. On an earlier occasion Jesus had interrupted a funeral in Nain to bring a corpse back to life (Luke 7:11-15). Is Martha expecting Jesus to do the same thing now for His good friend?

Against this possibility, however, are Martha's comments in verses 24 and 39. Those verses

Visual for
Lessons 7 & 11

Use this visual to probe your students' views on death. Do they really believe that death isn't final?

strongly imply that she does not really expect Jesus to help Lazarus at this point. Thus her words here are intended to show Jesus that she holds no grudge and has not lost faith in Him. He did not heal Lazarus, but of course that does not mean that Jesus is not a unique messenger of God.

Martha's remarkable faith in the face of grief is certainly commendable. She seems, however, to underestimate Jesus' power.

23, 24. Jesus saith unto her, Thy brother shall rise again. Martha saith unto him, I know that he shall rise again in the resurrection at the last day.

Many ancient Jews expect a final day of judgment, when the Messiah will appear in order to bring an end to this wicked world. At that time the righteous dead will be resurrected to enjoy eternal life. "And many of them that sleep in the dust of the earth shall awake, some to everlasting life, and some to shame and everlasting contempt" (Daniel 12:2).

Martha probably assumes that Jesus must be referring to the glorious occasion that the prophet Daniel mentions. So she interprets Jesus' remarks as words of pastoral comfort. It does not yet occur to her that Jesus will raise her brother much sooner than this. She is about to receive more than she expects.

25, 26. Jesus said unto her, I am the resurrection, and the life: he that believeth in me, though he were dead, yet shall he live: and whosoever liveth and believeth in me shall never die. Believest thou this?

Resurrection and eternal *life* are not blessings that we have to wait until the end of time to enjoy. Rather, we experience their hope right now through faith in Christ, who has all power over death.

The statements about death and life are powerful, aren't they? Believers who die physically (like Lazarus) will live eternally through Christ's power to save. If we choose in this life to believe in Jesus, we will *never die* spiritually in the sense that Christ grants us eternal life with Him in Heaven—even though our current bodies obviously will fail and decay. For more insight on our physical resurrection, see 1 Corinthians 15:12-55.

27. She saith unto him, Yea, Lord: I believe that thou art the Christ, the Son of God, which should come into the world.

Martha undoubtedly does not understand why Lazarus had fallen ill or why Jesus had waited before coming to Him. She undoubtedly does not understand (yet) what He means by saying that the dead will live.

Even so, Martha is firm in her understanding of one thing: she knows that Jesus is God's *Son.* This verse is John's equivalent of Peter's confession at Matthew 16:16: "Thou art the Christ, the Son of the living God." This kind of confession is a vital part of receiving eternal life.

Martha's confession touches on two key elements of John's portrayal of Christ. First, she seems to understand that Jesus is not just a political messiah. Rather, she realizes that He is the one who came from Heaven to reveal the Father to *the world* (John 1:14, 18; 3:13; 6:51; etc.).

Second, Martha's comment parallels John 20:31. That verse is often cited as the "purpose statement" of the Gospel of John that we noted in the lesson Introduction. Nowhere else in the Gospel of John do we see such a strong expression of faith, a fact that testifies to Martha's firm commitment in the face of grief. [See question #5, page 208.]

Conclusion

A. The Final Breath

Perhaps you think it strange that today's lesson text does not include the account of the actual resurrection of Lazarus (John 11:38-44). We all like to read "a happy ending," don't we? That resurrection itself is indeed marvelous. But by leaving out that event, today's lesson has forced us to examine the faith and emotions of Martha. It is a faith that knows something of Jesus but not everything. It is kind of an "in between" faith. It is the kind of faith that says, "Lord, I believe; help thou mine unbelief" (Mark 9:24). It's the kind of faith that many of us still have!

Jesus' question *Believest thou this?* in verse 26 is applicable not only to Martha but to all of us. It's easy to sit in a Bible study class and say, "Of course, I believe that Jesus can grant us eternal life"; it's harder to feel that way as we stand beside the grave of a loved one.

As we close the lid of the casket, or as we face serious health problems ourselves, how will we answer the question, *Believest thou this?* Do we really believe that Jesus has conquered death and that He has the power to grant eternal life? Real faith is tested at the final breath, whether ours or that of someone we love.

Several years ago the wife of a retired Bible college professor died. The funeral exhibited what a Christian funeral should: sadness and grief over the of loss of a loved one, but also a confident realization of an eternity with Jesus into which she had crossed. The husband she left behind said it best: "Of course I'm going to miss her. But let's face it—I haven't been preaching fairy tales all these years!" He had no doubt where she was. He had real faith that passed the test.

B. Prayer

Father, we do not want to die, and we do not want to lose people that we love. Help us find peace in the knowledge that Christ is the source of resurrection life. Help us share that peace with everyone who suffers grief. Give us the faith to really believe that Jesus has conquered death for us. In Jesus' name, amen.

C. Thought to Remember

Christ still has power over death.

Home Daily Bible Readings

Monday, Feb. 5—Christ Offers Eternal Life (Jude 17-25)
Tuesday, Feb. 6—The Way of Righteousness (Proverbs 8:22-32)
Wednesday, Feb. 7—Jesus Delays (John 11:1-6)
Thursday, Feb. 8—Jesus Goes to Bethany (John 11:7-16)
Friday, Feb. 9—I Am the Resurrection (John 11:17-27)
Saturday, Feb. 10—Jesus Comforts Mary (John 11:28-37)
Sunday, Feb. 11—Jesus Raises Lazarus (John 11:38-44)

Learning by Doing

This page contains an alternative lesson plan emphasizing learning activities. Classes desiring such student involvement will find these suggestions helpful.

Learning Goals

After this lesson, each student will be able to:

1. Describe the mind-sets of Jesus, the disciples, Mary, and Martha just before Lazarus's resurrection.

2. Explain how Martha is a model of faith in Jesus, as well as how her faith fell short.

3. Show how he or she can use Jesus' teaching to comfort someone in grief.

Into the Lesson

Read the following accounts to your class. Then discuss them with the aid of the questions that follow.

In the early seventeenth century, a certain Marjorie Elphinstone died and was buried. When grave robbers attempted to steal her jewelry, she shocked them by groaning. The robbers fled, and she revived. She walked home under her own power and outlived her husband by six years!

Marjorie Halcrow Erskine died in 1674 and was buried. The church officer (called a *sexton*) who buried her returned to the grave later to steal her jewelry. While the thieving sexton was trying to cut off her finger to get her ring, Erskine awoke. She lived many more years.

1. What was the mind-set of the robbers just before their intended victims awoke?

2. If you were a family member of one of these women, what would have been on your mind just before she walked through the door?

Tell your class that today's lesson deals with the reactions of loved ones to Lazarus's death and to Jesus' presence after that death.

Into the Word

Read aloud John 11:1-7, 17-27. Then divide your class into groups of four. Each group will choose one of three activities described below. Provide pens and paper for their work, or direct them to the student books for the exercises.

Group Activity A. Your group is the staff of a newspaper, the *Jerusalem Post*, covering the events surrounding the death of Lazarus. Write an article based on imaginary interviews with at least two of the following: Jesus, one of His disciples, or Mary. Using information from today's text, describe the state of mind each would have had before the resurrection.

Group Activity B. Your group is the reporting staff for Jerusalem television station WWJD. Write and present to the class an on-the-scene interview with at least two of the following: Jesus, one of His disciples, or Mary. Using information from today's text, describe the reaction each would have had before the resurrection.

Group Activity C. Your group is the editorial staff for a monthly religious magazine, *Judaism Today.* You've decided to do a story on Martha, a true believer in Jesus and the sister of Lazarus. Using information from John 11:20-27, describe Martha's strong faith as well as her spiritual doubts during the time of her brother's sickness and death.

Allow groups sufficient time to complete their activities. Then ask a volunteer "reporter" from each group to share that group's project with the entire class.

Into Life

Read the hypothetical situations described below. Ask your class to suggest scriptural answers, based on the principles Jesus expressed in His teaching before the raising of Lazarus. (This activity can also be found in the student book, if you are using that optional resource.)

1. A member of your congregation has just learned that he has inoperable cancer in an advanced stage. His doctors give him no hope of recovery. How do you help him and his family deal with this crisis?

2. A coworker has lost her teenage son in an auto accident. She and her husband are not Christians, and they are torn between seeking God and blaming Him for their son's death. What would be an appropriate way to minister to them in their time of grief?

3. Your friend's mother, a Christian, is reaching the end of her long life due to deteriorating health. She longs to go home to be with the Lord and end her suffering. How can you comfort both your friend and her mother?

4. Your neighbor, a longtime Christian, has been stricken by a mysterious disease that has left his doctors baffled and his faith shaken. He lies in a hospital bed, uncertain of his recovery and doubtful of his eternal destination. How do you reassure his faith?

Let's Talk It Over

The questions on this page are designed to promote discussion of the lesson
by the class and to encourage application of the lesson Scriptures. The answers
provided are only discussion starters. Let your class talk it over from there.

1. When Lazarus became seriously ill, his sisters Mary and Martha felt free to call upon Jesus to ask for His help. How will you form that kind of relationship with Christ? What things or attitudes in your life will be a help or a hindrance to this?

One definite help will be to make sure that our regular conversations with Jesus are filled with words of praise and celebration. These should be a natural part of expressing our innermost thoughts. When we build a lasting relationship with Him this way, we will avoid having what we may call a "spare tire" religion: "Use only in emergencies!"

Malachi 2:17 lists a possible hindrance: "Ye have wearied the Lord with your words. Yet ye say, Wherein have we wearied him? When ye say . . . Where is the God of judgment?" This verse should make us gasp! Undoubtedly part of the weariness that we bring to God stems from questions about His judgment—questions such as, "Why doesn't God *do something* about such and such?" Causing weariness in God will be a definite hindrance to prayer.

2. Our timetable isn't always the same as God's timetable. What are some reasons that God may have for not responding immediately to your prayer requests?

One good way to approach this question is by asking the reverse: What would the world be like if God responded to all prayer requests immediately? The results would be almost too bizarre to contemplate.

As is the case in today's text, God knows what is the best way to accomplish His purposes. Sometimes we ask for things that we are not really prepared to accept. What we think is good for us may not be good for others. What may benefit us in the short term may be harmful over the long haul. God is in the position to know all this.

Many of us can look back and say with all honesty, "I'm sure glad that God answered my prayer in *His* way instead of the way that *I* requested. I can see now that He knew some things that I didn't." Reflecting on how God has answered prayers in the past helps us understand how the Lord's way is better.

3. Jesus expects our faith and obedience even when (or especially when!) He doesn't reveal His plans to us. What was a time or circumstance that you can look back on and say, "Ah, now I see what God's plan was"?

This kind of question can lead to some lengthy and emotional stories. Be sure to ask this follow up question at the conclusion of each anecdote: "How did your faith grow stronger as a result of how God worked?"

4. Mary and Martha weren't alone when Jesus arrived—many were there to comfort them. What are some things we can do as a church or as a class to minister to those who have suffered the loss of a loved one?

Remember this principle: someone suffering grief needs your shoulder more than he or she needs your mouth. The presence of a friend can be of great comfort during a time when many emotions are vying for attention. Just to be there—and not say too much—is so important.

We can show care also by taking away the burdens of everyday chores. Acts such as bringing covered dishes and mowing the lawn flow from a servant's heart. For this kind of ministry to be most effective, your church needs to have an advance plan of ministry action. Having an ongoing plan to help during such times can ensure that the ministry is most effective when it is needed.

5. Martha's testimony expressed her confidence in the lordship of Christ, in spite of her grief. In what ways can you use tough times to reinforce your reliance on Jesus?

Several New Testament passages tell us to expect tough times (examples: John 16:1-4; 1 Peter 4:12-19). These times of trouble may refine us (1 Peter 1:7), they may help us serve as examples to others (1 Peter 2:21), or they may come as a test from Satan to determine how firmly committed we are to the Lord (2 Corinthians 12:7).

It is especially during tough times that we must keep our focus on Jesus. Others are watching to see how we handle ourselves during tough times. God may want our struggles to serve as a witness to how much we trust Him.

"I Am the Way, the Truth, and the Life"

DEVOTIONAL READING: Ephesians 4:17-24.

BACKGROUND SCRIPTURE: John 14:1-14.

PRINTED TEXT: John 14:1-14.

John 14:1-14

1 Let not your heart be troubled: ye believe in God, believe also in me.

2 In my Father's house are many mansions: if it were not so, I would have told you. I go to prepare a place for you.

3 And if I go and prepare a place for you, I will come again, and receive you unto myself; that where I am, there ye may be also.

4 And whither I go ye know, and the way ye know.

5 Thomas saith unto him, Lord, we know not whither thou goest; and how can we know the way?

6 Jesus saith unto him, I am the way, the truth, and the life: no man cometh unto the Father, but by me.

7 If ye had known me, ye should have known my Father also: and from henceforth ye know him, and have seen him.

8 Philip saith unto him, Lord, show us the Father, and it sufficeth us.

9 Jesus saith unto him, Have I been so long time with you, and yet hast thou not known me, Philip? he that hath seen me hath seen the Father; and how sayest thou then, Show us the Father?

10 Believest thou not that I am in the Father, and the Father in me? the words that I speak unto you I speak not of myself: but the Father that dwelleth in me, he doeth the works.

11 Believe me that I am in the Father, and the Father in me: or else believe me for the very works' sake.

12 Verily, verily, I say unto you, He that believeth on me, the works that I do shall he do also; and greater works than these shall he do; because I go unto my Father.

13 And whatsoever ye shall ask in my name, that will I do, that the Father may be glorified in the Son.

14 If ye shall ask any thing in my name, I will do it.

GOLDEN TEXT: I am the way, the truth, and the life: no man cometh unto the Father, but by me.—John 14:6.

Jesus Christ: A Portrait of God
Unit 3: Christ Guides and Protects
(Lessons 10-13)

Lesson Aims

After participating in this lesson, each student will be able to:

1. Describe Jesus' relationship to the Father.

2. Define what Jesus meant by *the way, the truth,* and *the life.*

3. Develop a plan for meditating on one of Jesus' miracles each day to increase belief.

Lesson Outline

Introduction

A. Famous Last Words

For some reason we attach special significance to the "last words" of a famous person. Good or bad, a person's final words often seem to summarize his or her life. The last words of U.S. President Dwight Eisenhower (1890–1969) were, "I've always loved my wife. I've always loved my children. I've always loved my grandchildren. I've always loved my country. I want to go. God, take me."

Nathan Hale (1755–1776), an American revolutionary spy, said, "I only regret that I have but one life to lose for my country," just before he was hanged by the British. Karl Marx (1818–1883), reflecting his prideful spirit, came to the

end of his life by saying, "Go on. Get out. Last words are for fools who haven't said enough."

As His crucifixion approached, Jesus had "yet many things to say" to His disciples (John 16:12). But He was no fool, as Marx's statement would suppose! Many of the final words of Jesus, recorded in John 13–17, are notable for their emphasis on the future.

B. Lesson Background

Our lessons in this series so far have focused on passages from the first 12 chapters of the Gospel of John. As we noted last week, this section is often called the Book of Signs because it highlights Jesus' public ministry of miracles and teachings; it portrays Jesus' actions as signs of His divine nature.

Yet despite all these great works, most people either did not believe Jesus or refused to confess their faith for fear of persecution (see John 7:13; 9:22). Following this rejection, Jesus met privately with His disciples on the last night of His life in an upper room. There they celebrated the Passover (John 13:1-3).

It is interesting to compare the Gospel accounts here. Matthew, Mark, and Luke focus mainly on the events surrounding the institution of the Lord's Supper (see Matthew 26:17-30; Mark 14:12-26; Luke 22:7-38). John, however, includes lengthy excerpts from Jesus' "farewell address"— His last words for the disciples before His arrest.

The farewell address occupies all of John 13–17. It focuses on the need for unity after Jesus' departure. This includes not only the disciples' unity with Christ but also unity with one another. In today's passage Jesus reminds the disciples that they can come to God only by believing in Him and following His example.

I. Ultimate Comfort
(John 14:1-4)

A. What to Do (v. 1)

1. Let not your heart be troubled: ye believe in God, believe also in me.

The original, Greek text of this verse can be translated in two different ways. One possibility is that Jesus could be urging the disciples to believe in both God and himself. Following this approach the *New International Version* reads, "Trust in God; trust also in me."

On the other hand, Jesus may be building on their already existing belief in God to encourage them to place complete faith in Him as well. The *King James Version* follows this approach: *ye* [already] *believe in God,* [now] *believe also in me.*

The *King James Version* seems to be the better translation. As Jews the disciples naturally believe in God and His power; now, however, Jesus asks them to trust in Him as well.

Jesus asks this knowing full well that the faith of the disciples will soon be tested by the shocking events of His arrest and crucifixion. The disciples should not lose faith even though most others do not believe. The disciples should maintain belief even when it looks like the forces of evil have won the day.

B. What Awaits (vv. 2-4)

2. In my Father's house are many mansions: if it were not so, I would have told you. I go to prepare a place for you.

The totality of Jesus' remarks undoubtedly give the disciples both comfort and alarm. The alarm comes with His announcement that He is going to leave them for a time. The alarm leads to confusion in the minds of the disciples when Jesus says that He is going to a place where they cannot come (John 13:33).

Peter, and apparently the others, take this to mean that He is going to go into hiding for a while. Peter then insists that he will follow Jesus even to death (13:37). Now Jesus assures the disciples that He is not leaving forever. He wants them to be with Him, so He must *prepare a place for* them in His *Father's house.*

This verse has caused a certain confusion about the nature of Heaven. The antique language of the *King James Version* says that the Father's house has *many mansions*, which suggests to twenty-first-century readers that Heaven is a place full of large, expensive country estates.

This mental picture, which builds on the imagery of the New Jerusalem in Revelation 21–22, perhaps places too much emphasis on the physical and not enough on the spiritual. We would do well to think of these "mansions" as something like "dwelling places"—special places within God's house. [See question #1, page 216.]

Believers have no permanent place in this world, which hates and persecutes the disciples (John 15:18; 16:1-3). We can take comfort, however, in the fact that Jesus has prepared places for us in God's house. Then we can be with Him forever in Heaven.

3. And if I go and prepare a place for you, I will come again, and receive you unto myself; that where I am, there ye may be also.

This is the good news: Jesus will not abandon His people. The word *go* clearly refers to His upcoming death, resurrection, and ascension. Jesus' death pays sin's penalty while His resurrection shows His mastery over death (Revelation 1:18). That is how Jesus is able to *prepare a place for* those who love Him.

Commentators are divided on the meaning of *come again.* Some argue that Jesus is referring to His appearances to the disciples after the resurrection, when He will give them further teaching. Others, however, suggest that the phrase *receive you unto myself* refers to our eternal home in Heaven (v. 2), so that *come again* must refer to Jesus' second coming. In either case Jesus stresses that a temporary departure will ultimately make it possible for believers to dwell with Him forever.

4. And whither I go ye know, and the way ye know.

Based on Jesus' ministry and teaching to this point, the disciples should understand who Jesus is and what is about to happen to Him. They should realize that His origin and destination is Heaven *(whither I go)* and that He must die *(the way)* in order to prepare their heavenly home. Jesus presumably intends to continue discussing that issue, but Thomas interrupts with a question that reveals a lack of understanding about Jesus and His mission.

II. Profound Truth
(John 14:5-11)

A. Know the Way (vv. 5-7)

5. Thomas saith unto him, Lord, we know not whither thou goest; and how can we know the way?

Jesus' popularity seems to ebb and flow. Jesus was at a height of popularity following the feeding of the 5,000 in John 6:1-14. But then Jesus' popularity in Galilee collapsed following His hard teachings (John 6:60-66).

The resurrection of Lazarus served to refocus attention on Jesus' indisputable power (John 11:45). A huge crowd has just welcomed Him to the Passover celebration in Jerusalem (John 12:12-18). Even the Pharisees are forced to admit that "the world is gone after him" (John 12:19).

It is against this backdrop that the disciples probably expect that Jesus will now take charge. Will He lead a revolt against Rome? Will He reform the temple? *Thomas* reveals some of this "earthly thinking" with his question. Exactly where is Jesus going and *how* are the disciples supposed to get there? Is Jesus going home to Galilee for a visit? Is He going into hiding so that He cannot be arrested (see John 10:39; 11:54; 12:9-11)?

Thomas's question shows a lack of spiritual discernment. It has not yet occurred to him that

Jesus may be talking about His death and return to Heaven. [See question #2, page 216.]

6. Jesus saith unto him, I am the way, the truth, and the life: no man cometh unto the Father, but by me.

The first part of Jesus' answer to Thomas's question features three nouns: *the way, the truth, and the life.* Jesus' statement that He is *the way* to God most directly answers Thomas's question in verse 5, "How can we know the way?" Jesus is *the truth* in that He defines correct beliefs about God. When we look at Jesus, we learn the truth about who God is, how He operates, and what He expects. For this reason, all people must accept Christ in order to come to a proper understanding of the Father.

Finally, Jesus is *the life* because He has life in himself (John 5:26). He is "the resurrection, and the life" (John 11:25). Jesus is "the true God, and eternal life" (1 John 5:20).

These facts mean that *no man cometh unto the Father, but by me.* Truly John 14:6 is one of the most important verses in the Bible! [See question #3, page 216.]

7. If ye had known me, ye should have known my Father also: and from henceforth ye know him, and have seen him.

Because Jesus is God's Son, and because He follows God's will perfectly, knowing Jesus gives us knowledge of God as well. The verb *know* goes beyond simple awareness that God exists; rather, it refers to a certain understanding of who God is, how He operates, and how we are to live as His people.

The disciples have learned (or should have learned) all that they need to know about these things through their experience with Jesus. The word *if* opens a criticism of the disciples' failure to understand adequately that Jesus is the true way to the *Father.* Now that Jesus has explained the matter more fully, He expects them *henceforth* to have a better comprehension.

B. Know the Father (vv. 8-11)

8. Philip saith unto him, Lord, show us the Father, and it sufficeth us.

Philip's innocent request reveals that he, like Thomas, is still having a hard time understanding Jesus' plan for the future. His request seems more unusual, however, in light of what Jesus has just said to Thomas.

As a result, students of the Bible are divided on Philip's intent. On the one hand, some believe that *Philip* harbors doubts about Jesus' claims to be the only way to God, and therefore Philip wants to see evidence to confirm his faith. Under this theory, the phrase *show us the Father* would thus be a request for some sort of visionary experience that would allow them to be certain of the truth of what Jesus is saying.

On the other hand it simply could be that Philip does not yet realize that Jesus' "Father" is not Joseph of Nazareth, but rather the eternal God in Heaven (compare John 6:42). If this is the case, then Philip perhaps thinks that Jesus is going back to Galilee to visit His parents. So Philip wants Jesus to explain exactly why He is going to do that. In either case Philip clearly does not yet comprehend fully that God the Father has made himself known in Jesus.

Show Me!

There are numerous phrases that mean, "Prove it!" One that was popular a few years ago was "Show me the money!" (from a movie). Enthusiastic talk is one thing. But when the impatient seller wants to close the deal, he or she may say, "Show me the money!" A similar phrase is, "Put your money where your mouth is!" Big talk is not enough.

This "prove it" attitude cuts across many areas of life. For several years I have been active in accrediting associations that review institutions of higher education. At one of our annual meetings a couple of years ago, the staff of the association sported buttons that proclaimed, "Show me the learning." It is not enough for a college to say they educate their students; they have to demonstrate that learning does in fact take place.

Our modern world is filled with demands of "Show me!" The same was true in ancient times, as we see in Philip's request. Jesus had identified

Visual for Lesson 12. *Point to this visual as you ask, "Why is this one of the most confrontational statements that Jesus could possibly make?"*

himself with the Father and said that the disciples had seen the Father in Jesus' activities. Yet even after three years, Philip still did not understand. "Show me," he demanded.

We are not much different. Our actions constantly request, "show me Your grace," "show me Your forgiveness," "show me Your love," "show me that You understand what I am going through." Before we make too many such requests of God, we should remember that Jesus *did* show us—on the cross.   —J. B. N.

9. Jesus saith unto him, Have I been so long time with you, and yet hast thou not known me, Philip? he that hath seen me hath seen the Father; and how sayest thou then, Show us the Father?

At this point in the Gospel of John, Jesus has spent some three years *(so long time)* with the disciples, teaching and working miracles. Over the course of His ministry, Jesus has explicitly discussed His unity with *the Father* and has said that He came to reveal God to the world.

Jesus is therefore dismayed at the lack of understanding in even His closest followers. They still do not really understand who He is. This is spiritual blindness.

10. Believest thou not that I am in the Father, and the Father in me? the words that I speak unto you I speak not of myself: but the Father that dwelleth in me, he doeth the works.

Jesus' question reflects His frustration. His words emphasize His complete unity with God—the Father is *in* Jesus, but Jesus is also *in the Father,* suggesting that the two think and act as one. This has been called a "mutual indwelling."

Jesus points to two areas of His ministry where this relationship should be obvious: the things He says and the things He does. Both Jesus' teachings and miracles reveal God to the world in an unprecedented way.

11. Believe me that I am in the Father, and the Father in me: or else believe me for the very works' sake.

Jesus did a tremendous miracle in John 6 when He fed the 5,000. But the result was that people sought Him out not because of the miracles but because they had had their fill (John 6:26). Jesus' miracles should prove that He is more than just a prophet, magician, or a bread king. These mighty deeds should lead people to understand that He reveals God in a new and unique way.

Jesus assumes that His works will eliminate any doubt about His own identity and the identity of His *Father.* If Philip can't understand

How to Say It

GALILEE. *Gal*-uh-lee.
GENTILES. *Jen*-tiles.
JERUSALEM. Juh-*roo*-suh-lem.
LAZARUS. *Laz*-uh-rus.
NAZARETH. *Naz*-uh-reth.
PENTECOST. *Pent*-ih-kost.
PHARISEES. *Fair*-ih-seez.

Jesus' teachings about himself, which seem to be obvious enough, perhaps he should ask himself what it means that Jesus could raise Lazarus from the dead! [See question #4, page 216.]

III. Extreme Promise
(John 14:12-14)

A. What We Can Do (v. 12)

12. Verily, verily, I say unto you, He that believeth on me, the works that I do shall he do also; and greater works than these shall he do; because I go unto my Father.

This verse presents us with some interesting challenges of interpretation. First, who is it that will do *greater works* than Jesus? Is it only the original apostles or is it all believers? The phrase *He that believeth on me* points to all Christians.

With that identity established we next need to ask, "In what sense will Christians be able to do greater works than Jesus?" The clue to answering this question is found in the last phrase *because I go unto my Father.* That exaltation will happen only after Jesus' death and resurrection. It is Jesus' sacrifice that launches a new era of power. None of Jesus' own miracles or teaching up to the point of the cross and empty tomb could bring about salvation.

Compare the power of the gospel before and after the cross. Even after more than three years of Jesus' teaching, preaching, and miracles, His most dedicated followers were relatively few in number. But after Jesus' resurrection comes the Day of Pentecost. Preceding that glorious day, there were only about 120 believers gathered in Jerusalem (Acts 1:15). Peter's sermon and the arrival of the Holy Spirit then add about 3,000 (Acts 2:41)!

Whereas Jesus' displayed His power only in a very limited geographical region, His followers eventually proclaim the gospel across the Roman Empire. Their efforts will reach a much larger number of people, including Gentiles. Christ empowers us to show everyone that He alone is the way to the Father. [See question #5, page 216.]

B. What Jesus Will Do (vv. 13, 14)

13, 14. And whatsoever ye shall ask in my name, that will I do, that the Father may be glorified in the Son. If ye shall ask any thing in my name, I will do it.

These verses must be interpreted both within their immediate context and within the larger context of the John's writings. Jesus has just told the disciples that believers will be empowered to do "greater works." In verses 15-17 (not in today's text), Jesus proceeds to tell His disciples that He will ask God to send "the Spirit of truth" to abide with them. The Spirit will give comfort in the face of persecution (John 14:26, 27) and will work with the disciples to convict the world of sin (16:8-14). Jesus clearly is speaking, then, of the power to proclaim the gospel. This is what brings glory to *the Father* (7:18; 8:50, 54; 12:28).

Consistent with this theme, 1 John 5:14, 15 states that God will answer prayers that we offer "according to his will"; in that context this apparently refers to prayers for those who have fallen away (1 John 5:16). Jesus is not saying, then, that we can expect God to grant our whims like some sort of heavenly Santa Claus. The emphasis, rather, lies in the phrase *in my name:* Through Jesus alone we come to God, and through Him God grants us power to proclaim the truth in a lost world.

ASK IN MY NAME

My father was a carpenter who spent most of his working years building houses for a contractor. While working on one project, he and his crew experienced significant harassment from the residents of a neighboring house. They threatened to sue because some of the workmen

had walked through a corner of their yard, damaging some grass. They refused to allow the workmen to get drinking water from an outside tap. They wanted a ridiculous amount of compensation because they said that the workmen had damaged some vegetables in the garden.

This hostile situation changed dramatically when the neighbors discovered that the workmen were under the contractor rather than under the developer. The neighbors had been cheated by the developer, but they had no grudge against the contractor. The name of the contractor was respected; the name of the developer was despised.

It is important to establish in whose name we operate, isn't it? If we come to God and request things in our own name, or on our own merits, we will not get much response. But when we ask in the name of Jesus according to His will, that's a different story! The name of Jesus opens us up to the marvelous power of God.   —J. B. N.

Conclusion

A. Mansion? Cottage?

The hymn "Mansion Over the Hilltop" by Ira Stanphill (1914–1993) is well known. Its lyrics compare the "cottage" the singer has on earth with the "mansion" that awaits in Heaven. But when the *King James Version* came into being in 1611, the word *mansion* simply meant an "abode" or "dwelling place" or a separate apartment that was not part of a larger building. In this sense a mansion in Heaven is the special place that God has prepared for those who are faithful to Him. Jesus does not emphasize the material comforts of this heavenly dwelling. Instead He focuses on the essential benefit that we will enjoy: God and Christ will be with us forever.

In the meantime Jesus calls us to live lives that show we are in fellowship with Him. As we do we have the confidence that He will give us the power we need to do all that He asks. This may be difficult, but a heavenly home awaits for those who remain faithful.

B. Prayer

Father, we live in a world of falsehood. Sometimes we have a hard time saying what the word *truth* means anymore. Please help us live lives that are pleasing to You. Give us confidence so that we can stand up for You and do the greater works that Jesus calls us to do. In Jesus' name, amen.

C. Thought to Remember

Believe in Jesus and find God.

Home Daily Bible Readings

Monday, Feb. 12—A New and Living Way (Hebrews 10:19-23)

Tuesday, Feb. 13—Jesus Testifies to the Truth (John 18:33-40)

Wednesday, Feb. 14—Jesus Has Brought Life (2 Timothy 1:8-14)

Thursday, Feb. 15—Turn from Darkness (Ephesians 4:17-24)

Friday, Feb. 16—Walking in the Truth (3 John 2-8)

Saturday, Feb. 17—Jesus Is the Way (John 14:1-7)

Sunday, Feb. 18—The Son Reveals the Father (John 14:8-14)

Learning by Doing

This page contains an alternative lesson plan emphasizing learning activities.
Classes desiring such student involvement will find these suggestions helpful.

Learning Goals

After participating in this lesson, each student will be able to:

1. Describe Jesus' relationship to the Father.
2. Define what Jesus meant by *the way, the truth,* and *the life.*
3. Develop a plan for meditating on one of Jesus' miracles each day to increase belief.

Into the Lesson

Distribute the following list of famous last words. Ask students to match each quote with its author. (If you use student books, you will find the exercise printed there.)

1. "How were the [circus] receipts today at Madison Square Garden?" 2. "I have offended God and mankind because my work did not reach the quality it should have." 3. "That was a great game of golf, fellers." 4. "All my possessions for a moment of time." 5. "Lord, help my poor soul." 6. "I . . . am now quite certain that the crimes of this guilty land will never be purged away but with blood!" 7. "Don't turn down the light. I'm afraid to go home in the dark." 8. "Last words are for fools who haven't said enough."

A. Bing Crosby; *B.* P. T. Barnum; *C.* O. Henry; *D.* Queen Elizabeth I, of England; *E.* John Brown (American abolitionist executed in 1859 for leading a raid); *F.* Leonardo da Vinci; *G.* Edgar Allan Poe; *H.* Karl Marx.

Answers: 1B; 2F; 3A; 4D; 5G; 6E; 7C; 8H

After going over the answers, ask students how these final quotes might reflect the character and lives of their authors. For example Edgar Allan Poe was an alcoholic who also suffered from severe depression for much of his adult life. John Brown was convinced that the only way to end slavery in the United States was to start a revolt. When you have finished your discussion, say, "Today's lesson will focus on some of Jesus' last words to His disciples. Those words will reveal important things about Him."

Into the Word

Each student will pair up with another to complete both activities below. Allow pairs several minutes to complete the first activity. Then discuss their conclusions as a class, using the lesson commentary to guide the discussion.

Follow the same procedure for the second activity. Provide pens and paper for students to use, or direct their attention to the student books where the activities are printed.

Activity A. Read John 14:1-14 and discuss with your partner the nature of Jesus' relationship with the Father by answering these questions: (1) What do Jesus' statements about preparing a place for us (vv. 2-6) tell us about His relationship to the Father? (2) What did Jesus mean when He said, "He that hath seen me hath seen the Father" (v. 9)? (3) What reason does Jesus give for the works that He will enable His disciples to do (v. 12)?

Activity B. Read John 14:6 and discuss with your partner what Jesus meant when He said, "I am the way, the truth, and the life." (1) How does Jesus constitute the only way to reach God? (Compare to John 10:9; Acts 4:12.) (2) What did Jesus mean when He called himself "truth"? (Compare to Ephesians 1:13; 1 John 2:4.) (3) In what ways does Jesus embody life for the believer? (Compare Matthew 16:25; 19:29; John 3:36; 6:35; Romans 5:10-18.)

Into Life

Using the commentary on John 14:12-14, explain the relationship among Jesus' miraculous works, the works of His disciples, and the Holy Spirit's use of those works to convict the world of sin. You may find that John's "purpose statement" in John 20:30, 31 will enrich your class discussion.

Next, ask each pair of students to write a brief meditation (100 words or less) on one of Jesus' miracles as recorded in John's Gospel. Assign each pair one of these passages: John 2:1-11; 4:43-54; 5:1-15; 6:1-15; 6:16-21; 9; 11:1-44. The meditations should answer these questions: (1) What did Jesus do? (2) What effect did the miracle have on the faith of those who witnessed or experienced it? (3) What effect should it have on our faith today?

Collect the meditations and compile them into a booklet. Distribute copies of the collection to your students at the next class period. Ask them to use them as part of their daily devotions for the week ahead. Suggest that they read one meditation each day.

Let's Talk It Over

The questions on this page are designed to promote discussion of the lesson by the class and to encourage application of the lesson Scriptures. The answers provided are only discussion starters. Let your class talk it over from there.

1. In what ways do you think our future, eternal dwelling places will contrast with our current, earthly homes?

It's tempting to focus on the physical as we imagine no more leaky pipes or balky furnaces to repair! The most important contrast, however, will be our new homes' nearness to the presence of God. God is ever with us now, of course. But His presence and nearness in eternity probably cannot be described!

2. What was a time in your life that you showed a lack of spiritual discernment? How did you grow from this experience?

The greatest challenge for most of us probably is realizing, on a continuous basis, that there is a spiritual reality that is more enduring than our current physical reality. If Satan can't get us to forget about the spiritual reality entirely, his other tactic is to get us to "compartmentalize" areas of our lives: spiritual stuff is for Sunday morning and grace before meals, while regular life is for all the other times.

When we slip into this kind of compartmentalizing, we do not allow Jesus to lead us in all areas. Which movies we watch, where we surf on the Internet, what kind of cars we buy—Jesus is interested in all of these areas. Our choices indicate spiritual discernment. Wouldn't it be great if we always knew for sure that we were making the choices that Christ wants us to make? Confusion in these areas may be reduced by greater attention to Bible study and prayer.

3. Suppose that you share John 14:6 with a skeptic. In response he or she says, "You're just being narrow-minded. Surely a loving God would make a way for those who have never heard of Jesus!" How do you prepare yourself in advance for this kind of reaction?

You may or may not be able to persuade the skeptic. Remember that even Jesus himself did not persuade everyone.

What is most important is that your own faith remain unwavering when you hear such arguments. Was Jesus himself narrow-minded? See Matthew 7:14: "Strait is the gate, and narrow is the way, which leadeth unto life, and few there

be that find it." Does God have any plan other than Jesus? See Acts 4:12: "Neither is there salvation in any other: for there is none other name under heaven given among men, whereby we must be saved."

God sent His Son to die for the sins of the world (John 3:16). You can't get more loving than that!

4. Make a list of some out-of-the-ordinary things that Jesus did in front of His disciples. Despite the miraculous things on this list, what made His disciples linger in their uncertainty about Jesus' identity and authority? How are your own doubts similar?

One reason for the disciples' wavering was that Jesus didn't fit their preconceived ideas about the Messiah. We see their misconception pop up again in the question that they ask right before His ascension (see Acts 1:6). Undoubtedly our own misconceptions also serve as roadblocks to unconditional acceptance of Jesus' authority. Perhaps a doubt that lingers in the back of our minds is, "Where is the promise of his coming?" This doubt is not new—see 2 Peter 3:4.

Doubts also arise because of our focus on the physical. The disciples could see the power of Rome all around them. But to realize that God's spiritual forces were more powerful required the eye of faith that they didn't quite have (compare 2 Kings 6:15-17). Similarly our vision often is limited only to the moment. We too quickly forget about God's power and what long-term benefits we can gain if we heed the teachings of His Word.

5. Jesus talked about others doing things even greater than He had done. How do you apply Jesus' expectations in your own life?

Jesus has general expectations of all believers (see Matthew 28:19, 20). Jesus also has expectations that tie in to our individual spiritual gifts (Romans 12; 1 Corinthians 12; and Ephesians 4). We learn of His expectations when we meditate on His Word. As we do we take care to notice that His promise to the disciples gave a purpose for their actions: "that the Father may be glorified in the Son" (v. 13). This is our motive as well.

"I Am the True Vine"

DEVOTIONAL READING: Psalm 1.

BACKGROUND SCRIPTURE: John 15:1-17.

PRINTED TEXT: John 15:1-17.

John 15:1-17

1 I am the true vine, and my Father is the husbandman.

2 Every branch in me that beareth not fruit he taketh away: and every branch that beareth fruit, he purgeth it, that it may bring forth more fruit.

3 Now ye are clean through the word which I have spoken unto you.

4 Abide in me, and I in you. As the branch cannot bear fruit of itself, except it abide in the vine; no more can ye, except ye abide in me.

5 I am the vine, ye are the branches. He that abideth in me, and I in him, the same bringeth forth much fruit; for without me ye can do nothing.

6 If a man abide not in me, he is cast forth as a branch, and is withered; and men gather them, and cast them into the fire, and they are burned.

7 If ye abide in me, and my words abide in you, ye shall ask what ye will, and it shall be done unto you.

8 Herein is my Father glorified, that ye bear much fruit; so shall ye be my disciples.

9 As the Father hath loved me, so have I loved you: continue ye in my love.

10 If ye keep my commandments, ye shall abide in my love; even as I have kept my Father's commandments, and abide in his love.

11 These things have I spoken unto you, that my joy might remain in you, and that your joy might be full.

12 This is my commandment, That ye love one another, as I have loved you.

13 Greater love hath no man than this, that a man lay down his life for his friends.

14 Ye are my friends, if ye do whatsoever I command you.

15 Henceforth I call you not servants; for the servant knoweth not what his lord doeth: but I have called you friends; for all things that I have heard of my Father I have made known unto you.

16 Ye have not chosen me, but I have chosen you, and ordained you, that ye should go and bring forth fruit, and that your fruit should remain; that whatsoever ye shall ask of the Father in my name, he may give it you.

17 These things I command you, that ye love one another.

GOLDEN TEXT: I am the vine, ye are the branches. He that abideth in me, and I in him, the same bringeth forth much fruit; for without me ye can do nothing.—John 15:5.

Jesus Christ: A Portrait of God
Unit 3: Christ Guides and Protects
(Lessons 10-13)

Lesson Aims

After participating in this lesson, each student will be able to:

1. Identify what Jesus meant by *vine, branches,* and *fruit.*

2. Explain why we must remain connected to Christ in order to bear fruit.

3. Correct one situation where he or she has failed to stay connected to the vine.

Lesson Outline

Introduction

A. You Can't Do It Alone

Whether we like it or not, there are many things a person can't do alone. You can't sing a duet alone; you can't run a relay race alone; you can't hold a conference alone; you can't do a group presentation alone; you can't play catch alone. As much as it may hurt our pride, there are some things that we can only do with the help and support of other people.

In our passage today Jesus adds something else to the list of things that we can't do ourselves: Jesus insists that we can't please God alone. This is the case because we draw our strength for service from our connection to Christ. God also commands us to love other peo-ple. We can't love others as long as we are focused on "going it alone."

B. Lesson Background

The three letters that John wrote (namely, 1, 2, and 3 John) reveal sobering news: the churches and people whom John addressed had experienced, or were just about to experience, serious internal crisis. John wrote his Gospel around AD 85–90 and the letters perhaps shortly thereafter. The 55 years or so since the death and resurrection of Christ allowed ample time for false doctrines and false Christs to spring up (compare 1 John 2:18, 22; 4:3; 2 John 7). Church splits were occurring (3 John 9, 10).

John's letters reveal that he wanted to correct these situations. A large part of the solution is found in John's Gospel. There John made sure to include Jesus' teaching about the vine and branches. This reminded believers that they must remain connected to the true Christ and to one another if they wished to please God.

I. Connected to Jesus
(John 15:1-11)

A. Pruning the Vineyard (vv. 1-3)

1. I am the true vine, and my Father is the husbandman.

Jewish readers would likely detect an allusion here to Isaiah's Song of the Vineyard. In Isaiah 5:1-7 the prophet compares Israel to a choice vineyard that God planted in the promised land. He tended it with special care. Of course God expected a good harvest for His work, as any farmer would. Instead the Israelites produced unrighteousness and injustice.

The vine imagery appears in other Old Testament passages as well (see Psalm 80:8-16; Isaiah 27:2, 3; Jeremiah 2:21; 12:10, 11; and Ezekiel 15). Here in John 15 Jesus now applies Old Testament imagery in a new way: the *true vine,* which will yield a faithful harvest, is Christ himself. Jesus replaces Judaism as the means by which people are connected to God, the keeper *(husbandman)* of the vineyard.

2. Every branch in me that beareth not fruit he taketh away: and every branch that beareth fruit, he purgeth it, that it may bring forth more fruit.

The imagery in this verse outlines God's work as the keeper of the vineyard. Jesus is the vine, and He now pictures the disciples as branches. When a *branch* withers or fails to produce *fruit,* it must be cut off from the vine to protect the overall health of the plant. In a similar way the disciples are forewarned that God expects them to be faithful; if they are not, they may lose their privileged position. Compare John the Baptist's dire warning in Matthew 3:10: "And now also the axe is laid unto the root of the trees: therefore every tree which bringeth not forth good fruit is hewn down, and cast into the fire."

On the other hand, the vine keeper also tends to the healthy branches by pruning them back in order to insure the maximum yield. This imagery possibly alludes to the persecution that Jesus will predict for the disciples in John 16:1-4. See also the discussion of God's discipline in Hebrews 12:3-11. Some will respond to suffering by losing their faith; others will become stronger and even more effective through these experiences. [See question #1, page 224.]

The exact nature of the fruit that Jesus has in mind is not defined here. He may be alluding back to John 14:15. There He said that those who love Him will keep His commandments; if this is the case, then the fruit here is similar to Paul's "fruit of the Spirit"—a Christian lifestyle characterized by "love, joy, peace, long-suffering, gentleness, goodness, faith, meekness, temperance" (Galatians 5:22, 23). [See question #2, page 224.]

Or it may be that Jesus is thinking more of John 14:30, 31, where He speaks of what the world must learn. If this is the case, the fruit would refer to the disciples' evangelizing efforts. Both meanings may be in view, and each is certainly an essential measure of spiritual health.

WHEN LESS YIELDS MORE

I grew up in suburbia in a family that had no interest in landscaping or beautification. I can't remember either of my parents ever planting any flowers or even maintaining houseplants. We had a happy home, but developing a green thumb was just not part of our family activities.

When my wife and I bought our first house, it was on a small lot in a major city, and the previous owner had planted a rosebush just in front of

---

How to Say It

ABRAHAM. *Ay*-bruh-ham.
EZEKIEL. Ee-*zeek*-ee-ul or Ee-*zeek*-yul.
GALATIANS. Guh-*lay*-shunz.
ISAIAH. Eye-*zay*-uh.
JEREMIAH. Jair-uh-*my*-uh.
JUDAISM. *Joo*-duh-izz-um or *Joo*-day-izz-um.
JUDAS. *Joo*-dus.

---

the house. I didn't know much about gardening. But even I could tell that the rosebush, which carried very few blossoms, was overgrown. The next spring I decided to cut back the plant. There were a lot of branches clustered in the center of the bush, and they were bending across each other.

So I cut out some of the excess branches in the center while thinning some of the outer branches. To my delight that summer the rosebush was covered with blossoms! There were far more blossoms than I would have assumed, even though I knew that was supposed to be the result.

That's the principle Jesus is talking about here. Even healthy plants need to be pruned for maximum productivity. Sometimes Jesus needs to cut some of the "stuff" out of our lives so that we can produce more and better results for His kingdom. We should expect Him to do so.

—J. B. N.

3. Now ye are clean through the word which I have spoken unto you.

The word *clean* refers back to the pruning process in verse 2. The disciples have been cleansed—prepared to serve and to witness—through their constant exposure to Jesus' teaching. Earlier, Jesus had referred to them as clean in order to distinguish them from Judas, whose motives obviously were impure and ungodly (John 13:10, 11).

B. Bearing Fruit (vv. 4-8)

4, 5. Abide in me, and I in you. As the branch cannot bear fruit of itself, except it abide in the vine; no more can ye, except ye abide in me. I am the vine, ye are the branches: He that abideth in me, and I in him, the same bringeth forth much fruit; for without me ye can do nothing.

The ideas of "that which should *abide in* us" and "whom we should abide in" are very important to the apostle John (see John 5:38; 14:17; 15:7; 1 John 2:14, 24, 27). The emphasis is on remaining faithful. This can come about only through closeness and unity with God.

The first statement in verse 4 is a promise to believers. A good paraphrase might be, "If you remain faithful to me, then I will remain faithful to you"—Christ will not abandon us. This charge is especially important in light of verse 2. Just as a branch cannot bear grapes without the nourishment provided by the vine, so believers cannot live lives that please God without the strength available through Christ.

If we lose that connection, then we lose our power to serve. And once we lose the power to serve and bear fruit, we are in great danger. The danger is not just in being pruned back a little but in being pruned away permanently (Luke 13:6-9). Jesus emphasizes this point here in verse 5 so that there can be no misunderstanding: *without me ye can do nothing.* [See question #3, page 224.]

6. If a man abide not in me, he is cast forth as a branch, and is withered; and men gather them, and cast them into the fire, and they are burned.

After the keeper of the vineyard prunes away the dead branches, he throws them into a pit and burns them. The wood from vines is useless for anything but burning (compare Ezekiel 15:1-5). Jesus alludes here to ultimate judgment of those who fall away: they are separated from the faithful and cast into eternal fire (compare Matthew 13:37-42).

7. If ye abide in me, and my words abide in you, ye shall ask what ye will, and it shall be done unto you.

Jesus informs His hearers of one way that He will continue to empower them: through His *words* or teachings. By learning what Jesus commanded while on earth, believers will know what they must do to please God. Is there anything more important than learning what Jesus desires of us?

It is important to stress both the context and the condition of the promise in this verse. First, in context Jesus is speaking about our ability to bear fruit through obedience to Him. Thus we are invited to ask for the power to serve, and

Visual for Lesson 13

Point to this image as you ask, "What have you found that helps keep you close to Jesus?"

Jesus will give it. We are not necessarily being promised that physical health or material blessings await just for the asking. In fact the reference to "pruning" in verse 2 may suggest that God will ask us to do without such things at times in order to increase our faith.

Second, the condition of our successful asking is stated in the first part of the verse: we must *abide in* Christ and allow His Word to abide in us. If we remain closely connected to Jesus and meditate on His teaching, then we can have a proper perspective on God's will for our lives. This perspective should focus our prayers on things that please Him rather than ourselves (compare James 4:3).

8. Herein is my Father glorified, that ye bear much fruit; so shall ye be my disciples.

God receives glory when we *bear much fruit* in the sense that our actions reveal His power at work in the world. When we do the right thing, our witness to others shows that we recognize God to be worthy of our service and worship. Jesus' entire earthly ministry has been focused on the glory of God (John 17:4). We show that we are His true followers when we attempt to do the same thing in our own lives.

CHANNELS OF PRODUCTIVITY

We all enjoy the result of fruit trees' productivity. Fruit, however, is not always automatic. I remember we had an old apple tree in our yard when I was a youngster. We did nothing to enhance the fruit, and the result was not very good. There were a lot of apples, but they were wormy, misshapen, blemished, and not worth eating.

Much later I learned that fruit trees require a good deal of care. Spraying controls the worms and blemishes. Pruning the trees helps production. Fertilizer and special applications aid the whole process. Fruit growers spend a lot of time and go to considerable expense to increase the yield of their trees.

But there is one thing that never happens in the process of producing fruit: the tree branches themselves don't have to go to extra effort to produce. Imagine tree branches hunkering down, grunting and groaning like a weight lifter doing a dead lift. Imagine tree branches working up a sweat while trying to increase the size of their fruit. Ridiculous, isn't it?

Yet we often attempt the same thing in trying to produce spiritual fruit. We strain as if the fruit comes from us. It doesn't. It only comes when we (the branches) are tapped into Jesus (the vine). Perhaps that's why Jesus says that *the Father* is glorified when we produce fruit. We aren't the producers—God is. We are channels of His productivity, if we allow ourselves to be.   —J. B. N.

C. Abiding in Love (vv. 9-11)

9. As the Father hath loved me, so have I loved you: continue ye in my love.

Love is the bond that unites *the Father* and the Son. It is also the bond that unites the branches with the vine. Jesus' entire ministry has been an expression of God's love for Him and for the world, and Jesus has shown the same love to the disciples. *Continue* is another translation of the Greek word for "abide": Jesus' love is our home, the place where we live. Verses 10 and 11 (next) will spell out two effects of this abiding love in our lives.

10. If ye keep my commandments, ye shall abide in my love; even as I have kept my Father's commandments, and abide in his love.

Jesus now explains exactly how it is possible to continue living in His *love*. When we see what Christ has done for us, we should respond by obeying His teachings. This could include all of His ethical commands, such as we see in the Sermon on the Mount. But the focus here is probably on the "new commandment" that Jesus has just spelled out at John 13:34. He will repeat it in 15:12, below—"love one another." By showing love for one another, we imitate Christ's love for us. (See also 1 John 5:2.)

11. These things have I spoken unto you, that my joy might remain in you, and that your joy might be full.

The thought of Christian service, love for others, and obedience to Christ's commands often seems overwhelming and impossible. Yet Jesus highlights the benefit of obedience: *joy*. The phrase *my joy* refers to the satisfaction that Jesus receives from knowing that He perfectly fulfills God's will, despite the difficulties He faces.

Such joy remains with us when we know that we also are following Christ's commands and bearing fruit despite circumstances. Of course this is not to say that we always will be happy in this life; we can, however, always be confident in the knowledge that God is pleased with our work. [See question #4, page 224.]

II. Connected to One Another
(John 15:12-17)

A. New Commandment (vv. 12, 13)

12, 13. This is my commandment, That ye love one another, as I have loved you. Greater love hath no man than this, that a man lay down his life for his friends.

Love one another is Jesus' "new commandment" of John 13:34, as noted above. Jesus' love is the model for the relationships we are to have with other believers.

Jesus illustrates this love by referring the disciples to what He has done for them already *(as I have loved you).* Up to this point in time, He has allowed them to enjoy a special, privileged relationship with Him. He has provided for their needs. He has protected them both physically and spiritually, as they have allowed Him to.

Jesus also illustrates the kind of love He is talking about by referring the disciples to what He is about to do in the very near future. He will provide the ultimate sacrifice by laying down *his life* for them on the cross.

Such sacrificial love is the purest expression of the fruit that Christ empowers us to bear. This does not mean that Jesus calls us to die upon a cross as He did. That was a one-time event, not to be repeated. Yet if the type of love that is evident in the cross is not evident in our lives as well, then we clearly are not drawing our power from the Christ, who died for sinners.

B. Friends of Christ (vv. 14-16)

14. Ye are my friends, if ye do whatsoever I command you.

The term *friends* is used to refer to people sharing the same social status in the ancient world. Viewed in this light the disciples must see this comment as something of a paradox. Technically, a servant (one who follows commands) is not a friend (an equal) to his or her master. We are friends of Christ in the sense that we are privileged to know His thinking, as was Abraham (2 Chronicles 20:7; Isaiah 41:8; James 2:23) and Moses (Exodus 33:11). See the next verse. [See question #5, page 224.]

15. Henceforth I call you not servants; for the servant knoweth not what his lord doeth: but I have called you friends; for all things that I have heard of my Father I have made known unto you.

The slave or *servant* does not need to understand the master's orders; he or she simply needs to obey them without asking questions. Jesus is our Lord, and He does not invite us to question His commands. At the same time, however, He has not simply left us with a code of laws and rules. Rather, Jesus has openly revealed the Father's will and purposes to the disciples. He has taught them the importance of revealing God's love to the world.

We should therefore be able to understand why it is so important for us to bear fruit and love one another. If we do not understand this, then we really cannot say that we understand anything that Jesus did or taught.

16. Ye have not chosen me, but I have chosen you, and ordained you, that ye should go and bring forth fruit, and that your fruit should remain; that whatsoever ye shall ask of the Father in my name, he may give it you.

While we can enjoy the privilege of friendship with Jesus, we must never forget that He is the boss. Christ is the one who initiates a relationship with us, and we should not take His offer lightly.

At the same time, however, we should feel secure in the knowledge that Jesus has not set us up to fail: He has not *ordained* that we should be pruned away and cast off (v. 2). He has cleansed us instead (v. 3). He tells us everything that we need to know to bear fruit. Because of our relationship with Him, we can expect not only God's favor but also His power for service.

C. New Commandment Reprised (v. 17)

17. These things I command you, that ye love one another.

Jesus closes by repeating the essential element in bearing fruit: that new commandment to *love one another.* By the time the apostle John writes his letters, this new commandment becomes an old commandment (2 John 5). Yet it bears repeating!

The disciples will have to depend on one another for support once Jesus is gone. The church will not be able to grow if it is divided. Strangely, Christians often take the command to love one's neighbor (Mark 12:31) more seriously than the command to love one another. That makes us prey to easy criticism from nonbelievers. Who wants to join a divided church?

Conclusion

A. Friends in High Places

Everyone knows that there are a lot of things we can't have access to unless we know people in "high places." I am devoted fan of NASCAR, and recently I was able to secure a garage pass to a race in Indianapolis. This pass allowed me full access to all the behind-the-scenes areas at the race. These included the garages where the cars are serviced and the areas where the drivers and crews meet to discuss strategy.

I saw many of my favorite drivers up close there, as well as some other celebrities who had come to the race. All this was possible solely because my cousin's husband works as a member of the crew on one of the NASCAR teams. Without his help I would have been watching from the stands or on television.

Our passage today applies that principle to our spiritual lives. If we follow Jesus' teaching, He treats us as "friends," and with Jesus, you really do have "a friend in high places"! With Him on our side, there is no limit to what we can do—provided that we stay connected.

How sad it is to see an unconnected Christian! Ironically, it seems sometimes that it is preachers who are in the most danger of losing their connection to the true vine. Preachers are under tremendous pressure to be involved in all the major and minor activities of the church. They scurry from one meeting to another, trying to keep all the programs going. Under all this time pressure, it's tempting for them to start cutting back on their prayer and devotional life.

The cure for the Christian who is relying on his or her own strength to get things done is Zechariah 4:6: "Not by might, nor by power, but by my Spirit, saith the Lord of hosts."

B. Prayer

Lord, we know that You have called us to love one another the way that You loved us. But sometimes our pride and feelings get in the way, and we don't treat each other the way that we know we should. Help us to see the importance of unity in Your church. Help us to bear fruit by staying closely connected to You and to one another. In Jesus' name, amen.

C. Thought to Remember

When we bear fruit and love one another we show that we understand Jesus.

Home Daily Bible Readings

Learning by Doing

This page contains an alternative lesson plan emphasizing learning activities.
Classes desiring such student involvement will find these suggestions helpful.

Learning Goals

After participating in this lesson, each student will be able to:

1. Identify what Jesus meant by *vine, branches,* and *fruit.*

2. Explain why we must remain connected to Christ in order to bear fruit.

3. Correct one situation where he or she has failed to stay connected to the vine.

Into the Lesson

Distribute the following quiz about common biblical metaphors (also printed in the student books). Correct answers are indicated in brackets, but distribute blanks for those. Challenge students to fill in the blanks without looking up the Scripture reference. Remind your class that a metaphor is a figure of speech containing a comparison in which a word or phrase normally used of one thing is identified with another. For example, "The sun is a bright, orange ball."

What's That Metaphor?

1. "I am the [bread] of life" (John 6:35).
2. "I am the [light] of the world" (John 8:12).
3. "I am the good [shepherd]" (John 10:11).
4. "Know ye not that ye are the [temple] of God, and that the Spirit of God dwelleth in you?" (1 Corinthians 3:16).
5. "The Lord is my [rock], and my fortress, and my deliverer" (Psalm 18:2).
6. "For our God is a consuming [fire]" (Hebrews 12:29).
7. "Ye are the [salt] of the earth" (Matthew 5:13).
8. "Ye are the [light] of the world" (Matthew 5:14).

Discuss the quiz. Then tell your students that this lesson will analyze three metaphors that Jesus used to describe a Christian's proper relationship to Him and to other Christians.

Into the Word

Before dividing your class for the two exercises in this portion of the lesson, use the lesson commentary to explain the background of John 15:1-17. Focus on the meaning and significance of the terms *vine, branch,* and *fruit.* Discuss the need to stay "connected" to Christ in order to serve effectively and keep heresy out of the church.

Divide the class into several small groups. Half of the groups will do the activities in Exercise #1. The other half will do the activities in Exercise #2. Provide blank paper and copies of each exercise for the groups you have created. (If you use the student books, you will still need to provide blank paper.) Allow 10 minutes for these exercises. Then ask each group to report its findings to the entire class.

Exercise #1

Activity A: Have someone in your group read aloud John 15:1-8. Identify what you think is the theme of this section.

Activity B: Write a paraphrase of John 15:1-8. "Translate," as much as possible, the key metaphors (vine, etc.) into plain speech.

Activity C: Discuss the following questions about the text: (1) In the church what are the respective roles of Jesus and the Father as vine and husbandman? (2) What will happen to those who do not produce fruit? (3) What constitutes fruit in Christ's kingdom?

Exercise #2

Activity A: Have someone in your group read aloud John 15:9-17. Identify what you think is the theme of this section.

Activity B: Write a paraphrase of John 15:9-17.

Activity C: Discuss the following questions about the text: (1) What are some aspects of the Father's love for His Son? (2) How does Jesus love us the same way? (3) How are we to love one another with this same love? (4) What must we do to remain in Christ's love? (5) What kind of joy comes from having this relationship with Christ?

Into Life

For each hypothetical situation described below, suggest scriptural ways to help these people reconnect with the Lord and His church.

1. Jennifer was a faithful Christian through her high-school years. When she went off to college, however, she drifted away from God. How can you help her reactivate her faith?

2. Bob is a member of your church, but he is inactive. His business is demanding, so he likes to use his Sundays to relax at home, do yard work, or play golf. He talks about returning to church but never seems to get around to it. What can you do to help him?

Let's Talk It Over

*The questions on this page are designed to promote discussion of the lesson
by the class and to encourage application of the lesson Scriptures. The answers
provided are only discussion starters. Let your class talk it over from there.*

1. In what ways have you noticed God "pruning" your life? What have you learned from this experience?

God seems to have various methods for pruning those who seek Him, doesn't He? We see some of those ways in the pages of Scripture (examples: Luke 18:28; 19:1-10). Some refused to be pruned, with sobering consequences (examples: Luke 18:18-23; 2 Timothy 4:10a).

Rather than wait for God's (possibly) severe pruning, perhaps some self-pruning is in order. "Don't confuse activity with accomplishment" is an old cliché, but it has a ring of truth. Some folks take on too many jobs at church, and their flurry of activity leaves them physically, mentally, and spiritually exhausted. A good start may be to consult with someone who knows you well and will give you frank answers. Ask, "What areas of my life do you think I need to prune back?" Then brace yourself—don't get defensive at an honest reply!

2. Bearing fruit (not just foliage) is vital. What kinds, qualities, and quantities of fruit do you think Jesus expects you to bear? How do you avoid the trap of perfectionism in this regard?

The first question should naturally bring to mind Paul's discussion of the fruit of the Spirit in Galatians 5:22-26. How those descriptions "play out" in everyday life can make for good discussion. Jesus said that ungodly people can be recognized by the fruit they bear (Matthew 7:15-20). Certainly a Christian's fruit should include bringing others to Christ.

The second question recognizes a real danger. One possible answer will include the idea of having an accountability partner or fellow members of a small group to help us see our motives properly.

3. Jesus' teaching on remaining faithful would become critical during the persecution that the first-century disciples were to face. What are some specific challenges that your church and her individual members face that cannot be overcome without complete faithfulness?

We sometimes hear that we live in the darkest days (spiritually) of history. But hasn't every generation of Christians said that? Zoning commissions may try to block construction of a church building because such a structure won't contribute to the local tax base; this is an issue that the first-century church didn't face. At the level of the individual, sin has always posed a challenge to holiness. Sin may be more apparent today, however, because we live in the Information Age. Pornography is all over the Internet, lurking and waiting to bring the believer to the gutter.

The media often ridicules churches or individual Christians who want to remain consistent to their Christian testimony. Our stories of trials, challenges, and temptations may not always be the same as those of our first-century brethren. But Jesus knows how to help each generation work through its unique issues.

4. How has obedience to Jesus brought joy to your life?

Jesus said, "My yoke is easy, and my burden is light" (Matthew 11:30). God never intended for obedience to be burdensome. Jesus is the one who took away our sin-stigma. Since Jesus manifested His love for us in this way, it should be easier to love one another and to know the joy that comes from being part of His family.

Two extremes regarding obedience must be avoided. *Legalism* brings back the law in a way that destroys the joy of salvation by grace (compare Galatians 3:10-14). *License,* or "do whatever you want," may seem fun for a time but will take us out of fellowship with Jesus (compare Jude 4).

5. Here Jesus refers to His disciples as friends. But in John 13:13-16, He affirms His role as Lord. How do you harmonize these? How do you fulfill your roles as both a servant and a friend of Jesus on a daily basis?

Analogies are defined and limited by their contexts. Jesus is God and we are not; in that sense He can be nothing other than Lord and Master. He, however, is not like an ordinary master; He grants us all we need to have, and He even dies for us! Ordinary, earthly masters simply don't do such things for their servants. We fulfill our roles as both servant and friend in gratitude of this fact.

Spring Quarter 2007

Our Community Now and in God's Future

Special Features

Lessons

Unit 1: Known by Our Love

Unit 2: A New Community in Christ

Unit 3: Living in God's New World

About These Lessons

An old saying goes, "Well begun is half done." Lessons 1–4 show us the key to beginning (and continuing) well: love. We love one another because God first loved us. It was God's love that sent Jesus to the cross (Lessons 5 and 6). That same love creates a new heaven and earth for our benefit (Lessons 7–13). What a great future! What an opportunity to show love *now*!

Mar 4
Mar 11
Mar 18
Mar 25
Apr 1
Apr 8
Apr 15
Apr 22
Apr 29
May 6
May 13
May 20
May 27

Quarterly Quiz

The questions on this page may be used in several ways: as a pretest at the beginning of the quarter; as a review at the end of the quarter; or as a review after each lesson. The questions are based on the Scripture text of each lesson (King James Version). **The answers are on page 228.**

Lesson 1

1. John said that it was just barely possible for someone to hate his brother yet still be in the light. T/F. *1 John 2:9, 11*
2. John wrote to young men because they were what? (strong? weak? rich?) *1 John 2:14*
3. "He that doeth the _____ of God abideth for ever." *1 John 2:17*

Lesson 2

1. We shall see Jesus as He is. T/F. *1 John 3:2*
2. What was the message from the beginning? (don't bother one another? love one another? have dinner with one another?) *1 John 3:11*
3. Cain, who killed his _____, is an example of unloving action. *1 John 3:12*

Lesson 3

1. God sent His Son to be the propitiation for our sins. T/F. *1 John 4:10*
2. John expects that we will have what on Judgment Day? (boldness? timidity? a good excuse?) *1 John 4:17*

Lesson 4

1. The one who overcomes the world is the one who believes that Jesus is the Son of God. T/F. *1 John 5:5*
2. Jesus came by water and what? (oil? fruit of the vine? blood?) *1 John 5:6*

Lesson 5

1. Jesus is Alpha and what? (Gamma? Delta? Omega?) *Revelation 1:8*
2. What two villages did Jesus approach on the outskirts of Jerusalem? (Bethphage and Bethany? Jericho and Bethlehem? Joppa and Bethany?) *Luke 19:29*

Lesson 6

1. Jesus is the first and the last. T/F. *Revelation 1:17*
2. When Mary Magdalene first saw the resurrected Christ, she thought He was a carpenter. T/F. *John 20:15*
3. What title did Mary Magdalene use when she recognized Jesus? (Rabboni? Son of Man? Emmanuel?) *John 20:16*

Lesson 7

1. The voice John heard in Heaven sounded like a what? (clarinet? harp? trumpet?) *Revelation 4:1*
2. The number of elders that John saw in Heaven was ___. *Revelation 4:4*

Lesson 8

1. The book or scroll was sealed with how many seals? (seven? seventy-seven? seventy times seven?) *Revelation 5:1*
2. What three ways is Jesus described? (Lion, Eagle, Branch? Lion, Root, Lamb? Lion, Lamb, Fox?) *Revelation 5:5, 6*

Lesson 9

1. Where are the servants of God sealed? (foreheads? hands? left ears?) *Revelation 7:3*
2. What three groups did John see worshiping God? (angels, elders, beasts? saints, angels, cats? angels, deacons, prophets?) *Revelation 7:11*

Lesson 10

1. How many beasts fell down and worshiped God? (0? 4? 24?) *Revelation 19:4*
2. John's vision announced the marriage supper of the Lamb. T/F. *Revelation 19:7, 9*

Lesson 11

1. In the new Heaven and earth, John saw a sea that was even bigger than the one before. T/F. *Revelation 21:1*
2. The holy city is also known as the new _____. *Revelation 21:2*
3. There will be no pain in Heaven. T/F. *Revelation 21:4*

Lesson 12

1. "The bride" is also the Lamb's wife. T/F. *Revelation 21:9*
2. The new Jerusalem, the holy city, has no temple. T/F. *Revelation 21:22*

Lesson 13

1. Jesus is the root and offspring of whom? (David? Artaxerxes? Jeremiah?) *Revelation 22:16*
2. What is the last word in the Bible? (amen? maranatha? Omega?) *Revelation 22:21*

Practice for Heaven

by Jonathan Underwood

OUR LOCAL CHRISTIAN RADIO STATION airs some short pithy statements in between the music and other programs at various times throughout the day. One of them is, "Practice for Heaven: love each other now!" The apostle John, the disciple whom Jesus loved, would have liked that statement. He had much to say about loving one another, and it is he who gives us the grand glimpse of Heaven that we know as the book of Revelation.

For the next three months, our attention will be on some of John's writings (with one text from Luke on Palm Sunday). In March our lessons come from 1 John. The longest of his three short letters near the end of our New Testament, its theme is love and how we practice it day by day. In April we'll make the transition to a study of Revelation with two lessons from the Gospels.

Our recall of the final week of Jesus' life and of His death and resurrection will draw us fittingly to a look at what the book of Revelation has to say about Heaven. And that's what we'll be doing for the remaining seven weeks of the quarter. We'll conclude with a prayer, "Even so, come, Lord Jesus."

Unit 1: March
Known by Our Love

Lesson 1 reveals "The Light of Love." Anyone who has risen in the night and stumbled over a chair or a stray shoe knows it's better to turn on a light before walking through a dark room. John tells us we likewise don't want to stumble in the darkness of a loveless relationship. To walk and live in the light, we need to walk in love.

In **Lesson 2** we are met with "The Test of Love." We can see that the Father himself passes this test, having lavished His love on us. Now it's up to us to pass the test in our relationships with each other. Our text includes the reminder that we cannot pass the test with words alone. True love is expressed in action.

Lesson 3, "The Source of Love," reminds us that love comes from God. If we are confronted with people who are hard to love, we may think we cannot love them. We can't—on our own. But we're not on our own! We are "born of God."

The unit concludes with **Lesson 4,** "The Way to Love." The title may lead some to expect a few easy steps to achieve a life of love. John says it's more basic than that. If you want to love, simply obey the commands of Christ. Obedience to a leader is usually identified more with faith than with love, but that's the point. When we practice our faith, we practice love.

Unit 2: April
A New Community in Christ

Lesson 5 launches a new unit and a new book for study: Revelation. But we'll use this lesson on Palm Sunday, so most of our text comes from Luke's account of Jesus' triumphal entry. The lesson is fittingly titled "Christ Is King"; it recalls how the people gave Jesus a king's welcome as He entered Jerusalem at the beginning of a momentous week that would end in Jesus' death and burial. It also recalls that the one who was heralded as a king in Jerusalem is in fact King of much more. He is the "Alpha and Omega, . . . the Almighty."

Lesson 6 will be used on Resurrection Sunday. It testifies that "Christ Is Risen" by laying John's account of Jesus' resurrection next to a few verses from Revelation. Both accounts give grand testimony to the fundamental truth that Jesus "was dead; and, behold, [is] alive for evermore." This is the foundation of our faith; nothing is more basic. If Jesus did not rise from the dead, then we might as well close the doors of our church buildings and put our Sunday school quarterlies in the trash. But, in fact, He did rise!

From **Lesson 7** on we devote ourselves wholly to texts from Revelation. The first is from Revelation 4 and declares that "Christ Is Worthy of Praise." All of Heaven adores Him and declares that He is worthy as creator. This attention paid to Him makes obvious another reason Christ is worthy of praise: He is worthy as Lord of Heaven. Actions in Heaven match the words; those who *say* Christ is worthy *act* as though He is worthy. That is an example worth noting.

Being Lord of creation and Lord of Heaven are reason enough for Jesus to receive our praise, but **Lesson 8** adds another: "Christ Is Able to Redeem." He is, in fact, not merely able—He has done it! People of every tribe and tongue and nation have been redeemed by His precious blood. Praise God that that includes us, because while Jesus is worthy of praise, we are not, of ourselves, worthy to praise Him! We would be separated from Him forever without His sacrificial grace. In the lesson text, every creature in Heaven bowed to worship the Lamb. In view of our redemption, can we do any less?

Lesson 9 promises "Christ Is Our Protection." This assurance should not be taken to mean Christians will have no trouble in life. Jesus himself warned that, in the world, we will have tribulation. But our text for Lesson 9 promises that this world will have to give an account for that tribulation. Judgment is sure, and it will be severe. But when God measures out His wrath on the wicked, we need not fear. Christ is our protection from God's wrath and punishment. Indeed, for us, "God shall wipe away all tears from [our] eyes."

Unit 3: May
Living in God's New World

In previous lessons we saw grand worship scenes in Heaven (especially from Revelation 4 and 5). In **Lesson 10**, "Taking Our Place at the Table," we see another—and yet there is something different here. Amid the *alleluias* for the Lord Jesus, we find that there is a place for us as well! We are not worthy to receive worship alongside Him, but we do have a place. He is the bridegroom and the host of the marriage feast. And we, the church, are the bride. We belong at His side. We are His beloved. "Blessed are they which are called unto the marriage supper of the Lamb."

Lesson 11 promises that we'll be "Finding a Home in Heaven." Our place at the table, then, is not merely as guests. Our dwelling place is there. The lesson text includes the dire warning that not everyone will share this place. There will be some whose place is in the fiery lake. They are the ones who reject the Lord in life. But we need not fear that place, that "second death." When we join the Lord in Heaven, we're there to stay!

Images and symbols are important in the book of Revelation, and many of them are taken from the Old Testament. The image of the temple is one of them. But John tells us he saw *no temple* in Heaven. In the Old Testament the temple, like the tabernacle that preceded it, symbolized God's presence with His people. Our text for **Lesson 12** tells us that in Heaven we need no symbol for that: we will literally be "Living in God's Presence."

Lesson 13 provides a fitting close to the unit and to the quarter with a focus on "Anticipating Christ's Return." With the grand visions of Heaven and its celestial worship, with the promises and reminders of redemption and protection and belonging, these lessons will already have made us look forward to the time when the promises are all fulfilled. So when we hear again the promise of Jesus, "Surely I come quickly," we reply with John, "Amen. Even so, come, Lord Jesus."

Who Will Be There?

In our lessons about Heaven we have focused primarily on our being in the presence of the Lord. Each one of us wants to see Him, to be with Him. As the song says, "Face to face with Christ my Savior, Face to face—what will it be? When with rapture I behold Him, Jesus Christ who died for me."

But it's not going to be just Jesus and me—it's Jesus and us, many of us, from every tribe and tongue and nation and people. It's people who speak a different language from mine and whose skin is a different color from mine. But it's also people very much like me, like the person I refused to speak to in church last week, or the person I argued with in Sunday school the week before that.

That's the reason we begin our studies this quarter with the unit on love. The early church was known for its love. Even the enemies of the cross had to admit that the Christians had a special love one for another. Surely John's writings were in part responsible for that behavior. So we look this quarter at some of those writings. Yes, we thrill at the scenes of glory and majesty in Revelation. But we are urged and prodded by His "old commandment which [we] had from the beginning." That commandment is simply, "Love one another."

As they say on the radio, "Practice for Heaven: love each other now!"

Answers to Quarterly Quiz
on page 226

Lesson 1—1. false; 2. strong; 3. will. **Lesson 2**—1. true; 2. love one another; 3. brother. **Lesson 3**—1. true; 2. boldness. **Lesson 4**—1. true; 2. blood. **Lesson 5**—1. Omega; 2. Bethphage and Bethany. **Lesson 6**—1. true; 2. false; 3. Rabboni. **Lesson 7**—1. trumpet; 2. 24. **Lesson 8**—1. 7; 2. Lion, Root, Lamb. **Lesson 9**—1. foreheads; 2. angels, elders, beasts. **Lesson 10**—1. 4; 2. true. **Lesson 11**—1. false; 2. Jerusalem; 3. true. **Lesson 12**—1. true; 2. true. **Lesson 13**—1. David; 2. Amen.

The last week of Jesus' life

Bethany
- Jesus is anointed

Mount of Olives and Jerusalem
- The Triumphal Entry

On the road between Bethany and Jerusalem
- Jesus curses the fig tree

Jerusalem
- Jesus cleanses the Temple

On the road between Bethany and Jerusalem
- Jesus and the disciples discuss the withered fig tree

Jerusalem
- Jesus' authority is questioned by the chief priest's and the elders
- Jesus teaches in the temple using parables and answers questions

Jerusalem
- Chief priest, scribes, and elders plot against Jesus
- Judas agrees to betray Jesus

Jerusalem
- Trials before Annas, Caiaphas, and the Sanhedrin
- Trials before Pilate and Herod; torture by Roman soldiers

Golgotha, outside Jerusalem
- Jesus' crucifixion and death

Joseph's Tomb
- Jesus' burial

Jerusalem, the Upper Room
- Preparation for the Passover meal
- The last supper with the disciples
- Jesus washes His disciples' feet
- Judas identified as the traitor
- The Lord's Supper instituted
- Jesus comforts and prays for the disciples and later believers

Gethsemane, on the Mount of Olives
- Jesus prays in the garden
- Jesus' betrayal and arrest

SAT
SUN
MON
TUES
WED
THURS
FRI

Our Community

(1 John, Revelation)

Known by Our Love

The meaning of God's love

A New Community in Christ

Community

Living in God's New World

Promises

The End

Making Sure It Is Right

by Ronald G. Davis

THIS QUARTER'S STUDY includes Jesus' well-known claim, "I am Alpha and Omega," the beginning and the end (Revelation 1:8, 11; 22:13). When He is allowed to be that in the individual disciple's life, the "ultimate" end definitely will be right.

Teachers naturally want their lessons to lead toward that good end. Yet the difference that a brief study of a Bible text makes in the life of a student is difficult to judge. That is why the consistent design of the lessons in this curriculum concludes with an "Into Life" segment.

Too often Bible teachers think that their task stops at explanation of text and context. Too often teachers are so rushed to "cover it all" that they ignore (or lop off) the end, the application step. Though Scriptures certainly are not obscure in their implications for life, most adults could use some encouragement and direction for the *So what?* stage of learning. The teacher's job is to help students see the truth's implications for life and point them to action. The teacher fulfills this responsibility with *reminders and reinforcers* and with a *call to action*.

Reminders and Reinforcers

Curriculum for children often includes take-home items. These are either products the children have produced in a learning activity or items the teacher or curriculum publisher have produced to correlate with truths studied. These are designed to give the learner "one more look" at the ideas (reminder) and/or an opportunity to communicate the lesson learned to someone else (reinforcement). The same learning concept holds true for adults: one more look—even a momentary notice—and an opportunity to share an idea learned with another person are valuable.

For example, the overriding emphasis in **Lessons 1** through **4** (from 1 John) is *love*. A constant reminder of love can take the form of a sticker, badge, or pin with a heart illustration to be worn week-to-week. This can, in turn, become the occasion for answering the likely inquiry, "Why are you wearing that heart emblem?"

As the series approaches Resurrection Sunday through **Lessons 5** and **6,** a teacher can encourage the learners to wear an emblem of Jesus'

death and resurrection. This would announce with godly pride, "I am a Christian. I have a living hope of resurrection and eternal life!" Suggest a simple *ET* badge to get attention. Curiosity can be answered, "It means *Empty Tomb*!" One can then explain that Jesus is the only true "extraterrestrial"; He is the only one to come to earth from Heaven, then go "back home" to prepare for His friends' arrival.

Lessons 7 through **13** deal with the end times and the glories of the new heaven and new earth. Simple "earth stickers," worn on an occasion or two, create the chance for remembering and revealing to others our hope: new earth and new Heaven. Some celebrate Earth Day on April 22 each year; your stickers can suggest a New-Earth Day to anticipate Jesus' return.

Here's another idea: establish an e-mail group to send out personalized key verses from week to week. For example, an e-mail following **Lesson 2** can read, "Hi, [student's name]. Isn't it great to know we are the beloved children of God? See 1 John 3:2." Or after **Lesson 10,** "Good morning, [student's name]. I hope you are starting this day with all God's servants praising our God. See Revelation 19:5, 7." One of your class members might enjoy doing this for the whole class each week of the quarter, if you would give her or him an example.

You can also make it easy for your learners to carry a copy of the Bible texts with them day to day. This will encourage a more-than-once look at God's Word. The *King James Version* can be copied freely for distribution. Passages from 1 John **(Lessons 1** through **4)** can be legibly copied onto the front and back of one sheet for ease in handling. Highlighting the printed texts will add emphasis. The texts for the studies from Revelation **(Lessons 5** through **13)** also can be copied onto two or three sheets. A suggestion to keep them handy at one's work station for examination during breaks or lunch may create a habit of regular Bible reading.

Call to Action

The Bible's *call to action* deals with both internal character and external deeds. Though righteousness (internal integrity) and righteous deeds (benevolent acts of kindness and faith) cannot truly be separated, some lesson texts emphasize the former, some the latter. As the apostle John notes, "In this the children of God are manifest . . . whosoever doeth not righteousness is not of God" (1 John 3:10). No righteous deeds, no character of true righteousness!

Consider, for example, **Lesson 2.** There the apostle says bluntly, "Whoso hath this world's good, and seeth his brother have need, and shutteth up his bowels of compassion from him, how dwelleth the love of God in him?" (1 John 3:17). You can use this text as opportunity for the class to make a collection and distribution to the needy. Try collecting gloves and mittens for the homeless, collecting money for one month's rent for a needy family, or initiating a drive for canned meat for the church's food pantry.

Calls to action can be presented in other ways as well. Many New Testament texts reveal the absolute standards of the Spirit for godly living, and when a disciple confronts them, he or she cannot but ask, "How am I doing?" Prime tasks of the teacher are to make sure the mirror of the Word is crystal clear and that it is squarely faced by every student. One strategy the teacher has in this regard is to present learners a "rating scale" to elicit a self-evaluation. The goal is to highlight needed improvements in one's character and thought life.

Consider, for example, **Lesson 7** as it emphasizes worship at the throne in Heaven. Who doesn't need to ponder a personal response to such statements as "I have proper fear and reverence for God"; "My understanding of God's holiness keeps me from choosing the unholy"; "God's eternal nature is a concept I fully appreciate"; "I believe that God created all things, and so I thank Him for all that is"; "My attire and demeanor when I join God's saints in worship is fully in honor of Him"; "Nothing that I have will I withhold from my worship of God"; and "I think about Heaven and its glories." Encouraging learners to choose *Always, Often, Sometimes,* or *Never* as responses will force a consideration of "What do I need to do now?"

A teacher also can offer simple fill-in-and-sign statements to challenge students to meet the Spirit's standards. **Lesson 9** and its picture of the saved at the throne of God could be accompanied by statements such as *I, _____, want to wear the white robe of the saved; I, _____, want to be sheltered by God's tent of love; I, _____, want to know the comfort of Heaven's satisfying provisions; I, _____, want to walk with the Lamb to the springs of living water.*

Action must include prayer, of course. This is one of the absolutely essential Christian disciplines. So the good teacher is always looking for ways to encourage prayer related to texts studied. Some of those prayers will be pure praise and thanksgiving to the worthy God.

The text of **Lesson 10** includes a call to God's people to praise Him (Revelation 19:5). A seven-day prayer stimulus card, distributed to each as he or she leaves class, can encourage remembrance of the study and a need to put those truths to work in Christian life. Consider the following, based on Revelation 19:1-10: *Monday:* Thank God for making things right (v. 2); *Tuesday:* Sing *alleluia* because the Lord our God Almighty reigns (v. 6); *Wednesday:* Humbly honor the Lord for allowing you to wear the fine linen of righteous deeds (vv. 7, 8); *Thursday:* Express your joy at receiving an invitation to the marriage supper of the Lamb (v. 9); *Friday:* Affirm your confident belief that the words of God are true and that you are privileged to hear and know them (v. 9b); *Saturday:* Thank God for the company of believers with whom you stand in worship (v. 10a); *Sunday:* Put feet on your prayer as you go to a place of worship today to worship God and Him only (v. 10b).

Praise is not the only way to pray, of course. Prayers of repentance and petition are also needed. For all adults there are "shadow moments" in which one's behavior is not fully characterized by love. **Lesson 1,** from 1 John 2:7-17, challenges every Christian to live in the light of love. Our shortfalls here call for heartfelt prayers of repentance and petition for God's help.

Though ultimately the teacher wants the students to word their own prayers, suggesting some prayers may be a step in that direction. For **Lesson 1,** offer this prayer: "Father who loves me, help me to be like You. When I am drawn to love the world and things in it, draw me back to You. By Your indwelling Spirit push aside my cravings, and lusts, and boastings. Help me to know and do Your will; I want to live forever. In Jesus' name, amen." Occasionally asking students simply to echo sincerely a prayer of yours will be effective.

The End

The end of every Bible study occurs after the study is over: in the daily life of each student. A concerned teacher of adults knows that and does what he or she can do to see that truths are carried from the place of study to the place of life and service. Only then does Jesus—the beginning and the end—have a true disciple.

The Light of Love

March 4
Lesson 1

DEVOTIONAL READING: 1 Peter 4:1-11.

BACKGROUND SCRIPTURE: 1 John 2:7-17.

PRINTED TEXT: 1 John 2:7-17.

1 John 2:7-17

7 Brethren, I write no new commandment unto you, but an old commandment which ye had from the beginning. The old commandment is the word which ye have heard from the beginning.

8 Again, a new commandment I write unto you, which thing is true in him and in you: because the darkness is past, and the true light now shineth.

9 He that saith he is in the light, and hateth his brother, is in darkness even until now.

10 He that loveth his brother abideth in the light, and there is none occasion of stumbling in him.

11 But he that hateth his brother is in darkness, and walketh in darkness, and knoweth not whither he goeth, because that darkness hath blinded his eyes.

12 I write unto you, little children, because your sins are forgiven you for his name's sake.

13 I write unto you, fathers, because ye have known him that is from the beginning. I write unto you, young men, because ye have overcome the wicked one. I write unto you, little children, because ye have known the Father.

14 I have written unto you, fathers, because ye have known him that is from the beginning. I have written unto you, young men, because ye are strong, and the word of God abideth in you, and ye have overcome the wicked one.

15 Love not the world, neither the things that are in the world. If any man love the world, the love of the Father is not in him.

16 For all that is in the world, the lust of the flesh, and the lust of the eyes, and the pride of life, is not of the Father, but is of the world.

17 And the world passeth away, and the lust thereof: but he that doeth the will of God abideth for ever.

GOLDEN TEXT: He that loveth his brother abideth in the light, and there is none occasion of stumbling in him.—1 John 2:10.

Our Community Now and in God's Future

Unit 1: Known by Our Love

(Lessons 1-4)

Lesson Aims

After participating in this lesson, each student will be able to:

1. List ways that people can benefit from the light of love.

2. Explain how the principle of love should act as a beacon to guide his or her life.

3. Articulate one way that the principle of love will guide his or her life in the week ahead.

Lesson Outline

INTRODUCTION
  A. Darkness and Light
  B. Lesson Background
 I. LIGHT'S ARRIVAL (1 John 2:7-11)
  A. What John Stresses (vv. 7, 8)
  B. What John Knows (vv. 9-11)
    Stumbling in Darkness; Walking in Light
 II. LIGHT'S RESULTS (1 John 2:12-14)
  A. Various Groups, Part 1 (vv. 12-13b)
  B. Various Groups, Part 2 (vv. 13c-14b)
    Guidance Still Needed?
III. WORLD'S DESIRES (1 John 2:15-17)
  A. Stark Choice (vv. 15, 16)
  B. End Result (v. 17)
CONCLUSIONS
  A. Ignoring the Light of Love
  B. Following the Light of Love
  C. Prayer
  D. Thought to Remember

Introduction

A. Darkness and Light

Cockroaches love the darkness. So do termites, slugs, and most kinds of mold and fungus. Some really disgusting stuff thrives in places where there is no light. Similarly, people who do evil deeds love the darkness (compare 1 Thessalonians 5:7). Physical darkness may hide misdeeds. Spiritual darkness is both the cause and increasing result of sin.

But God's people are to live in the light. When we live lives of love, we walk in the light. We have nothing to hide. We do not stumble in spiritual darkness. We are not corrupted by the love of the world and the lusts of the world. We gladly choose the ways of God. He is the one who said, "Let there be light!" He is the provider of both physical and spiritual light.

B. Lesson Background

Light and love are important themes in the writings of the apostle John. He writes near the end of his earthly days, after a long life as a leader of the church. In this first of three letters, he appears to address the church at large, warning people to avoid the darkness of false teaching and to embrace the light of love.

The time of John's writing is perhaps somewhere between AD 85 and 90. At this time near the end of the first century, the church began to be troubled by a false doctrine known as *gnosticism*. What we may call "full-blown gnosticism" doesn't really appear until the second century AD. So John was confronting an early version of that heresy. Gnostics thought that they knew more than other believers and that they alone would be saved. They taught that following Jesus was not enough to save. The gnostics claimed that believers had to learn secret knowledge. (See also our discussion of this heresy in Lesson 1 of the winter quarter.)

To set matters straight, John assured his readers that what they had received from the beginning was true. John's epistle, however, is far more than a warning against gnostic heresy. Its truths about light, love, and righteousness are needed in every age. Whenever a new false teaching or a new temptation confronts the church, this letter helps to keep us on course.

I. Light's Arrival
(1 John 2:7-11)

John wants his readers to know the truth and obey it. He begins his epistle with truth, asserting that he and the other apostles had heard and seen and touched Jesus personally. The second chapter continues to focus on truth—the true light that guides the church.

A. What John Stresses (vv. 7, 8)

7. Brethren, I write no new commandment unto you, but an old commandment which ye had from the beginning. The old commandment is the word which ye have heard from the beginning.

John calls his readers *brethren* since they share membership in God's community. As members of this community (the church), they must submit to all the commands of God. John reminds them that an important rule of behavior is a *command-ment* that is as *old* as Leviticus 19:18: "thou shalt love thy neighbor as thyself." (We will see John unpack the content and meaning of this commandment as our lesson continues.)

Unlike the false teachers who trouble the early churches, John has added nothing to this truth, which is part of the gospel of Christ (Matthew 19:19). John is merely reemphasizing the same command that Jesus gave, as we shall see (compare John 13:34; 1 John 3:23; 2 John 5, 6).

8. Again, a new commandment I write unto you, which thing is true in him and in you: because the darkness is past, and the true light now shineth.

The *commandment* of love is as old as the Law of Moses. It is as old as Jesus' earthly ministry, now some 55 or 60 years in the past as John writes. Yet it is as *new* as tomorrow's dawn. [See question #1, page 240.]

The command *is true in* Jesus, who demonstrated God's great love at the cross. The command is also true in the church, where believers live out divine love in their own lives. When love points the way, people no longer walk in *darkness*. The gloomy night of sin is over; the *light* of love accompanies the dawn of new life (compare Matthew 4:16). What was true in the life of Jesus is now being put into practice in the lives of believers (compare 1 John 2:5, 6).

The *true light* that *now shineth* is Jesus and truth about Him. The apostles have faithfully proclaimed this truth. Now false teachers are trying to extinguish that light. Their darkness must be rejected.

B. What John Knows (vv. 9-11)

9. He that saith he is in the light, and hateth his brother, is in darkness even until now.

The sharp contrast between light and darkness serves to reveal who a person "really is." Someone may claim to be *in the light*, but the darkness of attitude and actions will expose him or her. The one who *hateth his brother* is not at all like Jesus; such a person is more like Cain (compare

---

How to Say It

BATHSHEBA. Bath-*she*-buh.

DEMAS. *Dee*-mus.

GNOSTICS. *nahss*-ticks.

GNOSTICISM. *nahss*-tih-*sizz*-um (strong accent on *nahss*).

THESSALONIANS. *Thess*-uh-*lo*-nee-unz (strong accent on *lo*; *th* as in *thin*).

---

1 John 3:12). Actions speak louder than words. To God, the heart-attitudes that produce actions speak loudest of all. When a person's deeds show that he or she harbors hatred, that person loves the darkness (compare John 3:19-21). [See question #2, page 240.]

We should also remember that there is more than one way to hate. For many, hatred is shown by the absence of loving action. When they see their fellow Christians in need, they just do not care. When people who claim to be Christians fail to give anything—even a cup of water—in Jesus' name, they show clearly that they do not have God's love in their hearts (see Matthew 25:42, 43; 1 John 3:17). [See question #3, page 240.]

10. He that loveth his brother abideth in the light, and there is none occasion of stumbling in him.

The person who follows Jesus walks *in the light* of life. Such a person tries to imitate the greater love of Jesus, remembering how Jesus laid down His life for His friends (see John 15:13). The true believer does not step into the light only on special occasions; rather, such a person abides in the light permanently.

Because the light of love has opened that person's eyes to God's reality, there is no *occasion of stumbling in him* or her. This means that he or she will neither stumble nor be the cause of stumbling for others. The word that is translated *stumbling* originally referred to a trap of some kind. For deeper study you can explore how John uses this word in John 6:61; 16:1 (verb forms) and Revelation 2:14 (noun form). When we walk in the light with Jesus, we neither stumble nor serve as a trap for others to do so.

11. But he that hateth his brother is in darkness, and walketh in darkness, and knoweth not whither he goeth, because that darkness hath blinded his eyes.

The one who hates a fellow Christian is someone who perhaps still thinks of himself or herself as part of the fellowship of believers. But such a person actually walks *in darkness*. A person who makes this choice gives up the opportunity to walk safely with Jesus in the light. This person little knows (or cares) of the dangers that await in the darkness.

The false teachers whom John opposes make the darkness only worse. They have contempt, rather than love, for people who put their faith in Christ. They are quick to condemn anyone who does not have their "secret knowledge." These false teachers walk in darkness and do not know it because the darkness has *blinded* them to God's truth.

STUMBLING IN DARKNESS; WALKING IN LIGHT

Paris—the city of light! The city is famed for its brilliantly floodlit monuments and buildings that glow throughout the night. The cost for the lighting is considerable, but it pays for itself in quality of life for the residents and visitors. However, there is another side to Paris. A darker side.

In the city's fourteenth district, down 130 steps of a spiral staircase, one may enter "the empire of the dead." It is a dimly lit catacomb of several city blocks. There stacked in neat piles rest the skeletal pieces of 6 million people—the remains of those who died by plagues, the guillotine, and other causes of times past. For a fee one may walk a dimly lit path through the bones.

Two hundred years ago, the catacombs were totally dark and could be explored only by torchlight. The torch of one unfortunate explorer went out, and he stumbled along, lost in the darkness. Eleven years later his remains were found just a few feet from an exit. John reminds us that the times of darkness should be past because the gospel has come. It is a torch that never goes out.

Yet one can still stumble along in darkness voluntarily, bringing grief to self and others. A clue John offers as to whether we walk in light or darkness is whether we choose to make hatred or love the defining character of our lives.   —C. R. B.

II. Light's Results
(1 John 2:12-14)

The light of God and the love of God are not intended for a chosen few. God's light is for all people. By this light they can see the error of their ways and come to repentance (see 2 Peter

Visual for
Lesson 1

Post this chart to provide your students with a broad view this quarter's lessons.

3:9). As the following verses show, everyone can walk in this light and enjoy its results.

A. Various Groups, Part 1 (vv. 12-13b)

12. I write unto you, little children, because your sins are forgiven you for his name's sake.

Turning to a happier theme, John writes brief notes of celebration to various groups in the church. By using the address *children,* it is possible that John is referring either to those who are young in age or are young in the time they have been Christians. The address *little children* is a favorite of John's (see 1 John 2:1, 12, 18, 28; 3:7, 18; 4:4; 5:21). This may mean that John thinks of all who receive his letter as his own children in the faith.

In any case, John celebrates the fact that their *sins are forgiven*. The gnostics falsely tell them that they cannot have salvation until they know "secret truths." But John assures them that they are forgiven already. Moreover, this forgiveness is not a personal accomplishment. Rather, it is by Christ—all for God's great *name's sake*.

13a. I write unto you, fathers, because ye have known him that is from the beginning.

Next John turns specifically to the *fathers.* These are members of the church who are mature both in years and in faith. They have known Christ *from the beginning*—from the time the church was planted in their area. They know that their beliefs are the original truths. They can refute the assertions of the false teachers. God's community must always adhere to the apostolic truth preserved in the Bible, regardless of what false teachers present as a newer "truth."

We should pause to remember that Jesus cautioned against calling anyone on earth "father" (Matthew 23:9). The apostle John is not violating that restriction since he is not using the term *father* in the sense that Jesus forbids—a sense of a rival to the heavenly Father. For deeper study, you can explore how the New Testament uses this word in Luke 1:55; Acts 7:2; 22:1; Ephesians 6:4; Colossians 3:21; and 2 Peter 3:4.

13b. I write unto you, young men, because ye have overcome the wicked one.

Now John addresses the *young men*. As with "little children" of verse 12, *young* may refer to chronological or spiritual age (or both). The chief characteristic of young men is their vigor and strength. These young warriors for the faith *have overcome the wicked one,* the devil. Through Christ they have resisted temptation. Youth are particularly vulnerable to certain kinds of sin (2 Timothy 2:22). Blessed are the overcomers! [See question #4, page 240.]

B. Various Groups, Part 2 (vv. 13c-14b)

13c. I write unto you, little children, because ye have known the Father.

As if writing a second verse to a song, John addresses each group anew. He rejoices with the *little children* because they have come to know God. As the Gospel of John records, "This is life eternal, that they might know thee the only true God, and Jesus Christ, whom thou hast sent" (John 17:3). The first benefit of walking in the truth is knowing God.

14a. I have written unto you, fathers, because ye have known him that is from the beginning.

Again John addresses the *fathers*, repeating the same important truth. They are the ones who *have known Him that is from the beginning*. Walking in the light has given them the privilege of knowing Christ and serving Him for many years. Their ability to confirm and preserve the ancient truths makes them vital to the church.

14b. I have written unto you, young men, because ye are strong, and the word of God abideth in you, and ye have overcome the wicked one.

When John addresses the *young men* again, he adds two statements about them. Not only have they *overcome the wicked one* (repeated from v. 13b), they are *strong* and they have *the Word of God* abiding in them. They are not just casually acquainted with God's Word! Such are the benefits of belonging to the fellowship of believers.

GUIDANCE STILL NEEDED?

A generation ago, the baby boomers (those born between 1946 and 1964) entered adulthood. They wanted to "cut the apron strings." But in college they found they still needed guidance from adults—just not from their parents! So the Dean of Students office came to prominence in colleges to help guide students through academic life.

Now that the boomers' children are in college, the parents still want a level of involvement that colleges must learn to deal with. Thus, many universities have created a Coordinator of Parent Programs position to help parents learn to let go of their children who are becoming adults. The title of a *Wall Street Journal* article was "Tucking Them In—in the Dorm: Colleges Ward Off Overinvolved Parents" (July 28, 2005).

People of every generation have needs that they want addressed. When John writes to children, young men, and fathers, he is telling us the Word of God speaks to the needs of all. That Word helps us sort out the difference between *felt needs* and *real needs*. How will God's Word guide you today?   —C. R. B.

VISUALS FOR THESE LESSONS

The visual pictured in each lesson (example: page 236) is a small reproduction of a large, full-color poster included in the *Adult Resources* packet for the Spring Quarter. The packet is available from your supplier. Order No. 392.

III. World's Desires
(1 John 2:15-17)

Tragically, some people reject the light. Some reject it right from the start. Others reject the light after having first accepted it (see Hebrews 6:4-6).

A. Stark Choice (vv. 15, 16)

15. Love not the world, neither the things that are in the world. If any man love the world, the love of the Father is not in him.

Love should be our finest motive. It is to be a selfless devotion modeled after the nature of God. Yet some people direct their love to *the things that are in the world* rather than to *the Father*. Then love becomes an ugly thing—a distortion and a corruption. This was the problem of Demas (2 Timothy 4:10).

When John charges his readers to *love not the world*, he does not have in mind the world of humanity that God loved and sent His Son to save (see John 3:16). He means the fallen world as it continues defiantly to reject God (John 16:11; 1 John 4:3-5; 5:19).

To love the fallen world and its *things* is to prefer the company of sinners to the community of saints. It is to prefer living in fallen brokenness rather than being born anew. It is to be "of" the world rather than merely "in" it (John 17:11, 16). If a person loves the fallen world, he or she does not love God. We cannot have two masters (Luke 16:13). [See question #5, page 240.]

16. For all that is in the world, the lust of the flesh, and the lust of the eyes, and the pride of life, is not of the Father, but is of the world.

John has warned his readers not to love the world, and now he specifies what this means. The *lust of the flesh* is any craving that arises out of our selfish appetites. This includes the more obvious sins of gluttony, drunkenness, and sexual immorality. It also includes sins such as racism (selfishness for one's "own people") and contempt for the poor (selfishness for one's own social level). The *lust of the flesh* is the unholy desire to do any of the works listed in Galatians 5:19-21.

John's second warning is against the *lust of the eyes*. This refers to enticements that come through our sense of sight. The tree of the knowledge of good and evil in the Garden of Eden was "pleasant to the eyes" (Genesis 3:6). There was nothing wrong with the tree in and of itself. But Adam and Eve used it for an unholy purpose.

While there is often a sexual element in lust, as when David's eyes lingered on Bathsheba (2 Samuel 11:2), the primary focus here is materialism. Television, movies, and the Internet offer materialistic enticements to our eyes that did not exist in John's day. Believers must remember that their treasures are laid up in Heaven.

The third warning is against the *pride of life*. This is not pride in a positive sense, such as taking godly pride in doing the best we can. John refers, rather, to boastful arrogance. This describes those who think they are too good to honor God (see Romans 1:30). Such people become lovers of themselves (see 2 Timothy 3:2). They proudly list their virtues for God (see Luke 18:9-14). This is a fatal flaw of modern society, where status seekers care only about their public image, thinking, "It's all about me."

B. End Result (v. 17)

17. And the world passeth away, and the lust thereof: but he that doeth the will of God abideth for ever.

The fallen world is dying. Everything in the world passes *away*. Even the *lust* or desire for such things will finally die. Why should God's people care about carnal pleasures that do not bring lasting satisfaction? Why should we care about amassing goods, as did the rich fool (see Luke 12:16-21), only to die and lose it all? Why

should we care about our standing in the eyes of humanity, rather than our standing before God (see John 5:44)?

When life is done, only the one who does *the will of God* will endure. People who invested everything in the lust of the world will have nothing; God's people will have everything. The arrogant will perish in their carnal boasting; the meek will inherit the earth. So John warns his readers that love for the world brings failure. The wise choice is to walk in the light of love, to do the will of the Father, and to abide forever.

Conclusion

A. Ignoring the Light of Love

Over the centuries there have been many false teachers who have tried to lead God's people astray. Against this John issues a clarion call to the church to walk in the true light. This light is right for all ages and brings its special benefits to all ages. On the other hand, John warns that the one who chooses the darkness and the ways of the world will be exposed. The light of love is God's beacon to guide our lives.

B. Following the Light of Love

What does it mean to us today to follow the light of love? First, it means that to love God is to honor His truth. We must never let the "wisdom" of the world replace divine revelation. The light of love necessarily includes the love of truth. John clearly shows that love is not just a "feel good" emotion; it is inseparably intertwined with acting in accordance with truth. Truth matters!

A second application is found in the way we express love in the church. We can learn to love both from God's nature and from God's command. We get a foretaste of Heaven in a community of godly love. God's people are to be different from those controlled by worldliness. Our happiness does not lie in fulfilling the lust of the flesh; our eternal security does not lie in the size of our earthly estate. The only real satisfaction comes from walking with Jesus in the light—in the light of love.

C. Prayer

Father of love, we thank You for giving us the light. We rejoice that You have shown us Your unfailing love; now help us to show that kind of love to one another. In the name of Jesus, the light of the world, we pray, amen.

D. Thought to Remember

The ultimate folly is to reject the light.

Home Daily Bible Readings

Monday, Feb. 26—Partakers of the Divine Nature (2 Peter 1:5-11)

Tuesday, Feb. 27—Living in Love (Romans 12:9-21)

Wednesday, Feb. 28—Fulfilling the Law in Love (Romans 13:8-14)

Thursday, Mar. 1—Serve with Love (Galatians 5:13-26)

Friday, Mar. 2—Love Deeply (1 Peter 4:1-11)

Saturday, Mar. 3—Called to Live in Love (1 John 2:7-11)

Sunday, Mar. 4—Live for God (1 John 2:12-17)

Learning by Doing

This page contains an alternative lesson plan emphasizing learning activities.
Classes desiring such student involvement will find these suggestions helpful.

Learning Goals

After participating in this lesson, each student will be able to:

1. List ways that people can benefit from the light of love.

2. Explain how the principle of love should act as a beacon to guide his or her life.

3. Articulate one way that the principle of love will guide his or her life in the week ahead.

Into the Lesson

Display the following word-find puzzle as class begins (it also appears in the student book).

```
J E T A H O
H V H R N J
O O G H U K
N L I D R E
E S L A F N
W O D H O J
```

Say, "Four sets of John's contrasts can be found in this word puzzle. Check today's text and then find and mark the eight words." Allow time to find these words: DARK, FALSE, HATE, LIGHT, LOVE, NEW, OLD, TRUE. Say, "John uses simple terms to reveal profound truths." You may want to relate this truth to the lesson writer's discussion of the gnostic heresy of the first century.

Option. Perhaps you would like to introduce the entirety of the first unit (Lessons 1-4) of the series by displaying the following as class begins:

1 John 2:7-17	The ___ of Love	GHILT
1 John 3:1, 2, 11-24	The ___ of Love	ESTT
1 John 4:7-21	The ___ of Love	CEORSU
1 John 5:1-12	The ___ of Love	AWY

Ask the class to unscramble the letters at the end of each line to fill in the blank with the correct word: LIGHT, TEST, SOURCE, WAY.

Into the Word

Note to students that John is emphatically repetitious in his writing—he uses the same key words over and over. Then give them this list of words in a column: Because, Beginning, Brothers, Children, Command(ment), Dark(ness), Fathers, Hate, Light, Love, True/Truth, World, Write. Direct them to go through the text, 1 John 2:7-17, and make a tally of how many times each word (or form of a word) is used. Allow about five minutes, then ask for tallies. Don't get bogged down in disagreements; the point is to see how prevalent certain ideas are in the text.

Establish groups that you call "The Light Group" and "The Love Group." Duplicate the groups as many times as you need to keep each to no more than six people. Give each group a list from a concordance of 10 to 12 biblical references to *light* or *love*. (An exhaustive concordance will have hundreds of references, so you will need to be selective.) If you desire, you can choose from the following two lists.

Light: Genesis 1:3, 4; Exodus 10:21-23; Job 12:24, 25; 29:2, 3; Psalm 27:1; Isaiah 2:5; 5:20; 60:1-3; Daniel 2:22; Matthew 5:16; Luke 11:34-36; John 1:9; 3:19-21; 12:35, 36; Acts 26:17, 18; Ephesians 5:8; 1 Peter 2:9; Revelation 21:23.

Love: Exodus 20:6; Leviticus 19:18; Judges 5:31; Psalms 69:36; 97:10; Proverbs 10:12; 17:17; Jeremiah 31:3; Zephaniah 3:17; Luke 6:32; John 3:16, 19-21; Romans 12:10; 13:10; 1 Corinthians 8:3; Ephesians 4:1, 2; 1 Peter 1:22.

Say, "Cooperate on finding and reading the verses assigned. Note particularly how the key words are used, and then look at today's text in 1 John 2:7-17. Your task is to relate the verses you find to truths John expresses in today's text." If necessary, give this example: "Job 12:24 speaks of a contrast: that of spiritual darkness with light."

Allow the groups time to deliberate. Then ask volunteers to explain the connections they have made. Discuss.

Into Life

Either buy a package of lighthouse stickers or have an artistic class member sketch a simple lighthouse image onto peel-and-stick labels. Distribute one to each student.

Suggest that each student stick the image in a place where it will serve as a reminder to live and act in the light of God's love in the week ahead. Possible places are the bathroom mirror and the refrigerator door. Say, "When you are tempted by various sinful cravings or to boast of what you have or do, let the light of love show you a different way." Close with prayer.

Let's Talk It Over

The questions on this page are designed to promote discussion of the lesson by the class and to encourage application of the lesson Scriptures. The answers provided are only discussion starters. Let your class talk it over from there.

1. In Leviticus 19:18, God commands his people to love one another. The same imperative is before us with the coming of Christ. How can its "newness" be practiced today? What excuses do believers offer in failing to practice this?

First of all, we have an example to follow in our Lord Jesus. He didn't just talk about love, He demonstrated it! We will find that loving others is easier when we love out of gratitude for His life, death, and resurrection rather than out of mere obligation. As we do, we may discover a new aspect of love when others don't respond in kind. Despite that, the love that Jesus expects us to extend is far-reaching in scope. Helped by the Holy Spirit, we can love others as our Father in Heaven loves them.

Sometimes believers may excuse their lack of loving action because of the existence of government social programs. Someone needing food comes to the church door, and we direct him or her to a social service office to get some food stamps. What a lost opportunity to show the love of Jesus!

2. What happens when Christians "walk the walk" as well as "talk the talk"? How will you repair the damage for past inconsistencies in this regard?

Whether we like it or not, Christians are constantly being examined by the world. Others may be either threatened or intrigued by our insistence on the uniqueness of Christ; in either case, they are on alert for times when our behavior is inconsistent with our witness. When our lives reveal inconsistencies, we cause hardened hearts in those who observe us. Also, we make it difficult for other believers to witness because they are assumed to share the same faulty lifestyle that we demonstrate.

The Gospel message is bold in asserting that "there is none other name . . . whereby we must be saved" (Acts 4:12). To "talk" this assertion without "walking" it makes the claim seem laughable to unbelievers. But the damage can be repaired; the reinstatement of Peter is an example (John 21:15-19). If someone points out a real or imagined inconsistency, stay humble and admit the possibility of error.

3. What was a time in your life when, because of your faith in Christ, you changed your attitude toward someone from hatred or anger to love? How did things turn out?

Walking in the light of love is not something done occasionally. Rather, it is a mind-set, a consistent way of life. One who abides in the light accepts the circumstances of life as a way to demonstrate Christ to others. Experiencing hatred is one such circumstance; being able to return love is the challenge. The mature Christian is able to change his or her view of others to be able to do this (Luke 6:28).

4. The gospel is for all! Yet the devil tries to sow division in the church. What can we do to recognize, prevent, and heal such divisions?

One of the devil's tactics is to attempt division between old and young. Taking care to include both in church activities requires alertness and planning. Another satanic tactic targets relationships between the church board and the congregation. This may take the form of criticism as expressed in private murmurings. Asking the critics to bring their concerns directly to the people involved is important.

Prayer is effective against divisiveness. We often do not know where the enemy is attacking, but God does. People can build up animosity in the privacy of their thoughts, but God is aware of these. Speaking words of recognition and encouragement can help them to feel less isolated. The Holy Spirit can arrange the circumstances for this to happen, but we must be ready.

5. Give examples of *loving the world*. How does *love of the Father* provide an antidote?

Be sure to get the definitions straight. By "the world," John is referring to the culture of fallen humanity. This is a culture built upon the idols of human achievement, pleasure, self-absorption, and independence from God. A godly person may achieve fame and fortune in sports, politics, or business, yet not "love" any of those things in the sense of placing God in second place. On the other hand, a person may never achieve fame and fortune in sports, politics, or business, yet desires it so badly that he or she creates an idol.

The Test of Love

DEVOTIONAL READING: 1 Corinthians 13.

BACKGROUND SCRIPTURE: 1 John 3.

PRINTED TEXT: 1 John 3:1, 2, 11-24.

1 John 3:1, 2, 11-24

1 Behold, what manner of love the Father hath bestowed upon us, that we should be called the sons of God: therefore the world knoweth us not, because it knew him not.

2 Beloved, now are we the sons of God, and it doth not yet appear what we shall be: but we know that, when he shall appear, we shall be like him; for we shall see him as he is.

. . . .

11 For this is the message that ye heard from the beginning, that we should love one another.

12 Not as Cain, who was of that wicked one, and slew his brother. And wherefore slew he him? Because his own works were evil, and his brother's righteous.

13 Marvel not, my brethren, if the world hate you.

14 We know that we have passed from death unto life, because we love the brethren. He that loveth not his brother abideth in death.

15 Whosoever hateth his brother is a murderer: and ye know that no murderer hath eternal life abiding in him.

16 Hereby perceive we the love of God, because he laid down his life for us: and we ought to lay down our lives for the brethren.

17 But whoso hath this world's good, and seeth his brother have need, and shutteth up his bowels of compassion from him, how dwelleth the love of God in him?

18 My little children, let us not love in word, neither in tongue; but in deed and in truth.

19 And hereby we know that we are of the truth, and shall assure our hearts before him.

20 For if our heart condemn us, God is greater than our heart, and knoweth all things.

21 Beloved, if our heart condemn us not, then have we confidence toward God.

22 And whatsoever we ask, we receive of him, because we keep his commandments, and do those things that are pleasing in his sight.

23 And this is his commandment, That we should believe on the name of his Son Jesus Christ, and love one another, as he gave us commandment.

24 And he that keepeth his commandments dwelleth in him, and he in him. And hereby we know that he abideth in us, by the Spirit which he hath given us.

GOLDEN TEXT: Beloved, now are we the sons of God, and it doth not yet appear what we shall be: but we know that, when he shall appear, we shall be like him; for we shall see him as he is.—1 John 3:2.

*Our Community Now and
in God's Future*
Unit 1: Known by Our Love
(Lessons 1-4)

Lesson Aims

After participating in this lesson, each student will be able to:

1. Recite 1 John 3:16 from memory.

2. Compare and contrast John 3:16 with 1 John 3:16.

3. Commit to imitating Christ's love by sharing one possession with a Christian brother or sister in need.

Lesson Outline

INTRODUCTION

  A. Will We Be Tested on This?

  B. Lesson Background

 I. MAJESTY OF LOVE (1 John 3:1, 2)

  A. Our Present (v. 1)

  B. Our Future (v. 2)

    What Love Can Do

II. MESSAGE OF LOVE (1 John 3:11-15)

  A. Don't Be Like Cain (vv. 11, 12)

    The Opposite of Love

  B. Don't Be Surprised (v. 13)

  C. Don't Fail This Test (vv. 14, 15)

III. MEASURES OF LOVE (1 John 3:16-24)

  A. Practical Test (vv. 16-18)

  B. Inward Conviction (vv. 19, 20)

  C. End Result (vv. 21-24)

CONCLUSION

  A. Love: The Final Exam

  B. Love: The Commencement

  C. Prayer

  D. Thought to Remember

Introduction

A. Will We Be Tested on This?

A high-school teacher has spent hours preparing a special lesson. As she launches into her enthusiastic presentation, a hand goes up in the back row. The laziest student in the class raises the predictable question: "Will we be tested on this?" The implication is clear. If the material is not going to be on a test, then the student is not going to bother to learn it.

The apostle John wants his readers to know something for certain: they are going to be tested

on the subject of love. God has already shown them His love; now He expects them to show this same kind of undeserved, unearned love to one another.

"The royal law according to the Scripture" is "Thou shalt love thy neighbor as thyself" (James 2:8). Love is the defining mark of Jesus' followers. It is the first fruit of the Spirit (see Galatians 5:22); it is the crowning virtue to be added to a Christian's life (see 2 Peter 1:7). Love holds all the other virtues together; it is "the bond of perfectness" (see Colossians 3:14). Even when measured against faith and hope, the greatest of the three is love (see 1 Corinthians 13:13). The *King James Version* often uses the word *charity* for *love*.

B. Lesson Background

John wrote this epistle against a background of false teachers who came to be known as *gnostics*. Among other things, gnostics taught that it did not really matter if a person had morality or love—as long as he or she had "secret knowledge." To combat this false teaching, John emphasized the interconnection of right belief, right actions, and right love. To put it another way, it is the right involvement of head, hands, and heart. The child of God must believe the truth, obey the commands, and love the brethren.

Of these three areas, John's clear favorite is the emphasis on love (although they cannot really be separated). In last week's lesson John equated the life of love with walking in the light. Today he will examine God's love, the world's lack of love, and the saints' love that meets every test.

I. Majesty of Love
(1 John 3:1, 2)

Pure, unselfish love is a beautiful thing. The ultimate example of love is the love of God himself, which He showed when He invited unworthy people back into fellowship. John calls his readers to contemplate what kind of love this is and to imagine what the outcome of this love will be.

A. Our Present (v. 1)

1. Behold, what manner of love the Father hath bestowed upon us, that we should be called the sons of God: therefore the world knoweth us not, because it knew him not.

Look! What a wonder! Consider *what manner of love* God has offered! With these thoughts John calls his readers to ponder the degree of love it took for God to adopt us as His children. How can God love us when we have been sinful and unworthy? It is through Christ that God has forgiven us and welcomed us into His family. If we will only think about it, we will realize that it is not the having of merit or knowing secrets that will take us to Heaven. Rather, it is the love and grace of God.

The family of God must take note, however, that *the world* does not understand or approve of us. The fallen, unregenerate world refuses to know God, so it is only to be expected that the world will not look favorably on God's people. In spite of this, it is an eternal privilege for believers to be called *sons of God.* "But as many as received him, to them gave he power to become the sons of God, even to them that believe on his name" (John 1:12). [See question #1, page 248.]

B. Our Future (v. 2)

2. Beloved, now are we the sons of God, and it doth not yet appear what we shall be: but we know that, when he shall appear, we shall be like him; for we shall see him as he is.

As *the sons of God,* Christians have a glorious future. We are heirs of a Father who owns the whole universe. We as God's children will be changed (see 1 Corinthians 15:51-54), with bodies transformed into something far more glorious (see Philippians 3:21).

What we eventually *shall be* has not yet been disclosed fully. Even so, we do know this: when Jesus *shall appear* at His second coming, *we shall see him as he is.* At that time *we shall be like him,* with glorious bodies made eternal and incorruptible. Just as God made our bodies in the beginning and pronounced everything "very good," by His same power our bodies will be made even better.

God's immense love was poured out on people who deserved just the opposite. He invites us to come out of our rebellion to live in a heavenly home. The cost to God to issue this invitation was the life of His Son. When we consider the degree of love it took to do that, is God's command that we love one another so burdensome? The other person has not earned our love. But neither have we earned God's love.

How to Say It

COLOSSIANS. Kuh-*losh*-unz.
CORINTHIANS. Ko-*rin*-thee-unz (*th* as in *thin*).
GALATIANS. Guh-*lay*-shunz.
HEBREWS. *Hee*-brews.
PHILIPPIANS. Fih-*lip*-ee-unz.

WHAT LOVE CAN DO

George and Janet had been married for several years but were unable to start the family they so badly wanted. At last they were able to adopt a baby. But this baby had suffered from parental neglect. The little girl was a tragic sight to behold. Her skin was covered with lesions; her frail body bore the signs of abuse.

George and Janet came to visit their minister and his wife to show them the baby. The new parents proudly unwrapped the blankets and thrust the baby into the arms of the minister's wife with the words, "Isn't she beautiful?" The truth was that she *wasn't* beautiful physically; she showed the evidence of the former abuse. It was all the minister and his wife could do to feign an appreciation for a beauty they did not see. They could only state their joy that the three were now a family.

A few months later the family returned for another visit. This time there was no doubt: the baby was indeed beautiful! Tender care had transformed the infant from an object of neglect and abuse into a symbol of what happens when love does its wonderful work. God has brought us into His family, even though the spiritual abuse we suffer is self-inflicted. We cannot imagine how great the difference can be when we let His transforming love work its power on us!

—C. R. B.

II. Message of Love
(1 John 3:11-15)

God shows us the triumph of love at its best, but the fallen world shows us the failure to love at its worst. From a negative example we can learn what it is to reject the message of love.

A. Don't Be Like Cain (vv. 11, 12)

11. For this is the message that ye heard from the beginning, that we should love one another.

It was God's intention *from the beginning* that we should *love one another.* But what beginning is John talking about? Even before the church was established, Jesus proclaimed that "By this shall all men know that ye are my disciples, if ye have love one to another" (John 13:35). But John may intend the phrase *from the beginning* to go back even further, as the next verse shows.

12. Not as Cain, who was of that wicked one, and slew his brother. And wherefore slew he him? Because his own works were evil, and his brother's righteous.

Satan, the *wicked one,* tempted Eve and Adam to eat the forbidden fruit. More sin followed, bringing hatred and murder into the lives of their sons. When Cain's offering was rejected and Abel's was accepted, sin was at the door (Genesis 4:7). Refusing to listen to God's counsel, Cain allowed jealousy to overrule love. So he *slew his brother* out in the fields.

Cain was furious because his own offering from his garden did not win the approval of God while Abel's offerings from his flock did. Abel had made his offering "by faith" (see Hebrews 11:4). The same is not said of Cain's offering. Cain's *own works were evil*, but the works of his brother were *righteous* (compare Matthew 23:35). "The way of Cain" (Jude 11) is detestable. [See question #2, page 248.]

THE OPPOSITE OF LOVE

Graham Greene wrote the novel *The Quiet American* in 1956. The novel is set in about 1952, when France was fighting a war to hold on to its colonial power in Southeast Asia. In the novel, Thomas Fowler is a British journalist living with his mistress in Saigon. Alden Pyle, "the quiet American," disrupts Fowler's degenerate, opium-smoking, life at ease when he develops a romantic interest in Fowler's mistress. Using political ideology as his rationalization, Fowler conspires to have Pyle murdered.

The book and the movies that followed in 1958 and 2002 were subject to speculation about the author's political motivations. Regardless of the political spin, the story echoes the problem of allowing passion and self-interest to cause a person to hate and even murder.

It's a story as old as the one John reminds us of: Cain's attitude toward his brother and the murder that resulted. It is a topic that has timeless relevance. The ugliness of a lack of love in our hearts can cause us to gossip, condemn, backbite, or even do things much worse!   —C. R. B.

B. Don't Be Surprised (v. 13)

13. Marvel not, my brethren, if the world hate you.

Hatred is nothing new; it has existed in every generation. Therefore, John's readers should not *marvel* that this hatred is now directed against them. This is particularly true in light of what Jesus said to His disciples in the upper room: "If the world hate you, ye know that it hated me before it hated you" (John 15:18).

C. Don't Fail This Test (vv. 14, 15)

14. We know that we have passed from death unto life, because we love the brethren. He that loveth not his brother abideth in death.

The hatred of Cain is an old story, and the hatred of the world is probably not surprising. But what about hatred within the family of God? It is inconceivable! If a believer doesn't love *his brother* it signifies that such a person either has never come all the way into *life* or has gone back and now abides *in death*.

15. Whosoever hateth his brother is a murderer: and ye know that no murderer hath eternal life abiding in him.

To put it more bluntly, anyone who claims to be within the community of God yet hates a fellow believer *is a murderer*. Jesus said something similar in the Sermon on the Mount. The Law of Moses said "Thou shalt not kill," but Jesus added that "whosoever is angry with his brother without a cause" is in danger of the same judgment (see Matthew 5:21, 22). John shows the chilling twofold reality of this. First, the person who hates his brother is a murderer. Second, no murderer has *eternal life abiding in him*. Hatred and murder are in the same moral category.

III. Measures of Love (1 John 3:16-24)

Cain and the fallen world failed the test of love. But God's children can pass this test. In the following verses John outlines measures or tests of love. John presents this in a positive way, as if he expects his readers to live up to them. The theme is one of obedience.

A. Practical Test (vv. 16-18)

16. Hereby perceive we the love of God, because he laid down his life for us: and we ought to lay down our lives for the brethren.

The first measure of love is a practical test. *The love of God* is a love that we can *perceive* in action. When God loved the world, He sent Heaven's greatest gift. Jesus came and *laid down His life for us*—unrepentant enemies of God (see John 3:16; Romans 5:8, 10; Colossians 1:21, 22). Love like God's love could give nothing less. God's children should resemble their Father in this kind of love. We should be willing to do just about anything for our *brethren* (see John 15:12, 13).

17. But whoso hath this world's good, and seeth his brother have need, and shutteth up his bowels of compassion from him, how dwelleth the love of God in him?

Sometimes a person claims to be a loving member of the church, but that person's actions (or lack of actions) show otherwise. He or she may have plenty of *this world's good*, the material assets with which to help. But when a fellow Christian is in *need,* the person who is well off does not care.

In the vivid language of the *King James Version,* such a person *shutteth up his bowels of compassion.* In ancient times the stomach and intestines are thought to be the seat of emotion. To close these off means to have no pity or tender feeling toward a person in need. *How dwelleth the love of God* in such a person? [See question #3, page 248.]

18. My little children, let us not love in word, neither in tongue; but in deed and in truth.

Therefore, love must be put into action. Addressing his readers endearingly as *little children,* the aged apostle speaks as a loving father (compare 2 John 1). He urges his readers not to love merely *in word* or *in tongue,* paying mere lip service to the Lord's command (compare Matthew 7:21; James 1:22-25; 2:14-17). God wants His children to put their love to work *in deed and in truth.*

The earliest church in Jerusalem was a good example of this. In that community of love, no one said that any of "the things which he possessed was his own; but they had all things common" (Acts 4:32).

B. Inward Conviction (vv. 19, 20)

19. And hereby we know that we are of the truth, and shall assure our hearts before him.

The words *and hereby* link this verse to what has just been said. It is by our actions that *we know that we are of the truth.* If the Christian's loving actions are genuine and substantive, that is positive evidence of a right relationship to God. Knowing truly that we love produces confidence within our hearts, even to the extent that it will *assure our hearts* that we can stand before God at judgment. This is blessed assurance at its best!

20. For if our heart condemn us, God is greater than our heart, and knoweth all things.

But what if *our heart* should happen to *condemn us*? What if a tender conscience, manipulated by the devil, fills us with misgivings and doubts? The good news is that God himself is the final court of appeal; the devil cannot go over His head! We can rest assured that God, who knows *all things,* is well aware that we love Him and we are sincerely trying to love His children the best we can. [See question #4, page 248.]

C. End Result (vv. 21-24)

21. Beloved, if our heart condemn us not, then have we confidence toward God.

Visual for
Lesson 2

Point to this visual as you ask, "How do we recognize needs that God expects us to meet?"

Now John leads his *beloved* readers beyond the possible self-doubt of verse 20. *If our heart condemn us not*—and there is no reason that it should do so—then we can enjoy *confidence toward God.* Having this kind of confidence in the presence of our creator is not unreachable, especially when we remember that it is Jesus himself who makes it possible (Hebrews 4:14-16).

22. And whatsoever we ask, we receive of him, because we keep his commandments, and do those things that are pleasing in his sight.

John's focus on hands, head, and heart—in whatever sequence—is repeated frequently throughout his epistle. Moving from verses 20, 21 to verse 22 takes us from heart back to hands. When we keep God's *commandments,* that is, *do those things that are pleasing in His sight,* we are promised that we will receive whatever *we ask.*

Our loving Father will not withhold His blessings from His children. This presupposes, of course, that we ask in a spirit of love and that we ask for things that are according to His will. "And this is the confidence that we have in him, that, if we ask any thing according to his will, he heareth us" (1 John 5:14). Asking for blessings also presupposes that we ask with right motives. "Ye ask, and receive not, because ye ask amiss, that ye may consume it upon your lusts" (James 4:3).

23. And this is his commandment, That we should believe on the name of his Son Jesus Christ, and love one another, as he gave us commandment.

Now John moves us from hands to head in declaring what we must *believe.* Jesus was asked on one occasion, "What shall we do, that we might work the works of God?" He answered in these words: "This is the work of God, that ye believe on him whom he hath sent" (John 6:28, 29). Similarly, John says that God's *commandment* is simply this: *that we should believe on the name of his Son Jesus Christ.*

Added to this is the further commandment to *love one another* (compare Matthew 22:36-40). The right belief plus the right love fulfills God's demands. [See question #5, page 248.]

24. And he that keepeth his commandments dwelleth in him, and he in him. And hereby we know that he abideth in us, by the Spirit which he hath given us.

When God's child is obeying, believing, and loving as John has directed, then he or she is keeping God's *commandments* and dwelling in God. More than this, God is also dwelling in him or her. This closely parallels a promise of Jesus: "If a man love me, he will keep my words: and my Father will love him and we will come unto him, and make our abode with him" (John 14:23).

This divine presence in the life of the believer is identified in this verse as *the Spirit which He hath given us.* The abiding Spirit confirms to us that God is with us and in us (see Acts 2:33, 38; Romans 5:5; 8:14-16).

Conclusion

A. Love: The Final Exam

Love is a verb, not just a noun. It is an action, not just an emotion. We know that faith without works is dead (James 2:17). We could also say that love without works is dead. When John writes about love, he writes about *doing* more

than *feeling.* The command to love one another is a call to action.

God's "final exam" for His people on Judgment Day will not count how many church services were attended or how many verses were memorized. What He is interested in most of all is how our belief expresses itself in love. If we fail the test of love, we can never make up for it with any "extra credit" we may think we can gain from a flurry of religious activities.

B. Love: The Commencement

The context of 1 John suggests many ways that love can be put to work. We can show our love for God by committing ourselves to His Son and clinging to the truth of His Word. If we truly love God, we will not dishonor His Son by lazy discipleship (Hebrews 6:12). If we truly love God, we will not allow false teachings against His Word to stand (1 Timothy 6:3-5). Love and light must walk hand in hand.

We also show our love for God by loving His children. God wants us to combine our love for Him with our love for one another. This kind of shared love is what characterizes living in God's community—the church. Our love for one another is to be genuine and practical. Mere lip service cannot feed the hungry or clothe the naked. Real love is always ready to reach out.

Finally, we can show our love for God and His church by "talking up" our eagerness to go to Heaven. It is not a cop-out on this world to be eager to go to the next. When Jesus returns and we are suddenly, gloriously changed, we will live forever in fellowship with God, Jesus, and all our fellow saints. If we really treasure the reward of Heaven, we will want to bring the lost into the community of the saved. Inviting someone to join us on the road to Heaven is the ultimate expression of loving one another.

C. Prayer

Our Father, we cannot thank You enough for the love that has allowed us to be called Your children! Your people have rejected You time and time again over the course of many centuries. Yet You were working through it all to bring Your plan to fruition: the redemption of humans from the quagmire of self-inflicted sin.

Forgive us for sometimes treating Your great love so casually. Help us to honor Your love by reflecting it toward one another. In the name of Jesus, amen.

D. Thought to Remember

Love must act.

Home Daily Bible Readings

Monday, Mar. 5—Love Is Eternal (1 Corinthians 13)
Tuesday, Mar. 6—Jesus Commands Us to Love (John 13:31-35)
Wednesday, Mar. 7—A Widow's Gift of Love (Mark 12:38-44)
Thursday, Mar. 8—God Loves Us (1 John 3:1-5)
Friday, Mar. 9—Avoid the Wrong (1 John 3:6-10)
Saturday, Mar. 10—Evidence of New Life (1 John 3:11-15)
Sunday, Mar. 11—Love as Christ Loves (1 John 3:16-24)

Learning by Doing

This page contains an alternative lesson plan emphasizing learning activities.
Classes desiring such student involvement will find these suggestions helpful.

Learning Goals

After participating in this lesson, each student will be able to:

1. Recite 1 John 3:16 from memory.

2. Compare and contrast John 3:16 with 1 John 3:16.

3. Commit to imitating Christ's love by sharing one possession with a Christian brother or sister in need.

Into the Lesson

If you have access to a college bookstore, buy copies of the small "blue books" that schools typically use for written exams (they cost about ten cents apiece). Otherwise, prepare copies of a sheet with 20 numbered entries, an *A, B, C, D, E* by each number, and the word *TEST* prominently displayed at the top. Hand a copy to each student as he or she arrives. Also provide pens and pencils. Say nothing about your intentions.

As class begins say, "Please write your name at the top of the test sheet I have given you. While you are at it, also indicate at the top whether you will get a *pass* or a *fail.*" Give time for the grumbles and remarks and then say, "There is only one question on this test, and it is not multiple choice. It is a simple *yes* or *no.* Ready for the question? Here it is: 'Do you love as Jesus loves?'"

Discuss how this concept and this question relate to this lesson on "The Test of Love."

Into the Word

Make arrangement in advance for a musically talented member of your congregation to lead the class in singing "Behold, What Manner of Love" by Patricia Van Tine (© 1978 by Maranatha! Music). This song is based on 1 John 3:1. This song will set the tone for today's study: the true test of love in us is how closely we resemble the love God has shown to us in Christ.

Display the lesson writer's outline: I. Majesty of Love (1 John 3:1, 2), II. Message of Love (1 John 3:11-15), III. Measures of Love (1 John 3:16-24). Include in your display two columns conspicuously headed *FAIL* and *PASS.*

Lead a brief discussion of verses 1, 2. Then divide your class into two groups. Say, "Group #1, I want you to suggest a list of attitudes and deeds guaranteed to get the test taker a failing grade, based on verses 11-15 in today's text. Group #2, I want you to suggest a list of attitudes and deeds guaranteed to get the test taker a passing grade, based on verses 16-24 of today's text."

Allow time to examine the verses, then call for answers. Expect answers such as, "A person who hates fails" (v. 15); "Self-sacrifice for the good of others gets a passing grade" (v. 16); "One who cannot tolerate the success of others fails" (v. 12); and "Compassionate generosity passes" (v. 17). Write the two lists as answers are suggested.

Next, say "1 John 3:16 is an important verse, closely related to John 3:16. Let's dig into what 1 John 3:16 means." Then distribute four index cards that you have prepared in advance with the following phrases: *Card #1*—"How do we perceive the love of God?" *Card #2*—"Because He laid down His life for us"; *Card #3*—"So?" *Card #4*—"We ought to lay down our lives for the brethren!"

Give the four cards to individuals randomly chosen and not seated next to one another. Direct them to stand, say their phrases as quickly as possible, in order, and then hand their cards to another. Repeat the procedure five or six times. This will help class members fix this verse in their minds. Finish by reading 1 John 3:16 to the class.

Into Life

Say, "First John 3:17 describes what God did for us: saw us in need (sinners headed to Hell), felt compassion, and acted to meet our needs (sending Jesus as the pure and holy sacrifice to atone for and cover our sins). To be a true child of God, we must see, feel, and act in the same manner."

Give each student a small piece of paper. Indicate that you want each person to write on that paper the name and circumstances of someone in need. Suggest that it could be a young person needing help for a missions trip, a neighbor who has been victimized by fire or other disaster, or a senior saint struggling just to make ends meet.

Collect the papers and put them in a container. Place the container by the classroom exit. Suggest that your students take slips (without looking) as they leave and do their best to meet anonymously the needs identified.

Let's Talk It Over

*The questions on this page are designed to promote discussion of the lesson
by the class and to encourage application of the lesson Scriptures. The answers
provided are only discussion starters. Let your class talk it over from there.*

**1. What are some of the reasons the world
regards the church with suspicion? How should
we respond?**

Generally speaking, the world does not know
us because it does not know Jesus. It is natural
for people to question, or even hate and fear,
what they do not understand. When churches
meet in secret in some countries, they are suspected of plotting against the government. When
they attempt to win converts from another religion, religious leaders feel threatened; they may
put pressure on the state to declare proselytizing
a crime. Even in America, when Christians oppose legislation they consider unethical, they are
often accused of "shoving the Bible down the
throats" of those who disagree.

Our response is (at least) twofold. First, we ensure that our own conduct is always above reproach. Second, we view non-Christians as
potential converts to Christ.

**2. Many of us would disavow any connection
with Cain and dismiss him as "an extreme
case." Why is this a mistake? What can you
learn from the story of Cain that can help you in
your daily life?**

Remember that, "All Scripture . . . is profitable
for doctrine, for reproof, for correction, for instruction in righteousness" (2 Timothy 3:16). The
account of Cain is no exception. This account reminds us that all sin has a history. Cain had a
record of evil action before he murdered his
brother. This suggests the need to work continually to keep our thoughts and deeds acceptable to
God. Cain was warned by God before he became
a murderer, and the Lord provides warnings for
all of us. Sometimes the warning comes through
Scripture, sometimes through a faithful friend,
sometimes from a caring parent.

**3. You see a shabbily dressed man on a street
corner asking for money. His cardboard sign
says, "Homeless veteran. Hungry. What would
Jesus do?" How do you respond in a way that
demonstrates Christ's love?**

When a person is born again, he or she passes
from death into life. Such a person receives a
new nature in which loving is natural. So im-

pressed was the apostle John with this fact that
he was shocked at the idea of a Christian who
did not love a brother or sister. Even though John
was referring to help for fellow Christians, the
chance to help non-Christians with practical assistance is a great blessing! Some have called this
kind of benevolence *pre-evangelism* since it can
open a person's heart to the gospel.

For the homeless person in this case, dropping
money into his cup is probably not the best approach. Such a gift may be used for alcohol, etc.
You could instead keep some small boxes of
raisins on hand for on-the-spot assistance with
food. If your church has a benevolence program
in place, you can give the person a card telling
him where to go to get this help.

**4. How do you counsel a fellow Christian
who feels condemned by his or her own heart?
How will your counsel be flexible from person
to person?**

First, listen and don't talk too much! As you
do, you can help the person examine himself or
herself to uncover any personal sin. You may
discover that there is no specific sin causing the
guilt, but that the person is feeling guilty because
of unrealistic personal expectations (perfectionism). Help the healing by affirming the person's
decision to come to you. The devil loves it when
people keep personal anguish a secret.

**5. Love is probably written and sung about
more than any other emotion or action! In what
ways will your actions this week demonstrate
how the Christian concept of *love* differs from
what the world calls *love*?**

If we listen carefully to those shallow pop songs
about love, we discover a pattern: love is a "feeling" that finds its roots in "what you do for me."
Worldly love is often little more than a reciprocal
agreement of "you satisfy my needs and I'll satisfy
yours." When this self-centered system breaks
down, people end up in divorce courts or worse.

Christian love, on the other hand, is sacrificial. It puts aside its own preferences and conveniences in order to focus on Christ's desires. It is
from this foundation that Christian love serves
others (see 1 Corinthians 13).

The Source of Love

DEVOTIONAL READING: John 21:15-19.

BACKGROUND SCRIPTURE: 1 John 4:7-21.

PRINTED TEXT: 1 John 4:7-21.

1 John 4:7-21

7 Beloved, let us love one another: for love is of God; and every one that loveth is born of God, and knoweth God.

8 He that loveth not, knoweth not God; for God is love.

9 In this was manifested the love of God toward us, because that God sent his only begotten Son into the world, that we might live through him.

10 Herein is love, not that we loved God, but that he loved us, and sent his Son to be the propitiation for our sins.

11 Beloved, if God so loved us, we ought also to love one another.

12 No man hath seen God at any time. If we love one another, God dwelleth in us, and his love is perfected in us.

13 Hereby know we that we dwell in him, and he in us, because he hath given us of his Spirit.

14 And we have seen and do testify that the Father sent the Son to be the Saviour of the world.

15 Whosoever shall confess that Jesus is the Son of God, God dwelleth in him, and he in God.

16 And we have known and believed the love that God hath to us. God is love; and he that dwelleth in love dwelleth in God, and God in him.

17 Herein is our love made perfect, that we may have boldness in the day of judgment: because as he is, so are we in this world.

18 There is no fear in love; but perfect love casteth out fear: because fear hath torment. He that feareth is not made perfect in love.

19 We love him, because he first loved us.

20 If a man say, I love God, and hateth his brother, he is a liar: for he that loveth not his brother whom he hath seen, how can he love God whom he hath not seen?

21 And this commandment have we from him, That he who loveth God love his brother also.

GOLDEN TEXT: We love him, because he first loved us.—1 John 4:19.

Our Community Now and in God's Future
Unit 1: Known by Our Love
(Lessons 1-4)

Lesson Aims

After participating in this lesson, each student will be able to:

1. List the actions that God's love took on our behalf.

2. Explain the concept of *propitiation*, including how this doctrine alleviates fear in the life of the believer.

3. Write a prayer that asks God to help him or her replace fear with trust in His love.

Lesson Outline

INTRODUCTION
  A. Searching for the Source
  B. Lesson Background
 I. EXAMPLE OF LOVE (1 John 4:7-12)
  A. Our Pattern (vv. 7, 8)
  B. Our Salvation (vv. 9, 10)
  C. Our Challenge (vv. 11, 12)
    Stealing Jesus
 II. PROOF OF LOVE (1 John 4:13-16a)
  A. Spirit Was Given (v. 13)
  B. Son Was Sent (v. 14)
  C. Confession Is Made (vv. 15, 16a)
III. RESULTS OF LOVE (1 John 4:16b-18)
  A. Living in God (v. 16b)
  B. Bold at Judgment (v. 17)
  C. Freedom from Fear (v. 18)
IV. GRAND SUMMARY OF LOVE (1 John 4:19-21)
  A. God Was First (v. 19)
  B. God Commands Us (vv. 20, 21)
    Clean Hands and Loving Hearts
CONCLUSION
  A. Source of Love
  B. Channels of Love
  C. Prayer
  D. Thought to Remember

Introduction

A. Searching for the Source

Hernando de Soto was the first European to explore the Mississippi River. Despite all his courageous efforts, however, he only got as far up the river as modern-day Memphis, Tennessee. Little did he know that he was less than a third of the way up that mighty river! He died in 1542 of a fever, and his body was buried in the river that was too big for him to trace. David Livingstone was a Christian missionary and explorer of the Nile River in Africa. His final, most famous, journey was a search for that long river's source. When he died in 1873, he still had not found the elusive headwaters for which he was searching.

Sometimes searching for the source of a mighty river has been just too difficult. But what of the great river of love that flows in the community of God throughout the world and throughout history? What is its ultimate source? What inspired this love? The apostle John makes it clear in this lesson that the source of love is God. Love is part of His central nature; love flows from His heart. Whenever we act in love, we are reproducing what we learned first from Him.

B. Lesson Background

The apostle John is in some ways an unlikely person to be writing about love. He did not show much love when he and his brother wanted to call down fire from Heaven on a village in Samaria (Luke 9:54). He did not show much love when he and his brother tried to secure preferred seats of honor alongside Jesus (Mark 10:35-37). But while John did not show love very well in the beginning, he certainly received it—as "the disciple whom Jesus loved" (see John 21:20). John learned firsthand that we love because He first loved us. In the end John came to be known as *the apostle of love*.

Previously, we saw John demonstrate that love for fellow Christians is a test that reveals whether a person is really walking in the light. Now John goes further: love is also the test that reveals if a person actually is born of God. Since God is the ultimate source and embodiment of love, anyone who is genuinely born of God will reflect His characteristics. A person without love is a person who is not God's child. We will see John establish that such a person does not even know God.

I. Example of Love
(1 John 4:7-12)

A. Our Pattern (vv. 7, 8)

7. Beloved, let us love one another: for love is of God; and every one that loveth is born of God, and knoweth God.

John addresses his readers as people who are *beloved* in his eyes (see also 1 John 3:2, 21; 4:1, 11). John's urging that they *love one another* is a repeat of 1 John 3:11, 23. He is quick to supply a threefold reason. First, *love is of God;* that is, God is the source of this selfless emotion. Second, those who love show that they are *born of God;* they as genuine children resemble their Father in a vital way. Third, those who love show that they know God; they follow God's love as their pattern. [See question #1, page 256.]

8. He that loveth not, knoweth not God; for God is love.

John said previously that the one who lacks love walks in the darkness and abides in death (see 1 John 2:11; 3:14). If someone does not have love, John now asserts, he or she does not even know God. Since the very nature of God *is love,* the person unacquainted with love is unacquainted with God.

This is the same truth that Paul wrote to the Corinthians. Even if a person speaks in tongues, delivers prophecies, and exercises mountain-moving faith, it all means nothing without love (see 1 Corinthians 13:1-3). Love is the most excellent way because it is God's way. [See question #2, page 256.]

B. Our Salvation (vv. 9, 10)

9. In this was manifested the love of God toward us, because that God sent his only begotten Son into the world, that we might live through him.

God's love is not just an empty emotion. It is a mighty passion that impelled Him to bring salvation to those created in His image. It was *manifested,* or shown, in the way *God sent his only begotten Son* to take on human flesh and to die on the cross. This will forever be the world's greatest example of love (see John 15:13). God sent—and Jesus came—so *we might live through Him.* Exactly how Jesus' death can save us is the subject of the next verse.

10. Herein is love, not that we loved God, but that he loved us, and sent his Son to be the propitiation for our sins.

How to Say It

BOANERGES. *Bo*-uh-*nur*-geez (strong accent on *nur*).

CORINTHIANS. Ko-*rin*-thee-unz (*th* as in *thin*).

GALATIANS. Guh-*lay*-shunz.

HERNANDO DE SOTO. Er-*nan*-do da *So*-tow.

PROPITIATION. pro-*pih*-she-*ay*-shun (strong accent on *ay*).

SAMARIA. Suh-*mare*-ee-uh.

ZACCHEUS. Zack-*key*-us.

God is the source, the fountainhead, of love. It is *not that we loved God,* as if we had taken the first steps to make salvation possible. Rather, it is *that He loved us,* even when we were sinful and unworthy (see Romans 5:8). Love begins with God.

When God sent His only begotten Son into the world, He sent Him *to be the propitiation for our sins.* That word *propitiation* is vital for understanding how God forgives sin. God provided Jesus to be the sacrifice for sin. When Jesus gave His life, God accepted Jesus' suffering as payment for sin's penalty. This payment turned God's wrath away from us—God was propitiated. We could never have turned away God's wrath on our own (see also Romans 3:25; 1 John 2:2).

God does not just ignore our sins and pretend that they do not exist. His own holiness and justice do not allow this. Holiness and justice require than sin be punished. Yet in His great love for us, God took the necessary steps to deal with our sins. He sent Jesus, who was both infinite God and sinless man, to give His one great life in our place.

C. Our Challenge (vv. 11, 12)

11. Beloved, if God so loved us, we ought also to love one another.

The theme of love is repeated often in this epistle. God, the source of love, has *so loved us* that He gave Jesus for our salvation (John 3:16). Since we have been saved by this love, we ought to be ready to *love one another.* In view of what God has done for us in love, nothing less is acceptable (see also Matthew 18:33). [See question #3, page 256.]

STEALING JESUS

A few years ago a church in midtown Manhattan (New York City) was burglarized. It was a fairly predictable theft: an offering box and its contents were stolen. Three weeks later a more unusual theft took place: a four-foot plaster figure of Jesus, weighing 200 pounds, was stolen. Stranger yet was the fact that the statue was part of a crucifix, and the cross itself was left behind!

The church custodian commented, "They just decided, 'We're going to leave the cross and take Jesus.'" Think about the implications of that for a moment. Lots of people today like the idea of Jesus as an example of love. They even like the idea (theoretically, at least) of being a person who loves like Jesus. But, as John tells us, God showed His love for us by sending Jesus to be a propitiation for our sins.

If we're going to "take Jesus" as the model for our lives, then we're going to have to "take the cross" as a model as well. "If any man will come after me, let him deny himself, and take up his cross daily, and follow me" (Luke 9:23). Is this the model of love and service that directs your life?   —C. R. B.

12. No man hath seen God at any time. If we love one another, God dwelleth in us, and his love is perfected in us.

Adam heard the sound of God, Abraham heard the voice of God, and Moses stood on holy ground at the burning bush, but *no man* has ever seen God. Moses was even told that no man could see God's face and live. So on the mountain Moses was covered in the cleft of a rock when the presence of God passed by (see Exodus 33:20-23). Some were allowed to see various kinds of manifestations of God (Exodus 24:11). Yet the New Testament reaffirms that *no man hath seen God at any time,* both here and in John 1:18.

Even though we cannot see God, we can still have God's presence dwelling *in us.* God's very nature is love, so it is natural for Him to live in us if we have *love* for *one another.* This does not mean that we somehow "become" God—creator and creature are still distinct. Even so, we are able to reflect His love for each other. In this way His love *is perfected.* It reaches completion and fulfills its intended purpose.

II. Proof of Love
(1 John 4:13-16a)

A. Spirit Was Given (v. 13)

13. Hereby know we that we dwell in him, and he in us, because he hath given us of his Spirit.

Our knowledge *that we dwell in* God is not based on some mystic, mysterious experience. It is based on the fact that God has *given us of His Spirit* (Romans 8:9; 1 John 3:24). We know that we have the Spirit because God—who cannot lie (Hebrews 6:18)—has given us His firm promise (see Acts 2:38). Thus God's promise of the Spirit and our practice of love join together as proof that we are in Him and He is in us. Love is the first and greatest fruit that His Spirit produces in us (see Galatians 5:22).

B. Son Was Sent (v. 14)

14. And we have seen and do testify that the Father sent the Son to be the Saviour of the world.

When John says *we have seen and do testify,* he reemphasizes the truth of the opening verses of his epistle (see 1 John 1:1-3). He and the other apostles could testify because they knew firsthand that *the Father sent the Son* into the world. They had seen with their own eyes, heard with their own ears, and touched with their own hands the one sent *to be the Saviour of the world.* Jesus did not come just to teach, lead, and befriend—He came to rescue (John 3:17).

C. Confession Is Made (vv. 15, 16a)

15. Whosoever shall confess that Jesus is the Son of God, God dwelleth in him, and he in God.

God sent His Son to save humanity, and God has the right to set certain conditions for salvation. Specifically in this verse, God expects us to *confess that Jesus is the Son of God.* Jesus promised that if a person confesses Him before others, He will confess that person before the Father in Heaven (see Matthew 10:32).

Mere confession is not the entirety of the plan of salvation, of course. As John makes clear, loving action serves as proof that we belong to the truth (1 John 3:17-19). But confessing Jesus is a necessary condition.

16a. And we have known and believed the love that God hath to us.

John knows for certain that Jesus really came (v. 14), and because of this he also knows of the great love that God has for us. He and his readers have *known* this love and have *believed* it; they have put their trust and confidence in it.

III. Results of Love
(1 John 4:16b-18)

A. Living in God (v. 16b)

16b. God is love; and he that dwelleth in love dwelleth in God, and God in him.

God does not just "have" love, *God is love.* He embodies everything that is good about love and encompasses the entire range of love's expressions. God and love are so much identified with each other that to dwell *in love* is to dwell *in* God. Furthermore, when we dwell in this love, God himself also dwells in us.

B. Bold at Judgment (v. 17)

17. Herein is our love made perfect, that we may have boldness in the day of judgment: because as he is, so are we in this world.

When *our love* is *made perfect* or complete, the final result is that we will have *boldness* on Judgment Day. We will have nothing to fear when that day comes.

We will have this *boldness* before God because *as he* (Jesus) *is, so are we.* Just as Jesus is pure

(1 John 3:3) and righteous (1 John 3:7), by His blood we can also stand before the Father pure and righteous. Jesus abides in the Father (see John 17:21-26), and so can we. Although we live *in this world,* we can have confidence when our love has been made perfect through Christ. Even now, we can approach God's throne of grace in bold confidence (Hebrews 4:16).

C. Freedom from Fear (v. 18)

18. There is no fear in love; but perfect love casteth out fear: because fear hath torment. He that feareth is not made perfect in love.

Christians can have boldness in judgment, as the previous verse says, because there is *no fear in love.* This fear is not the kind of healthy awe that a person should have for God. Rather, the kind of fear in view is a paralyzing dread and terror. Love and that kind of fear simply have nothing to do with one another; they cannot coexist.

Therefore, love that is *perfect* or full grown will cast out fear. While fear paralyzes and has *torment,* genuine love confirms our salvation. The person who still lives in unhealthy fear of God is not yet mature. He or she is not yet *made perfect in love.*

IV. Grand Summary of Love (1 John 4:19-21)

A. God Was First (v. 19)

19. We love him, because he first loved us.

Now John sums up his grand teaching about love. God is the source of love. When *we love him,* it is only *because he first loved us.* Without God's initiative we would not have known genuine love; neither would we have known how to love. When we abide in God and His Spirit abides in us, divine love becomes a natural part of our lives.

We return to God the love He has shown us. At the same time, we pass on this kind of love on to our brothers and sisters in Christ.

B. God Commands Us (vv. 20, 21)

20. If a man say, I love God, and hateth his brother, he is a liar: for he that loveth not his brother whom he hath seen, how can he love God whom he hath not seen?

The practical test of love, as seen before, is that God's child must love the *brother* or sister in Christ. A person who says *I love God* but then hates a fellow Christian *is a liar.* There is a logical reason for this fact: we have been made in the image of God. Therefore, this brother or sister whom we should love bears a certain resem-

Visual for Lesson 3. *Point to this visual as you ask, "In what ways does our love for the heavenly Father drive out fear?"*

blance to God. We have *seen* this brother or sister, even though we have *not seen* God. If we cannot find anything attractive or lovable in our fellow Christian, then we will not find anything lovable in God. If we fail this practical test of love, our claims to love God are simply lies. [See question #4, page 256.]

CLEAN HANDS AND LOVING HEARTS

Millions of people suffer from food poisoning every year. A primary cause is the failure of food-service workers to wash their hands properly. Now "big brother" is here, this time for good! Ultraviolet light scanners developed to detect germs on meat in processing plants are being adapted to show whether we have washed our hands thoroughly. Imagine a parent saying to a child, "Johnny, put your hands under the scanner and let me see if you got them clean"!

Do we need to be reminded that what we can't see *can* hurt us? Yet there are ways to see the unseen, and ultraviolet scanning for germs is only one of them.

A much more important means of "scanning" for both the good and bad of life is found in today's text. John acknowledges that we can't see God. Even so, if we love God then our lives will be a confession of His existence. The Spirit living in us will help us to make this confession. The confession is more than just spoken words. It is also the testimony of our deeds each day of our lives as we exhibit godly character. We reflect God's love in the way we treat others. —C. R. B.

21. And this commandment have we from him, That he who loveth God love his brother also.

John concludes as he began: we must love one another. To love God and to love one's neighbor are inseparable. "On these two commandments hang all the law and the prophets" (Matthew 22:40).

Moreover, this is our Lord's *commandment*. It is not optional or negotiable. By observing this love in us, all people will be able to tell that we are Christ's disciples (see John 13:34, 35). [See question #5, page 256.]

Conclusion

A. Source of Love

Love does not just happen. It is a virtue of the highest order, created and demonstrated by God himself. If the world were merely an evolutionary accident and the law of the jungle demanded the survival only of the fittest, then there would be no room for self-sacrificing love. But just as God is the creator of the universe and the source of all life, so is He the source of true love.

Without our knowledge of God, searching for the source of love would be an impossible task. We would be like the early explorers who were hopelessly ill-equipped when they searched for the sources of great rivers. If we had only scientific observation to guide us, we would ultimately give up on love and agree with the law of the jungle: the strong devour the weak. If we had only the history of human empires as our guide, we might conclude that there is no real love to be found. It is only in the spiritual realm that we are able to trace love back to its divine source.

But unlike the source of a river, which becomes smaller and smaller as it is traced, the divine source of love becomes greater and greater as we draw nearer. Also unlike the source of a river, the source of love does not need to be increased by tributaries. God's love can never be diminished or depleted; it flows from God's infinite heart.

B. Channels of Love

When we recognize that God is the source of love, we next realize that He intends for us to be the channels of that love. We become the passageways through which the mighty river of God's love flows. This love will bless countless lives, but only as we allow it to flow through us.

God continues to be the dynamic source of the love that flows through us, but He has given us the responsibility to direct that love in ways that would please Him. For instance, we know that we should direct generous love toward the widows and the orphans (James 1:27). We should be channels of divine love toward those who are helpless, homeless, and hungry (Matthew 25:34-36).

To be like Jesus means being ready to extend God's love to children (Matthew 19:14), to social outcasts such as Zaccheus (Luke 19:1-10), and to people of other races such as the woman of Samaria (John 4:9). To be like Jesus means surprising people with the range of our love. To be like Jesus means also surprising people with the intensity of our love. Jesus' love for John marked that apostle for life. He never forgot that he was "the disciple whom Jesus loved."

Finally, we must remember that love begins at home. If we cannot love those who are nearby, we deceive ourselves to think that we can love those who are far away. It is in our own family and in our own church that love builds its foundation (Galatians 6:10; 1 Timothy 5:8). It bears repeating: How can we love the God whom we have not seen, if we do not love our brothers and sisters whom we have seen?

C. Prayer

Dear Father, thank You for showing us Your love even when we were sinners and enemies of Your kingdom. Help us to learn to love You better and to be channels of Your love to all our brothers and sisters. Thank You that there has never been a greater love than the love Jesus showed when He died in our place. Forgive us when we fail to love but let us learn from our failures. In the name of Jesus, the ultimate example of love, we pray, amen.

D. Thought to Remember

Focus on the source of love.

Home Daily Bible Readings

Monday, Mar. 12—Be Reconciled to God (Romans 5:1-11)

Tuesday, Mar. 13—Be Reconciled to One Another (Matthew 5:21-26)

Wednesday, Mar. 14—Care for One Another (John 21:15-19)

Thursday, Mar. 15—Investing in Eternity (1 Timothy 6:11-19)

Friday, Mar. 16—Knowing God Through Love (1 John 4:7-12)

Saturday, Mar. 17—God Is Love (1 John 4:13-17)

Sunday, Mar. 18—Love Brothers and Sisters (1 John 4:18-21)

Learning by Doing

This page contains an alternative lesson plan emphasizing learning activities.
Classes desiring such student involvement will find these suggestions helpful.

Learning Goals

After participating in this lesson, each student will be able to:

1. List the actions that God's love took on our behalf.

2. Explain the concept of *propitiation*, including how this doctrine alleviates fear in the life of the believer.

3. Write a prayer that asks God to help him or her replace fear with trust in His love.

Into the Lesson

Prepare 15 sheets of copier paper, each displaying one of the following letters or blanks. Put a number at the bottom of each sheet, as indicated.

S	O	N		O	F		T	H	U	N	D	E	R	!
1	10	8	15	11	6	3	14	7	13	9	2	4	12	5

On the back of these sheets of paper, print the following letters and blanks, inverted:

A P O S T L E   O F   L O V E

Affix the 15 sheets to the wall in a single line, with *Son of Thunder!* and numerals showing. Put masking tape along the top of the sheets so each can be lifted to reveal the letter on the back.

Refer to Luke 9:54, in which John and his brother suggested fire from Heaven to punish a village that refused hospitality to Jesus and His apostles. Refer to Mark 3:17, where Jesus gave these two brothers the nickname *Boanerges,* or "sons of thunder."

Lift the flaps in numerical sequence, taping the revealed letters upward. As letters are revealed, encourage students to identify at any time what the phrase on the reverse is. Once the puzzle is solved, ask, "How is it that one called a *son of thunder* became a messenger of love?" Be sure to mention that John, after being in Jesus' company for several years, felt so loved he would call himself the one "whom Jesus loved" (John 21:20).

Into the Word

Write all the following statements, drawn from the commentary, on slips of paper. Do not include either the sequence numbers or the verse numbers on the slips.

1. Genuine children resemble their Father in an important way (v. 7); 2. One who does not have love does not know God (v. 8); 3. God's love is a mighty passion (v. 9); 4. Jesus was the "propitiation" that restored God's favor (v. 10); 5. God took steps to deal with our sins (v. 10); 6. Nothing less than love for others is acceptable (v. 11); 7. We can have God's presence dwelling in us (v. 12); 8. We have the Spirit because God gave Him to us (v. 13); 9. The apostles knew firsthand that the Father sent the Son into the world (v. 14).

10. Jesus did not come just to teach—He came to rescue (v. 14); 11. If a person confesses Jesus, then God dwells in him or her (v. 15); 12. God embodies what is good about love (v. 16); 13. When we dwell in His love, God dwells in us (v. 16); 14. We have confidence to speak boldly in the presence of God (v. 17); 15. If our love is mature, then we can stand pure and righteous before the Father (v. 17); 16. Fear and love cannot coexist (v. 18); 17. The person who lives in unhealthy fear of God is not spiritually mature (v. 18); 18. Without God's initiative we would have not known genuine love (v. 19); 19. The practical test of love is that God's child must love others (v. 20).

20. If we cannot find anything lovable in another, then we will not find anything lovable in God (v. 20); 21. The two great commands of Jesus (love God; love one's neighbor) are inseparable (v. 21); 22. God is the source of love (v. 10).

Put the slips in a box and pass it around. Say, "Take one of the slips." (If your class is small, suggest each take two or three.) Then say, "Now turn to 1 John 4:7-21 and find the verse that best relates to the truth on your slip(s)."

As you read through the text, ask students to identify verses they have matched. Because of the emphatic repetition in John's style, students may associate statements with verses other than the ones identified above.

Into Life

Write the letters LFOEVAER on the board. Ask, "What's wrong here?" Once someone notices that the word *fear* is embedded in the word *love,* the answer will be obvious: 1 John 4:18! Ask the class to share in a prayer for God to make our love so perfect or whole that fear will disappear. Suggest that such a prayer is a worthy idea for the beginning of each new day. (A similar activity is in the student book.)

Let's Talk It Over

The questions on this page are designed to promote discussion of the lesson by the class and to encourage application of the lesson Scriptures. The answers provided are only discussion starters. Let your class talk it over from there.

1. Describe someone you know who excels at loving people. How will you follow his or her example?

Many of your students have relatives or friends whom they have witnessed loving unselfishly, even sacrificially. Sacrifice can be of both time and resources.

Some examples of lavish love can elicit warnings from well-meaning people, including Christians. For instance, those who care for foster children are warned that involvement in such a ministry will bring pain when the children are returned to their families. Those who minister to the urban poor are often warned of the dangers they face when they go out on the streets at night. Yet anytime we choose to put love into action on this fallen planet, we make ourselves vulnerable to pain. Jesus didn't let pain prevent Him from loving us. We follow His example!

2. Some may view church attendance and Bible study as good measures of a person's walk with God. What problems can that type of thinking create? Why is love a better test to discern authentic Christianity?

Church attendance and Bible study are spiritually nutritious activities. But thinking of those activities as standards by which to measure godliness confuses *means* with *ends*. When we grow spiritually through church attendance and Bible study (the means), the result should be to love as Jesus loves (the ends).

Loving others shows that a person understands the heart of the law . . . and the heart of God! "And thou shalt love the Lord thy God with all thy heart, and with all thy soul, and with all thy mind, and with all thy strength: this is the first commandment. And the second is like, namely this, Thou shalt love thy neighbor as thyself. There is none other commandment greater than these" (Mark 12:30, 31).

3. In what ways might you face (or have you faced) ridicule or social rebuff while expressing love as Jesus expects? How do you (or did you) react to such attacks?

People are generally tolerant, often approving, of small, convenient acts of charity. Writing a

check to a good cause or participating in a fundraiser for a cancer victim fit this idea. But should you offer to give up a vacation to go on a mission trip, you may find yourself met with looks of disbelief by family, coworkers, or even other Christians.

To love as Jesus loves means going beyond what is easy for others to understand. Loving an "outsider" can risk someone's "insider" social status. Yet connecting a person with a body of believers may provide a tangible way to experience the truth of God's love for eternity. What could be more important than that?

4. Verse 20 implies that "seeing" a person makes it easier to love him or her. Why is this true? What are some things that we can "see" in others that can help us love them?

We may think that seeing people is part of the problem rather than part of the solution, since some folks are about as huggable as a cactus. It helps to remember that love is more than an emotion—it's doing what's best for the one you love.

To do something that benefits another, we first have to see (or somehow be aware of) his or her needs. God himself doesn't need anything, but we can love Him by loving and serving the people He created. Jesus tells us that when we do loving things for others, He credits it to us as if we had done the deeds for Him personally (Matthew 25).

5. What was a time when it was difficult for you to love someone? What helped you to express loving action despite the difficulty?

It's not so hard to think of loving people if the people we are considering are our children, spouses, or close friends. But what about someone who is malicious? Can you act in a loving manner toward someone who is hateful to you? Jesus tells us that that is the mark of the children of God (Matthew 5:44-46). This type of love doesn't seem to be part of our human nature. It's possible, though, when we are filled up with God's love. Remembering that God loved us when we were unlovable can help us behave kindly toward those who are hard to love (Romans 5:8).

The Way to Love

DEVOTIONAL READING: **John 17:1-5.**

BACKGROUND SCRIPTURE: **1 John 5:1-12.**

PRINTED TEXT: **1 John 5:1-12.**

1 John 5:1-12

1 Whosoever believeth that Jesus is the Christ is born of God: and every one that loveth him that begat loveth him also that is begotten of him.

2 By this we know that we love the children of God, when we love God, and keep his commandments.

3 For this is the love of God, that we keep his commandments: and his commandments are not grievous.

4 For whatsoever is born of God overcometh the world: and this is the victory that overcometh the world, even our faith.

5 Who is he that overcometh the world, but he that believeth that Jesus is the Son of God?

6 This is he that came by water and blood, even Jesus Christ; not by water only, but by water and blood. And it is the Spirit that beareth witness, because the Spirit is truth.

7 For there are three that bear record in heaven, the Father, the Word, and the Holy Ghost: and these three are one.

8 And there are three that bear witness in earth, the spirit, and the water, and the blood: and these three agree in one.

9 If we receive the witness of men, the witness of God is greater: for this is the witness of God which he hath testified of his Son.

10 He that believeth on the Son of God hath the witness in himself: he that believeth not God hath made him a liar; because he believeth not the record that God gave of his Son.

11 And this is the record, that God hath given to us eternal life, and this life is in his Son.

12 He that hath the Son hath life; and he that hath not the Son of God hath not life.

GOLDEN TEXT: This is the record, that God hath given to us eternal life, and this life is in his Son.—1 John 5:11.

Our Community Now and in God's Future
Unit 1: Known by Our Love
(Lessons 1-4)

Lesson Aims

After participating in this lesson, each student will be able to:

1. Describe how love for God and love for others are related.

2. Give an example of how to show love for God and an example of how to show love for others.

3. Apply the two examples from lesson aim #2 in the week ahead.

Lesson Outline

INTRODUCTION
   A. The Way to Do It
   B. Lesson Background
 I. FOUNDATION OF GOD'S WAY (1 John 5:1-3)
   A. Faith and Love (v. 1)
   B. Love and Obedience (v. 2, 3)
     A Lost Score
 II. VICTORY OF GOD'S WAY (1 John 5:4, 5)
   A. An Overcoming Faith (v. 4)
   B. An Overcoming Savior (v. 5)
III. BASIS OF GOD'S WAY (1 John 5:6-10)
   A God's Witness to His Son (vv. 6-8)
   B. Our Response to His Son (vv. 9, 10)
IV. OUTCOME OF GOD'S WAY (1 John 5:11, 12)
   A. Ironclad Promise (v. 11)
   B. Ironclad Certainty (v. 12)
     Insurance or Assurance?
CONCLUSION
   A. Following the Way
   B. Prayer
   C. Thought to Remember

Introduction

A. The Way to Do It

"No, here's the way it's done." The father, a skilled craftsman, is teaching his son the right way to do a job. If the youngster is too stubborn to listen, he will be slow to make progress. But if he has confidence in his father's ability and pays careful attention, he will learn his lesson well.

God has tried to teach His children the way of love. At the beginning He provided generously for Adam and Eve. He even allowed them to exercise their freewill choice. Time and again in the history of Israel, He lovingly rescued His people from oppression. When they sinned, He corrected them. When they repented, He forgave them. When they prayed, He opened the windows of Heaven to pour out blessings on them. Most of all, He sent Jesus to die on the cross for them. No greater example of love has ever been known.

We have been shown the way to love. Will we be stubborn, or will we learn?

B. Lesson Background

This is the final chapter in John's first epistle, written near the end of the first century AD. The special problem of those who originally received the letter was a heresy called *gnosticism*, or at least an early version of it. This teaching placed little value on faith, love, or obedience. Instead, the gnostics said that secret knowledge was the way to Heaven. (The word *gnosis* means "knowledge" and is found within the English words *diagnosis* and *prognosis*.) As John brings his teaching to a conclusion, he puts all his emphasis on being in the right relationship with Jesus Christ. This includes having love for all God's children.

I. Foundation of God's Way (1 John 5:1-3)

Living God's way involves every part of our lives. As John has indicated previously in this epistle, this includes head, heart, and hands. With our minds we believe the truth; with our hearts we love God and His children; with our hands we do all that righteousness requires. The three areas are inseparably linked as God's design for us to live.

A. Faith and Love (v. 1)

1. Whosoever believeth that Jesus is the Christ is born of God: and every one that loveth him that begat loveth him also that is begotten of him.

John begins this section with a focus on faith. Anyone who is truly *born of God* will have faith that *Jesus is the Christ*. This faith is not merely an idle opinion about Jesus' identity. It involves sincere confession and commitment to Christ (see 1 John 4:2, 15). It is a trusting, ongoing faith (as shown by John's use of the present tense in the word *believeth*). True faith is vital for a lifelong relationship with Jesus.

Everyone who has the proper faith relationship with Jesus, within the biblical plan of salvation, is a child of God. John's immediate point here is that every such child should be an object of our love. After all, if we love *him that begat,* then we should also love anyone *that is begotten of him.* We remember what John has just said at the end of the previous chapter: "If a man say, I love God, and hateth his brother, he is a liar" (1 John 4:20).

B. Love and Obedience (vv. 2, 3)

2. By this we know that we love the children of God, when we love God, and keep his commandments.

John has said that if we love God we will love His children. And how do we know that *we love the children of God*? It is *when we love God* and when we *keep his commandments.* These ideas are reciprocal and complementary as they show both sides of an important truth: we honor God by loving His children; we love His children by loving God as we honor His commands.

The previous verse showed the inseparable connection between faith and love; this verse shows the connection between love and obedience. All three elements must be present to produce the Christian life.

3. For this is the love of God, that we keep his commandments: and his commandments are not grievous.

John sees nothing surprising in linking our *love* for God with our obedience to Him. It may truly be said that *the love of God* necessarily, even automatically, requires *that we keep his commandments.* This is the inherent truth of a right relationship with God. How could anyone think he or she loves God while ignoring or disobeying what God says? "If ye love me, keep my commandments" (John 14:15). [See question #1, page 264.]

John is quick to add that God's *commandments are not grievous.* Jesus himself said "my yoke is easy, and my burden is light" (Matthew 11:30). God's commandments have never been burdensome. This is borne out by Deuteronomy

---

How to Say It

COLOSSIANS. Kuh-*losh*-unz.
DEUTERONOMY. Due-ter-*ahn*-uh-me.
DOCETISM. Doe-*set*-iz-um.
EPHESIANS. Ee-*fee*-zhunz.
GALATIANS. Guh-*lay*-shunz.
GNOSTICISM. *nahss*-tih-*sizz*-um (strong accent on *nahss*).
GNOSTICS. *nahss*-ticks.
PHARISEES. *Fair*-ih-seez.

30:11, 14: "this commandment which I command thee this day . . . is very nigh unto thee, in thy mouth, and in thy heart, that thou mayest do it." It was the Pharisees who made obedience to God a burden. "They bind heavy burdens and grievous to be borne, and lay them on men's shoulders; but they themselves will not move them with one of their fingers" (Matthew 23:4). [See question #2, page 264.]

None of this should be construed that John is talking about salvation by works or salvation by law keeping. It comes down to motive. We obey God as a loving response to the salvation that is already ours. We do not obey in order to earn a salvation that God dangles in front of us.

A LOST SCORE

A Japanese music professor announced recently that part of a Bach wedding cantata had been found in the estate of a Japanese classical pianist. J. S. Bach (1685–1750) was a pioneer in classical music, and this cantata had been lost for 80 years. Musicologists believe "Wedding Cantata BWV 216" was copied by students Bach was teaching at the time he composed the piece.

The score contains only the alto and soprano portions of the cantata, and experts believe they were used in the original (and only) performance of the piece played at a wedding in 1728. Historians who specialize in Bach's music hope the lost score can help them reconstruct the full composition so it can be performed as it may have sounded originally.

We can draw a parallel in that the apostle John and the other New Testament writers have given us the "score" for a piece of divinely inspired "music." Believing in Jesus as God's Son, loving God, loving God's children, and keeping God's commandments are the recurrent themes in this composition. If we "lose" the score by neglecting to read it and meditate upon it, then we should not be surprised to find the themes missing from our lives. Those who truly love God will honor Him as a composer who deserves to have His "music" played the way He wrote it.

—C. R. B.

II. Victory of God's Way
(1 John 5:4, 5)

God's way—the way of love—is the right way. It is the way that brings victory. All the children of God will share in this victory because they have put their faith in Jesus, God's Son. Their faith is an overcoming faith, the kind of faith that trusts in an overcoming Savior.

A. An Overcoming Faith (v. 4)

4. For whatsoever is born of God overcometh the world: and this is the victory that overcometh the world, even our faith.

In context the phrase *the world* refers to the powers of evil that take their stand against God. This is what Jesus had in mind when He said, "I have overcome the world" (John 16:33).

By being *born of God*, we share in His *victory* over the world. As members of God's family, we have an overcoming *faith*. It is a faith that separates us from the fallen world and gives us victory over the temptations of the world. We live in this world in a physical sense, but we are not of the world in an ethical sense (see John 15:19; 17:6, 14-19). Even though we struggle on a daily basis to live godly lives, we can take heart in the fact that the victory has already been won. The outcome is already decided. We are on the winning side. [See question #3, page 264.]

B. An Overcoming Savior (v. 5)

5. Who is he that overcometh the world, but he that believeth that Jesus is the Son of God?

When we overcome *the world*, it is not because we ourselves are so powerful. The true source of our victory is the object of our faith: *Jesus the Son of God*. Through our faith in Him, we are assured that we overcome this world. "Thanks be to God, which giveth us the victory through our Lord Jesus Christ" (1 Corinthians 15:57).

Because we have put our trust and confidence in Jesus, "we are more than conquerors through him that loved us" (Romans 8:37). Even though we wrestle against the forces of spiritual darkness and wickedness (Ephesians 6:12), our final victory is secured. By faith we have chosen to join the victors.

III. Basis of God's Way
(1 John 5:6-10)

Christianity stands or falls with Jesus. Either He is who He claimed to be, or He is an imposter. If He is not God's Son, His moral teachings are groundless. If He has not risen from the dead, all Christian faith is in vain. Everything hinges on Jesus. For this reason John emphasizes the testimony to Jesus' identity as God's Son as well as the response to Jesus that we must make.

A. God's Witness to His Son (vv. 6-8)

6. This is he that came by water and blood, even Jesus Christ; not by water only, but by water and blood. And it is the Spirit that beareth witness, because the Spirit is truth.

Our Lesson Background notes the gnostic heresy that was beginning to emerge in the late first century AD. One element of gnosticism was another false teaching called *Docetism*. This word means "to seem" or "to appear to be." This false teaching denies that Jesus came in the flesh, only that Jesus *seemed* to appear in the flesh. John is very concerned about this kind of error: "Many deceivers are entered into the world, who confess not that Jesus Christ is come in the flesh. This is a deceiver and an antichrist" (2 John 7).

To counter such falsehood, John presents his own, firsthand evidence. From the beginning of Jesus' ministry to its very end, Jesus displayed His deity in bodily form (compare Colossians 2:9). Jesus *came by water* into His public ministry when He was baptized by John the Baptist in the Jordan River. Jesus came *by blood* to the conclusion of His ministry when He was nailed to the cross. The real humanity of Jesus is clearly shown by water and blood. [See question #4, page 264.]

In addition to the testimony of water and blood, the *Spirit* of God also bears *witness* to Jesus. When Jesus was baptized, the Holy Spirit descended from Heaven in the form of a dove and rested upon Jesus. It should not be overlooked that the Father testified about Jesus at that baptism (see Matthew 3:16, 17). The Father bore witness again by raising Jesus from the dead (Galatians 1:1), and the Spirit bore witness through the four Gospels. The veracity of the Gospels is assured by the Spirit who inspired them, for *the Spirit is truth*.

7, 8. For there are three that bear record in heaven, the Father, the Word, and the Holy Ghost: and these three are one. And there are three that bear witness in earth, the spirit, and the water, and the blood: and these three agree in one.

The earliest manuscripts of 1 John do not contain the words *in heaven, the Father, the Word, and the Holy Ghost: and these three are one. And there are three that bear witness in earth*. Even so, the phrasing is certainly true. The fact of the triune God—Father, Son, and Holy Spirit—is confirmed in several New Testament texts (see Matthew 28:19; Mark 1:10-12; 2 Corinthians 13:14; Ephesians 3:14-19). Jesus said, "I and my Father are one" (John 10:30). Jesus also closely identified the Holy Spirit with himself and His Father (see John 14:23-26).

The record borne by *the spirit, and the water, and the blood* is powerful! These three witnesses fulfill the requirements for legal testimony as stated in Deuteronomy 17:6; 19:15. Jesus had important things to say about the role of the Spirit, who followed after and confirmed Jesus' earthly ministry (see John 14:26; 15:26). Blood has the same meaning here as in verse 6. The blood signified both payment for sin and the reality of Jesus' flesh. *These three* give unanimous testimony; they *agree* as *one* voice. Jesus is the Son of God who came down to earth in human form.

B. Our Response to His Son (vv. 9, 10)

9. If we receive the witness of men, the witness of God is greater: for this is the witness of God which he hath testified of his Son.

The idea of testimony or bearing *witness* is important to John's thought (see John 5:31-34, 37; 8:18). Most people routinely *receive the witness of men,* especially in court cases. How much more necessary is it to accept *the witness of God!*

The Father *testified* to the identity of *his Son* on several occasions. We have already mentioned the Father's testimony at Jesus' baptism. At the transfiguration, God said, "This is my beloved Son: hear him" (Mark 9:7). Most important of all, God raised Jesus from the dead and exalted Him (see Acts 2:32, 33).

10. He that believeth on the Son of God hath the witness in himself: he that believeth not God hath made him a liar; because he believeth not the record that God gave of his Son.

The response that God requires is that we must believe in *the Son of God.* We are to trust Him, rely on Him, and put all confidence in Him. The one who does this is said to have *the witness in himself.* The person who does this has accepted the Father's testimony and put it in his or her heart. On the other hand, if a person does not believe what God has said about Jesus, then he or she pronounces God to be *a liar.* Such a person hears *the record that God gave of His Son* but rejects it as false. Ultimately, these are the only two responses we can make to the message of God: believe it as true or reject it as false.

IV. Outcome of God's Way (1 John 5:11, 12)

God's way promises the right outcome. Those who walk the path of faith and love have the promise of eternal life. Those who do not walk this way, however, receive a stern warning: because they have not chosen God's way, they will not have life.

A. Ironclad Promise (v. 11)

11. And this is the record, that God hath given to us eternal life, and this life is in his Son.

God's *record* or testimony about *His Son* reaches a wonderful conclusion: God has *given* the gift of *eternal life.* We do not earn or deserve this reward; it is a gift. Eternal life is not just an unending quantity of life. It is something far better. It is a whole new quality of life. It is life that is in His Son.

This life begins as a person comes to know God. It begins when he or she experiences God firsthand and enters a saving relationship with Him (see Acts 2:38; John 17:3). This is the testimony—the promise—of God.

B. Ironclad Certainty (v. 12)

12. He that hath the Son hath life; and he that hath not the Son of God hath not life.

John does not want his readers to be confused in any way by the false teaching they are hearing. Thus this verse is almost a repeat of John 3:36. John's readers can know this fact for a certainty: *he that hath the Son hath life.*

The believer can count on receiving life as the gift from God. But whoever has *not the Son of God* in heart and life should be warned of this fact: he or she has *not life.* The certainty of reward or punishment on Judgment Day is determined by whether or not a person follows Jesus. [See question #5, page 264.]

INSURANCE OR ASSURANCE?

Each area of the world has its distinct threats of natural disaster. In the American West, one of those threats is wildfires. Some years are worse than others for these disasters. October 2003 witnessed an especially terrifying fire season in San Diego County, California. The wildfires raged on

Visual for Lesson 4

Point to this visual as you ask, "How will the truth of this passage influence the way you live?"

several fronts for many days, consuming 2,400 houses in the process. The largest of the fires burned over 273,000 acres—that's more than 425 square miles!

The most expensive home to burn was a 20,000 square-foot structure valued at $4,366,000. The house contained the owner's vast art and music collections plus a movie theater. It was all fully insured, but the owner—a self-made millionaire—didn't bother to insure the house he owned next door because, as he later said, it contained only 4,000 square feet and was worth only $1,500,000!

Most of us don't have the kind of resources that enable us to be that blasé about our earthly possessions. But whether rich or poor in this life, our ultimate hope must be for riches in the life to come. Here is where John's message carries its real significance. God has offered us eternal life through Christ, His Son. If we have the Son, we have life. If we don't have the Son, we don't have life eternal. In that case, we don't really have much worth talking about, no matter how much we possess.   —C. R. B.

Conclusion

A. Following the Way

Jesus is the way. He is God's way, the right way. In fact, He is the way, the truth, and the life. No one comes to the Father except through Him (see John 14:6). If Christianity is criticized for claiming to be the only true religion, it is only repeating the claims of its founder. It may not be politically correct these days to say there is only one way to Heaven, but that is what the church must say to be faithful to her Lord.

Home Daily Bible Readings

Victorious faith enables us to love as Jesus loved. A review of today's text shows us what this includes. Verses 1 and 2 say that we should love all God's family. When Jesus walked this earth, He extended His love to all who would respond to God's call. We follow Jesus in this way of love.

Verse 3 says that we should keep all God's commandments. Jesus became obedient to the point of death on a cross (see Philippians 2:8). Although He was a Son, He learned obedience by what He suffered and He became the author of eternal salvation to all who obey Him (see Hebrews 5:8, 9). We remember that following the way of love includes obeying God's commands.

Verses 4 and 5 say that we are to have faith to overcome all this world's opposition. When Jesus faced opposition, He put His trust in the Father. He faced the temptations in the desert, for instance, by relying on God's Word. He faced the prospect of death on the cross by turning to God in prayer in the garden. We can be more than conquerors through this kind of overcoming faith.

Verses 6 through 10 say that we are to believe all God's testimony. When Jesus quoted Scripture, He showed that He believed it to be true. He used Adam and Eve to establish what is right in marriage (see Matthew 19:4-6). He used Noah and the flood to teach about the second coming (see Matthew 24:37). He used Jonah to teach about His own resurrection (see Matthew 12:40). Jesus accepted these accounts as true. We should have the same view of God's Word as Jesus did: "Scripture cannot be broken" (John 10:35).

Verses 11 and 12 say that the person of faith will receive God's reward. When Jesus put His trust in God and did as His Father told Him, God raised Him from the dead. He was then highly exalted and given the name above every name (see Philippians 2:9-11).

Today Jesus sits at the right hand of the Father in Heaven. We should take God at His Word and never doubt His promises. Then we will have eternal life in His Son.

B. Prayer

Father, we thank You for sending Jesus to live on earth as a man and to purchase our salvation. We praise You for the gift of eternal life we have in His name. Help us to have the faith to love as Jesus loved and to overcome this world. In Jesus' name, amen.

C. Thought to Remember

The way of love is the way to life.

Learning by Doing

This page contains an alternative lesson plan emphasizing learning activities.
Classes desiring such student involvement will find these suggestions helpful.

Learning Goals

After participating in this lesson, each student will be able to:

1. Describe how love for God and love for others are related.

2. Give an example of how to show love for God and an example of how to show love for others.

3. Apply the two examples from learning goal #2 in the week ahead.

Into the Lesson

Display several facsimile traffic signs as class begins: STOP, YIELD, NO U-TURN, ONE WAY, or others. Simple hand-drawn and colored ones will be adequate. Ask the class to note their reactions when they see such signs.

Next, direct students to make a quick read of 1 John 5:1-12 and select the sign that best makes a visual for today's study. Allow students to justify their choices with brief explanations. Example: someone may choose *One Way*, because of the exclusive nature of Jesus being the only way to Heaven (v. 12).

Into the Word

Make copies of today's text, with a space after each verse. Distribute one copy to each student. Say, "By now we all have noticed John's style: emphatic repetition of ideas and phrases. I want you to look at today's text and find phrases of three or more words that appear more than once. Circle them and draw a connecting line between the matches."

If students need a start, point out that "born of God" occurs in verses 1 and 4. Others they may find include "believeth that Jesus is the" (vv. 1, 5); "keep his commandments" (vv. 2, 3); "overcometh the world" (vv. 4 [twice], 5); "by water and blood" (v. 6 [twice]); "the witness of God" (v. 9 [twice]); "he that believeth" (v. 10 [twice]); "of His Son" (vv. 9, 10); "the Son of God" (vv. 5, 10, 12).

Have students call out their findings; make a list on the board. When the list is complete, go back through and ask how each phrase is completed in the text and what the implications are.

Label this next activity "Ask John" (write those two words on the board). Tell the class that you want them to be John. You will ask "John" questions and you want "John" to answer with one of the verses from today's text. For example, if you ask, "John, many say they are 'born again.' What is a first step to being born of God?" "John" should answer, from verse 1, "Whosoever believeth that Jesus is the Christ."

Here are some questions, in random order. "John, sometimes witnesses give conflicting testimony. Isn't that true regarding Jesus' humanity and deity?" (v. 8). "John, what is the most obvious result of loving God the Father?" (v. 1b). "John, how will I know that I truly love God's children?" (v. 2). "John, isn't belief simply a matter for the head? Isn't it only intellectual?" (v. 10a). "John, this world we are in sometimes just overwhelms me . . . with temptation, sickness, death. Can I get out alive?" (v. 4). "John, what is the secret to being an overcomer?" (v. 5). "John, aren't you being a bit exclusive when you say 'life is in his Son'?" (v. 12). "John, I've heard some claim that Jesus could not be both God and man. How do you respond to that?" (v. 6a). "John, I know that more than one witness is required in most legal systems. Do we have that regarding Jesus?" (vv. 7, 8). "John, the Old Testament is full of rules and regulations. How would you characterize God's commandments?" (v. 3b). "John, I know I should tell people that Jesus is the Christ, God's Son, but some won't believe me. What do I do?" (v. 9). "John, do I have to obey the Scriptures in order to love God?" (v. 3a). "John, some reject God's testimony regarding Jesus. What's the bottom line in that circumstance?" (v. 10b).

Into Life

Divide your class in two by saying, "I want those whose age is an odd number to help with the first list I am going to request. I want those whose age is an even number to help with the second. OK, here are the questions for our lists: (1) What can a person do this week to show love for God? (2) What can a person do this week to show love for others?"

As ideas are given, write the two lists on the board. Alternate between the two. When lists are completed, recommend that each student pick one entry from each list that is not in his or her typical lifestyle and try to implement both into the coming week of life and service.

Let's Talk It Over

The questions on this page are designed to promote discussion of the lesson by the class and to encourage application of the lesson Scriptures. The answers provided are only discussion starters. Let your class talk it over from there.

1. Some claim to believe in God, yet do not exhibit a lifestyle that acknowledges God's commands. How do you share with someone of this mind-set what a relationship with God really involves? How do you prepare yourself for a "judge not" response?

Mere mental assertion is so easy! Yet our faith in Christ must be more than this. Scripture tells us that even the demons believe there is a God (James 2:19).

Perhaps you can approach the person with an illustration: someone claims to be an employee of a company, but he or she never does any work there and knows nothing of that company's product line. Is he or she really an employee of that company? Scripture tells us that true faith and love for God is evidenced and expressed through obedience (James 2:20-24). After Jesus said, "Judge not" He also said, "by their fruits ye shall know them" (Matthew 7:1, 20).

2. John says God's commandments are not grievous (burdensome). Without giving trite, prepackaged answers, what would you say to a believer who is struggling with obedience in some area?

What we say to one who struggles with obedience can depend on the nature of the disobedience: giving up profanity may require a different approach from giving up an adulterous affair. It can also depend on whether or not the person seeks us out for counsel or we seek the person out for godly confrontation.

Modeling holy lives ourselves is a prerequisite in any case. Presenting oneself as an imperfect fellow struggler is also important. At our new birth, the Holy Spirit grants us a new nature that empowers us to obey, yet we know that we still struggle with sin (Romans 7:7-25). But we are not in the struggle alone: we have our fellow believers. God's Spirit changes our hearts, motives, and desires to the degree we allow Him to do so.

3. The next time you face temptation, how will it help you to know that everyone who is born of God overcomes the world?

There's nothing more empowering and encouraging than hearing "you can do it," as these verses proclaim. Other Scriptures confirm our ability to triumph over sin. Since we know that God always offers us a way out (1 Corinthians 10:13), we know to look for that escape. Since we know that we are in a battle and that God has equipped us with tools to fight Satan's attacks (Ephesians 6:10-18), we know to prepare for and expect temptations (1 Peter 5:8).

4. John writes these verses to refute a heresy that claimed Jesus had not come to earth "in the flesh." What other false ideas do we deal with today? What makes some false ideas more serious than others?

There is much historical evidence that Jesus walked the earth. Today we are more likely to find people who would deny Jesus' claim to deity rather than His humanity. Many struggle with the idea of virginal conception, six-day creation, and other biblical doctrines that science cannot explain.

Sometimes the most dangerous false ideas are not those that "subtract" from who Jesus was but those that "add" elements to His identity that are not found in the Bible. For example, one false doctrine acknowledges Jesus to be the Son of God while adding the idea that Jesus was also a spirit brother of Satan.

5. How does today's text help you witness to someone who believes in God but feels that insisting on Jesus as the only way is too exclusive? How do cultural trends lure people into this trap?

Some nonbelievers agree that Jesus puts forth the highest standards for morality. They recognize Him as a great moral leader, yet Jesus claims to be God. Would a great moral leader tell lies? Either He is God, or His moral teachings are hypocrisies, or He suffered from delusions.

Believing in God in the abstract is easy; believing in the God who walked the earth and looked at people eyeball to eyeball is threatening! Yet God himself offered dramatic validation of Jesus' divinity (Mark 9:7; Luke 3:22). God offers us no middle ground regarding who Jesus is. God allows each of us to choose or reject Jesus. He doesn't offer another way into His favor (John 14:6).

Christ Is King

DEVOTIONAL READING: Psalm 118:21-28.

BACKGROUND SCRIPTURE: Revelation 1:1-8; Luke 19:28-40.

PRINTED TEXT: Revelation 1:8; Luke 19:28-38.

Revelation 1:8

8 I am Alpha and Omega, the beginning and the ending, saith the Lord, which is, and which was, and which is to come, the Almighty.

Luke 19:28-38

28 And when he had thus spoken, he went before, ascending up to Jerusalem.

29 And it came to pass, when he was come nigh to Bethphage and Bethany, at the mount called the mount of Olives, he sent two of his disciples,

30 Saying, Go ye into the village over against you; in the which at your entering ye shall find a colt tied, whereon yet never man sat: loose him, and bring him hither.

31 And if any man ask you, Why do ye loose him? thus shall ye say unto him, Because the Lord hath need of him.

32 And they that were sent went their way, and found even as he had said unto them.

33 And as they were loosing the colt, the owners thereof said unto them, Why loose ye the colt?

34 And they said, The Lord hath need of him.

35 And they brought him to Jesus: and they cast their garments upon the colt, and they set Jesus thereon.

36 And as he went, they spread their clothes in the way.

37 And when he was come nigh, even now at the descent of the mount of Olives, the whole multitude of the disciples began to rejoice and praise God with a loud voice for all the mighty works that they had seen;

38 Saying, Blessed be the King that cometh in the name of the Lord: peace in heaven, and glory in the highest.

GOLDEN TEXT: Blessed be the King that cometh in the name of the Lord: peace in heaven, and glory in the highest.—Luke 19:38.

Our Community Now and in God's Future
Unit 2: A New Community in Christ
(Lessons 5-9)

Lesson Aims

After participating in this lesson, each student will be able to:

1. Explain the significance of the Palm Sunday events.

2. Understand how Jesus is king past, present, and future.

3. Determine a specific way to recognize the kingship of Jesus in his or her life.

Lesson Outline

INTRODUCTION
 A. Palm Sunday as Triumphal Entry
 B. Lesson Background
 I. CHRIST AS SOURCE AND GOAL (Revelation 1:8)
 II. CHRIST AS LORD TO BE SERVED (Luke 19:28-34)
 A. Disciples Given a Mission (vv. 28-31)
 B. Disciples Serve Their Lord (vv. 32-34)
 III. CHRIST AS KING TO BE PRAISED (Luke 19:35-38)
 A. Preparing the Way of the King (vv. 35, 36)
 BLEEX
 B. Praising God (v. 37)
 C. Blessing the King (v. 38)
 No P. T. Barnum, No April Fool
CONCLUSION
 A. Jesus the King: Past, Present, and Future
 B. Prayer
 C. Thought to Remember

Introduction

This week's lesson is the first in a set that begins to focus on Jesus as He is found in the book of Revelation. This lesson and the next come during two important days in the church calendar: Palm Sunday and Resurrection Sunday (Easter). These two Sundays bracket a period in Jesus' life called *Passion Week*—His final week leading up to the crucifixion.

The events of Passion Week are always worth studying and pondering anew. Taken together, the rest of the lessons for this quarter will allow students to see Jesus as more than the main character in the events of Passion Week; He is also the reigning Lord of all creation. This is the glorious picture found in the book of Revelation.

A. Palm Sunday as Triumphal Entry

The title and words of the old spiritual "Ride on, King Jesus" recall the day when Jesus was received into Jerusalem as king. The welcome of Jesus into the holy city on the Sunday before His crucifixion has long been called *the triumphal entry*. This event is found in all four of the Gospels, each having some unique details. Although the Gospels do not make any reference to this event as a "triumph," it does bear some relationship to the ancient custom of welcoming a victorious king or general back to his home city.

The city of Rome had a tradition of staging triumphal processions. This parade would include the Roman legions, enemy prisoners, wagons loaded with booty, and the victorious general in a special chariot. Sometimes a new triumphal arch would be created. This custom was revived by the French emperor Napoleon Bonaparte, whose *Arc de Triomphe* in Paris was commissioned in 1806 for the glory of the French army.

The triumphal entry of Jesus was a way of recognizing Him as king. What did it mean for those present to acclaim Jesus as king, and what does that mean for us today? This week's lesson will examine some of the implications involved in recognizing Jesus as king in our lives.

B. Lesson Background

Jewish law specified three important pilgrimage festivals for which all able-bodied Israelite men were expected to appear at the temple (see Deuteronomy 16:16). They were Passover (very closely associated with the Feast of Unleavened Bread), Pentecost (or Feast of Weeks), and Tabernacles. Passover came at the middle of the Jewish month of Nisan. This was in the spring, in March or April.

Passover was more than just a religious holiday. Since it marked the liberation of the Jews from Egyptian bondage, it was seen as a remembrance of the birth of their nation. Thus, it had strong patriotic and nationalistic overtones. It was ironic, then, to celebrate a national day of freedom when all Jews knew that their nation had again been subjugated, this time by the Romans. This surely made it a bittersweet holiday! As observant and loyal Jews, Jesus and His disciples were expected to celebrate Passover, and they did so willingly.

In Luke 9:51 we see that Jesus "steadfastly set his face to go to Jerusalem." For the next 10 chapters of that Gospel, Jesus and the disciples were on the pilgrim's journey to the temple city for the spring celebration of Passover. This was not a quick trip, and they were in no hurry. Traveling south from Galilee they passed through Jericho, a small city just north of the Dead Sea. This was a common route for travelers to Jerusalem from the north, and Jesus' band was doubtlessly a small part of thousands making the journey.

While in Jericho, Jesus was confronted by a blind man who understood Jesus' true identity. The man called out to Jesus as the "Son of David" (essentially the same as saying Messiah) and begged to be healed. This healing took place in the presence of the crowd, and they praised God (Luke 18:35-43). In Jericho Jesus also had a dramatic encounter with a height-challenged tax collector named Zaccheus. Jesus used this occasion to clearly state what He was about: "For the Son of man is come to seek and to save that which was lost" (Luke 19:10).

When His business in Jericho was finished, Jesus and His followers began the ascent to Jerusalem. Although Jericho is only about 15 miles from Jerusalem, there is a change in altitude of some 3,300 feet. It was a hot, dusty climb, but we can imagine the growing excitement of the pilgrim throng as it approached the beloved Jerusalem. This is the setting for the primary passage of today's lesson, Luke 19:28-38.

I. Christ As Source and Goal
(Revelation 1:8)

A fitting opening to today's study comes from the first chapter of Revelation. Here the apostle John is being introduced to the key figures in his heavenly visions. This includes God the Father

---

How to Say It

ALPHA. *Al*-fa.
ARC DE TRIOMPHE. Ark du treh-*onf*.
BETHANY. *Beth*-uh-nee.
BETHPHAGE. *Beth*-fuh-gee.
GOLIATH. Go-*lye*-uth.
JERICHO. *Jair*-ih-co.
MACCABEES. *Mack*-uh-bees.
MARDI GRAS. *Mar*-dee Grah.
NAPOLEON BONAPARTE. Nuh-*pole*-yun Bonuh-*part*.
NAZARETH. *Naz*-uh-reth.
NISAN. *Nye*-san.
OMEGA. O-*may*-guh.
PENTECOST. *Pent*-ih-kost.
PHILISTINE. Fuh-*liss*-teen or *Fill*-us-teen.
ZACCHEUS. Zack-*key*-us.
ZECHARIAH. *Zek*-uh-*rye*-uh (strong accent on *rye*).

---

and seven Spirits (Revelation 1:4). Jesus is introduced and described extensively in 1:5-7. Dramatically, He speaks for the first time to identify himself in the verse before us.

8. I am Alpha and Omega, the beginning and the ending, saith the Lord, which is, and which was, and which is to come, the Almighty.

It is striking to see that Jesus does not use the descriptive terms John has employed for Him in Revelation 1:5-7. Instead, Jesus uses the terms reserved for God in 1:4: *which is, and which was, and which is to come.* Revelation is never afraid to describe the risen Jesus in terms that remind us of Old Testament descriptions of God.

There are three parts to Jesus' self-description in the verse before us. First, He is *Alpha and Omega.* These are the first and last letters of the Greek alphabet, akin to our *A* and *Z.* Jesus is thus *the beginning and the ending.* He is the source and the goal for all of creation. Second, Jesus' claim that He is *the one which is, and which was, and which is to come* is an affirmation of His eternality; He is not bound by the constraints of time (compare Exodus 3:14; John 8:58).

Third, the verse before us refers to Jesus as *Lord* and as *the Almighty.* Often the Old Testament writers referred to God as "God Almighty" or "the Lord Almighty" (see Genesis 17:1). An equivalent title in the Old Testament is "the Lord of hosts" (see Jeremiah 50:34). It means that He is the commander of all the hosts of Heaven, all the armies of angels, and that no power in Heaven or earth can stand against Him. In the Old Testament, nothing is more powerful than the Lord of hosts. In the book of Revelation, nothing is more powerful than the risen Lord Jesus. [See question #1, page 272.]

II. Christ As Lord to Be Served
(Luke 19:28-34)

Peter preached that Jesus "went about doing good, and healing all that were oppressed of the devil" (Acts 10:38). As we move into Luke 19, that period is nearly over. Jesus has come to Jerusalem for the most sobering and important part of the plan for human redemption. Jesus alone is aware of what is about to happen, but His disciples play their parts by making preparations for His entry into the holy city.

A. Disciples Given a Mission (vv. 28-31)

28. And when he had thus spoken, he went before, ascending up to Jerusalem.

Jesus and His disciples leave Jericho to make the long climb to *Jerusalem.* This is a couple of days before what we call Palm Sunday, for they do not travel on the Sabbath (Saturday), and the trip is difficult to finish in a single day.

We can imagine a large throng of pilgrims making this climb, singing some of the joyous Psalms of Ascent (Psalms 120–134). One they may sing is Psalm 122:1, 2: "I was glad when they said unto me, Let us go into the house of the Lord. Our feet shall stand within thy gates, O Jerusalem."

29. And it came to pass, when he was come nigh to Bethphage and Bethany, at the mount called the mount of Olives, he sent two of his disciples.

Approaching from the east, the band first comes to two small villages near Jerusalem. We do not know the precise location of *Bethphage* (meaning "house of figs"). But *Bethany* ("house of misery" or "house of dates") is at the foot of the *mount of Olives,* less than two miles from Jerusalem. Bethany is the home of Mary, Martha, and Lazarus (John 11:1). This seems to be Jesus' "headquarters" for the coming week (see Matthew 21:17). Jesus probably arrives in Bethany just before the Sabbath begins (John 12:1).

30, 31. Saying, Go ye into the village over against you; in the which at your entering ye shall find a colt tied, whereon yet never man sat: loose him, and bring him hither. And if any man ask you, Why do ye loose him? thus shall ye say unto him, Because the Lord hath need of him.

The *village* to which the two disciples are sent is Bethphage (see Matthew 21:1, 2). The two men are asked to do something very puzzling: fetch *a colt* belonging to someone else. If accused of being thieves, they are to answer that Jesus, *the Lord,* needs to use the animal.

This request shows us two parts of Jesus' plan. First, Jesus' simple instructions indicate His authority. To steal a colt is a serious, punishable offense. But that is not what Jesus is doing, and the men obey with confidence. Second, Jesus acts in order to fulfill prophecy. Matthew 21:4 makes it clear that what is about to happen is a fulfillment of Old Testament predictions about Jesus' entry into Jerusalem (see Isaiah 62:11; Zechariah 9:9).

The fact that this animal has never been ridden has a dual significance. First, it offers a sense of holiness for the occasion. This is an ordinary animal but special in that it has never been mounted by any other person. Unknowingly, the owners have been preparing for Jesus' royal ride for many months. Second, Jesus' ability to ride an unbroken donkey is a way of demonstrating His lordship over all of creation. He is the prince of peace, whom even the untamed animals obey.

B. Disciples Serve Their Lord (vv. 32-34)

32. And they that were sent went their way, and found even as he had said unto them.

We can imagine the surprise and wonder of the obedient disciples when they find everything exactly as Jesus had predicted. There is no way to explain this except to believe in the supernatural knowledge and authority of Jesus. [See question #2, page 272.]

33, 34. And as they were loosing the colt, the owners thereof said unto them, Why loose ye the colt? And they said, The Lord hath need of him.

The details of Jesus' prediction even extend to a confrontation with *the owners* of *the colt.* Jesus' foreknowledge has already covered this, so the disciples answer as He had advised them. They give no long rationale such as, "Jesus of Nazareth is in town for Passover and needs to borrow a donkey because He wants to ride it into Jerusalem." They merely assert *The Lord hath need of him.* In so answering, they demonstrate both their confident obedience and their submission to the lordship of Jesus the Messiah.

III. Christ as King to Be Praised (Luke 19:35-38)

Artists have attempted to illustrate what Jesus' triumphal entry may have looked like. Composers too have worked to bring the event alive musically. All of these efforts fall short of the joyous, even riotous celebration that accompanies Jesus as He enters the holy city. This is shown by the reaction of Jesus' jealous opponents: "Master, rebuke thy disciples" (Luke 19:39). Jesus responds that if He did this, "the stones would immediately cry out" (Luke 19:40). This indicates that the joy of this occasion is inspired by God himself. If God is behind such rejoicing, who are humans to stifle it?

A. Preparing the Way of the King (vv. 35, 36)

35, 36. And they brought him to Jesus: and they cast their garments upon the colt, and they set Jesus thereon. And as he went, they spread their clothes in the way.

The word *him* refers to the borrowed animal. The crowd quickly joins the excitement of the celebration, improvising the best parade possible. There is no royal saddle for the donkey, so the disciples throw their outer *garments* up on the beast. These are their best clothes, their big-city, high holy day celebration clothes. There is no red carpet or newly paved street, so those in the crowd toss their cloaks to cover the dirt and give an air of elegance to the procession. This shows the size of the crowd, which may be sufficient to have garments that cover the mile or so of this march. Matthew 21:8 says the crowd is "very great." [See question #3, page 272.]

We are reminded that King Jesus does not receive the trappings of human royalty in the Gospel of Luke. At Jesus' birth, He is not laid in a royal bed in a palace but in a manger in a stable (2:7). He does not send out His emissaries with troops and lavish transportation but on foot with no money (10:4). Even so, they preach the kingdom of God (10:9). Jesus taught that His ideal kingdom members are not the rich and powerful of the world but those as little children (18:16).

BLEEX

BLEEX—no, that's not the sound of something getting bleeped out of a TV program. It's an acronym for **B**erkeley **L**ower **E**xtremities **EX**-oskeleton. The University of California developed the device to help people carry heavy loads. For example, firefighters can use a BLEEX as they struggle up the stairs of a building while carrying heavy rescue equipment.

BLEEX is not a hypothetical science-fiction gadget we have seen in *Star Wars*–type movies. BLEEX is real. It is a set of strap-on metal legs and power unit. Sensors and a hydraulic system assist the normal motions of the human body. As a result, the 100-pound exoskeleton and a 70-pound load can feel as light as 5 pounds. Imagine the superman impression one could make while transported by a BLEEX!

Had Jesus used something like a BLEEX to enter Jerusalem, the media undoubtedly would have focused on the contraption rather than on Jesus. By riding a humble beast such as a donkey, the attention was appropriately focused on Jesus himself. Jesus' significance came from who He was, not from the technology He used. That's important to remember. People today are enthusiastic about technology, and we use technological innovations at times to further the cause of Christ. But to allow technology to overshadow the message and identity of the king would be a grave mistake.   —C. R. B.

B. Praising God (v. 37)

37. And when he was come nigh, even now at the descent of the mount of Olives, the whole multitude of the disciples began to rejoice and praise God with a loud voice for all the mighty works that they had seen.

Our age is obsessed by the cult of celebrity worship. Many long to know every detail of the

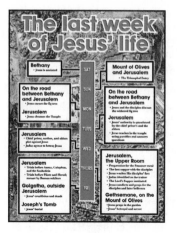

Visual for
Lesson 5

This chart will help your students see how the events of Jesus' final week all fit together.

lives of their favorite stars. We often witness the folly of assuming that famous people are wise and/or good examples. This verse shows us that the triumphal entry celebration is much more than celebrity glorification.

The crowd is not praising Jesus because He is famous. They *praise God* because in the ministry of Jesus they have seen the power of God displayed. This is the crowd that traveled with Jesus from Jericho, where He had dramatically healed a blind man just shortly before.

C. Blessing the King (v. 38)

38. Saying, Blessed be the King that cometh in the name of the Lord: peace in heaven, and glory in the highest.

Like the city of Rome, Jerusalem also knew of triumphal processions. The non-biblical passage 1 Maccabees 13:49-53 recounts a triumphal entry into the city with praise, palm branches, and music in 141 BC. Many centuries earlier, David returned to the city in triumph after slaying Goliath, the Philistine giant (1 Samuel 17:54; 18:6).

This type of victory procession is also reflected in Psalm 118. The psalm begins with a conversation between the king and his army as they approach Jerusalem, giving praise to God for the victory (vv. 1-18). In verse 19 they arrive at the gates of the temple and ask to be admitted. Once inside, they are filled with praise (v. 24). The celebration calls forth a blessing from the priest (v. 26). Then the king's sacrifice is accepted for the holy altar.

This mighty refrain is taken up by the crowds of Jewish pilgrims as Jesus enters the city: *Blessed be the King that cometh in the name of the Lord.* Although Jesus had won no military battles, they recognize and celebrate His kingship. [See question #4, page 272.]

Jesus' triumphal entry is characterized by more than a Mardi Gras–like party spirit, however. The crowd's spirit is one of worship. The acclamation is not at all inconsistent with that of the angels at Jesus' birth: "Glory to God in the highest, and on earth peace, good will toward men" (Luke 2:14). [See question #5, page 272.]

No P. T. BARNUM, No APRIL FOOL

Bridgeport, Connecticut's annual Barnum Festival is an upbeat civic event celebrating the life of P. T. Barnum (1810–1891). Barnum was the nineteenth-century circus king and was once the city's mayor. Barnum was called "The Prince of Humbug." He enjoyed playing hoaxes on people, all in the spirit of creative capitalism.

Barnum saw his sideshows as harmless ways of fooling people while giving them their money's worth in good, clean fun. His "Cardiff Giant," his "161-year-old nanny to George Washington," and his "Fejee Mermaid" are legendary. He even wrote a book entitled *Humbugs of the World* (see www.ptbarnum.org).

Jesus of Nazareth was no P. T. Barnum. There was no humbug, no hoax, no April fool in what Jesus offered the crowd that joined His entry into Jerusalem. He was not motivated by the idea of accumulating earthly possessions. Many had seen His miracles, heard His authoritative teaching, and witnessed His humility. Many people joined His procession that day; many probably deserted a few days later; some stuck with Him for the rest of their lives and into eternity. Will you follow Jesus today?   —C. R. B.

Home Daily Bible Readings

Monday, Mar. 26— Jesus Is the Cornerstone (1 Peter 2:4-10)

Tuesday, Mar. 27—Jesus, God's Son (Hebrews 3:1-6)

Wednesday, Mar. 28—Children Praise Jesus (Matthew 21:14-17)

Thursday, Mar. 29—Give Thanks (Psalm 118:21-28)

Friday, Mar. 30—The Lord Needs It (Luke 19:28-34)

Saturday, Mar. 31—Blessed Is the King (Luke 19:35-40)

Sunday, Apr. 1—Christ Will Return (Revelation 1:1-8)

Conclusion

A. Jesus the King: Past, Present, and Future

Several years ago, I was in a crowd that was addressed by Queen Elizabeth II, the reigning monarch of Great Britain. I was within a few dozen yards of the queen, and I saw and heard her clearly. She seemed to be a fine woman. The reality, though, is that her authority as queen is very limited. Our world no longer embraces the concept of hereditary monarchs who reign absolutely.

A central theme in the Bible is the kingship of Jesus. Jesus does not inherit a kingdom from an earthly father or win it through His accomplishments. His kingship is not bestowed upon Him by adoring citizens of the realm. He *is* king, has *always been* king, and will *always be* king. There will be challengers to His throne, but He will reign supreme (1 Corinthians 15:24, 25). Many rejected Him as king (see John 19:15), but in the end He will receive their acknowledgment (see Philippians 2:10, 11).

What are the personal implications of Jesus' kingship? Does He reign in your life? Consider the question this way: When you willingly disobey King Jesus, do you fear His wrath (see Revelation 6:16)? The New Testament teaches that those who reject the reign of the Lord will be crushed in "the winepress of the fierceness and wrath of Almighty God" (Revelation 19:15). Those who love Him, those who serve Him, will be those who obey Him. When Christ reigns in our lives, we can be free from the fear of God's mighty wrath (see 1 Thessalonians 1:10).

If you claim citizenship in the kingdom of God and of His Christ, is your allegiance absolute and consistent? Is your loyalty unwavering, even in the face of opposition? Are you able to let go of your own selfish desires to serve the King of kings without reservation? May God bless us as we each strive toward perfect and unreserved service, so that one day we will hear the words, "Well done, thou good and faithful servant: . . . enter thou into the joy of thy lord" (Matthew 25:21). [See question #6, page 272.]

B. Prayer

God in Heaven, we repeat the refrain: Blessed is He who comes in the name of the Lord! We thank You for sending Your Son, Jesus, to bring us salvation. May He reign supreme in our lives, now and forever. In His blessed name we pray, amen.

C. Thought to Remember

Celebrate the king!

Learning by Doing

This page contains an alternative lesson plan emphasizing learning activities.
Classes desiring such student involvement will find these suggestions helpful.

Learning Goals

After participating in this lesson, each student will be able to:

1. Explain the significance of the Palm Sunday events.

2. Understand how Jesus is king past, present, and future.

3. Determine a specific way to recognize the kingship of Jesus in his or her life.

Into the Lesson

To introduce today's lesson, provide hymnals for the class and lead your students in singing, "All Glory, Laud and Honor." If a certain class member is a good song leader, you may prefer to let him or her lead.

Next, ask your class to identify the New Testament event that is the basis of that hymn. If no one immediately guesses the triumphal entry or Palm Sunday, provide several clues: *Jerusalem, palm branches, a colt, "Hosanna!"* Once someone has guessed the event or you have revealed the answer, inform your class that today's lesson deals with the triumphal entry as it relates to Jesus' divine kingship.

Into the Word

Use the Lesson Background material to explain the setting of the lesson text. Then ask two class members to read Revelation 1:8 and Luke 19:28-38 aloud. One student will read the narration (Luke 19:28-30a, 32, 33a, 34a, 35-38a), the other the dialogue (Revelation 1:8; Luke 19:30b, 31, 33b, 34b, 38b) in the passages. (You may wish to recruit your readers ahead of time, so they have a chance to practice.)

After the reading, tell your students that these two texts highlight some qualities of King Jesus that point to Him as being unique among kings. To discover those qualities, have your students work independently to complete the matching exercise below. This activity also is printed in the student book. If you do not use the student book, you will need to make copies of the exercise to distribute to your class.

Each student should match the qualities with the corresponding verses. Mention that a passage may refer to more than one quality. Allow about 10 minutes to complete the quiz.

*Why We Call Him **King Jesus***

___1. Omniscient
___2. Fulfilled prophecy
___3. Accepted praise
___4. Commanded followers
___5. Pre-existed
___6. Inspired praise
___7. Eternal
___8. All-powerful

a. Revelation 1:8; b. Luke 19:29-34; c. Luke 19:37, 38; d. Luke 19:30, 31, 38 (Zechariah 9:9; Psalm 118:26); e. Luke 19:29-31. *(Correct answers: 1. b; 2. d; 3. c; 4. e; 5. a; 6. c; 7. a; 8. a.)*

After your students share their findings, use the lesson commentary and the discussion questions below to explore the text in more detail.

1. How do the terms *Alpha* and *Omega* indicate Jesus' eternal nature and His role in creation?

2. What is implied by the term *Almighty*?

3. How did Jesus' commands in verses 28-31 indicate His omniscience (total knowledge, even of the future) and His lordship? What was significant about the prophecies of Isaiah 62:11 and Zechariah 9:9 in this regard?

4. Why did people praise God at Jesus' arrival (v. 37)? Why did they quote Psalm 118?

Into Life

Divide the class into groups of three or four. Each group will work on the same hypothetical situation below, using information from the Gospel of Luke (not limited to chapter 19) to brainstorm a response designed to convince "Bob" that he should accept Christ as Savior.

Bob is willing to admit that Christianity is probably true. Nevertheless, he is unwilling to surrender his life to Christ. "I would have to give up too much," he says. "Why can't I be a Christian without changing my lifestyle?"

Ask groups to incorporate answers to the following questions: 1. Who is Jesus (His identity) that Bob should *worship* Him? 2. What power does He have (His attributes) that Bob should *submit* to His authority? 3. What has He done (His miraculous works) that Bob should *believe* in Him? 4. Why should Bob *trust* in Him?

Ask volunteers to share their conclusions with the class. Close with prayer, challenging your students to share Jesus with those like Bob.

Let's Talk It Over

The questions on this page are designed to promote discussion of the lesson by the class and to encourage application of the lesson Scriptures. The answers provided are only discussion starters. Let your class talk it over from there.

1. How does realizing that Jesus is almighty and eternal (the one who was, is, and is to come) have a positive effect on your faith? How should this realization affect your daily life as a Christian?

Some have credited their knowledge of the unchangeableness of Father, Son, and Holy Spirit as inspiration to keep going during difficult periods in their lives. Others are reminded that God worked positively through the events of history so that by Jesus He could unfold His plan for our salvation (Galatians 4:4, 5). Encourage students to share how their faith and Christian walk is enhanced through recognition of the unshakable faithfulness of God.

2. How will the faithfulness of those who followed the instruction of Jesus to retrieve the colt inspire you to be faithful in following His instructions?

We all struggle to walk by faith and not by sight, don't we? Yet we can be sure that Jesus knows all about the pressures and difficulties we face (Hebrews 4:14-16). He struggled as He lived a faithful life, and God rewarded Him (Philippians 2:1-11). When we follow Jesus' commands—even under threat of rebuke—we can be sure He will honor His promise to be with us and to use our work to bring glory to Him (see Isaiah 55:11; Matthew 6:33; 10:40-42). "Be thou faithful unto death, and I will give thee a crown of life" (Revelation 2:10).

3. How can you worship Jesus with significant gifts and by speaking up during hostile circumstances?

Those who greeted Jesus honored Him with more than song. They put their clothes in the path. They spoke publicly about Jesus in a location where such talk could have resulted in persecution. When faith costs a person something, there is a quick division between "Sunday-only Christians" and those who have truly given their lives to Jesus no matter the cost.

Ask class members to share times in which their faithfulness cost them something. Remind them that Christ notices all the sacrifices made on His behalf (Matthew 25:36).

4. Many who hailed Jesus as king undoubtedly were expecting Him to reestablish the realm of an earthly Jewish kingdom. What are some ways that you can safeguard yourself from being lulled into speculating about the events surrounding His second coming?

There are many theories about how end-of-time events will unfold. People create complicated second-coming timelines to try to satisfy their curiosity. People want to know!

Yet good students of the Scriptures cannot be led easily into endless, time-wasting speculation. Instead of majoring in unraveling mysteries, Christians are better off focusing their efforts on fulfilling the mission of the church: to seek and save the lost. This is our best safeguard.

5. It can be very difficult to reason with skeptics who prefer to focus on the imperfections of Christians. How can we turn the conversation away from criticisms of individual Christians to a focus on Jesus' right to be king of everything?

The Christian can ask the skeptic a question like, "Have you decided if Jesus is who He claimed to be?" or "When you stand before God, will Jesus claim you as one of His followers?" These are just two possibilities. Have the class list other questions that can be asked.

We also can be quick to acknowledge that being a Christian is not a ticket to perfection. Even though some boast that their behavior makes them Christians in good standing, God will be the final judge. Review with the class some steps of how to love your enemies as well as how to lead a person to Christ.

6. If you decided to live life with the kingship of Jesus always in view, how would your life change?

Christians like to think about being rescued and saved by a loving Savior. But Jesus is not just our redeemer; He is also Lord and King. Christians respond to the reality of His kingship with obedience and adoration. They kneel before His authority. Living in His kingdom is not like living in a democracy. Ask for specific examples (thoughts and actions) of how Jesus' kingship should direct a Christian's daily life.

Christ Is Risen

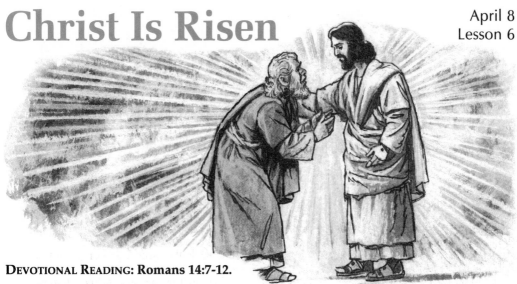

DEVOTIONAL READING: Romans 14:7-12.

BACKGROUND SCRIPTURE: Revelation 1:9-20; John 20:1-18, 30, 31.

PRINTED TEXT: Revelation 1:12a, 17, 18; John 20:11-16, 30, 31.

Revelation 1:12a, 17, 18

12a And I turned to see the voice that spake with me.

· · · · · · · · · · · ·

17 And when I saw him, I fell at his feet as dead. And he laid his right hand upon me, saying unto me, Fear not; I am the first and the last:

18 I am he that liveth, and was dead; and, behold, I am alive for evermore, Amen; and have the keys of hell and of death.

John 20:11-16, 30, 31

11 But Mary stood without at the sepulchre weeping: and as she wept, she stooped down, and looked into the sepulchre,

12 And seeth two angels in white sitting, the one at the head, and the other at the feet, where the body of Jesus had lain.

13 And they say unto her, Woman, why weepest thou? She saith unto them, Because they have taken away my Lord, and I know not where they have laid him.

14 And when she had thus said, she turned herself back, and saw Jesus standing, and knew not that it was Jesus.

15 Jesus saith unto her, Woman, why weepest thou? whom seekest thou? She, supposing him to be the gardener, saith unto him, Sir, if thou have borne him hence, tell me where thou hast laid him, and I will take him away.

16 Jesus saith unto her, Mary. She turned herself, and saith unto him, Rabboni; which is to say, Master.

· · · · · · · · · · · ·

30 And many other signs truly did Jesus in the presence of his disciples, which are not written in this book:

31 But these are written, that ye might believe that Jesus is the Christ, the Son of God; and that believing ye might have life through his name.

GOLDEN TEXT: When I saw him, I fell at his feet as dead. And he laid his right hand upon me, saying unto me, Fear not; I am the first and the last: I am he that liveth, and was dead; and, behold, I am alive for evermore, Amen; and have the keys of hell and of death.—Revelation 1:17, 18.

---

*Our Community Now and
in God's Future*
Unit 2: A New Community in Christ
(Lessons 5-9)

Lesson Aims

After participating in this lesson, each student will be able to:

1. Describe Mary Magdalene's role as a witness to the resurrection of Jesus.

2. Explain the importance of eyewitness testimony for the resurrection of Jesus.

3. Develop a personal faith-statement in Jesus, which is grounded in the biblical evidence for His resurrection.

Lesson Outline

INTRODUCTION

  A. The Cross and Easter

  B. Lesson Background

 I. DEATH IS UNLOCKED (Revelation 1:12a, 17, 18)

  A. Paralyzing Fear of Death (vv. 12a, 17)

  B. Encouraging Freedom from Death (v. 18)

    Not a Near-*Death Experience, But a . . .*

II. CHRIST IS RISEN (John 20:11-16)

  A. Weeping Without Christ (vv. 11-13)

  B. Meeting the Risen Christ (vv. 14, 15)

  C. Recognizing the Risen Christ (v. 16)

III. FAITH BRINGS LIFE (John 20:30, 31)

  A. Signs of Jesus (v. 30)

  B. Faith in Jesus (v. 31)

    Believing the Evidence

CONCLUSION

  A. Seeking a Dead Christ

  B. Prayer

  C. Thought to Remember

Introduction

A. The Cross and Easter

The cross is the most recognizable religious symbol on earth. It appears as jewelry, in logos, on buildings, in cemeteries, and in countless other places. Some churches often use a cross with Jesus included, called a *crucifix*. Other churches prefer an empty cross, symbolizing that Jesus' work on the cross is finished. Still other churches favor another symbol: an image of the risen Christ over the cross. This reflects an understanding that while Jesus' atoning sacrifice on the cross is essential to our salvation, it is His resurrection that validates that work and completes His mission on earth.

This week's lesson is for Resurrection Sunday (Easter). This has been celebrated by the church since her earliest days as the central event in all of human history. We will explore what it means to be a witness to the risen Christ and how such witnesses have continuing significance for us today.

B. Lesson Background

After His resurrection, Jesus appeared to some people but not to others. Why was that? We may not understand this completely, but the New Testament does give us some clues. First, we can see that Jesus appeared only to believers. There was no appearance to Pontius Pilate, to Caiaphas, or to the Roman emperor, as dramatic and powerful as such appearances might have been. He did appear to large groups, one group estimated by Paul to have been over 500 in number. But Paul calls these people *brethren*, meaning "fellow believers" (1 Corinthians 15:6). Therefore, the required condition to receive a visit from the risen Christ was faith.

The one possible exception to this first item (the condition of faith) was Jesus' startling appearance to Saul (later called Paul) on the road to Damascus (Acts 9). Yet the occasion was clear: Jesus had decided that this was the proper time to call this man of zeal to His service. Paul was a "chosen vessel" for the Lord (Acts 9:15).

Second, we see that Christ alone determined the occasions for His appearances. There was never a sense of Christ appearing at someone's command, like conjuring up a demon or a genie.

Third, the general purpose for Christ's appearances is also clear: He made himself known to those whom He wanted to be witnesses for Him. His parting words to the gathered disciples before His ascension served to commission them as "witnesses unto me" (Acts 1:8), meaning able to testify that Jesus was truly risen from the dead. A necessary qualification for replacing Judas as one of the 12 apostles was that the candidate be "a witness with us of his resurrection" (Acts 1:22). A central person in today's lesson is Mary Magdalene. After her early morning encounter with the risen Lord, she went "and told the disciples that she had seen the Lord" (John 20:18). The many such witnesses to the resurrection are what give us confidence that Jesus really did rise from the grave and that He has the power to save us from death.

John's account of the events of the Sunday morning of the resurrection of Jesus is full of unique details. One of these distinctive aspects is John's interest in the role of Mary Magdalene on that glorious morning. Luke records that Mary was an early follower of Jesus, having been delivered by Him from demon possession (Luke 8:2). In John, she is first introduced as one of several women who maintained a vigil at the cross (John 19:25). We can appreciate her great love for the one who freed her from spiritual bondage. We sympathize with her extreme anguish in seeing His suffering and death on a Roman cross.

The commitment of Mary to her Lord can be seen in that she was not just one of the last at the cross but also the first at the tomb. When most of the male disciples abandoned Jesus, Mary and the other women kept the deathwatch without regard to personal danger. While others slept on Sunday morning, Mary arose before daybreak to go to the tomb and finish the proper preparations of Jesus' corpse.

Upon arrival, Mary found the tomb open and empty, and she ran to Peter to report this. John makes it clear that she believed someone had removed Jesus' body (John 20:1, 2, 13, 14). As we study today's lesson, we experience Mary's crushing agony upon her discovery of the empty tomb and her mighty joy when she encounters her risen Lord. We share her emotions on this great day.

I. Death Is Unlocked
(Revelation 1:12a, 17, 18)

The book of Revelation is made up of a series of visions experienced by the apostle John while exiled on the prison island of Patmos. John signals to the reader the beginning of a new vision by writing that he is "in the Spirit" (Revelation 1:10; also 4:2; 17:3; 21:10). His first vision is of the risen Christ, whom he hears before he sees (1:10-12). This vision includes a description of

How to Say It

ARIMATHEA. *Air*-uh-muh-*thee*-uh (*th* as in *thin*; strong accent on *thee*).
CAIAPHAS. *Kay*-uh-fus or *Kye*-uh-fus.
HADES. *hay*-deez.
MAGDALENE. *Mag*-duh-leen or Mag-duh-*lee*-nee.
PATMOS. *Pat*-muss.
PONTIUS PILATE. *Pon*-shus or *Pon*-ti-us *Pie*-lut.
RABBONI. Rab-*o*-nye.
SHEOL. *she*-ol.

the Lord that is both awe-inspiring and full of allusions to the Old Testament.

A. Paralyzing Fear of Death (vv. 12a, 17)

12a, 17. And I turned to see the voice that spake with me. . . . And when I saw him, I fell at his feet as dead. And he laid his right hand upon me, saying unto me, Fear not; I am the first and the last.

We can easily understand the reaction of John. He is experiencing Jesus in all His heavenly glory. This includes a trumpet-like voice (Revelation 1:10). He sees eyes that burn like fire (1:14) and Jesus' countenance glowing like the sun (1:16). John is understandably filled with *fear*. Jesus taught that this fear is completely justified, for God is the one with ultimate power over a person's eternal destiny (Matthew 10:28). Fear of God is expected of everyone (Revelation 15:4).

John undoubtedly remembers a similar experience of over 60 years earlier, when he was one of three disciples allowed to witness the transfiguration of Jesus. The disciples had fallen down in fear (Matthew 17:6). At that time of deadly terror, Jesus' words had been, "Be not afraid" (Matthew 17:7). Here again, Jesus lays a comforting *hand* on the cowering John and tells him, "Fear not!" His life is not in danger. [See question #1, page 280.]

B. Encouraging Freedom from Death (v. 18)

18. I am he that liveth, and was dead; and, behold, I am alive for evermore, Amen; and have the keys of hell and of death.

Jesus gives John three powerful reasons not to fear, punctuating them with an *amen* (meaning "this is true"). First, Jesus reminds John of the event that changed history: Jesus' resurrection. John was likely one of those who helped take down Jesus' body from the cross. John was standing right there when the soldier pierced Jesus' side (John 19:34, 35). John knew, beyond any shadow of doubt, that Jesus' body had been devoid of all life. Yet he had also witnessed Jesus alive again. Jesus was *dead*, but God did not abandon Him in the grave (Acts 2:31, 32).

Second, Jesus was raised to eternal life. The Bible tells of several people who were brought back to life after dying (example: Lazarus in John 11). We assume, however, that all of these people eventually died a natural death again. Jesus' resurrection is quite different! He was truly dead, His body lying inert in the grave for days. When He came back to life, it was to be *alive for evermore*. [See question #2, page 280.]

Third, Jesus tells John that He has the *keys* to unlock the strongholds of *death*. The word *hell* as used in this verse does not necessarily refer to the place of ultimate punishment, the lake of fire (Revelation 20:10, 14). It is probably a general reference to the place of the dead, called *hades* by Greeks and *sheol* by Jews. To have the keys of death means that Jesus is able to lead us from death to life eternal. In this Jesus is the "captain" or pioneer of our salvation (Hebrews 2:10; 12:2), the one who has blazed the trail from death to life that we may follow.

When we as believers read these words, we should rejoice. Death has no power over us. We have been rescued from death and from the fear of death by Jesus, our Savior (Hebrews 2:15). Truly, we can sing with the apostle Paul, "Death is swallowed up in victory!" (1 Corinthians 15:54). [See question #3, page 280.]

NOT A *NEAR*-DEATH EXPERIENCE, BUT A . . .

Near-death experiences have been reported by many people. One devout Christian woman relates two such experiences. In both cases she had suffered a deep vein thrombosis that required emergency medical treatment to save her life. She tells of entering into a brilliant room where everything was intensely peaceful and where she was immersed in heavenly music.

These kinds of stories share similar themes. The book *90 Minutes in Heaven* is the story of a Christian minister who was the victim of a horrendous, head-on crash with a semitrailer truck. Rescue personnel found no pulse and declared him dead. Another minister arrived on the scene and prayed for him. Ninety minutes after the crash, the "dead" man showed signs of life and eventually recovered. During those 90 minutes, he saw himself at the gates of Heaven, surrounded by friends and relatives welcoming him home, but he was turned away before he could enter!

Do these stories reveal what actually happened, or do they merely describe the vivid imaginings of oxygen-starved brain cells? Regardless of what we make of these stories, they testify to the faith of Christians. Their faith is in the Lord who had not a *near*-death experience but a *through*-death experience. Our Lord is now alive forever. Death could not hold Him, and He has the keys to our death as well!   —C. R. B.

II. Christ Is Risen
(John 20:11-16)

The second Scripture for this week's lesson also comes from the apostle John. But this one is from his Gospel account of the life, death, and resurrection of Jesus. These verses focus on that momentous morning that inaugurated a new era for God's people.

A. Weeping Without Christ (vv. 11-13)

11. But Mary stood without at the sepulchre weeping: and as she wept, she stooped down, and looked into the sepulchre.

The previous verses of this chapter tell of how Mary had visited the tomb before dawn, found the tomb empty, returned to tell Peter, and then came back to the *sepulchre* herself. This is a moving, emotional time for Mary. Her grief brings tears and sobs. She is *weeping* because the shock of Jesus' missing body has rekindled all of the sorrow she felt at His death. It appears that she even has been denied the opportunity to do a final service to her Lord: full preparation of His body for its final rest. [See question #4, page 280.]

12. And seeth two angels in white sitting, the one at the head, and the other at the feet, where the body of Jesus had lain.

This type of tomb is not like the graves that we find in our cemeteries today. This one is a small room carved into the limestone hillside. In this cave-like room, there probably are several shelves or niches to lay newly deceased bodies. After a body is deposited, such a tomb is sealed with a large stone that has been shaped to fit the entrance snugly. The Gospels tell us that this particular tomb belongs to Joseph of Arimathea (Matthew 27:57-60) and that it has never been used for burial.

Looking inside, Mary sees something she does not expect: *two angels*. These visitors have just appeared because Peter and John found nothing in the tomb but empty grave linens, and then they went home (John 20:3-10). The appearance of these two angels thus is specially designed for Mary's benefit.

13. And they say unto her, Woman, why weepest thou? She saith unto them, Because they have taken away my Lord, and I know not where they have laid him.

The angels know what Mary doesn't: that this is a time for rejoicing, not weeping. Mary weeps because the great crush of events has overwhelmed her. Her master has been disgraced and executed as a common criminal. And now the final insult has come: His body has been *taken away*.

Mary's sorrow is so deep that she cannot even marvel at an angel manifestation. She can think only of one thing: find the missing body of her dead *Lord*, Jesus, and rescue it from those who would desecrate it.

B. Meeting the Risen Christ (vv. 14, 15)

14. And when she had thus said, she turned herself back, and saw Jesus standing, and knew not that it was Jesus.

Getting no answer from the angels (or perhaps not caring even to wait for an answer), Mary turns away from the entrance of the tomb. She is determined to find Jesus' body. Yet in the dim light of the dawn, she encounters another person. She finds Jesus' body but not in the way she expects.

15. Jesus saith unto her, Woman, why weepest thou? whom seekest thou? She, supposing him to be the gardener, saith unto him, Sir, if thou have borne him hence, tell me where thou hast laid him, and I will take him away.

The combination of Mary's extreme grief, tears that cloud her eyesight, and the scant light of early morning combine to prevent her from recognizing *Jesus*. He repeats the question of the angels, *why weepest thou?*

Mary, *supposing him to be the gardener*, asks the only question that seems reasonable at the time. Perhaps Jesus' body has been stolen. Or perhaps this gardener has moved it for some good reason. But neither idea is correct.

C. Recognizing the Risen Christ (v. 16)

16. Jesus saith unto her, Mary. She turned herself, and saith unto him, Rabboni; which is to say, Master.

Knowing that *Mary* has not recognized Him, *Jesus* speaks her name in a personal, revealing way. It all comes to her in a rush: Jesus is not dead! This is her Lord, her *Master* speaking to her. The realization of a split second changes her life forever.

Notice that Mary does not find the living Christ because of her seeking (remember: she is looking for a dead Christ). Rather, *the living Christ finds her!* This has huge significance for us today. The risen Jesus is alive still and is still seeking disciples. Jesus said He came to "seek and to save that which was lost" (Luke 19:10). If we make ourselves available, call on His name, and follow the biblical plan of salvation, Jesus finds us and changes us.

We will never be the same when this happens. We can be transformed from death to life (John 5:24). Our great fear of death no longer paralyzes us, for "now is Christ risen from the dead" (1 Corinthians 15:20) and "in Christ shall all be made alive" (1 Corinthians 15:22). Even if we die, we will be raised to eternal life and "so shall we ever be with the Lord" (1 Thessalonians 4:17). [See question #5, page 280.]

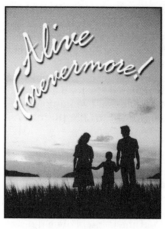

Visual for
Lessons 6 & 11

Use this visual to ask, "How is our new life in Christ like a sunrise?"

III. Faith Brings Life
(John 20:30, 31)

Have you ever wondered why the Gospels were written? The apostle John now gives his readers a clear statement of his purpose in writing: his purpose is evangelistic.

A. Signs of Jesus (v. 30)

30. And many other signs truly did Jesus in the presence of his disciples, which are not written in this book.

In John *signs* are the miracles of Jesus (see John 2:23; 4:48). The miracle accounts in John tend to be more extensive and detailed than in the other Gospels. John admits that he has been necessarily selective in choosing which miracles to recount (see John 21:25). How wonderful it would be to learn of some of those unrecorded miracles! Jesus' earthly life was not one of carefully chosen good deeds for a public-relations campaign. Rather, it was a pattern of healing and helping wherever He went.

B. Faith in Jesus (v. 31)

31. But these are written, that ye might believe that Jesus is the Christ, the Son of God; and that believing ye might have life through his name.

In fact, John does indeed tell us why he selects certain miracles and why he writes in general: he does this so *that believing ye might have life through his name.* John thinks his account of *Jesus* is adequate to make his case. The careful reader will see in Jesus the one who is God's *Son*, sent to redeem humanity (John 3:16). Such a reader will see the Lamb of God who takes away the world's sin (1:29). Such a reader will see God's chosen Messiah, who brings living water (4:14). Such a reader will see life and resurrection from the dead (11:25).

The one who believes in Jesus need not fear death, for He has conquered death. Those who believe are called to be faithful, even unto death, for they will receive a crown of life (Revelation 2:10). [See question #6, page 280.]

BELIEVING THE EVIDENCE

Juan Catalan was charged with the murder of a teenage girl in May 2003. He claimed that he had been with his daughter at Dodger Stadium in Los Angeles at the time of the murder, about 20 miles from the scene of the crime. Police did not believe him. Catalan had ticket stubs to the game, and family members testified to his innocence. But police had a witness placing Catalan at the murder site. Catalan's attorney obtained an official Dodger videotape of the game, but Catalan couldn't be identified.

Then the attorney discovered that HBO had also filmed a program at the stadium that evening. In footage that had been cut from the program, one scene clearly showed Catalan and his daughter eating hot dogs. The time codes on the tape were evidence that he had been at the stadium at the time of the murder. Cell phone records placed him near the stadium as well. Nearly six months after Catalan was jailed, the court threw his case out. Catalan was a free man.

Evidence is important! John wrote his Gospel to offer us evidence about Jesus. John says the evidence establishes the fact, without ambiguity, that Jesus is the Son of God and our Savior. Do you believe this evidence?   —C. R. B.

Conclusion

A. Seeking a Dead Christ

Some years ago there was a series of documentary programs produced for television entitled *The Long Search.* The shows examined the origins and beliefs of the world's great religions, including several varieties of Christianity. The premise of the series was that religion consists of the human search for God. This search turns out differently for different searchers, thus producing diverging faiths. In this way of thinking, religion is largely the product of human imagination and experience.

Biblical faith, at its core, is decidedly different. The Bible is not the record of humanity's search for God. It is much more the story of God's search to redeem His lost children. Yet there are those who, like Mary, still search for a dead Christ. Some seek Him as only a historical figure from 2,000 years ago. They find an enigmatic figure, a person very difficult to explain using the standard criteria of history.

Others seek Christ only in the pages of tradition. They see Him as the originator of a great system of ethical teaching: selflessness and service. Still others seek a Christ that fits their predetermined needs. They want a Savior according to their expectations, not according to His terms and demands. Therefore they seem to serve a dead Christ. He makes no impact on what they do, how they behave, or their future plans.

The great news of Resurrection Sunday is that we serve a risen Savior. He was alive on that morning when Mary visited the tomb. He is alive today and still seeking those who would serve Him, love Him, and be His disciples. As believers we can walk daily with the confidence of Jesus' presence in our lives. He is not dead! Hallelujah, He is risen indeed!

B. Prayer

God, our loving Father, we trust in Your promise that just as You did not abandon Your Son, Jesus, to the grave, so You will raise us to be with Him on the last day. May You take away our natural fear of death and replace it with the confidence of those who serve a risen Lord. We pray this in the name of the resurrected Christ, amen.

C. Thought to Remember

The risen Christ still offers eternal life.

Home Daily Bible Readings

Monday, Apr. 2—This Is My Body (Luke 22:7-23)

Tuesday, Apr. 3—Jesus Is Lord of All (Romans 14:7-12)

Wednesday, Apr. 4—Mary Finds an Empty Tomb (John 20:1-9)

Thursday, Apr. 5—Jesus Appears to Mary (John 20:10-18)

Friday, Apr. 6—Jesus Appears to His Disciples (John 20:19-23)

Saturday, Apr. 7—Jesus Appears to Thomas (John 20:24-31)

Sunday, Apr. 8—Jesus, the First and Last (Revelation 1:9-12, 17, 18)

Learning by Doing

This page contains an alternative lesson plan emphasizing learning activities.
Classes desiring such student involvement will find these suggestions helpful.

Learning Goals

After participating in this lesson, each student will be able to:

1. Describe Mary Magdalene's role as a witness to the resurrection of Jesus.

2. Explain the importance of eyewitness testimony for the resurrection of Jesus.

3. Develop a personal faith-statement in Jesus, which is grounded in the biblical evidence for His resurrection.

Into the Lesson

To open today's lesson, share the following riddle with your class (also printed in the student books). Ask students to guess the answer.

I am both first and last. In the course of time I was, and was not, and am again forever. Who am I?

List your students' suggested answers on the board, then ask them to read Revelation 1:12-18. They should recognize that the answer is *Jesus,* who is the first and the last, and who lived, died, and rose again to eternal life.

Next, use the commentary on verse 18 to sketch the three reasons why the Christian should not fear death. Then tell your class that today's lesson deals with the biblical evidence for believing that Jesus did indeed conquer death.

Into the Word

Share the following information with your class: George Rawlinson (1812–1902) was an English historian. He formulated guidelines for historians to follow to determine the value of historical writings. He proposed that (1) the writings of eyewitnesses generally have the highest degree of credibility, (2) the writings of those who get their information from eyewitnesses have the next highest degree of credibility, and (3) writers of a later age, who depend on word-of-mouth (oral tradition) for their information, have the lowest degree of credibility.

Using these guidelines and the questions below, your students should evaluate the historical credibility of the following biblical reports of the risen Jesus. (This exercise is also in the student books.) You can either divide your class into small groups and assign each group one or two passages, or investigate each passage with the entire class.

The passages are (A) John 20:11-20; (B) John 20:26-28; (C) John 21:1-14; (D) 1 Corinthians 15:3-8.

Questions for Each Passage

1. Was the author an eyewitness of the appearance of the resurrected Christ?

2. Did the author get the information from an eyewitness?

3. Did the author rely on word-of-mouth from an earlier age?

4. Taking the first three questions together, what degree of historical credibility should we assign to the passage in question?

Answers

Passages A, B, and C: The author, John, was an eyewitness of the resurrected Lord; see John 21:20-24 *(highest degree of credibility).*

Passage D. Paul and others were eyewitness of the risen Lord, though not all were witnesses to the same appearances; see Acts 9 *(highest degree of credibility).*

After you have analyzed each passage, discuss the implications this evidence has for a Christian's faith. Use the lesson commentary on John 20:30, 31 and the questions below to guide the discussion.

1. Why did John record so many miracles, especially the miracle of Jesus' resurrection?

2. Why is it important to have historical evidence of the highest credibility upon which to base one's faith in Jesus?

3. What assurance do we have that death has been defeated, based on the historical evidence we have for the resurrection of Jesus?

Into Life

Introduce the last exercise by saying, "It is important for each Christian to be able to explain why he or she believes in Christ. As Peter said, 'But sanctify the Lord God in your hearts: and be ready always to give an answer to every man that asketh you a reason of the hope that is in you, with meekness and fear' (1 Peter 3:15)."

Then ask students to use the paper you provided (or the space in their student books) to complete the following open-ended statement: "I believe that Jesus is the Christ, the Son of God, because . . ." Ask several volunteers to share their faith statements.

Let's Talk It Over

The questions on this page are designed to promote discussion of the lesson by the class and to encourage application of the lesson Scriptures. The answers provided are only discussion starters. Let your class talk it over from there.

1. In what ways has your healthy fear of God helped you to grow in Christ?

It is very appropriate to fear God because of who He is: all-knowing, all-powerful, the only judge, etc. Yet a healthy, reverential fear is not the same as a morbid, paralyzing fear. Ask the class to give examples of these two kinds of fear. One possibility is our reaction to the electricity in our houses. We have a healthy appreciation both for electricity's ability to harm and to power our appliances.

2. What are some typical reactions to death or the topic of death? In what ways does knowing of the resurrection of Jesus make facing death easier for you?

Reactions can be wide-ranging: resignation, shock, grief, avoidance, nervous humor, etc. Read 2 Corinthians 5:6-10 and ask students if they have ever experienced the same struggles the apostle Paul describes. Ask under what circumstances would students rather stay on earth and under what circumstances would they rather go to be with Jesus. Be prepared for a time of intense, emotional sharing.

3. Many believers who live in dire circumstances long to be with the Lord, while those who are well off sometimes put a lot of time and money into living on earth as long as possible. How can the church help both types stay focused on hope in Christ through His resurrection while remaining grounded in the present?

The mistake of both groups is to focus too much on the here and now. Those in dire circumstances dwell on what they lack; those who are well off may hold tightly to possessions and relationships as if they owned them.

Jesus prayed for His followers to be able to live in the world without becoming attached to the world (John 17:14-18). The church is to teach that believers have their citizenship in Heaven (Ephesians 2:19; Philippians 3:20) but are privileged to be witnesses for Jesus while living here.

4. How have the reactions of Mary and John in today's text been a help to you as you review your faith walk?

The feelings of Mary and John at different times included despair, fear, relief, and celebration. Even with John's years of personal experience with Jesus and years of walking by faith, John reacted with great fear when he saw Jesus in the vision. Help the class recognize that it is normal to have a variety of emotional reactions over time. Our strength returns when we refocus on the certainty of Christ's resurrection and all the power and assurance available to us (see Romans 6:5; Philippians 3:10, 11). Our confidence is in Him and not in our own strength. (Psalm 73 is a story of a similar struggle.)

5. Some say that Jesus did not come back to life. How can the church equip the average Christian to respond?

Some believe that quoting Scripture that asserts the resurrection of Christ will convince all skeptics. Still others can respond only by citing their personal experiences as proof that Jesus is alive. The church can teach specific techniques to raise the probability that a skeptic will consider what the Christian has to say. These techniques include showing patience and good listening skills to learn the skeptic's real issue (see Jesus' patience with both Mary and John in today's text). Being kind is vital. Introducing the skeptics to in-depth resources written by former skeptics can help doubters turn a corner (example: *The Case for Christ*, by Lee Strobel).

6. The meaning of Easter should not be any less important to the Christian than the meaning of Christmas. However, Christmas seems to have taken on more significance in many ways. How can the church help correct this imbalance?

If Jesus had merely visited earth and had not died taking our place to pay the penalty for sin, we would still be lost in that sin. If Jesus had not been resurrected, we would have no hope for our own resurrection (see 1 Corinthians 15). One way to help correct the imbalance is to bring the Easter themes into our Christmas celebrations, stressing that Jesus was born into the world in order to die for its sins. Ask the class to suggest other ways your congregation can have a positive impact in this area.

Christis Worthy of Praise

DEVOTIONAL READING: Psalm 111.

BACKGROUND SCRIPTURE: Revelation 4.

PRINTED TEXT: Revelation 4.

Revelation 4

1 After this I looked, and, behold, a door was opened in heaven: and the first voice which I heard was as it were of a trumpet talking with me; which said, Come up hither, and I will show thee things which must be hereafter.

2 And immediately I was in the Spirit: and, behold, a throne was set in heaven, and one sat on the throne.

3 And he that sat was to look upon like a jasper and a sardine stone: and there was a rainbow round about the throne, in sight like unto an emerald.

4 And round about the throne were four and twenty seats: and upon the seats I saw four and twenty elders sitting, clothed in white raiment; and they had on their heads crowns of gold.

5 And out of the throne proceeded lightnings and thunderings and voices: and there

were seven lamps of fire burning before the throne, which are the seven Spirits of God.

6 And before the throne there was a sea of glass like unto crystal. And in the midst of the throne, and round about the throne, were four beasts full of eyes before and behind.

7 And the first beast was like a lion, and the second beast like a calf, and the third beast had a face as a man, and the fourth beast was like a flying eagle.

8 And the four beasts had each of them six wings about him; and they were full of eyes within: and they rest not day and night, saying, Holy, holy, holy, Lord God Almighty, which was, and is, and is to come.

9 And when those beasts give glory and honor and thanks to him that sat on the throne, who liveth for ever and ever,

10 The four and twenty elders fall down before him that sat on the throne, and worship him that liveth for ever and ever, and cast their crowns before the throne, saying,

11 Thou art worthy, O Lord, to receive glory and honor and power: for thou hast created all things, and for thy pleasure they are and were created.

GOLDEN TEXT: Thou art worthy, O Lord, to receive glory and honor and power: for thou hast created all things, and for thy pleasure they are and were created.—Revelation 4:11.

Our Community Now and in God's Future
Unit 2: A New Community in Christ
(Lessons 5-9)

Lesson Aims

After participating in this lesson, each student will be able to:

1. Describe the praise offered to the Lord in the throne room scene.

2. Tell the significance of some of the elements of worship in Heaven as presented in Revelation 4.

3. Suggest one specific way to improve his or her personal approach to worship.

Lesson Outline

INTRODUCTION
    A. Worship in the Church Today
    B. Lesson Background
 I. PRELIMINARIES OF WORSHIP (Revelation 4:1)
    A. Door to Heaven (v. 1a)
    B. Invitation to Knowledge (v. 1b)
 II. CENTER OF WORSHIP (Revelation 4:2-5)
    A. Description of the Throne (vv. 2, 3)
       What Words Cannot Describe
    B. Elders Around the Throne (v. 4)
    C. Spirit of the Throne (v. 5)
III. WORSHIP IN HEAVEN (Revelation 4:6-11)
    A. Description of the Four Beasts (vv. 6-8a)
    B. Worship by the Four Beasts (vv. 8b-9)
       A Heavenly Menagerie
    C. Elders Cast Their Crowns (vv. 10, 11)
CONCLUSION
    A. The Nature of True Worship
    B. Prayer
    C. Thought to Remember

Introduction

A. Worship in the Church Today

Is it *worship* or is it *entertainment*? That's the question I have asked myself occasionally as I have participated in Sunday services at several hundred different churches in many different states, provinces, and countries. My judgment? Sometimes it's hard to tell the difference.

In many churches the worship time has evolved from hymns led by a song leader, accompanied by an organ and/or piano, to be a "worship set" led by a well-rehearsed team of singers and musicians. It is not uncommon to see 20 or more people on the stage of the church, leading in 30 minutes of singing, accompanied by lavish video projections of words to the songs. New songs are introduced on a weekly basis and repeated many times in order to allow the congregation to learn them. Auditoriums are now "worship centers," with adjustable mood lighting and fabulous sound systems. One church I visited even had fountains down the center aisle; these fountains exploded with water jets at the pinnacle of the worship set. The worship set is energetic. It's loud; it's emotional; it's invigorating.

This shift in styles has certainly added vitality to the worship experience long missing in some congregations. Churches with great worship attract visitors and may grow rapidly. Thus, some church strategists see investment in professionals to lead worship-with-excellence as a wise investment in a church's future.

Some have noticed, however, that the youngest generation of Christians has a different taste in worship. Their preference seems to lean toward acoustic rather than electronic instruments, subtle hand drums rather than booming drum sets, and simple vocals rather than elaborate vocal teams. Their music is quieter, more reflective. They see an emphasis upon professionalism in worship as phony and undesirable. They long to restore a sense of mystery and reverence to the worship time. One aspect of this has been the new generation's rediscovery of some old hymns such as "Be Thou My Vision," "O Sacred Head," and "Come, Thou Fount." Where this will lead the church of the future is yet to be seen.

The central question, however, remains: Is it worship or is it entertainment? As we examine Revelation 4, we will find biblical principles of the nature of worship that will help us guide our worship into being just that—worship.

B. Lesson Background

The book of Revelation has long been a source of controversy. It has been combed thoroughly as a source of prophecies concerning the future. Many different systems of interpretation for Revelation have been developed and passionately defended. Because of this controversy, some Christians avoid study of this book.

These controversies are unfortunate, for Revelation is much more than a book of prophecy. It is also the New Testament's great book of worship. In this regard, Revelation has much in common with the Psalms. Throughout the history of the church, writers of songs and hymns for worship have drawn from Revelation. Such varied pieces as Handel's "Hallelujah Chorus" (Revelation 19:1-6), Bridges and Thring's "Crown Him with Many Crowns" (19:12), Wesley's "O for a Thousand Tongues" (5:11, 12), Hoffman's "Are You Washed in the Blood?" (7:14), and Tomlin's "We Fall Down" (4:10) are drawn from Revelation.

Nearly half of the occurrences of the New Testament's Greek verb for *worship* appear in the book of Revelation (24 out of 60). We see in this book that Heaven is a place of worship. Scholars have identified seven hymns of praise and worship in Revelation. The songs of praise are spoken (4:8), sung (5:9), and cried out (7:10).

In the New Testament, the word *worship* implies "giving obeisance, bowing down." Thus worshiping can involve a physical position (see Matthew 4:9). Our English word *worship* has the connotation of "giving worth to someone," or "counting someone to be ultimately worthy." Worship is not an emotion; it is an acknowledgment and commitment. We worship that which is superior and worthy of our honor.

I. Preliminaries of Worship (Revelation 4:1)

The first three chapters of Revelation concern John's vision of the risen Christ and letters to the seven churches of Asia. It is helpful, though, to understand these letters as separate greetings to each of the seven churches. The rest of the book is the letter itself, and all of the churches are intended to receive its messages.

A. Door to Heaven (v. 1a)

1a. After this I looked, and, behold, a door was opened in heaven.

John understands his world like everyone else in antiquity. He sees the earth as being covered by a firmament, a large canopy that stretches over the earth (see Genesis 1:6-8; Isaiah 40:22). This firmament barrier prevents humans from seeing what is happening in the heavenly, spiritual realm. In his vision John sees a break in the firmament, a *door* into *heaven*. He sees what mortal eye is not normally allowed to see.

The fact that we now have traveled far beyond the sky into outer space diminishes neither the reality of Heaven nor the validity of John's vision. We still believe that Heaven exists as a definite place but not as a physical location that can be visited in a rocket ship. Heaven remains a place where mortals are normally denied access or viewing, but it is a real place just the same.

[See question #1, page 288.]

B. Invitation to Knowledge (v. 1b)

1b. And the first voice which I heard was as it were of a trumpet talking with me; which said, Come up hither, and I will show thee things which must be hereafter.

John is invited by an unnamed voice to view heavenly events. He knows this voice, however. It sounds like a *trumpet*, loud and brilliantly piercing. He has heard it before. It is the voice of the risen Christ (Revelation 1:10).

Christ warns John that what he is about to see in Heaven foreshadows future events. This is not to be an impromptu visit to God's throne to observe daily happenings. It is a vision designed to impart special knowledge of the future so John may share this with his fellow believers. Events in Heaven have an effect on us. People in the ancient world believe this, whether Jew, Roman, or Christian. Modern humanity tends to neglect the spiritual realm and dismiss the possibility that what happens in Heaven affects what goes on in our world. It is good for us to remember what is really the case: God is on His throne as the ruler of Heaven *and* earth.

II. Center of Worship (Revelation 4:2-5)

John's challenge is to use human language to describe the indescribable. So he paints wonderful word pictures, but we can be sure that the reality is far more glorious than what we are able to imagine. He begins his vision with a visit to the center of Heaven: the very throne room of God.

A. Description of the Throne (vv. 2, 3)

2, 3. And immediately I was in the Spirit: and, behold, a throne was set in heaven, and one sat on the throne. And he that sat was to look upon like a jasper and a sardine stone: and there was a rainbow round about the throne, in sight like unto an emerald.

Being *in the Spirit* means that a new vision has begun. This is very real to John. His spiritual eyes immediately focus on *the throne* of God itself. He describes the throne occupant as having the appearance of *jasper* (a gemstone that comes in a variety of colors) and *sardine* (also called *carnelian*, a bright red gemstone). He does not attempt any physical description of God because that would be sacrilegious. His choice of these two gemstones seems merely to indicate that God has a fiery, glowing appearance.

The throne itself looks like an *emerald* to John, a brilliant green color. It emanates color as well—a multihued *rainbow* radiance. Such marvelous colors surely overwhelm John's mind as they speak to him of the wonders of this place. Nothing on earth can compare with these marvels. [See question #2, page 288.]

WHAT WORDS CANNOT DESCRIBE

What is your favorite gemstone? For some, diamond is the first choice (possibly because of the jewelry industry's superb "diamonds are forever" marketing job). Others may name rubies or (as John does in our text) emeralds. John describes the emerald he saw as being like a rainbow—a description that reminds some people of opal.

A scientific description of opal is that "it is made up of layers of precipitated silica spheres . . . [that] sometimes produce a diffraction grating, that creates play of rainbow sparkling light from within the stone" (www.theimage.com). Such a description is pretty dull stuff until we get to the phrase "rainbow sparkling light." That grabs our attention! A cut-and-dried scientific description simply cannot do justice to the beauty of the opal (or most other gemstones, for that matter). You have to see it to believe it.

That's probably what John felt as he was trying to find words to describe for us what it was like to stand in front of the throne of God. Paper and ink descriptions of all of those wondrous phenomena give us only a faint hint of the glory we shall behold when we meet our Lord in Heaven. What a future we have!   —C. R. B.

B. Elders Around the Throne (v. 4)

4. And round about the throne were four and twenty seats: and upon the seats I saw four and twenty elders sitting, clothed in white raiment; and they had on their heads crowns of gold.

Home Daily Bible Readings

Monday, Apr. 9—Praise to a Gracious God (Psalm 145:8-12)

Tuesday, Apr. 10—Great Is Our God (Psalm 111)

Wednesday, Apr. 11—God's Eternal Purpose (Ephesians 3:7-13)

Thursday, Apr. 12—None Is Like God (Jeremiah 10:6-10)

Friday, Apr. 13—Live a Life of Love (Ephesians 4:25–5:2)

Saturday, Apr. 14—Endure Hardships (Revelation 2:1–7)

Sunday, Apr. 15—God Is Worthy of Praise (Revelation 4)

Surrounding God's throne are 24 *seats*, occupied by Heaven's *elders*. Who these elders are is not explained, but we have a few clues. They are not angels (see Revelation 7:11). Instead, they seem to be humans who have been installed into a position of honor. This is shown by their garb and their right to wear *crowns* in God's presence.

Numbers have special significance in Revelation. Twelve is the number for the people of God. Twelve was the number of the tribes of Israel (Exodus 24:4; 28:21). Twelve was also the number of disciples chosen by Jesus to be His apostles (Mark 3:14). Jesus himself had promised these 12 that they would be seated on thrones of judgment (Matthew 19:28). The number 24 is double 12. As a bit of speculation, this group of elders may therefore represent the combined peoples of God from the Old Testament and the New Testament: the faithful of Israel and the church.

C. Spirit of the Throne (v. 5)

5. And out of the throne proceeded lightnings and thunderings and voices: and there were seven lamps of fire burning before the throne, which are the seven Spirits of God.

In the book of Revelation, lightning and thunder are signs that a significant event is about to take place (compare Exodus 19:16). Such activity marks the last of the seven seals (Revelation 8:5), the seventh trumpet (11:19), and the seventh bowl of God's wrath (16:18). These supernatural fireworks are tied to the spiritual activity originating from *the throne*.

Seven is the number of perfection in Revelation (compare Zechariah 4:2). *The seven Spirits* represent the perfect Spirit, thus the Holy Spirit. John sees the Holy Spirit as attendant before the throne of God, ready to do God's bidding.

III. Worship in Heaven (Revelation 4:6-11)

The description of the scene of worship and its participants continues.

A. Description of the Four Beasts (vv. 6-8a)

6a. And before the throne there was a sea of glass like unto crystal.

The *sea* is seen in the ancient world as the most violent, uncontrollable force of nature. God's mastery of His created world is often symbolized by His ability to control the sea (see Psalm 89:9). So also Jesus' ability to calm the raging sea (Mark 4:39), and to even walk on its surface (Mark 6:48), are signs of His divinity and power. This sea in Heaven is in utter submission to God, with a surface as smooth as *glass*. This is a vivid symbol of God's power and authority.

6b. And in the midst of the throne, and round about the throne, were four beasts full of eyes before and behind.

The number *four* in Revelation is symbolic of the entire created world. These *beasts* are special creatures with *eyes* that observe everything. They are symbols of God's omnipresence (His presence everywhere) and omniscience (His knowledge of all things). They are able to give coverage to the four corners of the earth, to all of the created world (compare Revelation 7:1).

7, 8a. And the first beast was like a lion, and the second beast like a calf, and the third beast had a face as a man, and the fourth beast was like a flying eagle. And the four beasts had each of them six wings about him; and they were full of eyes within.

John notices individual differences in *the four beasts*. As with many of the things seen by John, the beasts are reminiscent of images from the Old Testament. In this case we are reminded of the four "living creatures" seen by the prophet in Ezekiel 1:5-15. The creatures in that vision each had four faces. The list of faces there is nearly the same as the list here, with the minor difference of Ezekiel's *ox* versus John's *calf*.

What do these beasts symbolize? A very old explanation ties them to the four Gospels. In this interpretation Matthew is the *lion*, the king of the beasts, because he presents Jesus as the king of the Jews. Mark is the *calf*, the dependable servant animal, because he presents Jesus as the servant of all humanity. Luke is the *man*, because he presents Jesus as the Son of Man. John is the *eagle*, the imperial symbol of the Romans, because he presents Jesus as the exalted Son of God. This explanation has been used to give a picture symbol for each of the Gospels (example: Matthew = lion).

A less complicated explanation is that the faces represent various qualities of God. Under this theory, the lion symbolizes God's power; the calf symbolizes God's faithfulness; the man symbolizes God's intelligence; and the eagle symbolizes God's sovereignty.

A more likely explanation is that these four creatures represent the general categories of creatures on the earth: wild animals (lion), domesticated animals (calf), human beings (man), and creatures of the sky (eagle). Thus, the picture is related to the number four, the symbol for the created world.

The detail of the *six wings* ties this vision to Isaiah's vision of Heaven (Isaiah 6). There the crea-

---

How to Say It

CARNELIAN. kar-*neel*-yun.

ISAIAH. Eye-*zay*-uh.

OMNIPRESENCE. *ahm*-nih-*prez*-ence (strong accent on *prez*).

OMNISCIENCE. ahm-*nish*-ence.

SERAPH. *sair*-uhf.

SERAPHIM. *sair*-uh-fim.

ZECHARIAH. *Zek*-uh-*rye*-uh (strong accent on *rye*).

---

tures above the throne are described as six-winged seraphim. A seraph is a heavenly creature.

B. Worship by the Four Beasts (vv. 8b, 9)

8b. And they rest not day and night, saying, Holy, holy, holy, Lord God Almighty, which was, and is, and is to come.

The four beasts have the function of ceaseless litany concerning the one seated on the throne. The threefold *Holy, holy, holy* is also found in Isaiah 6:3. This is an emphatic way of stressing God's unique holiness. (Interestingly, although the Bible says that "God is love," the Bible never describes Him as "love, love, love.")

John must be impressed that he is being allowed to view the center of all holiness. The words of the beasts tie this to John's initial description of God as the ageless one (Revelation 1:4). [See question #3, page 288.]

9. And when those beasts give glory and honor and thanks to him that sat on the throne, who liveth for ever and ever.

We now begin to understand the function of the four *beasts* more clearly. They serve as leaders of worship for the heavenly throng (especially when we see v. 9 and v. 10 together). There are four aspects to these words of worship. First, they give *glory* to God. The Bible teaches that we are to do this (see 1 Corinthians 10:31). To ascribe glory is to recognize God's greatness and power. Second, they *honor* God. To honor means to recognize sovereignty, to place oneself as a loyal vassal. Those in the ancient world are expected to honor the king (see 1 Peter 2:17). When we honor God, we are acknowledging His kingship in our lives.

Third, they give *thanks* to God. To give thanks is recognition of God's provisions for us and our dependence upon Him. Our need to give thanks to God will never end (see Psalm 30:12). Fourth, the four beasts recognize a central attribute of God: His eternality. God, the eternal one, lives *for ever and ever.*

Thou art worthy, O Lord, to receive glory and honor. —Revelation 4:11

Visual for Lesson 7. *Post this visual to start a discussion about the heart of worship. Ask, "Why is God, and only God, worthy of worship?"*

A HEAVENLY MENAGERIE

We humans have always found animals fascinating; this probably started when Adam first gave them names in the Garden of Eden. Just look at all the money we spend on our dogs and cats! From what we can learn of Solomon's knowledge and dealings with animals, we can speculate that he may well have had a royal zoo in Jerusalem (1 Kings 4:33; 10:22).

Modern zoo-keeping has been dated to 1752 with the establishment of the Imperial Menagerie in Vienna. It is still open to the public. Today every large city and many smaller ones have zoos or wild animal parks. What a delight it is to see the "zoo babies" every spring!

Do we find it surprising, then, that the God who created such a huge assortment of beasts in the first place would also take delight in having some of them serving Him around His heavenly throne? Whatever symbolism we see in this, one thing seems certain: in Heaven all of God's creatures will join in praising Him. Should the only creatures who are created in God's own image not praise Him daily?   —C. R. B.

C. Elders Cast Their Crowns (vv. 10, 11)

10. The four and twenty elders fall down before him that sat on the throne, and worship him that liveth for ever and ever, and cast their crowns before the throne, saying.

The 24 *elders* follow the lead of the beasts and now offer their own worship. They do this with a remarkable, unforgettable act: they bow and offer their *crowns*. In so doing they release any claim to their own separate authority and autonomy. They are completely devoted to the service of God.

11. Thou art worthy, O Lord, to receive glory and honor and power: for thou hast created all things, and for thy pleasure they are and were created.

The words of the elders are similar to those of the beasts, with a couple of additions. For one thing, they emphasize the elders' own *created* nature. [See question #4, page 288.] They are nothing without God. They would not even exist without a creator.

Another addition is the utterance *thou art worthy*. This is the very heart of worship: acknowledging the one who is worthy. In an absolute sense, God is the only one "worthy to be praised" (Psalm 18:3). When we understand worship as spiritual submission to God, we count Him as worthy of any possible praise. He is then our king and master, and we are His blessed servants.

Conclusion

A. The Nature of True Worship

Is the worship service at your church real worship or is it entertainment? Evaluate it by asking this question: is the congregation the *consumer* of worship or is it the *producer* of worship? In other words, are those gathered for worship thought of as the audience or as participants?

Worship, whether individual or corporate, should have the same purposes as given in the heavenly scene of Revelation 4. We can use this text to ask these evaluative questions: Is what we are doing in any way ascribing worthiness to God? Specifically, are we either giving God honor by our submission, giving God glory by our praise, or giving God thanks by the gratefulness of our hearts?

There is indeed an audience in the worship service, but it should be an audience of one: the Lord God. We may do other things at the weekly meeting time of a congregation, but let us not mistake them for worship. Let us renew our commitment to worship God "in spirit and truth" (John 4:24). [See question #5, page 288.]

B. Prayer

Mighty God of Heaven, who sits on the throne in power and glory, we worship You. May we lay our own personal crowns before You, submitting to Your will in every aspect of our lives. You alone are worthy. We pray this in the name of Your Son, Jesus, amen.

C. Thought to Remember

Worship of God is primary.

Learning by Doing

This page contains an alternative lesson plan emphasizing learning activities.
Classes desiring such student involvement will find these suggestions helpful.

Learning Goals

After participating in this lesson, each student will be able to:

1. Describe the praise offered to the Lord in the throne room scene.

2. Tell the significance of some of the elements of worship in Heaven as presented in Revelation 4.

3. Suggest one specific way to improve his or her personal approach to worship.

Into the Lesson

Distribute paper and pencils (or direct attention to the student books, if using those). Ask students to draw two pictures or write two descriptions. The first will be a picture or description of worship in Heaven as it is portrayed in popular culture. The second will be a picture or description of worship in Heaven as the student imagines it will be. Each picture or description should relate what the scene will look like, who will be there, and what they will be doing. (Caution your students not to attempt to draw a picture of God himself.)

When they finish, ask volunteers to display their artwork or read their descriptions to the class. Discuss the most common images (perhaps floating on clouds, playing harps, singing hymns) and ask your class why those images are so widely held. Then tell your students that today's lesson will deal with a vision of worship in Heaven described by John in Revelation 4.

Into the Word

Select 10 students to read Revelation 4 aloud. One will read the statements made by John (the "I" passages). Another will be the "voice like a trumpet." Four more will read, together, the words spoken by the four beasts. The remaining 4 students will represent the elders. If you have fewer than 10 students, use the same 4 students to represent the beasts and the elders.

After the reading, discuss the meaning of the text. Use your lesson commentary and the questions that follow to guide the discussion.

1. Whose was the voice like a trumpet (v. 1)? See Revelation 1:10-18.

2. Knowing that God is invisible (Colossians 1:14; 1 Timothy 1:17), what is the significance of John's description of His appearance and of the appearance of His throne in verse 3?

3. Who are the 24 elders? What is represented by their number and dress?

4. What is the significance of the thunder and lightning (v. 5)? Who are (or is) the seven spirits of God?

5. What is the meaning of the sea of glass in verse 6?

6. How similar are the four beasts to the creatures in Ezekiel 1:5-15? What do these beasts represent? What are the four aspects of their worship listed in verse 9?

7. Why did the elders cast their crowns before God's throne? How do their words of worship compare with those of the four beasts?

8. From this passage, what key elements or aspects of heavenly worship can we deduce? Why is each essential to proper worship?

As you discuss question eight, list this heading on the board: *Key Elements of Worship.* Under the heading, list the four aspects of worship mentioned in verses 9-11: *GLORY* (giving glory to God for His greatness and power); *HONOR* (honoring God for His sovereignty); *THANKS* (thanking God for His provision); *RECOGNITION* (recognizing God's eternality). Discuss.

Into Life

Say, "One of the initiatives of the sixteenth-century Reformation was the renewed emphasis on congregational involvement in worship, including congregational singing. Many believed the New Testament pattern for worship included the participation of every member of the congregation. With that in mind and in light of today's text, how do you respond to the following situations?"

1. Tim doesn't like to sing or participate in worship. He prefers to sit back and enjoy the music from the praise team, choir, and soloists. He just wants to be part of the audience and "soak it all in." How do you get him involved?

2. Jennifer loves to sing, and she considers that to be the "real" worship in the worship service. She doesn't see a reason to read Scripture in church ("We do enough of that in Bible school"), and she thinks the sermons are boring. Prayer is for private devotions, not public worship. How would you correct her misconceptions?

Let's Talk It Over

*The questions on this page are designed to promote discussion of the lesson
by the class and to encourage application of the lesson Scriptures. The answers
provided are only discussion starters. Let your class talk it over from there.*

**1. In what ways do you think your walk with
Christ would be affected if you, like John, could
get a personal glimpse through the door of
Heaven? Why is it probably a good idea for God
not to give you that glimpse?**

Ask the class to describe their imagined features of Heaven and what people will do there.
Note how hard it is to describe God and Heaven
given the limitations of human vocabulary in this
regard.

A glimpse into Heaven may fire us with renewed passion to take as many there with us as
possible. On the other hand, a personal glimpse
into Heaven may make us so impatient to get
there *right now* that we would even go so far as to
think of suicide! (Notice that Jesus waited until
John was very elderly before allowing him this
vision.) Such a glimpse would also make our
Christian walk more by sight than by faith since
we actually would have seen Heaven. God expects us to walk by faith based on the evidence
He's already given us.

**2. What cautions should be given to readers
in terms of how the different images of this text
are interpreted?**

Some authors have used many pages to speculate about the meaning and/or application of each
descriptive phrase. And others have spent many
years trying to determine the sequence of end-
times events.

One real possibility is that John did not have
an adequate vocabulary to explain in clear detail
everything he saw. But his description is adequate for us to know that God is in charge and
will carry out His plan to call His people to be
with Him for eternity. This encourages us to devote our energy into living daily for Christ and
proclaiming His saving message whenever we
have the opportunity.

**3. Today's lesson might tempt one to assume
that the complete spiritual emphasis in Heaven
means that secular issues on earth are totally
unimportant! How do you resist the temptation
to think this way?**

In earthly terms, the elders and beasts in God's
presence "put in a good day's work" every day.

We, however, cannot be in a special spiritual location 24 hours a day on earth. We must spend a
lot of time earning a living, doing chores around
the house, etc.

Yet doing our work as if to the Lord and as if
the Lord is our boss (which He is) can be worshipful. While working to honor Him, our bodies become "a living sacrifice, holy, acceptable
unto God" (Romans 12:1). We honor God by
keeping His commands (see John 14:15; 1 Corinthians 6:20).

**4. How can we arrange the content and style
of our worship to honor God adequately for all
His great deeds?**

Be careful not to let this question turn into a
gripe session about the current way your church
conducts worship. We can worship in many
ways. One of the ways of honoring God in the
Old Testament was to recite over and over the
great deeds of God (example: Exodus 15:1-21).
Perhaps you can think of a way to review the
events of Jesus' life to show how His lineage, His
power, His wisdom, and His character all accomplish what Jesus wanted: to demonstrate the nature of God.

Most of all we would want our words and actions to agree with Scripture to make sure that all
could see the fullness of God (see 1 Corinthians
12:6; 15:28). It should be our goal to worship
Him for His pleasure rather than just trying to
gratify our whims and preferences.

**5. If your church organized its worship to
match the worship pattern in Heaven, what
would change? How do you think the changes
would be accepted?**

Before we think about changing a current pattern or routine, perhaps we should think first
about changing our *awareness*. Are we aware
that in worship we are talking and singing to
God as our audience?

When that awareness takes hold, we will not
fret as much over songs or styles of music that
we don't like personally. We may even end up
being much less aware of those around us because our focus will be on God. We want Him to
receive all the glory!

Christ Is Able to Redeem

DEVOTIONAL READING: Psalm 107:1-9.

BACKGROUND SCRIPTURE: Revelation 5.

PRINTED TEXT: Revelation 5:1-5, 8-14.

Revelation 5:1-5, 8-14

1 And I saw in the right hand of him that sat on the throne a book written within and on the back side, sealed with seven seals.

2 And I saw a strong angel proclaiming with a loud voice, Who is worthy to open the book, and to loose the seals thereof?

3 And no man in heaven, nor in earth, neither under the earth, was able to open the book, neither to look thereon.

4 And I wept much, because no man was found worthy to open and to read the book, neither to look thereon.

5 And one of the elders saith unto me, Weep not: behold, the Lion of the tribe of Judah, the Root of David, hath prevailed to open the book, and to loose the seven seals thereof.

. . . .

8 And when he had taken the book, the four beasts and four and twenty elders fell down before the Lamb, having every one of them harps, and golden vials full of odors, which are the prayers of saints.

9 And they sung a new song, saying, Thou art worthy to take the book, and to open the seals thereof: for thou wast slain, and hast redeemed us to God by thy blood out of every kindred, and tongue, and people, and nation;

10 And hast made us unto our God kings and priests: and we shall reign on the earth.

11 And I beheld, and I heard the voice of many angels round about the throne, and the beasts, and the elders: and the number of them was ten thousand times ten thousand, and thousands of thousands;

12 Saying with a loud voice, Worthy is the Lamb that was slain to receive power, and riches, and wisdom, and strength, and honor, and glory, and blessing.

13 And every creature which is in heaven, and on the earth, and under the earth, and such as are in the sea, and all that are in them, heard I saying, Blessing, and honor, and glory, and power, be unto him that sitteth upon the throne, and unto the Lamb for ever and ever.

14 And the four beasts said, Amen. And the four and twenty elders fell down and worshipped him that liveth for ever and ever.

Apr
22

GOLDEN TEXT: Thou art worthy to take the book, and to open the seals thereof: for thou wast slain, and hast redeemed us to God by thy blood out of every kindred, and tongue, and people, and nation.—Revelation 5:9.

Our Community Now and in God's Future
Unit 2: A New Community in Christ
(Lessons 5-9)

Lesson Aims

After participating in this lesson, each student will be able to:

1. List the three titles of Jesus as found in Revelation 5.

2. Identify how the titles of Jesus explain His power and authority to redeem.

3. Design a worship service that incorporates the titles of Christ.

Lesson Outline

INTRODUCTION
  A. Jesus as the Lamb
  B. Lesson Background
I. LAMB REVEALED IN HEAVEN (Revelation 5:1-5)
  A. Scroll (v. 1)
  B. Crisis (vv. 2-4)
  C. Lion and Root (v. 5)
    Navajo Code Talkers
II. LAMB WORSHIPED IN HEAVEN (Revelation 5:8-14)
  A. Beasts and Elders (v. 8)
  B. New Song (vv. 9, 10)
  C. Host of Angels (vv. 11, 12)
  D. Universal Chorus (vv. 13-14)
    Heavenly Music
CONCLUSION
  A. Jesus in Christian Worship
  B. Prayer
  C. Thought to Remember

Introduction

A. Jesus as the Lamb

"Behold the Lamb of God!" proclaimed John the Baptist (John 1:29, 36). This introduces a major theme in John's Gospel: Jesus as our Passover lamb. The apostle John (who is not the same as John the Baptist) ties the death of Jesus closely to the celebration of the Passover in Jerusalem (see John 13:1; 19:14, 15).

The lamb of Passover was a tradition the Jews had observed for over a thousand years by the time Jesus arrived on the scene. It was at the center of the feast of Passover, a commemoration of God's deliverance of Israel from Egyptian slavery. In Egypt the children of Israel had been commanded to kill lambs and smear their blood outside their doors. This act of faith caused God's agent of death to "pass over" marked dwellings and not inflict God's final plague: the death of the household's firstborn son.

Paul wrote that, "Christ our passover is sacrificed for us" (1 Corinthians 5:7). When we look at the regulations for the Passover lamb, some striking parallels to Christ are found. The lamb was to be without blemish or defect (Exodus 12:5); the apostle Peter described Jesus as "a lamb without blemish and without spot" (1 Peter 1:19). The Passover lamb was to have no bone broken (Exodus 12:46); John included this detail into his account of Jesus' death, telling us that His legs were not broken by the Roman executioners (John 19:36).

The most remarkable parallel is that, according to Jewish tradition, the Passover lambs were killed by priests within the Jerusalem temple precincts, and then taken to homes for the feast. At 3 PM on Passover day, the high priest would slaughter the final lamb, saying, "It is finished." If we combine Mark 15:34 and John 19:30, we can see that it was at 3 PM on (what we call) Good Friday when Jesus uttered the words "It is finished" as He died for the sin of the world.

The designation of *Lamb* is the most common way of referring to the risen Jesus in the book of Revelation, used some two dozen times there. A marvelous picture emerges if we examine these verses: the Lamb shares the judgmental wrath of God (Revelation 6:16); the Lamb's blood cleanses His people from sin (7:14); the Lamb is the author of the book of life (13:8); the Lamb has a song akin to the song of Moses (15:3); the Lamb leads the victorious armies of Heaven (17:14); and the Lamb will be the light of new Jerusalem (21:23). A central, climactic event in Revelation is the marriage supper of the Lamb, where He takes His bride, the church (19:7-9).

The Passover lambs of the Jews symbolized purity, sacrifice, and escape from God's wrath. The book of Revelation uses all of these attributes in drawing its picture of the Lamb. The book adds truths that the Christ-Lamb is victorious over death and over the enemies of God. This mighty image deserves our study!

B. Lesson Background

Last week's lesson looked at the opening scene of John's vision of Heaven. We found a breathtaking tableau of worship before the throne of God, led by the 4 creatures that attend the throne. The worship was joined by 24 honored elders. Study of this scene allowed us to understand the heart of true worship. This week's lesson continues in that vein, but worship has ceased temporarily. The reasons for its pause and for its resumption are key elements of Revelation 5.

A central item in this chapter is a certain scroll (compare Isaiah 29:11). This scroll represents the mystery of God's gracious salvation and of His judgmental wrath. The scroll is closed by seven seals.

The breaking of each seal in the following chapters brings about symbolic events tied to the grim judgments of God. While the images are terrifying, we who are in Christ can rest assured that God's punishing anger will not be visited upon us. Our names are written in the Lamb's book of life. We have overcome by the blood of the Lamb (Revelation 12:11).

I. Lamb Revealed in Heaven (Revelation 5:1-5)

As children, my friends and I sent messages to each other using secret codes. Sometimes we used toy decoder rings; other times we made up codes. The modern world of text messaging has created a new kind of code. For example, ICQ means "I seek you," a request to have an online conversation. Code language is great if you know the code but frustrating if you don't.

The first part of Revelation 5 focuses on a mysterious scroll. We are not told where it originated. We (like John) desire to know its hidden meanings. But we cannot know the scroll's content unless it is revealed and "decoded" for us.

A. Scroll (v. 1)

1. And I saw in the right hand of him that sat on the throne a book written within and on the back side, sealed with seven seals.

Although the text says *book,* we should not think that this is a book in a modern sense. Modern books have leaves stacked and bound on one side, creating pages. That type of book (called a codex) will not come into common use for another hundred years from John's perspective.

How to Say It

ANTIPAS. *An*-tih-pus.

CORINTHIANS. Ko-*rin*-thee-unz (*th* as in *thin*).

DOMITIAN. Duh-*mish*-un.

EZEKIEL. Ee-*zeek*-ee-ul or Ee-*zeek*-yul.

ISAIAH. Eye-*zay*-uh.

NAVAJO. *Na*-vuh-ho.

The book in view here is a scroll. It has leaves sewn end to end and rolled around a wooden rod. This makes it possible to seal the outer edge. This is similar to what we find on a new roll of paper towels, where the beginning of the roll is stuck to the main body and must be peeled away for use. Another theory is that the *seven seals* are found one after the other, in a sequence, as the scroll is unrolled a little at a time.

The *seven seals* give a high sense of the importance to the scroll's contents. The book of Revelation uses the number *seven* 55 times. Seven is this book's number for perfection. The number *seven* here tells us that the scroll contains the perfect message of God. It awaits its revelation to John and the rest of the heavenly audience.

A further intriguing detail is that the scroll has been *written* on both sides. We can imagine the practical difficulties in using a scroll that has text on both sides, so this is not the common practice of ancient scribes. Usually a scroll has writing only on the inner side for ease of use. Writing on both sides gives the sense that the scroll is crammed with very important information, more data than a normal scroll can contain (compare Ezekiel 2:9, 10). This heightens our desire to know the contents.

B. Crisis (vv. 2-4)

2. And I saw a strong angel proclaiming with a loud voice, Who is worthy to open the book, and to loose the seals thereof?

The book (or scroll) cannot be opened without breaking *the seals.* The seal on government correspondence in the ancient world is more than a way of keeping the document closed. The nature of the seal determines who has the authority to break it and read the document. For example, a document sealed with the emperor's imprint can be viewed only by an official of the highest level (compare Esther 3:12; 8:10).

This scroll is rated top secret, and not just anyone can break its seals. The one who opens it must have the proper authority—that is, must be found *worthy.* This question of worthiness is tied to worship in these chapters. The one with ultimate authority is worthy, and therefore properly deserving of worship.

3. And no man in heaven, nor in earth, neither under the earth, was able to open the book, neither to look thereon.

Presumably, the one seated on the throne (God) can *open the book.* But He is the one who has prepared and sealed it in the first place. God waits for someone with adequate authority to come for it, someone having authority approved by Him. John is aware that none of his fellow creatures, whether human or angelic, has the requisite authority to break the seals and open the book. This is because none of them is worthy.

4. And I wept much, because no man was found worthy to open and to read the book, neither to look thereon.

The facts of verse 3 cause what we may deem to be a strange reaction in John: weeping. He feels the crisis deeply. We can infer that he is sad for two reasons. First, he has a strong desire to know the contents of the scroll, both for himself and so that he may be able to share the contents with his fellow believers (see Revelation 1:1). When that happens, humans may know better how to proceed with God's plans. [See question #1, page 296.]

Second, John realizes that no human is *worthy* of this task, not even him. Much like Isaiah, John is overwhelmed by his own unworthiness (Isaiah 6:5). God has established the standard of worthiness, and apparently no one measures up to it.

C. Lion and Root (v. 5)

5. And one of the elders saith unto me, Weep not: behold, the Lion of the tribe of Judah, the Root of David, hath prevailed to open the book, and to loose the seven seals thereof.

John's weeping is short-lived. There is indeed one worthy to break the seals and unroll the scroll. He is called the *Lion of the tribe of Judah* (compare Genesis 49:9) and the *Root of David.* Both of these are obvious titles for the Messiah, the risen Christ. However, the exact phrase *Root of David* is not found in the Old Testament (see Isaiah 11:10, "root of Jesse," realizing that Jesse was King David's father). Sometimes the Old Testament prophets refer to the Messiah as the branch of David who originates from David's dynasty (see Jeremiah 23:5; 33:15). This was true of the earthly Jesus, a rightful descendant of David (Matthew 1:1).

But in His eternal fullness, the Messiah is not derivative of the house of David. Rather, just the reverse is true: that house is dependent upon Him. The preexistent Christ is the source of the promise to David. This was taught by Jesus when He pointed out that David prophetically referred to the Messiah as "my Lord" (Luke 20:41-44).

NAVAJO CODE TALKERS

Navajo code talkers took part in every U.S. Marine battle in the Pacific between 1942 and 1945. Fewer than 30 non-Navajos could speak the language at the time. One of them was Philip Johnston, son of a missionary who grew up on a Navajo reservation. He persuaded the U.S. government that Navajo was the perfect code language (www.history.navy.mil). An unwritten language, Navajo uses a very complex syntax and tonal system.

To make the code work, a series of unrelated Navajo words were first translated into English equivalents. Then the first letters of the equivalents were used to spell English words. To make the code even harder to crack, most English letters could be signified by more than one Navajo word. The skilled Japanese code breakers couldn't break this one!

Some have seen the Bible as a book of codes— codes that we should try to "break." Indeed, the idea of *mystery* or *secret* is found in many places in the Bible (examples: Daniel 2:18, 19, 27, 30; Romans 11:25; 16:25; Colossians 1:26, 27). The secrets of the book that John saw revealed were more inscrutable than those protected by any human code. We should not be surprised that only God can reveal those secrets. This might also be good advice to heed when someone offers the supposedly "one-and-only true" interpretation of the book of Revelation!   —C. R. B.

II. Lamb Worshiped in Heaven (Revelation 5:8-14)

The Messiah now appears. But He is not as a muscle-bound superhero. He is a lamb. He is not a cute, docile lamb, however, but a powerful, bold being. He has the appearance of having been slaughtered (Revelation 5:6, not in today's text), probably meaning His white wool is smeared with blood. He has seven horns, symbolizing perfect, absolute authority. He also has the seven spirits, the Holy Spirit of God, at His disposal (again, 5:6). His authority and worthiness are unquestioned. The enthroned God gladly allows Him to take the scroll in preparation for its opening (5:7).

A. Beasts and Elders (v. 8)

8. And when he had taken the book, the four beasts and four and twenty elders fell down before the Lamb, having every one of them harps, and golden vials full of odors, which are the prayers of saints.

With the appearance of *the Lamb* on the scene, the worship resumes. Now, however, the Lamb himself is the object of worship as signified by the *elders* bowing before Him. There are two added elements: *harps* and *vials.* Now we can imagine the beautiful strains of a heavenly harp orchestra. Present in the vials are *the prayers* of

believers, which add the aroma of sweet incense
to the worship (compare Psalm 141:2).

B. New Song (vv. 9, 10)

**9. And they sung a new song, saying, Thou art
worthy to take the book, and to open the seals
thereof: for thou wast slain, and hast redeemed
us to God by thy blood out of every kindred,
and tongue, and people, and nation.**

Further evidence of the level of worship given
the Lamb is found in the singing of *a new song*.
In the Old Testament, the new song was always
sung to God as an act of worship (Psalm 33:3;
40:3; 96:1; 98:1; 144:9; Isaiah 42:10). [See question #2, page 296.]

Two things motivate this great worship celebration for the Lamb. Most basic, He appears in
Heaven as the redeemer for the people of God.
He has been slain as an atoning sacrificial victim.
The price of His blood has brought redemption
to many, both Jew and Gentile. [See question #3,
page 296.] Jesus' death is not seen as a defeat but
as a victory (Revelation 5:5, He has "prevailed").
Second, He is acclaimed because His triumphant
sacrifice has made Him worthy to solve the current crisis: break the *seals* and *open* the *book*.

**10. And hast made us unto our God kings and
priests: and we shall reign on the earth.**

The idea of a priestly kingdom has already
been introduced (Revelation 1:6; compare
1 Peter 2:5, 9). This was the ideal for Israel as
God's holy nation (see Exodus 19:6). The
promises we see here are encouraging to John's
first readers, who are under persecution from
the Roman Empire.

C. Host of Angels (vv. 11, 12)

**11. And I beheld, and I heard the voice of
many angels round about the throne, and the
beasts, and the elders: and the number of them
was ten thousand times ten thousand, and thousands of thousands.**

The song of the elders is now joined by a seemingly infinite host of heavenly *angels*. Saying *ten
thousand times ten thousand* is not a precise
mathematical formula but is more like our exuberant expression "gazillions." They are innumer-
able (compare Daniel 7:10; Hebrews 12:22). This
glorious scene is beyond our imagination.

**12. Saying with a loud voice, Worthy is the
Lamb that was slain to receive power, and riches, and wisdom, and strength, and honor, and
glory, and blessing.**

The worship from the angels is sevenfold, the
perfect combination. It encompasses vitally important qualifications for worthiness: *power* (abil-

Visual for Lesson 8. *This visual can remind your
students that there are more than six billion people
on the earth. Ask, "How will we reach them?"*

ity), *riches* (wealth), *wisdom* (intellect), *strength*
(might), *honor* (esteem), *glory* (majesty), and
blessing (approval). See 1 Chronicles 29:11, 12.

D. Universal Chorus (vv. 13, 14)

**13, 14. And every creature which is in heav-
en, and on the earth, and under the earth, and
such as are in the sea, and all that are in them,
heard I saying, Blessing, and honor, and glory,
and power, be unto him that sitteth upon the
throne, and unto the Lamb for ever and ever.
And the four beasts said, Amen. And the four
and twenty elders fell down and worshipped
him that liveth for ever and ever.**

The worship chorus is now joined by *every
creature*. The celebration is so great that even
heaven cannot contain it! The acclamation of the
creatures is fourfold, symbolic of the entire
world, repeating four of the items from the angelic song.

This song is also reminiscent of the original
song of God's worthiness in Revelation 4:11,
with one key difference: the worship now includes *the Lamb*—Jesus Christ, the risen one.
The redeemer of humanity is worthy of worship,
and no human king is similarly deserving. The
scene ends on a high note with the worship by
the 4 *beasts* and the 24 *elders*. They worship unreservedly, counting the Lamb as worthy as the
one who sits on the *throne*.

This powerful, moving description of heavenly worship is as inspiring today as it was when
John first wrote it. We see in it the great esteem
and worthiness that all Heaven accords to the
risen Jesus, our redeemer and Lord. [See question #4, page 296.]

HEAVENLY MUSIC

Is there any piece of music composed by a human being that would be worthy of being sung before the very throne of God? Some believe that the "Hallelujah Chorus" could be it!

Handel composed this chorus in 1741 as part of his famous *Messiah* oratorio. That was a difficult year for Handel. He was trying to get by on a very small income and it was bringing him to despair. Creditors were hounding him. But one day he received a thick envelope from Charles Jennens, a wealthy admirer of Handel's music. Inside the envelope was page after page of carefully chosen Scripture passages that Jennens thought should be set to music.

Handel was inspired! Over the next few weeks he worked day and night on the piece of music that was burning in his soul. When he had finished, he exclaimed, "I do believe I have seen all of Heaven before me and the great God himself!" Audiences since Handel's day have seemed to agree, especially given the tradition of rising to one's feet during the "Hallelujah Chorus." We may be sure that the great chorus of praise in Heaven will be even more glorious!   —C. R. B.

Conclusion

A. Jesus in Christian Worship

One of the burning issues of John's day was the danger of worshiping false gods. Under the reign of Emperor Domitian, citizens were required to do a yearly act of worship to the "genius" of the emperor—something Christians refused to do. For this they were persecuted, some even to death. John knew that one of the seven churches of Asia had suffered the martyr-

---

Home Daily Bible Readings

Monday, Apr. 16—Thanks for Redemption (Psalm 107:1-9)

Tuesday, Apr. 17—Serving the Living God (Hebrews 9:11-15)

Wednesday, Apr. 18—Life in Holiness (1 Peter 1:13-21)

Thursday, Apr. 19—Praise for Redemption (Psalm 40:1-5)

Friday, Apr. 20—That Your Love May Overflow (Philippians 1:3-11)

Saturday, Apr. 21—The Scroll Is Opened (Revelation 5:1-5)

Sunday, Apr. 22—Worthy Is the Lamb (Revelation 5:11-14)

---

dom of a faithful member named Antipas (Revelation 2:13). Revelation tells the horrible story of people who worshiped a false god. This may be code language for emperor worship (see Revelation 19:20; 20:4). [See question #5, page 296.]

There are two sides to the coin of worship. On one side is the principle that *worship is for God and only for God*. If there is another recipient of worship, worship has become idolatry, the most grievous sin in the Bible. When John falls down to worship an angel, he is admonished, "Do it not . . . worship God!" (Revelation 19:10). This is an absolute in the Bible. There is only one God, and He alone is worthy of worship.

The other side of the coin is that *acts of worship clearly reveal who a person's god is*. We may claim to worship God, but the way we live our lives will show what we really count as worthy. It may be ourselves. It may be a political philosophy. It may be wealth and pleasure. We see Paul's awareness of this when he writes of those "whose God is their belly" (Philippians 3:19).

With these principles in mind, we are confronted with a difficult dilemma. If there is only one God, and He alone is worthy of worship, where does Jesus, the redeeming Lamb, fit in? If we worship God and His Son, are we guilty of worshiping two Gods?

We may not have an exhaustive answer to this question because it hinges on the mystery of the Trinitarian nature of God. The doctrine of the Trinity defies human logic, because it claims in a certain sense that $1+1+1=1$. Some have therefore had an aversion to doing anything that seems like direct worship of Jesus.

This is not what we find in the picture of worship supplied by John. Once the Lamb enters the scene, worship is directed, unreservedly, to the one sitting on the throne (God) *and* to the Lamb (Revelation 5:13). This combination appears several times in the book (example: Revelation 22:1). It is proper and fitting to worship Jesus the Lamb, who redeemed us by taking away our sin. This is the Jesus we have a relationship with today. He is seated at the right hand of God in Heaven. Jesus should be counted as worthy in our hearts and in our worship.

B. Prayer

To God, the one who sits on the throne, we offer our praise, our honor, and our blessings. To the Lamb, our redeemer, we offer our deepest thanks and devotion. In Jesus' name, amen.

C. Thought to Remember

Honor Jesus in your worship.

Learning by Doing

This page contains an alternative lesson plan emphasizing learning activities.
Classes desiring such student involvement will find these suggestions helpful.

Learning Goals

After participating in this lesson, each student will be able to:

1. List the three titles of Jesus as found in Revelation 5.

2. Identify how the titles of Jesus explain His power and authority to redeem.

3. Design a worship service that incorporates the titles of Christ.

Into the Lesson

To begin today's lesson, ask your students to match each U.S. president listed below with his nickname or description. Also ask your students if they can explain the origin of each nickname. This exercise also is found in the student book.

__ 1. John Adams	a. Old Hickory
__ 2. Andrew Jackson	b. Peanut Farmer
__ 3. W. H. Harrison	c. Ol' Tippecanoe
__ 4. Abraham Lincoln	d. Comeback Kid
__ 5. James A. Garfield	e. His Rotundity
__ 6. Theodore Roosevelt	f. Emancipator
__ 7. Harry Truman	g. The Gipper
__ 8. Jimmy Carter	h. Preacher
__ 9. Ronald Reagan	i. Rough Rider
__10. Bill Clinton	j. Haberdasher

Answers: 1e. Adams was chubby! 2a. Jackson was a strict military disciplinarian, "as hard as hickory"; 3c. Harrison won the battle of Tippecanoe in 1811; 4f. Lincoln, The Great Emancipator, authored the Emancipation Proclamation to free slaves; 5h. Before his entrance into politics, this Preacher President was a Disciples of Christ minister; 6i. Roosevelt led the Rough Riders during the Spanish-American War; 7j. "Haberdasher Harry" Truman was co-owner of a hat store following World War I; 8b. Carter owned a peanut farm; 9g. Reagan played George Gipp in the film *Knute Rockne, All American;* 10d. Clinton was defeated following his first term as governor of Arkansas but then came back to win reelection to several more terms.

After you review answers, say, "Today's lesson includes three titles or descriptions of Jesus found in Revelation 5. Presidents' nicknames are related to their accomplishments, background, etc. So too Jesus' titles are related to His accomplishments and background."

Into the Word

Introduce this section with a brief lecture on Revelation 5:1-5, using both the Lesson Background and the commentary. Focus on the significance of "Lion of . . . Judah" and "Root of David."

Next, divide your class into small groups. Each group will research the title "Lamb of God." Distribute the following questions and Scripture passages to each group (or direct their attention to the student book). Suggested answers follow each question, but don't distribute those.

1. For what sacrifices and rituals did the Old Testament specify the use of a lamb? See Exodus 12:21; 13:1-16; Leviticus 4:32-35. *(For Passover; to redeem the firstborn; for sin offerings.)*

2. What were important characteristics of such a lamb? See Exodus 12:5, 46. *(Had to be without blemish and could not have its bones broken.)*

3. What characteristics did Jesus have in common with the sacrificial lambs of the Old Testament? See John 19:36; Acts 8:32-35; 1 Peter 1:19. *(Bones were not broken on the cross; had no blemish [sin]; was led to slaughter [cross].)*

4. What did Jesus accomplish by His death that relates to the title *Lamb of God?* See John 1:29; Colossians 1:14; Hebrews 9:11-15, 28; 1 Peter 1:18, 19; 1 John 1:7; Revelation 5:9, 10. *(Redeemed us from sinful lives by securing forgiveness for our sins.)*

Ask for volunteers to share answers. Next, direct your students' attention to Revelation 5:8-14. Have a student read the passage aloud and then ask the class how the beasts, elders, and angels around the throne react to the appearance of the Lamb. Why do they worship Him? How significant is this, considering that John was commanded to worship only God (Revelation 19:10)?

Into Life

Ask your small groups to design a worship service to honor Christ as the Lamb of God. Provide hymnals or chorus books; have each group choose Scriptures to be read and songs to be sung that reflect that theme. Challenge your students to design creative ways to praise the Lamb with skits, poems, responsive readings, etc.

Have groups share their results. Choose one, or a combination of two or more, to offer to your church's leadership for use.

Let's Talk It Over

The questions on this page are designed to promote discussion of the lesson by the class and to encourage application of the lesson Scriptures. The answers provided are only discussion starters. Let your class talk it over from there.

1. In what ways could an observer tell by your actions that your heart has ached because God's plans were seemingly thwarted and that He was not being glorified as He deserves?

John was moved to tears because the scroll could not be opened. He was upset that God's plan and purposes seemingly could not proceed. People reveal their spiritual maturity by the things that they allow to upset them. Some are distraught that their church is not giving to them what they want in terms of preferred music, worship times, décor, etc. Others become upset with God when He does not answer their prayers the way they desire (see James 4:1-3).

Such concerns are quite shallow in contrast with John's reaction! John was upset because God was not going to be glorified since (apparently) His plan could not proceed as planned. A Christian who is deeply saddened because God is not being honored is a person who is more likely to work hard to fulfill God's purposes on this earth.

2. Do you think we should limit the types of our praise to the model found in the book of Revelation? Why, or why not? (In addition to Revelation 5, see also chapters 4 and 7.)

The style and type of worship in Heaven is focused. It is clear that God is above all and deserves honor for who He is and what He has done, especially in providing salvation for us through Christ. Our attention and worship likewise should be directed to Him. Our songs can be diverse in nature, but they should always honor Him. God can be honored in many ways, including when we live in a manner that matches His commands (Hosea 6:6).

3. How can your church use the imagery of Jesus' sacrifice to persuade young people to enter missionary service? How hard would it be for you personally to see your child go overseas for missionary work?

Sometimes it is difficult to talk to people about becoming missionaries because many desire lives of ease and comfort instead of lives of sacrifice. Yet the image of Jesus is one of sacrifice in bringing us the message and means of salvation.

Ask your students what their lives would be like today if God had not given up Jesus to become a missionary to us. Then explore ways your church can encourage her young people to go into mission work. This may begin with encouraging young people to go to Bible college. Some in the class may have relatives or children who are already in mission work. Encourage them to share their perspective and emotional struggles.

4. There is no doubt: Christians have specific preferences about how worship should be conducted! How can we help one another become more open to different ways of worship?

Christians who become angry because corporate worship time is not conducted according to their preferences (volume, pace, style, etc.) can become a thorn in the side of a congregation. They may hinder the effectiveness of that church in various ways.

Conducting an in-depth study of the worship practices from the book of Revelation may help. Showing video clips of different worship practices around the world may also be beneficial. Spiritually mature Christians may need to mentor those individuals. Church leadership must not allow the expressions of different preferences for worship to become divisive (Romans 16:17, 18; Titus 3:10).

5. How does today's text provide you hope to face ongoing struggles? In what ways does it help you resist the temptation to follow another religion and the temptation to trust materialism instead of Christ?

The text assumes the background of the full history of the life of Christ on the earth. While on earth, He faced oppression from His enemies. He was tempted by Satan to give up His mission and focus on self, wealth, and power (Matthew 4:1-11). Jesus even had to deal with dissension among His followers.

Yet in the face of all these difficulties, Jesus remained faithful to His calling. Every Christian can dedicate himself or herself to live faithfully through the tough times just as Jesus did. Eternity with Him will be worth it.

Christ Is Our Protection

DEVOTIONAL READING: Psalm 121.

BACKGROUND SCRIPTURE: Revelation 7.

PRINTED TEXT: Revelation 7:1-3, 9-17.

Revelation 7:1-3, 9-17

1 And after these things I saw four angels standing on the four corners of the earth, holding the four winds of the earth, that the wind should not blow on the earth, nor on the sea, nor on any tree.

2 And I saw another angel ascending from the east, having the seal of the living God: and he cried with a loud voice to the four angels, to whom it was given to hurt the earth and the sea,

3 Saying, Hurt not the earth, neither the sea, nor the trees, till we have sealed the servants of our God in their foreheads.

. . . .

9 After this I beheld, and, lo, a great multitude, which no man could number, of all nations, and kindreds, and people, and tongues, stood before the throne, and before the Lamb, clothed with white robes, and palms in their hands;

10 And cried with a loud voice, saying, Salvation to our God which sitteth upon the throne, and unto the Lamb.

11 And all the angels stood round about the throne, and about the elders and the four beasts, and fell before the throne on their faces, and worshipped God,

12 Saying, Amen: Blessing, and glory, and wisdom, and thanksgiving, and honor, and power, and might, be unto our God for ever and ever. Amen.

13 And one of the elders answered, saying unto me, What are these which are arrayed in white robes? and whence came they?

14 And I said unto him, Sir, thou knowest. And he said to me, These are they which came out of great tribulation, and have washed their robes, and made them white in the blood of the Lamb.

15 Therefore are they before the throne of God, and serve him day and night in his temple: and he that sitteth on the throne shall dwell among them.

16 They shall hunger no more, neither thirst any more; neither shall the sun light on them, nor any heat.

17 For the Lamb which is in the midst of the throne shall feed them, and shall lead them unto living fountains of waters: and God shall wipe away all tears from their eyes.

Apr
29

GOLDEN TEXT: These [who are arrayed in white robes] are they which came out
of great tribulation, and have washed their robes, and made them white
in the blood of the Lamb.—Revelation 7:14.

Our Community Now and in God's Future
Unit 2: A New Community in Christ
(Lessons 5-9)

Lesson Aims

After participating in this lesson, each student will be able to:

1. Describe the image of Christ as our protector as given in Revelation 7.

2. Explain how Christ serves as his or her protector now.

3. Write a prayer of thankfulness for Christ's protection.

Lesson Outline

INTRODUCTION
A. The History of Blood
B. Lesson Background
I. SEAL OF PROTECTION (Revelation 7:1-3)
A. Angels Controlling Nature (v. 1)
B. Angel with God's Seal (vv. 2, 3)
Extreme Makeovers
II. PANOPLY OF THE PROTECTED (Revelation 7:9-12)
A. White-Robed Multitude (vv. 9, 10)
Symbols
B. Heavenly Throng (vv. 11, 12)
III. BLOOD OF PROTECTION (Revelation 7:13-17)
A. Washed in Blood (vv. 13, 14)
B. Fulfilled in God's Service (v. 15)
C. Protected by the Mighty Lamb (vv. 16, 17)
CONCLUSION
A. Cleansing and Protecting Blood
B. Prayer
C. Thought to Remember

Introduction

A. The History of Blood

Blood is a "hot commodity" today—the Red Cross always seems to need blood donors. Yet blood is a dangerous fluid because of medical risks. As a diabetic who travels frequently, I have experienced the discomfort many people feel at the thought of my blood touching them if they have to deal with my blood-soaked testing strips. We know of basketball players ordered off the floor because a little blood was seen. The HIV/AIDS crisis has made us wary of contact with anything tainted by blood. Yet there is no substitute for whole blood and blood derivatives for many medical procedures. We are scared by blood, but we need it.

In the religions of the ancient world, blood was viewed as sacred. Some ancients saw blood as containing the life principle, even the soul. They did not understand the function of blood in the body. The fact that blood circulated in the body was not well understood until William Harvey's conclusions in about AD 1615.

Blood was widely consumed as a food in the first century AD. This practice was abhorrent to the Jews (Leviticus 7:26; 17:12, 14; 19:26) and was forbidden by the early church (Acts 15:20). Like many of their contemporaries, ancient Jews believed a person's blood contained his or her life. If the blood drained from a person, they knew that that person would die.

Thus life and blood were tightly linked (Deuteronomy 12:23). This helps us understand the frequent phrase *innocent blood*. From our modern, scientific point of view, we cannot imagine blood itself being guilty or innocent any more than hair can be. Yet *innocent blood* conveys the idea of the violent death of an innocent person. To slay an innocent person would bring "blood" or "bloodguilt" upon the perpetrator (see Deuteronomy 19:10; compare Psalm 106:38).

The Old Testament taught that human blood was not to be shed in violence (see Genesis 9:6, part of the covenant with Noah). Murder was more than a criminal act; it was an offense against God. There was a sense, then, that all the human blood belonged to God and that humans had no right to abuse it (see Genesis 4:10).

Yet animal blood was an integral part of the Jewish religious system. A dramatic example of this is found in Exodus 24:3-8, Moses' ceremony of the blood of the covenant. In this ceremony of commitment, Moses took fresh animal blood and sprinkled it on the crowds of people (warning: don't try this at your church!). Thus their vow was sealed. The Old Testament taught that blood purifies, as summarized in the New Testament passage Hebrews 9:22: "without shedding of blood is no remission [of sins]." [See question #1, page 304.]

Blood—on the one hand, so abhorrent; on the other hand, so important. Today's lesson looks at Revelation 7, which gives a spectacular picture of the importance of the blood of Jesus for John's readers and for us today.

B. Lesson Background

Last week's lesson (Revelation 5) saw a crisis in Heaven resolved by the appearance of the redeeming Lamb of God, the risen Christ. He was deemed worthy to break the seven seals of the mysterious scroll held by God. The Lamb could unroll the book to reveal its contents.

Revelation 6 is the account of the breaking of the first six seals. When a seal is broken, various symbolic things happen. The first seal, the white horse, represents the lust for conquest; a good example of this is the Roman Empire (Revelation 6:1, 2). The second seal, the red horse, symbolizes war; this is both the ancient and modern plague of humanity (6:3, 4). The third seal, the black horse, stands for famine; this is a usual consequence of war (6:5, 6). The fourth seal, the pale horse, denotes death; this is the ultimate result of war (6:7, 8). These four seals are a distinct set, sometimes referred to as the Four Horsemen of the Apocalypse.

The fifth seal (Revelation 6:9-11) presents a question from the people of God, "How long, O Lord?" (6:10). The answer is that they must wait "for a little season," that is, a little longer (6:11). While they wait, their confidence is found in the way they address God: "O Lord, holy and true" (6:10).

The sixth seal (Revelation 6:12-17) is summed up in the statement, "wrath is come" (6:17). It presents a frightening picture of cosmic upheaval when the wrath of God and of the Lamb is unleashed on sinful humanity. Those caught in this cataclysm ask, "Who shall be able to stand" against it? (6:17). The answer is not given but is obvious: no one can withstand the unleashed fury of God. This is the day of God's final vindication of His righteousness (see Amos 5:18-20).

The seventh seal does not come until Revelation 8:1. It does not have a distinct event attached to it. Rather, it is the beginning of the next series, the seven trumpets. Chapter 7, our focus in this lesson, is an interlude between the terrifying images of the first six seals and that next sequence. It comes back to answer for the people of God the question, "Who shall stand?"

The people of God are the saints pictured in the fifth seal. While no one can withstand God's wrath, there is a protection for the people of God so that they will not have to face it. This protection comes through the blood of the Lamb, our blessed Savior, Jesus Christ.

I. Seal of Protection
(Revelation 7:1-3)

Can you spot a Christian by appearance alone? Do we look different from non-Christians? While some styles of dress may identify persons as non-believers, most Christians look and dress like their non-Christian neighbors. This text teaches that there is a spiritual seal on God's people that somehow marks them.

A. Angels Controlling Nature (v. 1)

1. And after these things I saw four angels standing on the four corners of the earth, holding the four winds of the earth, that the wind should not blow on the earth, nor on the sea, nor on any tree.

The number *four* symbolizes the whole *earth* in Revelation. This may be represented by the *four angels* charged with the earth, *the four corners* or quarters of the land (see Revelation 20:8), or *the four winds* that blow upon the earth (compare Jeremiah 49:36; Ezekiel 37:9; Daniel 7:2; Mark 13:27). The four angels seem to be stewards of the earth. Their actions demonstrate a pause in the furious activities of the previous chapter.

B. Angel with God's Seal (vv. 2, 3)

2. And I saw another angel ascending from the east, having the seal of the living God: and he cried with a loud voice to the four angels, to whom it was given to hurt the earth and the sea.

Another angel enters the scene like the rising sun *(ascending from the east)*, symbolizing the dawning of a new stage in the drama. This angel possesses God's *seal,* giving him the ability to place a spiritual mark on people. This angel also has authority over the four earth-steward *angels* and is able to command them.

3. Saying, Hurt not the earth, neither the sea, nor the trees, till we have sealed the servants of our God in their foreheads.

The spiritual seal of *God* is pictured as a mark on the *foreheads* of God's *servants.* Any destruction to be done by the four earth-steward angels is "on hold" until the project of marking all servants of God is accomplished.

This *seal* on the forehead is a repeated image in this book (see Revelation 9:4; 14:1; 22:4; compare Ezekiel 9:4). It stands in contrast to the "mark of the beast," a type of sealing done on those who are not covered by the blood of the Lamb, whose names are not written in the Lamb's book of life (see Revelation 14:9; 16:2). This mark is equivalent to having worshiped the false god of the beast. The lake of fire awaits those who do (19:20; 20:10, 15).

What is this seal? We should not understand it as a physical mark, like a tattoo or brand. It is spiritual in nature. Many Bible students have equated the sealing with the act of baptism. Paul taught that when we are baptized, we "put on

Christ" (Galatians 3:27). Baptism into Christ is connected with receiving the gift of God's Holy Spirit (Acts 2:38); having the Holy Spirit is a type of seal for believers (see Ephesians 1:13).

Those who maintain their trust in Christ are not in danger of having the mark of the beast stamped on their souls. As the next verses show, Christians are protected by the blood of the Lamb.

EXTREME MAKEOVERS

Just a few years ago, *Extreme Makeover* was a popular television program. The concept was to take a person who was "aesthetically challenged," so to speak, and provide cosmetic surgery to help change that person's looks and outlook on life.

One of the people featured on the show was Ray Krone. He had been wrongfully convicted of a murder not once but twice! His first conviction, in 1992, carried the death penalty. But it was overturned because of procedural errors. At his second trial, in 1996, he was again convicted but given a life sentence. DNA testing in 2002 exonerated Krone.

A key piece of the evidence against Krone in both of his convictions was his crooked smile, which supposedly matched bite marks on the victim. That was the feature that led to his being called "the snaggle-tooth killer." So Krone was a perfect candidate for an "extreme makeover"—dental work, hair transplant, nose job—so no one would misidentify him again.

The seal on the foreheads of the righteous is probably not a physical feature. Yet it symbolizes the "extreme makeover" that God does to our spirits when we accept Christ and become His disciples. From that time on, we are different people with a new outlook on life. No one should be able to call us by any of those old epithets we carried when we were rebellious sinners.   —C. R. B.

II. Panoply of the Protected
(Revelation 7:9-12)

Revelation 7:4-8 (not in today's text) introduces the concept of God's people numbering 144,000. This is not to be taken literally, as if Heaven were run by census takers. The number 12, which occurs 35 times in Revelation, is an important number relating to God's people. (See the discussion of the 24 elders of Revelation 4:4 in Lesson 7.) The number 144,000, or 12 times 12,000, refers to the ultimate, multiplied people of God. These are pictured as coming from the nation of Israel, but they are not alone.

A. White-Robed Multitude (vv. 9, 10)

9. After this I beheld, and, lo, a great multitude, which no man could number, of all nations, and kindreds, and people, and tongues, stood before the throne, and before the Lamb, clothed with white robes, and palms in their hands.

Added to the 144,000 is a countless crowd. The crowd defies any attempt to *number* it. This *multitude* comes from all the families and peoples of the earth, not just Israel. They are uniformly *clothed* in *white robes* (which will be explained later).

They are also carrying palm fronds. This reminds us of Palm Sunday and Jesus' triumphal entry into Jerusalem (John 12:13). It is customary in the ancient world to carry palm branches at celebrations (see Leviticus 23:40 and the nonbiblical 1 Maccabees 13:51).

SYMBOLS

A white robe is the customary baptismal garb in many churches. The color white has long symbolized purity.

One of the grim ironies of life is how symbols of goodness and holiness have been misappropriated by the forces of evil. An example is how white robes became a symbol of virulent racism. After America's Civil War, men dressed in white robes and wearing white hoods brought a reign of terror on African-American citizens.

Such ideology continues to have influence even in the early twenty-first century. How ghastly it is that some members of such organizations even thought of themselves as "good Christians." Some even were ministers!

In today's text John sees a multitude of God's people dressed in white standing before His throne. Their robes are a symbol of the righteousness they had found in Christ; their robes are not cloaks for evil deeds and attitudes. Can you think of other ways in which holy symbols are misappropriated to disguise sin?   —C. R. B.

10. And cried with a loud voice, saying, Salvation to our God which sitteth upon the throne, and unto the Lamb.

How to Say It

APOCALYPSE. Ah-*pock*-uh-lips.
DEUTERONOMY. Due-ter-*ahn*-uh-me.
EPHESIANS. Ee-*fee*-zhunz.
EZEKIEL. Ee-*zeek*-ee-ul or Ee-*zeek*-yul.
GALATIANS. Guh-*lay*-shunz.
LEVITICUS. Leh-*vit*-ih-kus.

Home Daily Bible Readings

Monday, Apr. 23—Thanks for Faithful Followers (Colossians 1:3-8)

Tuesday, Apr. 24—The Lord Will Keep You (Psalm 121)

Wednesday, Apr. 25—God Is Our Deliverer (Psalm 3)

Thursday, Apr. 26—God Is Good (Psalm 34:1-10)

Friday, Apr. 27—Protection in Trials (Revelation 3:7-13)

Saturday, Apr. 28—Salvation Belongs to God (Revelation 7:1-3, 9, 10)

Sunday, Apr. 29—The Lamb on the Throne (Revelation 7:11-17)

The Palm Sunday cry of "Hosanna" meant "God, save us!" Understandably, the Jews of Jesus' day were hoping for God's miraculous saving of their nation. The cry *Salvation to our God* is a fulfillment of that Palm Sunday appeal. In Heaven the people of God shout "Salvation!" to celebrate an accomplished fact. They are the multitude of the saved, and the salvation is attributed both to God and to *the Lamb.*

B. Heavenly Throng (vv. 11, 12)

11. And all the angels stood round about the throne, and about the elders and the four beasts, and fell before the throne on their faces, and worshipped God.

The multitude of the saved is now joined by the heavenly cast of characters who worship. We saw *angels, the elders,* and *the four beasts* back in chapters 4 and 5. As before, they assume a prostrate posture of worship. [See question #2, page 304.]

12. Saying, Amen: Blessing, and glory, and wisdom, and thanksgiving, and honor, and power, and might, be unto our God for ever and ever. Amen.

The throng sings a sevenfold worship chant. It is like their earlier praise song (Revelation 5:12) with the change of riches to *thanksgiving. Amen* means "it is true." The long-anticipated salvation of God is now finalized.

III. Blood of Protection (Revelation 7:13-17)

Most men are not experts at doing laundry. If they are like me, they end up with white sheets tinged pink because they washed them with a new red T-shirt. However, even the worst launderer knows that you need clean water to get clean clothes. You cannot wash white linens in muddy water and make them bright white. Yet Scripture offers an amazing image: robes washed in blood that become purest white.

A. Washed in Blood (vv. 13, 14)

13. And one of the elders answered, saying unto me, What are these which are arrayed in white robes? and whence came they?

John again draws the attention of one of the *elders* (see Revelation 5:5). Perhaps John looks confused at this vast array of white robes, so the elder poses a question that is already in John's mind: What's going on with all these white-robed people?

14. And I said unto him, Sir, thou knowest. And he said to me, These are they which came out of great tribulation, and have washed their robes, and made them white in the blood of the Lamb.

John wisely lets the elder answer his own questions. The robed persons have survived *great tribulation.* [See question #3, page 304.] Some interpreters see this as referring to a specific tribulation period related to Christ's second coming, but that is probably not what is meant. These are the saints who have endured to the end. [See question #4, page 304.] They have been faithful unto death (Revelation 2:10); they have received their crown-of-life reward. This reward is pictured here as the privilege of wearing a *white* robe. It is white, the symbol of purity, because of the cleansing power of the *blood* of Jesus.

We therefore have a startling picture: washing a robe in red, staining blood and having it come out the purest white. The blood of Jesus was the price for our sins. The Bible teaches that blood must be shed for sins to be forgiven (Hebrews 9:22). The blood of Jesus is thus a divine means for our forgiveness. The shedding of Jesus' blood paid the price that God decreed for sin's punishment. We can have our guilt taken away (Hebrews 10:19; 12:24; 1 John 1:7).

B. Fulfilled in God's Service (v. 15)

15. Therefore are they before the throne of God, and serve him day and night in his temple: and he that sitteth on the throne shall dwell among them.

This is not simply a picture of future bliss in Heaven. This can also be seen as a possibility for us today. Worship is our acknowledgment of the Holy God and submission to Him. We don't need to wait for the afterlife in order to *serve him day and night.* Do it now!

C. Protected by the Mighty Lamb (vv. 16, 17)

16, 17. They shall hunger no more, neither thirst any more; neither shall the sun light on them, nor any heat. For the Lamb which is in the midst of the throne shall feed them, and shall lead them unto living fountains of waters: and God shall wipe away all tears from their eyes.

This too is not simply a picture of future bliss. Much of this is a spiritual image of our lives today. We are sheltered by our Savior. We suffer no eternal damage from the natural world. We live with the comfort of *God* in our lives. We do indeed suffer the daily sorrows of life, but God overcomes these.

We now live lives of protection and purpose. The center of the throne is *the Lamb,* and the Lamb is the center of our lives (compare Isaiah 49:10). Our purpose is to trust, obey, and follow Him (John 21:22). Jesus bids us follow Him today and every day (Matthew 16:24). We thus die to self and rejoice in our service to Him (1 Corinthians 15:31). [See question #5, page 304.]

Conclusion

A. Cleansing and Protecting Blood

From a medical perspective, blood has several functions for our bodies. It protects us in that it contains white cells that fight against invasive infections. Blood carries away wastes created by the various cells and allows the kidneys and other organs to eliminate them. Sometime a person administering first aid will allow a small wound to bleed a little in order to "clean" it, that is, flush out some impurities.

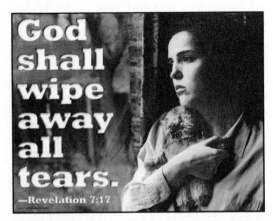

Visual for Lesson 9. *You can use this visual as a lead-in to question #5 on page 304. Ask, "How will God lead you through your tears today?"*

Paul taught that since we are justified by Christ's blood, we are saved from God's wrath (Romans 5:9). Peter wrote that we have been redeemed from futile lives by the blood of Jesus (1 Peter 1:18, 19). The author of Hebrews advised his audience that the blood of Christ purifies us so that we can worship God (Hebrews 9:14). In John's opening statements of Revelation, he affirmed that the blood of Jesus makes us free from the enslavement of sin (Revelation 1:5).

These are just a few of the rich ways that the New Testament authors use the image of the blood of Christ to help us understand how our salvation has been made secure. And this is not just "any blood" of Jesus. If Jesus had had a bad hangnail that bled and we possessed the bloody rag that He wrapped it in, this would have no more spiritual value than any other historical curiosity. The blood of Jesus had no magical properties. It did not glow in the dark or have sparkly glitter in it. It is what that blood represents that is important: Jesus' atoning death on the cross for our sins.

Paul put it very plainly when he said "Christ died for our sins according to the Scriptures" (1 Corinthians 15:3). As Robert Lowry (1826–1899) wrote in the hymn "Nothing But the Blood,"

> What can wash away my sin?
> 　Nothing but the blood of Jesus;
> What can make me whole again?
> 　Nothing but the blood of Jesus.
> Oh! precious is the flow
> 　That makes me white as snow;
> No other fount I know,
> 　Nothing but the blood of Jesus.

Without the blood of Jesus, we would be overwhelmingly dirty because of our sin. As we consider God's marvelous provision, may we offer thanks to the one who still sits on the throne and to the Lamb who gave His blood for us.

"Dear dying Lamb, Thy precious blood shall never lose its pow'r. Till all the ransomed Church of God be saved, to sin no more."

—William Cowper (1731–1800)

B. Prayer

O Jesus, Your blood, Your blood, Your cleansing blood! It is a mystery and a marvel to us; what power it has! Father we thank You for providing our salvation through the blood of Your only Son, Jesus, in whose name we pray, amen.

C. Thought to Remember

Our eternal protection
is the blood of the Lamb.

Learning by Doing

This page contains an alternative lesson plan emphasizing learning activities.
Classes desiring such student involvement will find these suggestions helpful.

Learning Goals

After participating in this lesson, each student should be able to:

1. Describe the image of Christ as our protector as given in Revelation 7.

2. Explain how Christ serves as his or her protector now.

3. Write a prayer of thankfulness for Christ's protection.

Into the Lesson

Put the following quiz in students' chairs. They can begin to work on them as they arrive. If you use student books, you will find the quiz printed there.

1. Which cells defend against infection? a. Red blood cells; b. White blood cells; c. Platelets. *2.* Which cells carry oxygen? a. Red blood cells; b. White blood cells; c. Platelets. *3.* Which plays the most vital role in the blood-clotting process? a. Red blood cells; b. White blood cells; c. Platelets. *4.* What is the life span of red blood cells? a. 3 to 4 weeks; b. 3 to 4 months; c. 3 to 4 years. *5.* Red blood cells get their color from what? a. Hemoglobin; b. Oxygen; c. Plasma. *6.* The adult body contains about how many quarts of blood? a. 5; b. 10; c. 15. *7.* What are the four basic blood types? a. A, B, C, D; b. A, B, A+, B–; c. A, B, AB, O. *8.* Blood cells are produced by which of these? a. Heart; b. Kidneys; c. Bone marrow.

Answers: 1b; 2a; 3c; 4b; 5a; 6a; 7c; 8c.

After your students complete the quiz and you have graded it together, say, "Today's lesson will focus on the importance of Jesus' blood to those who trust in Him for salvation."

Into the Word

To begin exploring today's text, prepare a brief lecture on the history of blood using the Lesson Background. Your lecture should cover:

1. Why eating blood was forbidden by the early church (Acts 15:20).

2. The meaning of the terms *innocent blood* and *bloodguilt* (Deuteronomy 19:10).

3. The reasons for the prohibition against murder (Genesis 4:10; 9:6).

4. The role of animal blood in the Jewish religious system, especially in covenant-making and purification (Exodus 24:3-8; Hebrews 9:22).

5. The identification or purpose of the six seals in Revelation 6.

After you finish the lecture portion of this lesson, lead a discussion of Revelation 7:1-3, 9-17. Use your lesson commentary and these questions: *1.* What do the four angels symbolize in this passage? *2.* What is the purpose of the seal on the foreheads of God's servants? What protection does it offer? *3.* Who are the 144,000 and the great multitude? What is the significance of their white robes? Why are they carrying palm fronds? *4.* What is the significance of their cry, "Salvation"? *5.* Why do those around the throne say, "Amen"? *6.* How were the robes made white? *7.* To what service does Jesus call those who have washed their robes in His blood? What protection does He offer?

Distribute slips of paper with the following references (or direct the class to the student books where they are listed): Romans 3:25; 5:9; Ephesians 1:7; Hebrews 9:12-14; 13:11, 12; 1 Peter 1:18, 19; 1 John 1:7; Revelation 1:5, 6. Ask that these Scriptures be read aloud. Comment on each in turn, as appropriate, using your lesson commentary and the remarks below.

Romans 3:25; 5:9—Jesus turned away God's wrath by taking the punishment we deserved; *Ephesians 1:7; 1 Peter 1:18, 19*—Jesus bought us back from slavery to sin by offering His blood as the purchase price; *Hebrews 9:12-14; 13:11, 12*— Jesus' blood accomplished what no animal blood could: purification; *1 John 1:7; Revelation 1:5, 6*—Only the blood of Jesus has the power to cleanse us from all sin.

Into Life

Ask your students to write either a prayer, hymn, or chorus (their personal choice) of less than 10 lines; it is to praise Christ for the forgiveness and protection we have through the power of His blood. For inspiration, direct them to hymns and choruses such as "There Is a Fountain," "Nothing but the Blood," "But for the Blood," "The Blood Will Never Lose Its Power," "There Is Power in the Blood," and "Are You Washed in the Blood?" If you don't use student books, provide pens and paper along with the hymnals or chorus books. Ask volunteers to share their work.

Let's Talk It Over

The questions on this page are designed to promote discussion of the lesson by the class and to encourage application of the lesson Scriptures. The answers provided are only discussion starters. Let your class talk it over from there.

1. For the church to talk about the blood of Christ may seem "uncivilized" to some. How would you defuse this problem before it arises? Or have you found this even to be a problem?

There is a certain delicate balance here. The blood that Jesus shed for us is a stark reality. We are to teach this in a way that is understandable. If we sugarcoat this fact too much, however, the message may be lost.

One approach is to help the listener understand the Old Testament teaching about the purpose of blood sacrifices. These point to the seriousness of sin and how great its penalty must be. Yet those sacrifices were not capable of paying sin's penalty. That is why we needed the death of Jesus to satisfy the price of redemption (Romans 3:21-26).

2. There will be unity in Heaven among all people, creatures, and angels! How does that fact inspire you to build up the kingdom of Christ and work for the unity on earth for which Jesus prayed (John 17:20, 21)?

Divisions and bickering among God's people can be detrimental to a person's growth in faith. Whenever those who disagree over some understanding of God's Word get together, it would be good that they first rejoice over the beliefs they have in common. Then they can calmly discuss their points of difference, seeking to learn from each other to remove spiritual blind spots.

Remembering that God is the final judge can help keep tempers calm. Such a congenial, unified spirit will make looking forward to unity in Heaven much easier. Even in the face of those who would want to argue and divide, maintaining a focus on the disagreement as being temporary can be inspiring to the Christian life (Colossians 1:10-14).

3. How can we pray for fellow Christians who are being persecuted? Do you think God listens to generalized prayers such as "O Lord, please help all the suffering Christians"? Why, or why not?

Spiritually mature Christians naturally have tender hearts for one another. Who would want a fellow believer to become discouraged and give up the faith he or she has in Christ? Praying for those afflicted by war, poverty, and persecution is the least we can do. The best prayers are the ones that are as specific as possible.

Prayer for those suffering can result in our hearts being burdened to find tangible ways to help. This may involve providing for the physical and spiritual needs of those who are suffering because of Christ. See James 1:27 for a definition of *pure religion*. See also Proverbs 19:17; 21:13; 22:9; 29:7; 31:9, 20; James 2:16.

4. The church can teach Christians how to remain faithful during times of persecution and ridicule. But will the same techniques work during times of great prosperity, when the temptations of "the good life" on earth distract us? Explain.

Facing situations of life and death can force us to ask, "What will happen to me if I die?" That question can increase our determination to be faithful under any circumstance. Prosperity, however, lures people away from thinking much about life after death. Prosperity convinces some that their good fortune is from their own efforts (compare Daniel 4:30). Trusting in riches or in oneself is opposed to an active and abiding faith in God.

We can resist this problem by remembering that God owns everything and that we are stewards. Studying the passages that deal with being rich can help us keep everything in proper perspective (Matthew 19:16-30; James 2:1-13; 5:1-6).

5. In what ways have you found that the promise of God taking care of your needs in Heaven has helped you deal with the tough spots in life on earth?

The following analogy may help. Often students facing final assignments and exams in the last two weeks of the spring semester look forward to school being over so they can just stop and relax. Since they know that easier times are coming, they often say to themselves, "I can do anything for two weeks." The Christian has an additional advantage: the Christian knows that he or she has the Lord's strength to undergird his or her personal efforts.

Taking Our Place at the Table

DEVOTIONAL READING: Psalm 148:1-14.

BACKGROUND SCRIPTURE: Revelation 19.

PRINTED TEXT: Revelation 19:1-10.

Revelation 19:1-10

1 And after these things I heard a great voice of much people in heaven, saying, Alleluia; Salvation, and glory, and honor, and power, unto the Lord our God:

2 For true and righteous are his judgments; for he hath judged the great whore, which did corrupt the earth with her fornication, and hath avenged the blood of his servants at her hand.

3 And again they said, Alleluia. And her smoke rose up for ever and ever.

4 And the four and twenty elders and the four beasts fell down and worshipped God that sat on the throne, saying, Amen; Alleluia.

5 And a voice came out of the throne, saying, Praise our God, all ye his servants, and ye that fear him, both small and great.

6 And I heard as it were the voice of a great multitude, and as the voice of many waters, and as the voice of mighty thunderings, saying, Alleluia: for the Lord God omnipotent reigneth.

7 Let us be glad and rejoice, and give honor to him: for the marriage of the Lamb is come, and his wife hath made herself ready.

8 And to her was granted that she should be arrayed in fine linen, clean and white: for the fine linen is the righteousness of saints.

9 And he saith unto me, Write, Blessed are they which are called unto the marriage supper of the Lamb. And he saith unto me, These are the true sayings of God.

10 And I fell at his feet to worship him. And he said unto me, See thou do it not: I am thy fellow servant, and of thy brethren that have the testimony of Jesus: worship God: for the testimony of Jesus is the spirit of prophecy.

GOLDEN TEXT: I heard as it were the voice of a great multitude, and as the voice of many waters, and as the voice of mighty thunderings, saying, Alleluia: for the Lord God omnipotent reigneth.—Revelation 19:6.

Our Community Now and in God's Future
Unit 3: Living in God's New World
(Lessons 10-13)

Lesson Aims

After participating in this lesson, each student will be able to:

1. Describe the hope that is available for God's faithful as John reveals it.

2. Explain the imagery that John uses to describe how the faithful can have confidence in their future.

3. Be able to correct false popular ideas of what worship should be.

Lesson Outline

INTRODUCTION
    A. "Senioritis"
    B. Lesson Background
 I. GOD DESTROYS (Revelation 19:1-5)
    A. Praise for Justice (vv. 1, 2)
    B. Praise for Complete Punishment (v. 3)
    C. Praise for Victory (vv. 4, 5)
        Deserved Praise
II. GOD PROVIDES (Revelation 19:6-10)
    A. Everybody Loves a Wedding (vv. 6-8)
        Dressed for the Wedding
    B. Everybody Loves a Meal (v. 9)
    C. Only God is to Be Worshiped (v. 10)
CONCLUSION
    A. We Have What It Takes
    B. Prayer
    C. Thought to Remember

Introduction

A. "Senioritis"

A few years ago, I had a very capable senior-level student in my class—let's call him Jason—who simply could not bring himself to complete one last, easy, two-page assignment. Jason had a case of *senioritis*. If you know a student, then you've no doubt heard that term. Right when it counts the most, college and high-school seniors find that the repetition and hard work begin to take their toll.

As a professor, I see this all the time at this time of year. Even our very best students can succumb to the effects of senioritis. Their hard work begins to wear on them, they lose the plot,

they take their eyes off the prize of graduating. Before long we have bad grades, missed classes, and a halfhearted effort that characterizes their work.

Jason's senioritis caused him to think that such a small assignment wouldn't really matter. But while it was only a small assignment, it was still very much a part of the course and thus the degree. And you can't graduate without completing all of your courses.

Jason and his parents were horrified to find out the day before graduation that he was going to fail the course and thus not graduate. He had family coming in from around the country to celebrate his accomplishments, and his friends assumed everything was fine. Sadly, Jason failed to achieve what he had worked hard for. It was all because he lost his focus and thus his motivation.

The daily rigors of life take a toll on our ability to stay the course. It may be finances, relationships, or "everything in general"; all of us sometimes find that we just want to give up. And, of course, this is only too true of our spiritual journeys. The terrain becomes difficult to traverse and we begin to falter and fall. We often don't want to get up again.

But there is a solution. The same solution that enables students to complete their requirements is what can help us continue our spiritual journeys. That solution is a confident expectation of the future. Students keep working because they *know* that if they stay the course, they'll earn a degree. And we can keep going in our spiritual lives because we *know* that there is an eternal reward waiting for those who are able to stay the course.

B. Lesson Background

As we come to the next stage in our discussion of the book of Revelation, let's consider where we've been so far. John's Revelation has been a story of hope. John repeatedly makes the same point throughout Revelation: if you are faithful to God, then you will be a part of God's eternal victory.

In the chapters previous to Revelation 19, we encounter Babylon, the great whore. Historically speaking, the early church used *Babylon* as a way to refer to Rome (1 Peter 5:13). The reason for this was that Babylon, in the history of Israel, was a place that brought about the destruction of many of God's people. Babylon thus stood as an icon of human arrogance, a place that put itself before God in its pursuit of worldly pleasure and success (even though God used it as His instrument). The early Christians referred to Rome as

Babylon because they believed it represented the same sort of worldly values.

Worldly pleasures—fame, possessions, money, etc.—appeal to virtually all of us on some level, don't they? And this appeal is characterized as the lure of a prostitute; thus we have Babylon as the great whore who lures people away from God. As we look into the next part of the story in chapter 19, we find John using this image of the great whore to contrast the virtuous character of the bride of Christ.

I. God Destroys
(Revelation 19:1-5)

A. Praise for Justice (vv. 1, 2)

1, 2. And after these things I heard a great voice of much people in heaven, saying, Alleluia; Salvation, and glory, and honor, and power, unto the Lord our God: for true and righteous are his judgments; for he hath judged the great whore, which did corrupt the earth with her fornication, and hath avenged the blood of his servants at her hand.

These two verses comprise the first of a series of praises. Note that the praise has two components. Verse 1 shows us the worshipful attitude of those who belong to God. This praise is a personal statement of acceptance of God's authority and an appreciation for His provision. Worship at its core is the recognition of the nature of our reigning God.

Verse 2 provides us with the reason that God's creation should praise and give honor to Him: *For true and righteous are His judgments.* Thus we worship God because of who He is (v. 1) as we recognize that a central feature of God's nature is His justice (v. 2).

As John pens these words, it is easy for Christians of his day to think of Babylon from chapters 17–18 as a reference to Rome. The *great whore* of the pagan Roman culture tempts and ravages the people of God. However, the fact that John uses another, very broad figure of speech *(corrupt the earth)* to describe unholy ef-

fects indicates a concern for any influence that leads people away from their heavenly Father. In the final analysis, Babylon and the great whore thus can refer to anyone or anything that opposes God's purposes. So this first praise is recognition for the way God destroys any who work against His mission of salvation for His people.

Anyone who does not submit to God's authority is an opponent of God. There is no neutral ground in the spiritual world (see John 1:5; 12:46; Ephesians 5:8; 1 Thessalonians 5:5; 1 John 1:5-7). Verse 2 emphasizes the fact that God's destruction of the great whore is a just act.

It is important, however, not to take this as a morbid celebration of death. Instead, John is emphasizing the way God is proven to be who He claims to be: a just and righteous God. John does this to show his original readers, who are under persecution, that God is all-powerful and able to keep His promises.

If we remain faithful to Him, then God will save us for all eternity. The multitudes of Heaven see the destruction of the great whore for what it really is: a magnification of the power of the God who is faithful to keep His promises to those who are faithful to Him.

B. Praise for Complete Punishment (v. 3)

3. And again they said, Alleluia. And her smoke rose up for ever and ever.

The praise for God's victory over His opponents continues. John uses repetition to bring home the point: God is truly victorious and thus truly worthy of our praise! The phrase *for ever and ever* emphasizes the idea of completeness and permanence (compare Isaiah 34:10). The destruction of those who reject God's authority will be just that.

C. Praise for Victory (vv. 4, 5)

4. And the four and twenty elders and the four beasts fell down and worshipped God that sat on the throne, saying, Amen; Alleluia.

Following the "much people" of verse 1, *the four and twenty elders and the four beasts* are two more groups who praise God for His victory. We were introduced to the elders and the beasts in Revelation 4 (Lesson 7). They are always found giving special recognition to God.

The mention of four beasts in the *King James Version* could be a little off-putting to some, since we tend to think of "beast" in a satanic way. Clearly, these four beasts are not satanic beings. The Greek word underneath the English is a general term for "living beings" or "creatures."

How to Say It

BABYLON. *Bab*-uh-lun.
EPHESIANS. Ee-*fee*-zhunz.
ISAIAH. Eye-*zay*-uh.
OMNIPOTENT. ahm-*nih*-poh-tent.
SENIORITIS. seen-your-*eye*-tuss.
THESSALONIANS. *Thess*-uh-*lo*-nee-unz (strong accent on *lo; th* as in *thin*).

The emphasis of the word is on the fact that they are living.

Again, this worship of God emphasizes that God really is victorious. Those who appreciate that fact will have eternal blessing. [See question #1, page 312.]

5. And a voice came out of the throne, saying, Praise our God, all ye his servants, and ye that fear him, both small and great.

The throne always refers to the presence and authority of *God* (examples: Psalm 9:7; 11:4; 45:6; 47:8; Hebrews 1:8). The voice we hear from the midst of God's presence issues a direct call to all the faithful to yield *praise*. If we understand the true nature of God, then we can still praise Him even in the midst of our deepest sorrow and toughest trial. We can do this because we understand that He is worthy. [See question #2, page 312.]

We also offer praise because we know that His purposes are eternal, that His salvation is sure, and that His victory is guaranteed and complete. We have a hope that transcends our temporary, earthly existence and daily difficulties. How marvelous is His eternal salvation and deliverance! How can we not worship? Worship in spirit and in truth reflects the fact that we understand the true nature and purposes of God. *Fear of the Lord* is related to our praise of Him in Psalm 22:23.

DESERVED PRAISE

A cartoon showed two teenage slackers reading a newspaper. The headline read, "Asian Students Superior to Americans in Science and Math." The caption to the cartoon has one teenager saying, "That may be, but I'll hold our self-esteem up against theirs any day!" This points up an ongoing debate within American culture concerning how to motivate children, how to bring out the best in them. The relationship among praise, self-esteem, and accomplishment is frequently debated.

Culture makes an idol out of self-esteem. We praise children disproportionately for minor accomplishments, assuming this will create high self-esteem and make the children successful. We outlaw comparisons between children in order to save the self-esteem of underachievers. A few years ago, schools in Nashville, Tennessee, decided to do away with honor rolls. Low academic achievers might be embarrassed to see their names missing!

We can debate the role that praise plays in the lives of youngsters. But there is no debate about God's worthiness to receive praise! Such praise is not an attempt to manipulate an underachiever into thinking well of himself. God is not an underachiever, and He suffers no self-esteem problems. Praise will be offered by a multitude who have experienced the greatness of God because He has saved them from their sins. He deserves our praise.

—C. R. B.

II. God Provides
(Revelation 19:6-10)

A. Everybody Loves a Wedding (vv. 6-8)

6. And I heard as it were the voice of a great multitude, and as the voice of many waters, and as the voice of mighty thunderings, saying, Alleluia: for the Lord God omnipotent reigneth.

The praise that results from the command in verse 5 is indeed loud! The sounds *of a great multitude, and as the voice of many waters, and as the voice of mighty thunderings* overlap to create a sense that this is an intense moment of praise.

And why not? This is the moment all the faithful have been waiting for, as verse 7 will show. It is the moment when the faithful servants of God enter into eternal, heavenly fellowship with their Savior, Jesus Christ. Such joy! This will be the time when all of God's work throughout history moves toward its magnificent conclusion.

And all this can come about because the God we serve is *omnipotent* (all-powerful). His power is demonstrated by the overwhelming and complete victory over His opponents; now His all-powerful nature brings His promises to their completion.

Thus John shows us why we can have courage to be faithful, even in the midst of great trouble: our God reigns over all and will always be able to deliver us. No wonder the praise from the multitude is thunderously loud! How can it be anything less? [See question #3, page 312.]

7a. Let us be glad and rejoice, and give honor to him: for the marriage of the Lamb is come.

John now shifts to a picture of a wedding. Using our "sanctified imaginations," we can see that our spiritual lives parallel the practice of getting married. We may say that the cultural practice of becoming engaged parallels the occasion when we first give our lives to Christ. Then the period between the engagement and the wedding parallels the period in which we faithfully await and prepare for the Lord's return. The wedding itself parallels the time when the faithful are finally with Christ for all eternity.

The groom here is identified as *the Lamb*. A pure and spotless lamb has always been the ideal sacrifice offered to God. The Passover, in particular, celebrated God's deliverance with the slaughter of a lamb (Exodus 12:21; 2 Chronicles 30:15; 35:1; Luke 22:7).

John the Baptist referred to Jesus as "the Lamb of God" (John 1:29). The apostle Peter said that Jesus was "a lamb without blemish and without spot" (1 Peter 1:19). And in Revelation, the apostle John frequently uses the term *Lamb* to refer to Jesus (Revelation 5:6; etc.). The idea of Christ as the sacrificial lamb lies at the very heart of our redemption and our salvation.

7b. And his wife hath made herself ready.

John also draws our attention to the fact that the *wife* of the Lamb has been busy getting *herself ready*. She is the community of the redeemed. She consists of the faithful who have submitted themselves to Christ's authority. Their faithfulness is their preparation. Thus the marriage that John now describes unites the Christ, who sacrificed His life for humanity, with all those who accepted this sacrifice.

But let us pay attention to the implicit warning in this verse: there will be no person at the wedding who is not ready to be there. Jesus used the image of a wedding to warn about the need to be ready. Matthew 25:1-13 offers the Parable of the Ten Virgins, five of whom were unprepared for the groom's arrival and so failed to enter into the wedding celebration. When they begged to be let in, the groom's response was "Verily I say unto you, I know you not" (Matthew 25:12). Jesus also told the Parable of the Marriage Feast. One man who had not made himself ready through proper attire was thrown out (Matthew 22:1-14).

8. And to her was granted that she should be arrayed in fine linen, clean and white: for the fine linen is the righteousness of saints.

This verse develops the previous verse's idea of the bride's readiness for the Lamb. The nature of the clothing projects an image of purity: *fine linen, clean and white* (compare Isaiah 1:18; Revelation 3:4, 5; 6:11; 7:9-14). This wedding attire is not something the bride herself could have acquired. Instead, as John says, it is *granted* to her to dress in this manner.

The final phrase of verse 8 reveals that the description of the fine wedding outfit reflects the *righteousness of the saints*. We don't have a righteousness of our own. Rather, it is the sacrifice of the Lamb of God that enables the bride to present herself in the white and clean wedding dress (compare Philippians 3:9). The imagery of Isaiah 61:10 is powerful: "He hath clothed me with the garments of salvation, he hath covered me with the robe of righteousness." (See also Romans

Visual for
Lesson 10

Jesus the lamb is also Jesus the rock! Point to this visual as you ask, "How has Jesus been your rock?"

1:17; 3:21, 22; 5:17-21; 1 Peter 2:24.) [See question #4, page 312.]

DRESSED FOR THE WEDDING

Brides usually spend a great amount of time and money getting ready for the ceremony. Choosing the attendants, musicians, and menu for the reception demands attention. Not to be overlooked are personal elements—getting rid of those extra pounds, choosing a good hair style, etc., will make everything "just perfect."

But the centerpiece of all the preparations is the bridal gown. White seems to be an enduring color of choice. Years ago, a wedding advice columnist observed that while white wedding gowns were traditional, gowns in off-white and other colors had gained in popularity. Even so, the color white has shown its staying power.

The purity of the bride of Christ is an important, vivid image in this Bible text. Her "fine linen, clean and white" signifies this purity. But the bride of Christ doesn't have to try to construct her own gown. We can't make ourselves pure enough; our faith in the Lamb is the means by which His purity becomes ours. Thus we are counted worthy of the pure white linen robes He shall provide.   —C. R. B.

B. Everybody Loves a Meal (v. 9)

9. And he saith unto me, Write, Blessed are they which are called unto the marriage supper of the Lamb. And he saith unto me, These are the true sayings of God.

The "wife" of verse 7 is an image of the faithful who join Christ forever. Now John refers to the same group as *they which are called.*

There is a slight change in the dynamics of the story here because now John tells us that he has been asked to write *the true sayings of God*. While all Scripture has its origins in God, John now draws even more attention to the vital nature of the message. His readers must know of the utter reliability of the point that anyone who is faithful to God, and thus participates in this *marriage supper of the Lamb,* is truly *blessed.*

We recall that John's original readers are in the midst of suffering and are in desperate need of maintaining hope. John helps them, and us, with a reminder of the reliability of God's promises. This is a major theme of the book of Revelation: God is faithful and true to those who are faithful and true to Him. The book of Revelation is thus a source of hope for all Christians of all centuries who suffer and experience attacks against their relationship with God.

C. Only God Is to Be Worshiped (v. 10)

10. And I fell at his feet to worship him. And he said unto me, See thou do it not: I am thy fellow servant, and of thy brethren that have the testimony of Jesus: worship God: for the testimony of Jesus is the spirit of prophecy.

We may think that the apostles were not prone to make mistakes, but here John reveals his own error. John is so overcome by the magnificence of God's blessing of His people that he attempts *to worship* the angel who is delivering the message. The angel rebukes John for the mistake but also helps John to understand the problem (see also Acts 10:25, 26; 14:11-18; Revelation 22:9). [See question #5, page 312.]

The final statement *for the testimony of Jesus is the spirit of prophecy* is difficult. There are numerous explanations that attempt to take in the various ways of dealing with the original language. For example, does the phrase *testimony of Jesus* (used twice) mean "testimony that comes from the lips of Jesus" or "testimony that is about Jesus" or both?

Perhaps the best way to approach this is to note first that the angel recognizes that he is a *fellow servant* of the *brethren that have the testimony of Jesus.* We take the word *brethren* to refer to all faithful believers, understanding that they represent Christ to the world. These faithful people have a *testimony* or *witness* about Jesus that results in their persecution (Revelation 6:9; 12:11; 20:4).

The word *prophecy* also can cause confusion. It is important to understand that the word translated *prophecy* does not always signify "telling the future." The idea, rather, is one of "speaking on behalf of God" (it's just that sometimes God speaks about the future). So, speaking on behalf of God in testimony is prophecy. The angel thus is talking about the faith of the saints as they live out their relationship to Christ. The Holy Spirit enables them (us) to do so.

Conclusion

A. We Have What It Takes

The Christian life is filled with challenges that wear us down and threaten our ability to remain faithful. Satan knows all our weaknesses, and he doesn't hesitate to exploit them. The book *The Screwtape Letters* by C. S. Lewis offers us a hypothetical account of demons trying to figure out the best ways to tempt humans. We may see ourselves as willing victims on every page!

If we understand the true nature of God—that He really is victorious, destroying His enemies and blessing His faithful—then we have what it takes to remain steadfast, even in the face of suffering. If we are steadfast in our faith, then we will be ready for the groom's arrival. Our eternal future is under His protection. What a reason for praise this is!

B. Prayer

Our mighty and gracious Father, we thank You for the hope You have given us through the sacrifice of the Lamb. Help us to remain steadfast and faithful to You as we await Your return. To be with Jesus for all eternity will be worth it all. In Jesus' name, amen.

C. Thought to Remember

Be ready for the wedding feast.

Home Daily Bible Readings

Monday, April 30—Parable of the Wedding Banquet (Matthew 22:1-14)

Tuesday, May 1—The Song of the Lamb (Revelation 15:1-5)

Wednesday, May 2—He Will Reign Forever (Revelation 11:15-19)

Thursday, May 3—The Heavens Praise (Psalm 148:1-6)

Friday, May 4—The Earth Praises (Psalm 148:7-14)

Saturday, May 5—Hallelujah! (Revelation 19:1-5)

Sunday, May 6—Give God Glory (Revelation 19:6-10)

Learning by Doing

This page contains an alternative lesson plan emphasizing learning activities.
Classes desiring such student involvement will find these suggestions helpful.

Learning Goals

After participating in this lesson, each student will be able to:

1. Describe the hope that is available for God's faithful as John reveals it.

2. Explain the imagery that John uses to describe how the faithful can have confidence in their future.

3. Be able to correct false popular ideas of what worship should be.

Into the Lesson

Ask each student to take a piece of paper (or use the student book) and draw or describe something he or she really wished for as a child, as an adolescent, and as an adult. (This could be one, two, or even three different things.) Ask volunteers to share their answers. Were any of these dreams fulfilled? Why, or why not? How did your students feel when their dreams were fulfilled or not fulfilled? How are we affected by such gratifications and disappointments?

Transition by saying, "Today's lesson deals with the fulfillment of every Christian's greatest hope and the effect it should have on our faith."

Into the Word

Pair off your students to answer the following questions (also listed in the student books). Assign the first five questions to half of your pairs and the last four to the other half. (Suggested answers are italicized; don't distribute those.)

1. Why is the multitude praising God (vv. 1, 2)? *(His judgments are true and righteous.)*

2. Who is the great whore who corrupted the earth (vv. 1, 2; see also Revelation 17:1, 18; 18:1, 2)? *(Babylon, or any influence that leads people away from their heavenly Father.)*

3. What will happen to those condemned by God (v. 3)? *(Their destruction will be certain.)*

4. The 24 elders and the 4 beasts represent what 2 groups (v. 4; also Revelation 4:1-11 in Lesson 7)? *(The elders signify all believers and the beasts point to all the creatures of the world.)*

5. Why did the multitude praise God (vv. 6, 7)? *(Because God reigns over all and has all power to accomplish His will.)*

6. What is the wedding of the Lamb? To whom is He to be married (v. 7; see also Revelation

18:23; 21:2, 9; 22:17)? *(The Lamb's bride is the church, those who have submitted themselves to Christ's authority.)*

7. What does fine linen represent? How do people receive it (v. 8; see also Isaiah 61:10)? *(It represents the righteousness of the saints, which comes from Christ on the basis of His sacrifice; Christ gives the clothing to His bride.)*

8. Why are those called to the marriage supper considered "blessed"? On what basis are they invited to the supper (v. 9; Matthew 22:1-14)? *(They are blessed because they have God's promise of eternal life if they remain faithful to Christ. They are those who accepted Christ as Lord.)*

9. Whom did John attempt to worship (v. 10)? Why was he rebuked? *(John tried to worship an angel but was rebuked because all worship should be directed only to God.)*

After pairs have finished their research, reassemble the class to discuss their findings. Focus especially on verses 7-11 and what is involved in being invited to the marriage supper of the Lamb. Be sure that students grasp the importance of this question: Why should knowing that our righteousness is not self-achieved increase our confidence in God's promise of eternal life?

Into Life

Ask each pair from the previous exercise to write a brief response to one of the viewpoints below. Make sure to assign all viewpoints.

1. Dave thinks that the weekly worship service is a form of entertainment. If the music is great and the sermon keeps his attention, he considers it real worship. Otherwise, it's a waste of his time. What would you say to him?

2. Jennifer believes that every worship service should be geared to meet the needs of "seekers." She was converted at such a service and feels that any other focus fails to fulfill the Great Commission (Matthew 28:19, 20). How would you respond to her?

3. Ted doesn't understand why the church bothers to include an invitation in every service. "After all, nearly everyone's going to be saved anyway, so why should we worry? Let's just focus on praising God," he says. How do you respond to Ted?

Allow time to discuss suggestions.

Let's Talk It Over

The questions on this page are designed to promote discussion of the lesson by the class and to encourage application of the lesson Scriptures. The answers provided are only discussion starters. Let your class talk it over from there.

1. What are some of the victories for which we should fall down and worship God, both as individuals and corporately as the church? Why do we fail to do this as often as we should?

We often get so caught up in some of the trials of life that we fail to appreciate the triumphs. Our personal salvation is a matter for which we can worship and praise God daily. We have a reason to rejoice in victory as new people are added to the church. God has helped us overcome specific sins in our lives. And we can fall down and worship God for the hope we have for the future victory over death. Here's an idea: for every defeat you are tempted to dwell on, think of two victories God has granted you.

2. How do you praise God when you are going through tough times?

God desires that we continually praise and worship Him through both good times and bad. It is important that we realize that temptations in life are not from God (James 1:13, 14). God does permit us to go through temptations and trials, but He is always faithful to prevent us from being tempted beyond what He knows we can bear (1 Corinthians 10:13). Because of this promise we can praise Him. We know that God can bring good out of these tough times (Romans 8:28).

3. In what ways have you experienced God's awe-inspiring power at work? How do you know when the power at work is from God and not your own ability?

Can anyone doubt that God's power, His omnipotence, has been demonstrated in many ways? God's power is readily visible in His creation. The heavens declare His glory and power (Psalm 19:1); the earth demonstrates His handiwork (Genesis 1). God's omnipotent power is also seen in His re-creation of bringing people from death to life through the new birth.

But God's power is seen in the small things as well—the gentle touch of a trusted friend at just the right time or the word fitly spoken by a Spirit-led teacher or preacher. It often is only after the fact that we recognize God's power at work. Taking time to reflect upon our lives is time well spent, as it allows us to see God's work. A journal in which we write reflections of our daily lives can lead us to see more readily God's power at work in us.

4. What can we do as a church, as the bride of Christ, to make ourselves ready for His return? What mistakes do churches sometimes make in this regard?

Some churches place much attention and emphasis on strategic plans, policy and procedure manuals, constitutions, and by-laws. The idea is to be ready for anything that may come up in the day-to-day operation of the church. Too much emphasis here, however, will make the church more of a corporation and less of a living body.

Readiness for the "grand tomorrow" of the coming of the bridegroom requires purity in our teaching (1 Timothy 4:16) as well as how we apply that teaching to our lives (James 1:22). A focus on fulfilling both the Great Commandment to love (Matthew 22:36-38) as well as the Great Commission to go (Matthew 28:19, 20) is required. Neither is to be stressed at the expense of the other.

5. We readily say that Jesus alone is Lord and that only He is to be worshiped and praised. But like John, we too can be guilty of falling down and worshiping the wrong one. In what ways have you done this? How have you guarded yourself against this error?

There are times when a preacher or former preacher is so venerated that he becomes the object of adoration in a church. Perhaps a program he began cannot be eliminated, even if it is no longer effective, because it was "a program begun by Brother So-and-so." Sometimes we are guilty of idealizing (if not worshiping) the past. A church may continually try to recreate that past to reclaim the old "days of glory."

Some have such a preference for certain TV preachers that they neglect their own local church while supporting those other ministries. Christians may end up pouring their offerings into ministries that can "do no wrong" while their own church struggles financially. This is at least a wrong priority and at most idol worship.

Finding a Home in Heaven

DEVOTIONAL READING: 2 Peter 3:10-18.

BACKGROUND SCRIPTURE: Revelation 21:1-8.

PRINTED TEXT: Revelation 21:1-8.

Revelation 21:1-8

1 And I saw a new heaven and a new earth: for the first heaven and the first earth were passed away; and there was no more sea.

2 And I John saw the holy city, new Jerusalem, coming down from God out of heaven, prepared as a bride adorned for her husband.

3 And I heard a great voice out of heaven saying, Behold, the tabernacle of God is with men, and he will dwell with them, and they shall be his people, and God himself shall be with them, and be their God.

4 And God shall wipe away all tears from their eyes; and there shall be no more death, neither sorrow, nor crying, neither shall there *God also un area* be any more pain: for the former things are passed away.

5 And he that sat upon the throne said, Behold, I make all things new. And he said unto me, Write: for these words are true and faithful.

6 And he said unto me, It is done. I am Alpha and Omega, the beginning and the end. I will give unto him that is athirst of the fountain of the water of life freely.

7 He that overcometh shall inherit all things; and I will be his God, and he shall be my son.

8 But the fearful, and unbelieving, and the abominable, and murderers, and whoremongers, and sorcerers, and idolaters, and all liars, shall have their part in the lake which burneth with fire and brimstone: which is the second death.

May 13

GOLDEN TEXT: I heard a great voice out of heaven saying, Behold, the tabernacle of God is with men, and he will dwell with them, and they shall be his people, and God himself shall be with them, and be their God.—Revelation 21:3.

Our Community Now and in God's Future

Unit 3: Living in God's New World

(Lessons 10-13)

Lesson Aims

After participating in this lesson, each student will be able to:

1. Identify the Alpha and Omega.

2. Contrast the first heaven and earth with the second.

3. Teach one unbeliever about the differences between the first heaven and earth and the second heaven and earth.

Lesson Outline

INTRODUCTION

   A. Thank the Lord for Solid Ground

   B. Lesson Background

 I. NEW HEAVEN AND EARTH! (Revelation 21:1-5)

   A. Changed Reality (vv. 1, 2)

     Something Really *New*

   B. Dwelling with God (vv. 3-5)

II. NEW LIFE OR SECOND DEATH? (Revelation 21: 6-8)

   A. Life for the Godly (vv. 6, 7)

     Better or Bitter?

   B. Death for the Ungodly (v. 8)

CONCLUSION

   A. What Our Homes Lack

   B. Prayer

   C. Thought to Remember

Introduction

A. Thank the Lord for Solid Ground

I grew up in Australia, and thus it was practically required that I have a passion for surfing. But any person who has ever had the pleasure of enjoying the sea is a person who also knows the wonderful security of *terra firma*: solid ground!

On a stormy day in 1989, I learned to appreciate solid ground in a way I never had before. The reports of cyclones (hurricanes) and helicopter rescues made others sense danger. But all my best mate and I could think about was big, fun waves. After only a few minutes in the surf, we realized that we had misjudged the situation!

Having drifted three-quarters of a mile up the coast, we were no longer staring back at the golden sands of the beach but at an unforgiving rocky wall. I suddenly lost all interest in surfing and developed a very healthy interest in just staying alive.

We struggled against the current and the waves for about two hours; the sun had set, the waves becoming only silhouettes. We were about a quarter of a mile offshore and could see only a few lights here and there. A huge set of waves loomed in the distance, blackening what was left of the horizon.

My friend made it over the waves, but I did not. The lip of one wave picked me up and slammed me down through the water and onto the rocky ocean floor. Somehow I made it back up to the surface only to have two more waves crash down and do the same thing all over again.

I genuinely thought I was going to die right there in the dark water. I decided all I could do was to make a desperate swim straight for the lights on the shore. Whether it was all rocks or sand, I didn't care. I just wanted something solid and secure. My friend and pieces of my surfboard were waiting for me there as I crawled onto the beach. I laughed nervously at escaping death but then fell down and hugged and kissed the shore. It was so good! At that moment in my life there was simply nothing better than wonderfully solid ground.

Today's lesson offers a similar message. The world is fraught with danger and suffering. But we know the shore is there, even though it is hard to see. If we persevere, by the grace of God we will emerge from the struggle victorious. The things causing our suffering will be put behind us in the end. We will stand firmly for all eternity on wonderfully solid ground.

B. Lesson Background

In Revelation 20 we read of Satan's final downfall. Anyone who has ever suffered has felt the power of Satan, because all suffering finds its origin in Satan's influences. That began with the fall of humanity in the Garden of Eden. Satan has set himself up in this world as the enemy of God. Satan actively seeks to destroy us all (1 Peter 5:8). Jesus came to put an end to Satan's project (1 John 3:8). For all who experience Satan's influences through our suffering, pain, and trials, the book of Revelation is a great comfort.

God understands what it means for us to suffer. Jesus, as "the Lamb as it had been slain" (Revelation 5:6), knows what it means to suffer and experience trial (also Mark 1:13; Luke 22:41, 42). He knows our pain (Hebrews 4:15). The book of Revelation is His Word, and this book shows us that we are given what is necessary to overcome. In the book of Revelation, God tells us that He knows that we suffer. But He promises to destroy the source of our suffering: Satan. Those who embrace Jesus and this promise are able to remain faithful; they surely will be delivered to an eternal life—a life free from the trials and sufferings that Satan brings.

I. New Heaven and New Earth! (Revelation 21:1-5)

A. Changed Reality (vv. 1, 2)

1. And I saw a new heaven and a new earth: for the first heaven and the first earth were passed away; and there was no more sea.

Our passage begins with an important contrast between what is *new* and what is *first*. As we consider what this image conveys, we should note that the word *heaven* as used here is a reference to what we call "the skies." This is very much along the lines of the word *firmament* in Genesis 1:8. The image thus presents a contrast between what we see when we look out the window right now (what John calls the *first*) and what will be *new*.

The word translated *new* in our text can be interpreted in two ways. One way is as a reference to time, like when a recently purchased second-hand car is called "new." (I may say that such a car is "new to me.") Another way is to take *new* as a reference to quality, like when someone buys a brand new car that no one has ever owned before. Such a car has the quality of never having been used—it is "factory fresh."

This particular word for *new*, based on the way John uses it, refers to quality. So when John uses the image of a *new earth*, we're not to take that as a reference to an updated version of our own current earth. Rather, it refers to a new kind of earth altogether. The word *new* signals this

How to Say It

ABRAHAM. *Ay*-bruh-ham.
ALPHA. *Al*-fa.
EZEKIEL. Ee-*zeek*-ee-ul or Ee-*zeek*-yul.
GALILEE. *Gal*-uh-lee.
ISAIAH. Eye-*zay*-uh.
JEREMIAH. Jair-uh-*my*-uh.
JERUSALEM. Juh-*roo*-suh-lem.
LEVITICUS. Leh-*vit*-ih-kus.
OMEGA. O-*may*-guh.
PATMOS. *Pat*-muss.
ZECHARIAH. *Zek*-uh-*rye*-uh (strong accent on *rye*).

change from corruptible to eternal (see also Isaiah 65:17; 66:22; 2 Peter 3:13).

The sea figures prominently as a symbol in Revelation. About 40 percent of all the references to the sea in the New Testament are in this book (if we don't count "Sea of Galilee," which is actually a lake). The sea in the ancient world is a place of mystery, danger, and vulnerability. Those of John's day use the sea for industry and travel, but it is a strange place that is thought by some to span the gap between the worlds of "gods" and humans. Revelation uses the ancient ideas of the sea as both the thing between God and humans (Revelation 4:6), and as a place of great evil and fear (13:1). Revelation also uses the image of sea to show God's absolute power over all evil (10:1-6). Jesus used the image of the disturbance of the sea as a sign of great turmoil (Luke 21:25).

So the comment *there was no more sea* makes a lot of sense in the context of the ancient culture. With the final passing away of this first, temporary world, the new world will be a place without fear and danger that the sea represents. [See question #1, page 320.]

SOMETHING *REALLY* NEW

The newspaper ad of a house for sale read, "3br, 2ba, newer kitch, ocn vu." Anyone familiar with real-estate jargon can translate *3br* into "three bedrooms" and *2ba* into "two bathrooms." *Ocn vu* is plain enough: it means that if you climb on a chair in one of the bathrooms and look out of the upper corner of the window, you can view the ocean in the distance—easily adding $10,000 to the price!

But what is a "newer kitch"? *Kitch* stands for kitchen, of course. But what about that slippery word *newer*? Newer than what? That bit of real-estate jargon means that the kitchen is not as old as the rest of the house. Thus it signifies that the house has had its kitchen redone sometime in the indefinite past.

John tells us that the dwelling place he saw in his vision will not be merely *newer*—as a piece of real estate that had been updated a while back. Rather, it will be *qualitatively* new—different in every important way from what we have known before. Everything that could remind us of the pain and sadness of this old, fallen world will be completely gone. Our new, heavenly dwelling place will be *really* new!   —C. R. B.

2. And I John saw the holy city, new Jerusalem, coming down from God out of heaven, prepared as a bride adorned for her husband.

John's use of geographic locations to depict the coming new world becomes more focused in this verse. As with the new heaven and new earth, the reference here is not to the renewal of the Jerusalem that exists in John's day or even now. It is a reference to a brand *new Jerusalem*. There are two important points made about this new kind of Jerusalem: it comes *from God* and it is *prepared*.

The earthly Jerusalem has a special place in the history of God's people. But as Christianity developed, early believers increasingly used the name *Jerusalem* to refer to the coming promise. For example, Paul can use the word *Jerusalem* to refer both to the city of his day and to the Jerusalem "which is above" (Galatians 4:25, 26). The author of Hebrews uses the term *Jerusalem* in this latter sense (see Hebrews 12:22).

The reason Jerusalem is thought of in this way by first-century Christians is that this city was known in the Old Testament as the place of God's temple, where God put His name (2 Chronicles 6:4-6). This was a place where God was present with His people in a special way. The early Christians drew upon this idea; thus *Jerusalem* could refer to the promise of eternal life with God. John uses the term in this way Revelation 3:12 (compare Isaiah 52:1; Hebrews 11:10, 16).

John further defines the idea of the new Jerusalem by saying that it is *prepared as a bride*. We came across this concept in the previous lesson. Revelation 19 uses wife or bride imagery to refer to the faithful. Here *bride* means the same thing. That is, the new Jerusalem that comes from God is in fact the gathering of the faithful who dwell with God in eternal peace. It is *we* who are the holy city of God.

B. Dwelling with God (vv. 3-5)

3. And I heard a great voice out of heaven saying, Behold, the tabernacle of God is with men, and he will dwell with them, and they shall be his people, and God himself shall be with them, and be their God.

Essentially, *tabernacle* is a repetition of the ideas "holy city" and "new Jerusalem" mentioned in the previous verse. God had given very specific instructions to Moses to set up a tabernacle and its furnishings (Exodus 26–27, 35–38). It was to be a focal point of God's presence (Exodus 29:44-46). After Moses had carried out all that the Lord asked of him, "the glory of the Lord filled the tabernacle" (Exodus 40:34). God was with His people in a special way.

It has been God's desire all along to live with His people (compare Leviticus 26:11, 12; Ezekiel 37:27; Zechariah 2:10; 2 Corinthians 6:16). Putting these ideas together reveals that John is making a point that is similar to his point in the previous verse: *we* are the dwelling place of God!

4, 5. And God shall wipe away all tears from their eyes; and there shall be no more death, neither sorrow, nor crying, neither shall there be any more pain: for the former things are passed away. And he that sat upon the throne said, Behold, I make all things new. And he said unto me, Write: for these words are true and faithful.

With the passing of the first heaven and earth will also come the passing of Satan's power and influence. And this is the hope to which we all cling: this world and its suffering are only temporary. Suffering tempts us to lose our focus on the eternal. Thus it is a great tool used by Satan to distract God's people and tempt them to question their relationship to Him.

People often find cause to blame God for their suffering. But in reality, suffering comes to all of us because we live in a world that has fallen to Satan's temptation and is therefore subject to decay (Genesis 3:1-19; Romans 8:18-22). When a loved one is dying from a terrible disease, who does not long for that person's healing? When we suffer physically, our perspective swiftly turns toward the physical and temporary. The tragedy of suffering drives our minds to obsess about the physical. Thus we become prime targets for the temptation to allow the temporary to dominate our thinking and values. [See question #2, page 320.]

John's solution is to help us understand that our future with the Lord is utterly free from suffering (compare Isaiah 25:8; 35:10; 65:19). And because John understands the deep and eternal significance of this for us, he reminds us that these are not his *words* but the Lord's. The words are of the one who sits *upon the throne*!

We can have absolute confidence in our future, new life because *these words are true and faithful*. It is worth noting that John emphasizes the reliability of the message three times toward the end of this book (here and in Revelation 19:9; 22:6).

II. New Life or Second Death? (Revelation 21:6-8)

A. Life for the Godly (vv. 6, 7)

6. And he said unto me, It is done. I am Alpha and Omega, the beginning and the end. I will give unto him that is athirst of the fountain of the water of life freely.

In this verse John again emphasizes the reliability of the message, only from a different angle. This time he embeds into the story the point of God's activity in history. God is the one speaking, and he refers to himself as *Alpha and Omega*. Those are the first and the last letters of the Greek alphabet. So when God calls himself *the beginning and the end* we understand it to be a repetition of Alpha and Omega. (You can see what an Alpha and an Omega look like in today's Scripture art at the beginning of the lesson.) God is not, however, admitting that He himself has a beginning and an end. Rather, He announces that all beginnings and ends are in His control (Isaiah 44:6; 46:9, 10; 48:12).

The second part of this verse offers two important ideas: a certain problem (spiritual thirst) and its solution *(water of life)*. These two concepts are not unique to Revelation. They are found throughout the Bible (examples: Psalm 65:9; Isaiah 41:17, 18; 55:1; Jeremiah 2:13; Zechariah 13:1). For clarity we can look to John's Gospel. In John 7:37, 38, Jesus speaks to the problem of spiritual thirst and then offers the solution in terms of believing on Him. Here, those who are *athirst* are those who understand their need for Jesus. See also John 4:13, 14. [See question #3, page 320.]

7. He that overcometh shall inherit all things; and I will be his God, and he shall be my son.

He that overcometh is mentioned both here and in each of the seven "letters" of Revelation 2 and 3. The phrase comes from the Greek word for "the one who is victorious." In Revelation 2 and 3 the overcomer is the person who has been able to remain faithful in spite of opposition to his or her faith. And the concept of overcoming is a key to the entire book of Revelation. We could even say that a purpose of Revelation is to enable its readers to overcome.

To overcome is the essence of faithfulness. The primary biblical example of this (other than Jesus) is Abraham. Abraham's trust in God was repeatedly challenged. But Abraham's unwavering belief that God would deliver on His promises proved Abraham to be faithful and the father of all who are faithful (Genesis 12:1–25:8; Romans 4:16-22). Faithfulness means overcoming any challenge to one's relationship with the Lord. Thus the overcomer is the person who does not melt away when faith is under fire (1 Peter 4:12-19). Such a person stands firm, knowing that the Lord will always win.

But we must not assume that challenges to faith always come in the obvious form of persecution. Faith is tested by anything that threatens our relationship with God. Money problems,

Visual for
Lessons 6 & 11

Probe your students' understanding by asking, "How does the work of Christ assure us of life?"

family issues, health problems, etc. can all erode the foundation of that relationship. In short, *all of us* are constantly being challenged in our faith. The good news is that every time we withstand a challenge, we become stronger in our faith. In this way we become true overcomers who remain faithful to God. Thus we will inherit all things and be forever God's children. [See question #4, page 320.]

BETTER OR BITTER?

Louise Ashby, age 21, had a dream of becoming an actress and model. So she moved to Hollywood, California. That is the place where such dreams are supposed to come true. But it is also a place where physical beauty often is required for success.

Suddenly her dream crashed—literally—in a head-on auto accident. Following the brain surgery that saved her life, Ashby was in a coma. A week later came a lengthy surgery that started the reconstruction of her face. Her first look in a mirror revealed an unrecognizable person with a watermelon-sized head. Fourteen reconstructive surgeries and 238 small titanium plates later, she ended up with a million-dollar face. She was once more a physical beauty. You would never guess what she has had to overcome.

But today the beauty goes deeper. Ashby still models and acts, but she also became involved with an organization that offered counsel and financial help to children who need surgery to correct facial birth defects. She began to make frequent visits to UCLA's Craniofacial Clinic, encouraging the patients there by telling them what she had overcome.

Ashby affirms that her ordeal made her stronger. That's what happens when we overcome obstacles, whether in a physical or spiritual sense. Whatever spiritual challenges we must overcome in this life, we become stronger with the help of God. Rather than becoming bitter, we can become better—fit for eternity. Blessed are the overcomers!   —C. R. B.

B. Death for the Ungodly (v. 8)

8. But the fearful, and unbelieving, and the abominable, and murderers, and whoremongers, and sorcerers, and idolaters, and all liars, shall have their part in the lake which burneth with fire and brimstone: which is the second death.

This list of those who are doomed to an eternal *death* is another encouragement to readers. Removal of evil people removes their persecutions of Christians as well (compare Matthew 25:41). To the degree that the unbelieving will be doomed forever, those who are faithful will be blessed forever.

This list of ungodly people works like many lists in the New Testament: we are better off taking it as a whole rather than scrutinizing it on a point-by-point basis. As we read the list, we're supposed to get an impression of the *kind* of person who is doomed to eternal death. These are people who live in rebellion against God.

Further, we must not forget that the book of Revelation was originally written to people suffering physical persecution. John himself is a prisoner in exile on the island of Patmos as he writes. In such a circumstance we can easily appreciate how the announcement of doom for those who bring pain and suffering to Christians will help strengthen the faith of the readers. That is, if you are being persecuted but you know that in the end you will be delivered and your persecutor will be punished, then it becomes a way for you to endure.

The *second death* idea is the counterpart of "the first heaven and the first earth" in verse 1. But note that John does not call this death a *new death*—he says *second death*. John will often use synonyms to refer to similar things in order to create a sense of distinct value. For example, John describes in Revelation 11 two witnesses of God. John uses "forty and two months" (11:2) to describe a time of persecution and "a thousand two hundred and threescore days" (11:3) to refer to the time of their prophecy.

John describes this same time period in two different ways to show how the Christian experience is double-sided. On the one hand, we serve Christ and experience His peace; on the other hand, we live in a temporary world filled with pain and suffering. Thus the second death is an eternal death to which the unfaithful must go in the same way that the new heaven and earth is an eternal destiny for the faithful. [See question #5, page 320.]

Conclusion

A. What Our Homes Lack

When we look at our earthly homes, we often think in terms of what they don't have—we dwell upon what they lack. "It doesn't have central air." "It doesn't have a basement." "It doesn't have an attached garage." "It doesn't have a sun room." Too much thinking like this can lead to envy and unhappiness.

But what our heavenly homes will lack will be glorious indeed: these homes will lack all the evil people, attitudes, and practices that we see in Revelation 21:8. There won't be any bad neighbors in Heaven! What a glorious encouragement this is.

B. Prayer

Lord, we are grateful for John's glorious vision of future hope. We thirst for You and the hope of an eternity in Your presence. We trust that You will deliver us. Help us to realize that kind of trust in this present life. In this way we will walk with You each day, and we will overcome all that tries to challenge our relationship with You. In Jesus' name, amen.

C. Thought to Remember

Our final home is our final hope.

Home Daily Bible Readings

Monday, May 7—Our Citizenship Is in Heaven (Philippians 3:17-21)
Tuesday, May 8—The Coming of the Kingdom (1 Corinthians 15:20-28)
Wednesday, May 9—Our Heavenly Dwelling (2 Corinthians 5:1-10)
Thursday, May 10—Longing for a New Home (Hebrews 11:10-16)
Friday, May 11—The Day of the Lord (2 Peter 3:10-18)
Saturday, May 12—New Heavens and a New Earth (Isaiah 65:17-19, 23-25)
Sunday, May 13—God Will Dwell Among Us (Revelation 21:1-8)

Learning by Doing

This page contains an alternative lesson plan emphasizing learning activities.
Classes desiring such student involvement will find these suggestions helpful.

Learning Goals

After this lesson each student will be able to:

1. Identify the Alpha and Omega.

2. Contrast the first heaven and earth with the second.

3. Teach one unbeliever about the differences between the first heaven and earth and the second heaven and earth.

Into the Lesson

As your students arrive, give each one a copy of the following agree/disagree exercise (or direct their attention to the student book, where it is printed).

1. Old hymns are much better than new praise choruses. Agree or disagree?

2. Younger preachers are better speakers than older preachers. Agree or disagree?

3. Older church buildings have a more worshipful atmosphere than newer church buildings. Agree or disagree?

4. Life 50 years ago was better than it is today. Agree or disagree?

After you discuss their answers, tell your students that today's lesson deals with the contrast between the old heaven and earth and the new. (Feel free to change any questions you think will be too controversial!)

Into the Word

Distribute "The New Resident's Guide to Heaven" set forth below (also printed in the student book); do not include the parenthetical answers. Then read Revelation 21:1-8 aloud. Ask students to indicate who/what is either present or absent from Heaven, as indicated.

The New Resident's Guide to Heaven

What/Whom You Will Find There: v. 1 (newness); v. 2 (new Jerusalem); v. 3 (tabernacle of God; God himself); v. 6 (fountain of water of life); v. 7 (overcomers).

What/Whom You Won't Find There: v. 1 (sea); v. 4 (tears; death; sorrow; crying; pain; former things); v. 8 (the fearful; the unbelieving; the abominable; murderers; whoremongers; sorcerers; idolaters; liars; lake of fire/second death).

When your students have completed the guides, use the following questions to discuss their answers.

1. What is "new" about the new heaven and earth, compared to the old?

2. Why is there no sea in heaven?

3. What is the new Jerusalem, and why is it compared to a bride?

4. What does verse 3 mean by "the tabernacle [or dwelling] of God is with men"?

5. How will God do away with all suffering?

6. What does the reference *Alpha and Omega* signify?

7. What is the water of life? How does someone who is spiritually thirsty drink from it?

8. What does it mean to be an overcomer?

9. What is the second death? Who will suffer it? Why? Compare Revelation 21:8 with 1 Corinthians 6:9-11. What does Paul say about those who will or who won't inherit the kingdom of God?

Into Life

Divide your class into pairs or groups of three, depending on how many students you have. Assign one of the following scenarios to each pair or trio. Say, "Write a brief letter to the character in the scenario, using today's text to challenge him or her to follow Christ." Have several volunteers share their suggestions.

1. Jim no longer believes in God. He has been suffering from inoperable brain cancer and endures such pain that he can rarely leave his bed. Jim sees life as nothing more than torture, with death as the only release from that agonizing existence. What hope can you offer him?

2. Sharon is into the occult. She relies on her daily horoscope for guidance, she worships nature with a group of pagans, and she spends much of her free time digesting occult literature and films. How can you reach her with the truth?

3. Dave belongs to a cult that teaches that the only way to reach God is through special meditation. They consider all religions to be equally valid. No matter what faith one chooses to follow, that religion will lead to salvation as long as one meditates properly. How do you respond?

4. Rachel claims to be a Christian but is notoriously dishonest. She cheated to get through school, she lies to her friends and family, and she steals from her employer. She admits to these offenses, but considers them justifiable means to an end. How can you convince her to change?

Let's Talk It Over

The questions on this page are designed to promote discussion of the lesson by the class and to encourage application of the lesson Scriptures. The answers provided are only discussion starters. Let your class talk it over from there.

1. What are some of the figurative "seas" of life that you face now? How does anticipation of the great, last day help you overcome these?

We look forward to a day when there will be no more "sea"—that is, no more evil or fear. Fear can be a paralyzing emotion, rendering us useless physically, emotionally, and spiritually. Satan and his demons throw many things into our lives to cause fear and stop us dead in our tracks of Christian service.

At times we are faced with the fear of false teaching; we get so concerned about false teaching in the world that we become defensive and fail to reach the world with the truth of God's Word. Sometimes we fear someone not liking something we are seeking to do in the church; thus the fear of conflict causes many churches to fail to move forward in effective ministry. There is the fear of being rejected; so instead of sharing our faith with others we keep it to ourselves. God's love drives out fear!

2. How do you as a Christian deal with death and sorrow? What help do you need in this regard? How have you helped others?

Knowing that the words of God are faithful and true assures us that death and sorrow will pass away. Even so, we need to be careful not to deny the reality of sorrow or try to gloss it over. Sorrow is real, even though God exists. Stressing the reverse is even more helpful: God exists even though sorrow exists as well. In the midst of pain, we continue to acknowledge that God is still God. He is on His throne. Our hope is strengthened as we remember that God will one day claim the ultimate victory.

Knowing "the end of the story" can carry us through the epic battles we face. We do not grieve as does the world, which does not know Christ. But we do grieve. As Christians we provide comfort to one another in these times of grief (2 Corinthians 1:3, 4).

3. What are some inadequate ways you sought to have your spiritual thirst quenched in the past? What turned you around?

There are plenty of spiritual hucksters in the world ready to sell us "water" that will never sat-isfy the thirst we have. Their wares may come in the form of pop Christian psychology, retreats filled with a lot of emotionalism, or the power of positive thinking. The "name it and claim it" evangelists are still around.

We may sometimes think that our spiritual thirst is satisfied when we are happy and comfortable in our spiritual walk, when really what God has called us to be is holy and committed. The thirst is properly satisfied as we follow the teaching of Scripture to seek God's will first, when we live lives of holiness, and when we trust in God with all our hearts.

4. What are some ways that our heavenly inheritance differs from an earthly inheritance? How do these differences comfort you?

It is an ugly scene when family members gather around the bed of a dying father just waiting for him to leave this world so they can fight over their inheritance. It is a touching scene as others gather around the deathbed of their father wanting really nothing more than for their father not to leave them.

With regard to our heavenly inheritance, we will receive all that God has to offer, especially His continual presence. Being reunited with our friends and loved ones in the Lord who have gone on before us is another great thing. And to know that death and sorrow and pain will no longer be part of our lives is a gift beyond our comprehension.

5. When we read verse 8, we rejoice in the ultimate victory of God and the defeat of all evil. What are some other things this verse should cause us to do—or not do?

First, we can be careful not to be smug and filled with pride at the defeat of these enemies of God. We must recognize that it is only by God's grace that we stand complete in His presence and will not face the same end. Humility and thankfulness are to mark us as we consider the words here. The knowledge that many will face this second death should break our hearts and challenge our lives to the point of wanting to share the message of hope and salvation with these murderers, idolaters, liars, and the like.

Living in God's Presence

DEVOTIONAL READING: Ephesians 1:15-23.

BACKGROUND SCRIPTURE: Revelation 21:9–22:5.

PRINTED TEXT: Revelation 21:9-11; 21:22–22:5.

Revelation 21:9-11, 22-27

9 And there came unto me one of the seven angels which had the seven vials full of the seven last plagues, and talked with me, saying, Come hither, I will show thee the bride, the Lamb's wife.

10 And he carried me away in the spirit to a great and high mountain, and showed me that great city, the holy Jerusalem, descending out of heaven from God,

11 Having the glory of God: and her light was like unto a stone most precious, even like a jasper stone, clear as crystal.

. . . .

22 And I saw no temple therein: for the Lord God Almighty and the Lamb are the temple of it.

23 And the city had no need of the sun, neither of the moon, to shine in it: for the glory of God did lighten it, and the Lamb is the light thereof.

24 And the nations of them which are saved shall walk in the light of it: and the kings of the earth do bring their glory and honor into it.

25 And the gates of it shall not be shut at all by day: for there shall be no night there.

26 And they shall bring the glory and honor of the nations into it.

27 And there shall in no wise enter into it any thing that defileth, neither whatsoever worketh abomination, or maketh a lie: but they which are written in the Lamb's book of life.

Revelation 22:1-5

1 And he showed me a pure river of water of life, clear as crystal, proceeding out of the throne of God and of the Lamb.

2 In the midst of the street of it, and on either side of the river, was there the tree of life, which bare twelve manner of fruits, and yielded her fruit every month: and the leaves of the tree were for the healing of the nations.

3 And there shall be no more curse: but the throne of God and of the Lamb shall be in it; and his servants shall serve him:

4 And they shall see his face; and his name shall be in their foreheads.

5 And there shall be no night there; and they need no candle, neither light of the sun; for the Lord God giveth them light: and they shall reign for ever and ever.

GOLDEN TEXT: There shall be no night there; and they need no candle, neither light of the sun; for the Lord God giveth them light: and they shall reign for ever and ever.—Revelation 22:5.

Our Community Now and in God's Future

Unit 3: Living in God's New World

(Lessons 10-13)

Lesson Aims

After participating in this lesson, each student will be able to:

1. Recite ways that life in God's eternal presence will provide peace.

2. Contrast the security of Heaven with the insecurity of earthly life.

3. Describe one way to bring the peace of Heaven into daily life.

Lesson Outline

Introduction

A. A Run in the Country

I have no trouble admitting that I'm a city person. I love the country, but the fact is it does scare me. I grew up where the streetlights came on as soon as the natural light faded. I grew up close to convenience stores, hospitals, fire houses, and police stations. It was an ordered, safe, and predictable environment.

Recently my wife and I decided to get out into the country. So we drove up to "Amish country" in central Ohio. There we stayed in an old log cottage located at the back of a working farm. Fortunately the cottage had satellite TV, a weather radio alarm, fire extinguishers, a tele-phone, smoke and carbon-monoxide detectors, security lights, and all the conveniences of the city—right there in the country!

While enjoying the country life late on the first afternoon, I thought I would go out for a run through the woods at the back of the farm. I was a long way out when I realized that the sun had almost set. I found myself running along an old isolated road in the dark and not really sure of where I was. My idea was to keep running and hope I didn't miss the gap in the trees that I had come out of an hour earlier.

I did, of course, miss that gap. So I ran and walked for a few hours. Every time I saw a house light, I'd run up and find that I was not in the right place. There were no shops to stop at, no water fountains to drink from, no food that was not still alive. Dogs ran after me, strange noises freaked me out, and I thought I saw a bear (in central Ohio?!). In short I was terrified. Suddenly I had a new appreciation for the city.

Although the city comes with its own dangers, my run in the country taught me something about John's world. In today's lesson John contrasts being inside with being outside the city to show us the security and abundance that will come when we enjoy the eternal presence of God in the new Jerusalem.

B. Lesson Background

We must always remember that Revelation was written to encourage first-century Christians who were being persecuted for their faith. Like all biblical prophecy, its primary value is in its original context. So our interpretation of Revelation must begin with the original readers.

The figures of speech that John uses come from the world of the first century AD. They are strange to us, and so we often miss the real value of the imagery. In Revelation 21–22, we have John's description of Heaven as he experiences his revelation. Yet for John to describe the vision, he has to use images and terms from the then-current, physical world. He wrote Revelation so that his readers could appreciate the next world in such a way that it would make a difference in how they were living out their lives at the time.

John's description of Heaven helps us appreciate its wonders. We should be cautious about taking the descriptions of our eternal home too literally, however. To make this mistake would be to limit Heaven to only the earthly things that we can imagine are valuable.

For example, consider how John describes the foundations of the wall of the city (Revelation 21:19, 20). City walls were valuable things in the ancient world, because they were physical barriers against enemies—it is an impression of security. Today, however, very few cities depend on walls for safety. Instead, we may think of safety in terms of early-warning radar (both military and weather). John uses ideas from his first-century world to create the most meaningful impression he can. When we allow John's intended impression to shape our hearts, we will fall at the feet of Jesus in praise.

I. People of God
(Revelation 21:9-11)

A. Their Status (v. 9)

9. And there came unto me one of the seven angels which had the seven vials full of the seven last plagues, and talked with me, saying, Come hither, I will show thee the bride, the Lamb's wife.

We have already considered the image of *the bride, the Lamb's wife* in earlier lessons; in Revelation 19:7 and 21:2, we saw this terminology used as a reference to all who belong to God. The focus was on the bride's preparation, the way the faithfulness of those who belong to God prepared them for eternal life. When John refers to the Lamb, he draws attention to the fact of whose we are.

The counterpart of the bride is the great whore of Revelation 17:1. The purity of the bride is in sharp contrast to the filthiness of the great whore (compare Revelation 19:7, 8 with Revelation 17:2). Mention of *the seven angels which had the seven vials full of the seven last plagues* harks back to the judgment of God in chapters 15 and 16.

B. Their Future (vv. 10, 11)

10. And he carried me away in the spirit to a great and high mountain, and showed me that great city, the holy Jerusalem, descending out of heaven from God.

In order for John to see divine things, he must see them from a spiritual perspective. John started off his experiences "in the Spirit" (Revelation 1:10). Then when he was called into the presence of God, he also was "in the Spirit" (4:1, 2). When John was shown the demise of the unfaithful, it too was "in the spirit" (17:1-3). Now for him to see the future of the faithful, it likewise must be *in the spirit* (compare Ezekiel 40:2).

The significant point of this passage is what John sees while he is in the spirit: *that great city, the holy Jerusalem, descending out of heaven from God.* In the previous verse the angel said that he was going to show John the bride, the Lamb's wife. What John subsequently sees

means that the bride of verse 9 is the same thing as the holy Jerusalem of verse 10.

11. Having the glory of God: and her light was like unto a stone most precious, even like a jasper stone, clear as crystal.

John uses breathtaking language to describe what he sees. What makes this city so beautiful is God's presence among His people. John sees the future of all who have remained faithful and how they manifest God's glory.

The glory of God is more than mere *light*. The glory of God is also what He achieves, what He does, and what represents Him (compare Isaiah 60:1, 2, 19). The opening word *having* indicates that the community of the faithful (the new Jerusalem) shows God's glory by being in this place with Him forever. [See question #1, page 328.]

The image of precious stones creates a sense of a value beyond measure. And if you read this and feel like jumping up and down with excitement, you should! This is a place beyond compare, and we the faithful really will all be there one day.

II. City of God
(Revelation 21:22-27)

A. Living in the Light (vv. 22-26)

22. And I saw no temple therein: for the Lord God Almighty and the Lamb are the temple of it.

John uses images that reflect important ideas for our understanding of eternity. The first is that there is *no temple.* The original audience of Revelation lived in a world where temples were the norm. Temples were thought to be the way to communicate with your god. Even those who served the true God in Solomon's time and thereafter understood that if you wanted to be closest to God you should go to the temple in Jerusalem.

As John writes, the Jerusalem temple has lain destroyed for at least 20 years. But John emphasizes that there is no need for a temple because the faithful will live in the presence of God. The truth of this is seen in the descriptions of city, bride, and tabernacle up to this point.

John's reference to *the Lamb* should remind us that we are forever dependent upon Christ's sacrificial work. Our future abundance already has been secured through the cross; what is necessary for us to have eternal life Jesus already has provided! We can live a victorious life *now.*

23. And the city had no need of the sun, neither of the moon, to shine in it: for the glory of God did lighten it, and the Lamb is the light thereof.

A pre-electricity world is a dark world. And darkness naturally hides all sorts of dangers. Since the ancient world relied more on natural light than we do today, the difference between *light* and dark has greater significance to the ancients. The New Testament writers use this significance in their writings. Their light *vs.* dark imagery contrasts people who belong to God (those in the light) and people who do not (those in the dark); see examples in John 8:12; Ephesians 5:8-13; Colossians 1:12, 13; 1 Thessalonians 5:4-8; and 1 John 1:5-7.

This is also a contrast in the Old Testament; see examples in Job 29:3; 30:26; and Isaiah 5:20. The light that Jesus is said to bring in Matthew 4:15, 16 is a quotation of Isaiah 9:1, 2. [See question #2, page 328.]

GOD'S BRIGHT IDEA

A composite photo taken from space shows the world at night glowing with light from thousands of cities. Yet well-ordered artificial illumination has been developed only within the last two centuries. In 1807 London could boast of the first gas street lamps. By the 1880s electric lighting was replacing gas lighting.

But with progress comes problems, and eventually the first blackout occurred. That happened in New York City on October 14, 1889. Headlines read, "A Night of Darkness—More than One Thousand Electric Lights Extinguished." However, it wasn't a power failure that caused the darkness; it was the outraged mayor who ordered all the lights shut off!

Streets of the time were illuminated by high voltage, carbon arc lights fed through a tangle of overhead wires. Several people had been accidentally (and publicly) electrocuted by the poorly maintained system. Something better was needed, and eventually the shift was made to safer technology. As a result, we can live in the relative security of lighted homes, streets, and public buildings.

We take light for granted, but the new Jerusalem will be illuminated by a light more brilliant than anything we have experienced. This light will be so bright that sunlight will no longer be needed. This light will never be dimmed by power failure, will never cause pain or death, and will signify absolute safety and security. There will be no danger of blackouts. What a bright idea that is!   —C. R. B.

24-26. And the nations of them which are saved shall walk in the light of it: and the kings of the earth do bring their glory and honor into it. And the gates of it shall not be shut at all by day: for there shall be no night there. And they shall bring the glory and honor of the nations into it.

The reference to the open *gates* and the absence of *night* reinforces the idea of security. Further, John now specifies that it is the *nations* that *shall walk in the light of it.* The important concept of *nations* is woven throughout biblical history. [See question #3, page 328.] A key part of God's plan of salvation came into being when He called Abraham to be the father many nations (Genesis 17:5).

In particular, Abraham became the father of the nation of Israel. That nation bore the responsibility of preparing itself to usher in the Messiah, who would bring God's light to the rest of the world (Acts 13:47, quoting Isaiah 49:6). Today, the church functions as a kind of new Israel as she communicates the light of the gospel to those in darkness (compare Acts 26:17, 18).

The allusion to this final gathering of the saved from among the nations is clear in Isaiah 60:1-5. While Isaiah 60:5 refers to humans bringing their "forces," John magnifies the idea by saying that *kings* bring their *glory and honor.* This glory they bring or offer has always belonged to God in the same way that all power has always belonged to God. This is the ultimate point of the Isaiah passage: any power, wealth, or "forces" that seem to belong to us truly belong to God. The faithful will surrender it all to Him.

B. Promise and Warning (v. 27)

27. And there shall in no wise enter into it any thing that defileth, neither whatsoever worketh abomination, or maketh a lie: but they which are written in the Lamb's book of life.

John's Revelation is for those believers struggling to live in this world, to give us the hope we need to endure trials. But as we saw in Revela-

---

How to Say It

COLOSSIANS. Kuh-*losh*-unz.
CORINTHIANS. Ko-*rin*-thee-unz (*th* as in *thin*).
EPHESIANS. Ee-*fee*-zhunz.
EZEKIEL. Ee-*zeek*-ee-ul or Ee-*zeek*-yul.
ISAIAH. Eye-*zay*-uh.
JERUSALEM. Juh-*roo*-suh-lem.
PHILIPPIANS. Fih-*lip*-ee-unz.
SOLOMON. *Sol*-o-mun.
THESSALONIANS. *Thess*-uh-*lo*-nee-unz (strong accent on *lo*; *th* as in *thin*).

tion 16–18, this book is not good news for everyone. John issues a warning for anyone who would dare to reject what God has provided.

On the one hand, we see a promise to the faithful that their future in the presence of God will not be compromised by His enemies. On the other hand, we see a warning that is especially pertinent to modern culture. Many seem to believe that they can avoid the consequences of their actions. But John's message is clear: God will not overlook those who have rejected Him. We see similar warnings in Isaiah 52:1 and 1 Corinthians 6:9, 10. [See question #4, page 328.]

The *book of life* belongs to the Lamb because it is Christ's work that saves us. Those who are covered by Christ's blood are those whose names are written in that book (compare Psalm 69:28; Exodus 32:32, 33; Daniel 12:1; Philippians 4:3).

III. Peace of God
(Revelation 22:1-5)

A. Eternal Abundance (vv. 1, 2)

1. And he showed me a pure river of water of life, clear as crystal, proceeding out of the throne of God and of the Lamb.

As John moves the book toward its close, he brings together many of his previous points to help us understand the message. Thus he reintroduces the *water of life* image discussed previously (Revelation 21:6). The point of the image is that those who worship God will never have any want. John sees this abundant supply of our needs to originate from the presence *of God*. John's frequent reference to *the Lamb* is a constant reminder that our eternity will always be founded upon Christ's sacrifice.

2. In the midst of the street of it, and on either side of the river, was there the tree of life, which bare twelve manner of fruits, and yielded her fruit every month: and the leaves of the tree were for the healing of the nations.

A *river* sustains life, and John describes the "pure river of water of life" (v. 1) as the sustainer of *the tree of life* (compare Genesis 2:9). The images are overlapped in order to reinforce the message: our eternal home will be abundantly supplied with all that we need.

John's world is not technologically advanced. As a result, the food supply in his day is much less predictable than in ours. A bad harvest to John's contemporaries means everyone will be dieting. Famine, common to the ancient world, is almost unheard of in Western democracies today. This fact can make it difficult for us to appreciate John's point. This tree has not one but

Home Daily Bible Readings

Monday, May 14—The Hope of Our Calling (Ephesians 1:15-23)

Tuesday, May 15—The Glory of the Lord (Isaiah 60:18-22)

Wednesday, May 16—An Unshakable Kingdom (Hebrews 12:22-28)

Thursday, May 17—The Hope of Glory (2 Corinthians 3:7-18)

Friday, May 18—John Sees the Heavenly City (Revelation 21:9-14)

Saturday, May 19—God Will Be the Light (Revelation 21:22-27)

Sunday, May 20—Blessings to Come (Revelation 22:1-5)

twelve kinds of *fruit*, and these twelve kinds of fruit aren't produced just annually but *every month*! It's always harvest time in Heaven, and the crop is always bountiful. [See question #5, page 328.]

STENCH OF DEATH, PROVISION OF LIFE

God has created some very unusual plants! Do you suppose He did this for His own amusement or for our amazement? One of the strangest examples is known as *titan arum*—the "corpse flower." It gets that name because its fragrance (if that is the right term!) is reminiscent of rotting flesh. The reason for the smell is that it attracts carrion beetles to pollinate the plant. Such beetles normally feed on—you guessed it—rotting flesh.

The plant was discovered in the jungles of Sumatra in 1878. Horticulturists subsequently brought the plant to botanical gardens in the western world. The tuber from which the blossom grows may weigh 170 pounds; the blossom can be from 6 to 10 feet tall and lasts only 2 days.

The blossom is rare in cultivated examples of the plant, but huge crowds will visit exhibits in spite of (or maybe because of) the smell. In 2003, some 16,000 visitors came to see the two-day bloom at the United States Botanic Garden in Washington, D.C.

How different this flower is from the trees that John saw! There will be no smell of death in Heaven. Instead, the tree of life will delight us with its unending provision.   —C. R. B.

B. Eternal Security (vv. 3-5)

3a. And there shall be no more curse: but the throne of God and of the Lamb shall be in it.

The Lord God giveth them light: and they shall reign for ever and ever.
—Revelation 22:5

Visual for Lesson 12. *Point to this visual as you ask, "In what ways does God give you a light* right now *that is better than sunlight?"*

In this one remark John spans the entirety of history, from the fall in the Garden of Eden to the final redemption. The fall of humanity occurred when Adam and Eve decided to privilege their own interests over God's (Genesis 3:6). The resulting *curse* was not so much the hard work and pain (Genesis 3:16-19) as it was being banished from God's presence (Genesis 3:22-24).

What happened after that is the long story of the Lord preparing for our return to His presence. That could come about only via the redemption from the effects of our sin. And now John makes this point: a time comes when the curse is finally gone. We will at last be back with our creator, where we should have been all along.

In the end, there will be no separation from God's presence as there is in this fallen, temporary world. We cannot fail to note that John refers once more to *the Lamb*. It is the work of Christ that has rescued us from the effects of the curse.

3b. And his servants shall serve him.

Being in the presence of God is an experience we cannot fully comprehend. But John tells us that our natural joyful response will be to *serve* God.

4. And they shall see his face; and his name shall be in their foreheads.

John's world does not have the experience of televised images or photographs. So for him and his original readers, the only practical way to see people's faces is to be in their presence. Thus seeing God's *face* repeats the previous point that we shall be in the presence of God (compare Psalm 17:15; Matthew 5:8).

By saying that God's *name* will be *in their foreheads*, John reinforces that the future of the faithful will be abundant and secure. That is be-

cause we will be in the presence of God. A name or identity written on the forehead is a powerful image (compare Exodus 28:36-38; Ezekiel 9:4-6; Revelation 13:16; 14:9; 17:5). A mark on a forehead designates a certain identity; in this case, it identifies someone as belonging to God. God knows who we are, and we know we belong to Him. We will forever be designated as God's and thus forever enjoy His presence, His abundance, His protection. What a comfort!

5. And there shall be no night there; and they need no candle, neither light of the sun; for the Lord God giveth them light: and they shall reign for ever and ever.

John reemphasizes the point that he has been making all along: the faithful shall experience the presence of God and enjoy the eternal security and protection that His presence affords. While it's impossible for us to fathom exactly what John sees, we can still get the message from our limited perspective. Even though we may suffer now, even though our relationship with God may be tested, even though we may have fear now, our faithfulness will ultimately lead us to eternal security and abundance. "The saints of the Most High shall take the kingdom, and possess the kingdom for ever, even for ever and ever" (Daniel 7:18).

Conclusion

A. No Gray Areas

If you ever take a class in ethics at a secular university, you may discover that the teaching is absorbed with the so-called *gray areas.* These are areas where right and wrong are determined by the individuals in the particular situation under consideration—and almost all situations are thought to be gray areas in some way!

Make no mistake: there will be no gray areas when it comes to determining who will live in God's presence and who won't. God knows those who are His and those who aren't. The choice to stay within the love of Christ or reject Him confronts us daily. What does your choice today say about where you intend to spend eternity?

B. Prayer

Father, we praise You for the victory that You have already secured through the death and resurrection of Christ. We pray that we would have the strength to make that victory true even now in our present lives. In Jesus' name, amen.

C. Thought to Remember

Anticipate eternity!

Learning by Doing

This page contains an alternative lesson plan emphasizing learning activities.
Classes desiring such student involvement will find these suggestions helpful.

Learning Goals

After participating in this lesson, each student should be able to:

1. Recite ways that life in God's eternal presence will provide peace.

2. Contrast the security of Heaven with the insecurity of earthly life.

3. Describe one way to bring the peace of Heaven into daily life.

Into the Lesson

Distribute pencils and paper and ask students to design the safest home they can imagine. It should protect their families from intruders, accidents, and disasters. Give your students the choice of drawing a blueprint of the home or simply listing the safety features. (This activity is also found in the student books.)

When your students finish their drawings or lists, ask for volunteers to share their ideas. List these on the board. Some safety features they may mention include burglar alarms, smoke and carbon-monoxide detectors, childproof locks, fire-retardant building materials, deadbolt locks, and ground-fault interrupters on electrical outlets. Ask your class which safety features provide them with the most peace of mind.

Make a transition by saying that today's lesson will draw a sharp contrast between the insecurity of this life versus the security of Heaven.

Into the Word

Divide your class into small groups. Half of your groups will complete Exercise #1; the other half will complete Exercise #2. If you do not use the student books, instruct your students to use paper and pencils from the previous activity.

Exercise #1: Life's Trials. Read the following passages and briefly describe the trials faced by Christians in the late first century AD: 3 John 9, 10; Revelation 2:9, 10, 13; 6:9, 10; 12:13-17; 13:5-7. Next, discuss within your group the questions that follow.

A. What do these trials have in common with those faced by Christians today?

B. What trials did early Christians face that we may not have to endure today, if any?

C. What trials do we face today that early Christians may not have endured, if any?

Exercise #2: Heaven's Security. Read Revelation 21:9-11, 22-27; 22:1-5. What are the images of security that the faithful Christians will enjoy in Heaven?

When the groups finish their research, ask each to share its findings. Potential responses for Exercise #1 include (A) martyrdom (in some parts of the world) and enemies within the church; (B) widespread and overt persecution (absent at least in Western democracies); (C) subtle discrimination and harassment—being passed over for job promotions, being excluded from social groups, being denied government grants, etc.

Potential responses for Exercise #2 include the safety of the walled city; the city's illumination against the evils of darkness; the presence of God and the Lamb; exclusion of all the unholy; no hunger or thirst for the saved; permanent absence of the curse of sin. Ask those who did the second exercise to choose which "security measures" they consider most important—that is, which features of Heaven will make them feel most secure about being there.

Into Life

To close today's lesson, ask each student to complete the following statements. (Space is provided in the student books.)

1. I feel secure in my faith because _____.

2. Because I, as a Christian, enjoy the promise of Heaven, I no longer fear _____.

3. Because I no longer fear _____, I can do _____ for God. (Note: ask for specifics in the last two questions. Do not allow answers such as "anything" or "all things"!)

Allow a minute or two for your students to complete their work. Then ask for volunteers to share their answers to each statement. Make a list of these answers on the board, then discuss the implications of their answers. In particular, focus on their answers to the third statement, discussing what they can do for God because they have the promise of Heaven. Encourage your class to be bold in their daily service of Christ because they have His promise of heavenly security.

Close with prayer, thanking God for the promise of Heaven and the comfort that promise brings in your lives.

Let's Talk It Over

The questions on this page are designed to promote discussion of the lesson by the class and to encourage application of the lesson Scriptures. The answers provided are only discussion starters. Let your class talk it over from there.

1. The church, the people of God, will reflect God's glory in the new Jerusalem, the heavenly city. But how can we reflect His glory while here on earth?

According to an old saying, "We can become so heavenly minded that we are of no earthly good." God's glory is revealed as we offer the cup of cold water in His name, as we comfort the afflicted, clothe the naked, and care for the destitute. Having hearts of compassion instead of hearts of stone reflects the image and glory of God. This happens when the church becomes involved in deeds of goodness and kindness, in Jesus' name, here on earth as we fulfill the Great Commission. To be content to sit back in our church services or Bible studies, merely enjoying the company of one another, is not an option in God's sight.

2. In what ways has the church in general— or your church in particular—lost her "shine" for God? How can she get it back?

The light of Christ provides the only light we will need in Heaven, and Jesus wants to shine through His people today to provide light in a darkened world (Matthew 5:14). Often churches keep this light inside the church walls. Sometimes the church loses its shine by becoming conformed to the world instead of being transformed. Sometimes in the desire to be culturally relevant the church loses its godly uniqueness. Some solutions can be found in 1 John 3:18; 2 John 4-11; 3 John 11; Revelation 2:5, 16, 25; 3:3, 11, 18.

3. The nations will be gathered together as one in the new Jerusalem! What impact should that fact have on your church today?

Living out our faith includes seeking to build bridges with various ethnic, social, and age groups. The church is to take care not to become so segmented that she loses the image of being a family. No family is made up of people of all the same age with the same tastes in all matters. The church growth concept of "targeted demographics" is a bit troubling in this regard. Christ's kingdom is for everyone.

In Heaven we will all dwell together. On earth we can "practice" for that coming day! Christ expects no less.

4. How has the warning given in verse 27 affected the church in both negative and positive ways?

This verse makes clear that not everyone will be saved. The fact that Scripture teaches that many will be lost to an eternal Hell can cause some to try to point those people out, thus becoming the judges of the world. Sadly, there are even some who seem to revel in consigning people to eternal damnation. There have even been Web sites created that portend to count how many "days in Hell" a certain deceased person has spent there.

But for many others the thought of anyone going to an eternal Hell motivates them to become evangelists instead of judges. A heart motivated by the love of God will be motivated to share that love with others.

5. God ensures that the tree of life produces fruit constantly in Heaven. He also wants us to produce fruit constantly and He empowers us to do so. How effective are you at producing the fruit of new souls? How can you do better?

It is vital that the church learn the difference between *means* and *ends*. In other words, we can get so caught up in the *process* that we forget the *purpose*. This was the problem of first-century Jewish leaders. They forgot that the nation of Israel existed to usher in the Messiah. Instead, they worried that "If we let him [Jesus] thus alone, all men will believe on him; and the Romans shall come and take away both our place and nation" (John 11:48).

One mistake is to focus on having activities in our church to the exclusion of fulfilling the Great Commission. Are we keeping the same programs and activities year after year, but neglecting to evaluate if they are effectively fulfilling God's purpose? To state this problem as a bit of a cliché, we end up doing church work instead of doing the work of the church.

One possible solution is to decide that every church program comes with a "sunset clause" attached. This means that programs are automatically canceled after one year unless the church leadership decides otherwise. This plan encourages frequent reviews for effectiveness.

Anticipating Christ's Return

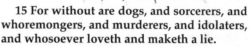

DEVOTIONAL READING: John 16:17-24.

BACKGROUND SCRIPTURE: Revelation 22.

PRINTED TEXT: Revelation 22:6-21.

Revelation 22:6-21

6 And he said unto me, These sayings are faithful and true: and the Lord God of the holy prophets sent his angel to show unto his servants the things which must shortly be done.

7 Behold, I come quickly. Blessed is he that keepeth the sayings of the prophecy of this book.

8 And I John saw these things, and heard them. And when I had heard and seen, I fell down to worship before the feet of the angel which showed me these things.

9 Then saith he unto me, See thou do it not: for I am thy fellow servant, and of thy brethren the prophets, and of them which keep the sayings of this book: worship God.

10 And he saith unto me, Seal not the sayings of the prophecy of this book: for the time is at hand.

11 He that is unjust, let him be unjust still: and he which is filthy, let him be filthy still: and he that is righteous, let him be righteous still: and he that is holy, let him be holy still.

12 And, behold, I come quickly; and my reward is with me, to give every man according as his work shall be.

13 I am Alpha and Omega, the beginning and the end, the first and the last.

14 Blessed are they that do his commandments, that they may have right to the tree of life, and may enter in through the gates into the city.

15 For without are dogs, and sorcerers, and whoremongers, and murderers, and idolaters, and whosoever loveth and maketh a lie.

16 I Jesus have sent mine angel to testify unto you these things in the churches. I am the root and the offspring of David, and the bright and morning star.

17 And the Spirit and the bride say, Come. And let him that heareth say, Come. And let him that is athirst come. And whosoever will, let him take the water of life freely.

18 For I testify unto every man that heareth the words of the prophecy of this book, If any man shall add unto these things, God shall add unto him the plagues that are written in this book:

19 And if any man shall take away from the words of the book of this prophecy, God shall take away his part out of the book of life, and out of the holy city, and from the things which are written in this book.

20 He which testifieth these things saith, Surely I come quickly: Amen. Even so, come, Lord Jesus.

21 The grace of our Lord Jesus Christ be with you all. Amen.

GOLDEN TEXT: He which testifieth these things saith, Surely I come quickly: Amen. Even so, come, Lord Jesus.—Revelation 22:20.

*Our Community Now and
in God's Future*

Unit 3: Living in God's New World

(Lessons 10-13)

Lesson Aims

After participating in this lesson, each student will be able to:

1. Identify the main purpose of the book of Revelation.

2. Summarize how Revelation 22 describes Christ's return.

3. Suggest one specific area of life in which he or she will focus to keep "the sayings of the prophecy" of Revelation.

Lesson Outline

INTRODUCTION

  A. The Bigger Picture

  B. Lesson Background

 I. TRUST THIS MESSAGE (Revelation 22:6-10)

  A. Nature of the Message (vv. 6-9)

  B. Urgency of the Message (v. 10)

    Coming Sooner, or Later?

II. CHOOSE YOUR DESTINATION (Revelation 22: 11-15)

  A. Beyond the Point of No Return (v. 11)

  B. Before the Point of No Return (v. 12)

III. EXPECT CHRIST (Revelation 22:13-15)

  A. Identity of Him Who Comes (v. 13)

  B. Identity of the Blessed (v. 14)

  C. Identity of the Cursed (v. 15)

IV. LISTEN TO THE FINAL WORDS (Revelation 22: 16-21)

  A. Testimony (v. 16)

  B. Plea (v. 17)

  C. Warning (vv. 18, 19)

  D. Affirmations (vv. 20, 21)

    No Asterisk

CONCLUSION

  A. Amen

  B. Prayer

  C. Thought to Remember

Introduction

A. The Bigger Picture

Everything seemed normal early on September 11, 2001, when a certain passenger jet took off. But soon a group of terrorists seized control of the plane and directed it toward Washington, D.C. The plan apparently was to ram the jet into the White House, the symbol of U.S. freedom and power. This was to be the last of four planes scheduled to wreak death and destruction on U.S. values and infrastructure that day.

When passengers began receiving cell phone calls from concerned family members, those aboard the plane soon realized that this hijacking was not motivated by the desire to extort money. This was an attack against the U.S. itself. A group of ordinary citizens began to see their present situation in light of the bigger picture. They decided to ignore their self-preservation instincts and attack the attackers. The result was a jet that crashed into a field in Pennsylvania rather than into a building in Washington, D.C.

We often get so busy with our lives that we let our busyness drown out the bigger picture of life. Yet every now and then something makes us look up and see that picture. Once the passengers aboard that jet became aware of the bigger picture, they made right decisions because they understood what was at stake.

Today's lesson focuses on the end of the book of Revelation. It calls Christians everywhere to "look up." It is a call to get out of the smallness of our individual circumstances and start acting with reference to the magnitude of eternity.

B. Lesson Background

The point at the end of the book of Revelation is the same point that John has made all the way through: the Lord's victory is certain. His future return is the hope that enables us to remain faithful in the face of trial. It is important, though, that we understand the meaning of *hope*. In modern English this word often means something like "wishful thinking," as in "I hope I win a new car." But *hope* in biblical contexts means something more like "expectation." Christian hope is not wishful thinking but rather is confident expectation. As the writer of Hebrews notes, "Now faith is the substance of things hoped for, the evidence of things not seen" (Hebrews 11:1).

Thus, Christian hope is our certainty that the Lord will indeed return. If we know friends are coming for dinner, we are expecting them and that means action is required. An important aspect of expectation is the way that our awareness of what is to happen affects how we prepare for that event. Christian hope reveals its true colors in how we live our lives in the here and now.

The book of Revelation helps the reader develop this true Christian hope. As John comes to the end of the book, all his points will support this major thrust.

I. Trust This Message
(Revelation 22:6-10)

A. Nature of the Message (vv. 6-9)

6. And he said unto me, These sayings are faithful and true: and the Lord God of the holy prophets sent his angel to show unto his servants the things which must shortly be done.

The point John now makes is one he has made before: the Word of the Lord is reliable. It is *faithful and true* (compare Revelation 3:14; 19:11; 21:5). Christians of all eras can stake their lives on the truth of this prophecy!

While all of Revelation is faithful and true, the context requires us to observe what the angel has in mind specifically at this point. The angel is about to show John *the things which must shortly be done.* The idea of *shortly* (mentioned four times in Revelation 22) normally can refer either to a brief interval of time (as in "soon" or "without much delay") or to speed (as in "quickly" or "swiftly"). Here, however, it is likely that John is simply suggesting that these things will certainly occur. Thus he communicates to his readers a sense of urgency. It's another way of saying that something must indeed take place.

We recall that "one day is with the Lord as a thousand years, and a thousand years as one day" (2 Peter 3:8). This cautions us against imposing our view of time on God. Rather than computing time lines, we will do well to focus on how faithful and true the Lord's words are.

7. Behold, I come quickly. Blessed is he that keepeth the sayings of the prophecy of this book.

It is possible to be confused by a potential reference to speed in the phrase *I come quickly.* What was true of *shortly* in the previous verse is true of *quickly* here. The Greek words in these two instances have the same root and should be read in essentially the same way. The overall point is that Jesus will certainly return. [See question #1, page 336.]

We should note carefully the implicit warning in this verse. The person for whom Jesus' return will be a *blessed* occasion is the person who is prepared. Such a person pays attentions to and keeps the message of the *book* of Revelation. For anyone not prepared, Jesus' return undoubtedly will be "too quick" (compare Matthew 25:1-13).

8, 9. And I John saw these things, and heard them. And when I had heard and seen, I fell down to worship before the feet of the angel which showed me these things. Then saith he unto me, See thou do it not: for I am thy fellow servant, and of thy brethren the prophets, and of them which keep the sayings of this book: worship God.

John is overcome by the experience and makes the mistake of attempting *to worship . . . the angel.* Even given all that the apostle John has seen and experienced, he still makes big mistakes! Even when we try our best, we too will make mistakes.

John undoubtedly knows of the occasions when Cornelius bowed down to Peter (Acts 10:25, 26) and when villagers tried to offer sacrifices to Paul and Barnabas (Acts 14:11-18). Thus it is interesting that John makes his mistake not once but twice (see Revelation 19:10).

John's mistakes come from the overwhelming nature of his experience. Even when we have the best of intentions, even when our heart is just right, we can still make significant mistakes that contradict the nature of our faith. A person may be *sincere* while being *sincerely wrong.* Just because we mean well does not mean that our actions are correct. [See question #2, page 336.]

B. Urgency of the Message (v. 10)

10. And he saith unto me, Seal not the sayings of the prophecy of this book: for the time is at hand.

Interestingly, this is the exact opposite of the instructions given to the prophet Daniel. After receiving a magnificent vision, that prophet was told, "But thou, O Daniel, shut up the words, and seal the book, even to the time of the end" (Daniel 12:4). The directions that John receives speak to the very heart of the book of Revelation: it is a *revelation* from God for us. We bear a responsibility to study this message and gain from it what the Lord wants to give to us.

That John refers to the *time* being *at hand* should not mislead us into thinking in terms of "soon." As in the previous verses, the word *time* here has a qualitative value. The author of Hebrews refers to "these last days" (Hebrews 1:2). The apostle John speaks of his day as "the last time" (1 John 2:18). If we don't sort through this issue carefully, we may end up asking arrogantly, "Where is the promise of his coming?" (2 Peter 3:4).

How to Say It

BARNABAS. *Bar*-nuh-bus.
COLOSSIANS. Kuh-*losh*-unz.
CORNELIUS. Cor-*neel*-yus.
EPHESIANS. Ee-*fee*-zhunz.
ISAIAH. Eye-*zay*-uh.
THESSALONIANS. *Thess*-uh-*lo*-nee-unz (strong accent on *lo; th* as in *thin*).

A mistake of some readers of the Bible is to think that they can predict when the Lord will return. Every one of them has failed (see Matthew 24:36; Acts 1:7; 1 Thessalonians 5:1, 2). The point is that it *will* happen. Thus our appropriate response is not to guess when but to be ready for it. We are to expect it!

COMING SOONER, OR LATER?

In one sense, time is *static:* it moves forward second by second for everyone. But in another sense, time seems to be *relative:* the pace of life has not always moved as rapidly as it seems to do for most of us today.

Think about automobile speeds. In the early twentieth century when the automobile was a new invention, people were amazed at how fast they could go. The fact that this was not very fast was demonstrated in 2003 by a cross-country parade of Model T Fords in celebration of the Ford Motor Company's one-hundredth anniversary. Fifty of the antique cars traveled from southern California to Dearborn, Michigan, taking 19 days to do so. Their top speed was 45 miles per hour.

Today we routinely travel much faster when we are able to break free from the gridlock of large cities. Yet in the early 1900s, some speculated that people would die, perhaps from a heart attack or asphyxiation, if they were to exceed 60 miles per hour. We chuckle at such quaint ideas.

The insistence of some that Christ will return soon—meaning "by such-and-such a date"—is an example of how rapidly we expect things to move. The fact that 2,000 years have elapsed since Christ's first coming makes some folks impatient. That seems like a long time, relatively speaking. Yet church history has proven the folly of trying to solve our impatience with date-setting. Christ may not be coming tomorrow, but He *is* coming *certainly*!   —C. R. B.

II. Choose Your Destination
(Revelation 22:11, 12)

A. Beyond the Point of No Return (v. 11)

11. He that is unjust, let him be unjust still: and he which is filthy, let him be filthy still: and he that is righteous, let him be righteous still: and he that is holy, let him be holy still.

If we're not paying attention, we can easily misread this verse to mean that God has no interest in allowing people to be transferred out of "the power of darkness" and "into the kingdom of his dear Son" (Colossians 1:13). John is seeing the final outcome of all things; there will be at a certain, particular point in the history of salva-

tion no opportunity for second thoughts. It will all be finished.

The end result of those who are not faithful, who prefer to be *unjust,* is that they remain unjust. The end result of the faithful, who are made *righteous,* is that they also remain in that state. This verse thus views eternal destinies from a perspective that is past the point of no return.

If in this life we obstinately chose to be spiritually *filthy,* then we will forever be condemned as unjust. If, however, we deny ourselves and prefer to serve Christ and His purposes in this world, then we will forever be justified.

B. Before the Point of No Return (v. 12)

12. And, behold, I come quickly; and my reward is with me, to give every man according as his work shall be.

John starts by repeating the *quickly* (or "certainty") theme, and then he moves to the subject of Jesus' *reward.* The point is that the certainty of Jesus' return will be accompanied by the certainty that He will repay each *according as his work shall be.* This is not "works salvation" but is a recognition that our works demonstrate our faith—or lack thereof (James 2:14-26).

The idea of reward or recompense occurs frequently in the Bible (Psalm 28:4; 62:12; Isaiah 40:10; 59:18; 62:11; Ephesians 6:8; etc.). And before we assume that all is well for us in this area personally, let's give close attention to Matthew 25:31-46. There Jesus offers a clear warning to those who think that they are serving God when in reality they are not.

III. Expect Christ
(Revelation 22:13-15)

A. Identity of He Who Comes (v. 13)

13. I am Alpha and Omega, the beginning and the end, the first and the last.

For the last few verses, John has described the final outcome of the decisions we make in this life. Now John puts the spotlight on the God of history; this is the God who declares "the end from the beginning" (Isaiah 46:10; compare 44:6; 48:12). He knows our past, present, and future. This imagery reaffirms the power of God to do exactly what He says He will do: repay all people according to the choices made in this life. (We discussed *Alpha and Omega* in Lesson 11.)

B. Identity of the Blessed (v. 14)

14. Blessed are they that do his commandments, that they may have right to the tree of life, and may enter in through the gates into the city.

While John's vision is in the spirit and of the future, everything he writes is for the benefit of his readers in this world. We've now read that the Lord will certainly come. By the time the end comes there will be no chance of changing our minds. He will certainly repay us according to our choices in this life. [See question #3, page 336.]

Thus we understand the significance of the verse before us: we will be blessed if we choose the Lord now while we have a choice. For those who remain faithful, their reward from Jesus will be the blessing of the *tree of life* and entrance into the holy *city*. This means eternity with our creator, never to be separated again.

C. Identity of the Cursed (v. 15)

15. For without are dogs, and sorcerers, and whoremongers, and murderers, and idolaters, and whosoever loveth and maketh a lie.

Here we have the flip side of the situation. Those who persist in making unholy choices in this life will not enter the eternal city. They will not experience abundance and security. They will not experience the eternal presence of God. If you choose God in this life, then your identity will be blessed. But if you choose yourself and your own desires in this life, then you will be identified for all eternity as having made that choice.

IV. Listen to the Final Words (Revelation 22:16-21)

A. Testimony (v. 16)

16. I Jesus have sent mine angel to testify unto you these things in the churches. I am the root and the offspring of David, and the bright and morning star.

Most of the announcements in Revelation come from divine messengers sent from God. But this is one of the occasions in which the Lord himself speaks. It is further confirmation for the reader that this is a reliable message. This brings Revelation full circle, since it is a repetition of how the book began (Revelation 1:1, 2).

During Christ's earthly ministry, people generally expected that if He were the Messiah, then He would mount some kind of political or military campaign (compare Acts 1:6). That He did not do so probably was a disappointment to many. However, when Jesus now announces that He is *the root and the offspring of David*, His kingship is beyond doubt. We have to appreciate that the culture of the ancient Jews understands this phrase to be a reference to a warrior Messiah.

The reference begins in Isaiah 11:1-10, where the prophet refers to a new growth springing up from Jesse, the father of King David. The image there is of a felled tree, most likely referring to the apparent end of David's line of kings. But there is still life in these roots and they allow for the growth of a successor: the Messiah. "The root of David, hath prevailed" (Revelation 5:5). Jesus is indeed a victorious warrior, but not in the way many in the first century expect.

The title *bright and morning star* has been rather difficult for many commentators to explain. It seems best to understand this title as being based on Numbers 24:17. That verse was understood by Jews to be a reference to a coming Messiah who would destroy God's enemies. Thus, both of these titles refer to Jesus as a victorious, conquering Messiah. This divine warrior-king blesses those who accept Him, but He also punishes those who don't.

B. Plea (v. 17)

17. And the Spirit and the bride say, Come. And let him that heareth say, Come. And let him that is athirst come. And whosoever will, let him take the water of life freely.

Much has already been said to the reader of Revelation, and much has been repeated for emphasis. Throughout the book we've heard the warnings of eternal death that come with rejecting the truth of Christ. We've heard of eternal blessings that are available for all who embrace that truth. What is our obvious response? Here in the final verses of the book we are told that we respond correctly when we *come*.

The book of Revelation is a message of hope. Hope enables us to remain faithful, and our faithfulness ensures our hope. Our hope is in Christ's ability to secure us for eternity. Our

---

Home Daily Bible Readings

Monday, May 21—Pain Becomes Joy (John 16:17-24)

Tuesday, May 22—Jesus Overcomes (John 16:25-33)

Wednesday, May 23—One Body, One Spirit (Ephesians 4:1-6)

Thursday, May 24—May Christ Rule Your Hearts (Colossians 3:12-17)

Friday, May 25—Worship God (Revelation 22:6-11)

Saturday, May 26—The Reward for Faithfulness (Revelation 22:12-16)

Sunday, May 27—The Invitation (Revelation 22:17-21)

hope is in Christ and His victory over sin and death. This is what impels us to come and to *say, Come* to others who are *athirst*. Who can turn away from such a plea?

C. Warning (vv. 18, 19)

18, 19. For I testify unto every man that heareth the words of the prophecy of this book, If any man shall add unto these things, God shall add unto him the plagues that are written in this book: and if any man shall take away from the words of the book of this prophecy, God shall take away his part out of the book of life, and out of the holy city, and from the things which are written in this book.

To ignore *the words* of the *book* of Revelation is bad enough. How much worse will it be for the one who hears the words of Revelation then obscures or abuses that message! Such a person will be cursed. [See question #4, page 336.]

D. Affirmations (vv. 20, 21)

20, 21. He which testifieth these things saith, Surely I come quickly: Amen. Even so, come, Lord Jesus. The grace of our Lord Jesus Christ be with you all. Amen.

We come to the last words of the Bible. The final point is that the one who is behind the revelation of this message will certainly *come* again. (Note our earlier discussion concerning *shortly* and *quickly*.) The importance of this fact is embedded deeply within the fabric of this book. The Lord really will return, and all that we have read really will come about. We do well to expect His return and prepare for it through our faithfulness. [See question #5, page 336.]

Visual for Lesson 13. *Use this visual to introduce discussion question #5 on page 336. Ask, "Do we really want Jesus to 'come quickly'?"*

NO ASTERISK

On September 24, 1919, Babe Ruth hit home run number 28 of the season. That feat broke a record that had stood for 35 years. In 1920 and 1921 he raised that single-season record to 54 and 59, respectively. Ruth's final record came in 1927, when he hit 60 homers. His record held until 1961, when Roger Maris hit 61. However, Maris's feat was brought into question by the fact that 8 games were added to the schedule.

Mark McGwire broke Maris's record in 1998, hitting 70 homers. Barry Bonds passed McGwire in 2001 with 73. But these records are tainted by scandals relating to the alleged use of drugs to enhance performance. So the argument among baseball fans has been, "Does scheduling additional games or ignoring rules against drug use disqualify later records? Shouldn't we add an asterisk to those later records, with a note of explanation at the bottom, to say 'maybe, maybe not'?"

In the eternal scheme of things, arguments about baseball records mean little. However, John writes a warning that is of eternal significance: the revelation he received is God's message and its provisions do not change. We are either with Christ or against Him. As a result of this choice, a person's name is either written in the book of life or it is not. There is no asterisk, either there or after the last *Amen* in the Bible, to say "maybe, maybe not."   —C. R. B.

Conclusion

A. Amen

The very last word in the Bible is *Amen*. With that word the aged apostle John finished his earthly writing ministry before the Lord called him home. Yet the challenges offered by what John wrote are ever new. We worship and serve the Lamb because the Lamb is worthy. We tell others about the Lamb for the same reason.

There comes a time when the eternal destiny of a person is "locked in," never to change. That day comes either when a person dies or, for those still living, when Jesus returns. Eternity beckons. What is your choice?

B. Prayer

Lord, help us to prepare the world for the hope that You have for us. In our own lives help us to use the message of Revelation to overcome all that stands between us and serving You and Your people. In Jesus' name, amen.

C. Thought to Remember

Christ's return is certain.

Learning by Doing

This page contains an alternative lesson plan emphasizing learning activities.
Classes desiring such student involvement will find these suggestions helpful.

Learning Goals

After participating in this lesson, each student will be able to:

1. Identify the main purpose of the book of Revelation.

2. Summarize how Revelation 22 describes Christ's return.

3. Suggest one specific area of life in which he or she will focus to keep "the sayings of the prophecy" of Revelation.

Into the Lesson

Open today's lesson by sharing the following notorious predictions of the end of the world: In 793, Beatus, abbot of Liébana, Spain, prophesied on Easter day of the end of the world. His prediction started a riot. In 1719, Jacques Bernoulli, a famous Swiss mathematician, predicted the return of a comet that passed the Earth in 1680. This time the comet was supposed to strike and destroy the planet.

The July 20, 1993, issue of a supermarket tabloid predicted that asteroid "M-167" would strike the Earth on November 11, 1993, and possibly end all life on the planet. There is no asteroid M-167. In 1999, a self-proclaimed prophet warned that solar flares would strike the Earth in April of that year and kill most of the population.

Ask your students to complete the following open-ended sentence (also printed in the student books): *If I knew for certain that the world would end next week, I would . . .*

Ask several volunteers to share their answers. Then say, "As you may have guessed by now, today's lesson deals with the return of Christ and the end of the world."

Into the Word

Divide your class into groups of three or four. Direct the groups to the activity "The Return of Christ" in the student book. If you don't use the student books, provide paper and pencils; then assign each team one of the following passages: Revelation 22:6-10; Revelation 22:11-15; Revelation 22:16-21.

Instruct each group to write a brief, two- or three-sentence paraphrase of its assigned passage. Then each group is to answer the following questions about its assigned text.

Revelation 22:6-10

1. How could John have been told that Jesus is coming "quickly" (v. 7) if it has been nearly 2,000 years since that revelation? 2. Why was John told not to worship the angel (vv. 8, 9)? 3. What do you think verse 10 means when it says, "the time is at hand"?

Revelation 22:11-15

1. What do you think verse 11 means when it talks about a person remaining unjust/filthy or righteous/holy? 2. What is the most important work that we are called to do? (See also John 6:29.) 3. Who identifies himself as "Alpha and Omega" in verse 13? (See also v. 16.) Why is this significant in light of Revelation 21:5, 6? 4. What is signified by the tree of life (v. 14)?

Revelation 22:16-21

1. How does Jesus identify himself in verse 16? Recall the lesson on Revelation 5. What is significant about Jesus' descent from David? (See Isaiah 11:1-10; Matthew 22:42-45.) 2. Who are the Spirit and the bride (v. 17)? What invitation do they offer? 3. What will happen to those who attempt to modify the book of Revelation? Why?

When your teams finish their studies, use your lesson commentary and the questions above to discuss findings. Especially emphasize the lesson writer's key to understanding the entire book of Revelation: The Lord's victory is certain. His future return is the hope that enables us to remain faithful in the face of trial.

Into Life

Remind your students of their answers to the first exercise in today's lesson. Then direct the class to the two open-ended statements below. (Write them on the board.)

1. If I knew for certain that Jesus would return one week from today, I would . . .

2. Because I believe the New Testament's promise that Jesus will return someday, and I know that it could be today, I will . . .

Ask for volunteers to share their thoughts. Stress why answers to the second statement are much more important than answers to the first. Pray with your class for the faith to expect the return of Christ, the wisdom to prepare for that return, and the resolve to live with that expectation in mind.

Let's Talk It Over

The questions on this page are designed to promote discussion of the lesson by the class and to encourage application of the lesson Scriptures. The answers provided are only discussion starters. Let your class talk it over from there.

1. The Lord's return is spoken of in Scripture as being *shortly* or *quickly*. How will you live your life with this fact in mind? What mistakes will you be careful to avoid?

Many have attempted to calculate the exact date of Jesus' second coming; all have failed. Some who think they have pinpointed that date have even quit jobs, sold homes, and gathered together to wait idly, only to be sadly mistaken and disappointed. Most of us can remember a certain amount of "end-time frenzy" as the year 2000 approached.

The *fact* or *certainty* of Christ's future return is what stimulates the Christian to action! Constant vigilance is to mark our lives as we wait for that return (Mark 13:35-37). Constant vigilance doesn't mean standing around looking up at the sky (Acts 1:11); it does mean that we want to be found faithful until our death or until the return of Christ (Matthew 24:36-51).

2. The angel was quick to tell John not to worship him. In what ways have other messengers of God failed to follow the example of this messenger, this angel? How do you recognize and steer clear of this kind of problem? When does praise and admiration cross the line?

Many cult leaders have started out as believers in Jesus and have sought to lead people toward the way of truth. But when people began to praise and admire those leaders, pride took root.

But it is not just cult leaders who are guilty. Preachers, youth ministers, or Christian musicians all can get caught up in the moment and begin to revel in the praise they receive. Although this may not be outright worship of the person, it is a short step from there to pride that leads to the fall of the servant of God.

The servant or messenger of God, as well as the follower, has a responsibility to keep this problem in check. First, the follower must not become so caught up in admiration of the leader that God is forgotten. And the leader must make sure that praise received is not producing pride. An accountability partner can help.

3. What are some ways that keeping the commandments of Christ has enriched your life?

One view says that people do good works in order to earn God's favor or to avoid His wrath. But changing our motivation from fear to love makes a big difference! We faithfully fulfill the commands of Christ because His love for us causes us to *want* to do so. We return love for love. The desire to want to fulfill Christ's commands motivates us to be alert to opportunities for service.

4. Verses 18, 19 present a sobering warning! How do you make sure that you are not adding to or subtracting from the Bible? Was there ever a time when you slipped up in this regard? How did you get back on track?

Every sentence in the Bible occurs within the framework of a larger paragraph. Every paragraph occurs within the framework of a larger book. Every book occurs within the framework of either the New or the Old Testament. Valid interpretations (meaning those that neither add to nor subtract from the authors' original intent) will honor all these frameworks.

Remember that Satan is a master deceiver and father of lies. He will take a Scripture and twist it in our minds to the point where we miss the true meaning and significance of the passage. Following this *framework principle* is an important safeguard.

5. Can you honestly say, "Come, Lord Jesus" as if you wanted Him to return today? Why, or why not?

Sometimes we fear we have not done enough good to be ready for Heaven. Though we look forward to Heaven and we long to live with God for eternity, there is always that fear of the unknown. We may also be reluctant to pray for Christ to return now because we know someone who would be lost for eternity.

In the first area of reluctance, we can be assured that we are never "good enough" to merit Heaven. Instead, we trust the promise of God for salvation through Christ to the faithful. And as for our concern for those who are without Christ, the possibility of Christ's return tomorrow can motivate us to share the message with them now!

Summer Quarter 2007

Committed to Doing Right
(Prophets, Lamentations, and 2 Kings)

Special Features

Lessons

About These Lessons

To commit means "to obligate or pledge oneself." Many people have no problem doing that when it comes to signing a contract for a car loan. But to commit one's life to God—that can be a different story! Yet nothing is more important. This quarter's lessons show us why.

Jun 3
Jun 10
Jun 17
Jun 24
Jul 1
Jul 8
Jul 15
Jul 22
Jul 29
Aug 5
Aug 12
Aug 19
Aug 26

Quarterly Quiz

The questions on this page may be used in several ways: as a pretest at the beginning of the quarter; as a review at the end of the quarter; or as a review after each lesson. The questions are based on the Scripture text of each lesson (King James Version). ***The answers are on page 340.***

Lesson 1

1. One of the great sins of the house of Israel was taking bribes. T/F. *Amos 5:12.*

2. Things were so bad in the day of Amos that the prudent would do what? (wring their hands? faint? keep silence?) *Amos 5:13*

3. The Day of the Lord "is ____, and not ____." *Amos 5:18*

Lesson 2

1. What three things did the inhabitants of the land lack? (pity, knowledge of God, pride? truth, mercy, knowledge of God? honest scales, solemn oaths, shrewdness?) *Hosea 4:1*

2. The occupation of a person who uses "balances of deceit" is that of a ____. *Hosea 12:7*

Lesson 3

1. God compared the rulers and people of Israel to what two cities? (Rome, Babylon? Sodom, Gomorrah? Nineveh, Babylon?) *Isaiah 1:10*

2. Just about the only thing that the Lord found pleasing in Judah were the new moon and Sabbath observances. T/F. *Isaiah 1:13*

3. The Lord offered the people a chance to have their sins made white as ____. *Isaiah 1:18*

Lesson 4

1. The Lord promised that those who would come to Him would be able to buy what two things without money? (bread and meat? wine and milk? cheese and crackers?) *Isaiah 55:1*

2. "Seek ye the Lord while he may be ____, call ye upon him while he is ____." *Isaiah 55:6*

Lesson 5

1. The Lord accused the leaders of Israel of a kind of cannibalism. T/F. *Micah 3:2, 3*

2. The Lord said He would be pleased if the Israelites increased the amount of their offerings. T/F. *Micah 6:7*

Lesson 6

1. The Lord compared the princes and judges of Judah with bears and tigers. T/F. *Zephaniah 3:3*

2. The Lord promised that the earth would be devoured by the fire of His what? (love, irritation, jealousy?) *Zephaniah 3:8*

Lesson 7

1. The one who is condemned builds a town by what? (blood? sweat? tears?) *Habakkuk 2:12*

2. The knowledge of the ____ of the Lord shall fill the earth. *Habakkuk 2:14*

Lesson 8

1. The people of Jerusalem needed to place more trust in the temple of the Lord. T/F. *Jeremiah 7:4*

2. What false gods were the people of Jerusalem burning incense to? (Shiloh? Neptune? Baal?) *Jeremiah 7:9*

Lesson 9

1. Jeremiah wrote a letter to those who had been taken captive from Jerusalem to Babylon. T/F. *Jeremiah 29:1*

2. The Lord advised the captives in Babylon to start a bloody revolt. T/F. *Jeremiah 29:7*

3. The Lord's thoughts toward the captives were of ____ and not of evil. *Jeremiah 29:11*

Lesson 10

1. King Zedekiah successfully escaped from the Babylonians (Chaldees). T/F. *2 Kings 25:5-7*

2. To wait quietly for the salvation of the Lord is a bad thing because it shows a lack of initiative. T/F. *Lamentations 3:26*

Lesson 11

1. God grants life to the wicked who turn from their sins. T/F. *Ezekiel 18:21, 22*

2. God desires that people have a new heart and a new ____. *Ezekiel 18:31*

Lesson 12

1. Darius reigned during the time of Zechariah. T/F. *Zechariah 1:1*

2. The Lord scattered His people with a what? (earthquake? whirlwind? fire?) *Zechariah 7:14*

Lesson 13

1. Malachi said that it is not possible to weary the Lord. T/F. *Malachi 2:17*

2. The Lord promised that the coming day would burn as what? (sheol? a snakebite? an oven?) *Malachi 4:1*

Back to Basics

by Doug Redford

A SERIES OF STUDIES on *doing right* may seem a bit pointless. Isn't it kind of like reinventing the wheel? Shouldn't we be studying something deeper or more challenging?

The sobering truth is that God's people have always had to guard against compromising their commitment to doing what is right in His eyes. As someone once observed, too many Christians are like thermometers, merely reflecting the moral and spiritual temperature around them. Often the problem is not that we become engaged in blatant, outright sin; rather, we simply lose our first love (see Revelation 2:4). We compromise our standards and are no longer committed to doing right.

Instead of being thermometers, we are to resemble thermostats, setting (with God's help) the moral and spiritual standards. We do this by word and example, encouraging others to pursue a God-honoring lifestyle.

Perhaps no group of people can shake us out of spiritual apathy better than the Old Testament prophets. Most of the Scripture texts this quarter are drawn from the books that record the timeless messages of these courageous men of God (with additional passages from the books of 2 Kings and 2 Chronicles). This series of lessons encourages us to rekindle the commitment to doing right—even when wrong appears to be the more popular choice.

Unit 1: Life as God's People

Lesson 1, "Committed to Justice," is taken from the prophet Amos. The key verse for this lesson is Amos's oft-quoted exhortation to "let judgment run down as waters, and righteousness as a mighty stream" (Amos 5:24). However, we must not forget his earlier commands to "seek good, and not evil" and to "hate the evil, and love the good" (Amos 5:14, 15). We cannot pursue what is just and right unless we let God determine what those terms mean.

Lesson 2, "Recommitted to God's Ways," comes from the prophet Hosea. He uses the language of the courtroom to describe how the Lord had a "controversy" with His people (Hosea 4:1). One cannot read his description of people who "break out" from God's standards (Hosea 4:2) without reflecting on how modern society lives, as if there were no God to whom we must give

account. We who are Christians must ask ourselves, "Have we compromised our spiritual values for the sake of accommodating secular standards? Would the Lord have a 'controversy' with us?"

Lesson 3 challenges us to be "Committed to True Worship" by using exhortations from the prophet Isaiah. The subject of worship continues to be a hot button issue in many churches. People can be quite passionate about it—and so is God! Consider His words: "Bring no more vain oblations; incense is an abomination unto me; . . . Your new moons and your appointed feasts my soul hateth: they are a trouble unto me; I am weary to bear them" (Isaiah 1:13, 14).

God's primary concern with worship is the gap that His people sometimes create between what they say in worship and how they live. Today we must bridge that gap. Reaching a lost world depends on it.

Lesson 4, the final lesson in this unit, is also taken from Isaiah. It encourages seeking God. To become a Christian is not the end of a search; it is a never-ending adventure, and it must be carried out on God's terms, not ours. Isaiah's use of hunger and thirst to picture spiritual longing (Isaiah 55:1, 2) is similar to Jesus' language in the Beatitudes about hungering and thirsting after righteousness (Matthew 5:6).

Unit 2: What Does God Require?

The first lesson in this unit, **Lesson 5,** is drawn from the prophet Micah, who poses the question, "What doth the Lord require of thee?" (Micah 6:8). There may be many opinions about this matter, but Micah's is the final answer: God has always wanted obedience.

Even in the New Testament, Jesus made obedience a key test of His followers' love for Him: "If ye love me, keep my commandments" (John 14:15). Note that this lesson will be taught on the Sunday before the Fourth of July; this will provide an opportunity for American Christians to remind themselves that freedom involves responsibility, whether the subject is political or spiritual freedom.

Lesson 6, entitled "Committed to Righteousness," comes from the book of Zephaniah. An important theme of this lesson is God's judgment. Judgment is not a popular topic today. A victim mentality encourages everyone to excuse personal behavior by proclaiming, "It's not my fault!" But a day of reckoning is unavoidable: "It is appointed unto men once to die, but after this the judgment" (Hebrews 9:27).

The theme of **Lesson 7** is "Committed to Hope," from the prophet Habakkuk. Habakkuk recognized that hard times for God's people were on the horizon, for the Babylonians were posing an increasingly ominous threat to Judah. But Habakkuk found hope in seemingly hopeless times by declaring, "The just shall live by his faith" (Habakkuk 2:4). So can we.

The focus of **Lesson 8** is accountability. Drawn from passages in Jeremiah and 2 Kings, it should strike a responsive chord with many students. *Accountability groups* and *accountability partners* are often used by churches today as a means of providing support, encouragement, and (when necessary) rebuke. Yes, God will hold accountable those who reject Him; but He will also richly bless all who answer His plea, "Amend your ways" (Jeremiah 7:3) and turn back to Him in repentance.

Lesson 9 is entitled "Committed to Trusting God." It includes the contents of a letter that the prophet Jeremiah sent to those who already had been taken captive to Babylon.

Jeremiah instructed the people there to build houses, plant gardens, and start families (Jeremiah 29:5, 6). They would not be coming home soon in spite of what some false prophets were claiming (Jeremiah 28:1-9).

However, in God's own time, after seventy years had passed, He would "visit" His people and bring them home (Jeremiah 29:10). God always has the last word, and it is the best word.

Unit 3: How Shall We Respond?

Whereas Habakkuk in Lesson 7 looked ahead to the coming onslaught of the Babylonians against God's people in Judah, **Lesson 10** chronicles the tragic fulfillment of Habakkuk's words. Verses from 2 Kings 25 record the event itself; verses from the book of Lamentations record Jeremiah's expressions of grief over what has befallen his land and his countrymen.

But Lamentations is more than just laments. There are invitations to hope throughout the book as well. Consider Lamentations 3:26: "It is good that a man should both hope and quietly wait for the salvation of the Lord."

In **Lesson 11** we see the prophet Ezekiel confronting the efforts of some of God's people to avoid taking responsibility for their actions. Ezekiel ministered to those who already had

been taken captive to Babylon, some of whom had expressed the attitude (noted earlier), "It's not my fault!"

The road to reconciliation with God begins with the acknowledgment that we are sinners. Without that confession, we are left in a prison of our own making.

The final lessons of the quarter are taken from two of the postexilic prophets, Zechariah and Malachi. While God had disciplined His people through the Babylonian captivity, that incident was meant to be a *comma*, not a *period*, in His plan for them. Through Zechariah **(Lesson 12)**, God's loving invitation was "turn ye unto me . . . and I will turn unto you" (Zechariah 1:3). This invitation is echoed in the New Testament in the words of James 4:8: "Draw nigh to God, and he will draw nigh to you."

Lesson 13, from Malachi, highlights another phase of God's plan—not only for His people but for the entire world. It is a thrilling climax to this quarter of studies. The Lord had sent messengers time and again to convey His love for His people and to warn them of coming catastrophe (2 Chronicles 36:15, 16). Malachi added a prediction of a day when "the Lord, whom ye seek, shall suddenly come to his temple, even the messenger of the covenant" (Malachi 3:1). That messenger of a new covenant—a new and superior way to God—is Jesus Christ. He who was fully committed to doing right and who committed no sin against God went to the cross so that we could be made right with God.

Today we Christians are God's messengers on behalf of that messenger—commissioned to be His witnesses to a world that desperately needs to follow the right way. May we be faithful to the task before us!

Answers to Quarterly Quiz on page 338

Lesson 1—1. true. 2. keep silence. 3. darkness, light. **Lesson 2**—1. truth, mercy, knowledge of God. 2. merchant. **Lesson 3**—1. Sodom, Gomorrah. 2. false. 3. snow. **Lesson 4**—1. wine and milk. 2. found, near. **Lesson 5**—1. true. 2. false. **Lesson 6**—1. false. 2. jealousy. **Lesson 7**—1. blood. 2. glory. **Lesson 8**—1. false. 2. Baal. **Lesson 9**—1. true. 2. false. 3. peace. **Lesson 10**—1. false. 2. false. **Lesson 11**—1. true. 2. spirit. **Lesson 12**—1. true. 2. whirlwind. **Lesson 13**—1. false. 2. an oven.

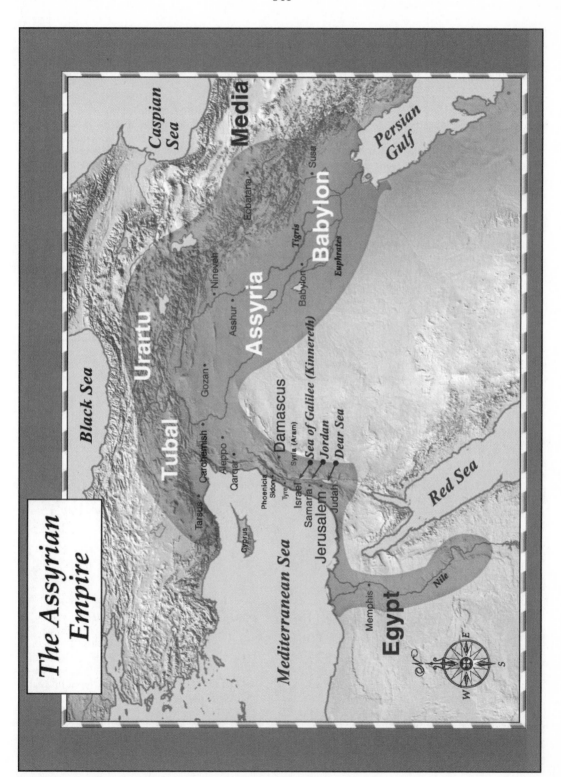

The Assyrian Empire

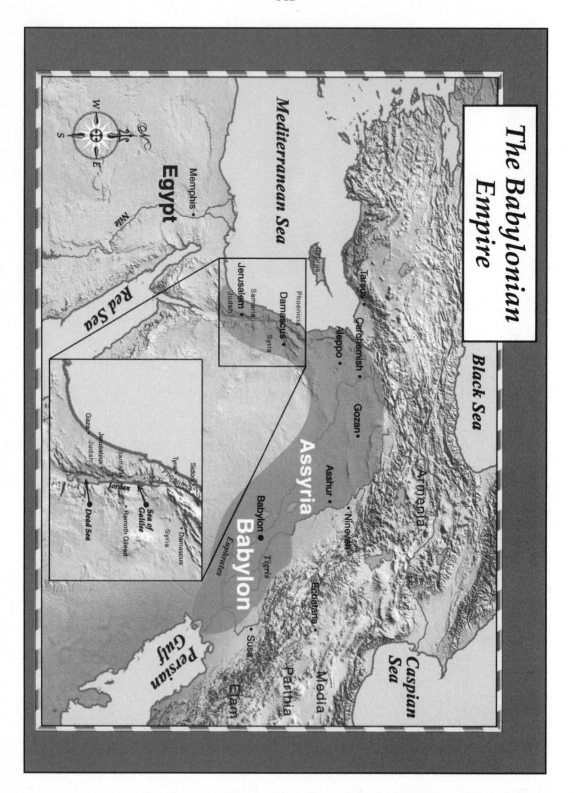

The Babylonian Empire

Committed to Justice

June 3
Lesson 1

DEVOTIONAL READING: **Psalm 82.**

BACKGROUND SCRIPTURE: **Amos 5:10-24; 8:4-12; 2 Kings 13:23-25.**

PRINTED TEXT: **Amos 5:10-24.**

Amos 5:10-24

10 They hate him that rebuketh in the gate, and they abhor him that speaketh uprightly.

11 Forasmuch therefore as your treading is upon the poor, and ye take from him burdens of wheat: ye have built houses of hewn stone, but ye shall not dwell in them; ye have planted pleasant vineyards, but ye shall not drink wine of them.

12 For I know your manifold transgressions and your mighty sins: they afflict the just, they take a bribe, and they turn aside the poor in the gate from their right.

13 Therefore the prudent shall keep silence in that time; for it is an evil time.

14 Seek good, and not evil, that ye may live: and so the LORD, the God of hosts, shall be with you, as ye have spoken.

15 Hate the evil, and love the good, and establish judgment in the gate: it may be that the LORD God of hosts will be gracious unto the remnant of Joseph.

16 Therefore the LORD, the God of hosts, the Lord, saith thus; Wailing shall be in all streets; and they shall say in all the highways, Alas! alas! and they shall call the husbandman to mourning, and such as are skilful of lamentation to wailing.

17 And in all vineyards shall be wailing: for I will pass through thee, saith the LORD.

18 Woe unto you that desire the day of the LORD! to what end is it for you? the day of the LORD is darkness, and not light.

19 As if a man did flee from a lion, and a bear met him; or went into the house, and leaned his hand on the wall, and a serpent bit him.

20 Shall not the day of the LORD be darkness, and not light? even very dark, and no brightness in it?

21 I hate, I despise your feast days, and I will not smell in your solemn assemblies.

22 Though ye offer me burnt offerings and your meat offerings, I will not accept them: neither will I regard the peace offerings of your fat beasts.

23 Take thou away from me the noise of thy songs; for I will not hear the melody of thy viols.

24 But let judgment run down as waters, and righteousness as a mighty stream.

GOLDEN TEXT: Let judgment run down as waters, and righteousness
as a mighty stream.—Amos 5:24.

Committed to Doing Right
Unit 1: Life as God's People
(Lessons 1-4)

Lesson Aims

After participating in this lesson, each student will be able to:

1. Describe the evils that Amos condemned.

2. Compare and contrast the evils cited in today's text with those seen in modern society.

3. Make a plan for his or her church to help correct one societal injustice.

Lesson Outline

INTRODUCTION
  A. The Price of Telling the Truth
  B. Lesson Background
I. BEWARE OF SOCIAL SINS (Amos 5:10-15)
  A. Indictment (vv. 10, 11)
  B. Warning (vv. 12, 13)
    Taking a Bribe
  C. Plea (vv. 14, 15)
II. BEWARE THE DAY OF THE LORD (Amos 5:16-20)
  A. There Will Be Weeping (vv. 16, 17)
  B. There Will Be Darkness (vv. 18-20)
    The Frying Pan
III. BEWARE OF SPIRITUAL SINS (Amos 5:21-24)
  A. False Feasts (vv. 21, 22)
  B. Insincere Songs (v. 23)
  C. Blessed Behavior (v. 24)
CONCLUSION
  A. Speak Up or Stay Silent?
  B. Prayer
  C. Thought to Remember

Introduction

A. The Price of Telling the Truth

Have you ever had to tell someone an unpleasant truth? Have you ever paid a price for telling the truth? Amos, the prophet who delivered the message of today's lesson text, was a truth-teller. He paid the price of ridicule, even direct repudiation (Amos 7:12, 13).

Telling the truth was dangerous in Amos's world. Even today, a person with a message like Amos's might be dismissed or killed. Yet what the world needs today are more people like Amos, willing to stand up for the truth when it is inconvenient or even dangerous.

Amos is often ignored in the contemporary church. This might be understandable if we had solved all the problems Amos talked about, but we haven't. Maybe we ignore Amos today for the same reason people ignored him in his own time—he hit too close to home.

B. Lesson Background

Amos is one of what are often called *the Minor Prophets*. These prophets are not called minor because their books are insignificant. They are called minor because the books are relatively short. The Minor Prophets are collected in a group of 12 books that could be contained on a normal-sized scroll. Amos is third on the list.

Amos prophesied around 760 BC. He prophesied to the northern kingdom of Israel, about 38 years before it fell to Assyrian invaders. During the time of Amos's preaching, Jeroboam II was king in that northern kingdom while Uzziah was king in the southern kingdom of Judah (Amos 1:1). It appears that Amos prophesied around the same time as Hosea and Zechariah, perhaps a little before Isaiah and Micah. Those desiring to know more about those times should study 2 Kings 14:23–15:7 and 2 Chronicles 26.

Amos is, in certain respects, a rather unusual choice to deliver prophecy. First, Amos himself confessed that he was not a trained prophet, nor was he related to any prophet (Amos 7:14). In some places in the ancient world, there were schools for prophets, where groups of men studied under a prophet. Other places had a notion of succession—that children of those who prophesied might well be prophets themselves. Amos had neither of these credentials. He was a simple farmer and shepherd. Yet God had written on Amos's heart a message he could not suppress (Amos 7:15).

Second, Amos was from Tekoa, a small town about 20 miles south of Jerusalem (Amos 1:1; compare 2 Chronicles 11:6). That makes him a Judean, yet he was called to go northward from Judah to Israel. There was friction between the two nations, and the northern kingdom was quite resistant to a prophet from the south calling them to account (Amos 7:10-13). Yet God gave Amos a burden. Thus Amos had to speak up.

To the casual observer, it seemed that things in Israel were going quite well at the time. It was a time of general prosperity, and many had become quite wealthy. But Amos looked beneath the veneer and saw great social and religious corruption. The real picture was one of decadence (Amos 2:8; 4:1; 6:1-6), immorality (2:7), and—worst of all—idolatry (8:14).

In chapters 1 and 2, Amos indicts eight regions for their sins. These areas are Damascus, Gaza, Tyre, Edom, Ammon, Moab, Judah, and Israel. At the end of the book, chapters 7–9 relate certain visions that Amos received. They contain images of grasshoppers, fire, a plumb line, fruit, and God and the altar. All of these visions relate to Israel's judgment.

In the middle of the book, chapters 3–6 appear to contain three sermons. Scholars have different methods by which to distinguish the three. One common method separates the sermons by the phrases "hear this word" and "hear ye this word" in Amos 3:1; 4:1; and 5:1. So the first sermon is chapter 3; it deals with the sinful affairs in Israel. The second sermon is chapter 4; it speaks of Israel's past, sinful conduct. The third sermon is chapter 5; it warns of Israel's punishment if they do not change.

Today's lesson comes from this third sermon. This entire section of Amos 5:1-17 is also called a lament (see v. 1). The tone of the sermon in chapter 5 is set in verse 5. There Amos warned the people not to go to Bethel. Bethel was historic; it was the place where Jacob saw the vision of angels (Genesis 28:10-22). Nevertheless, Amos did not want the Israelites to go there because of corrupted worship in that place. People had turned Bethel into a substitute for Jerusalem. The worship in Bethel was blatantly idolatrous.

This fact leads Amos to condemn Bethel, Gilgal, and Beersheba as a group. Amos looks for evidence of genuine worship in these places and finds none (compare Hosea 4:15; Amos 8:14). This condemnation continues through Amos 5:6. In verse 7 the concern switches from one of false religion to one of false justice. With the tone of the sermon now set, we break in at Amos 5:10.

How to Say It

ASSYRIAN. Uh-*sear*-e-un.
BEERSHEBA. Beer-*she*-buh.
BETHEL. *Beth*-ul.
EPHRAIM. *Ee*-fray-im.
HOSEA. Ho-*zay*-uh.
JEROBOAM. Jair-uh-*boe*-um.
MALACHI. *Mal*-uh-kye.
MANASSEH. Muh-*nass*-uh.
OBADIAH. O-buh-*dye*-uh.
TEKOA. Tih-*ko*-uh.
UZZIAH. Uh-*zye*-uh.
ZECHARIAH. *Zek*-uh-*rye*-uh (strong accent on *rye*).
ZEPHANIAH. Zef-uh-*nye*-uh.

I. Beware of Social Sins
(Amos 5:10-15)

A. Indictment (vv. 10, 11)

10. They hate him that rebuketh in the gate, and they abhor him that speaketh uprightly.

We catch Amos in the middle of a strong indictment against the behavior of God's people. This verse deals with a court situation because legal proceedings are held at the city *gate*. That is where many business and legal transactions take place. It is where the city elders meet (examples: Deuteronomy 21:18-21; Ruth 4:1-11).

Him that rebuketh is someone in authority who renders verdicts. Amos thus charges his listeners with being completely uninterested in justice and truth. In modern terminology we could say that people don't want honest judges or witnesses (compare Proverbs 24:23-25; Isaiah 29:21).

11. Forasmuch therefore as your treading is upon the poor, and ye take from him burdens of wheat: ye have built houses of hewn stone, but ye shall not dwell in them; ye have planted pleasant vineyards, but ye shall not drink wine of them.

The rich have robbed *the poor* of their livelihood. Tying in with verse 10, the picture is of the rich abusing the court system to steal grain from the poor. There will be punishment! Though the rich may build fine *houses,* one day they will stand empty. Though the rich may plant *vineyards,* one day they will stand unpicked. The ancient curse of Deuteronomy 28:30 is about to be fulfilled! [See question #1, page 350.]

B. Warning (vv. 12, 13)

12. For I know your manifold transgressions and your mighty sins: they afflict the just, they take a bribe, and they turn aside the poor in the gate from their right.

God's anger is justified because the people have committed such injustice. One of the *mighty sins* is the rich giving bribes to those who pass judgment. Thus the rich use the court system to deprive *the poor* of their livelihood. If the legal system is corrupted so that those who can afford a bribe can get the outcome they want, then there is no hope for the poor. Denial of justice is specifically forbidden in the covenant (Exodus 23:1-8; Deuteronomy 16:18-20). The penalty for such denial is severe (see Isaiah 10:1-4; 29:20, 21).

TAKING A BRIBE

In the 1980s a major American city was hit by *Operation Greylord,* an effort to expose corruption among public officials. The facts disclosed were awesome and frightening. Corrupt lawyers conspired to request bribe money from their clients to pay off cooperative judges. In the corridors of the court building, courtroom personnel often bickered over the split of the bribes that were flowing into the judge's chambers.

A young state's attorney took $50 from misdemeanor defendants on the "understanding" that they would not be prosecuted vigorously. A secret FBI recording caught one judge requesting help from city politicians to get a different assignment, promising to help support the proposed political slate of new judges. One judge accepted $10,000 to acquit a man accused of assassinating a labor union official. Another judge was accused of "fixing" at least three murder trials. His payoffs were $4,000, $10,000, and $100,000.

By the time the investigation ended, 92 individuals were indicted. They consisted of 17 judges, 48 lawyers, 8 policemen, 10 deputy sheriffs, 8 court officials, and 1 member of the state legislature (www.fbi.gov).

Amos would not have been surprised by such revelations. Even in his time, officials afflicted the just, accepted bribes, and denied the poor their rights. Amos calls these "manifold transgressions" and "mighty sins." What do we call them?   —J. B. N.

13. Therefore the prudent shall keep silence in that time; for it is an evil time.

This seems to be a strange verse at first glance. Aren't we supposed to speak up when we see injustice and not *keep silence*?

Amos is merely describing the situation as it exists at the time as he observes it. He is not recommending that people stay quiet—he himself certainly hasn't! He is illustrating that things have become so corrupt that even sensible people are afraid to speak the truth. Things have become so bad that *prudent* people just keep quiet. They don't want to make trouble for themselves. They live in a society that does not reward tellers of truth—it punishes them.

C. Plea (vv. 14, 15)

14. Seek good, and not evil, that ye may live: and so the LORD, the God of hosts, shall be with you, as ye have spoken.

The people think that *God* is with them. But Amos points out that God is with them only if they decide to pursue *good*.

Often in the Old Testament we see variations of the expression *the Lord, the God of hosts*, but we forget the impact. This host is an army—a heavenly army. God is its commander (1 Samuel

1:3, 11; Isaiah 37:16). Those who pervert justice have a powerful enemy!

15. Hate the evil, and love the good, and establish judgment in the gate: it may be that the LORD God of hosts will be gracious unto the remnant of Joseph.

Not only are the people to pursue *the good*, they also are to *hate the evil* (compare Romans 12:9). This suggests that the commitment to righteousness, while involving the behavior of the people, finds its source ultimately in the heart. [See question #2, page 350.]

The phrase *remnant of Joseph* hearkens back to Amos 5:6, which has "house of Joseph." Joseph was father to Ephraim and Manasseh, after whom 2 of the 12 tribes are named (Joshua 14:4). The dire predictions against the house of Joseph in verse 6 are balanced against a promise of hope. It's not too late to repent!

II. Beware the Day of the Lord (Amos 5:16-20)

A. There Will Be Weeping (vv. 16, 17)

16. Therefore the LORD, the God of hosts, the Lord, saith thus; Wailing shall be in all streets; and they shall say in all the highways, Alas! alas! and they shall call the husbandman to mourning, and such as are skilful of lamentation to wailing.

Amos paints a word picture of a nation that will be in total despair. There will be *wailing* in the city *streets* as well as on the country roads. Everyone will cry out, from the city dweller to the simple farmer to the professional mourner (one who is *skilful of lamentation to wailing*).

17. And in all vineyards shall be wailing: for I will pass through thee, saith the LORD.

What makes the judgment all the more poignant is that the *wailing* will take place as God walks through their midst. [See question #3, page 350.] Leviticus 26:6 speaks of what happens when people obey the Lord—it is a time when "neither shall the sword go through your land." The case before us is just the opposite.

The defeat that will come shortly in 722 BC will indeed be severe (2 Kings 17).

B. There Will Be Darkness (vv. 18-20)

18. Woe unto you that desire the day of the LORD! to what end is it for you? the day of the LORD is darkness, and not light.

The phrase *day of the Lord* appears about two dozen times in the Bible. It is a popular concept at various times in the history of prophecy. In addition to Amos, the prophets Isaiah, Jeremiah, Ezekiel, Joel, Obadiah, Zephaniah, Zechariah, and Malachi use this phrase.

The Day of the Lord is that time when God balances the scales and defeats the enemies of His people. Usually the ancient Israelites anticipate this to be a great day. But Amos warns that that day will be bad news for all who oppose God, even if they are of Jewish descent. What Amos's audience fails to see is that the Day of the Lord is a time for God to judge sins. (In the New Testament, see Acts 2:20; 1 Corinthians 5:5; 2 Corinthians 1:14; 1 Thessalonians 5:2; 2 Peter 3:10.)

19. As if a man did flee from a lion, and a bear met him; or went into the house, and leaned his hand on the wall, and a serpent bit him.

Amos uses two figures of speech to illustrate what happens on the Day of the Lord. The images could be almost humorous were it not for the real tragedy that awaits. Think about it: first *a man* flees from a *lion* only to run into a vicious *bear*. The one who escapes from the lion must feel a sense of relief. "Whew, that was close!" he says. But this is a false sense of security.

The second figure is of a man who makes it to what he thinks is the safety of his home. The sharp pain of a snakebite then jolts him out of his false sense of security!

OUT OF THE FRYING PAN

The old adage *out of the frying pan, into the fire* is familiar, sometimes painfully so. This adage applies when people try to get out of a very negative situation only to discover themselves in an even worse one.

The 1964 movie *Father Goose* demonstrates this. Cary Grant plays Walter Eckland, an unshaven runaway from Western civilization who is forced into the role of a coast watcher for the Royal Navy in the South Pacific in World War II. (Fire #1: he escapes civilization and winds up in the middle of a war.)

Then Grant is asked to remove a fellow coast watcher from another island. Instead, he rescues a diplomat's daughter (played by Leslie Caron) and seven school children, all girls. (Fire #2: he

The Assyrian Empire

Visual for Lesson 1. *Keep this map of the Assyrian Empire posted for several lessons to help your students gain a geographical perspective.*

avoids capture by the Japanese but winds up responsible for eight females.) The list of fires goes on!

Father Goose is a charming comedy, but the situation Amos describes is neither charming nor funny. Fleeing a lion, you meet a bear; safe at home, you're bitten by a snake. You survive the travails of life only to experience the Day of the Lord—finding yourself in a time of darkness, rather than light. God's judgment will not be what many delude themselves into believing! Are you ready for it?   —J. B. N.

20. Shall not the day of the LORD be darkness, and not light? even very dark, and no brightness in it?

The ancient Israelites may assume that only the non-Jews have anything to fear on the Day of Judgment. But Amos says, "Not so fast." When God passes judgment, He will have to do so on the people of God themselves. To Amos this is more than just a *maybe*—it is a *certainty*. Darkness stands for distress and trouble in many Old Testament passages (examples: 1 Samuel 2:9; Job 5:14; Psalm 35:6).

III. Beware of Spiritual Sins (Amos 5:21-24)

A. False Feasts (vv. 21, 22)

21. I hate, I despise your feast days, and I will not smell in your solemn assemblies.

God established three yearly pilgrimage celebrations (see Exodus 23:14-17; 34:22-25; Deuteronomy 16:10-16). God also established Sabbath days, new moon festivals, etc. (see Nehemiah

10:33; Hosea 2:11). God now hates what the people have done to those *days*. God hates the very things the people think are pleasing to God. The people have made a mockery of God's holy days.

22. Though ye offer me burnt offerings and your meat offerings, I will not accept them; neither will I regard the peace offerings of your fat beasts.

The opening chapters of Leviticus established various kinds of *offerings*. God himself is the author of what those offerings are to be and what they are to represent.

Yet Amos says that these offerings have become completely unacceptable to God. God has not "canceled" the offerings in and of themselves in Amos's day. Rather, it is improper motives and unholy lives of the people who offer false acts of worship that disgust God. [See question #4, page 350.]

B. Insincere Songs (v. 23)

23. Take thou away from me the noise of thy songs; for I will not hear the melody of thy viols.

Music is a vital part of Old Testament worship (Ezra 2:65; Psalm 150; etc.). Usually God delights in our music of praise but not if offered insincerely. *Songs* of praise that don't match holiness in one's life are so displeasing to the Lord that He demands they be removed from His presence.

Many churches are struggling these days over styles of worship and music. While that concern is understandable, a greater concern should be the kind of person the music comes from rather than the kind of music that comes from the person. [See question #5, page 350.]

C. Blessed Behavior (v. 24)

24. But let judgment run down as waters, and righteousness as a mighty stream.

This may well be the most familiar verse in the book of Amos. The great civil rights leader Martin Luther King, Jr. quoted it. The verse describes what God wants: justice and righteousness to permeate the land like *a mighty stream* bringing life-giving water to the people. Justice *(judgment)* must flow continually—day and night. Justice cannot be an intermittent, three times out of four, proposition.

Conclusion

A. Speak Up or Stay Silent?

Amos was not a professional prophet. He was not even a citizen of the northern kingdom of Israel. He might well have contented himself with pruning the fruit trees and watching sheep. But he could not keep silent. He chose to tell the people the truth, an unpopular truth at that.

The people's complacency was exactly why they needed a prophet like Amos. Gary Smith says that Amos's challenge was much like a doctor telling a patient he has a terminal disease. Sometimes people get angry with the messenger. Instead of being angry with the messenger, they need to take the cure. Amos did not just diagnose, he also prescribed. The problem is that the people did not want the prescription.

Amos drew a lot of attention when he came north. His activities were reported to the king himself (Amos 7:10-12). By coming north and condemning the worship in Bethel, he was coming to the center of idolatrous religion in the northern kingdom. Amos caught the ire of the lead priest at Bethel. That man told Amos to go home and prophecy to his own people if he was determined to preach (Amos 7:12, 13).

We know that Amos's prophecy was true, for history reveals Amos was right. We don't know if Amos remained a prophet for the rest of his life or if he went back to farming. One thing is sure: his message has not been forgotten. Or has it?

B. Prayer

Dear Father, help me to be concerned about the things that concern You. Help me to live in a way that reflects my commitment to You. In my worship let not my rituals be isolated from my behavior and my devotion of the heart. In the name of Jesus, amen.

C. Thought to Remember

Repentance, not ritual.
Commitment, not complacency.

Home Daily Bible Readings

Learning by Doing

This page contains an alternative lesson plan emphasizing learning activities.
Classes desiring such student involvement will find these suggestions helpful.

Learning Goals

After this lesson, each student will be able to:

1. Describe the evils that Amos condemned.

2. Compare and contrast the evils cited in today's text with those seen in modern society.

3. Make a plan for his or her church to help correct one societal injustice.

Into the Lesson

Prepare and post three bold and garish signs that say *BEWARE!* One of the signs should be at the entrance to your learning space. When students voice some interest or concern, explain that the lesson writer outlines today's study with three *bewares*. Encourage the adults to figure out the three dangers for which they are to be on the alert. (You will be returning to these words of warning in the Into Life section of today's study.)

Have also a *NO MINORS ALLOWED!* sign near your room's entrance. After the *beware* introduction, point the class's attention to the other sign to introduce the *Minor Prophets*, books from which most of this quarter's texts are drawn. Be certain the learners know in what way these Old Testament books are "minor" and what ways they are not. The lesson writer has an explanatory note in the Lesson Background.

Into the Word

List the following phrases and ideas on separate sheets of paper, perhaps as cartoon dialogue balloons:

> *Hate the message? Kill the messenger!*
> *You cannot have your cake and eat it too*
> *Under the table and out the door*
> *A time to speak*
> *What are you looking for?*
> *It's a love-hate relationship*
> *Crocodile Tears*
> *Passing Through*
> *Some wanted things are not desirable*
> *It couldn't get any worse, could it?*
> *Dark? How dark was it?*
> *A holding-the-nose stench*
> *Is a gift truly given if it is not accepted?*
> *Some music is nothing more than noise*
> *No muddy water here*

These phrases are designed to summarize a truth of each verse of today's text, from verse 10 ("Hate the message . . . ") to verse 24 ("No muddy . . . "), respectively.

You may choose to display all the above statements at once (in random order), or you may shuffle them and display them one at a time. Say, "Look at Amos 5:10-24 and decide to which verse each of these ideas best relates." If students see a relationship to a verse other than the one intended, ask for an explanation.

To help your students see the sins that brought God's words of wrath and condemnation, identify these items as drawn from the lesson writer's outline: the social sins of Israel (vv. 10-15), bad doctrine regarding the Day of the Lord (vv. 16-20), and spiritual sins (vv. 21-24). Ask the class, "What are these sins?"

For social sins, expect such responses as rejection of truth, hatred, oppression of the poor, self-centeredness, sensuality, prejudice, and cowardly silence. For bad doctrine regarding the Day of the Lord, expect responses such as expecting God to overlook sins because the Israelites were "His people" plus believing that everything was going to be all right when the Lord comes, even though their sins were blatant and persistent. For spiritual sins, expect such responses as ritualism substituting for true worship, hypocritical songs, and unrighteousness.

Into Life

From an office supply store, buy sheets of stick-on lettering for the letter *B*. Give each student one or more of the letters; tell them that it is their *B-wear!* as you stick one to your own lapel. Suggest they "wear their Bs" to heighten their sensitivity to *Beware!* of the three elements highlighted in today's study: social sins, doctrine about the Day of the Lord, and spiritual sins. A short discussion of how these dangers are seen in personal lives and society will enhance the value of the letters as they are worn.

Read the Golden Text in unison with the class. After the recitation, ask, "How well are we doing in letting that happen in our community?" Following the responses, ask, "What can we do as a class and individually to enhance the free flow of justice?" Make the list and then ask, "What steps can we take to make these happen?" Create an action plan from this list.

Let's Talk It Over

*The questions on this page are designed to promote discussion of the lesson
by the class and to encourage application of the lesson Scriptures. The answers
provided are only discussion starters. Let your class talk it over from there.*

**1. Jesus said, "For ye have the poor always
with you" (Matthew 26:11). What are some proper and improper ways to react to this verse?**

We may see the poor as lazy and apathetic.
Sometimes that is true (compare 2 Thessalonians
3:10). But often it is not true. In reality, it may be
that we have become lazy and apathetic in carrying out the teachings of Scripture concerning
ministry to the poor!

We make a mistake when we use Matthew
26:11 to justify that there is no use bothering to
minister to the poor since there's so many of
them. That interpretation violates James 1:27.
Some have neglected to minister to the poor because they think that the poor deserve what they
are getting. We fear also that someone who presents himself as poor is conning us, and we don't
want to be taken advantage of. Therefore, we
allow fear to restrict us from taking care of some
who may have real needs.

**2. Why do you find it difficult at times to hate
the evil and love the good? How do you overcome this difficulty?**

The issue may have to do with what is ingrained in our nature. As prince of this world,
Satan deludes our minds. Our eyes see the pleasures of the world, and this tends to override the
greater spiritual reality that is unseen. At times
that which is evil seems to provide the most pleasure, so we follow our feelings instead of the
principles of God's Word. We try to stand for that
which is morally right, but the tide of evil against
us makes us think, "What's the use?" Thus godly,
countercultural behavior often seems to fail us.

**3. If God were to come walking through the
garden of your life or the life of your church, in
what areas would He find you lamenting your
state of affairs? What would you confess to Him?
How do you think He would respond?**

Often we get our priorities out of order. Instead of seeking the kingdom of God first (Matthew 6:33), we pursue those things that give us
the greatest pleasure or meet our "felt needs." In
the church we can be so focused on attaining
numbers that we fail to make true, spiritually-deep disciples.

The use of money on wrong priorities, both individually and as a church, can be an area where
we may be convicted if God were to come into
our midst. The important thing to remember,
though, is that God is continually walking among
us, and the conviction of sin is to be a continual
part of our lives.

**4. In what ways do our twenty-first-century
offerings and assemblies please and displease
God? How can we do better?**

Sometimes we are guilty of bringing to God
gifts that are more of a legalistic act than a love
offering. We can also be very rigid in the conduct
of our worship assemblies, while failing to express love to those gathered. We may present our
offerings or gather for our worship for the purpose of trying to gain favor with God rather than
trying to glorify God. Also, our worship and giving may be done simply to absolve our conscience rather than to advance the kingdom.
When this is the attitude, we have failed to realize the true purpose of our giving and our assembling. God is not pleased as a result.

Here's a very practical idea for making your
Sunday morning worship more meaningful to
both God and you: make sure you get enough
sleep the night before. To stay up "all hours" on
Saturday night only to drag your sleepy self to
worship on Sunday morning is quite pointless!

**5. How will your songs offer worship that is
acceptable to God?**

Churches continue to experience battles over
music styles, volume, and the use of various
kinds of instruments. The problem with these
"worship wars" is that they begin at the wrong
starting point.

Worship that is acceptable to God does not
start with the outer aspects of the worship but
with the heart of the worshiper. Worship music
that is acceptable to God comes from a heart that
is dedicated to God and to accomplishing His
will. It is music that focuses on glorifying and
honoring God. It is also music that is for edification as we teach and admonish "one another in
psalms and hymns and spiritual songs" (Colossians 3:16).

Recommitted to God's Ways

DEVOTIONAL READING: Hosea 14.

BACKGROUND SCRIPTURE: Hosea 4:1-4; 7:1, 2; 12:1-9; 14:1-3; 2 Kings 15:8-10.

PRINTED TEXT: Hosea 4:1-4; 7:1, 2; 12:6-9; 14:1.

Hosea 4:1-4

1 Hear the word of the LORD, ye children of Israel: for the LORD hath a controversy with the inhabitants of the land, because there is no truth, nor mercy, nor knowledge of God in the land.

2 By swearing, and lying, and killing, and stealing, and committing adultery, they break out, and blood toucheth blood.

3 Therefore shall the land mourn, and every one that dwelleth therein shall languish, with the beasts of the field, and with the fowls of heaven; yea, the fishes of the sea also shall be taken away.

4 Yet let no man strive, nor reprove another: for thy people are as they that strive with the priest.

Hosea 7:1, 2

1 When I would have healed Israel, then the iniquity of Ephraim was discovered, and the wickedness of Samaria: for they commit falsehood; and the thief cometh in, and the troop of robbers spoileth without.

2 And they consider not in their hearts that I remember all their wickedness: now their own doings have beset them about; they are before my face.

Hosea 12:6-9

6 Therefore turn thou to thy God: keep mercy and judgment, and wait on thy God continually.

7 He is a merchant, the balances of deceit are in his hand: he loveth to oppress.

8 And Ephraim said, Yet I am become rich, I have found me out substance: in all my labors they shall find none iniquity in me that were sin.

9 And I that am the LORD thy God from the land of Egypt will yet make thee to dwell in tabernacles, as in the days of the solemn feast.

Hosea 14:1

1 O Israel, return unto the LORD thy God; for thou hast fallen by thine iniquity.

GOLDEN TEXT: Hear the word of the LORD, ye children of Israel: for the LORD hath a controversy with the inhabitants of the land, because there is no truth, nor mercy, nor knowledge of God in the land.—Hosea 4:1.

Lesson Aims

After participating in this lesson, each student will be able to:

1. Describe the conditions that Hosea saw in his society.

2. Compare and contrast the conditions of Hosea's society with conditions today.

3. Identify one area in his or her own life to conform to God's ways.

Lesson Outline

INTRODUCTION
  A. Order in the Court
  B. Lesson Background
I. SERIOUS CHARGES (Hosea 4:1-4)
  A. Absence of Goodness (v. 1)
  B. Presence of Wickedness (v. 2)
    Rogue's Harbor
  C. Presence of Mourning (v. 3)
  D. Absence of Integrity (v. 4)
II. SPURNED OFFER (Hosea 7:1, 2)
  A. Healing Was Rejected (v. 1)
  B. Repentance Was Rejected (v. 2)
III. STERN COMMAND (Hosea 12:6-9; 14:1)
  A. Turn for a Blessing (v. 6)
    Axels or U-Turns?
  B. Turn for Perspective (vv. 7, 8)
  C. Turn or Face Judgment (v. 9; 14:1)
CONCLUSION
  A. Holy God, Sinful People
  B. Prayer
  C. Thought to Remember

Introduction

A. Order in the Court

Have you ever noticed how many courtroom dramas are on TV? From *Perry Mason* in the 1950s and 1960s to today's *Law & Order,* this is an enduring staple of secular entertainment. An entertainment-oriented culture even looks upon such shows as *Court TV* as a source of reality-based amusement.

Hosea wasn't a scriptwriter for a courtroom drama. His book wasn't designed to be entertaining. Hosea wasn't a lawyer, but he could have been. Much of his teaching is like an indictment that would be presented in court. It is a bill of particulars confronting Israel for sin.

Hosea's focus in both the positive and negative sections of his book is on the relationship between God and His people. The prophet Amos talked about God, Israel, and the surrounding nations, but Hosea largely focused on the theme of God and Israel. (In this context, *Israel* refers to the northern kingdom of God's divided people as distinct from the southern kingdom of *Judah*.)

B. Lesson Background

To put Hosea's words in context, it will be helpful to understand what the people of Israel had done to their religion. In some cases they had rejected God and their traditions outright. In other cases they had merged the religion of the one true God with a regional religion that worshiped a god named *Baal* (Hosea 2:8). This greatly disturbed Hosea and the other prophets.

Hosea probably began his prophetic ministry just as Amos's ministry (last week's lesson) was drawing to a close. Hosea thus prophesied between about 760 BC and the fall of the northern kingdom in 722 BC.

This period of time seemed like a golden age to the people living in it (compare Isaiah 2:7; 3:16). Yet Hosea saw it, as did Amos and Isaiah, as anything but a golden age. Yes, there was prosperity, but the rich took advantage of the poor. Yes, there were religious observances, but they were corrupted by paganism and sensuality.

Hosea's name means "salvation," and he certainly preached that the people were in need of that! Yet the people did not see themselves as vulnerable—"Salvation from what?" they probably asked themselves. The relatively stable reigns of Uzziah in the south and Jeroboam II in the north bred complacency.

But the prophets of God were not fooled. Just as Amos had seen the truth, so did Hosea. As a patriotic dweller of the north, he warned the people of the problem. And his warning would later prove to be valid.

In some ways Hosea is the most intriguing prophet in the Old Testament. Hosea's tumultuous family life, as noted in Hosea 1:2-11; 3:1-3, became almost a metaphor of what was happening between God and His people. God had commanded Hosea to marry a woman who would prove to be unfaithful. This was so that Hosea's family could be an example of God's willingness to love and take back His faithless people. Thus Hosea's own family became a kind of object lesson of human faithlessness and God's forgiveness.

The book of Hosea itself can be studied in three divisions. The first division, chapters 1–3, describes the personal information about Hosea and his family life.

The second division is chapters 4–13; this contains the oracles, or sermons, of Hosea. These messages are very tough condemnations of what was going on in Israel. The lesson for today is taken primarily from this section.

The final section is chapter 14. It deserves its own designation because, while it also contains sermonic material from Hosea, a bit of hope is introduced. Even so, no more than 10 percent of the book of Hosea deals with God's blessings. The book is overwhelmingly a message of condemnation and punishment.

I. Serious Charges
(Hosea 4:1-4)

A. Absence of Goodness (v. 1)

1. Hear the word of the LORD, ye children of Israel: for the LORD hath a controversy with the inhabitants of the land, because there is no truth, nor mercy, nor knowledge of God in the land.

The opening phrase *hear the word of the Lord* begins the indictment. What follows is a bill of particulars about things the people are lacking. We may call these *sins of omission.*

First, the Lord says *there is no truth.* The word used for *truth* carries the idea of faithfulness, fidelity, honesty, or reliability (compare Genesis 24:49; 47:29; Exodus 18:21; Joshua 2:12, 14).

Neither is there any *mercy* in the land. *Mercy* is one of the most beautiful and interesting words in the Old Testament. It is sometimes translated *love, loving-kindness, goodness,* etc. (examples: Psalm 36:7; Jeremiah 9:24). The Hebrew words translated *truth* and *mercy* in this

---

How to Say It

AMOS. *Ay*-mus.

BAAL. *Bay*-ul.

BETH-AVEN. *Beth-ay*-ven (strong accent on *ay*).

BETHEL. *Beth*-ul.

EPHRAIM. *Ee*-fray-im.

HOSEA. Ho-*zay*-uh.

ISAIAH. Eye-*zay*-uh.

JEROBOAM. Jair-uh-*boe*-um.

JERUSALEM. Juh-*roo*-suh-lem.

UZZIAH. Uh-*zye*-uh.

ZEPHANIAH. Zef-uh-*nye*-uh.

---

passage occur together (translated in various ways) in dozens of other Old Testament passages. One interesting example is Exodus 34:6: "The Lord, the Lord God . . . abundant in goodness and truth." What the Lord himself abounds in is precisely what His people disdain!

Third, Hosea says there is no *knowledge of God.* This does not mean that there is no knowledge that God exists. Rather, the word *knowledge* is used to describe an intimate mindfulness of God and His requirements under the covenant. In place of this knowledge, the people have substituted meaningless ritual. "For I desired mercy, and not sacrifice; and the knowledge of God more than burnt offerings" (Hosea 6:6).

Do we see any of these omissions in our own age? Truth is certainly under attack. [See question #1, page 358.] There is too little mercy. While there are few genuine atheists in the world, there is still a dearth of the knowledge of God. God has made knowledge of himself available, but many suppress it (Romans 1:18-23).

B. Presence of Wickedness (v. 2)

2. By swearing, and lying, and killing, and stealing, and committing adultery, they break out, and blood toucheth blood.

Here Hosea describes the presence of serious sins. We would call these *sins of commission.* He describes a decay that is illustrated by the people's ignoring basic morality and decency, such as what is prescribed in the Ten Commandments (Exodus 20:1-17; Deuteronomy 5:6-21).

At least four of those commandments are mentioned here by use of the words *lying, and killing, and stealing, and committing adultery.* The word *swearing* probably does not refer to using obscenities but to pronouncing a curse on someone. *Break out* is the idea of violating boundaries (compare 1 Samuel 25:10). The expression *blood toucheth blood* probably means that one murder quickly follows another.

This corrupt society can trace its problems to a single cause: the rejection of God. The kinds of qualities that are missing (v. 1) are foundational to a healthy society. The serious sins that are present inevitably serve to weaken a society. Since Hosea is a resident of the land, this must fill him with both anger and sorrow.

ROGUE'S HARBOR

Peter Cartwright (1785–1872) spent several decades as a frontier Methodist circuit-riding preacher, first in Kentucky and then in Illinois. In 1856 he wrote his autobiography, which has become a classic on the history of frontier religion.

Cartwright was still a child when his parents moved from Virginia to Kentucky, much of which was untamed wilderness at the time. Logan County, where his parents settled, was known as *Rogue's Harbor.* It was the home of many individuals who came to escape justice or punishment. Law could not be enforced. Murderers, horse thieves, highway robbers, and counterfeiters formed a majority of the population. Honest citizens tried to prosecute them, but the outlaws just provided alibis for each other and always escaped justice.

Finally the law-abiding citizens formed a group known as the Regulators to establish their own code of bylaws. One day the two groups met in town and a battle ensued, fought with knives, pistols, and clubs. Many were wounded, some were killed. The rogues were victorious and drove the Regulators out of town.

Sound like a nice place to live and raise your family? It is similar to the situation Hosea described: a community of killing, lying, adultery, and murder after murder. That is the result of a community that does not know God. When there is no knowledge of God, morals and social stability disappear just as quickly as the outward formalities of religion. This may lead you to reflect on how much knowledge of God remains in your city.   —J. B. N.

C. Presence of Mourning (v. 3)

3. Therefore shall the land mourn, and every one that dwelleth therein shall languish, with the beasts of the field, and with the fowls of heaven; yea, the fishes of the sea also shall be taken away.

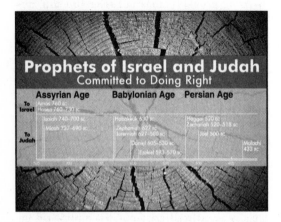

Visual for Lesson 2. *Use this visual as a discussion starter by asking, "What do tree rings and the dating of the prophets have in common?"*

The faithlessness of God's people is to be punished by a drought—that is a secondary meaning of the word *mourn* in this context. This same Hebrew verb is used in Jeremiah 4:28; 12:4; Joel 1:10; and Amos 1:2. Hosea's description is of an environment in the process of ruination. All creatures that live in the land will waste away or, literally, wither. Even *the fishes of the sea* are threatened.

Isn't it interesting that God associates judgment for sin as being the occasion for general decline even in the realm of nature? Paul speaks of creation groaning as a result of sin (Romans 8:20-22).

D. Absence of Integrity (v. 4)

4. Yet let no man strive, nor reprove another: for thy people are as they that strive with the priest.

The first line of this verse is difficult to interpret. At first glance you would think that God is forbidding the readers to *reprove* one another with regard to the moral decay—which is exactly what we need to do! The idea, rather, is that finger-pointing and blaming others will not solve the problems. Great revivals begin not when we put the spotlight of the sins of others but when we dare to indict ourselves.

The last line is also difficult to interpret. Is Hosea condemning his readers for being the kind of people who would dare to bring charges even against a *priest*?

Considering how angry Hosea is toward the priests, that is not likely (Hosea 4:6-9; 5:1; 6:9; 10:5). Many commentators say the verse should be seen as an encouragement to confront the priests. Under this theory, it might be read as, "Your people should be as they who bring charges against a priest." A different theory is that this is another reference to finger-pointing, as in, "Any problems are the fault of the priesthood, not me!"

II. Spurned Offer
(Hosea 7:1, 2)

A. Healing Was Rejected (v. 1)

1. When I would have healed Israel, then the iniquity of Ephraim was discovered, and the wickedness of Samaria: for they commit falsehood; and the thief cometh in, and the troop of robbers spoileth without.

The name *Ephraim* is another way to refer to the northern kingdom of *Israel.* Ephraim is a prominent tribe in the northern kingdom. Adding the word *Samaria* to the mix serves to emphasize the entirety of the 10 tribes that are situated north of Judah. God is saying to them that He is willing to heal all Israel. But as God makes this attempt, the sins of the people become even more apparent.

The primary way God attempts to heal Israel is by sending them prophets. Rather than causing the people to repent, the work of the prophets just reveals more and more sin and guilt. The prophets are persecuted (Amos 7:10-13), not welcomed (compare Acts 7:52). [See question #2, page 358.]

The last line speaks of being robbed inside one's own house *(the thief cometh in)* as well as while out on the city streets *(the troop of robbers spoileth without)*. While committing *falsehood* may be a sneaky, somewhat hidden crime, other kinds of banditry are all too clear. There is no social justice anywhere.

B. Repentance Was Rejected (v. 2)

2. And they consider not in their hearts that I remember all their wickedness: now their own doings have beset them about; they are before my face.

The people of Israel erroneously assume that God does not know or care about the evil they are doing. How often human beings have deceived themselves into thinking they can hide their sins from God! Yet God does not suffer from Attention Deficit Disorder. Nor does He have a faulty memory (Leviticus 26:42; Psalm 105:8). [See question #3, page 358.]

III. Stern Command
(Hosea 12:6-9; 14:1)

A. Turn for a Blessing (v. 6)

6. Therefore turn thou to thy God: keep mercy and judgment, and wait on thy God continually.

This verse follows a discussion of Jacob's encounter with God at Bethel (Hosea 12:2-4; compare Genesis 28:10-22; 35:1-15). Hosea is highly critical of what has been going on at Bethel. See Hosea 10:5, which refers to *Beth-aven*, a sarcastic name for Bethel. While *Bethel* means "house of God," *Beth-aven* means "house of wickedness."

In Hosea 12:4, the prophet reminds his audience that Bethel was once a holy place. The people need to return to the kind of religion first celebrated there.

Turning *thou to thy God* involves repentance. [See question #4, page 358.] The people are also to *wait* on *God*. Why the delay? They need for God to bless them again. They need the blessing that God once gave to Jacob. [See question #5, page 358.]

Axels or U-Turns?

Normally the word *turn* brings to mind a change in direction. But not all turns are alike. In figure skating there is a maneuver known as an *axel*, named after Norwegian figure skater Axel Paulsen (1856–1938). The axel features a jump with a turn in the air that results in the skater still going in the same direction upon landing. It is just for show. Though the axel takes a good deal of skill, it does not result in a change of direction.

Curves on an interstate highway sometimes do not take any effort on the part of the driver. The road may be banked sufficiently for the car to change direction almost by itself. The turn is done by the road conditions, not by the driver.

Then there is a U-turn. This is a 180-degree change of direction. It occurs only when the driver takes a very deliberate action. There is nothing happenstance or accidental about it. It is a conscious effort by the driver to follow a new course.

When Hosea urged the people to turn to God, he was not talking about a showy axel that would impress others. Nor was he talking about a situation where the people were turned merely by force of external circumstances, without any conscious effort on their part. Hosea confronts his audience (and us) with the need to make a deliberate change of direction—a U-turn.   —J. B. N.

B. Turn for Perspective (vv. 7, 8)

7. He is a merchant, the balances of deceit are in his hand: he loveth to oppress.

The Hebrew word translated *merchant* is literally *Canaanite*. Canaanites are known as shrewd traders, thus the translation *merchant* captures the sense very well. Canaanites inhabited the promised land before the Israelites arrived (Exodus 3:8).

Greedy merchants are known for their dishonest balance scales *(balances of deceit)*. This is very offensive to God (Deuteronomy 25:13-16; Proverbs 11:1; 20:23). The children of Israel think they are quite superior to the previous inhabitants of the area, but the message is that they have become the same as them. They love *to oppress*.

8. And Ephraim said, Yet I am become rich, I have found me out substance: in all my labors they shall find none iniquity in me that were sin.

In a state of arrogant pride, *Ephraim* believes itself to be *rich* and righteous. The people are indeed rich in a material way in the manner of unjust merchants. Not only do they see themselves as rich, they do not see that they had committed any *sin.* "What harm did we do in accumulating these riches?" the Israelites ask themselves.

They have so manipulated the laws that they can maintain that technically they are not guilty (compare Mark 7:9-13). *They shall find none iniquity in me* is an arrogant, self-righteous confidence. Yet God knows better (Amos 6:1-7). Several decades after Hosea writes, the message to Jerusalem to the south will be about the same (Zephaniah 1:11-13).

C. Turn or Face Judgment (v. 9; 14:1)

9. And I that am the LORD thy God from the land of Egypt will yet make thee to dwell in tabernacles, as in the days of the solemn feast.

The word *tabernacles* refers to the tents that the Israelites lived in while in the wilderness wanderings after they had left *the land of Egypt.* Thus the Lord promises a severe reduction in Israel's standard of living: they will give up their cozy houses for tents.

The *solemn feast* here probably refers to the Feast of Tabernacles. During this festival, people set up booths or tents as a reminder of wilderness wanderings (Leviticus 23:33-44). How sad: the Israelites will return to tents not as a memorial but as a punishment.

14:1. O Israel, return unto the LORD thy God; for thou hast fallen by thine iniquity.

We should be glad that the book of Hosea has a fourteenth chapter! It is in this chapter that hope is restored. That hope is more evident in the verses that follow (not in today's text). There are only seven "blessings sections" in Hosea, and this is one of them.

It is the sin of the people that causes them to stumble. If they *return* to God, He can lift them up and help them walk in the right paths. This is a note of hope in an otherwise very dark book.

Yet it is not the only note of hope. Remember that in Hosea's own experience he bestows forgiving love to an errant wife (Hosea 3). Thus Hosea uses his own life as an example that God also can forgive the people who have been unfaithful to Him.

Conclusion

A. Holy God, Sinful People

Hosea taught that evil can become pervasive. Evil affects the fabric of society. We see in Hosea God's sense of hurt, betrayal, and disappointment. God suffers when His people sin. Hosea also discovered and taught that God is both holy and merciful. God thundered against sin, but He could be warm and forgiving to the repentant sinner.

Here is where we need to remind ourselves of Hosea's marital situation. Hosea sought out his wife, bought her out of prostitution, and took her back into his household (Hosea 3). Hosea could not understand how Israel could so callously choose not to love the God who had loved them so much.

Combining his own personal insight and hurts with God's revelation, Hosea realized the depth of the meaning of *unfaithfulness.* Unfaithfulness toward another human and toward God can be forgiven, but it takes sincere repentance and profound love. Hosea's love for his wife was a picture of God's love for His people.

No Christian looking at this can fail to see that Jesus did something similar for us. He paid a price to bring us back home. He did this even though we did not deserve it. "While we were yet sinners, Christ died for us" (Romans 5:8).

This is why some people say that Hosea begins to put into our minds what will come into sharper focus in the New Testament: the doctrine of grace. "For the law was given by Moses, but grace and truth came by Jesus Christ" (John 1:17).

B. Prayer

Forgive me, O God, for breaking Your heart. That fact would be overwhelming to me if not for the message of Your grace. Even in Your anger there is love, and even in the midst of pain You can pardon. In the name of Jesus, who embodied this truth, amen.

C. Thought to Remember

Repentance required!

Home Daily Bible Readings

Monday, June 4—The Fourth Generation (2 Kings 15:8-12)

Tuesday, June 5—Repentance Brings Blessing (Hosea 14)

Wednesday, June 6—God's Love for Israel (Hosea 11:1-5)

Thursday, June 7—God Cares (Hosea 11:6-11)

Friday, June 8—A Nation Sins (Hosea 4:1-5)

Saturday, June 9—Evil Deeds Remembered (Hosea 7:1-7)

Sunday, June 10—Return to Your God (Hosea 12:5-10)

Learning by Doing

This page contains an alternative lesson plan emphasizing learning activities.
Classes desiring such student involvement will find these suggestions helpful.

Learning Goals

After this lesson, each student will be able to:

1. Describe the conditions that Hosea saw in his society.

2. Compare and contrast the conditions of Hosea's society with conditions today.

3. Identify one area in his or her own life to conform to God's ways.

Into the Lesson

Invite a man of your congregation who enjoys drama to present the following as an opening monologue. Ideally, costume your actor as an Old Testament figure.

I am Hosea, a heartbroken man and God's prophet to Israel.

My nation is a lawless place where kings are assassinated and the assassin is also murdered. The Israelites seem bent on destroying themselves, all the while considering themselves to be the privileged and protected people of Almighty God. Assyria licks her lips. Egypt slyly says, "Let us help."

God named my children after the tragedy of Israel. My daughter Lo-ruhamah—you would know her as *Not Pitied*. There is also Lo-ammi, God's declaration that Israel was no longer His people. You could have called Israel *Not Mine!*—an illegitimate child.

I am Hosea, God's heartbroken prophet. "Ephraim hath hired lovers." But God continues to love, and so must I. So must I!

Conclude with any other background information you see as essential.

Into the Word

Questions are important in God's confrontation with Israel (see Hosea 6:4; 9:5; 11:8; 13:10). As noted by the lesson writer, much of Hosea's teaching is like a courtroom indictment, a lawyer and judge asking the accusatory questions of wrongdoers.

Prepare the following pairs of questions (Q) and follow-up questions (FQ) on 12 separate slips of paper, one pair for each verse of the text. Distribute them to class members.

Q: What are the first three indictments God makes against Israel in Hosea 4:1? *FQ:* How many violations of the Ten Commandments are represented in the indictment?

Q: In Hosea 4:2, what is meant by the statement, "They break out"? *FQ:* How does the expression relate to John's declaration, "Sin is the transgression of the law" (1 John 3:4)?

Q: How is drought in Hosea 4:3 an excellent figure for spiritual weakness and ruin? *FQ:* In what sense is deterioration of natural environmental systems related to sin?

Q: In Hosea 4:4, what common practice is alluded to that occurs often when things go wrong? *FQ:* What recent examples of finger-pointing can you name?

Q: What crime does Hosea 7:1 reveal, a crime common in the world's sinful cities? *FQ:* How is the frequency of robbery a good indication of general sinfulness?

Q: What does Hosea 7:2 say will happen even when people refuse to believe that God sees their sin? *FQ:* How common is the belief that God sees all that we think and do?

Q: What significant Old Testament event is described by Hosea before he calls for repentance in Hosea 12:6? *FQ:* What is it that every believer is waiting for when he or she "waits for God"?

Q: Why would Hosea highlight the sin of a dishonest merchant as he does in 12:7? *FQ:* In what ways do you see "dishonest scales" in modern business practices?

Q: How common is the self-deceit we see in Hosea 12:8? *FQ:* What is the root of self-deceit when it comes to sin and its consequences?

Q: As 12:9 affirms, how can living in tents be a good thing? *FQ:* How can thinking about an earlier, even harder time help one's spiritual life?

Q: How is Hosea 14:1 the fundamental message of the prophets? *FQ:* How is 14:1 the message every evangelist must use with every sinner?

Ask students holding questions to ask them aloud, pausing for answers between *Q*s and *FQ*s.

Into Life

Say, "People fall away from the church and from Christ for various sinful reasons. How do we intervene when that happens? How do we make sure that we are not being hypocritical in this regard?" Discuss a preventive plan for both questions. Be cautious about mentioning names!

Let's Talk It Over

The questions on this page are designed to promote discussion of the lesson by the class and to encourage application of the lesson Scriptures. The answers provided are only discussion starters. Let your class talk it over from there.

1. Though Christians claim to believe the truth, what are some ways in which it may appear that we do not have the truth? How can we do better?

A danger of those who claim to be loyal followers of the New Testament is to be very strong in *orthodoxy* (right teaching or doctrine) while being weak in *orthopraxy* (right practice). Church leaders who preach one thing but do the opposite can find themselves in public scandal. There is a word for this: hypocrisy.

Jesus reserved some of His strongest criticism for those who neglected right practice (Matthew 23:23). Faith is dead if it is not put to work (James 1:22; 2:17). Notice that the third Learning Goal for each of these lessons focuses on application. That could be a good place to begin to match doctrine and practice!

2. What are some ways that you rejected the healing that God desired to provide? How did you turn this around?

God sent prophets to Israel to warn them and lead them to repentance, and He also raises up preachers and teachers in the church today to challenge us. But as Israel ended up attacking the messenger, we can do the same. Some preachers feel pressure to avoid preaching on certain sins because people may be offended. If those messages are suppressed, that can end up being a rejection of the healing that God wants to provide.

Similarly, we can be guilty of surrounding ourselves with teachers who say what we prefer to hear instead of what we need to hear (compare 2 Timothy 4:3, 4). Self-delusion can be difficult to break down! The solution begins with brokenness before God.

3. What factors can cause us to think we can hide our sins from God? How do you avoid this trap?

Though we intellectually know from our study of Scripture that God is everywhere and that He knows all things, we can still fool ourselves into believing that God will not care about our sin. One way we do this is simply to deny that what we have done is sin. We have ways of rationalizing sins to the point where we feel we have not

sinned. We convince ourselves of this, and thereby think we've convinced God.

Sometimes we hide behind the feeling that we have not committed a "major" sin. As long as our sin is not as bad as someone else's, we are OK. We can also try to hide our sins by making ourselves the victims, blaming others for "driving us to it" instead of taking responsibility for our own actions. Discussing our situation with a spiritually mature Christian can be the first step toward correction.

4. In what areas do you need to repent? How did you receive God's blessings at a time you repented?

Failure to make God first in our lives and in our churches calls for repentance; anything less is idolatry. For some, buildings, budgets, and plans have become more important than making disciples and practicing spiritual disciplines.

God has been known to withdraw His blessings because of "sin in the camp" (see Joshua 7). To truly repent and thereby receive the blessings of God may mean, in severe cases, that church leaders stand before the congregation and confess that they have not led the church in maintaining the proper priorities. It may mean going to those who are not like us in skin color or economic class and confess that we have judged them improperly (James 2:1-4). This list can be long!

5. What are some ways that God has provided for you? for your church?

God is able to bless us abundantly beyond what we can ever ask or imagine (Ephesians 3:20). He has sustained His people, His church, through 2,000 years.

There have been congregations seemingly on the verge of extinction, but God, by His grace, has pulled them through. As God led Israel through the wilderness wandering, so He leads us through our difficult times. God has led us out of our "Egypt"—out of our bondage to sin—and is faithfully leading us to the promised land of Heaven. God has even provided for us in His promise that this tabernacle in which we live, this tent, this body of flesh, will one day be redeemed and we will receive a new body.

Committed to True Worship

DEVOTIONAL READING: Isaiah 58:6-12.

**BACKGROUND SCRIPTURE: Isaiah 1:10-20;
2 Kings 15:32-35.**

PRINTED TEXT: Isaiah 1:10-20.

Isaiah 1:10-20

10 Hear the word of the LORD, ye rulers of Sodom; give ear unto the law of our God, ye people of Gomorrah.

11 To what purpose is the multitude of your sacrifices unto me? saith the LORD: I am full of the burnt offerings of rams, and the fat of fed beasts; and I delight not in the blood of bullocks, or of lambs, or of he goats.

12 When ye come to appear before me, who hath required this at your hand, to tread my courts?

13 Bring no more vain oblations; incense is an abomination unto me; the new moons and sabbaths, the calling of assemblies, I cannot away with; it is iniquity, even the solemn meeting.

14 Your new moons and your appointed feasts my soul hateth: they are a trouble unto me; I am weary to bear them.

15 And when ye spread forth your hands, I will hide mine eyes from you: yea, when ye make many prayers, I will not hear: your hands are full of blood.

16 Wash ye, make you clean; put away the evil of your doings from before mine eyes; cease to do evil;

17 Learn to do well; seek judgment, relieve the oppressed, judge the fatherless, plead for the widow.

18 Come now, and let us reason together, saith the LORD: though your sins be as scarlet, they shall be as white as snow; though they be red like crimson, they shall be as wool.

19 If ye be willing and obedient, ye shall eat the good of the land:

20 But if ye refuse and rebel, ye shall be devoured with the sword: for the mouth of the LORD hath spoken it.

GOLDEN TEXT: Learn to do well; seek judgment, relieve the oppressed, judge the fatherless, plead for the widow.—Isaiah 1:17.

Committed to Doing Right
Unit 1: Life as God's People
(Lessons 1-4)

Lesson Aims

After participating in this lesson, each student will be able to:

1. Identify worship attitudes and practices that Isaiah said pleased the Lord and those he said did not.

2. Explain the relationship between attitude and practice in worship.

3. Identify one area in his or her life that hinders true worship and make a plan to change it.

Lesson Outline

INTRODUCTION
    A. Surprised by Trouble
    B. Lesson Background
I. DEFENDANTS SUBPOENAED (Isaiah 1:10)
    Hear!
II. PLAINTIFF READS CHARGES (Isaiah 1:11-15)
    A. Disgusting Sacrifices (vv. 11-13a)
    B. Insufferable Gatherings (vv. 13b, 14)
    C. Disregarded Prayers (v. 15)
III. JUDGE OFFERS A CHANCE (Isaiah 1:16-20)
    A. Stop the Bad (v. 16)
    B. Start the Good (v. 17)
    Inner Mission
    C. The Only Chance (vv. 18-20)
CONCLUSION
    A. A Show of Real Reality
    B. Prayer
    C. Thought to Remember

Introduction

A. Surprised by Trouble

As a child, I once came cheerily into the house, only to be confronted by my parents. They clearly were upset with me. My mother said, "Well, it looks to me like he is ready for a spanking!" I do not remember what wrong I had done. I do not even remember what happened thereafter. However, I do remember vividly that my heart began pounding and my toothy grin dissolved. I came in thinking everything was great; but suddenly I was surprised by trouble.

In today's text, Judah is also surprised by trouble. Isaiah had a message from the Lord that was designed to wipe the grins off their smug faces, as though saying, "It looks to me like they are ready for punishment." Isaiah 1 is a vision designed to move people to repentance.

B. Lesson Background

Isaiah 1:1 allows us to date Isaiah's lengthy prophetic ministry between 740 and 680 BC. Last week we saw Hosea, an older contemporary of Isaiah, tell the northern kingdom of Israel to repent and recommit their ways to the Lord. Sadly, they refused. Within a few years after Hosea's ministry, the northern kingdom was defeated and dispersed. That happened in 722 BC.

Isaiah's ministry to the southern kingdom of Judah had only slightly better prospects. The Lord told Isaiah that his preaching to Judah would also fall on deaf ears. But though they would also be taken into exile, the Lord would preserve a small remnant (Isaiah 6:9-13).

Isaiah's book contains glorious passages of this restoration of Judah, one of which is the text for next week. Apparently the original readers latched on to the good news and ignored the warnings and calls for repentance. They mistook the miraculous deliverance from the Assyrian army in 701 BC as a sign that God would never allow Judah to fall. By seeing the temple as something of a good-luck charm, they deviated from true worship (compare Jeremiah 7:4).

Isaiah 1:2-31 introduces the entire book of Isaiah. Therefore it was probably written after 701 BC, when the people clearly had failed to understand the Lord's message. So the Lord presents to Isaiah a vision in a form of a lawsuit.

Ancient law courts were different from modern ones, but many roles are similar. It is important to identify the role that each character may represent (judge, plaintiff, defendant, witness, etc.) and the purpose for the scene (to level charges, to prove guilt, to announce a verdict, to impose a sentence). Within the drama of the trial, both the Lord and the prophet may take more than one role. When the prophet steps out of the drama, he speaks to the reader.

Isaiah 1:10-20 forms the central part of the trial scene. The author seems to interrupt the trial drama with interludes, something like a reporter may do. Here is one possible way to identify the back-and-forth of Isaiah 1:

Trial Scenes	Prophetic Interludes
2, 3	4
5-8	9
10-20	21-23
24-26	27, 28
29-31	

In verse 10, where we begin today, the defendants are called to trial. Charges are leveled in verses 11-15. Then the trial motif takes an unusual turn: the offer of a chance for a stay of sentence in verses 16-20.

I. Defendants Subpoenaed
(Isaiah 1:10)

10. Hear the word of the LORD, ye rulers of Sodom; give ear unto the law of our God, ye people of Gomorrah.

Sodom and *Gomorrah* are used figuratively for Judah. These cities were destroyed because of extreme wickedness (Genesis 19). The references to both the *rulers* and the *people* show the same to be true of Judah. The Lord threatens punishment because His chosen people are sinful at all levels of society. *The word of the Lord* is parallel to *the law of our God*, both referring to the specific charges in the next section. [See question #1, page 366.]

HEAR!

As I get older (don't we all!), more and more infirmities come my way. I won't bore you with the whole organ recital, but a recent concern has been my hearing. I still believe my hearing is good. No family member, friend, or medical professional has suggested I need a hearing aid. Certain loud noises, however, give me a headache, and I avoid them.

Another problem is background noise. This can take the form of road noise in a car, conversations at adjacent tables in a restaurant, or even other conversations during a social gathering. All this can prevent me from really hearing what a person is saying. I sometimes have to say, "I'm sorry; I can't hear you." But technically, that's a matter of definition. In the sense that the sounds being made are registering on my eardrum, I ac-

---

How to Say It
ASSYRIAN. Uh-*sear*-e-un.
BABYLON. *Bab*-uh-lun.
DEUTERONOMY. Due-ter-*ahn*-uh-me.
EZEKIEL. Ee-*zeek*-ee-ul or Ee-*zeek*-yul.
GOMORRAH. Guh-*more*-uh.
HOSEA. Ho-*zay*-uh.
ISAIAH. Eye-*zay*-uh.
JUDEANS. Joo-*dee*-unz.
LEVITICUS. Leh-*vit*-ih-kus.
NAHUM. *Nay*-hum.
SODOM. *Sod*-um.

---

tually can hear the other person. But I can't decipher these sounds sufficiently to understand the words being used. It helps to remove the distracting noise and concentrate on the speaker.

The same applies in the spiritual realm. When the Lord speaks to us, there sometimes are so many other background noises that we do not hear with enough clarity for the message to register in our consciousness. We may then need to eliminate the distracting noises and concentrate on the speaker. "Hear the word of the Lord!"   —J. B. N.

II. Plaintiff Reads Charges
(Isaiah 1:11-15)

A. Disgusting Sacrifices (vv. 11-13a)

11. To what purpose is the multitude of your sacrifices unto me? saith the LORD: I am full of the burnt offerings of rams, and the fat of fed beasts; and I delight not in the blood of bullocks, or of lambs, or of he goats.

The Lord begins His testimony with a rhetorical question—a question that actually makes a statement. The exact expression in Hebrew (literally, "for what to me?") occurs only two other times in the Old Testament: Genesis 27:46 and Job 30:2. In all three cases the phrase has to do with importance or value.

The problem is not the number of sacrifices (a *multitude* of them) nor the type of sacrifices (*burnt offerings* prescribed in the law). Neither is the quality of the animals at issue. The phrase *fed beasts* is merely descriptive of the good quality of the animals (compare 2 Samuel 6:13; 1 Kings 1:9).

It must shock the readers to learn that even though they offer sacrifices that are plentiful, correct, and good in and of themselves, God is not pleased. When the Lord says *I am full*, it is as if He is saying, "Your offerings make me sick—I am fed up!" (Compare Proverbs 28:19.) [See question #2, page 366.]

12. When ye come to appear before me, who hath required this at your hand, to tread my courts?

To appear before refers to the offering of the sacrifices mentioned in verse 11. The Lord is saying that He has not demanded them *to tread* His *courts*. The treading may be that of the animals, but more likely it is the unfitness of the worshipers themselves.

13a. Bring no more vain oblations; incense is an abomination unto me.

Oblations is a general term for sacrifices, both grain and animal. The adjective *vain* is the same word used in the Third Commandment (Deuteronomy 5:11) in connection with the use of

God's name. *Incense* can refer generally to spices (Exodus 30:1, 7-9) or to specific sacrifices. But here it probably refers to sacrifices generally (as in Psalm 66:15) that are supposed to be as pleasant to the Lord as incense.

The nation's offerings are useless; worse, they are all an *abomination* to the Lord. He is disgusted with them all.

B. Insufferable Gatherings (vv. 13b, 14)

13b. The new moons and sabbaths, the calling of assemblies, I cannot away with; it is iniquity, even the solemn meeting.

Observances of *new moons and sabbaths,* along with various other *assemblies,* were established by God himself (Exodus 20:8; Leviticus 23; Numbers 10:10; 28:11, 14). These are various religious gatherings under the Law of Moses.

Even though God had established these observances, He now says *I cannot away with;* this expression means that the Lord cannot bear, abide, or endure the way His people conduct these events. In short, *it is iniquity!* The Lord cannot tolerate any sacred assembly that is characterized by wrong motives and evil intent. [See question #3, page 366.]

14. Your new moons and your appointed feasts my soul hateth: they are a trouble unto me; I am weary to bear them.

The blistering indictment continues with strong statements of the Lord's contempt. He hates the *appointed feasts.* Such feasts have become a source of *trouble* to Him. The Lord is *weary* of enduring these gatherings. On page after page of Scripture, we can see the Lord's patience. But His patience has limits.

Visual for Lesson 3. *Use these five elements of true worship as discussion starters. For each ask, "What is a specific way to implement this one?"*

C. Disregarded Prayers (v. 15)

15. And when ye spread forth your hands, I will hide mine eyes from you: yea, when ye make many prayers, I will not hear: your hands are full of blood.

To *spread forth your hands* refers to the visible component of prayer, the physical postures. Here the arms are extended, probably to Heaven or to the most holy place, with palms up, as in a plea to receive from God. But no matter the physical posture, the Lord intends to *hide His eyes.*

Does it surprise you that the Lord doesn't always heed prayer? The Lord explains that the people themselves are the problem: *your hands are full of blood.* This can mean the guilt for various kinds of killings (Deuteronomy 19:10; 22:8). Here it probably refers more broadly to all kinds of injustice that harm others (compare Isaiah 33:15; Ezekiel 9:9; Nahum 3:1).

All their acts of worship (sacrifices, religious gatherings, prayers) are detestable because the people are guilty of sin against others; they refuse to connect ritual with obedience. They expect God somehow to have "selective vision"—seeing their pious sacrifices while ignoring the daily injustice they practice. Such arrogance! [See question #4, page 366.]

III. Judge Offers a Chance (Isaiah 1:16-20)

A. Stop the Bad (v. 16)

16. Wash ye, make you clean; put away the evil of your doings from before mine eyes; cease to do evil.

The verse offers specific commands to the people. To *wash* can be used of simple bathing or of ceremonial washing. The context requires this to refer to the ceremonial. We see ceremonial washing in the New Testament in Matthew 27:24; John 13:1-17; etc.

Make clean has a moral sense in the Old Testament. Thus *wash* refers to more than mere ritual washing; moral cleansing must be involved (compare Luke 11:39). God's faithful people will actively pursue both a genuine inward and outward righteousness because they love their God and want to be like Him.

B. Start the Good (v. 17)

17. Learn to do well; seek judgment, relieve the oppressed, judge the fatherless, plead for the widow.

The Lord now gives five positive commands concerning the character of the true worshiper. These move from general to specific, the last three being applications. *To do well* may mean "to be pleasing," "to be skillful," or "to do what is moral or ethical." The context of unethical behavior makes clear that the Lord means the latter. *Learn* implies growth. The readers are surprised by trouble because they are very shallow in their understanding of what it means to relate to God. Changing one's moral fiber is going to involve will and effort.

The word *judgment* often makes modern readers think of condemnation. Though the word can mean this, in the *King James Version* it refers more broadly to setting things right according to God's standard, as in "work for justice" or "promote justice." The people of Judah are to promote justice in dealings with one another. Deuteronomy 16:20 insists that the people are to promote that which is "altogether just" as a condition for inheriting the land.

The application *relieve the oppressed* seems clear enough, but another translation is possible. The Hebrew word translated *oppressed* occurs only here in the Old Testament, though the same root occurs in one other place, namely Psalm 71:4: "Deliver me, O my God, out of the hand of the wicked, out of the hand of the unrighteous and cruel man." There this root occurs behind the word *cruel*. This fact leads some to believe that *relieve the oppressed* here in Isaiah 1:17 may be translated something like "rebuke the oppressor." Surely the Lord expects both!

The next two applications involve the protection of the powerless of society: *judge the fatherless* (again *judge* means "to show justice toward") and *plead for the widow* (make sure they get justice as well). When we see cases of injustice in today's society, God's faithful people will seek to deal ethically with all people and pursue justice. Christians may not be able to rectify all wrongs. Yet we are to seek justice for all and protection for the defenseless at every level of society. This is a continuing battle. [See question #5, page 366.]

INNER MISSION

Johann Wichern (1808–1881) was a German minister who was moved by the suffering of children in the impoverished sections of the city of Hamburg. Convinced that something ought to be done for them, he helped organize the Rough House as a home for boys in 1833. This was similar to an orphanage but based on the principles of family education to provide for both spiritual and physical needs.

Under Wichern's expert organizational skills, the Evangelical Church in Germany formed the Inner Mission in 1848. It supervised 1,500 various charitable activities of the German Protestants. Ultimately this Inner Mission included nursing centers, prison reform activities, orphanages, and homes for those afflicted with mental retardation. Before the Nazis closed down the system in 1938, there were 3,800 institutions under the umbrella of the Inner Mission.

Similar to Wichern is the story of George Mueller (1805–1898), a German who came to London in 1829. In 1832 he established an orphanage in Bristol that ultimately cared for more than 2,000 children. These are just two examples of the kind of thing God pleads for through Isaiah: "relieve the oppressed, judge the fatherless, plead for the widow." They are examples that speak to us—and convict us—yet today.—J. B. N.

C. The Only Chance (vv. 18-20)

18a. Come now, and let us reason together, saith the LORD.

Properly understanding this well-known verse requires that the reader remember that the Lord is still speaking in His role as judge. When He says to Judah, *Come now, and let us reason together*, He does not mean to invite these people to sit down over coffee and doughnuts to discuss things. This is not a give-and-take negotiation. Rather, the Lord is challenging them in court to consider the truth of what He has been saying, to realize the peril in which they find themselves!

18b. Though your sins be as scarlet, they shall be as white as snow; though they be red like crimson, they shall be as wool.

After confronting His people with the reality of their sin, the Lord now holds out the hope of the good they may experience. He then lays out the condition for that good (v. 19) and warns them of the punishment for failure to repent (v. 20).

The colors *scarlet* and *crimson* are synonyms. *Scarlet* may be used positively, as in parts of the tabernacle (Exodus 25:4; 26:1; etc.), of good quality clothing (Proverbs 31:21), or even the color of beautiful lips (Song of Solomon 4:3). It may be used neutrally simply of thread (Genesis 38:28, 30). However, *scarlet* thread also is used in a purification ritual (Leviticus 14:4, 6, 49, 51, 52; Numbers 19:6) and may also have the suggestion of sin, as it clearly does here.

Yet there is good news: the scarlet color of sin can change to *be as white as snow*! Snow is used here to describe the degree of whiteness, as a symbol of moral purity that also is found in Psalm 51:7. Likewise *wool* is used as a descriptor of whiteness parallel to that of snow in Daniel 7:9 and Revelation 1:14.

Though not named, it is clear that only the Lord can transform the impure into pure. Under the new covenant, the purity is first and foremost a righteousness that the Lord declares and provides (Romans 3:21-26). This results in the transformation of our lives (Romans 12:1, 2). The Lord offers hope for true renewal. However, the Lord leaves a vital part for us to play: choice.

19. If ye be willing and obedient, ye shall eat the good of the land.

The conditions for blessing are that the people *be willing and obedient*. The willingness involves consent to obey the Lord.

The phrase *eat the good of the land* occurs elsewhere only in Ezra 9:12. Both there and here it means "to live well from the land, to prosper." This blessing from the Lord is that the Judeans remain in the land of promise. Their role, as God's chosen people, is to bring the Messiah into the world. All the punishments that Isaiah has been preaching can be avoided if they repent.

Sadly, we know from history that this repentance didn't happen. The people had to go into exile in Babylon. Yet even after that exile is finished, Ezra 9:12 reaffirms this promise. God is a God of second chances!

20. But if ye refuse and rebel, ye shall be devoured with the sword: for the mouth of the LORD hath spoken it.

To *refuse and rebel* is the opposite of being willing and obedient. To refuse the Lord's will has serious consequences! Notice what happened after Pharaoh's refusal to let Israel worship (Exodus 12:29). The idea of refusal is found numerous times in Jeremiah. Most refer to the refusal of the people to admit their sin or repent (Jeremiah 8:5; 9:6; etc.).

Home Daily Bible Readings

Monday, June 11—Praise for God's Goodness (Psalm 65:1-8)

Tuesday, June 12—Doing Right in God's Sight (2 Kings 15:32-36)

Wednesday, June 13—Here Am I; Send Me (Isaiah 6:1-8)

Thursday, June 14—The Fast That Pleases God (Isaiah 58:6-12)

Friday, June 15—Comfort for God's People (Isaiah 40:1-5)

Saturday, June 16—Not Desiring Sacrifices (Isaiah 1:10-14)

Sunday, June 17—Learn to Do Good (Isaiah 1:15-20)

The word *rebel* should remind the readers of both Moses and Aaron not being allowed to enter Canaan because of their respective rebellions (Numbers 20:10-12, 24; 27:14). Very commonly, the idea of rebellion is applied by the prophets to God's people (examples: Isaiah 3:8; 63:10).

The opposite of "eat the good of the land" in verse 19 is to *be devoured with the sword*. Judah was delivered miraculously from Assyria in 701 BC. It had seemed like certain disaster. Now the Lord is warning them that unless their ritual is accompanied by a heart that proves its love for Him, they will suffer even greater devastation in war. They can prove their love by obedience in their personal lives and in their behavior toward others. The threat is real because *the Lord hath spoken it.*

Conclusion

A. A Show of Real Reality

The rage on television these days is the "reality show." The idea is to show people in states of raw emotion by placing them in very stressful circumstances. Other than that, though, this type of show has very little to do with what we may call *everyday reality*. But even *everyday reality* is not the same as *ultimate reality*. The sacrifices, gatherings, and prayers that the people of Judah were participating in were "real" in the sense that they happened. But these things were not genuine or sincere.

God's people today must be genuine. Giving money to good causes (even to the church), going to church, and praying do not prove that a person has a genuine relationship with the Lord. Real relationship means that these actions will be accompanied by a heart and lifestyle consistent with the character of God himself. The Old and New Testaments both bear witness to the fact that God is not mocked; no person can manipulate the Lord to get into Heaven.

B. Prayer

Dear Lord, we thank You for counting us as purer than snow. We love You because You first loved us. May our love for You drive us to examine honestly our deepest thoughts and motives, that in the end our scarlet lives may become white as snow. At all times we rely on Your grace to save us in spite of our shortcomings. In the name of Jesus our Savior, amen.

C. Thought to Remember

"To obey is better than sacrifice" (1 Samuel 15:22).

Learning by Doing

This page contains an alternative lesson plan emphasizing learning activities.
Classes desiring such student involvement will find these suggestions helpful.

Learning Goals

After participating in this lesson, each student will be able to:

1. Identify worship attitudes and practices that Isaiah said pleased the Lord and those he said did not.

2. Explain the relationship between attitude and practice in worship.

3. Identify one area in his or her life that hinders true worship and make a plan to change it.

Into the Lesson

Display the word *WORSHIP* vertically on the board. As class begins ask, "What are the components of true worship? Use the letters of the word to develop your list." Allow learners to express their own ideas, but you can expect such responses as *willingness, orderliness, reverence, relationship, songs, submission, heart, head, honesty, integrity, prayer, praise.* (A similar activity is included in the student book.)

Transition to a study of the text by saying, "In Isaiah 1:1-10, Isaiah and God are describing the defective practice of worship seen in the land. As we study, contrast our list with what is found there. How many 'opposites' do we see?"

Into the Word

Prepare the following 12 "quotes" of bad attitudes on separate slips and distribute them to various people. *1.* "Well, I don't live in Amsterdam or San Francisco; I'm one of God's children" (v. 10). *2.* "I give more than 10 percent to the church, plus all the good jobs I do there. What more do you want?" (v. 11). *3.* "Every time the church door is open, you'll see me there" (v. 12). *4.* "No one has more prayer candles lit than I do" (v. 13a). *5.* "I'm here at church for all the special events, in addition to all the regular services" (vv. 13b, 14). *6.* "My hands are up, my head is down, my tears flow, my prayers are constant. What more could you ask?" (v. 15). *7.* "Well, we're all sinners. So we all carry a few sins into every worship assembly. No big deal" (v. 16). *8.* "My time is limited. As for projects like painting at the children's home and visiting shut-ins, I'll leave those to others. But I always have time for the Lord" (v. 17). *9.* "I listen to what God says in His Word; it's just that sometimes I kind of dis-

agree with His decisions" (v. 18a). *10.* "Hey! My sins are all small and hardly noticeable. They're in the barely-stained range" (v. 18b). *11.* "I want it all, especially God's blessings, but He's going to have to overlook some things; I am just human" (v. 19). *12.* "You don't really believe God is going to punish anyone, do you? What kind of God is that?" (v. 20).

Introduce the exercise by saying, "Deeds are important! Yet God's rejection of Israel's worship as pictured in Isaiah 1:10-20 focused on attitudes and motives. Their defective character and lack of submission were primary." Assign to other students the verses and verse portions indicated on the slips. Ask those holding the "quotes" to stand one at a time at random and say their quotes with the implied emphasis. Then ask for the one who has the Scriptural "match" to stand and read his or her verse or verse segment.

Verse numbers are given after each "quote" for confirmation, but, of course, those should not be read with the quote. Your goal is to draw students' attention to the text and its implications.

Next, return to the Into the Lesson acrostic activity. Ask students for contrasts between the positive attributes of their definition and the negative characteristics rampant among the Judean worshipers.

When students suggest opposites, expect such items as the sincerity of true worship in contrast with the hypocrisy of false worship; the willing nature of true worship in contrast with the mechanical nature of the false; the preoccupation with forms and quantity of prayer in Israel's worshipers contrasting with the heartfelt passion and quality of prayer in proper worship.

Into Life

Return to the attitude "quotes" from above. Have students read these again. Suggest to the group that as the quotes are read, each should prayerfully ponder how often the sentiment or a similar one runs through their minds and even over their lips.

The Been There, Heard That activity in the student book also has a list of expressed (bad!) attitudes that could be used, or you as teacher may prepare another list reflecting attitudes you have heard and seen.

Let's Talk It Over

The questions on this page are designed to promote discussion of the lesson by the class and to encourage application of the lesson Scriptures. The answers provided are only discussion starters. Let your class talk it over from there.

1. How can you better prepare yourself to hear the Word of the Lord? What progress have you made in this regard?

It has been said that understanding God's Word is like a bank account: you get out of it what you put into it. A true hearer of the Word of God must invest time and effort into the task. Proverbs 8:34 says one way we hear is by watching and waiting daily. It is not just listening to a message one day a week, but daily taking time to read and hear God's Word.

Ecclesiastes 5:1 says that we need to "be more ready to hear, than to give the sacrifice of fools." The *sacrifice of fools* in this context is about speaking many words *about* or *to* God while failing to hear words *from* God (compare Matthew 6:7, 8). We hear God's Word best when we hear it for what it actually is and not what we want it to be (2 Timothy 4:4).

2. What offerings have you brought to God in the past that you think He was dissatisfied with? How did you get back on the right track?

We can offer God the sacrifice of praise with our lips without giving Him our hearts (Isaiah 29:13). We can be guilty of going through the motions of worship and praise to the person of God while lacking commitment to the will of God.

When we offer our financial gifts as a means of trying to appease God instead of honoring Him, He is not pleased. When we bring our offerings to God while at the same time having dissension with a brother or sister in Christ, God is not satisfied with that offering (Matthew 5:23, 24). Some Christians focus so much on giving a specific percentage of their income that their families go without necessities (compare 1 Timothy 5:8).

These problems may be spiritual blind spots to us. Sometimes the intervention by another Christian is necessary to make us aware.

3. How might our assemblies become iniquities in the eyes of God? What safeguards can we implement?

In some of the same ways that our offerings can be a dissatisfaction to God, so can our worship be an iniquity to Him. When we neglect worship that is in spirit and truth, we have offered improper worship. Worship that is done as a show that seeks to please people instead of God is an iniquity to Him.

Paul pointed out that when created things are worshiped instead of God the creator, abomination results (Romans 1:25). In some parts of the world, this happens literally where people hold certain animals to be sacred. The problem presents itself in Western democracies when material things occupy the throne of our heart where God should be instead.

Worship that does not offer God our best is a problem. Leftovers in regard to time, energy, or finances are displeasing to Him. Examining our levels of commitment (or overcommitment) in other areas can help us avoid giving God leftovers.

4. What can you do to assure that God hears your prayers? Conversely, how do you make sure that nothing hinders your prayers?

Some people feel that their prayers are rising no higher than the ceiling. Part of the problem may be that the prayer is not being answered in the way the one praying wants it to be or as quickly as he or she would like for it to be. To be open to the Lord's will, to ask the Lord's will to be done, and then to be patient for Him to do things His way in His time are all important.

Prayers also may be ineffective because of unrepented sin. The fervent prayer of the righteous person is effective (James 5:16). Thus, there may be a need for true repentance and godly sorrow prior to presenting our requests to God. Praying more for others and for the work of God and less for personal and selfish ends is vital (James 4:3).

5. What are some ways your church can help the oppressed, the fatherless, the widow, and the widowers? What should your own part be in this ministry?

There are many possibilities. A starting point is to examine why more hasn't been done so far. Often we fail to help these people because we have become blind to them. We can be guilty of being involved in a "holy huddle" where we fail to look outward to those to whom we are called to minister. To develop a mind-set of *go and share* rather than strictly *come and see* is a start.

Committed to Seeking God

DEVOTIONAL READING: 2 Corinthians 9:10-15.

BACKGROUND SCRIPTURE: Isaiah 55:1-11.

PRINTED TEXT: Isaiah 55:1-11.

Isaiah 55:1-11

1 Ho, every one that thirsteth, come ye to the waters, and he that hath no money; come ye, buy, and eat; yea, come, buy wine and milk without money and without price.

2 Wherefore do ye spend money for that which is not bread? and your labor for that which satisfieth not? hearken diligently unto me, and eat ye that which is good, and let your soul delight itself in fatness.

3 Incline your ear, and come unto me: hear, and your soul shall live; and I will make an everlasting covenant with you, even the sure mercies of David.

4 Behold, I have given him for a witness to the people, a leader and commander to the people.

5 Behold, thou shalt call a nation that thou knowest not, and nations that knew not thee shall run unto thee because of the LORD thy God, and for the Holy One of Israel; for he hath glorified thee.

6 Seek ye the LORD while he may be found, call ye upon him while he is near:

7 Let the wicked forsake his way, and the unrighteous man his thoughts: and let him return unto the LORD, and he will have mercy upon him; and to our God, for he will abundantly pardon.

8 For my thoughts are not your thoughts, neither are your ways my ways, saith the LORD.

9 For as the heavens are higher than the earth, so are my ways higher than your ways, and my thoughts than your thoughts.

10 For as the rain cometh down, and the snow from heaven, and returneth not thither, but watereth the earth, and maketh it bring forth and bud, that it may give seed to the sower, and bread to the eater:

11 So shall my word be that goeth forth out of my mouth: it shall not return unto me void, but it shall accomplish that which I please, and it shall prosper in the thing whereto I sent it.

GOLDEN TEXT: Seek ye the LORD while he may be found, call ye upon him while he is near.—Isaiah 55:6.

Committed to Doing Right
Unit 1: Life as God's People
(Lessons 1-4)

Lesson Aims

After participating in this lesson, each student will be able to:

1. Tell what Isaiah says God expects of a holy people.

2. Compare the moral climate called forth in Isaiah 55 with the moral climate of his or her own society.

3. Create a prayer list of people who need to heed the invitation to accept Christ.

Lesson Outline

INTRODUCTION
   A. The Dream Team
   B. Lesson Background
I. BLESSINGS OFFERED (Isaiah 55:1-5)
   A. Invitation (vv. 1, 2)
     Buy Without Money
   B. Benefits (v. 3)
   C. Agent (vv. 4, 5)
II. ACCEPTANCE URGED (Isaiah 55:6, 7)
   A. Seeking Required (v. 6)
   B. Forsaking Required (v. 7)
III. UNFAILING WORD AFFIRMED (Isaiah 55:8-11)
   A. Thoughts and Ways (vv. 8, 9)
     His Thoughts, And Ours
   B. Intent and Outcome (vv. 10, 11)
CONCLUSION
   A. "You Can't Miss It"
   B. Prayer
   C. Thought to Remember

Introduction

A. The Dream Team

The film *The Dream Team* is a 1989 comedy about mental patients who meet for group therapy. When their psychiatrist takes them on an outing, he witnesses a slaying and is nearly killed by the perpetrators. The group, not knowing what happened to their doctor, is left in New York City alone. They soon learn they are wanted both for the slaying and for the attempted murder of their doctor, who has ended up in a hospital.

The humor results from the need of this "dream team" to grapple with reality. How will they find their way out of the trouble they are in? In our days of psychiatrists and psychologists, support groups, and abundance of self-help books, it sometimes makes us wonder where previous generations got mental and emotional help. What did Christians do in all those centuries before professional Christian counselors came along?

Once I came across an ancient work entitled *Conferences*. It was written by John Cassian, a monk who lived about AD 365–433. In this book, monastery leaders are portrayed as meeting with Cassian in groups to discuss issues of how to live the Christian life. In other words, they would counsel together for the spiritual benefit of themselves and for those to whom they ministered. Those with greater spiritual maturity could help guide others.

Today's lesson also offers us a picture of members of a group coming together for counseling. Chief among the group members are the future Jewish exiles. The prophet Isaiah writes 100 years before the Babylonian exile, but Isaiah knows that the Judeans will find themselves in deep trouble. They will not know where to turn.

The counselor, however, is the Lord himself. His wisdom and knowledge are infallible. We often wonder, as though in a dream, where to turn in times of trouble. God often uses our Christian friends who are wise enough to help us deal with reality. At other times He provides those with professional training to help. But behind any of these counselors must be the wisdom of the Lord, who alone can bring hope from despair.

B. Lesson Background

In last week's text, the Lord sought to shock Judah into repentance. Their acts of worship were in vain unless their lives demonstrated inward purity and outward righteousness. Isaiah's ministry was a call to repentance. Failure to repent meant destruction. Isaiah was told two things about Judah. First, since his preaching would fall on deaf ears, destruction would occur. (In fact, it did in 586 BC.) Second, in order to keep His covenant, the Lord would preserve a remnant of faithful people in spite of this destruction (Isaiah 6:8-13). This remnant was the exiles surviving the Babylonian captivity, which ended in 539 BC. This week's lesson stresses that message again.

The first section of Isaiah, chapters 1–39, is mostly judgment. The second section, chapters 40–66, is mostly blessing; almost all of it is poetry (except for 66:17-24), which means there is much use of figures of speech. Commentators have proposed many different outlines of these last 27 chapters, but most see 3 units of 9 chapters each. Isaiah 55 falls within the second unit, namely Isaiah 49–57. One way to look at these chapters is as a group discussion involving five parties: the Lord, the Messiah, Isaiah, Zion, and the Gentile nations.

The fourth party requires a little discussion. *Zion* can refer specifically to the city of Jerusalem, but also may be used to refer to the nation as a whole. In this part of Isaiah, *Zion* probably refers to the faithful remnant in the (to them, future) Babylonian exile. This remnant is idealized in those who accept the Messiah.

During the course of the discussion, the Lord reveals the fact, method, and scope of His salvation. In Isaiah 55, the reader must identify speakers and those being addressed by carefully noting the pronouns and then identifying the main point.

I. Blessing Offered
(Isaiah 55:1-5)

A. Invitation (vv. 1, 2)

1. Ho, every one that thirsteth, come ye to the waters, and he that hath no money; come ye, buy, and eat; yea, come, buy wine and milk without money and without price.

The phrase "come unto me" in verse 3 (below) leaves no doubt that it is the Lord speaking. He is the one offering the covenant. The people of Judah are the ones being addressed as the plural pronoun *ye* shows (*King James Version* along with the Hebrew).

The first address, to *every one that thirsteth*, describes those who are invited to come *to the waters;* those who have need will be satisfied (compare Revelation 21:6; 22:17). The second address, to the one who *that hath no money,* refers to those who are in abject poverty; they will need no money to buy what they need. What a future the Lord promises!

The word *wine* is used in both positive and negative ways in the Old Testament. Isaiah 56:12 offers us a negative sense, but in the verse before us the image is plainly positive. *Milk* also symbolizes great blessing (compare Exodus 3:8). Wine and milk are found together in Song of Solomon 5:1 as a great delicacy. The Lord is calling His people to buy these desirable things at no cost to them, a symbol of plenty provided by the Lord.

Guaranteed *water* is comfort for the poor and needy (Isaiah 41:17-20); wine is a part of the feast that celebrates for all people the end of death forever (Isaiah 25:6-8); milk is a symbol of blessing in the promised kingdom of the one born of a virgin (Isaiah 7:14, 22). Isaiah 55:2, 3 (below) make clear that these are symbols here as well. To recognize these as figures of speech is not to make them unreal. On the contrary, what they symbolize is very real and very important.

Though water, wine, and milk will have literal significance for the future returnees from the Babylonian exile, Isaiah can use these images to symbolize spiritual blessing. The return from the Babylonian exile many years after Isaiah writes will indeed be a blessing for God's people.

The church age, inaugurated at Christ's first coming, is the beginning of a much more profound period of blessing. Being saved from the guilt and sickness of sin is something no one has money enough to buy. Thanks be to God for His gracious free gift that saves us from our spiritual poverty! [See question #1, page 374.]

BUY WITHOUT MONEY

There was a time in my younger days when I had a powerful financial fantasy. We were struggling with money problems, as happens often to young couples raising a family on one income.

My fantasy was that I had become a personal friend to the owner of a major department store, and I had been given a special card that permitted me to enter the store at any time. I could take whatever I wanted and never be charged for it. All my money problems would magically disappear, since I could now acquire whatever I needed (or wanted!) and never have to pay for it.

Then I realized that some people believe they have a card like this. It's called *a credit card.* They can go into any store, acquire whatever they need (or want!) and not have to pay for it. The major difference, however, is that ultimately they do have to pay for it. That's the reality of credit cards.

But Isaiah describes a situation much more like my original fantasy. God gives us a situation where we can buy without money. In fact, the items do not even have prices and there will never be a monthly statement. God supplies all the spiritual items we could ever need or want, and His credit covers them all. Do you live with that truth in mind?   —J. B. N.

2. Wherefore do ye spend money for that which is not bread? and your labor for that which satisfieth not? hearken diligently unto me, and eat ye that which is good, and let your soul delight itself in fatness.

To *spend money* or exert one's own *labor* summarizes the human pursuit for happiness. The Lord uses a rhetorical question to stress that these yield what is not really *bread.* Whatever the Judeans are striving for is not food that truly nourishes. It *satisfieth not* the deepest human need. [See question #2, page 374.]

The command to *hearken diligently* means to understand and heed. The structure of the Hebrew indicates that both of the next two statements will be the results of obeying Him. First, the readers will *eat . . . that which is good.* Second, they will experience *delight* in the plenty *(fatness)* of the land.

These images may be taken in a physical sense, since the future exiles will return physically to "the land of milk and honey" that the Lord provides. But as figures of speech the implications are much more profound: godly living will bring great spiritual blessings. To take the promise merely in a physical sense would be to miss the main message.

B. Benefits (v. 3)

3. Incline your ear, and come unto me: hear, and your soul shall live; and I will make an everlasting covenant with you, even the sure mercies of David.

Every parent knows the frustration of giving instructions and warnings to a child, only to have the child blithely skip off to do whatever he or she wants to do anyway. That must be how God feels on occasion. His prophets must feel the same way as well (compare Ezekiel 33:31, 32). The people will behave sinfully right in the midst of the exile itself! Yet the result of their coming back to the Lord will be that He *will make an everlasting covenant.*

The phrase *the sure mercies of David* is quoted in Acts 13:34. There the phrase is applied to the resurrection of the Messiah. The name *David* usually refers to the human king in historical writings. *David* may also stand for his royal descendant. However, *David* is sometimes used by

the prophets in an ultimate sense as a title for the Messiah (see Jeremiah 30:9; Ezekiel 34:23, 24; 37:24, 25; Hosea 3:5). The next two verses offer clues as to which the Lord intends here.

C. Agent (vv. 4, 5)

4. Behold, I have given him for a witness to the people, a leader and commander to the people.

The tense of *have given* does not rule out an event later than the time of writing; the context is future. Therefore the historical King David cannot be in view. A strictly human king of the line of David could be possible, except that no such ruler is ever the cause of the actions in verse 5, below.

Therefore, the name *David* as used in verse 3 (*him* here in v. 4) seems to refer to the ideal, ultimate one: the Messiah. As *witness* to the love of God, the Messiah will make plain God's love to His people. As *leader and commander,* the Messiah is qualified to rule *the people.*

5. Behold, thou shalt call a nation that thou knowest not, and nations that knew not thee shall run unto thee, because of the LORD thy God, and for the Holy One of Israel; for he hath glorified thee.

As we work through our lesson text, remember that we are trying to figure out who is speaking and who is being spoken to at every point. Here the words *thou* and *thee* may refer to Zion being spoken to. If so, then the Lord's future kingdom, redeemed Zion, will call a nation it previously did not know. This seems to look forward to the time when redeemed Zion is the church.

If *thee* and *thou* refer ultimately to the church, then *shalt call* refers to the preaching of the gospel to the world by the church, and *shall run* refers to the Gentiles' inclusion into the church. From Isaiah's perspective, this will happen *because of the Lord thy God.* From our perspective, this has indeed happened and continues to happen.

The phrase *for he hath glorified thee* probably also refers to redeemed Zion and to the church. Isaiah 46:13 predicts the glorification of redeemed Zion (Israel; see also Isaiah 61:3). Romans 11:11-24 describes the glorification of the church in terms of a restored relationship between God and all believers, both Jewish and Gentile.

We should realize, however, that it is also attractive to understand *thou* as indicating that the Lord now turns to speak to "David," meaning the Messiah, while in the presence of Zion. If this is the case, then it is the Messiah who will call nations to the Lord; the nations will run to the Lord because He will have *glorified* His Son (see Acts 3:13; Hebrews 1:1-3).

How to Say It

BABYLONIAN. Bab-ih-*low*-nee-un.
EZEKIEL. Ee-*zeek*-ee-ul or Ee-*zeek*-yul.
GENTILE. *Jen*-tile.
HOSEA. Ho-*zay*-uh.
ISAIAH. Eye-*zay*-uh.
JUDEANS. Joo-*dee*-unz.
MESSIAH. Meh-*sigh*-uh.
ZION. *Zi*-un.

Hebrews 5:5 implies that the Son was glorified by the Father. Under this idea, the divine Messiah calls a nation that *thou knowest not* and nations *that knew not thee* in the sense of establishing relationships.

The Messiah will indeed have that relationship with the Gentiles under the new covenant. That relationship was not really a part of the old covenant (Hosea 1:10; 2:23; both quoted in Romans 9:25, 26; see also 1 Peter 2:10).

II. Acceptance Urged
(Isaiah 55:6, 7)

A. Seeking Required (v. 6)

6. Seek ye the LORD while he may be found, call ye upon him while he is near.

The speaker is now the prophet Isaiah. This is indicated in verse 7 (below), where he refers to "our God." The idea in the verse before us is not that the readers should *seek* God before God moves away and becomes distant. Rather, the idea is for the readers to seek God while their hearts are soft and willing to believe. They need to seek Him and grow in their faith.

In Hebrew poetry, the center of a poem often is the main point. Isaiah's urge to Zion is the center of the chapter. Therefore, this appeal to seek *the Lord* is the main point.

B. Forsaking Required (v. 7)

7. Let the wicked forsake his way, and the unrighteous man his thoughts: and let him return unto the LORD, and he will have mercy upon him; and to our God, for he will abundantly pardon.

Isaiah tells Zion that two things are involved in seeking the Lord. First, *the wicked* must *forsake his way;* that means that unrighteous lifestyles are to be left behind. Second, *the unrighteous man* must forsake *his thoughts;* this is a challenge to abandon the internal sins of the heart. These are summarized with the challenge to *return unto the Lord . . . and to our God.* The results of returning to the Lord are twofold: first, the Lord *will have mercy upon* the one who does so. Second, the Lord *will abundantly pardon.*

What comfort this must bring the exiles while they are suffering! They will be in exile some 70 years, without temple or homeland. When that time comes (in about 100 years from Isaiah's perspective), many will see no hope of restoration. The years will drag on and on. Well may they wonder, "Has the Lord rejected us forever?"

The Lord affirms that there is abundant forgiveness. Even so, every individual outside of

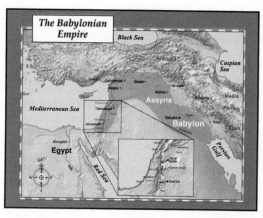

Visual for Lessons 4 & 5. *Keep this map of the Babylonian Empire posted for several lessons to help your students gain a geographical perspective.*

Christ today is God's enemy. Once one learns the reality and depth of the life of sin—a life governed by self without God—one asks the same question, "Is there no hope for what I have done in rejecting God?" The good news is that there is the "wonderful grace of Jesus, greater than all my sin." [See question #3, page 374.]

III. Unfailing Word Affirmed
(Isaiah 55:8-11)

A. Thoughts and Ways (vv. 8, 9)

8, 9. For my thoughts are not your thoughts, neither are your ways my ways, saith the LORD. For as the heavens are higher than the earth, so are my ways higher than your ways, and my thoughts than your thoughts.

Clearly the Lord has resumed as speaker because it is the Lord's *thoughts* that are unsurpassed. That He is speaking to Zion is clear because the pronoun *your* in Hebrew is plural.

The fact that God's thoughts are so far beyond ours has at least two applications. First, this fact can give us hope when we see no way out of trouble. God can see a way out when we can't. Second, this fact should make us humble about our own ability to know. When we are "sure" that we know the motives of others who have hurt us, we ought to remember that only God truly knows the human heart (Jeremiah 17:9, 10). [See question #4, page 374.]

HIS THOUGHTS, AND OURS

Enrico Fermi (1901–1954) was an Italian immigrant and nuclear physicist who played an important role in building America's atomic bomb.

His brilliance was evident early in his career. He received his PhD in 1922 at the age of 21. At his graduation ceremony he gave a lecture that put some of his professors to sleep; it was more intricate than they could follow.

He was present at the explosion of the first atomic bomb on July 16, 1945. With others, he was safely some distance away at the moment of explosion. Most of the witnesses were transfixed by the nature of the explosion itself. But Fermi was focused on determining the amount of power that the explosion released. Fermi dropped pieces of paper before, during, and after the passage of the blast wave. By measuring the displacement of the pieces, he was able to estimate the strength of the blast.

We can see the grandeur of God's creation, and that is well and good as far as it goes (Psalm 19:1). Yet we can miss the power and force of His values if we're not careful. His thoughts and ways are indeed far beyond our own, and one of His highest values is the repentance of the sinner and the power of forgiveness. Though none of us saw the crucifixion and resurrection of Jesus, the immeasurable power of the cross still reaches us.

—J. B. N.

B. Intent and Outcome (vv. 10, 11)

10, 11. For as the rain cometh down, and the snow from heaven, and returneth not thither, but watereth the earth, and maketh it bring forth and bud, that it may give seed to the sower, and bread to the eater: so shall my word be that goeth forth out of my mouth: it shall not return unto me void, but it shall accomplish that which I please, and it shall prosper in the thing whereto I sent it.

Home Daily Bible Readings

The Lord illustrates the certainty of His word by referring to *rain* and *snow from heaven* in relationship to what gives life on *earth*. *Returneth not thither* brings out the point that the precipitation does not go back into heaven without having a useful effect.

Verse 11 is the lesson to be learned from the illustration. Precipitation from above corresponds with the Lord's Word *that goeth forth out of* His *mouth*. He sends it down to earth through His prophets, but His Word does not return to Him without effect. Rather, it accomplishes what He intends. [See question #5, page 374.]

Conclusion

A. "You Can't Miss It"

I do not have a reputation in my family for always being able instinctively to find my way around while traveling. Since I know this, I (unlike many men) do not have any qualms about stopping to ask directions.

However, some people are better at giving directions than others. Upon finishing the description, he or she may utter those often-heard words, "You can't miss it." Since on occasion I have indeed "missed it," those words do not offer me much comfort!

However, the Lord is saying to the exiles who will experience His punishment, "If you listen to what I say, if you give up trusting in your own ways, and if you seek me, then restoration will occur. Its scope will be beyond anything you can imagine. And this restoration is as certain as my Word: you can't miss it."

His directions are clear: seek Him. This always leads home. This was comfort to the faithful remnant. It is comfort to all who seek the Lord today. No one is too far away to come to the Lord. One does not have to be free from sin to do this (otherwise no one would come). One has to be willing only to stop demanding to be the boss of one's life and let the Lord be the boss.

B. Prayer

Dear Father, We thank You for being absolutely trustworthy and effective. For all the times we still struggle with wanting to run our own lives apart from You, we ask Your forgiveness. We, the most defiled, thank You for the relationship You have built with us through Christ, the Messiah, in whose name we pray, amen.

C. Thought to Remember

"Behold, what manner of love the Father hath bestowed upon us" (1 John 3:1).

Learning by Doing

This page contains an alternative lesson plan emphasizing learning activities.
Classes desiring such student involvement will find these suggestions helpful.

Learning Goals

After participating in this lesson, each student will be able to:

1. Tell what Isaiah says God expects of a holy people.

2. Compare the moral climate called forth in Isaiah 55 with the moral climate of his or her own society.

3. Create a prayer list of people who need to heed the invitation to accept Christ.

Into the Lesson

Because this week's lesson is a bold and gracious invitation from the Lord to Israel, send special "invitations" to your class members in advance. Inexpensive party invitations can usually be found at the dollar-or-less stores. Or you could recruit a computer-literate class member to design and send the invitations.

If mailing costs are prohibitive, have the invitations ready to be handed to each student upon arrival. On the invitation put the usual *when* and *where* information but incorporate key words such as "Eats!" "Delights!" and "Free Gifts!"

Into the Word

Duplicate and distribute the following list of two-word expressions: *Big Thoughts; Caller Waiting; Exit Evil; Free Food; Heaven's Highway; Listen Up! National Race; People's Leader; Rat Race; Water Cycle; Word Works.* (These are to be related to vv. 8, 6, 7, 1, 9, 3, 5, 4, 2, 10, and 11, respectively, of Isaiah 55.)

Say, "Look at each of these two-word headings. Decide which verse from today's text can best be labeled with each. Put the verse number before each phrase for consideration." Give time for consideration and then come back to confirm the relationships. If a student has made connections other than those noted, let him or her explain the rationale.

Say, "Isaiah 55 may be considered a kind of evangelism study. It is one of God's great invitations to seek and find Him." Divide your class into 3 groups of no more than 6 each. (If your class is larger than 18, duplicate the assignments.)

Say this to the group(s) you will call *Needs:* "Look at Isaiah 55:1-11 and make a list of basic human needs that you can identify from those verses." To the group(s) you will label *Provisions*

say, "From Isaiah 55:1-11 make a list of all the blessings God offers to the one who responds to Him." For the group(s) you will call *Evangelism,* give this direction: "Look at Isaiah 55:1-11 and decide what that text offers to the one who would invite the unsaved to a meeting with God and His Son."

Allow about five minutes for deliberation. Then ask for a report from each group. Expect some of the following items to be included. *Needs* group: water; food; satisfying work; covenants—that is, agreements of various sorts; a leader and commander who knows the right way; mercy and forgiveness. *Provisions* group: delights for the soul as well as the body; a covenant with God; a witness to who God is; mercy; pardon; a predictable science; God's Word. *Evangelism* group: meaning for an otherwise dreary existence (purpose for being); God's Word as life for the soul; Jesus as our wise leader and commander; mercy and pardon readily available; possibility of a new direction in life.

Into Life

Recruit a member of the class who enjoys computer work to produce for each class member a foldable sheet as a card. It will have a simple front page reading, "Come!" The inside right should also be simple, reading this way:

Dear _____,
 This is a simple invitation, sent by God himself. If you are feeling _____, consider that Isaiah affirms _____ in Isaiah 55:___. God will welcome you to His celebration, and He will provide all the gifts! Hoping you can join us for the delights.
  Signed, _____

Distribute these with the following directions: "Consider someone you know who needs to hear God's invitation. Write in his or her name, then identify the 'feeling' that may be keeping him or her from the Lord. Consider the elements introduced in our small group discussions and add a note of blessing that Isaiah affirms. You may not actually want to send this invitation. But use it as a prayer and action stimulus to become God's ambassador to that person."

Let's Talk It Over

*The questions on this page are designed to promote discussion of the lesson
by the class and to encourage application of the lesson Scriptures. The answers
provided are only discussion starters. Let your class talk it over from there.*

1. How has God quenched your own spiritual hunger and thirst? Did you find this surprising? Explain.

Our generous God indeed pours His grace upon us! He satisfies our spiritual thirst as we heed His Word. This Word is strong meat for our spiritual nourishment (Hebrews 5:12, 14). Jesus, the Word in the flesh (John 1:14), is also our spiritual bread as well as the water of life (John 6:35).

God provides for us as well through the promises of the spiritual drink and spiritual manna for those who overcome (Revelation 2:7, 17). The gift of salvation sustains our souls (John 4:10). The promise of Heaven does so as well. There we will drink freely of the water of life (Revelation 22:17).

2. What are some ways that people today spend money for that which does not satisfy? How can we guard ourselves against stumbling into such foolishness?

We know all too well that people are guilty of accumulating "treasures of wickedness" (Proverbs 10:2). But even people who accumulate money honestly can trap themselves into thinking that possessions will bring happiness.

We can make the mistake of doing much the same thing spiritually. Some Christians spend money attending seminar after seminar or going to numerous conferences on spiritual growth. They pay for "knowledge" of how to grow spiritually, but fail to practice basic disciplines for spiritual growth such as Bible reading and prayer.

Churches, for their part, may spend lots of money on feel-good activities, such as taking trips to theme parks, while at the same time failing to invest money in evangelistic activities or benevolent ministries. The former are not bad as long as the latter are not neglected.

3. Was there a time when God restored you after you returned to Him? Explain.

Estrangement from God may lead to sinful practices such as alcohol and drug abuse, which harm the body. As we come back to God and leave these practices behind, we are restored. There is restoration even though we may still carry some of the marks of those sins in our lives.

At other times, our problem may be financial. Neglecting our stewardship to God may be part of this. Returning to God and becoming good stewards will bring blessings from Him. We can sin against one another, hold grudges, and refuse to forgive. When we are convicted of those sins and return to God, He restores relationships.

4. What are some specific areas in which you have had to admit that God's thoughts and ways surpass those of your own? What happened when you finally made that admission?

Admitting that God is superior to us in thinking and acting should be a given. But sometimes we still believe that we should be able to provide a sound answer to all issues of existence. For example, some try to explain exactly *how* creation occurred. Some even set a date for *when* it occurred. Other times we try to explain the concept of the Trinity even though full explanation eludes us; all of our analogies break down at some point. We stumble as we try to explain why bad things happen to good people, or why good things happen to bad people.

At the tragic death of a small child we may say that God just wanted another little voice in His heavenly chorus; that runs the risk of assigning blame to God. Sometimes the best thing to do is to say that we don't know the answer to a question, and yet, by faith, we still believe that God is good and His plans cannot be undermined.

5. What purposes of God's Word are being accomplished right now in your life? in your church?

Sometimes we may live our lives as if God were not really doing much of anything through us or through the church. We may place blame on a world that is hostile to Christianity, on the busyness of people and lack of concern about the things of God, or on Satan.

It is important to see in Isaiah 55:11 that for God to accomplish His purpose, His Word goes forth. When God's Word does go forth, faithfully proclaimed by His people, souls come to Jesus and lives are renewed. When we live out God's Word to seek first His kingdom and His righteousness, our needs are supplied (Matthew 6:33).

Committed to God's Requirements

DEVOTIONAL READING: **Hebrews 12:6-12.**

BACKGROUND SCRIPTURE: **Micah 2:1-4; 3:1-5, 8-12; 6:6-8.**

PRINTED TEXT: **Micah 3:1-4; 6:6-8.**

Micah 3:1-4

1 And I said, Hear, I pray you, O heads of Jacob, and ye princes of the house of Israel; Is it not for you to know judgment?

2 Who hate the good, and love the evil; who pluck off their skin from off them, and their flesh from off their bones;

3 Who also eat the flesh of my people, and flay their skin from off them; and they break their bones, and chop them in pieces, as for the pot, and as flesh within the caldron.

4 Then shall they cry unto the LORD, but he will not hear them: he will even hide his face from them at that time, as they have behaved themselves ill in their doings.

Micah 6:6-8

6 Wherewith shall I come before the LORD, and bow myself before the high God? shall I come before him with burnt offerings, with calves of a year old?

7 Will the LORD be pleased with thousands of rams, or with ten thousands of rivers of oil? shall I give my firstborn for my transgression, the fruit of my body for the sin of my soul?

8 He hath showed thee, O man, what is good; and what doth the LORD require of thee, but to do justly, and to love mercy, and to walk humbly with thy God?

GOLDEN TEXT: He hath showed thee, O man, what is good; and what doth the Lord require of thee, but to do justly, and to love mercy, and to walk humbly with thy God?—Micah 6:8.

Committed to Doing Right
Unit 2: What Does God Require?
(Lessons 5-9)

Lesson Aims

After participating in this lesson, each student will be able to:

1. Summarize Micah's rebuke of evil in his society and his call to do what God requires.

2. Compare and contrast what the Lord requires in Micah 6 with what the Lord requires in the new covenant.

3. State one specific way he or she can better "walk humbly with thy God."

Lesson Outline

INTRODUCTION
    A. The Walk of Humility
    B. Lesson Background
  I. LOVING EVIL (Micah 3:1-4)
    A. Mistake #1: "God Won't Judge" (vv. 1-3)
      Cannibalism
    B. Mistake #2: "God Ignores My Evil" (v. 4)
 II. LOVING JUSTICE AND MERCY (Micah 6:6-8)
    A. Correct Action #1: Worship God (vv. 6, 7)
      The Price of Love
    B. Correct Action #2: Obey God (v. 8)
CONCLUSION
    A. An Out-of-Balance Life
    B. The Well-Rounded Life
    C. Prayer
    D. Thought to Remember

Introduction

A. The Walk of Humility

At his inauguration in 1977, incoming American President Jimmy Carter used the historic Bible that had been employed by George Washington at his own inauguration. Carter said, "Here before me is the Bible used in the inauguration of our first President, in 1789, and I have just taken the oath of office on the Bible my mother gave me a few years ago." Carter then read Micah 6:8, his key verse. Carter thus recognized that even the most powerful men on earth are called "to do justly, and to love mercy, and to walk humbly."

Yet humility, in particular, seems to be in scarce supply these days. We see a seemingly un-

limited procession of people seeking to become famous celebrities. In the last century, a famous boxer was widely known for boasting, "I am the greatest!" More recently, we have seen the rise of so-called "reality" television, where ordinary people are thrust into a celebrity-type spotlight. In the 1960s, pop philosopher Andy Warhol predicted, "In the future, everyone will be famous for fifteen minutes." Warhol later reversed this line to say, "In fifteen minutes, everybody will be famous." The lists of famous celebrities seem to become increasingly crowded.

The Bible teaches us that "before honor is humility" (Proverbs 15:33). The humbled/exalted paradox is that those who strive to be honored will not succeed in God's eyes, but those who serve humbly, without concern for applause, will be honored. Those seeking celebrity status should remember this warning: "God resisteth the proud, but giveth grace unto the humble" (James 4:6). Humility, then, is not an occasional choice. For the Christian it must be a *walk*, a lifestyle (compare Philippians 2:3).

As we seek to serve the Lord, we should begin by asking, "What does God expect?" Fortunately, we do not have to guess the answer to this question. One source of information for us is found in the writings of God's prophets. These men left a marvelous record of their messages: Bible texts that provide a clear picture of what God demands from His people.

B. Lesson Background

Micah is one of the great eighth-century prophets of Israel. That was also the time frame of Isaiah, Hosea, and Amos. Micah 1:1 records that he prophesied during the reigns of Jotham, Ahaz, and Hezekiah, kings of the southern kingdom of Judah. However, this verse also tells us that his prophecies were for both Judah (with its capital city of Jerusalem) and the northern kingdom of Israel (with its capital in Samaria).

The reign of those three kings spanned the period of approximately 750–690 BC, roughly 60 years. This was a tumultuous time for the people of God. Micah lived through the destruction of the northern kingdom in 722 BC by the Assyrians (2 Kings 18:9-11). About 20 years later, he was probably an eyewitness to a similar threat to Jerusalem in 701 BC. That time, however, God miraculously delivered Judah from the Assyrian menace by destroying 185,000 members of the Assyrian army (2 Kings 19:35).

There are strong connections between Micah and Isaiah, indicating they may have been colleagues. For example, Isaiah 2:2-4 and Micah 4:1-

3 are nearly identical texts. Both prophets share messages of the necessity for the people of God to repent and work for justice. Both preach the future hope of God's coming Messiah. We also know that the ministry of Micah influenced the later prophets of Judah (see Jeremiah 26:18, 19).

Micah's words are both forceful and eloquent. He was well aware of the empowerment of God's Spirit to give him his prophetic message (Micah 3:8). He also knew that his message was not well received by some, and that there were those who wanted to silence him (Micah 2:6, 7). He indicted Israel with God's "controversy," meaning God's charge of Israel's failure to uphold the covenant of obedience and righteousness (Micah 6:1, 2). This "controversy" with His people was not unique to Micah (see Jeremiah 25:31; Hosea 4:1; 12:2).

Micah's plea was that God's people must realize that if they did not seek justice in their society, then God would purge them of evil by allowing their destruction. While Christians are not citizens of Micah's Israel, that prophet's call for holiness and righteousness sounds a needed plea to the church today.

I. Loving Evil
(Micah 3:1-4)

The idea of *loving evil* seems detestable to most Christians. That idea is something that characterizes those "other people," the unbelievers. In our world, where sinfulness is not hidden but celebrated, we can find many examples of people who seem to seek wickedness passionately in every possible form.

Yet God, who knows our hearts completely, can see that this is sometimes true of all of us. For Micah, even the apparently respectable leaders of Israel had been judged by their actions and found to love evil more than good (compare Psalm 52:3). Micah points out two fundamental flaws in their thinking that have caused this circumstance.

A. Mistake #1: "God Won't Judge" (vv. 1-3)

1. And I said, Hear, I pray you, O heads of Jacob, and ye princes of the house of Israel; Is it not for you to know judgment?

The British historian Lord Acton (1834–1902) commented, "Power tends to corrupt, and absolute power corrupts absolutely." History is full of examples of leaders who acted as if they were above the law rather than stewards of the law. Acton also said, "Remember, where you have a concentration of power in a few hands, all too frequently men with the mentality of gangsters get control."

It seems to be in this light that Micah thunders at the leaders of Judah and Israel the provocative question *Is it not for you to know judgment?* In other words, "Do you believe that you are above the law, that you can administer or withhold justice at your own whim?" (Remember: *judgment* often means the same as *justice* in the KJV). Those who think they can administer justice this way are in for a shock. The book of Revelation pictures a time when the wealthiest and most powerful people on earth will quiver in fear at the judgmental wrath of God (Revelation 6:15-17).

This admonition is not only for the rich and powerful, however. It is for the father who tyrannizes his family behind closed doors. It is for the boss who exploits his or her employees at the workplace. It is for the shoplifter who believes that petty theft can be done secretly and without consequence. It is for those of us who believe we can get away with private sins of lust or pride. God is the perfect judge, and no one escapes His all-seeing eye.

2, 3. Who hate the good, and love the evil; who pluck off their skin from off them, and their flesh from off their bones; who also eat the flesh of my people, and flay their skin from off them; and they break their bones, and chop them in pieces, as for the pot, and as flesh within the caldron.

Micah employs some of the most violently graphic language of the Old Testament to drive home his point. God says that the leaders of Israel have exploited *my people.* These people are the very ones the leaders should have been protecting. Micah uses the horrific language of cannibalism, saying, in effect, "You have eaten my precious children."

How to Say It

ASSYRIAN. Uh-*sear*-e-un.
BYZANTINE. *Bih*-zen-teen.
CONSTANTINOPLE. *Kahn*-stan-ten-oh-puhl.
HAGIA SOPHIA. *Hag*-ee-uh So-*fee*-uh.
HEZEKIAH. Hez-ih-*kye*-uh.
HOSEA. Ho-*zay*-uh.
ISTANBUL. *Is*-tun-bull.
JOTHAM. *Jo*-thum.
LEVITICUS. Leh-*vit*-ih-kus.
MESSIAH. Meh-*sigh*-uh.
MICAH. *My*-kuh.
SAMARIA. Suh-*mare*-ee-uh.
ZECHARIAH. *Zek*-uh-*rye*-uh (strong accent on *rye*).

This does not refer to actual cannibalism, but to the relentless economic oppression of the poor people of Israel by the rulers. Those in power have manipulated the system to seize the property (and therefore the livelihood) of the lower classes (Micah 2:2). They have been consumed by greediness and wickedness (Micah 2:1).

CANNIBALISM

Most cultures regard cannibalism as repulsive. In spite of its hideous qualities, however, it has occurred repeatedly in history. Usually it occurs in situations where people are facing utter starvation, and it is a last resort to secure food.

One famous instance was the Donner Party, traveling to California in 1846. They were just a day late trying to cross the Sierra Mountains before snow blocked the passes. Only 1,000 feet from the top, a snowstorm caught the 81 travelers. In a desperate attempt, 15 people hiked out. They became lost. As some died of malnutrition, others butchered them for food (labeling the packages so no one would have to eat a relative). Survivors finally stumbled into civilization and relief parties went back to save the others. Cannibalism had occurred even in the main camp. Nearly half the people died (www.pbs.org).

Cannibalism is hard to conceive of, even in situations involving starvation. But Micah describes a situation in which the princes of Israel practiced economic cannibalism on their own people by choice, not by necessity. They had figuratively devoured their people. It is no wonder that Micah 3:4 says the Lord would hide His face from the perpetrators in their own time of need!

—J. B. N.

B. Mistake #2: "God Ignores My Evil" (v. 4)

4. Then shall they cry unto the LORD, but he will not hear them: he will even hide his face from them at that time, as they have behaved themselves ill in their doings.

A difficult reality is that sometimes the consequences for sins are not immediately evident. For example, adultery can eat away at a marriage like a cancer, although the symptoms of that relationship cancer may take a long time to appear. Just because we are not incinerated by a lightning bolt every time we sin does not mean that God fails to notice or that God is indifferent.

A hard lesson that the people of Israel have to learn is that God is not endlessly forgiving. There comes a time when God acts with decisive justice. God offers salvation by grace through Jesus, yet a time is coming when God's wrath will be poured out on the disobedient (Ephesians 5:6).

Two centuries after Micah, the prophet Zechariah explains God's judgment in a similar way. He notes that God's prophets had called repeatedly for social justice but had been met by hardheartedness. Eventually God responds this way: "Therefore . . . as [I] cried, and they would not hear; so they cried, and I would not hear" (Zechariah 7:13). God does not offer infinite opportunities to repent. The time for repentance is always now. [See question #1, page 382.]

II. Loving Justice and Mercy (Micah 6:6-8)

To be sure, Micah has harsh words for those who have spurned God's standards, loving evil. But Micah balances this with encouragement for those seeking to live lives pleasing to God.

A. Correct Action #1: Worship God (vv. 6, 7)

6a. Wherewith shall I come before the LORD, and bow myself before the high God?

In examining our relationship with God, an important starting point is the issue of worship. The most foundational meaning of worship in the Old Testament is to "*bow* down before." To do so is to acknowledge that God is great and worthy of honor and devotion (see Psalm 95:6). [See question #2, page 382.]

Another key aspect of Old Testament worship is sacrifice. To sacrifice is to relinquish freely something of value back to God. Sacrifice for us today may be in the form of monetary offerings for the work of the church. Sacrifice in the Old Testament often takes the form of agricultural produce and livestock, things that can be used for food.

Any person's worship should include acts of sacrifice in order to be complete. Micah, however, drums a common beat of the prophets: that sacrifice without an attitude of submission to God is empty and worthless. God takes no delight in meaningless sacrifice; He refuses to acknowledge such hollow acts (see Amos 5:22). The following verses expand on this.

6b, 7. Shall I come before him with burnt offerings, with calves of a year old? Will the LORD be pleased with thousands of rams, or with ten thousands of rivers of oil? shall I give my firstborn for my transgression, the fruit of my body for the sin of my soul?

Micah checks off possible sacrifices in a list of accelerating value. He begins with simple burnt offerings, which could be as lowly as a small bird (see Genesis 8:20). This proceeds to a yearling calf, an animal of considerable value. Micah then moves to a kingly sacrifice, namely *thousands of rams* (see 1 Kings 8:63). He next mentions a sacrifice that moves beyond the potential of even the wealthiest person: a myriad of flowing *rivers of* olive *oil*. This is an offering of unimaginable value.

Micah ends the list with an unspeakable offering: human sacrifice of a *firstborn* child. This has dual significance for the Israelites of Micah's time. First, they are aware of God's testing of Abraham, who was commanded to offer his beloved son Isaac as a burnt offering (Genesis 22:2). The lesson of that story, however, is that while God has a right to demand the sacrifice of that which is most precious to us, He does not condone human sacrifice at our initiative. Second, Micah's imagery also reminds the Israelites of their pagan neighbors, who sacrificed children to false gods. This is abhorrent to the Lord (Leviticus 20:2; Jeremiah 7:31; 19:5; 32:35).

Micah leaves questions unanswered, but the expected response is clear. We cannot earn God's favor by our sacrifices, no matter how lavish they may be. Sacrifice can be empty or self-serving, and God does not desire such acts.

THE PRICE OF LOVE

What kind of gift does it take to demonstrate the value of love and devotion? Merchants want us to go overboard at Christmas. To convince a spouse of the depth of our love, we are encouraged to purchase expensive diamonds. Middle-aged husbands now receive advertising that tells them, "Now that the tight financial years of early marriage are past, purchase a ring that will tell her how much you really love her!"

The old Christmas carol *The Twelve Days of Christmas* also goes a bit overboard. "On the first day of Christmas, my true love gave to me a partridge in a pear tree," it says. And then come turtledoves, French hens, calling birds, etc. The list also becomes cumulative. That is, a partridge in a pear tree is given *each* of the 12 days, and all the other gifts also repeat on all later days. On the twelfth day there are 78 gifts given, for a grand total of 364. All to demonstrate true love!

Wouldn't one carefully chosen, thoughtful gift be more appropriate? Enough with all your birds and leapers! Rather than the quantity of sacrifices, God is more interested in the quality of love and devotion demonstrated in service.

—J. B. N.

B. Correct Action #2: Obey God (v. 8)

8a. He hath showed thee, O man, what is good; and what doth the LORD require of thee.

Visual for Lessons 4 & 5. *Keep this map of the Babylonian Empire posted for several lessons to help your students gain a geographical perspective.*

Micah 6:8 is one of the most important verses in the Bible. It has been called the "key to the prophets." It is a concise summary of what God demands from His people. It is not a list of actions, but rather a trio of attitudes that will result in behavior that is pleasing to God. While this verse is addressed to the people of Israel, it still retains value for Christians who desire to live lives that are in accordance with God's will.

Micah is not teaching anything new to the people of Israel. He begins the verse by reminding them that they have been shown these things in the past. The requirements for goodness in the eyes of God can be boiled down to three things.

8b. But to do justly.

To do justly includes the concepts of justice in the society and righteousness in one's personal life. God's "controversy" with Israel is that the government of God's people is not just. Instead, it exploits and oppresses the poor and downtrodden for the advantage of the rich and powerful.

God wants a nation that flows with justice for all (Amos 5:24). The Lord has made it clear that sacrifice without justice is not what He wants (Proverbs 21:3). God wants leaders who will protect the most vulnerable members of their community, often symbolized by widows and orphans in the Old Testament (see Isaiah 1:17; compare James 1:27).

Personal righteousness is also required. Righteousness is right actions, doing the right thing. The people of ancient Israel are to be guided by the Law of Moses, which clearly defines right behavior. As Christians we understand that we are righteous through our faith in Christ, not by keeping the law (Philippians 3:9). But this does not diminish God's expectation that we will strive for holiness in our lives, to live righteously (1 Timothy 6:11). [See question #3, page 382.]

8c. And to love mercy.

The word translated *mercy* here may be the most significant doctrinal term in the Old Testament. It is sometimes translated *loving-kindness* and is seen as a supreme characteristic of God. The loving-kindness of God is to be valued more than life itself (Psalm 63:3). The mercy of the Lord prevents us from being consumed (Lamentations 3:22).

On both the level of the society and on the personal level, the quest for justice must be tempered with mercy. When we seek righteous judgments, we must do so with the loving heart of the Father. As with justice, sacrifices and worship from those without mercy are not pleasing to God. Jesus was quick to quote Hosea 6:6 to His critics, reminding them that God desired mercy above sacrifice (see Matthew 9:13; 12:7).

8d. And to walk humbly with thy God?

The third requirement is a necessary companion to the first two. God is not impressed by those who do acts of justice and mercy in order to gain credit and call attention to themselves (compare Matthew 6:1-4). Humility demands that we behave in a godly manner because it is the right way to act, not because we will be rewarded for it. Virtue truly becomes its own reward. The humble person will do the right thing consistently, even when no one else is aware of his or her action.

The opposite of humility is pride. Peter advised his readers to "be clothed with humility," because "God resisteth the proud, and giveth grace to the humble" (1 Peter 5:5). As a spirited

---

Home Daily Bible Readings

Monday, June 25—Fear the Lord (Deuteronomy 10:12-22)

Tuesday, June 26—The Disciplined Life (Hebrews 12:6-12)

Wednesday, June 27—Human Plans and God's (Micah 2:1-5)

Thursday, June 28—Sins Denounced (Micah 3:1-7)

Friday, June 29—Micah Speaks Out (Micah 3:8-12)

Saturday, June 30—Promise of Peace (Micah 4:1-5)

Sunday, July 1—What Does God Require? (Micah 6:3-8)

---

stallion must be "broken" to be useful, so we must be broken and humble before God if He is to use us for His service (see Matthew 18:4). This brokenness and humility is our finest sacrifice to God (Psalm 51:17). [See question #4, page 382.]

Conclusion

A. An Out-of-Balance Life

One of the grandest church buildings in the world is the *Hagia Sophia* in Istanbul (ancient Constantinople). It was built by the Christian Emperor Justinian in the sixth century AD.

Justinian was perhaps the greatest ruler of the Byzantine Empire, and the *Hagia Sophia* was his supreme accomplishment. Justinian established a court system that dispensed justice for centuries. He was merciful to his people and lavished his largesse upon them. Yet he wanted his *Hagia Sophia* to exceed the grandeur of the temple of Jerusalem. Upon seeing the finished building, it is said that Justinian exclaimed, "O Solomon, I have outdone thee!" Justinian loved justice and mercy, but he failed the last of Micah's three great standards: to walk humbly with his God.

B. The Well-Rounded Life

The well-rounded life is measured by all three of Micah's cardinal virtues: *justice, mercy,* and *humility.* These three form an interlocking grid, and the absence of one will yield a life without proper balance.

Studying Micah gives us an opportunity for self-evaluation. Do we seek justice and righteousness? Are there unrighteous elements in our lives with which we have become complacent? Do we really love being people of mercy? Have we become tired of kindness, "weary in well doing" (2 Thessalonians 3:13)? How would we evaluate our personal humility? Are we proud and boastful? Do we expect others to acknowledge our acts of service? Or are we content in knowing that we have done the right thing, whether or not we ever receive praise for it? [See question #5, page 382.]

C. Prayer

God of mercy, God of justice, we come to You in humility. May You help us have victory over pride. May You help us be merciful, just as You have been merciful to us. May You help us long for righteousness and justice according to Your standards. We pray these things in the name of your Son, Jesus Christ, the righteous one, amen.

D. Thought to Remember

Practice God's requirements.

Learning by Doing

This page contains an alternative lesson plan emphasizing learning activities. Classes desiring such student involvement will find these suggestions helpful.

Learning Goals

After this lesson, each student will be able to:

1. Summarize Micah's rebuke of evil in his society and his call to do what God requires.

2. Compare and contrast what the Lord requires in Micah 6 with what the Lord requires in the new covenant.

3. State one specific way he or she can better "walk humbly with thy God."

Into the Lesson

Pair off your students. Ask each pair to discuss these questions: (1) "What do people (both Christians and non-Christians) think God expects from them?" (2) "What does God actually require?" Allow your students several minutes to discuss the questions, then call for conclusions. Write their responses on the board.

After you hear from several volunteers, tell your class that today's lesson from the book of Micah explains the difference between what those in the prophet's day *thought* God expected of them and what God *actually* required.

Into the Word

Divide your class into an even number of groups by combining student pairs from the previous exercise. Each group should have four to six students. Assign each group a number. The odd-numbered groups will answer questions one and three. The even-numbered groups will answer questions two and four.

Appoint a discussion leader for each group or let each choose its own leader. If you do not use the student books, you will need to copy and distribute the questions and instructions below.

Question #1: What angered God in Micah's day?

Read Micah 3:1-4. Compare what Micah says there with Micah 1:5-7; 2:1, 2; and 2 Kings 17:1-17. Of what sins were the people guilty? What happened to the people as a result? Why was God angry about these sins?

Question #2: What did God expect?

Read Micah 6:6-8 and compare it with Proverbs 21:3; Jeremiah 22:1-5; Hosea 6:6; and Amos 5:21-24. What did God expect? Why would God reject the Jews' sacrificial offerings if He commanded them to be made in the first place? (See Leviticus 26, especially v. 31.)

Allow the groups a few minutes, then discuss their findings. Especially discuss the meaning of the commands in Micah 6:8 to "do justly," "love mercy," and "walk humbly with thy God." When you have finished this discussion, tell your groups to move on to questions three and four.

Question #3: What do Christians do today to anger God?

Read Matthew 25:14-30; 1 Corinthians 6; and Hebrews 10:26-31. Why are the sins mentioned here particularly offensive to God? How do they compare with the sins committed in Micah's day? What will happen to those who continue committing these sins?

Question #4: What does God expect of Christians today?

Read Ephesians 5:1–6:9; Philippians 2:3-5; 1 Timothy 6:3-11; James 2:8-17; and 1 John 3:16-18. How does God expect Christians to behave today? Especially, how are we to treat one another? How does this compare with God's expectations for His people in Micah's day? What does it mean for a Christian today to do justice, love mercy, and walk humbly with God?

Allow the groups a few minutes to answer, then discuss their findings.

Into Life

Display the following headings on the board: *Do Justice; Love Mercy; Walk Humbly with God.*

Ask each group to choose one of the categories for this last exercise. Make sure each category is chosen by at least one group. When each group has selected its category, group members should work together to write several introspective questions that will help an individual evaluate how well he or she is carrying out that command. For instance, a question for the category *Love Mercy* may be, "Do I make a regular effort to visit the sick, the elderly, and the poor?"

Instruct each group to write at least five questions. Next, ask for volunteers to suggest questions to the entire class. Write these on the board. Finally, tell your students to take a few minutes to ask themselves these questions and to look for areas in their lives that need improvement. They need not share their answers.

Close with a prayer for God to guide your students as they try to keep these commands.

Let's Talk It Over

*The questions on this page are designed to promote discussion of the lesson
by the class and to encourage application of the lesson Scriptures. The answers
provided are only discussion starters. Let your class talk it over from there.*

**1. What steps need to be taken to teach people
that God has limits to His patience? Why is the
church sometimes negligent in doing so?**

The pendulum of the church's message seems
to have swung back and forth between extremes
throughout history. Sometimes we see an emphasis on wrath and holiness to the exclusion of His
love. Sometimes it's the other way. In an age in
which bumper stickers proclaim *God is Love* and
God Loves You, there is the possibility that believers and nonbelievers alike will assume that
God will always be patient and forebearing. The
church is to have a balanced message. God does
indeed love everyone; He is not willing for any to
perish. But God also says He cannot tolerate sin.

The church can show that God's judgment
sometimes comes quickly (Genesis 3; Acts 5:1-
11). At other times judgment follows many warnings (the prophets warned both the northern and
southern kingdoms for decades). A review of
God's judgment on the seven churches in Revelation 2–3 can be helpful here. See commentaries
that discuss what eventually happened to fulfill
God's warnings to those churches or their cities.

**2. Many attend church looking for "what the
church can do for me." What steps can your
church take to teach individuals about the
importance and priority of worship?**

"Today's church service did nothing for me" is
the uncomfortable refrain of some. If all worshipers would arrive having prepared themselves
to give genuine honor to God, then they would
depart having received something very special.

Think about it: churches don't really teach
many classes on how or why to worship! Such instruction could undoubtedly include the idea of
leaving the consumer mentality at home. The
church can also stress that meaningful worship is
not limited to the confines of a specific building.
A life of worship honors God seven days a week.
This happens through our devotional and prayer
lives, by how we live, and by how we treat others.

**3. People see corrupt behavior from business
or political leaders, yet may feel powerless to do
anything. How can the church encourage
Christians not to settle for the status quo?**

Prayer comes first. The church then can encourage Christians to be informed, speak out,
and vote. Christians can learn how to collect evidence to be used against sinful officials, how to
involve other government officials to bring about
change, and how to organize citizens to insist on
just treatment of all people, especially the poor.

At least two cautions are in order. First, working for social justice should never be allowed to
supplant fulfilling the Great Commission (Matthew 28:19, 20). Second, preachers should be extremely careful about giving the appearance of
endorsing political candidates or political parties
from the pulpit while in the process of addressing social concerns.

**4. Suppose you were in charge of producing 3
videos, of 20 minutes each, designed to instruct
the young people of your church how they can
live out the three principles in Micah 6:8. What
would you include in each video to illustrate
how a Christian is *to do justly, to love mercy,*
and *to walk humbly with thy God*?**

Encourage your students to be specific about
appropriate ways to live out these principles.
Challenge your students to answer not only *what*
but *why*. Ask class members which action steps
each will incorporate into his or her life during
the coming week.

**5. What parallels, if any, are there between
how the people responded to God in the text
and how young people today respond to
parental authority? If you see a problem, what
solutions can you offer?**

Some of today's young people are well behaved in the presence of their parents but live rebellious lives when they are away from the eyes
of adults. Some young people will give all the
right answers in a church youth meeting yet disobey those same precepts when with their peers
later on.

The church's challenge is to demonstrate how
obedience honors God, whose very nature includes holiness and righteousness. The church
can be careful not to give lists of rules without
also passing along knowledge of the one who
breathed the rules into existence (2 Timothy 3:16).

Committed to Righteousness

DEVOTIONAL READING: Psalm 27:7-14.

BACKGROUND SCRIPTURE: Zephaniah 3:1-13; 2 Chronicles 34:1-3.

PRINTED TEXT: Zephaniah 3:1-9.

Zephaniah 3:1-9

1 Woe to her that is filthy and polluted, to the oppressing city!

2 She obeyed not the voice; she received not correction; she trusted not in the LORD; she drew not near to her God.

3 Her princes within her are roaring lions; her judges are evening wolves; they gnaw not the bones till the morrow.

4 Her prophets are light and treacherous persons: her priests have polluted the sanctuary, they have done violence to the law.

5 The just LORD is in the midst thereof; he will not do iniquity: every morning doth he bring his judgment to light, he faileth not; but the unjust knoweth no shame.

6 I have cut off the nations: their towers are desolate; I made their streets waste, that none passeth by: their cities are destroyed, so that there is no man, that there is none inhabitant.

7 I said, Surely, thou wilt fear me, thou wilt receive instruction; so their dwelling should not be cut off, howsoever I punished them: but they rose early, and corrupted all their doings.

8 Therefore wait ye upon me, saith the LORD, until the day that I rise up to the prey: for my determination is to gather the nations, that I may assemble the kingdoms, to pour upon them mine indignation, even all my fierce anger: for all the earth shall be devoured with the fire of my jealousy.

9 For then will I turn to the people a pure language, that they may all call upon the name of the LORD, to serve him with one consent.

GOLDEN TEXT: My determination is to gather the nations, that I may assemble the kingdoms, to pour upon them mine indignation, even all my fierce anger: for all the earth shall be devoured with the fire of my jealousy.—Zephaniah 3:8.

Committed to Doing Right
Unit 2: What Does God Require?
(Lessons 5-9)

Lesson Aims

After participating in this lesson, each student will be able to:

1. List at least three sins that characterized the moral conditions of Josiah's Jerusalem.

2. Explain why God has a right to be angry at unholy behavior.

3. Praise God that He tempers His wrath with grace through Jesus Christ.

Lesson Outline

INTRODUCTION
 A. Moral Choices in an Immoral Society
 B. Lesson Background
 I. GOD SEES MORAL FILTH (Zephaniah 3:1-5)
 A. Polluted, Disobedient City (vv. 1, 2)
 B. Insatiable, Greedy Rulers (v. 3)
 C. Haughty, Profane Priests & Prophets (v. 4)
 D. Righteous, Unfailing Judge (v. 5)
 II. GOD PUNISHES CORRUPTION (Zephaniah 3:6, 7)
 A. Coming Destruction (v. 6)
  Scorched Earth
 B. Persistent Corruption (v. 7)
 III. GOD RESTORES HIS PEOPLE (Zephaniah 3:8, 9)
 A. Waiting on God's Wrath (v. 8)
 B. Serving God in Unity (v. 9)
  Unity in Service
CONCLUSION
 A. The Mighty Day of the Lord
 B. Prayer
 C. Thought to Remember

Introduction

A. Moral Choices in an Immoral Society

A recent claim of some genetic researchers is that the DNA of men is programmed for infidelity. In other words, the males of the human species are not created in the image of God but are more like bread mold, which exists to spread its spores everywhere.

If this were true, then the Bible's teaching about confining sexual activity to marriage would seem to be fighting a losing battle against the irresistible forces of nature. While this may be welcome news to some in our society, it contradicts the picture of morality found in the Bible.

Is there such a thing as *biblical morality*? The answers to this question range from *yes*, to *not really*, to *who cares*? Increasingly, there are large segments of the population that want to get away from *moral* versus *immoral* distinctions. They prefer to see things from an *amoral* perspective—a perspective that does not recognize any absolute standards of right and wrong. Under amorality, what may seem wrong to one person becomes enjoyable and right to another. This worldview is becoming more common, even within the church.

Yet the Christian who believes that the teachings of the Bible are from God will never be comfortable with attempts to paint morality a neutral gray. If we come from the perspective of biblical morality, then *amoral = immoral*, a violation of God's standards. We seek to live as God's people in a society that does not recognize God. We are moral people in an immoral world.

In the ancient world there were plenty of people who rejected God's standards, even within God's chosen people of Israel. God continually raised up prophets to proclaim His demands for justice and righteousness. The prophets' call for reform was accompanied by a dire warning: God would not allow wickedness to go unpunished forever. There would be a day when the righteous would be rewarded and the evil would be purged. Zephaniah was the ideal prophet for this message.

B. Lesson Background

King Josiah was the last righteous king to rule in Jerusalem before the destruction of the city by the Babylonians. He reigned from about 640 to 609 BC. The Bible teaches that there was "no king before him, that turned to the Lord with all his heart, . . . neither after him arose there any like him" (2 Kings 23:25).

Josiah came to the throne under very difficult circumstances. Manasseh, his grandfather, was king for 55 years and can be judged to be the most evil king in the history of Judah (see 2 Kings 21:9, 16; 24:3). Josiah's father, King Amon, continued in the evil ways of Manasseh. Amon reigned only two years before being killed in a palace coup (2 Kings 21:23). This brought Josiah to become king at age 8 (2 Kings 22:1).

Despite his heritage of evil and his tender age, Josiah eventually was responsible for many reforms in Judah. While Josiah was king, Hilkiah the high priest found the book of the law while making repairs in the temple. Josiah and his advisors used this book as the basis for reforms that purged Judah of its pagan practices and reinstituted the worship of God (see 2 Kings 23:24).

These reforms "didn't take," however. They only delayed the downward spiral of Judah. Josiah was killed in battle with the Egyptians about 608 BC (2 Kings 23:29). His successors were not of his moral stature, and God allowed the Babylonians to dominate Judah. The cream of the crop of Hebrew young men (like Daniel) was carried into captivity. Eventually the city of Jerusalem was destroyed in 586 BC, roughly 20 years after the death of Josiah.

Zephaniah was one of the three great prophets of the last days of Jerusalem before its destruction. The other two, Habakkuk and Jeremiah, will be studied in the following lessons. Zephaniah preached the coming doom of Judah because of its deep sin. Although Zephaniah prophesied at the time of Josiah's godly reforms, he saw the coming demise of Judah after those reforms were rejected. But Zephaniah also gave a picture of God's future restoration.

Zephaniah was a spokesman for the concept of *the day of the Lord,* a future point in time when God would move powerfully to punish wickedness and redeem the righteous. *The day of the Lord* found fulfillment in the history of Judah with its exile and return but also looks forward to a future day of God's final judgment of all humanity.

I. God Sees Moral Filth
(Zephaniah 3:1-5)

Nations do not rise above the moral level set by their leaders. Under Manasseh, wickedness flourished among the people of God and permeated every aspect of the society.

Unrighteousness was not confined to religious practices. It extended to business practices and to the integrity of public leaders. This was the moral situation that confronted the reformer king, namely Josiah. It is a situation into which God's prophet Zephaniah speaks.

A. Polluted, Disobedient City (vv. 1, 2)

1. Woe to her that is filthy and polluted, to the oppressing city!

A *woe* is the opposite of a blessing. As such, a woe is equivalent to a curse. Moses had promised that God would give blessings if the people of Israel were obedient and curses if they were disobedient (Deuteronomy 11:26-28). So the verse before us is not a blessing. Jerusalem is not the "holy city." Indeed, it is characterized by moral filth and by *oppressing* mistreatment of its citizens by the rulers. [See question #1, page 390.]

2. She obeyed not the voice; she received not correction; she trusted not in the Lord; she drew not near to her God.

Zephaniah outlines four primary charges against Jerusalem: general disobedience, defiance in the face of *correction,* lack of trust in God, and willful abandonment of relationship with God. All of these accusations hit home with the society fostered by King Manasseh; for half of a century, he had led Jerusalem away from the Lord.

The era of Manasseh had endured so long that the vast majority of citizens knew nothing else. How faith survived in persons like Jeremiah, Hilkiah, Josiah, and Zephaniah is a testimony to the providential power of God.

B. Selfish, Greedy Rulers (v. 3)

3. Her princes within her are roaring lions; her judges are evening wolves; they gnaw not the bones till the morrow.

Zephaniah uses vivid metaphor to give a stark condemnation of the leaders of Judah. The government officials *(princes)* are like *roaring lions,* a picture of the wild beast hunting for prey that may be eaten. The *judges,* those who should be stewards of the law, are like *wolves* after the kill. They don't even leave the *bones* of their victims uneaten.

God expects the leaders of the people to protect the innocent and preserve justice. Those leaders should defend the orphan and plead for the widow (see Isaiah 1:17). In God's plan people are not given authority in a government structure so that they may enrich themselves and increase their power. Yet the leaders of Zephaniah's Jerusalem are like wild, ferocious beasts. They terrify the citizens and are relentless in satisfying their own desires for wealth. The citizenry is not their field of duty but their hunting ground.

C. Haughty, Profane Priests & Prophets (v. 4)

4. Her prophets are light and treacherous persons: her priests have polluted the sanctuary, they have done violence to the law.

After indicting the government leaders, Zephaniah turns his attention to the religious leaders, the *prophets* and *priests.* A prophet in the Old Testament is not just a person who gives accurate predictions of the future. Prophets are primarily tasked with demanding repentance from the people of God and calling out for justice and righteousness in the nation. Zephaniah is unconcerned as to whether or not the prophets of his day know the future. He condemns them because their words are *light,* meaning something like "arrogant recklessness."

These prophets have turned a blind eye and a deaf ear to the widespread sin of the city. They have treacherously refused to speak against it. They are in cahoots with those who profit from sins, and this has stilled their tongues from speaking right words.

The priests are responsible for the purity of Judah's religious practices, particularly in the Jerusalem temple. Yet they had stood silently (or even cooperated) when Manasseh had defiled the temple by building altars to pagan gods within its courts (2 Kings 21:4, 5). Zephaniah sees this as more than mere neglect. By allowing God's house to be spiritually polluted, the priests have *done violence to the law.*

These priests had torn God's covenant book out of the heart of Israel and hidden it from the people. This is seen by the fact that during the reign of Josiah the high priest "found" the book of the law in the temple (2 Kings 22:3–23:3). This would be like someone "finding" a copy of the Constitution of the United States (or any other country) after 50 years of neglect.

Zephaniah implies that the "losing" of the law was not an accident. It was planned deliberately. The only surprising detail is that it had not been destroyed altogether, to disappear without a trace. [See question #2, page 390.]

D. Righteous, Unfailing Judge (v. 5)

5. The just LORD is in the midst thereof; he will not do iniquity: every morning doth he bring his judgment to light, he faileth not; but the unjust knoweth no shame.

In contrast to the wicked leaders, Zephaniah lifts up the perfect judge: the *Lord* God himself.

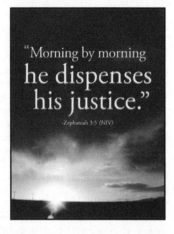

Visual for Lesson 6

"Morning by morning **he dispenses his justice.**"
-Zephaniah 3:5 (NIV)

Point to this visual as you ask, "How has God been merciful to you this morning?"

The prophet points out three characteristics of God's judgments. First, they are untainted by sin, for God *will not do iniquity.* Second, they are not hidden judgments, but are in the *light* for all to see. God standards are clear, and we are not left in the dark as to what His judgments will be. Third, God never avoids making judgments. He does not decline to rule on the hard cases. Instead, He renders judgment in an unfailing, consistent manner. [See question #3, page 390.]

These worthy characteristics of God the judge are compared with corrupt human judges in a simple statement: they know *no shame.* Shame is a powerful influence for social control. A shamed person has acted inappropriately and brought dishonor to himself or herself. Avoidance of public disgrace is a strong motivator.

If, however, a person has become immune to feelings of shame, then outrageous behavior carries no social stigma. A judge with no shame has little reason to act with integrity and justice. Instead, favorable judgments are sold to the highest bidder. The immorality of judicial corruption becomes amoral and a matter of opportunity. [See question #4, page 390.]

God will not stand for this. Injustice is always injustice, no matter who the defendant is. Dishonesty from the bench of the judge is particularly grievous to the Lord.

II. God Punishes Corruption (Zephaniah 3:6, 7)

The focus now shifts to the future activity of God. At the time of Zephaniah, it may seem as if Josiah's reforms had put the nation back on track. Yet the prophet Jeremiah, Zephaniah's contemporary, revealed that the sins of Manasseh were so deep and pervasive that God had already made the decision to cleanse Judah through the exile to Babylon (see Jeremiah 15:4). The downfall of Jerusalem is coming. It is just a matter of time.

A. Coming Destruction (v. 6)

6. I have cut off the nations: their towers are desolate; I made their streets waste, that none passeth by: their cities are destroyed, so that there is no man, that there is none inhabitant.

God first reminds the people that He has acted in the past to wipe out evil *nations,* including the northern kingdom of Israel. Such lands were depopulated, and their grand buildings became rubble. Today, the Near East is full of ruins of dead civilizations. Once thriving cities lie under layers of dirt and waste.

SCORCHED EARTH

Occasionally an invading army will follow a policy of *scorched earth;* this means to inflict utter devastation. This is a policy that ancient Rome eventually followed in dealing with its major rival Carthage.

These two rivals clashed in three conflicts known as *the Punic Wars.* The first war (264–241 BC) began as a squabble over Sicily, where both Rome and Carthage had colonies. The second war (218–202 BC) began in Spain, where both powers again had interests.

Despite the brilliant tactics of Hannibal, Carthage's general, the Romans ultimately prevailed in that second war. Yet Carthage eventually proved to be an economic and military threat to Rome yet again. The Roman statesman Cato ended every speech in the Senate by declaring, "Carthage must be destroyed."

In the third war (149–146 BC), Rome attacked the city of Carthage directly. The army went from house to house, systematically slaughtering the citizens. The city was demolished, and salt was sown into the ground to render it infertile. Carthage became a desolate site.

The Punic Wars had not yet been fought when Zephaniah wrote. Yet that prophet was well aware of what God's plans of *scorched earth* would mean for various nations, particularly Judah. It is a sobering policy, indeed! Have you read Revelation 8:7 recently?   —J. B. N.

B. Persistent Corruption (v. 7)

7. I said, Surely, thou wilt fear me, thou wilt receive instruction; so their dwelling should not be cut off, howsoever I punished them: but they rose early, and corrupted all their doings.

God's frustration with His people is supremely evident here. No matter how dire the warnings or how persistent His prophets, Judah has continued to ignore God's pleadings. Zephaniah gives the startling picture of an inability to sleep late due to the desire to rise *early* in order to get to the work of corrupt wickedness.

What must God do to get our attention? We are reminded of Jesus' parable of the wicked tenants (Mark 12:1-9). In this story, the owner is unable to get the rent payment from those who have leased his vineyard. Servants who are sent to collect are abused, even killed. In an act of utter exasperation, the owner sends his son, saying, "They will reverence my son."

Yet they kill the son too, leading the vineyard owner to come and destroy them. This pattern is found elsewhere in the Bible and still has application today. Sometimes God uses extraordinary

How to Say It

AMON. *Ay*-mun.
BABYLONIANS. Bab-ih-*low*-nee-unz.
DEUTERONOMY. Due-ter-*ahn*-uh-me.
HABAKKUK. Huh-*back*-kuk.
HILKIAH. Hill-*kye*-uh.
JOSIAH. Jo-*sigh*-uh.
JUDAH. *Joo*-duh.
MANASSEH. Muh-*nass*-uh.
OBADIAH. O-buh-*dye*-uh.
PUNIC. *Pyu*-nik.
ZEPHANIAH. Zef-uh-*nye*-uh.

circumstances to wake us from our sinful daze. But there are those for whom no amount of prodding from the Lord will turn them back from their deserved destruction.

III. God Restores His People (Zephaniah 3:8, 9)

Zephaniah pictures God as the ultimate force behind the rise and fall of nations. Greek, Roman, British, Russian—history is littered with empires that have collapsed and disappeared, including the kingdom of Judah.

A. Waiting on God's Wrath (v. 8)

8. Therefore wait ye upon me, saith the LORD, until the day that I rise up to the prey: for my determination is to gather the nations, that I may assemble the kingdoms, to pour upon them mine indignation, even all my fierce anger: for all the earth shall be devoured with the fire of my jealousy.

The picture of God gathering *the nations* shows Zephaniah's understanding of God's mighty power. The Lord God is not just the God of Israel. He is the one God and the master of every human government.

God's motivation for national destruction is pictured here as red-hot *jealousy.* This is not the petty jealousy of a girlfriend who observes her boyfriend looking at another girl for a little too long. This is the righteous jealousy of the wrath of God. He is unwilling to share devotion with any man-made gods and false religions (Exodus 34:14). Why should He? There is no other God! [See question #5, page 390.]

B. Serving God in Unity (v. 9)

9. For then will I turn to the people a pure language, that they may all call upon the name of the LORD, to serve him with one consent.

From this litany of wrath and destruction emerges a bright ray of hope. Zephaniah looks forward to a restoration of the unity of humanity under God. He sees three specific elements.

First, there will be *a pure language*. This is an image of atoning for sin (compare Isaiah 6:5-7) or purity of worship (compare Psalms 16:4; Hosea 2:17). Second, there will be a united effort to *call upon the name of the Lord*. This is a way of referring to worship from the earliest days of humanity (Genesis 4:26). Unity of worship eliminates anyone calling upon a false god (see 1 Kings 18:24); this ties in to the purity of worship idea.

Third, humanity will *serve* God with *one consent*. The idea of *serve* includes worship; numerous passages place the two concepts alongside one another as almost inseparable ideas (Daniel 3:28; Luke 4:8; etc.). True believers will serve and worship God in unity. [See question #6, page 390.]

UNITY IN SERVICE

Thomas Campbell (1763–1854) had a burning desire for the union of all Christians under the simple authority of the New Testament. Born in northern Ireland, as a young man he joined a denomination that reflected many of the sectarian divisions then rife in the British Isles. Thomas Campbell became an Old Light, Anti-Burgher, Seceder Presbyterian, Protestant kind of a Christian. He immigrated to America in 1807, hoping to find an atmosphere that would foster unity.

Campbell was rebuffed by his denomination. So in 1809 he and some friends formed the Christian Association of Washington. Campbell wrote its constitution and bylaws, "Declaration and Address." In this document he laid out some general principles that would guide their activities.

His first proposition was that "the church of Christ on earth is essentially, intentionally, and constitutionally one." All divisions, he contended, came either from neglecting part of God's Word or adding human teaching on top of Scripture. He believed that if everyone accepted the teachings of Scripture and followed the precedents of the New Testament church—no more and no less—then we could have unity.

Today Campbell's spiritual descendants still try to follow his twin commitments to Christian unity and scriptural authority. The dream of Campbell is similar to the vision of Zephaniah. That prophet foresaw a time when the people would speak a pure language, turn to the Lord, and serve Him in unity. It is an ideal that is yet to be realized.   —J. B. N.

Conclusion

A. The Mighty Day of the Lord

Zephaniah has been called the prophet of *the day of the Lord*. That phrase occurs several times in his little book.

The day of the Lord is a concept with strong biblical roots (see Isaiah 2:12; Joel 2:31 [quoted in Acts 2:20]; Obadiah 15; and Zechariah 14:1 for a few examples). Old Testament prophets foresaw this as a future day when God would intervene in history to punish evil and reward righteousness. This was accomplished in an unexpected way when Israel and Judah both suffered destruction at the hand of foreign invaders.

That destruction was only what we call a "type" of the ultimate day of the Lord, however. In the New Testament it is synonymous with Christ's second coming (1 Thessalonians 5:2). The New Testament authors see this as a day of finality, when there will be a destruction of heavens and earth (2 Peter 3:10). This too will be a pouring out of the wrath of God (see Revelation 6:17).

The day of the Lord can be either terrifying or comforting, depending on one's relationship to God. May we, as believers, take comfort in the assurance that God sees us as righteous because of the blood of Jesus. We have nothing to fear.

B. Prayer

God of all nations, we pray for the day when our speech will become pure, and we will worship You with one voice. We pray this in the name of Jesus, our soon and coming king, amen.

C. Thought to Remember

God is always righteous,
whether in punishment or deliverance.

Home Daily Bible Readings

Monday, July 2—Prayer for Help (Psalm 27:7-14)

Tuesday, July 3—The Day of the Lord (Isaiah 2:12-22)

Wednesday, July 4—God's Eternal Counsel (Psalm 33:1-11)

Thursday, July 5—Young Josiah's Reforms (2 Chronicles 34:1-7)

Friday, July 6—Woe to Wrongdoers (Zephaniah 3:1-7)

Saturday, July 7—Deliverance Will Come (Zephaniah 3:8-13)

Sunday, July 8—The Call to Rejoice (Zephaniah 3:14-20)

Learning by Doing

*This page contains an alternative lesson plan emphasizing learning activities.
Classes desiring such student involvement will find these suggestions helpful.*

Learning Goals

After participating in this lesson, each student will be able to:

1. List at least three sins that characterized the moral conditions of Josiah's Jerusalem.

2. Explain why God has a right to be angry at unholy behavior.

3. Praise God that He tempers His wrath with grace through Jesus Christ.

Into the Lesson

Below are several statements about morality from the pens of famous writers. Ask your students to critique the quotations.

1. "I know only that what is moral is what you feel good after and what is immoral is what you feel bad after" (Ernest Hemingway); *2.* "Morality is simply the attitude we adopt toward people whom we personally dislike" (Oscar Wilde); *3.* "Morality is the best of all devices for leading mankind by the nose" (Friedrich Nietzsche); *4.* "What is morality in any given time or place? It is what the majority then and there happen to like and immorality is what they dislike" (Alfred North Whitehead); *5.* "Morality is the theory that every human act must be either right or wrong, and that 99 percent of them are wrong" (H. L. Mencken).

When you finish your discussion, explain that today's lesson deals with upholding God's moral standards in an immoral society.

Into the Word

Divide the class into pairs. Ask each to read Zephaniah 3:1-9 and answer these questions:

1. What does the word *woe* signify in verse 1? *2.* The people were guilty of what four sins, according to verse 2? *3.* What do the images of lions and wolves tell us about how the rulers treated their people? *4.* In what way could the Judean prophets be guilty of treachery? *5.* How did the priests pollute the sanctuary and do violence to the law? (See 2 Kings 21:4, 5.) *6.* How did God bring His judgment to light? How did the unjust respond to these revelations? *7.* What nations had God destroyed before that time? (See Deuteronomy 3:1-11; Joshua 10; etc.) *8.* How had God warned Jerusalem concerning sin and impending destruction (v. 7)? How had the people

responded? *9.* What warning did God give the nations? What promise did He make to the people? *10.* What is the contrast between the promised "pure language" of verse 9 and the treachery of the false prophets in verse 4?

When your pairs have completed the exercise, discuss their answers. Also explain (from the lesson Conclusion) the concept of the "day of the Lord" in Zephaniah and the other prophets. Then ask your students to read 1 Thessalonians 4:13–5:15. Use these questions to discuss that passage. Answers are indicated in parentheses.

1. To what event does Paul link the day of the Lord? *(the return of Christ) 2.* What will happen to those who are not ready for His return? *(they will be destroyed; see Matthew 24:36-44; 25:31-46) 3.* How will Christians escape the wrath of God? *(through the death of Christ; see also Romans 5:6-11) 4.* Knowing all this, how should Christians behave? (with self-control, living by faith, love, and hope; we encourage one another)*

Into Life

Ask your students to return to the quotations from the Into the Lesson exercise. Below are summary statements of the quotes and a criticism of each based on today's lesson. Tell students to turn to their student books and do a three-way match: each author with a summary statement and a criticism. (If you don't use the student books, reproduce the text below as necessary.)

A. Morality is just the opinion of the majority; *B.* Morality is based on personal feelings; *C.* Morality is just a means of controlling others; *D.* Morality is just a theory that most human behavior is bad; *E.* Morality is a means to criticize people we dislike.

a. Biblical morality is about self-control, so that we are ready for Christ's return; it is not about controlling others; *b.* Christians are to use morality to encourage one another to be like Christ, not simply to condemn people; *c.* Only behavior that contradicts God's Word is evil; *d.* Morality is based on God's nature and His Word, not on human feelings; *e.* Morality is based on God's nature and His Word, not on majority opinion. *(Answers: 1Bd, 2Eb, 3Ca, 4Ae, 5Dc.)*

Discuss answers and relate them to question four of the 1 Thessalonians exercise.

Let's Talk It Over

The questions on this page are designed to promote discussion of the lesson by the class and to encourage application of the lesson Scriptures. The answers provided are only discussion starters. Let your class talk it over from there.

1. How can we speak so that both believers and nonbelievers can appreciate the contrast between the holiness of God and the awfulness of sin? Should we use different language to the two groups in this regard? Explain.

Nonbelievers may tune us out when their sinful behavior is described as filthy and polluted. Yet if sinful behavior is allowed to be perceived as normal, then it is hard for individuals to examine it from another perspective.

Perhaps one way to begin is to focus on the holiness of God and how His commandments flow from this characteristic. Anything short of that standard fails miserably by comparison.

2. How can leaders in the church stumble into following the bad example of the religious leaders described in our text? How do we guard against this?

There are many historical examples of religious leaders who followed the customs of the day rather than being beacons directing people to God. For example, many of the church leaders in the time of Hitler gave in to the fear of punishment, while many others actively supported the rising philosophy of nationalism and hate of others.

Church leaders today can choose several paths to guard themselves. Accountability to others is vital. Daily prayer and devotions keep the leader's heart in tune with God. Spiritual retreats and seminars promote maturity.

3. If the average Christian lived life with the action of God in verse 5 in mind, what difference would it make?

People are often asked to evaluate how they would act if Jesus were standing beside them. But what if we turned that idea around? If we watched God as He worked in the midst of sinful situations as He tried to bring people back to Him, we could have a guide on how to do the same.

4. How can the church teach young people—or indeed anyone—that shame, guilt, and remorse are appropriate reactions to sin?

We are surrounded by a generation of young people who seem not to be embarrassed about seeing or participating in any activity. There will

be no shame, guilt, or remorse where sin is not recognized as sin. Helping people see the truth of this concept is thus vital.

If your class is made up of older individuals, this question may lead them into rehearsing a long list of the things the younger generation does that really irritates them. But a mannerism or behavior by one person that irritates another isn't necessarily sinful in the eyes of God.

5. What descriptive models can we create to communicate an accurate picture of the awesome force of God's anger? Or should we just say what the Bible says and not be too "creative" in this regard?

Lead the class in formulating a list of possible ways to explain God's reactions of anger and judgment; then help them evaluate the effectiveness of these models in today's culture. One potential problem is using modern disasters as examples of His anger. We cannot be sure if they were judgments from God or just occurrences of nature. Passages such as Revelation 8:6–9:19 are powerful enough without embellishment!

6. What safeguards can the church put in place to keep the focus on winning the lost rather than fighting over interpretations of prophecies?

The fulfillment of the prophecy in verse 9 has been explained variously as (1) the return of the Jewish people to rebuild Jerusalem, (2) the unity developed as the church began, (3) a set of circumstances that will unfold just before the second coming of Christ, and (4) the final unity in Heaven. Rather than immediately focusing on disagreement, it is undoubtedly better to focus on what all Christians can agree with: God is in charge and His plans will be revealed in His time frame.

Yet we need not merely stop at that point, sweep our disagreements under the rug, and say, "God will work it out; let's not worry about it." We can dig deeper to see if there are further areas of agreement. For example, another thing we can agree upon is that in prophecy more than one interpretation *may* be true in a "double fulfillment" kind of way.

Committed to Hope

Devotional Reading: Psalm 37:27-34.

Background Scripture: Habakkuk 2:1-20; 2 Kings 23:35-37.

Printed Text: Habakkuk 2:1-14.

Habakkuk 2:1-14

1 I will stand upon my watch, and set me upon the tower, and will watch to see what he will say unto me, and what I shall answer when I am reproved.

2 And the LORD answered me, and said, Write the vision, and make it plain upon tables, that he may run that readeth it.

3 For the vision is yet for an appointed time, but at the end it shall speak, and not lie: though it tarry, wait for it; because it will surely come, it will not tarry.

4 Behold, his soul which is lifted up is not upright in him: but the just shall live by his faith.

5 Yea also, because he transgresseth by wine, he is a proud man, neither keepeth at home, who enlargeth his desire as hell, and is as death, and cannot be satisfied, but gathereth unto him all nations, and heapeth unto him all people:

6 Shall not all these take up a parable against him, and a taunting proverb against him, and say, Woe to him that increaseth that which is not his! how long? and to him that ladeth himself with thick clay!

7 Shall they not rise up suddenly that shall bite thee, and awake that shall vex thee, and thou shalt be for booties unto them?

8 Because thou hast spoiled many nations, all the remnant of the people shall spoil thee; because of men's blood, and for the violence of the land, of the city, and of all that dwell therein.

9 Woe to him that coveteth an evil covetousness to his house, that he may set his nest on high, that he may be delivered from the power of evil!

10 Thou hast consulted shame to thy house by cutting off many people, and hast sinned against thy soul.

11 For the stone shall cry out of the wall, and the beam out of the timber shall answer it.

12 Woe to him that buildeth a town with blood, and stablisheth a city by iniquity!

13 Behold, is it not of the LORD of hosts that the people shall labor in the very fire, and the people shall weary themselves for very vanity?

14 For the earth shall be filled with the knowledge of the glory of the LORD, as the waters cover the sea.

Golden Text: The earth shall be filled with the knowledge of the glory of the LORD, as the waters cover the sea.—Habakkuk 2:14.

Committed to Doing Right
Unit 2: What Does God Require?
(Lessons 5-9)

Lesson Aims

After participating in this lesson, each student will be able to:

1. Name two challenges faced by Habakkuk in relaying God's coming judgment on the nation of Judah.

2. Explain how the knowledge of the glory of the Lord is a valuable hope.

3. Express his or her eternal hope through one act of kindness in the coming week.

Lesson Outline

INTRODUCTION
    A. Reformation Key
    B. Lesson Background
  I. WAITING FOR GOD'S ANSWER (Habakkuk 2:1-3)
    A. Habakkuk Prepares to Hear (v. 1)
      Watchtowers, Then and Now
    B. God Prepares to Respond (vv. 2, 3)
 II. HEARING GOD'S ANSWER (Habakkuk 2:4-13)
    A. Pride and Faith (v. 4)
    B. Behavior and Attitudes (vv. 5, 6a)
    C. Thievery and Woe (v. 6b)
      Robber Barons
    D. Reactions and Consequences (vv. 7, 8)
    E. Covetousness and Woe (vv. 9-11)
    F. Violence and Woe (vv. 12, 13)
III. HOPING FOR GOD'S GLORY (Habakkuk 2:14)
CONCLUSION
    A. Living by Faith
    B. Prayer
    C. Thought to Remember

Introduction

A. Reformation Key

The great reformer Martin Luther (1483–1546) was of humble birth. His father, Hans, was a copper miner. Hans used his modest wealth to educate Martin, with plans for him to become a lawyer. So the son progressed in his studies and entered law school. But God dealt with him in mighty ways, and he left legal studies to take vows as a monk.

Luther progressed rapidly to ordination as a priest at age 23, to a doctor of theology degree at age 29, and to a teaching post at the University of Wittenberg that same year. He quickly became the most popular teacher at the university. His lectures on Psalms, Romans, Galatians, and Hebrews brought standing-room-only crowds.

Yet Luther was not satisfied with this sparkling career. He had no peace in his soul. He was overwhelmed by his sense of sinfulness before a holy, righteous God. The then-current practice of penance did not relieve this feeling but only added to it. This young man, idolized by hundreds as a Bible expositor, was wracked by his own sense of inadequacy and sin.

The religious teachers of the Middle Ages instructed that people were bound to God by their love. This love must reveal itself in deeds of righteousness—"saving works of merit." For Luther such deeds were not a bad thing, but they did not relieve his feelings of personal sin.

Luther found his answer in Scripture. He discovered a verse from the ancient prophet Habakkuk that the apostle Paul used: the righteous person shall live by faith (Habakkuk 2:4; Romans 1:17; Galatians 3:11). Luther thus discovered that salvation was founded on faith!

This was the key that set in motion the reformation of the sixteenth century. No longer could the medieval church attempt to control salvation, allowing access because of sufficient good deeds. Luther may not have understood everything perfectly, but he broke the back of a doctrinal monopoly that had made salvation a tool of the church rather than a gift of God.

The Bible teaches that we cannot earn salvation, for it is a gift (Ephesians 2:8, 9). Salvation through faith (as opposed to works) was not invented by Luther; he found it in Paul's writings. But Paul did not coin the concept either; he found it in Habakkuk. This is not just a New Testament or an Old Testament concept. It is a Bible concept. This lesson will look at the roots of this way of understanding salvation by examining Habakkuk in its original context.

B. Lesson Background

There is no clear indication in the book of Habakkuk as to when that man of God wrote or exactly when he served as a prophet. Outside the Bible there is a tradition that Habakkuk was a priest and prophet from the tribe of Levi. This tradition places him in Judah during the later career of Jeremiah and the early days of Daniel. This was a time when the Babylonians had begun to dominate Judah but had not yet destroyed Jerusalem and the temple. That destruction took place in 586 BC.

The message of Habakkuk fits very well into this period, approximately 600–590 BC. We know that the ancient Jews held Habakkuk in high esteem. One of the most famous of the Dead Sea Scrolls is a commentary on the book of Habakkuk, dated two centuries before Christ.

The form of the book is unusual among the prophets and more like the book of Job. The first two chapters are a dialogue between the prophet and the Lord. Much like Job, Habakkuk challenges God with some primary issues: Why do the righteous people of the world suffer? Why does God wait to punish evil? And how could God use an ungodly people like the Babylonians to punish Israel, His chosen people? The third and final chapter is a poetic prayer of praise and faith.

Habakkuk begins with the prophet's complaint to God: Why does lawlessness prevail (Habakkuk 1:2-4)? In the pagan world the answer to this question was easy: there are good gods and evil gods. But among the people of Israel, with their belief in one holy God, it was much more difficult. If there is one God—a good and holy God—then why is there still evil?

God's answer to Habakkuk is found in the next section (Habakkuk 1:5-11). God asserts that He is about to do something. He is about to bring the Chaldeans (another name for the Babylonians) to punish wayward Israel.

Habakkuk responds to this with amazement (1:12–2:1). How can the Lord link himself with the tyranny of a conqueror? How can a holy God use such evil people in this way? In other words, Habakkuk is saying that the Judeans might have been naughty, but that doesn't compare with the overwhelming evil of the Babylonians. This second question sets the stage for the second answer of God, which is where our lesson text begins.

I. Waiting for God's Answer (Habakkuk 2:1-3)

In the Old Testament, one of the answers to the problem of evil is that we must "wait on the Lord" (see Psalm 37:34). When the righteous are in distress, they must wait for God to save them (Proverbs 20:22). In chapter one, Habakkuk thinks he has asked God a very difficult question. He now waits for His answer.

A. Habakkuk Prepares to Hear (v. 1)

1. I will stand upon my watch, and set me upon the tower, and will watch to see what he will say unto me, and what I shall answer when I am reproved.

Habakkuk has gone to his watchtower to wait for the answer to his question, "God, how can You think of using the evil, violent Babylonians against Your people?" Habakkuk expects that God should protect His nation from foreign threats, not support the aggressors. He admits his confusion and ponders what he should say to God when the answer comes.

It is common for us to have tough questions about God and faith. Many people have wished they could speak to God directly, to get simple, satisfying answers. It doesn't work that way, however. As Job said, "For he is not a man, as I am, that I should answer him, and we should come together in judgment" (Job 9:32). We should remember that God is under no obligation to *answer* us. He does not dance to our tune. [See question #1, page 398.]

WATCHTOWERS, THEN AND NOW

Watchtowers have played crucial roles in the history of defense and communication. Consider the Greek island of Chios (Kios in Acts 20:15), in the eastern Aegean Sea. There a series of about 50 watchtowers, called *viglas*, were built around the perimeter of the entire island. From the top of each vigla, the watcher could see the next two viglas, one on each side. Any sighting of pirates or other enemies could be communicated quickly to the entire island (www.chiosonline.gr).

The southern coast of Spain was also once a prime target for pirates. During the Middle Ages, the Moors built a system of watchtowers. These towers could communicate with each other using smoke signals by day and fires at night. Seashells could be blown to warn the local populace.

When the Christians conquered the territory, they kept the tower system and even strengthened it. The system worked surprisingly well and could transmit news over large distances in a relatively short period of time. Watchtowers helped the populace avoid nasty surprises.

How to Say It

BABYLONIANS. Bab-ih-*low*-nee-unz.
CHALDEANS. Kal-*dee*-unz.
CHIOS. *Ki*-as (*i* as in *eye*).
GALATIANS. Guh-*lay*-shunz.
HABAKKUK. Huh-*back*-kuk.
HEBREWS. *Hee*-brews.
JERUSALEM. Juh-*roo*-suh-lem.
JUDAH. *Joo*-duh.
LEVI. *Lee*-vye.
WITTENBERG. *Wi*-ten-berg or *Vi*-ten-berk.

Habakkuk is not looking for an enemy attack while he is in his watchtower. Rather, he is alert for communication from the Lord. Each of us would do well to make Habakkuk's choice our own. We can climb into our own, private watchtowers, meaning we make time for daily devotions when we're alone with God and His Word. This will make us more sensitive to His leading. This kind of a watchtower will give us the isolation and perspective to perceive His will more clearly. In a roundabout way, using our own watchtowers in this manner can keep us alert to attacks by Satan. —J. B. N.

B. God Prepares to Respond (vv. 2, 3)

2, 3. And the LORD answered me, and said, Write the vision, and make it plain upon tables, that he may run that readeth it. For the vision is yet for an appointed time, but at the end it shall speak, and not lie: though it tarry, wait for it; because it will surely come, it will not tarry.

The Lord does indeed respond! But before the actual answer, God gives the prophet two instructions. First, He wants Habakkuk to *write* the answer in straightforward, unmistakable language. The image of one who *may run* is the image of a herald who travels quickly with news; thus the message must be shared with others. This emphasizes the importance of the forthcoming message.

Second, God warns Habakkuk that he may need patience in order to see God's plan worked out. Even though there may be a delay, it will surely come, God says. As Paul would say, "This is a faithful saying" (see Titus 3:8). Our impatience does not require that God alter His plan. [See question #2, page 398.]

II. Hearing God's Answer (Habakkuk 2:4-13)

The response of God is a comparison between two kinds of people. This is followed by three *woes* or curses against the proud person.

A. Pride and Faith (v. 4)

4a. Behold, his soul which is lifted up is not upright in him.

The Lord's answer is to contrast two human reactions to the dilemma. The first reaction is that of a person whose *soul . . . is lifted up.* This refers to the proud, self-sufficient person. God says this person is *not upright,* meaning that his or her life is out of sync with the will of God.

4b. But the just shall live by his faith.

The second reaction God describes is the kind He is seeking. The person with the outlook men-

Home Daily Bible Readings

Monday, July 9—The Lord Loves Justice (Psalm 37:27-34)

Tuesday, July 10—Judah Becomes Egypt's Vassal (2 Kings 23:31-37)

Wednesday, July 11—Habakkuk's Complaint (Habakkuk 1:12-17)

Thursday, July 12—The Lord Answers (Habakkuk 2:1-5)

Friday, July 13—Woes Reported (Habakkuk 2:6-14)

Saturday, July 14—The Lord Will Act (Habakkuk 2:15-20)

Sunday, July 15—The Lord Is Our Strength (Habakkuk 3:13-19)

tioned here does not trust in his or her own power. Instead, this person lives by an ongoing *faith* in God. Even in the face of trouble and seeming injustice, even in the shadow of looming national disaster, this person is unwavering in this regard. This is the person who surrenders the need to have all questions answered. This person falls back on the simple belief that God is in control and that God cares for him or her.

The effect of this answer is to rebuke Habakkuk and any who are like-minded. If we determine the questions that God must answer, then we have assumed the position of judge and inquisitor of God. God will not allow this. We are called to *live* by *faith,* in full realization that we do not understand why everything happens. We take hope from our trust in God. [See question #3, page 398.]

B. Behavior and Attitudes (vv. 5, 6a)

5, 6a. Yea also, because he transgresseth by wine, he is a proud man, neither keepeth at home, who enlargeth his desire as hell, and is as death, and cannot be satisfied, but gathereth unto him all nations, and heapeth unto him all people. Shall not all these take up a parable against him, and a taunting proverb against him.

The language of this description is difficult to understand. But if we examine it carefully, we can identify five characteristics of the person who displeases God. First, this person is a drunkard. [See question #4, page 398.] Second, this person is publicly proud. Third, he or she is restless and does not stay *at home.*

Fourth, this person's greed is as big *as hell* (the grave); the person's greed is insatiable—it *cannot be satisfied.* Fifth, this kind of person desires to dominate other *people* and *nations;* thus the greed is not just for material things but for power as well. All of this describes the leaders of Judah, who are deserving of condemnation.

C. Thievery and Woe (v. 6b)

6b. And say, Woe to him that increaseth that which is not his! how long? and to him that ladeth himself with thick clay!

The first woe describes a dishonest businessman. He barters in *that which is not his,* meaning stolen property. The reference to being laden with *thick clay* probably is an idiom that implies involvement in extortion. He is "thick as thieves," because he is one of them.

ROBBER BARONS

The Robber Barons is the title of a 1934 book that examines the "captains of industry" of the late nineteenth century. These captains included Andrew Carnegie (steel), John D. Rockefeller (oil), Cornelius Vanderbilt (railways), as well as financiers such as Jay Gould and J. Pierpont Morgan. Their entrepreneurial methods were often questionable and sometimes downright illegal.

For example, Rockefeller made secret agreements with various railroad companies in order to create an oil monopoly. He and fellow refiners in the Standard Oil Trust had their freight rates sharply reduced while competing refiners saw their own freight rates increase dramatically. The railroads then kicked back to Standard Oil a large part of that increase. Within just a few months, many competitors yielded to Rockefeller and joined Standard Oil. He was then able to control the price for all oil sales throughout the United States.

Vanderbilt was able to consolidate several rail lines into one, also using dubious tactics. Once when questioned about the legality of his business methods, he responded, "What do I care about the law? Ain't I got the power?"

By squeezing out competitors, these aggressive business leaders were able to gouge the public without regard to ethics. They enriched themselves by taking advantage of powerless people. As Habakkuk phrases it, they were increasing what was not theirs. But the Lord still watches, even in the twenty-first century AD.   —J. B. N.

D. Reactions and Consequences (vv. 7, 8)

7, 8. Shall they not rise up suddenly that shall bite thee, and awake that shall vex thee, and thou shalt be for booties unto them? Because thou hast spoiled many nations, all the remnant of the people shall spoil thee; because

of men's blood, and for the violence of the land, of the city, and of all that dwell therein.

God says that the problem will not continue for long. Eventually the victims will *bite* back, and the thief will become their booty or plunder. God promises that this person will get his or her just deserts. Those whom such a person has abused will eventually turn the tables and repay the scoundrel.

E. Covetousness and Woe (vv. 9-11)

9. Woe to him that coveteth an evil covetousness to his house, that he may set his nest on high, that he may be delivered from the power of evil!

The second woe is directed to the covetous person. In this context, this person seeks to remove himself or herself from the problems of society by setting a *nest* (home) *on high.* This person thus wants to live in the fortress enclave of wealth, untouched by the poor and needy of the community.

10. Thou hast consulted shame to thy house by cutting off many people, and hast sinned against thy soul.

From the safety of a fortress-home, the covetous person continues to oppress the poor by *cutting* them *off* from their livelihoods. In so doing, God says this person commits a serious sin. In other words, such a person truly sells his or her own *soul.* Therefore, that person's life is now forfeit.

11. For the stone shall cry out of the wall, and the beam out of the timber shall answer it.

Habakkuk warns metaphorically that the components of this person's house will bring the accusation. This is because that lavish home has been built with ill-gotten wealth. Mighty *stone* walls are paid for by cheating the innocent. Massive ceiling beams are financed from the proceeds of criminal activity.

F. Violence and Woe (v. 12, 13)

12. Woe to him that buildeth a town with blood, and stablisheth a city by iniquity!

The third woe is a general condemnation against the violent, wicked person of power. *A city* built on crime and injustice cannot endure and will never be blessed by God.

13. Behold, is it not of the LORD of hosts that the people shall labor in the very fire, and the people shall weary themselves for very vanity?

The exploitative, ruthless leaders have driven the workers of their land without rest. The great city they have built (namely, Jerusalem) is for *vanity,* because its destruction is coming from the Babylonians. Thus the people's labor is only for the *fire*, meaning it will be burned up and not endure. Even so, God hears the cries of His people, just as He heard their cries in Egypt as they labored to build the great cities for the pharaohs (see Exodus 3:7).

These series of woes explain God's anger toward Judah. His holy people have perverted God's gift of the land of Israel. Rather than use it for God's glory and for His service, they have allowed human greed and pride to reign supreme. God has been very patient with them, but His patience has run its course. Now the only hope for correction is destruction of Judah by the Babylonians. This will cleanse it of this pervasive sin.

III. Hoping for God's Glory (Habakkuk 2:14)

Like many passages from the prophets, the predictions of doom and gloom are not the last word. Habakkuk ends this section with a word of hope, looking forward to a time when there will be universal acknowledgment of the Lord God.

14. For the earth shall be filled with the knowledge of the glory of the LORD, as the waters cover the sea.

Although often overlooked, this verse is one of the great texts of the Old Testament. It pictures in marvelous symbolic language a time when *the earth* will be flooded *with the knowledge of the glory of the Lord*. This spiritual deluge will engulf all people. There will be no holdouts who continue to deny the greatness and majesty of God.

A theme found throughout Scripture is the coming day of universal recognition of our glorious God. Isaiah saw a future time when all would come and see God's glory (Isaiah 66:18). Isaiah also looked forward to the day when every knee would bow to God and every tongue would acknowledge Him (Isaiah 45:23). This scenario is repeated by Paul in Philippians 2:10, 11.

In the last chapter of his book, Habakkuk looks forward to a time when God's glory will cover the heavens and the earth will be filled with His praise (Habakkuk 3:3). This promise comforts the suffering saints of Habakkuk's day and gives hope to Christian believers today. Centuries later, the apostle Peter will offer similar hope when he writes that we "are partakers of Christ's sufferings; that, when his glory shall be revealed, [we] may be glad also with exceeding joy" (1 Peter 4:13). [See question #5, page 398.]

Conclusion

A. Living by Faith

Habakkuk ends his book with a grim look at the bleakness of many people's lives. He knows there are times when "the fig tree shall not blossom, neither shall fruit be in the vines; . . . and the fields shall yield no meat; the flock shall be cut off from the fold, and there shall be no herd in the stalls" (Habakkuk 3:17). Even in these times, however, Habakkuk exclaims, "I will rejoice in the Lord, I will joy in the God of my salvation. The Lord God is my strength, and he will make my feet like hinds' feet, and he will make me to walk upon mine high places" (3:18, 19).

The life of faith means utter trust in God. It means that we serve Him diligently. And, yes, it means that we work hard and enjoy life. But at the end of the day we continue in hope without fear, for we know that God controls the future, and we rest secure in Him. This is what it means to live by faith.

Most of all, living by faith means that we trust in God for salvation. We do not fear judgment, for Jesus our Savior has prepared a place for us in Heaven (John 14:3). Martin Luther said that "the only saving faith is that which casts itself on God for life or death." May we have that faith!

Visual for
Lesson 7

"The earth shall be filled with the knowledge of the glory of the LORD, as the waters cover the sea."
-Habakkuk 2:14

Point to this visual as you ask, "How has today's lesson increased your knowledge?"

B. Prayer

God of Glory, may it be said of us as it was of King Hezekiah, "He trusted in the Lord." Forgive us when we doubt. Strengthen us when we believe. We pray this in the name of Jesus Christ, Your only Son, amen.

C. Thought to Remember

Live by faith, especially in the midst of evil.

Learning by Doing

This page contains an alternative lesson plan emphasizing learning activities.
Classes desiring such student involvement will find these suggestions helpful.

Learning Goals

After this lesson, each student will be able to:

1. Name two challenges faced by Habakkuk in relaying God's coming judgment on the nation of Judah.

2. Explain how the knowledge of the glory of the Lord is a valuable hope.

3. Express his or her eternal hope through one act of kindness in the coming week.

Into the Lesson

Distribute copies of the survey below as your students enter the classroom (or direct them to this exercise in the student books). The instructions should read, "Rank-order the following tasks from most difficult to least difficult, with 1 being the hardest. If you can think of a task more difficult than one of these, include it in your list."

___ *Notifying someone of a death in the family*
___ *Laying off an employee*
___ *Telling someone that she is terminally ill*
___ *Confessing to a loved one that you have broken a possession precious to that person*
___ *Admitting to your parents or spouse that you are in trouble with the law*
___ *Telling a child that his parents are divorcing*
___ *(your choice)* _____

After several minutes, ask volunteers to share their conclusions. What other difficult tasks did they list? What makes some tasks especially difficult? Ask your students what help or encouragement they would need to be able to fulfill such difficult responsibilities. Then inform the class that today's lesson explains how the prophet Habakkuk dealt with God's command to prophesy judgment and destruction upon Judah.

Into the Word

Develop a brief lecture from the Lesson Background and the commentary on Habakkuk 2:1-3. Explain the difficulties Habakkuk faced in announcing God's coming judgment upon Judah.

When you have finished your mini-lecture, divide your class into groups of three or four students each. Give each group a copy of the following questions (or direct your students' attention to their students books, if using those, where they can find this exercise printed).

What Kind of Person Does God Want in a Crisis?
Read Habakkuk 2:4-14 to answer these questions: *1.* What does Habakkuk mean in verse 4 when he says that a prideful person's soul is "not upright"? *2.* What is the guiding principle in the life of a just, or righteous, person? *3.* What are the sinful characteristics of a proud person (vv. 5, 6)? *4.* What is significant about the term *woe* in verses 6, 9, and 12? *5.* What is the meaning of the expression "ladeth himself with thick clay"?

6. What are the crimes of the covetous person (vv. 9-11)? What will accuse such a person of his or her crimes? *7.* Why is God angry with those who built Jerusalem (vv. 12, 13)? What is the meaning of the word *vanity*? *8.* Despite the doom prophesied, what is the predicted outcome of God's judgment (v. 14)? Why should that information be important to the righteous person who tries to live by faith?

Call your groups back together and discuss their conclusions.

Into Life

Use the illustration of Martin Luther and Habakkuk 2:4 ("The just shall live by his faith") to introduce this portion of the lesson. Stress Luther's reliance on the Bible and its emphasis on faith (as contrasted with works) to receive God's gift of salvation. Remind your class that Luther was able to deal with a crisis in his spiritual life by drawing upon God's Word to change his attitudes about God, sin, and salvation.

Next, distribute the following open-ended statements (or direct attention to the student books, where they are reprinted). Ask each student to write at least one response to each statement. Encourage complete honesty, since no one else will see their work.

My Crisis of Faith
In order to respond to a crisis of faith, I predict that I would need to
  Change my attitude by . . .
  Remember these biblical truths:
  Avoid these sins and stumbling blocks:

After allowing several minutes, challenge your class to make these issues a matter of prayer this week. Then close the session with a prayer of commitment.

Let's Talk It Over

The questions on this page are designed to promote discussion of the lesson by the class and to encourage application of the lesson Scriptures. The answers provided are only discussion starters. Let your class talk it over from there.

1. On a scale from one to ten, how would you rate yourself in the category of "waiting on the Lord" for a patient answer to the questions you have asked Him? What steps can you take to improve your score?

Allow students time to rate themselves. Some who want God to show His power and glory or to bring immediate justice might rank themselves very low. They may criticize themselves for their lack of patience.

This may not actually be a bad kind of impatience. If we are eager for God to be justified through demonstration of His power, we are really on His side and acting as His cheerleaders. This is not the same as being frustrated with God because He will not act the way we desire for meeting selfish requests (see James 4:1-3). As we focus on doing the work God assigned to us, we will grow in patience, allowing God to do His work on His own timetable.

2. When we pray we often have in mind the answer we want God to give us. Is that a good thing? Why, or why not? What guidelines will help us be ready for God's answer if it does not agree with our expectation?

Habakkuk is a good example. He was convinced that God would answer. He did not know when or how, but he prepared himself to listen. He continued in his faithfulness to God in every way. He also got ready to respond if God surprised him. He was ready to do the specific work God assigned him to do, no matter what.

3. What secrets (if that is the right term) need to be passed along to younger Christians about walking by faith versus trusting self to do it all?

The danger of trusting self can lead easily to the tendency to use inadequate or sinful means (cheating, violence, undue fear, etc.) to reach the desired results. The servant who buried his one talent is an example (Matthew 25:25).

In contrast, walking by faith means listening carefully to God's instructions and taking steps to follow those instructions. We may find this easier as we become familiar with the ways faithful individuals in the Bible struggled and succeeded in their walk with God. Many of us will also find

it easier if we venture out one step at a time while experiencing God's providential care as new situations unfold. Keeping a journal of the faithfulness of God in our lives will provide reminders over time that God can be trusted in all things.

4. How would you respond to someone who says that the use of wine (or any alcoholic beverage) could never become a problem in his or her life?

The Bible does not condemn wine as such (compare 1 Timothy 5:23). Sin does not come in a bottle. Yet the Scripture is very clear about the dangers that alcohol use poses. It can quickly affect a person's judgment, actions, and witness. Wine is cast in a negative light in Habakkuk 2:5 (also see vv. 15, 16).

Researchers (not to mention police officers!) have long known of the connection between the use of alcohol and domestic violence, traffic accidents, lost jobs, and impulsive decisions. Therefore the safest advice to anyone is either to abstain totally or to use alcohol only as Scripture implies.

5. How does knowing that God's plan will ultimately be fulfilled help you deal with situations in life in which evil seems to be in control? How do you need to grow spiritually in this regard?

Righteous people have always had to endure the negative aspects of living in a fallen world. While desiring to have a good life here for our 70 or so years on the earth is understandable, Christians must realize that we were created primarily to live eternally with God.

Therefore we are to be ready to remain faithful in the face of very difficult circumstances as we make our way toward living forever in eternity. Adopting a fatalistic approach—"what will be, will be"—is not productive. Yet being attuned to what God wants us to do to improve (not just endure) a situation requires spiritual maturity. Sometimes just pausing for a few minutes to reflect on the concept of eternity can help us keep a perspective. With that perspective, the Christian may be better able to detect doors of opportunity that God may be opening.

Committed to Accountability

DEVOTIONAL READING: 2 Chronicles 7:11-16.

**BACKGROUND SCRIPTURE: Jeremiah 7;
2 Kings 23:36, 37.**

**PRINTED TEXT: Jeremiah 7:1-4, 8-15; 2 Kings
23:36, 37.**

Jeremiah 7:1-4, 8-15

1 The word that came to Jeremiah from the LORD, saying,

2 Stand in the gate of the LORD's house, and proclaim there this word, and say, Hear the word of the LORD, all ye of Judah, that enter in at these gates to worship the LORD.

3 Thus saith the LORD of hosts, the God of Israel, Amend your ways and your doings, and I will cause you to dwell in this place.

4 Trust ye not in lying words, saying, The temple of the LORD, The temple of the LORD, The temple of the LORD, are these.

. . . .

8 Behold, ye trust in lying words, that cannot profit.

9 Will ye steal, murder, and commit adultery, and swear falsely, and burn incense unto Baal, and walk after other gods whom ye know not;

10 And come and stand before me in this house, which is called by my name, and say, We are delivered to do all these abominations?

11 Is this house, which is called by my name, become a den of robbers in your eyes? Behold, even I have seen it, saith the LORD.

12 But go ye now unto my place which was in Shiloh, where I set my name at the first, and see what I did to it for the wickedness of my people Israel.

13 And now, because ye have done all these works, saith the LORD, and I spake unto you, rising up early and speaking, but ye heard not; and I called you, but ye answered not;

14 Therefore will I do unto this house, which is called by my name, wherein ye trust, and unto the place which I gave to you and to your fathers, as I have done to Shiloh.

15 And I will cast you out of my sight, as I have cast out all your brethren, even the whole seed of Ephraim.

2 Kings 23:36, 37

36 Jehoiakim was twenty and five years old when he began to reign; and he reigned eleven years in Jerusalem. And his mother's name was Zebudah, the daughter of Pedaiah of Rumah.

37 And he did that which was evil in the sight of the LORD, according to all that his fathers had done.

GOLDEN TEXT: Go ye now unto my place which was in Shiloh, where I set my name
at the first, and see what I did to it for the wickedness of my people Israel. . . .
And I will cast you out of my sight, as I have cast out
all your brethren.—Jeremiah 7:12, 15.

Committed to Doing Right
Unit 2: What Does God Require?
(Lessons 5-9)

Lesson Aims

After participating in this lesson, each student will be able to:

1. List at least five sins for which God held His people accountable.

2. List at least five modern behaviors that are parallel to the sins of the ancient Judeans.

3. Examine his or her life for signs of these sins and take measures to resist them.

Lesson Outline

Introduction

A. Trusting in Lies

"If you tell a lie big enough and keep repeating it, people will eventually come to believe it." This was the strategy of Adolf Hitler's minister of propaganda, Joseph Goebbels. Goebbels and the Nazis perfected the modern art of misinformation, the concept of *the big lie*. Goebbels thought that the more outrageous the lie, the better, because the populace would think it was too extreme to be false.

As strange as that theory may seem to us, the Nazi propaganda machine successfully deceived the German people for over a decade. Yet the *big lie* technique did not originate with the Nazis. The history of human governments is littered with examples of lying kings and conquerors. Jeremiah the prophet was incensed by the ongoing deception of God's people by the leaders of Judah.

Jeremiah was particularly enraged by the deceptions of those who claimed to be speaking for God. He denounced this as villainy. As a true prophet of God, Jeremiah revealed God's displeasure: they "have spoken lying words in my name, which I have not commanded them" (Jeremiah 29:23). Jeremiah also castigated the people who trusted "in lying words, that cannot profit" (Jeremiah 7:8).

We as believers are called to be discerning of the truth. We have confidence that the Word of God is truth (John 17:17). Scripture is given to us as a measuring stick for all matters in life. Scripture is "the word of truth" (2 Timothy 2:15).

While some leaders in government are more truthful than others, history promises that the future holds more lying leaders. Today's *Honest Abe* may be replaced by tomorrow's *Deceiver*. The unfailing Word of God stands above all of this. God is the God of truth (Deuteronomy 32:4). God's Word is not a mixture of truth, opinion, and falsehood. It is all truth, and it has the power to transform and change us (2 Corinthians 6:7). The more we study God's Word and incorporate its teachings into our lives, the less likely we are to trust in lies.

B. Lesson Background

The writings contained in the book of Jeremiah are drawn from his four-decade ministry as a prophet of God to the nation of Judah. The book opens with prophecies from the thirteenth year of Josiah's reign, approximately 627 BC (Jeremiah 1:2). The book closes with events surrounding the destruction of Jerusalem by the Babylonians in 586 BC (39:2). The book is somewhat unusual for the prophets, for it contains both *oracles* (the words of the prophet delivered to the people) and *narrative* (accounts of historical events during this period).

The book of Jeremiah bears testimony that that prophet suffered a great deal for his prophetic ministry. Although he was assured by God that he was chosen even before birth, he protested about his inadequacy (Jeremiah 1:5, 6). Later he complained that his prophecies had made him an object of derision in public (20:7, 8).

Yet when Jeremiah tried to ignore God's prophetic voice in his life, it was as if his bones were on fire and he could not hold the words in (Jeremiah 20:9). This prophet's words caused him to be beaten and thrown into prison (37:15).

Later he was thrown into a dungeon-like cistern, where he wallowed in the smelly mire (38:6).

Most of Jeremiah's words are sharp and condemning. This has caused him to be seen as the prophet of doom and gloom. Because of this, we have adopted the English word *jeremiad,* meaning an angry tirade. In English literature, *a Jeremiah* is symbolic of a person who is a persistent and vocal pessimist.

Yet Jeremiah also has a hopeful side. One of the most stirring passages in all the Old Testament is Jeremiah's vision of the new covenant. He foresaw this as a time when the law of God would be a matter of the heart, not just observance (Jeremiah 31:33), and that the sin of the people would no longer be remembered by God (Jeremiah 31:34). Jeremiah's vision of fresh, new beginnings was adopted by the author of Hebrews to explain the new covenant that has been given to the church as the people of God (see Hebrews 8).

This week's lesson is drawn from one of the prophet's warnings against evil among the people of Judah. It is a biting condemnation of hypocrisy, particularly in worship.

I. False Security
(Jeremiah 7:1-4)

A. Hearing the True Word (vv. 1, 2)

1, 2. The word that came to Jeremiah from the LORD, saying, Stand in the gate of the LORD's house, and proclaim there this word, and say, Hear the word of the LORD, all ye of Judah, that enter in at these gates to worship the LORD.

How to Say It

ASSYRIANS. Uh-*sear*-e-unz.
BAAL. *Bay*-ul.
BABYLONIANS. Bab-ih-*low*-nee-unz.
CANAANITES. *Kay*-nun-ites.
CHALDEANS. Kal-*dee*-unz.
DIOGENES OF SINOPE. Die-*ah*-jin-eez of Suh-*no*-peh.
EPHRAIM. *Ee*-fray-im.
JEHOIAKIM. Jeh-*hoy*-uh-kim.
JEREMIAD. jair-uh-*my*-ud.
JOSIAH. Jo-*sigh*-uh.
MANASSEH. Muh-*nass*-uh.
NEBUCHADNEZZAR. *Neb*-yuh-kud-*nez*-er (strong accent on *nez*).
PEDAIAH. Peh-*day*-yuh.
PHILISTINES. Fuh-*liss*-teens or *Fill*-us-teens.
ZEBUDAH. Ze-*bu*-duh.

Routines and habits provide a sense of security. We put out the trash on Wednesday, mow the grass on Friday, do laundry on Saturday, and go to church on Sunday. We work the same job and live in the same house for many years. What happens when the routine is disrupted—our trash day is changed to Monday, the washing machine breaks down, and we lose our job? Such changes can make us feel insecure.

Jeremiah wants his people to know that routine does not equal a strong, secure relationship with God. We may appear religious because we do certain things on a regular basis, yet be far from the will of God. Our relationship may be empty and false. This is as true today as it was in Jeremiah's time.

God does not call Jeremiah to evangelize the pagan masses of the ancient world. His message is for the (supposed) people of God, the citizens of Jerusalem. His target audience is even more selective as shown by the location for preaching given to him: he is to stand at *the gate of the Lord's house,* meaning the main entry point of the temple in Jerusalem. Those he is to address are not coming for business, education, or meetings. They are coming *to worship* in the house of *the Lord.* They are following their routine, just as many attend church services each Sunday without much thought. [See question #1, page 406.]

The gate is more than a doorway into the temple. It is an impressive structure that is more like a pass-through building than a simple wall opening. Gates in the ancient world can have rooms and open areas. They serve as gathering places. In the cities of ancient Israel, gates are places where judges dispense justice to the public (see Amos 5:15). Jeremiah's cry at the gate of the temple is to be a call for justice and righteousness and truth in worship.

B. Rejecting Soothing Lies (vv. 3, 4)

3. Thus saith the LORD of hosts, the God of Israel, Amend your ways and your doings, and I will cause you to dwell in this place.

Jeremiah's message is a warning with a promise: Quit sinning and *God* will let you continue to live in the land *of Israel.* Jeremiah is calling for a change in hearts and in practices. Empty ritual is not acceptable worship. Idolatrous practices are not tolerable for God (see Jeremiah 8:19).

Some of the hearers must wonder what is so wrong. Aren't they being faithful to worship at the house of the Lord? Aren't they wearing their best temple-go-to-meetin' clothes? Don't they bring their offerings? Don't they sing the temple praise songs? Haven't they repeated the proper prayers? Why is this prophet haranguing them?

4. Trust ye not in lying words, saying, The temple of the LORD, The temple of the LORD, The temple of the LORD, are these.

Jeremiah's prophecy of doom for Judah is not new. It has been preached since the time of Isaiah. Yet through decades of national crisis and foreign threat, the southern kingdom of Judah has survived. *The temple* is some 300 years old by this time. It has survived threats from enemies such as the Assyrians, the Egyptians, and the Chaldeans (Babylonians).

But that is exactly the point for Jeremiah: the presence of this house of worship has given the people a false sense of security! They believe that the temple is a sign of God's continued favor and protection. Jeremiah mocks the temple worshipers by repeating their falsely confident refrain, "This is *The temple of the Lord, The temple of the Lord, The temple of the Lord.*" Tradition, history, and edifices count for nothing when hearts are false. [See question #2, page 406.]

II. Delusional Duplicity (Jeremiah 7:8-15)

A. Double Life of Worship (vv. 8-10)

8. Behold, ye trust in lying words, that cannot profit.

Trusting in a lie does not make it the truth, for a lie will always be a lie. False security is just that: false. There is no value in accepting untruth, no matter how sincere and passionate the liar may be. Lies will always fail. They cannot protect us.

Visual for Lesson 8. *Use this visual to challenge your students to name actions for which they suffered immediate or delayed consequences.*

There is a story about Diogenes of Sinope, who comes along some 200 years after Jeremiah. The story pictures him as wandering around ancient Greece with a lantern in daylight, unsuccessfully searching for an honest man. Earlier in his book, Jeremiah also had searched Jerusalem for a person who was on the side of truth and justice (Jeremiah 5:1). God hoped for such a person, for this would be reason to spare Jerusalem. But Jeremiah's quest was as futile as that of Diogenes. How sad it is when truth is seen as optional, and we find ourselves loving lies!

9, 10. Will ye steal, murder, and commit adultery, and swear falsely, and burn incense unto Baal, and walk after other gods whom ye know not; and come and stand before me in this house, which is called by my name, and say, We are delivered to do all these abominations?

Jeremiah's complaint now gets very specific. He charges that the people of Judah have violated six of the Ten Commandments (Deuteronomy 5:7-21). They are thieves (Commandment Eight). They have committed *murder* (Commandment Six). They are adulterers (Commandment Seven). They have given false witness (Commandment Nine). They have worshiped *other gods* and made idols of them (Commandments One and Two).

Jeremiah warns that God knows of these *abominations.* God does not overlook them just because the people are going through the motions of worship at the temple. Most offensive to God is the mix of His worship with the worship of false gods like Baal of the Canaanites. This false worship is a sure way to bring about the wrath of the Lord (see Judges 2:13, 14). [See question #3, page 406.]

PROBABILISM

A theory of moral theology known as *probabilism* came into being in the seventeenth century AD. The main idea is that if you can find a good ethical motive behind an action, even if it is highly improbable, then the action can be defended as allowable.

For example, if a merchant cannot sell his wine at a fair profit, he can add water to it and sell it as pure in order to make the profit. If servants are not being paid a proper wage by their master, they may take property from the master that will make up the difference. If necessity forces a person to take wood from someone else's pile, he is not obligated to restore it. If someone has committed a crime, he may swear in a loud voice, "I have not done this crime" and then in a subdued voice add, "today." Thus the total statement is true, and he is exonerated from falsehood.

The result of probabilism is to take moral laws and turn them inside out. Jeremiah condemned this kind of thinking centuries before Christ. This condemnation still stands. —J. B. N.

B. Den of Robbers (v. 11)

11. Is this house, which is called by my name, become a den of robbers in your eyes? Behold, even I have seen it, saith the LORD.

Jeremiah now brings a devastating charge against Judah: the hypocritical dishonesty of the leaders has found a home within the temple precincts. This has made the house of the Lord *a den of robbers.*

This charge likely has to do with the commerce going on in the temple courts, the location of a financial center for the nation. Rather than conduct business with integrity and truth, dealing is done with deception and greediness. This will also be a problem during the time of Jesus several centuries later. He will cleanse the temple of His day by running out the money changers and merchants (see Mark 11:15-17). [See question #4, page 406.]

C. Disaster of Shiloh (vv. 12-15)

12. But go ye now unto my place which was in Shiloh, where I set my name at the first, and see what I did to it for the wickedness of my people Israel.

Shiloh was the original location in the promised land of the house of the Lord. This was the tabernacle transported by Israel through the wilderness. The tabernacle at Shiloh had become a more permanent structure than the tent of the exodus and was sometimes referred to as the temple (see 1 Samuel 1:9).

Although we do not have details, the Old Testament hints in several places that God allowed this former sanctuary to be destroyed, perhaps by the Philistines (see Psalm 78:60). The ruins of this temple are still around in Jeremiah's day. Those ruins should serve as a warning that building a house for God does not guarantee God's favor.

13. And now, because ye have done all these works, saith the LORD, and I spake unto you, rising up early and speaking, but ye heard not; and I called you, but ye answered not.

Jeremiah's final accusation at this point is that the people of the temple repeatedly have turned a deaf ear to God's pleas for change. Although they are regular worshipers, they have forgotten the one whom they worship.

What we call *worship time* can easily become a noisy series of presentations designed to please the audience. We should remember that God is present at our worship efforts, and He may be *speaking* to us. By this we do not mean that we should expect an audible voice coming from Heaven. Rather, the idea is to expect our hearts to be touched through Scripture and prayer and praise. When God's Holy Spirit is prompting us to change our lives, to admit and abandon the love of sinful practices, then we should listen. [See question #5, page 406.]

14, 15. Therefore will I do unto this house, which is called by my name, wherein ye trust, and unto the place which I gave to you and to your fathers, as I have done to Shiloh. And I will cast you out of my sight, as I have cast out all your brethren, even the whole seed of Ephraim.

History has a habit of repeating itself, even in tragic ways. Jeremiah reminds the hearers that God had *cast out all* their *brethren, even the whole seed of Ephraim* (signifying the northern kingdom of Israel) on account of persistent sin and rebellion.

God also has abandoned an earlier temple of Israel, the sanctuary at *Shiloh.* God will do it again with the southern kingdom of Judah and the Jerusalem temple. And, let us be forewarned, God can do it with any church that tolerates and grows comfortable with a hypocritical lifestyle and empty, meaningless worship practices. The warnings in Revelation 2 and 3 are important to heed!

TRANQUILITY?

In Hebrew, the word *Shiloh* means "tranquility, rest." When the Israelites conquered the land of Canaan, they set up the tabernacle at Shiloh. This remained the seat of worship for some time. The tabernacle was still there in the early years of Samuel.

When the Philistines returned the Ark of the Covenant after its capture, it was not returned to Shiloh. Instead, it ultimately was sent to Jerusalem. The town of Shiloh began to decline; this continued into the days of Jeremiah. How interesting that a place named *tranquility* would come to represent desolation.

Because of its positive Old Testament connotations, many churches have been named *Shiloh.* One of the most interesting was a small country Methodist church in southern Tennessee near a spot on the Tennessee River called Pittsburgh Landing. A major battle of the American Civil War was fought there on April 6 and 7, 1862.

Much of the battle swirled around the church building itself. Some 100,000 soldiers fought there, suffering over 23,000 casualties. How ironic that a place whose name means "tranquility" would be the scene of such horrible violence and death.

Yet that is a message of Jeremiah. God has been patient, but ultimately He will wreak vengeance upon the faithlessness of His people. Shiloh was desolate, and Jerusalem would be destroyed. Such is eventually the case with all who abandon God's paths to seek their own way.   —J. B. N.

III. Failed Leadership
(2 Kings 23:36, 37)

36, 37. Jehoiakim was twenty and five years old when he began to reign; and he reigned eleven years in Jerusalem. And his mother's name was Zebudah, the daughter of Pedaiah of Rumah. And he did that which was evil in the sight of the LORD, according to all that his fathers had done.

The historical record of the Old Testament shows that Judah did not heed Jeremiah's dire warnings. King *Jehoiakim began to reign* in 609 BC, and he was the son of the reformer King Josiah (Jeremiah 22:18). But the son did not continue his father's efforts to bring Israel back to an obedient relationship with the Lord. Instead, he chose the path of Manasseh and did *evil*. Jeremiah tells us that Jehoiakim went so far as to burn, out of contempt, a scroll of prophetic warnings (36:22, 23, 28).

In 2 Kings 24:1-5 (which may have been written by Jeremiah) we learn that Jehoiakim arrogantly rebelled against Babylonian King Nebuchadnezzar. The result was disaster, for that king had been sent by God. Nebuchadnezzar

looted the temple and physically humiliated Jehoiakim (2 Chronicles 36:6, 7). God's will, as proclaimed by Jeremiah, was accomplished. God's will shall always be accomplished!

Conclusion

A. Hypocrites I Have Known

We do not live in ancient Jerusalem. We do not worship at Solomon's temple. We need not fear Nebuchadnezzar and the Babylonian army. But Jeremiah's word should still be heard in our churches today. Are our efforts to worship God motivated by a true heart, or are they the empty acts of self-serving hypocrites?

As one who has ministered in many different churches for several decades, I have observed various hypocrites in action: the church staff member who complained about the miserly giving of the congregation, yet didn't give proportionately himself; the elder who griped about the rambunctious behavior of the youth group while having an affair with his secretary; the worship leader who focused the singing time on herself, then grumbled that the people weren't singing; the Sunday school teacher who carried the biggest Bible I've ever seen, yet was so dishonest in his business dealings that no one in the church would patronize his store; the committee member who had just paid cash for a new SUV, yet moaned when a missionary asked for funds to replace his 10-year-old van, which had in excess of 300,000 miles on it.

But I know the biggest hypocrite even more intimately. He is the one who wants Sunday worship only according to his tastes, not for God's glory. He is the one who gives far less than he could because he spends so much on his own whims. He is the one who looks down on those who don't know the Bible as well as he, but often turns a deaf ear to Scripture that confronts his life. That hypocrite is me.

B. Prayer

Heavenly Father, God of ancient Israel and of the church, have patience with us. Please don't give up on reminding us of our hypocrisy and sin. Give us the spiritual strength to change and the joy that comes from serving You with clean hands and a pure heart. We pray this in the name of the one who never acted with hypocrisy, Jesus Christ Your Son, amen.

C. Thought to Remember

God holds us accountable
to serve Him without hypocrisy.

Home Daily Bible Readings

Monday, July 16—Pay Greater Attention (Hebrews 2:1-4)

Tuesday, July 17—Forgiveness Is Possible (2 Chronicles 7:11-16)

Wednesday, July 18—Choices of Consequences (1 Kings 9:1-9)

Thursday, July 19—Disaster Is Coming (Jeremiah 19:1-6)

Friday, July 20—Downfall Threatened (Jeremiah 26:1-6)

Saturday, July 21—Amend Your Ways (Jeremiah 7:1-7)

Sunday, July 22—Judgment of the Wicked (Jeremiah 7:8-15)

Learning by Doing

This page contains an alternative lesson plan emphasizing learning activities. Classes desiring such student involvement will find these suggestions helpful.

Learning Goals

After participating in this lesson, each student will be able to:

1. List at least five sins for which God held His people accountable.

2. List at least five modern behaviors that are parallel to the sins of the ancient Judeans.

3. Examine his or her life for signs of these sins and take measures to resist them.

Into the Lesson

Say, "Sometimes we can get a false sense of security about our daily environment." To illustrate this point, ask your students to rank-order these creatures according to how many people they kill each year in the United States: bears; cougars; dogs; insects and spiders; sharks; and snakes. (This activity is also in the student book.)

Answers are: 1. insects and spiders (50 to 150 deaths per year, not counting deaths from illnesses borne by mosquitoes); 2. dogs (about 15 deaths per year); 3. snakes (10 to 12); 4. sharks (2); 5. bears (fewer than 1); 6. cougars (fewer than 0.5).

After you have discussed their answers, say, "Sometimes the things we may fear the most, such as sharks and bears, are far less dangerous to us than things we take for granted, such as insects or dogs. Today's lesson deals with Judah's failure to realize the danger of their shallow religious routines."

Into the Word

Deliver a brief introductory lecture from the Lesson Background to help your students understand Jeremiah's ministry. This will set the stage for the passages they will be studying.

Next, distribute copies of the following true-false statements (or direct your students to their student books, where this quiz is also found). Tell your students to read Jeremiah 7:1-4, 8-15, and 2 Kings 23:36, 37 to find the answers to this quiz. (Answers are provided in parentheses, but don't distribute those.)

1. God told Jeremiah to preach in the gate of Solomon's temple in Jerusalem *(true, Jeremiah 7:1)*; 2. God ordered the Jews to amend their ways *(true, v. 3)*; 3. Jeremiah instructed the Jews to chant the phrase "the temple of the Lord" *(false, v. 4)*; 4. Jeremiah accused the Jews of burning incense to the false god Dagon *(false, v. 9)*; 5. God accused the Jews of making the temple a den of robbers *(true, v. 11)*; 6. God said that He had set His name (located His tabernacle) first at Shiloh *(true, v. 12)*; 7. God warned Judah that He would destroy the temple, just as He had destroyed the tabernacle at Shiloh *(true, v. 14)*; 8. God also warned that He would remove Judah from the land, just as He had removed Ephraim *(true, v. 15)*; 9. Jehoiakim was 30 years old when he became king of Judah *(false, 2 Kings 23:36)*; 10. Jehoiakim was a great religious reformer like his father, Josiah *(false, v. 37)*.

When your students have completed the quiz, review the correct answers and discuss the meaning of the text. Use the following questions for discussion:

1. Why would Jeremiah stand in the gate of the temple to deliver his message? *2.* What offer did God make to the Jews if they changed their ways? *3.* How were the people given a false sense of security by the existence of the temple? *4.* Of what specific sins were the Jews guilty? *5.* How had the Jews made the temple a den of robbers? (Remember that Jesus leveled the same charge; Mark 11:15-17.) *6.* What punishment did God threaten against Judah? *7.* How would they know God's threat was genuine? *8.* Who was Jehoiakim? What happened to him?

Into Life

Reproduce this chart to give to your students:

Judah's Sins	Our Sins
1. Trust in the temple	
2. Theft	
3. Murder	
4. Adultery	
5. False gods	

Ask your students to note one or two sins common today that are comparable to the sins of Judah. For example, they could list *tax fraud* in place of *theft* or *abortion* in place of *murder*.

Next, instruct your students to turn to 1 Corinthians 6:9-11 and 1 John 1:8–2:2 to see what God expects us to do about such sins today. Ask them to write a brief summary of God's instructions. Discuss the fact that God still offers forgiveness for people who return to Him through Christ.

Let's Talk It Over

The questions on this page are designed to promote discussion of the lesson by the class and to encourage application of the lesson Scriptures. The answers provided are only discussion starters. Let your class talk it over from there.

1. What are some innovations in the activities or schedules of your church that would be valuable in helping people hear God's messages?

If your students need something to jumpstart their thinking on this question, ask them what has been helpful from the past in allowing a fresh look at the depths of God's Word (examples: lakeside services, conferences, retreats). Some ideas they may suggest include moving the place or time of worship once a month, having the minister preaching on the steps of the church as people arrive, or showing appropriate clips of movies that illustrate secret sins.

2. What misconceptions, routines, slogans, and habits do people hold onto today that parallel the comfortable lies and behavior of the Jewish people in the text? How do today's lies hamper the effectiveness of the church? What do we do to expose those lies?

As the church builds bridges into the surrounding culture, secular thinking can get into the church as a result. A two-way street is inevitable in this regard. It is not uncommon to hear people at church repeating slogans they heard from movies and to see those slogans become part of their lives. The primary difficulty arises when these snippets of pop psychology lead people to trust in something other than God.

Certain church traditions, which may have served valid purposes in the past, can become pointless routines at best and delusions at worst. People who find undue comfort in a saying, setting, or tradition place themselves in danger. Discuss how individuals as well as entire congregations can be lulled into spiritual sleep through false trust in these areas.

3. If God sent a specific message to Christians today, what list of sins do you think He would give to expose how people act one way in worship and another way the rest of the week?

Put your students' answers into two lists: a list of sins of *commission* (lying, stealing, murder, etc.) and the sins of *omission* (failing to help those in need, neglecting use of spiritual gifts, etc.). Include both the spiritual and social consequences in the discussion.

For those who live in consumer-driven democracies, a pointed discussion on covetousness (the Tenth Commandment) will be in order. Bring in some glossy ads from the Sunday paper and discuss how these entice people to want more. Discuss how covetousness ties with idolatry (Colossians 3:5).

4. In what ways could God refer to today's church as a "den of robbers"? What can the church do to rectify this situation?

Methods of corruption exist today that did not exist in the first century AD. One example is a person who hands to the church treasurer a check made out to the church, then asks for a lesser amount in change—in order to claim on his or her income tax return the full amount of the check as an offering.

A second situation would be shady business leaders who attend church to give themselves an aura of respectability and to make business contacts. The result is to use the church in a way that God does not intend. A third possibility could be a church's decision to pour its funds overwhelmingly into buildings and stained glass while the physical needs of the community's poor are ignored. (There is nothing wrong with stained glass, but a certain balance is called for!) There are many other examples.

5. If you were asked to be a spiritual accountability partner by another Christian, what steps would you take to help your friend ensure that his or her worship does not become an empty ritual?

An accountability partner should be good at both gentle encouragement and the ability to ask pointed questions. Some examples are, "How is your prayer life?" "How are you really doing in your private worship?" "What did you do yesterday to draw closer to God?" "In your responses to me, have you been less than fully open and honest on any of your answers?"

The accountability partner's goals include celebrating growth, inquiring about weak spots, and helping one's friend find ways to enhance his or her walk with the Lord. Every class and church can encourage members to have such partners.

Committed to Trusting God

DEVOTIONAL READING: Psalm 145:13b-21.

BACKGROUND SCRIPTURE: Jeremiah 28, 29.

PRINTED TEXT: Jeremiah 29:1-14.

Jeremiah 29:1-14

1 Now these are the words of the letter that Jeremiah the prophet sent from Jerusalem unto the residue of the elders which were carried away captives, and to the priests, and to the prophets, and to all the people whom Nebuchadnezzar had carried away captive from Jerusalem to Babylon;

2 (After that Jeconiah the king, and the queen, and the eunuchs, the princes of Judah and Jerusalem, and the carpenters, and the smiths, were departed from Jerusalem;)

3 By the hand of Elasah the son of Shaphan, and Gemariah the son of Hilkiah, (whom Zedekiah king of Judah sent unto Babylon to Nebuchadnezzar king of Babylon) saying,

4 Thus saith the LORD of hosts, the God of Israel, unto all that are carried away captives, whom I have caused to be carried away from Jerusalem unto Babylon;

5 Build ye houses, and dwell in them; and plant gardens, and eat the fruit of them;

6 Take ye wives, and beget sons and daughters; and take wives for your sons, and give your daughters to husbands, that they may bear sons and daughters; that ye may be increased there, and not diminished.

7 And seek the peace of the city whither I have caused you to be carried away captives, and pray unto the LORD for it: for in the peace thereof shall ye have peace.

8 For thus saith the LORD of hosts, the God of Israel; Let not your prophets and your diviners, that be in the midst of you, deceive you, neither hearken to your dreams which ye cause to be dreamed.

9 For they prophesy falsely unto you in my name: I have not sent them, saith the LORD.

10 For thus saith the LORD, That after seventy years be accomplished at Babylon I will visit you, and perform my good word toward you, in causing you to return to this place.

11 For I know the thoughts that I think toward you, saith the LORD, thoughts of peace, and not of evil, to give you an expected end.

12 Then shall ye call upon me, and ye shall go and pray unto me, and I will hearken unto you.

13 And ye shall seek me, and find me, when ye shall search for me with all your heart.

14 And I will be found of you, saith the LORD: and I will turn away your captivity, and I will gather you from all the nations, and from all the places whither I have driven you, saith the LORD; and I will bring you again into the place whence I caused you to be carried away captive.

Jul
29

GOLDEN TEXT: I know the thoughts that I think toward you, saith the LORD, thoughts of peace, and not of evil, to give you an expected end.—Jeremiah 29:11.

Committed to Doing Right
Unit 2: What Does God Require?
(Lessons 5-9)

Lesson Aims

After participating in this lesson, each student will be able to:

1. Outline Jeremiah's letter to the captives.

2. Outline a letter that a modern Jeremiah could write to people of his own society.

3. Suggest one or two ways that he or she can seek the Lord more wholeheartedly on a daily basis.

Lesson Outline

Introduction

A. Desperate Living

I saw her again the other day. She was in the frozen-food section at the supermarket. This time she was tall and very thin. She had dark hair and a light complexion. At first I thought her face was dirty. Then I realized that even her heavy makeup could not hide the bruises. Her eyes were downcast, her expression blank.

But our eyes met for just an instant as our shopping carts passed, and I was stunned by her look of fear and pain. Who had beaten her? Boyfriend? Husband? Father? I realized that I had seen her too many times. Sometimes she had been short and blond. Other times her skin had been dark. She was the woman betrayed by a man who should have protected her, and she saw no way out of her wretched situation. She finished her shopping and returned to her world of horror.

Henry David Thoreau (1817–1862) wrote, "The mass of men lead lives of quiet desperation." This is still true. We drag ourselves through each day, overwhelmed by commitments, bills, and worries. We live vicariously through pop celebrities, sports heroes, or other media creations. When we are asked how we are doing, we automatically say, "Fine." But we aren't "fine." In our heart of hearts, many of us have given up hope and see nothing in the future but playing out a life of drudgery.

This is not what God intends for us, though. God wants us to be people of hope, not fear. God created us to live with confident assurance, not daily desperation and aimless distraction. Today's lesson gives a clear view of the irrefutable fact that God intends the very best for His people. He asks that we trust Him and obey Him. He will give us full, rich lives.

B. Lesson Background

It is difficult to imagine a more desperate time in history than the Jerusalem of Jeremiah's day. Religious and moral confusion reigned in the city and the surrounding countryside (Jeremiah 5:1; 11:13). The city was under constant danger from foreign invaders (1:15; 6:1). The threat of God's wrath was against the city (4:4); the Lord Almighty promised to lay the city in ruins (6:8; 9:11). Jeremiah constantly preached that the future for Jerusalem was dismal (see 13:16).

In spite of these dire warnings from Jeremiah and other prophets such as Zephaniah and Habakkuk, the leaders of the nation did not respond. Instead, they continued in ways of rank wickedness (see Jeremiah 22:17; 29:19). The few who understood the implications of Jeremiah's condemnation must have felt powerless, helpless, and without hope. National disaster would destroy them too even if, individually, they heeded Jeremiah's call to repent.

The Babylonians controlled Judah for many years before the destruction of Jerusalem in 586 BC. This control began about 605 BC, after the Babylonians defeated the Egyptians at the epic Battle of Carchemish (Jeremiah 46:2). After that, the Babylonians were the masters of the ancient world, including Jerusalem and Judah.

Three distinct groups of citizens from Judah were transported to Babylon (Jeremiah 52:28-30). Daniel was likely a member of the first group, taken about 605 BC. Ezekiel was a member of a group that was transported after the capture of Jerusalem in about 597 BC. The largest group was taken after Jerusalem's destruction in 586 BC. Jeremiah himself was not taken to Babylon but ended up in Egypt after the city was destroyed.

Jeremiah is often portrayed as a prophet of doom. Yet his book also offers hope for the future. Although Judah would be devastated, virtually ceasing to exist, God planned to gather a remnant of faithful people to rebuild the city (Jeremiah 23:3). This would be the cause of great rejoicing (31:7-14). This ray of hope shines brightly in Jeremiah 29, the focus of today's lesson.

I. Communication in Captivity
(Jeremiah 29:1-3)

In the tense periods between Nebuchadnezzar's initial deportation of hostages and exiles (605 BC), the capture of Jerusalem (597 BC), and the city's destruction (586 BC), Jeremiah works actively as a spokesman for God. In that role he interprets these judgmental events for the nation. His ministry even involves communication with the leaders in exile, those who had been transported to Babylon in 597 BC or earlier.

A. Judah Is Uprooted (vv. 1, 2)

1. Now these are the words of the letter that Jeremiah the prophet sent from Jerusalem unto the residue of the elders which were carried away captives, and to the priests, and to the prophets, and to all the people whom Nebuchadnezzar had carried away captive from Jerusalem to Babylon.

How to Say It

CARCHEMISH. *Kar*-key-mish.
ELASAH. *El*-ah-sah.
EUPHRATES. You-*fray*-teez.
GEMARIAH. Gem-uh-*rye*-uh (G as in get).
HABAKKUK. Huh-*back*-kuk.
HILKIAH. Hill-*kye*-uh.
JECONIAH. *Jek*-o-*nye*-uh (strong accent on *nye*).
JEHOIAKIM. Jeh-*hoy*-uh-kim.
SABAOTH. *Sab*-a-oth.
SHAPHAN. *Shay*-fan.
ZEDEKIAH. Zed-uh-*kye*-uh.
ZEPHANIAH. Zef-uh-*nye*-uh.

If you were to travel straight across the desert from *Jerusalem* to ancient *Babylon,* the distance would be about 500 miles. But following the northern route, through the Babylonian administrative center of Riblah and down the Euphrates River valley, would make the distance more like 880 miles.

This is a well-traveled road in Jeremiah's day, and it takes six to eight weeks to make the journey. In the period between Jerusalem's capture and its destruction, those left in the city seem to communicate regularly with their exiled brothers and sisters in Babylon. Jeremiah's ability to send the exiles a *letter* is a confirmation of this.

2. (After that Jeconiah the king, and the queen, and the eunuchs, the princes of Judah and Jerusalem, and the carpenters, and the smiths, were departed from Jerusalem.)

Jeconiah was the son of Jehoiakim. His surrender of Jerusalem in 597 BC allowed Nebuchadnezzar to sack the city and loot the temple (see 2 Kings 24:11-15). This verse thus dates the prophecy we are studying between 597 and 586 BC, during the reign of King Zedekiah in Jerusalem. Daniel and Ezekiel, who are in Babylon, are among the possible recipients of this letter. (See Daniel 9:2, which shows his acquaintance with the writings of Jeremiah.)

B. Judah Is Not Forgotten (v. 3)

3. By the hand of Elasah the son of Shaphan, and Gemariah the son of Hilkiah, (whom Zedekiah king of Judah sent unto Babylon to Nebuchadnezzar king of Babylon) saying.

King *Zedekiah* uses two emissaries to communicate with his master, King *Nebuchadnezzar.* These men, *Elasah* and *Gemariah,* also serve the purpose of carrying Jeremiah's letter to the proper recipients in exile. [See question #1, page 414.] The people in Jeremiah's target audience have been displaced. But he has not forgotten them.

II. Waiting in Captivity
(Jeremiah 29:4-9)

The actual content of the letter begins with Jeremiah 29:4.

A. Build Lives While Waiting (vv. 4-6)

4. Thus saith the LORD of hosts, the God of Israel, unto all that are carried away captives, whom I have caused to be carried away from Jerusalem unto Babylon.

The letter begins with two titles for God. First, He is the *Lord of hosts.* Another way of saying this is Lord Sabaoth (compare Romans 9:29), meaning "master of the hosts of heavenly armies." It is a strong affirmation of the power of God.

Second, He is the *God of Israel*. The capture of Jerusalem and exile of its leaders do not mean that God has ceased to be Israel's God. He is still in control and has even *caused* the captivity according to His plan.

5, 6. Build ye houses, and dwell in them; and plant gardens, and eat the fruit of them; take ye wives, and beget sons and daughters; and take wives for your sons, and give your daughters to husbands, that they may bear sons and daughters; that ye may be increased there, and not diminished.

Even after tragedy, life goes on. After disaster, you must recover, pick up the pieces, and keep living. God is telling Israel not to wait for some kind of quick solution and a return to Jerusalem. They need to understand that they are there for many years, so they should make the best of it. God still cares for them. His will is that their lives improve *(be increased)* and that they have opportunities to flourish. He is still their God and wants to bless them. [See question #2, page 414.]

TIMING

Timing is everything may be a bit of an overstatement but not by much! Often knowing *when* to do something is at least as important—if not more so—than knowing *how* to do it. During the American Civil War, Union General George B. McClellan was a genius when it came to organization and discipline but a failure at timing.

McClellan had overwhelming superiority during the Peninsular Campaign of 1862. But he was hesitant to attack. Ultimately, Confederate General Robert E. Lee took the initiative and forced McClellan out of Virginia. Later at Antietam, McClellan had a copy of Lee's battle plan. But still McClellan hesitated. He never threw all his forces into the battle. There is a time to be cautious, but there is also a time to attack. McClellan never seemed to know the difference.

When Grant faced Lee two years later, he knew it was time to attack. So he moved his army south. Even after the bloody battles of the Wilderness and Spotsylvania, Grant moved south. When it was time for movement, he moved. When it was time for trench warfare at Petersburg, he dug in. When the Confederate line cracked and Lee pulled out, Grant followed him and forced his surrender. Grant understood timing.

The Jews hungered for a return to Jerusalem, but Jeremiah knew that that was premature; return would occur decades later. Jeremiah was sensitive to God's timetable. Are we?   —J. B. N.

B. Seek Peace While Waiting (v. 7)

7. And seek the peace of the city whither I have caused you to be carried away captives, and pray unto the LORD for it: for in the peace thereof shall ye have peace.

Peace is a loaded term in the Old Testament. Coming from the word *shalom*, it means much more than simple absence of warfare. It has the added sense of prosperity and welfare.

God's message for the exiles is that they should desire and *pray* for the peace and prosperity of their new community (Babylon), even though they have been brought there against their will. As Babylon prospers, so they will prosper. When Jeremiah writes, the prosperity of the exiled Jews is dependent upon the peace of this *city*, not the peace of Jerusalem.

C. Reject Deception While Waiting (vv. 8, 9)

8. For thus saith the LORD of hosts, the God of Israel; Let not your prophets and your diviners, that be in the midst of you, deceive you, neither hearken to your dreams which ye cause to be dreamed.

There are *prophets* among the exiles who are telling them that freedom is just around the corner. Their dreams and longings are focused on going home. The mighty God of Israel warns against this deception. This can be either self-deception *(your dreams)* or an attempt to deceive the exiles by false prophecy.

9. For they prophesy falsely unto you in my name: I have not sent them, saith the LORD.

The false prophet is a long-standing problem in the nation of Israel. Such people have contributed to circumstances leading to the capture of Jerusalem. The false prophets blamed the captivity in Babylon on the wrong reasons; they failed to pronounce that God was punishing Judah for its iniquity (Lamentations 2:14). Ezekiel, who prophesies in Babylon at about the same time Jeremiah is working in Jerusalem, sees the core problem when he says these prophets invoke the name of the Lord "when the Lord hath not spoken" (Ezekiel 22:28).

A true prophet speaks for God, with God's authority. The nature of this position makes it easily susceptible to abuse and fakery. Even today, we should be careful whenever we encounter someone claiming to speak directly for God as a prophet. God has given us His Scripture to measure such words. The biblical pattern is that true prophets usually point out sin and call for repentance rather than tell people that prosperity is just around the corner (Jeremiah 6:13, 14). [See question #3, page 414.]

III. Promised Freedom from Captivity (Jeremiah 29:10-14)

Having warned against the false prophets and having given strategies for the survival of the exile, Jeremiah now lays out a set of four promises from the Lord for the future of His people.

A. Promise of Return (v. 10)

10. For thus saith the LORD, That after seventy years be accomplished at Babylon I will visit you, and perform my good word toward you, in causing you to return to this place.

Jeremiah begins with a promise of *return* to Jerusalem. This is a classic good news/bad news message. The good news? The exile will not last forever. The bad news? Most adults hearing this will not live to see it, for it will be two or three generations down the road.

The prophecy of 70 years proves to be accurate. The first group of exiles (including Daniel) was taken to *Babylon* when Nebuchadnezzar became the king, about 605 BC. The Babylonian empire falls to King Cyrus of Persia in 538 BC. Cyrus serves as God's battle-axe to break the power of the Babylonians (see Jeremiah 51:20). Cyrus then grants permission for the Jews to return to Jerusalem and rebuild the temple. That return begins in about 536 BC (see Daniel 9:2).

B. Promise of Prosperity (v. 11)

11. For I know the thoughts that I think toward you, saith the LORD, thoughts of peace, and not of evil, to give you an expected end.

We should understand *thoughts* as future plans that God has for Israel. God plans that the exiles will see *peace,* meaning future prosperity rather than new devastation. They will gain *an expected end*, meaning the future they hope for. This will be a return to the land of their inheritance (Judah), to their holy city (Jerusalem). There they will rebuild the house of the Lord (the temple). This is the second promise, the promise of future prosperity for Israel.

Although this promise was made to the exiles of ancient Judah, it still has application for us today. God's desire is that we prosper. Our Lord is not a vengeful, cruel God who delights in punishing us. He waits for our trust and obedience so that He may bless us with His bounty. [See question #4, page 414.]

CAPTIVES

Captives. The word itself has a quite negative ring to it. The immediate word-picture is that of people confined and held against their will,

probably herded off to some distant place they don't want to go.

History is filled with stories of captives. The Romans took many captives from their conquered lands, using their muscle power as the fuel to drive the empire. People from Africa were captured, sold into slavery, and transported to the New World. One of my ancestors was a 7-year-old running the streets of London in 1750. He woke up one morning on a ship bound for America. He had been kidnapped and was then sold as an indentured servant in colonial Virginia.

Many people are "captives" of their jobs, economically dependent on their employment but disliking every moment spent at work. We are captives of our culture, the values of our generation rather than those of previous or future generations. The fact is, we are all captives in one way or another. That's why the words of hope and comfort that Jeremiah speaks to those held captive centuries ago can apply to us today. —J. B. N.

C. Promise of Accessibility (vv. 12-14a)

12-14a. Then shall ye call upon me, and ye shall go and pray unto me, and I will hearken unto you. And ye shall seek me, and find me, when ye shall search for me with all your heart. And I will be found of you, saith the LORD.

To *call upon* the Lord is Bible language for earnest prayer. It particularly refers to calling upon God for assistance in the time of need. This practice began in the book of Genesis (Genesis 4:26). The psalmist taught that God was near to those who called upon Him, but only if they did so in truth (Psalm 145:18). Another

"I know the plans ... to prosper you ... plans to give you hope and a future."
—Jeremiah 29:11 *(NIV)*

Visual for Lesson 9. *Use this visual to introduce this question: "How do you think God is planning for you to prosper in His service?"*

principle taught in Psalms is that God turns a deaf ear to our pleas if we cherish sin in our hearts (Psalm 66:18).

After the time of Jeremiah, the prophet Zechariah will teach that God refused to hear the pleas of Israel during the Babylonian period because of their hard hearts (Zechariah 7:13). Israel's restoration needs to involve more than temple reconstruction. It needs to include a restored relationship with God, a time of renewed prayer and worship. This is the third promise, the promise of renewed accessibility to God in prayer (compare Zephaniah 3:9).

D. Promise of Restoration (v. 14b)

14b. And I will turn away your captivity, and I will gather you from all the nations, and from all the places whither I have driven you, saith the LORD; and I will bring you again into the place whence I caused you to be carried away captive.

God ends this section by reminding the exiles of His sovereignty. It was God who scattered the Israelites, first by the Assyrians and then by the Babylonians (see Jeremiah 50:17). It is only God, then, who can restore Israel (see 27:22). This is the fourth promise, a promise of restoration.

In the big picture of the Bible, Israel is to be restored for more than simply rebuilding the city of Jerusalem and its temple. Restored Israel is to be the nation that produces God's Messiah. This will bring "salvation unto the end of the earth" (Isaiah 49:6).

The nation of Israel, whether in exile or restored, is not an end unto itself. It is intended by God to be the vehicle that allows for His Messiah to come and restore humanity to Him. This is God's ultimate plan to give peace and well-being.

Home Daily Bible Readings

Monday, July 23—The Goodness of the Lord (Psalm 145:13-21)

Tuesday, July 24—God Restores (Jeremiah 30:18-22)

Wednesday, July 25—Loved with an Everlasting Love (Jeremiah 31:1-9)

Thursday, July 26—Shepherd of the Flock (Jeremiah 31:10-14)

Friday, July 27—They Shall Be My People (Jeremiah 31:33-37)

Saturday, July 28—Jeremiah Writes the Exiles (Jeremiah 29:1-9)

Sunday, July 29—God's Good Plans (Jeremiah 29:10-14)

The message of the New Testament is that we can be at peace with God through Jesus Christ (Romans 5:1).

Conclusion

A. Hardship and Hope

Reading Jeremiah allows us to take "the long view." We can see beyond temporary adversity to a time of restoration and blessing. We can get through tragedy without doubting God's love for us. We can pray to God in our times of need, knowing that He is listening and gives us hope.

The horror of Jerusalem's destruction is almost incomprehensible to us today. The survivors of this catastrophe wept uncontrollably when they arrived in Babylon (Psalm 137:1). Most of us have faced personal tragedy that left us feeling the same way. Think of a time when you endured great pain and sorrow. Maybe some are in this state now, this week.

In this dark night of the soul, it is easy to think that we will never be happy again. This is particularly true when misfortunes come at us in waves. Will this never stop? Why is this happening to me? What did I do wrong?

We should be careful not to see every bad thing in our lives as God's punishment for sin. Bad things sometimes happen to good people because our world is full of sin, and this sin affects us directly and indirectly. We can, however, see that every tragedy will be followed eventually by God's blessings and peace. We are, after all, children of the light (1 Thessalonians 5:5).

Even after the horrific events of Jerusalem's destruction in 586 BC, Jeremiah saw hope in the future (see Lamentations 3:21-24; written by Jeremiah). His hope was based on eternal promises. First, God's compassion and mercy are inexhaustible; His fountain of blessings never runs dry. Second, God's faithfulness is great and continually renewed. We can depend on God, for He never betrays our trust. This is our antidote for the sickness of hopelessness. These promises are ours too. [See question #5, page 414.]

B. Prayer

God of hope, God of truth, we trust You with our futures. We trust You when our lives are challenging, for in You we have hope. May You give us the strength always to depend on You. We pray this in the name of Your instrument of hope and peace, Jesus Christ, amen.

C. Thought to Remember

When feeling defeated, look up!

Learning by Doing

This page contains an alternative lesson plan emphasizing learning activities.
Classes desiring such student involvement will find these suggestions helpful.

Learning Goals

After participating in this lesson, each student will be able to:

1. Outline Jeremiah's letter to the captives.
2. Outline a letter that a modern Jeremiah could write to people of his own society.
3. Suggest one or two ways that he or she can seek the Lord more wholeheartedly on a daily basis.

Into the Lesson

As your students arrive, give each one a copy of the following exercise. (It is also printed in the student book.) Ask your students to read the quotations and write either *agree* or *disagree* in response to each:

1. "A mind troubled by doubt cannot focus on the course to victory" (Arthur Golden). *2.* "He who despairs over an event is a coward, but he who holds hope for the human condition is a fool" (Albert Camus). *3.* "Worries go down better with soup than without" (Jewish proverb). *4.* "If you can solve your problem, then what is the need of worrying? If you cannot solve it, then what is the use of worrying?" (Shantideva). *5.* "Character cannot be developed in ease and quiet. Only through experience of trial and suffering can the soul be strengthened, ambition inspired, and success achieved" (Helen Keller). *6.* "Pain is inevitable; suffering is optional" (M. Kathleen Casey). *7.* "The mass of men lead lives of quiet desperation" (Henry David Thoreau).

Discuss your students' answers. Then tell your class that today's lesson will draw a clear, scriptural contrast between the daily desperation that many people endure and the hope and assurance that God intends for His people to enjoy.

Into the Word

Introduce this section with a brief lecture on the ministry of Jeremiah, using both the Lesson Background and the lesson commentary. Make sure you mention that although Jeremiah prophesied doom and destruction for Judah, he also foretold the reestablishment of the Jewish nation from the remnant that would survive.

Next, divide your class into pairs. Each pair will study Jeremiah 29:1-14 and create an outline of the passage, placing the phrases below into their proper location in the outline grid. (If you do not use the student books, you will need to reproduce both the grid and phrases.)

I. _____ (29:1-3)
  A. _____ (vv. 1, 2)
  B. _____ (v. 3)
II. _____ (29:4-9)
  A. _____ (vv. 4-6)
  B. _____ (v. 7)
  C. _____ (vv. 8, 9)
III. _____ (29:10-14)
  A. _____ (v. 10)
  B. _____ (v. 11)
  C. _____ (vv. 12-14a)
  D. _____ (v. 14b)

Phrases: *Build Lives While Waiting; Communication in Captivity; Judah Is Not Forgotten; Judah Is Uprooted; Promise of Accessibility; Promise of Prosperity; Promise of Restoration; Promise of Return; Promised Freedom from Captivity; Reject Deception While Waiting; Seek Peace While Waiting; Waiting in Captivity.*

When your students have finished their outlining, ask for volunteers to share answers. Write each line on the board as it is completed. Use the text to resolve disagreements.

Into Life

Ask your pairs from the previous exercise to outline a letter that a modern Jeremiah could write to people of our society. Each letter should include the following elements: a listing of and denunciation of the sins prevalent in modern society (see 1 Corinthians 6:9-11; Galatians 5:19-21); a warning of judgment from God because of those sins (Matthew 24:36-51; 2 Peter 3:3-13; Revelation 20:7-15); an offer of salvation (Acts 2:36-40; 3:17-26); and a promise of restoration to those who are faithful to God (Hebrews 10:23-31; Revelation 22:12-17).

When the pairs have completed their work, have each share the results. Challenge your students to identify privately any sins that are a continuing problem in their lives. Remind each one that he or she needs to confess those sins to God (1 John 1:7–2:2). Close with prayer for your society's repentance and your students' continuing commitment to Christ.

Let's Talk It Over

The questions on this page are designed to promote discussion of the lesson
by the class and to encourage application of the lesson Scriptures. The answers
provided are only discussion starters. Let your class talk it over from there.

1. Name some individuals in your life who brought you the Word of God even though they seemed to have been working behind the scenes. In what ways are you doing the same for someone else?

The identities of Elasah and Gemariah would not be known to us if they had not undertaken the task of taking Jeremiah's letter to the captives in Babylon. The message was a blessing to all who heard it. Ask the class to share stories about individuals who have been a special inspiration and blessing because they brought God's Word.

Next, ask the class to mention the names of those they are blessing through the Word. Discuss ways class members can take the good news of Jesus to many more. Talk about specific methods that can be used (examples: helping a neighbor take care of an elderly person, babysitting for a non-Christian single mom).

2. What steps do you need to take so you can adjust your purposes to God's purposes in your current situation?

Personal expectations of "the way things should be" can cause us to miss some of the blessings that God has in store for us while we're in the middle of very uncomfortable situations. The exiled people wanted to return to their homeland. But God said they could be blessed if they would settle down in the new place and live their lives as if they were back in Judah. God is very capable of bringing blessings to us wherever we are.

One specific step to take is to choose to focus on God rather than the problem or the person that is causing you difficulty. Maintain this focus by regular prayer and devotions. Scripture that deals with the power and sovereignty of God can be particularly helpful.

3. How can your church help fortify Christians so they can discern between God's message and the messages of false teachers?

Christians can be warned that people have a tendency to seek out the messengers who will tell them what they *want* to hear rather than what they *need* to hear (2 Timothy 4:1-4). The challenge of every congregation is to communi-cate the entirety of God's Word clearly, no matter how uncomfortable that may be.

Beyond that, Christians can be taught ways to study the Scriptures productively. If we could narrow down Bible study principles to a single, most-important idea, that idea would be *context*. Much doctrinal error springs from failing to pay attention to immediate and larger contexts.

Learning to discern the characteristics of false teachers is also important. Such folk may insist that they are the only correct teachers, requiring listeners to accept only their words. They will resist examining what other Christians have taught through the centuries, and they will be good at playing to the whims of the audience (compare Matthew 7:15; 3 John 9, 10; Jude 4, 12).

4. How do you encourage those who have lost trust in God because God did not respond in the way they expected?

One way to dislodge conclusions reached while playing the blame game ("This is all God's fault") is to ask the person how he or she arrived at those conclusions. Hearing their own reasoning bounce off the wall and come back into their thinking can cause some people to question their own conclusions.

Asking the person to list all the possible ways and timings that God could use to bless them is another way to disrupt this all-or-nothing thinking. Sharing the focus of today's text may help them see that God may bless them in a much larger context than simply providing a short-term answer for them.

5. How can the account of God's actions with Judah serve as a model for parents as they deal with the misbehavior of their children?

There should be clear communication about expectations and the consequences if those expectations are not met. When punishment begins, there must be an indication of the ending time of the punishment. This picture should include a description of what a full restoration of privileges will look like. The possibility of a fully restored fellowship with the parent is vital. The goal of child-rearing is to raise a responsible, Christian adult. This "long view" is crucial.

Committed to Hope Even in Pain

DEVOTIONAL READING: Psalm 23.

BACKGROUND SCRIPTURE: 2 Kings 25:1-7;
Lamentations 3:25-58.

PRINTED TEXT: 2 Kings 25:1, 2, 5-7; Lamentations 3:25-33, 55-58.

2 Kings 25:1, 2, 5-7

1 And it came to pass in the ninth year of his reign, in the tenth month, in the tenth day of the month, that Nebuchadnezzar king of Babylon came, he, and all his host, against Jerusalem, and pitched against it; and they built forts against it round about.

2 And the city was besieged unto the eleventh year of king Zedekiah.

. . . .

5 And the army of the Chaldees pursued after the king, and overtook him in the plains of Jericho: and all his army were scattered from him.

6 So they took the king, and brought him up to the king of Babylon to Riblah; and they gave judgment upon him.

7 And they slew the sons of Zedekiah before his eyes, and put out the eyes of Zedekiah, and bound him with fetters of brass, and carried him to Babylon.

Lamentations 3:25-33, 55-58

25 The LORD is good unto them that wait for him, to the soul that seeketh him.

26 It is good that a man should both hope and quietly wait for the salvation of the LORD.

27 It is good for a man that he bear the yoke in his youth.

28 He sitteth alone and keepeth silence, because he hath borne it upon him.

29 He putteth his mouth in the dust; if so be there may be hope.

30 He giveth his cheek to him that smiteth him: he is filled full with reproach.

31 For the Lord will not cast off for ever:

32 But though he cause grief, yet will he have compassion according to the multitude of his mercies.

33 For he doth not afflict willingly nor grieve the children of men.

. . . .

55 I called upon thy name, O LORD, out of the low dungeon.

56 Thou hast heard my voice: hide not thine ear at my breathing, at my cry.

57 Thou drewest near in the day that I called upon thee: thou saidst, Fear not.

58 O Lord, thou hast pleaded the causes of my soul; thou hast redeemed my life.

Aug
5

GOLDEN TEXT: It is good that a man should both hope and quietly wait for the salvation of the LORD.—Lamentations 3:26.

Committed to Doing Right
Unit 3: How Shall We Respond?
(Lessons 10-13)

Lesson Aims

After participating in this lesson, each student will be able to:

1. Retell at least one expression of faith that resulted from the fall of Jerusalem.

2. Explain how experiences of deprivation and despair provide opportunities for strong expressions of hope.

3. Write a prayer to use for the next severe trial in his or her life.

Lesson Outline

INTRODUCTION
   A. Tragedy Theology
   B. Lesson Background
 I. SIEGE OF JERUSALEM (2 Kings 25:1, 2, 5-7)
   A. Dates Determined (vv. 1, 2)
   B. Disasters Described (vv. 5-7)
II. STATEMENTS OF JEREMIAH (Lamentations 3:25-33, 55-58)
   A. Reminders in Suffering (vv. 25-27)
     Gain from Pain
   B. Reactions to Suffering (vv. 28-30)
   C. Reassurances in Suffering (vv. 31-33)
   D. Responses by God (vv. 55-58)
     Low Cotton
CONCLUSION
   A. Alone?
   B. Prayer
   C. Thought to Remember

Introduction

A. Tragedy Theology

The tsunami tragedy of December 26, 2004, resulted in massive loss of life. So did the earthquake on the Pakistan-India border of October 8, 2005. Many organizations and nations responded by providing immediate and continuing aid for the ones who survived but who had lost homes, possessions, and their means of livelihood.

Tragedies of such proportions affect everyone psychologically. The enduring question is *Why?* Accounts from the tsunami and earthquake tragedies tell of individuals or groups that were spared through various circumstances. Did that mean that God was with them more than He was with the ones who lost their lives?

God knows when tragedies occur, for He knows when even a sparrow falls to the ground (Matthew 10:29). The fact that death can come at any age or in any circumstance confirms that an individual must be prepared for that possibility at all times. Every day there are accidents and acts of terror. No one is guaranteed that he or she will be alive tomorrow.

Thousands around the world die each year because of the fact that they are Christians. They lose their lives simply because they give expression to their faith by assembling together, distributing literature, or even using charitable acts as methods of evangelism. In many parts of the world it is just expected that a Christian will suffer. Yet the ultimate purpose of life for the Christian is to die in Christ. Family members who survive have a loss, but they are blessed with expectation of reunion. They also have examples of how a Christian handles the trials of life. God is with His people in both life and death.

B. Lesson Background

Nebuchadnezzar became the king of Babylon when his father died in the summer of 605 BC. The Babylonians had just defeated the Egyptians, and to demonstrate that there was a new power in the region, Nebuchadnezzar took captives from Jerusalem. They included the prophet Daniel. Nebuchadnezzar allowed Jehoiakim to remain on the throne of David.

Nebuchadnezzar returned in the summer of 597 BC to put down a rebellion initiated by Jehoiakim. But Nebuchadnezzar found that Jehoiakim's son, Jehoiachin, had been reigning for three months. Nebuchadnezzar therefore took Jehoiachin and 10,000 others captive. He then placed Zedekiah (Jehoiakim's brother) on the throne (2 Kings 24:14-17). The prophet Ezekiel was among the captives taken to Babylon then.

Zedekiah, Judah's last king, was therefore a puppet king under Nebuchadnezzar. Zedekiah was not a good puppet, however. At the beginning of his reign he sponsored a gathering of messengers from other nations. They came to Jerusalem to plan rebellion (Jeremiah 27:1-3).

On that occasion Jeremiah was instructed by the Lord to put a yoke on his neck and to announce to the delegates that Nebuchadnezzar was God's servant, and that all the lands were given by God into Nebuchadnezzar's hand (27:4-6). To prophesy this submission did not seem very patriotic, but it was in the best interests of the nations involved. Would Jerusalem obey?

I. Siege of Jerusalem
(2 Kings 25:1, 2, 5-7)

King Zedekiah made a trip to Babylon in the fourth year of his reign (about 594 BC; Jeremiah 51:59). It is sometimes thought that he and others who plotted against Babylon were compelled to make this journey in order to give personal expressions of allegiance to Nebuchadnezzar.

A few years later, however, Zedekiah rebelled (2 Kings 24:20). Nebuchadnezzar then moved to subjugate the disloyal nations, and Judah was first on his list.

A. Dates Determined (vv. 1, 2)

1, 2. And it came to pass in the ninth year of his reign, in the tenth month, in the tenth day of the month, that Nebuchadnezzar king of Babylon came, he, and all his host, against Jerusalem, and pitched against it; and they built forts against it round about.

The tenth month is in winter. This shows Nebuchadnezzar's determination as he begins the military blockade of *Jerusalem*. Polite warfare (if there is such a thing) in ancient times waits until spring and the beginning of the dry season. To move an army and its equipment into position in the rainy, cold months of winter is a hardship. [See question #1, page 422.]

The conditions inside Jerusalem are not pleasant during the long months of siege. There is the constant thought that the enemy outside is waiting for you to surrender or starve. In the meantime the Babylonians patiently work to break through the defenses. Undoubtedly, there is a lot of "foxhole faith" inside Jerusalem at this time. [See question #2, page 422.]

Jeremiah's message is that the lives of the people and the city itself can be saved only by surrender (Jeremiah 38:17, 18). Some of the officials of the city attempt to have Jeremiah killed for

---

How to Say It

ASSYRIANS. Uh-*sear*-e-unz.
BABYLONIANS. Bab-ih-*low*-nee-unz.
CHALDEES. *Kal*-deez.
JEHOIACHIN. Jeh-*hoy*-uh-kin.
JEHOIAKIM. Jeh-*hoy*-uh-kim.
MICAH. *My*-kuh.
NEBUCHADNEZZAR. *Neb*-yuh-kud-*nez*-er (strong accent on *nez*).
RIBLAH. *Rib*-luh.
TSUNAMI. su-*nah*-me.
ZEDEKIAH. Zed-uh-*kye*-uh.

---

discouraging the men of the city with these words. The food supply eventually becomes so critical that some women eat their children (Lamentations 2:20; 4:10).

This time there is not a miracle to save Jerusalem, unlike the threat by the Assyrians over 100 years prior (see 2 Kings 19:34, 35). In July of 586 BC, the Babylonians finally force their way into the city.

B. Disasters Described (vv. 5-7)

5. And the army of the Chaldees pursued after the king, and overtook him in the plains of Jericho: and all his army were scattered from him.

Zedekiah and others attempt to flee from the wrath of the besieging army, but the tactic does not work. The *Chaldees* (Babylonians) capture the fleeing *king* on *the plains of Jericho*. The soldiers who are pledged to defend the king abandon him. It is every man for himself!

6. So they took the king, and brought him up to the king of Babylon to Riblah; and they gave judgment upon him.

Zedekiah is closely related to the three prior kings of Judah. But his royal pedigree is of no value. He is just a prisoner, walking many miles to the north to meet *the king of Babylon*, whom he has betrayed. Every step is difficult, and the anticipation of the outcome only increases the anxiety.

7. And they slew the sons of Zedekiah before his eyes, and put out the eyes of Zedekiah, and bound him with fetters of brass, and carried him to Babylon.

The last thing that *Zedekiah* is allowed to see is the death of his *sons*. [See question #3, page 422.] Then he is blinded, perhaps with hot coals. He will never rebel again. Several years earlier, Ezekiel had made an interesting prophecy about Zedekiah: he was to be brought *to Babylon*, but he was not to see it (Ezekiel 12:13). The judgment on him by Nebuchadnezzar fulfills the prophecy. Other leaders of Judah also experience death at Riblah (2 Kings 25:18-21; Jeremiah 39:6).

II. Statements of Jeremiah
(Lamentations 3:25-33, 55-58)

Jeremiah is traditionally thought to be the author of the book of Lamentations. The theme of the book is the desolation that accompanies the destruction of Jerusalem.

It has now been some 40 years since Jeremiah was called to prophesy. In one sense Jeremiah probably considers himself a failure. His nation is gone, and the majority in Judah did not heed his message. In God's sight, however, Jeremiah is a faithful prophet who preaches even when he does not wish to do so (Jeremiah 20:9). Future generations regard him highly. His is one of the names given to Jesus when He asked His disciples how others identified Him (Matthew 16:13, 14).

The first four chapters of Lamentations are alphabetic acrostics: the 22 letters of the Hebrew alphabet are used consecutively to begin the verses. Here in chapter three there are three verses for each letter. In two places the letters are transposed, and no one knows why. Some think that this method of writing may increase the ability to remember, demonstrate the carefulness of the writer, or perhaps show that the subject is covered completely.

A. Reminders in Suffering (vv. 25-27)

25. The LORD is good unto them that wait for him, to the soul that seeketh him.

This verse and the two following not only begin with the same letter of the Hebrew alphabet, but in the Hebrew they also begin with the same word—*good.* Its position as first in the sentence indicates its importance.

First, Jeremiah reminds the reader that the Lord really is good to the ones who have hope or expectations concerning God's promises. God fulfills His word, whether it is the destruction of a sinful nation or the revival of a nation that is considered dead.

The careful student will also notice that the triad of verses immediately before this one provides the background for one of the great hymns of the faith, namely, "Great Is Thy Faithfulness." Most people who sing the words do not realize

Home Daily Bible Readings

Monday, July 30— Promise of Deliverance (Isaiah 30:15-19)
Tuesday, July 31—Jerusalem Destroyed (2 Kings 25:1, 2, 5-7)
Wednesday, Aug. 1—God Is Our Hope (Psalm 33:12-22)
Thursday, Aug. 2—My Soul Waits (Psalm 130)
Friday, Aug. 3—God Is Faithful (Lamentations 3:19-24)
Saturday, Aug. 4—Wait for the Lord (Lamentations 3:25-33)
Sunday, Aug. 5—God Hears My Plea (Lamentations 3:55-59)

the depths of faith that Jeremiah was expressing when he wrote them. It is almost inconceivable that Jeremiah can say that God's mercies are new every morning (v. 23). The experiences of Jerusalem's siege are still vivid in his mind, but he can still see the blessings. He has confidence in the plan of God.

26. It is good that a man should both hope and quietly wait for the salvation of the LORD.

The latter part of this verse is difficult for many. Today's generation wants immediate gratification. Action is thought to be much better than quietly waiting for anything. To *quietly wait* also means that complaining or murmuring is not present. It is *good* that faith and faithfulness combine to eliminate impatience with God's timetable concerning the fulfillments of His promises (compare 2 Peter 3:4-9). [See question #4, page 422.]

27. It is good for a man that he bear the yoke in his youth.

To *bear the yoke* is a figure of speech that means someone has been placed under a burden, similar to an animal that wears a yoke. It is a forced place of service. It indicates humiliation.

The person who experiences tough times later in life is usually better able to accept them if they were also part of his or her earlier years. Pain and suffering are never desirable, but there may be valuable lessons for the ones who endure them.

The exhortations of this verse and the previous one add a different dimension to the laments. These are positive expressions, and they say much about handling the traumas of life.

GAIN FROM PAIN

Some parents try to bring up their children in a "risk-free" world. They try to protect them from all emotional pain or hardship. Yet going through emotional pain can have a positive result. The same is true physically. Exposure to certain less-severe viruses can build immunity against those that are even worse.

The discipline of children is an area in which some parents have abandoned the responsibility of administering healthy doses of pain or hardship. The TV show *Nanny 911* makes this all too clear: children run riot in the home as parents attempt to be their buddies rather than their, well, parents. Scripture reminds us that tough discipline, though not pleasant at the moment, has ultimate value (Hebrews 12:11).

In our spiritual lives, times of pain and trial may have a good ultimate result if we will allow God to use them for that purpose. Paul reminds us that "our light affliction, which is but for a moment, worketh for us a far more exceeding and eternal weight of glory" (2 Corinthians 4:17). None of us would make the request, "Bring on the pain, let the bad times roll." Yet we do know that God can bring good out of our patient endurance in times of trouble, hardship, and pain. The key is to allow Him to do so.   —A. E. A.

B. Reactions to Suffering (vv. 28-30)

28. He sitteth alone and keepeth silence, because he hath borne it upon him.

Jeremiah's words in the next three verses seem to combine the thought of the previous verse (bearing a yoke) and the suffering that accompanied Jerusalem's siege and destruction. There is no question this time about the source of the sorrows. The Lord is the one who has placed the burden on His people.

One of the frequent questions in negative experiences is, "What did I do to deserve this?" In many cases the answer is that nothing was done; some things just happen. Sometimes there are accidents, and no one is to blame. For Judah, however, the causes are known. It is therefore simply better to maintain *silence.* Asking questions only intensifies the sense of guilt and loss.

God uses the Babylonians to punish Judah, and the Babylonians are certainly not considered more righteous than Judah. Would that be a good question to raise with God? The prophet Habakkuk addressed that same issue approximately 20 years before Jerusalem fell: How could God use such a sinful nation to punish Judah?

God's response is one of the outstanding verses of the Bible. Regardless of what happens, the just shall live by faith (Habakkuk 2:4; see also Romans 1:17; Galatians 3:11). Oh, yes, God will also take care of the Babylonians. (See Lesson 7.)

29. He putteth his mouth in the dust; if so be there may be hope.

The figures of speech showing humiliation or abasement continue, and this one is distinctive. It is similar to "lick *the dust,*" as given in Micah 7:17. It is also reminiscent of a conqueror's putting his foot on the neck of the one conquered (Joshua 10:24). [See question #5, page 422.]

The one who is treated in this way, however, does not surrender *hope.* His or her spirit is not broken. Such a person anticipates that with God's help there will be better days ahead.

30. He giveth his cheek to him that smiteth him: he is filled full with reproach.

The mistreatment moves from humiliation to physical violence. It is possible to view this verse figuratively. If that is the case, then it is a recog-

nition that God is behind the abasement that takes place.

We must remember that many who read these laments are righteous survivors of the catastrophe of 586 BC. For them, Jeremiah's words are spiritual encouragement. It is extremely difficult to accept punishment when you are innocent of wrongdoing, but sometimes it must be endured.

C. Reassurances in Suffering (vv. 31-33)

31. For the LORD will not cast off for ever.

It is always easier to endure present suffering if one knows that it is only temporary. Here Jeremiah provides assurance that being *cast off* is not a permanent situation. Its real purpose is to purge and purify a sinful nation. Comparisons may be made to surgical procedures. These are painful for the present, but the promise of healing enables one to look past the pain and discomfort.

32. But though he cause grief, yet will he have compassion according to the multitude of his mercies.

The strong medicine of discipline may not taste good, but it is good for the recipient. The *compassion* of God leads Him to bring a restoration that is based on the qualities that a thoughtful person should expect God to have. God is holy, and sin must be punished; but He is also prompted by His abundant mercy to do what is best for those who serve Him. After all, "God so loved the world," not just one person or nation.

33. For he doth not afflict willingly, nor grieve the children of men.

The word *willingly* is interesting, for in the Hebrew it literally says "from his heart." This also says much about the character of our God. He is not a sadist who finds joy in torture. The writer of Hebrews expresses a parallel thought when he says, "for whom the Lord loveth he chasteneth, and scourgeth every son whom he receiveth" (Hebrews 12:6).

D. Responses by God (vv. 55-58)

55. I called upon thy name, O LORD, out of the low dungeon.

The verses immediately before this section show that Jeremiah is vividly recalling the time when he personally was the object of violence. See Jeremiah 38:6-13.

LOW COTTON

Being reared in an area where cotton was grown, I became familiar with the idea of someone being *in low cotton.* This spoke of the person who had to pick cotton in a field where the stalks were not very high, thus he or she had to stoop way over to pick the cotton. The reason for the low cotton was that the field was not producing well. But the cotton would grow higher in a good growing season, therefore the picker did not have to stoop so low. Thus to be *in high cotton* meant that times were good, but to be *in low cotton* meant times were tough.

We all go through tough times—times when it seems we are about as low as we can get. God's people are not exempt. Remember Daniel: he was in pretty low cotton when he was in the lion's den. Joseph was not much better off when he was cast into a pit by his brothers then sold into slavery.

But no matter how low we may go, the good news is we can never go so low that God cannot hear us or see us. We know we have victory through Jesus in the low times. The words of that great Easter hymn help us to recall this: "Low in the grave he lay, Jesus my Savior, waiting the coming day, Jesus my Lord. Up from the grave He arose." Jesus knows what it means to be in low cotton, and He knows how to lift us out of that state. —A. E. A.

56. Thou hast heard my voice: hide not thine ear at my breathing, at my cry.

This is Jeremiah's testimony: the Lord *heard* his prayer and his *cry* for help. The old saying, "Where there's life, there's hope!" comes to mind. Jeremiah is almost saying that since he is able to pray, then he is confident that he is heard.

57. Thou drewest near in the day that I called upon thee: thou saidst, Fear not.

Jeremiah recognizes answered prayer: *Fear not.* The Christian today also has a blessed assur-

ance in several ways. Centuries after Jeremiah, Jesus will promise to be with His followers to the end of the age (Matthew 28:20). The apostle Paul affirms that through Christ we conquer all things, no matter the peril (Romans 8:37-39). Take a look at those words again; they proclaim that there is hope even in pain.

58. O Lord, thou hast pleaded the causes of my soul; thou hast redeemed my life.

The final response that is expressed by Jeremiah is the joy that the Lord has *redeemed* his *life.* The word *redeemed* is a special word for the Hebrew. It is the word for the relative who can avenge a death (Numbers 35:19), redeem a kinsman from slavery (Leviticus 25:47-49), retrieve a family inheritance that had been sold, or marry a widow of a close relative who has no sons. In this case it is Jeremiah's life that has been redeemed. This is a source of joy!

Conclusion

A. Alone?

One preacher testifies that in the past he often battled depression on Monday morning if things had not gone as he desired on Sunday. The cure was very simple: go to a local discount store! Merely being with and meeting people, many of whom he knew, would compel him to smile. Soon the depression would vanish. We are made for relationships!

To attempt to handle the trials of life alone is difficult for most people. One of the responsibilities of Christians is to help bear the burdens of others (Galatians 6:2). Even the apostle Paul expressed concern when he had to face his trials alone. When others deserted him, it was not pleasant (2 Timothy 4:16).

Some people will resist offers of help, but fellowship is important. If a person can conquer pride and actually ask for assistance, then everyone involved benefits. After all, it is not good for us to dwell alone!

B. Prayer

Almighty God in Heaven, thank You for the blessings of redemption, daily bread, and friends in Christ. None of us seek trials and pain, but we can thank You for the steadfastness, character, and hope through the suffering that those trials and pain produce. In the name of the Son who suffered so much, amen.

C. Thought to Remember

"I can do all things through Christ which strengtheneth me" (Philippians 4:13).

Visual for
Lesson 10

Use this montage to challenge your students to name an unending sequence of God's blessings.

Learning by Doing

This page contains an alternative lesson plan emphasizing learning activities. Classes desiring such student involvement will find these suggestions helpful.

Learning Goals

After participating in this lesson, each student will be able to:

1. Retell at least one expression of faith that resulted from the fall of Jerusalem.

2. Explain how experiences of deprivation and despair provide opportunities for strong expressions of hope.

3. Write a prayer to use for the next severe trial in his or her life.

Into the Lesson

As your students arrive, give each a copy of the following matching quiz. (The quiz is also printed in the student books.)

(In)Famous Disasters
____ 1. January 15, 588 BC
____ 2. August 24, AD 79
____ 3. November 1, 1755
____ 4. October 8, 1871
____ 5. May 31, 1889
____ 6. April 15, 1912
____ 7. December 7, 1941
____ 8. September 11, 2001
____ 9. December 26, 2004
___ 10. August 30, 2005

A. Pearl Harbor attacked by military forces of Imperial Japan; B. the World Trade Center destroyed by terrorists; C. a tsunami hits Indonesia and 275,000 die; D. ancient Jerusalem is besieged by Babylonians; E. the Titanic sinks; F. Vesuvius erupts, destroying Pompeii, Italy; G. an earthquake, tsunami, and fires level Lisbon, Portugal, killing between 60,000 and 100,000; H. Hurricane Katrina floods New Orleans, Louisiana; I. the Great Chicago Fire destroys much of that city, leaving one-third of the inhabitants homeless; J. a flood in Johnstown, Pennsylvania, kills 2,200 people.

(Answers: 1D, 2F, 3G, 4I, 5J, 6E, 7A, 8B, 9C, 10H)

Correct quizzes together as a class. Then say, "Today's lesson deals with one of these infamous events: the siege of Jerusalem by the Babylonians and its aftermath, which began in 588 BC."

Into the Word

To introduce your class to today's Bible texts, hand out copies of the quiz below (or direct your class to the student books, where the quiz also is found). Students may use their Bibles to find the answers in 2 Kings 25:1, 2, 5-7 and Lamentations 3:25-33, 55-58. Correct answers are indicated in parentheses.

Besieged by Babylon

1. Jerusalem was attacked in the ____ year of Zedekiah's reign. *(ninth)*

2. The Babylonians were led by King _____. *(Nebuchadnezzar)*

3. The Babylonians captured King Zedekiah in the plains of _____. *(Jericho)*

4. King Zedekiah was taken to Nebuchadnezzar at _____. *(Riblah)*

5. Zedekiah's ____ were put out. *(eyes)*

6. It is good to wait quietly for the Lord's ___. *(salvation)*

7. It is good to bear the _____ while young. *(yoke)*

8. A suffering man ____ alone, keeps _____, and puts his mouth in the ___. *(sits, silence, dust)*

9. He turns his _____ to the one who would hit him. *(cheek)*

10. The Lord will not _____ off forever. *(cast)*

11. Though he causes _____, he will have _____ according to his _____. *(grief, compassion, mercies)*

12. He does not _____ willingly nor grieve the children of ____. *(afflict, men)*

13. Jeremiah called upon God from the low _____. *(dungeon)*

14. God heard Jeremiah's _____. *(voice)*

15. God did not hide his ear at Jeremiah's _____, his _____. *(breathing, cry)*

16. God told Jeremiah, "_____ not." *(Fear)*

17. God redeemed Jeremiah's _____. *(life)*

When your students have completed their work, correct their quizzes together. This can be a small-group exercise. Use the answers as a springboard for your discussion of the lesson text.

Into Life

Provide pencil and paper. Ask each student to use today's lesson as inspiration to write a brief statement or prayer of faith that he or she can share with others in a time of trial or despair. (This exercise is also printed in the student books.)

Let's Talk It Over

The questions on this page are designed to promote discussion of the lesson by the class and to encourage application of the lesson Scriptures. The answers provided are only discussion starters. Let your class talk it over from there.

1. What may be some reasons that God would allow an adversary to "pitch against" your church today? What corrective action do you need to take?

We often feel that if we are meeting regularly on the Lord's Day, taking the Lord's Supper, giving our offerings, and carrying on the other activities of the church, then we are pleasing God. But just going through the rituals and motions of Christianity—doing "church things"—is not what God is looking for. God looks deeper.

When we get together but fail to meet needs, God is displeased. When we give our money without giving our hearts, we are unfaithful. When we practice ritual without practicing righteousness, God may allow His church to be refined through the fire of persecution from an enemy.

2. How do some practice "foxhole faith" today? How do we avoid this?

The old saying is, "There are no atheists in foxholes." When the bullets start whizzing overhead in time of war, suddenly everyone believes in God and starts praying! America saw church attendance rise dramatically following the terrorist attacks of 9/11. The rise subsided rapidly in a matter of weeks.

This type of "faith" is evident when people do religious exercises for the purpose of trying to please God during difficult times. Life may seem good at first, with no need for God. So a person stops going to church. Then problems set in. A person may feel that he or she has offended God and therefore needs to get back into church to appease Him.

During such times, God may answer a person's prayers—or maybe He won't. It depends on the person's heart (compare Deuteronomy 1:45; Zechariah 7:13; John 9:31; Acts 17:27; Hebrews 11:6; etc.). Maintaining a heart for God continuously will eliminate a need for foxhole faith.

3. How do you respond to someone who questions the goodness of God when he or she reads passages such as 2 Kings 25:7?

Passages such as 2 Kings 25:7 must be set alongside texts that speak of the patience of God (example: Nehemiah 9:30). Throughout the Old Testament, God had given directives to Israel, and then gave them chance after chance to do what was right. He warned them over and over concerning the consequences of failing to be faithful to His way. God is simply being true to His Word when He allows the enemies to overtake those who have abandoned Him. The God who grants the breath of life to people has the right to take it back.

Even so, we must be careful not to leave the impression that every time something bad happens that it is caused by God. We live in a fallen world and are subject to its problems.

4. What are some ways that God has rewarded your patience?

God has promised that in all situations He will continue to work for good for those who are the called according to His purpose (Romans 8:28). Also it is in waiting patiently that we receive strength (Isaiah 30:15). When we pray, we often want quick answers. Yet God teaches us to wait. If we wait faithfully, He provides the right answer at the right time. Our finances may be in shambles, and so we pray for help. It may not come immediately, but in His time God provides.

Churches sometimes need to search for a preacher or church leaders. If they grow tired of waiting and hurriedly place people in those positions, then they will suffer for their haste. But churches that patiently wait for God to bring together the right circumstances are blessed with strong biblical leaders.

5. Why do some find it so hard to practice abasement when in the valley of despair?

Many of us live in cultures that teach that we should have all of our needs met and have them met immediately. A consumer culture makes us think that whatever we desire we should have, even when (or especially when) in the valley of despair.

The political process in democracies feeds this drive. When we are continually told to demand our rights, toot our own horns, and strive to be "empowered," then it can be difficult to practice humility. The valley of despair should drive us closer to God, not closer to politicians.

Committed to Taking Responsibility

DEVOTIONAL READING: Psalm 18:20-24.

BACKGROUND SCRIPTURE: Ezekiel 18.

PRINTED TEXT: Ezekiel 18:4, 20-23, 30-32.

Ezekiel 18:4, 20-23, 30-32

4 Behold, all souls are mine; as the soul of the father, so also the soul of the son is mine: the soul that sinneth, it shall die.

. . . .

20 The soul that sinneth, it shall die. The son shall not bear the iniquity of the father, neither shall the father bear the iniquity of the son: the righteousness of the righteous shall be upon him, and the wickedness of the wicked shall be upon him.

21 But if the wicked will turn from all his sins that he hath committed, and keep all my statutes, and do that which is lawful and right, he shall surely live, he shall not die.

22 All his transgressions that he hath committed, they shall not be mentioned unto him: in his righteousness that he hath done he shall live.

23 Have I any pleasure at all that the wicked should die? saith the Lord GOD: and not that he should return from his ways, and live?

. . . .

30 Therefore I will judge you, O house of Israel, every one according to his ways, saith the Lord GOD. Repent, and turn yourselves from all your transgressions; so iniquity shall not be your ruin.

31 Cast away from you all your transgressions, whereby ye have transgressed; and make you a new heart and a new spirit: for why will ye die, O house of Israel?

32 For I have no pleasure in the death of him that dieth, saith the Lord GOD: wherefore turn yourselves, and live ye.

GOLDEN TEXT: I have no pleasure in the death of him that dieth, saith the Lord GOD: wherefore turn yourselves, and live ye.—Ezekiel 18:32.

Lesson Aims

After participating in this lesson, each student will be able to:

1. State the basic concepts of responsibility for Old Testament Israel as given by Ezekiel.

2. Compare and contrast Ezekiel 18:20 with Exodus 20:5; 34:7.

3. Eliminate one behavior in his or her life that profanes God's name.

Lesson Outline

INTRODUCTION
   A. Always an Alibi
   B. Prophets in the Context of Exile
   C. Lesson Background
  I. GOD'S PRINCIPLES (Ezekiel 18:4, 20)
   A. Absolute #1: God Is Sovereign (v. 4a)
     A Sense of Belonging
   B. Absolute #2: Sin Brings Death (vv. 4b, 20a)
   C. Absolute #3: Each Is Responsible (v. 20b)
 II. GOD'S PROMISES (Ezekiel 18:21-23, 30a)
   A. God's Conditions (v. 21)
   B. God's Commitment (v. 22)
   C. God's Joy (v. 23)
   D. God's Judgment (v. 30a)
     Tough Love
III. GOD'S PLEADINGS (Ezekiel 18:30b-32)
   A. Decide About Sin (v. 30b)
   B. Discard Sin (v. 31a)
   C. Desire a New Heart (v. 31b)
   D. Delight in Life (v. 32)
CONCLUSION
   A. The Anger of Guilt
   B. Prayer
   C. Thought to Remember

Introduction

A. Always an Alibi

He was a very pleasant teenager. You could count on him to assist the elderly, to carry babies or diaper bags for young parents, or to do those extra tasks for teachers in the classrooms. His desire to please others and to be recognized by them did have one negative dimension: he sometimes followed troublemakers in their devious schemes in an attempt to please. When confronted with his wrong decisions, however, he always used the same alibi to explain his latest misdeed.

With tears—perhaps genuine tears—he would tell his story, and those who were in places of authority were ready to forgive him. His tale of suffering included the facts that his father had been killed in an accident when he was young, and he often had lived with his grandparents. This generation gap was just too big, and his life had been filled with woe. His grandparents just did not understand. They wanted to go to bed early, and he wanted to stay up late. They arose early in the morning, and he wanted to sleep until noon.

One day, however, he met a counselor who responded in a different way. After listening patiently, the counselor told the young man that if he was intelligent enough to blame his grandparents, then he was intelligent enough to accept the consequences for his actions. If he was not responsible for what he did, then there were institutions in the state where such people were sent.

This congenial young man had just encountered the doctrine of individual responsibility. He was learning that each person is responsible for what he or she does. As it says in Romans 14:12: "So then every one of us shall give account of himself to God." It is a lesson the ancient Judeans had to learn as well.

B. Prophets in the Context of Exile

Daniel, Jeremiah, and Ezekiel—each prophet had a definite place in God's plan for the people of Judah during the final days and exile of that nation. Daniel's place of service was to the kings of Babylon, especially to King Nebuchadnezzar.

Jeremiah's primary ministry was to the people in Judah and Jerusalem before the main exile began. In that role he offered hope in affirming that the Lord would bring His people back from Babylon after 70 years were completed (Jeremiah 29:10). That period is usually determined in one of two ways: it was approximately 70 years from the time that the first captives were taken (605 BC) until the time of the first return (538 BC); it was also about 70 years from the destruction of the temple (586 BC) to the dedication of the new temple some 20 years after the first wave of people returned from captivity (515 BC; Ezra 6:15).

Those in exile were given the prophet Ezekiel as a fellow captive. The exiles had attitudes that had to be corrected, and Ezekiel was the man to do it. We are fairly certain that Ezekiel was among the 10,000 captives taken from Judah and Jerusalem in 597 BC (2 Kings 24:14).

C. Lesson Background

Like Jeremiah, Ezekiel was a priest (Jeremiah 1:1; Ezekiel 1:3). The first verse of Ezekiel's book is usually interpreted to mean that Ezekiel was 30 years old when he received a special revelation of God's glory. It was mid-summer of 593 BC, and Ezekiel had been a captive for about 4 years. Working the year 593 BC back to 605 BC means that Ezekiel was about 18 when he saw Daniel and his friends taken away by Nebuchadnezzar's army. Eight years later, Ezekiel himself was compelled to leave his home and his native land.

In his formative years, Ezekiel must have looked forward to reaching the age of 30. That's when he would qualify to function fully as one of the priests; the service of all priests and Levites began at that age (Numbers 4). The Lord had a ministry for Ezekiel starting at age 30, but it was not the one Ezekiel had anticipated. He was to be God's prophet in Babylonia, not a priest in Jerusalem.

One survey indicates that many people would not like to live next door to a conservative Christian. Ezekiel's neighbors may have thought about moving, for some of his actions were certainly strange. He spoke only when he had a message from God (Ezekiel 3:26, 27). The rest of the time he was silent and unable to give expression to the rebukes of his heart.

Ezekiel's strange actions and object-lesson sermons must have been the talk of the exilic community, and that is what God intended. Here are some examples. After Ezekiel's initial call, he played "toy soldier" with a tile or brick (Ezekiel 4:1, 2). He sketched an outline of the city of Jerusalem, and he portrayed the implements used in a siege against the city—that was not what the exiles wanted to happen to their beloved city! This was combined with his lying on one side or the other for over 14 months, and his occasional preaching against Jerusalem (Ezekiel 4:7).

During most of this time, Ezekiel's daily diet reflected the conditions of a city under siege: about eight ounces of bread from several grains (indicating the scarcity of food) and approximately two-thirds of a quart of water. These happened at the beginning of his prophetic ministry.

I. God's Principles
(Ezekiel 18:4, 20)

The lesson this week focuses on one aspect of Ezekiel's ministry: an attitude adjustment. It is a message that he gives after he completes a series of bizarre actions and before the next dated message of 591 BC (Ezekiel 20:1).

In the interval he declares that Jerusalem definitely will be destroyed (Ezekiel 14:12-23). The response of the people is normal: they look for someone to blame. The proverb that the people quote shifts the blame by stating that their fathers ate sour grapes, but it was the children's teeth that were set on edge (Ezekiel 18:2). The people in Judah, some 880 miles away, are using the same proverb to lament their own circumstances (Jeremiah 31:29, 30). It is a familiar expression that provides an alibi.

Ezekiel 18:1-3 indicates that God will not accept this alibi. Today many use alibis to blame society, parents, chromosomes, or overpowering compulsions for deviant behavior. The passage under consideration therefore flies directly against any culture that desires a no-fault society in which everyone is a victim and no one is to be blamed personally for anything. God is ready to pronounce profound truths that are ancient yet almost revolutionary in their implications.

A word of caution must also be sounded. While it is true that a person reaps what is sown (Galatians 6:7), this must not lead to a type of "retribution theology" that says that every tragedy in life is a direct, cause-and-effect payback for sin. The book of Job gives a rebuttal to applying the retribution concept universally. See also Luke 13:1-5.

A. Absolute #1: God Is Sovereign (v. 4a)

4a. Behold, all souls are mine; as the soul of the father, so also the soul of the son is mine.

The first absolute is that every person belongs to God. This is more than ownership; it is an expression of the sovereignty of God. He has the right and the power to work with both nations and individuals to accomplish His purposes. [See question #1, page 430.]

A SENSE OF BELONGING

In a sitcom dialogue in 1984, comedian Bill Cosby reflected on the exasperations of fatherhood when he told his "son" on the show, "I am your father. I brought you into this world, and I can take you out." A son who receives this type of message from a father may not feel very wanted!

Our heavenly Father can say to us, "I brought you into this world." Psalm 139 reminds us that God was forming us even in our mother's womb. It is only because of the creative power of God that we exist. For those who have accepted Jesus, God has become Father in another sense: in our re-creation in Jesus Christ. God is both our creator for our physical birth and redeemer for our spiritual rebirth. He will also be with us when we leave this world. We are exhorted in Revelation to be faithful, even to the point of death, and then we will receive the crown of life (Revelation 2:10).

It is encouraging to realize that our Father in Heaven knows us personally, that He has created us and re-created us. And it is a source of hope to know that He will make us new again when we pass from this life. We anticipate the day when He will give us that new, glorified body in Heaven (2 Corinthians 5:4, 5). What can create any better sense of belonging than this?—A. E. A.

B. Absolute #2: Sin Brings Death (vv. 4b, 20a)

4b. The soul that sinneth, it shall die.
20a. The soul that sinneth, it shall die.

The second absolute is that sin brings death. Ezekiel declares unequivocally that sin produces a punishment, and the punishment is death. This is true whether or not the individual acknowledges God. This same assertion is repeated in the New Testament in Romans 6:23. It is sad that so many live their lives in such a way that this absolute does not seem to be a controlling factor in what they do or say. There is a payday, and that is absolute truth. [See question #2, page 430.]

The careful student will quickly observe that there are several verses between the two parallel statements. These verses contain three scenarios that represent God's responses to three generations. The first (vv. 5-9) tells of an upright man who walks in righteousness, and the sentence is pronounced that he will live. The second setting is that of a son of the righteous man, and the son's life is full of wickedness. This time the judgment is that the son will surely die (vv. 10-

13). The third illustration is of a righteous grandson who does all things well, and again it is stated that he will live. On each side of the three incidents, however, are the sobering words that death is the sentence for the sin.

C. Absolute #3: Each Is Responsible (v. 20b)

20b. The son shall not bear the iniquity of the father, neither shall the father bear the iniquity of the son: the righteousness of the righteous shall be upon him, and the wickedness of the wicked shall be upon him.

The third absolute is that each individual's situation is his or her own. There is no generational transfer of either sin or *righteousness*. The consequences of just or unjust deeds may fall on others, but the guilt is nontransferable. [See question #3, page 430.]

Those who are quoting the parable we see in Ezekiel 18:2 may be misusing Exodus 20:5 and its parallel in Deuteronomy 5:9. Those passages warn that God extends His punishment for a father's sin to the children down to "the third and fourth generation." But when harmonized with other Scripture, those passages simply indicate that God's wrath on the fathers is bound to have some indirect or collateral effect on their children.

II. God's Promises
(Ezekiel 18:21-23, 30a)

Such sobering thoughts! What God desires is a response that will bring a person's life to where it should be.

A. God's Conditions (v. 21)

21. But if the wicked will turn from all his sins that he hath committed, and keep all my statutes, and do that which is lawful and right, he shall surely live, he shall not die.

The first two words of the verse show that God's promises are conditional. Two conditions are expressed: (1) the individual must *turn* from the present way of living, and (2) that person must begin doing *all* that God has prescribed. It is not just a matter of entering into a covenant relationship with God; it is also imperative that the terms of the covenant be kept. Jesus said the same thing in the Great Commission: Jesus' disciples are to be taught to obey everything that He has commanded (Matthew 28:20).

If a person does change *from all* the ways of wickedness, then the righteous should rejoice and provide encouragement. Sometimes it is tempting to want to get even, but forgiveness is to be extended instead. It is also true that the one

---

Home Daily Bible Readings

Monday, Aug. 6—One God and One Mediator (1 Timothy 2:1-6)

Tuesday, Aug. 7—God Rewards the Righteous (Psalm 18:20-24)

Wednesday, Aug. 8—God Judges Each One's Ways (Ezekiel 33:12-20)

Thursday, Aug. 9—Those Who Sin Will Die (Ezekiel 18:1-4)

Friday, Aug. 10—The Righteous Will Live (Ezekiel 18:5-9)

Saturday, Aug. 11—Those Who Repent Will Live (Ezekiel 18:19-23)

Sunday, Aug. 12—God Judges Each of Us (Ezekiel 18:25-32)

who repents will do whatever he or she can to make restitution for wrongs committed.

B. God's Commitment (v. 22)

22. All his transgressions that he hath committed, they shall not be mentioned unto him: in his righteousness that he hath done he shall live.

God promises to provide no reminders of sin. The person who has been forgiven probably remembers them all too well, and he or she does not need to be reminded. This is different from the individual who maintains a mental or written account of the shortcomings of someone else—in case he or she ever wants to use them in an attack. Love does not even think of such things (1 Corinthians 13:5). Such a list may be necessary when building a court case against someone, but the situation here is forgiveness, not litigation. [See question #4, page 430.]

C. God's Joy (v. 23)

23. Have I any pleasure at all that the wicked should die? saith the Lord GOD: and not that he should return from his ways, and live?

God does not find *pleasure* in giving sinners what they deserve. The implication is that He does find joy in forgiving so that *the wicked* may *live*. He is not willing that any should perish, but that all should repent and turn from their evil *ways* (2 Peter 3:9).

D. God's Judgment (v. 30a)

30a. Therefore I will judge you, O house of Israel, every one according to his ways, saith the Lord GOD.

God forgives all who repent. But here is the sobering reminder that each person will be judged *according to his ways*. It is not wise to try to take advantage of God's goodness. Peter warns that the righteous are scarcely saved (1 Peter 4:18). It has been stated that the gospel contains facts to be believed, commands to be obeyed, warnings to be heeded, and promises to be enjoyed. The words in the first part of this verse constitute a warning to be heeded.

TOUGH LOVE

Some organizations encourage parents to adopt a *tough love* policy in dealing with their adolescent children. The idea behind this is to take strong steps to counter aberrant behavior. There can be a need for this in marital relationships as well.

Dr. James Dobson says that one of the major culprits of relationship problems is disrespect of one person toward another. Whether it is a child's

attitude toward a parent or one spouse toward the other, disrespect must be dealt with in a firm way. It can't be allowed to continue. It is not enjoyable or easy to practice tough love in this regard. But failure to do so will only make things worse—the cycle of bad behavior and disrespect will spiral downward, out of control.

God practices tough love with His children. The discipline He exerts (Hebrews 12:6-11) is not pleasurable at the time for either the giver or the receiver. But God knows it is a necessary part of the transformation of His children. Parents may say to their children when disciplining them, "This hurts me more than it hurts you." Children never quite understand that until they become the ones who have to discipline their own children.

We do well to remember this when God has to discipline us. He finds no pleasure in it. It even pains Him to do so, but in the end it is for the best. It is tough redemptive love.   —A. E. A.

III. God's Pleadings
(Ezekiel 18:30b-32)

God expects action and response. He is clear about what those should involve.

A. Decide About Sin (v. 30b)

30b. Repent, and turn yourselves from all your transgressions; so iniquity shall not be your ruin.

The apostle Peter makes a similar statement on the occasion of his healing the lame man in the temple. His message after the healing includes the challenge that his audience repent and be converted so that their sins could be blotted out. Only then would times of refreshing come over them (Acts 3:19). [See question #5, page 430.]

It is important to notice that God permits freedom of choice. That is one of the main thrusts of this lesson—that each person is to take responsibility for his or her own eternal destiny. That has ever been God's message. In the Garden of Eden it was by freewill choice that the first man and woman ate of the forbidden fruit. After Israel conquered Canaan, it was Joshua's challenge to the nation to "Choose you this day whom ye will serve" (Joshua 24:15). The person who hears the conditions of the gospel (John 3:16; Acts 2:38; etc.) and does not respond cannot blame others. Each person must decide about sin.

B. Discard Sin (v. 31a)

31a. Cast away from you all your transgressions, whereby ye have transgressed.

The discarding of sinful deeds must follow repentance from sin. No one can claim repentance of stealing a car if he or she continues to drive it without the rightful owner's consent!

C. Desire a New Heart (v. 31b)

31b. And make you a new heart and a new spirit: for why will ye die, O house of Israel?

The sins to be discarded may include attitudes and language that are not pleasing to God. Such things are sometimes considered "little" sins, but the command to discard includes any sinful practice. Sin in any form is not acceptable.

The way to rid oneself of sin is to develop *a new heart* that will look on life with a new perspective. The writer of Hebrews affirms that without holiness no one will see God (Hebrews 12:14; compare Matthew 5:8). Therefore everything one does will be centered on the fact that God is holy. Having a new perspective means changing the way that a person thinks about life, and this is the new heart that God demands. It

Visual for Lesson 11. *Point to this visual as you challenge your students to name a time when God granted them a new start after they repented.*

also involves the mind, for Jesus stated that the first commandment is to love God with all the heart, soul, and mind (Matthew 22:37).

D. Delight in Life (v. 32)

32. For I have no pleasure in the death of him that dieth, saith the Lord GOD: wherefore turn yourselves, and live ye.

Again we see that *God* has *no pleasure in the death of* any person (see v. 23). This is confirmed by what is called the Golden Text of the Bible, John 3:16. The verse states that God so loved that He gave His Son. The purposes are that mankind may believe and no one would have to perish. God desires that everyone choose to *live* for Him.

The contrast in this verse is vivid: life or death. The challenge of the verse is the heart of the lesson: being committed to taking responsibility for one's spiritual destiny. It is a personal choice, and it cannot be delegated.

Conclusion

A. The Anger of Guilt

Today's lesson encourages everyone to accept responsibility for personal actions. Each should acknowledge that there are basic principles that God has set forth concerning the consequences of sin. We should be prepared, however, for a certain reaction from those confronted with their wrong deeds: anger.

This kind of anger often is directed toward the person who is trying to provide the correction. If a person is told that homosexuality is sin, one response is to point fingers at the messenger. Members of a congregation may be reminded that the ministries of the church need greater financial support; a person in the church who reacts with anger probably is guilty of inadequate giving. Yet anger does not bring about the righteous life that God desires (James 1:20). That principle is true for nations, churches, or individuals.

Sin—it produces many consequences in our lives. Yet God is willing to forgive. But before a person may be right *with* God he or she must repent and turn *to* God.

B. Prayer

Almighty God, I resolve today to have the correct responses as Your Word convicts me of sin, righteousness, and the judgment to come. In Jesus' name, amen.

C. Thought to Remember

"Every one of us shall give account of himself to God" (Romans 14:12).

Learning by Doing

This page contains an alternative lesson plan emphasizing learning activities.
Classes desiring such student involvement will find these suggestions helpful.

Learning Goals

After participating in this lesson, each student will be able to:

1. State the basic concepts of responsibility for Old Testament Israel as given by Ezekiel.

2. Compare and contrast Ezekiel 18:20 with Exodus 20:5; 34:7.

3. Eliminate one behavior in his or her life that profanes God's name.

Into the Lesson

To begin class, share these creative excuses with your students, or substitute some that you have heard (or used!). (These examples are printed in the student books.)

I can't come in to work; it's Friday the thirteenth, and I'm really superstitious. I won't be in to work today because my dog has to have emergency cataract surgery. I didn't meet the deadline because I couldn't find matching socks. I'm locked in my car, and I have to go to the dealership so they can get me out. There was a bomb scare at my office building, and I couldn't call the personnel manager for my phone interview. I can't help it, officer; someone hypnotized me to park illegally.

Next, ask your students to share some excuses they have heard or used. After you have heard several examples, tell your students that today's lesson deals with taking responsibility for our behavior and not making excuses to God.

Into the Word

Develop a mini-lecture from the Lesson Background to introduce today's text. After this introduction, divide your class into three small groups of three to five students each. For larger classes create additional groups in multiples of three. Each group will cover one section of the lesson text. Distribute the following instructions, along with pencil and paper (or direct attention to the student book). Allow several minutes for each group to complete its activity.

Group #1. Read Ezekiel 18:4, 20. Identify three absolute principles stated by God in these verses. For each principle write down at least one excuse that is invalidated by that principle.

Group #2. Read Ezekiel 18:20-23, 30a. Compare verse 20 with Exodus 34:6, 7. How can both passages be true? Identify three promises that God offers to the repentant sinner in Ezekiel 18:21-23, 30a. Also identify any conditions connected with those promises. What reason does God give for offering the promises?

Group #3. Read Ezekiel 18:30-32. List the steps God required for the ancient Israelite to move from spiritual death to life and to avoid God's judgment. Explain what was involved in each step and why it was essential.

When your groups have completed their work, discuss their findings. Be sure to address the implications for evangelism, missions, and preaching today.

Into Life

Assign one of the following scenarios to each group from the previous exercise. Each team is to write a brief plan of action. The plans will use today's text to challenge the recipient(s) to take responsibility for personal actions and to allow God to renew a relationship with Him.

Scenario #1. Kim and her two young children occasionally attend worship services at your church. She wants her boy and girl to have some religious training, since she never received any from her own parents. Kim has never been married but currently lives with her boyfriend. He is not the father of her children. She blames her parents for her situation because they showed her little affection as a child. What would you say to help her?

Scenario #2. Dave is despondent about his lifestyle. He has been in and out of treatment centers for alcohol abuse but can't kick the habit for good. Dave's friends and coworkers try to encourage him to stay sober but he blames them for his addiction because they drink socially. Now he's come to your church for help. What can you do for him?

Scenario #3. Bill and Stacy have a troubled marriage. They fight often and have separated on several occasions. They have no children. Stacy blames Bill for not wanting a family, for being gone from home too often, and for failing to meet her emotional needs. Bill blames Stacy for spending too much money so that he has to work a second job to pay the bills. How can you help this troubled couple?

Let's Talk It Over

The questions on this page are designed to promote discussion of the lesson by the class and to encourage application of the lesson Scriptures. The answers provided are only discussion starters. Let your class talk it over from there.

1. How does the knowledge that God owns your very being affect how you live? What changes do you need to make?

The fact of creation makes God the owner. Scripture also reminds us that we have been bought back from sin by the blood of Christ; therefore we glorify God in body and spirit (1 Corinthians 6:20). All this means that we are not to be the servants of others in a sense of allowing them to have ultimate authority over us (1 Corinthians 7:23). We seek God's will above all else.

Our minds belong to God; therefore we are to let only holy thoughts enter. Our eyes belong to God; therefore we are to keep them from lingering over those things that bring unholy thoughts into our minds. Our time also belongs to God; therefore we are to be sure that we use our hours in ways that honor Him.

2. In what ways have you been guilty of circumventing or disavowing your personal sin? How have you made positive changes in this regard?

The Scottish singing group *The Proclaimers* has a song entitled "Everybody's a Victim." That title pretty much says it all, doesn't it? A common cultural response to an accusation of wrongdoing is for a person to claim that he or she is a victim and thus not responsible. The song bemoans the fact that the singer's country (presumably Scotland) is becoming like America in that regard.

The comedian Flip Wilson was famous for his tagline, "The devil made me do it." Scripture speaks against this view, saying that sin is the fault of the sinner (James 1:14, 15). Another way we try to alleviate personal responsibility for sin is by rationalizing. The idea is that if we are "not as bad" as someone else, then we must be relatively OK. We attempt to justify greed and bitterness by telling ourselves that at least we did not steal or kill. But Jesus said that if we ponder certain things in our hearts, then we are as guilty as if we had actually committed the sin (Matthew 5:21, 22).

3. Though sin guilt is not passed from parent to child, the consequences may be. What are some ways that the consequences of one's sins may be visited upon another? Conversely, what are some ways that the consequences of one's holy actions may be a benefit to another?

A mother who has been a drug addict may give birth to a baby who suffers birth defects caused by the addiction. A father who spends all his money on drinking binges is not able to provide properly for the needs of his family. If a child overhears a parent complaining about things in the church, the children may develop a cynical attitude toward Christianity. Acts of mercy and compassion, on the other hand, serve as a witness (1 Timothy 4:12; Titus 2:7).

4. God neither keeps a record of a Christian's sins nor remembers them. How do you use this fact to develop a godly nature?

Reminders of our past sin come from three sources: Satan, other people, and self. Learning to let go of the past and not hold on to guilt can be difficult when these three sources keep bombarding us with reminders! Recognizing the source of the discouragement is important. One thing is certain: the source is not God.

Another challenge we have is to hold no sins of others against them. When someone has repented and is trying to put his or her life back together, we as brothers and sisters in Christ are to do all we can to affirm and assist in the restoration process. God expects us to be part of the solution, not part of the problem.

5. Repentance leads to a restored relationship with God. What other benefits of repentance have you noticed in your life?

Salvation is, of course, the ultimate good that comes from repentance. But there are other benefits for us while still living out our faith on earth. Turning from sexual sins can lead to the avoidance of disease. Turning from sins of abusiveness restores relationships; if there was physical abuse, then there is now safety for those who were being abused.

Repentance or turning from a sin today makes it easier to resist another temptation tomorrow. It has been said that in repentance we do not become sinless, but we do sin less and less.

Committed to Returning to God

DEVOTIONAL READING: Isaiah 12.

BACKGROUND SCRIPTURE: Zechariah 1:1-6; 7:8-14; 8:16-23.

PRINTED TEXT: Zechariah 1:1-6; 7:8-14.

Zechariah 1:1-6

1 In the eighth month, in the second year of Darius, came the word of the LORD unto Zechariah, the son of Berechiah, the son of Iddo the prophet, saying,

2 The LORD hath been sore displeased with your fathers.

3 Therefore say thou unto them, Thus saith the LORD of hosts; Turn ye unto me, saith the LORD of hosts, and I will turn unto you, saith the LORD of hosts.

4 Be ye not as your fathers, unto whom the former prophets have cried, saying, Thus saith the LORD of hosts; Turn ye now from your evil ways, and from your evildoings: but they did not hear, nor hearken unto me, saith the LORD.

5 Your fathers, where are they? and the prophets, do they live for ever?

6 But my words and my statutes, which I commanded my servants the prophets, did they not take hold of your fathers? and they returned and said, Like as the LORD of hosts thought to do unto us, according to our ways, and according to our doings, so hath he dealt with us.

Zechariah 7:8-14

8 And the word of the LORD came unto Zechariah, saying,

9 Thus speaketh the LORD of hosts, saying, Execute true judgment, and shew mercy and compassions every man to his brother:

10 And oppress not the widow, nor the fatherless, the stranger, nor the poor; and let none of you imagine evil against his brother in your heart.

11 But they refused to hearken, and pulled away the shoulder, and stopped their ears, that they should not hear.

12 Yea, they made their hearts as an adamant stone, lest they should hear the law, and the words which the LORD of hosts hath sent in his Spirit by the former prophets: therefore came a great wrath from the LORD of hosts.

13 Therefore it is come to pass, that as he cried, and they would not hear; so they cried, and I would not hear, saith the LORD of hosts:

14 But I scattered them with a whirlwind among all the nations whom they knew not. Thus the land was desolate after them, that no man passed through nor returned: for they laid the pleasant land desolate.

GOLDEN TEXT: Thus saith the LORD of hosts; Turn ye unto me, saith the LORD of hosts, and I will turn unto you, saith the LORD of hosts.—Zechariah 1:3.

Committed to Doing Right
Unit 3: How Shall We Respond?
(Lessons 10-13)

Lesson Aims

After participating in this lesson, each student will be able to:

1. Cite at least one attitude and one behavior that the postexilic Judeans needed to eliminate from their lives in order to receive God's favor.

2. Name at least one attitude and one behavior that hinder people from having God's favor today.

3. Eliminate one attitude and one behavior that hinder his or her fellowship with God.

Lesson Outline

INTRODUCTION
  A. Turning Takes Effort
  B. Lesson Background
 I. LORD'S CALL TO REPENTANCE (Zechariah 1:1-6)
  A. Appeal by Words (vv. 1-3)
  B. Appeal by Example (vv. 4-6a)
  C. Application to Life (v. 6b)
II. LORD'S CALL TO ACTION (Zechariah 7:8-14)
  A. What to Do (vv. 8, 9)
  B. What Not to Do (v. 10)
    Of Dos *and* Don'ts
  C. People's Decision (vv. 11, 12)
  D. Lord's Discipline (vv. 13, 14)
    Losing (the) Ground
CONCLUSION
  A. As If We Had Never Left
  B. Prayer
  C. Thought to Remember

Introduction

A. Turning Takes Effort

At the time I learned to drive, one of the vehicles that my family owned was a 1957 Chevrolet. It had a gearshift on the steering column and no power steering. Needless to say, turning the wheel required what seemed at times to be a Herculean effort. Both hands were needed, yet there were times when one hand had to do because the other had to be free to shift gears.

What a far cry from the convenience of today's vehicles! Power steering now allows one to negotiate hairpin turns while sipping hot coffee or talking on a cell phone. (Some drivers, no doubt, could replace the *or* in the previous sentence with *and*!)

Today's text from the prophet Zechariah focuses on the idea of turning from sin to the Lord. That is often easier said than done. While we may intend to make such a turn, there may be a variety of factors (peer pressure, family members, pleasures of the world, intellectual doubts, etc.) that serve as unseen hands trying to steer us in the opposite direction.

For those who earnestly seek to turn to Him, however, the Lord provides encouragement. Through His Word, His Spirit, and the support of those who have already learned how to negotiate the turn, He gives us the power steering needed to defeat the efforts of those who would keep us on the same dead-end road.

The words of today's text are still the Lord's promise: "Turn ye unto me, . . . and I will turn unto you" (Zechariah 1:3).

B. Lesson Background

Zechariah was a postexilic prophet. This means he prophesied after the Babylonian exile had occurred and after God's people had been allowed to return home as a result of the decree of King Cyrus of Persia (2 Chronicles 36:22, 23). That journey home took place in the year 538 BC.

Those who returned to Judah were initially excited to be home—back in the land that God had promised would be the place where Abraham's descendants would live. One of the first orders of business was to rebuild the temple. This was an essential part of Cyrus's decree: "The Lord God . . . hath charged me to build him a house at Jerusalem" (Ezra 1:2).

The work proceeded smoothly at first. Within two years of their arrival, the people had completed the foundation of the new structure. The Bible records the mixed emotions that were expressed at the dedication of the foundation. Many shouted with joy at this significant step; however, those who could remember the grandeur of Solomon's temple and who recognized that this new temple would in no way measure up to it began to weep (Ezra 3:12, 13).

Perhaps the disparity in response to the rebuilding began to dampen enthusiasm to complete the project. Ezra 4:1-5 notes the rise of opposition from without; because of this, "Then ceased the work of the house of God. . . . So it ceased unto the second year of the reign of Darius king of Persia" (Ezra 4:24). That was 520 BC. Thus from approximately 536 to 520 BC (16 years), the temple of the Lord lay unfinished—a sad witness to a discouraged people.

I. Lord's Call to Repentance
(Zechariah 1:1-6)

The Lord raised up two prophets, namely Haggai and Zechariah, in about 520 BC to awaken the people out of their apathy and spur them on to finish what they had begun. Both prophets are mentioned in Ezra 5:1. We see the impact of their ministries in Ezra 5:2: the leaders of God's people at this time (Zerubbabel and Jeshua, also called Joshua) "began to build the house of God."

A. Appeal by Words (vv. 1-3)

1. In the eighth month, in the second year of Darius, came the word of the LORD unto Zechariah, the son of Berechiah, the son of Iddo the prophet, saying.

The second year of Darius is also mentioned in Ezra 4:24. As noted previously, this is 520 BC. This particular Darius is Darius Hystaspes, who ruled the Persian Empire from 522 to 486 BC.

The phrases *in the eighth month . . . came the word of the Lord* are standard language in prophetic books. They indicate the source of the prophet's message. As 2 Peter 1:21 states, "The prophecy came not in old time by the will of man: but holy men of God spake as they were moved by the Holy Ghost."

2. The LORD hath been sore displeased with your fathers.

Many today are quick to describe God's love in glowing terms. At the same time, they are fearful of mentioning His wrath lest someone be offended. Not Zechariah! He wastes no time in getting right to the point: *The Lord hath been sore displeased with your fathers.*

The term *fathers* can be used in a literal sense, or it can be used with a broader meaning to include previous generations, as in "forefathers."

How to Say It

BERECHIAH. Bair-uh-*kye*-uh.
CYRUS. *Sigh*-russ.
DARIUS HYSTASPES. Duh-*rye*-us Hiss-*tas*-pus.
EZEKIEL. Ee-*zeek*-ee-ul or Ee-*zeek*-yul.
HAGGAI. *Hag*-eye or *Hag*-ay-eye.
HOSEA. Ho-*zay*-uh.
MICAH. *My*-kuh.
NEBUCHADNEZZAR. *Neb*-yuh-kud-*nez*-er (strong accent on *nez*).
PERSIA. *Per*-zhuh.
ZECHARIAH. *Zek*-uh-*rye*-uh (strong accent on *rye*).
ZERUBBABEL. Zeh-*rub*-uh-bul.

The people addressed by Zechariah are 66 years removed from the time when the Babylonian captivity took place in 586 BC. Some had experienced the devastation of the downfall of Jerusalem and the burning of the temple, but many had not. Yet God was displeased not only with that generation but with previous generations as well. Those generations had rejected His call to repentance as issued through His prophets.

God's anger is not something that erupts suddenly as a fit of rage. Rather, it is His holy hostility toward sin. He had warned His people repeatedly of this and of the bitter consequences they would face. But, as the succeeding verses of our text show, they refused to listen.

3. Therefore say thou unto them, Thus saith the LORD of hosts; Turn ye unto me, saith the LORD of hosts, and I will turn unto you, saith the LORD of hosts.

The Lord's appeal to His people is remarkably simple: *Turn ye unto me, . . . and I will turn unto you.* James 4:8 issues a similar call: "Draw nigh to God, and he will draw nigh to you." God's people had returned to the land some 18 years earlier, in 538 BC. But have they returned to the Lord? The Lord gives us the freedom of choice—a truth reflected in the various "whosoever" passages of the Bible (John 3:16; Romans 10:11; Revelation 22:17). [See question #1, page 438.]

B. Appeal by Example (vv. 4-6a)

4. Be ye not as your fathers, unto whom the former prophets have cried, saying, Thus saith the LORD of hosts; Turn ye now from your evil ways, and from your evildoings: but they did not hear, nor hearken unto me, saith the LORD.

Zechariah's reference to *the former prophets* may indicate that he has other generations of God's people in mind beside "the fathers" of those he is addressing. The term *former prophets* could include eighth-century BC prophets such as Amos, Hosea, and Micah. These men of God came from a variety of backgrounds, and God used a variety of circumstances to speak through them.

All of them, however, conveyed essentially the same message, prefaced with the authoritative words *Thus saith the Lord.* Sadly, the response to the prophets' appeals was also essentially the same: *They did not hear, nor hearken.*

5. Your fathers, where are they? and the prophets, do they live for ever?

The answers to these questions are obvious. Both the *fathers* and *the prophets* (that is, the audience and the messengers of the Lord who addressed them) are but a memory in Zechariah's day. They have passed from the scene of history.

True, the prophets were holy men of God (2 Peter 1:21), but they were subject to death as is every human being (Hebrews 9:27).

6a. But my words and my statutes, which I commanded my servants the prophets, did they not take hold of your fathers?

Because the prophets spoke as servants of the Lord and proclaimed His *words* and His *statutes*, their message cannot die (and has not died to this day). The prophets' enemies may silence the messengers, but any effort to stifle or squelch their message is doomed to fail.

Zechariah asks, concerning the Lord's words and statutes, *did they not take hold of your fathers?* The term *take hold* can imply affecting someone in a life-changing way. Here, however, the meaning is more likely "overtake," in the sense of "catching up with" those who had neglected the message. The message held them accountable. A person can run from God's Word, but he or she cannot hide!

C. Application to Life (v. 6b)

6b. And they returned and said, Like as the LORD of hosts thought to do unto us, according to our ways, and according to our doings, so hath he dealt with us.

Is Zechariah describing how the fathers responded to the prophets' appeal, or is he recording his contemporaries' repentance before the Lord? Since Zechariah describes how the prophets' words "overtook" the people's fathers (first half of v. 6), it appears that this text relates the response of Zechariah's audience.

Some of these individuals, now listening to Zechariah, had witnessed the fall of Jerusalem. They recall the anguish of being forced to travel to a pagan land. They do not want to repeat the mistakes of the previous generation(s). They agree that they are "guilty as charged." They deserved the Lord's judgment.

The road to restoration lies in conforming our thinking and acting to God's standards, not in trying to create excuses for ourselves or lowering those standards. Like the prodigal son, we must determine to say to our Father, "I have sinned against heaven, and before thee" (Luke 15:18).

[See question #2, page 438.]

II. Lord's Call to Action (Zechariah 7:8-14)

According to Zechariah 7:1, the message in verses 8-14 comes to the prophet in the "fourth year of king Darius, . . . in the fourth day of the ninth month." This is a little over two years after the message that constitutes the first part of our printed text. This *fourth year* is thus 518 BC.

The seventh chapter begins by describing a delegation of men sent to ask the priests and the prophets about whether they should continue to "weep in the fifth month" as they had been doing "these so many years" (7:3). Most likely this weeping refers to a time of fasting, since this is a part of Zechariah's response in verse 5. In verse 4, Zechariah notes, "Then came the word of the Lord of hosts unto me." Though many priests and prophets are present at this time, only Zechariah is empowered to reply to the question they raise.

Because the temple in Jerusalem had been ravaged by the Babylonians in the fifth month of the nineteenth year of Nebuchadnezzar of Babylon (2 Kings 25:8, 9), some Jews had begun a fast in that month to commemorate the tragic event. According to Zechariah 7:5, that fast had been going on for nearly 70 years—in other words, ever since the city had fallen in 586 BC.

In response, Zechariah rebukes the people for their shallow acts of worship. They are shallow because those acts have not been accompanied by lives devoted to the principles that God wants to see demonstrated by His covenant people.

A. What to Do (vv. 8, 9)

8. And the word of the LORD came unto Zechariah, saying.

According to verse 4, *the word of the Lord came unto Zechariah* earlier. A series of questions from the prophet in verses 5-7 follows. Perhaps Zechariah pauses to give the people time to reflect on those questions before speaking once again the Lord's message.

9. Thus speaketh the LORD of hosts, saying, Execute true judgment, and show mercy and compassions every man to his brother.

The commands given here are in keeping with the kind of conduct that the Lord has always required of His people. *Judgment* (or justice) may be considered to be treating people the way God would treat them. The ideals of *mercy and compassions* are an essential part of this.

B. What Not to Do (v. 10)

10. And oppress not the widow, nor the fatherless, the stranger, nor the poor; and let none of you imagine evil against his brother in your heart.

This verse moves from the more abstract ideals of verse 9 to specific groups who need more than high ideals—they need to see the actions of flesh and blood put on those ideals! These groups include *the widow, the fatherless, the stranger,* and *the poor.* The individuals in these groups are frequently taken advantage of because their circumstances leave them vulnerable. Churches today often have opportunities to exhibit the love of Jesus by initiating ministries to those who would be considered, in Jesus' words, "the least of these" (Matthew 25:40, 45; see also James 1:27).

Notice that this verse also addresses our inner motives: *let none of you imagine evil against his brother in your heart.* Sometimes people view the Old Testament as concerned more with outward actions to the minimization of one's thoughts and motives. That is clearly not the case, as is apparent in the Tenth Commandment (covetousness). Also, we think of passages such as Proverbs 4:23: "Keep thy heart with all diligence; for out of it are the issues of life." [See question #3, page 438.]

OF *DOS* AND *DON'TS*

As I write these words, we are just two weeks removed from Hurricane Katrina, which devastated the gulf coast of the United States in late August 2005. One area greatly affected was the city of New Orleans. Since that city is below sea level, levees had been built to protect it from flooding. But the levees failed, and most of the city was under water.

Since New Orleans is noted for a party atmosphere and unholy events, there were some Christians quick to say that this was God's judgment on that city. They said that the city was suffering punishment for violating God's *don'ts.* But the number who said this was low in relation to the number of Christians who responded by providing various kinds of assistance to the evacuees.

Sometimes Christianity is known as a religion that focuses primarily on *don'ts.* The *don'ts* are indeed important—for example, the Ten Commandments are primarily worded that way. But the *dos* are important too!

The best way to counteract the charge of being primarily a religion of negative rules, a religion of *don'ts,* is to do positive things by showing mercy and compassion. Rick Rusaw and Eric Swanson have the right idea: "Externally focused churches have the advantage of deploying people into the community where they can be church to people through their love and service. Their light is not hidden under a bushel" (*The Externally Focused Church*, page 28).   —A. E. A.

C. People's Decision (vv. 11, 12)

11. But they refused to hearken, and pulled away the shoulder, and stopped their ears, that they should not hear.

The *they* in this verse apparently refers to the former generations who were exposed to the pleas of the "former prophets" (7:7, 12), mentioned previously in Zechariah 1:4. What stubbornness the people had exhibited!

12. Yea, they made their hearts as an adamant stone, lest they should hear the law, and the words which the LORD of hosts hath sent in his Spirit by the former prophets: therefore came a great wrath from the LORD of hosts.

The phrase *adamant stone* describes an extremely hard material, most likely flint or a harder substance. Note the language used in Ezekiel 3:9, where God tells that prophet, "As an adamant harder than flint have I made thy forehead: fear them not, neither be dismayed at their looks, though they be a rebellious house."

The law and the *prophets* are the two primary vehicles of revelation during the Old Testament period. The two terms came to be used in such a way as to designate the equivalent of the entire Old Testament (Luke 16:16; John 1:45; Romans 3:21). The influence of God's *Spirit* upon the prophets is also noted (see also Nehemiah 9:30). The Lord's *great wrath* is similar to His being "sore displeased" in Zechariah 1:2. [See question #4, page 438.]

D. Lord's Discipline (vv. 13, 14)

13. Therefore it is come to pass, that as he cried, and they would not hear; so they cried, and I would not hear, saith the LORD of hosts.

Earlier we read the Lord's invitation in Zechariah 1:3: "Turn ye unto me, . . . and I will turn unto you." The verse before us states the negative side of this truth: God will not respond if we

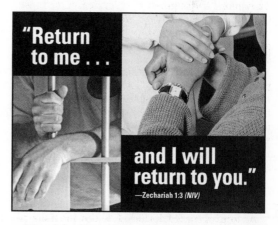

"Return to me . . . and I will return to you."
—Zechariah 1:3 *(NIV)*

Visual for Lesson 12. *Use this visual as a discussion starter by asking, "What are some ways that people intentionally move away from God?"*

repeatedly ignore His appeals or merely cry out to Him only as a last resort. [See question #5, page 438.]

14. But I scattered them with a whirlwind among all the nations whom they knew not. Thus the land was desolate after them, that no man passed through nor returned: for they laid the pleasant land desolate.

This verse describes the consequences of the people's refusal to heed the Lord's message through His prophets. The impact on God's people was that they were *scattered . . . among all the nations*. As Adam and Eve had been evicted from their paradise in Eden, God's people were ousted from their home in fulfillment of His word—a warning issued since the time of Moses (Leviticus 26:27-35; Deuteronomy 28:36, 37).

The impact on *the land* is also noted. The land that had once flowed with milk and honey is here described as *desolate* and as a place where no one *passed through nor returned* to. In other words, normal activities could not be carried out because of the extent of the devastation.

Tragic as these circumstances were, God's people had no one to blame but themselves. They—God's chosen people—were responsible for making the pleasant land desolate.

LOSING (THE) GROUND

Because of sin, the ancient Israelites ended up losing the very ground that God had given them, the promised land. Losing this ground in a physical sense was preceded by losing it spiritually. Instead of growing in obedience to God, the Israelites rebelled against His will. Instead of being a pure and holy people, they became defiled by the nations around them.

Home Daily Bible Readings

Monday, Aug. 13—How to Return to God (James 4:6-10)

Tuesday, Aug. 14—God's Everlasting Love (Psalm 103:8-18)

Wednesday, Aug. 15—God Is My Salvation (Isaiah 12)

Thursday, Aug. 16—Return to God (Zechariah 1:1-6)

Friday, Aug. 17—The People Refuse God (Zechariah 7:8-14)

Saturday, Aug. 18—Divine Deliverance for God's People (Zechariah 8:1-8)

Sunday, Aug. 19—Come to the Lord (Zechariah 8:14-17, 20-23)

This is part of a disturbing pattern. The Roman Empire, for example, also "lost it all." A few reasons cited for the fall of this great empire include political corruption, urban decay, increased military spending at the expense of other vital needs, and a decline in morals. Rome's downfall seems to have been predicted in Daniel 2:33, 34.

It is easy to take pride in our own nation. But pride leads to a fall. We do well to remember that, "Righteousness exalteth a nation: but sin is a reproach to any people" (Proverbs 14:34). Failure to practice righteousness can still lead nations into "losing ground" physically. For the individual, failure to practice righteousness may also mean losing the promised land of Heaven.

—A. E. A.

Conclusion

A. As If We Had Never Left

America's civil war ended in 1865. President Abraham Lincoln faced a particularly explosive issue: what was to be done with the southern states that had seceded from the Union to form the Confederacy? Some demanded a stiff punishment for what they considered treason against the United States. Lincoln, however, advocated a much more conciliatory policy. His eloquent response to the matter of how to treat the states in question was that it would be "as if they had never left."

Today's lesson has called attention to God's gracious invitation to forsake sinful ways and return to Him. He has done all He can do to remove whatever obstacles exist. The most daunting obstacle, sin, has been addressed at the cross through God's provision of His Son, Jesus, as an atoning sacrifice. If we choose to accept that sacrifice and respond to the Father's invitation to come home, He will forgive us completely and make us new creatures.

It will indeed be as if we had never left.

B. Prayer

Father, thank You for the opportunity to leave the life of sin and return to You. We are so unworthy of such an opportunity, yet in Your grace You have opened up a way through Your Son, Jesus. Help us to see that whatever we give up in the process of returning to You will be far, far outweighed by what You have in store for us. In Jesus' name, amen.

C. Thought to Remember

God is now—and always has been—ready for you to return.

Learning by Doing

This page contains an alternative lesson plan emphasizing learning activities.
Classes desiring such student involvement will find these suggestions helpful.

Learning Goals

After participating in this lesson, each student should be able to:

1. Cite at least one attitude and one behavior that the postexilic Judeans needed to eliminate from their lives in order to receive God's favor.

2. Name at least one attitude and one behavior that hinder people from having God's favor today.

3. Eliminate one attitude and one behavior that hinder his or her fellowship with God.

Into the Lesson

Give to each student a copy of the following Things to Eliminate quiz (or direct your students' attention to the quiz in the student book, if you're using those). Ask students to match the things they would eliminate with solutions.

1. To put out a fire, eliminate ___.
2. To avoid heartburn, eliminate ___.
3. To overcome insomnia, eliminate ___.
4. To avoid a broken leg, eliminate ___.
5. To avoid excessive debt, eliminate ___.
6. To avoid verbosity, eliminate ___.
7. To finish a task, eliminate ___.
8. To reduce the threat of heart disease, eliminate ___.

A. nonessential words; B. oxygen; C. worries that fill your mind; D. spicy foods. E. credit cards; F. ice on the sidewalk; G. procrastination; H. smoking. *(Answers: 1B, 2D, 3C, 4F, 5E, 6A, 7G, 8H)*

Grade the quizzes together. Then tell your class that this lesson deals with eliminating barriers that keep us separated from God.

Into the Word

Use the Lesson Background to introduce today's lesson text, then have two students read the text aloud. One will read Zechariah 1:1-6; the other will read Zechariah 7:8-14.

Next, divide your class into pairs. Half the pairs will study the text from Zechariah 1; the other half will study the text from Zechariah 7. Give each pair a copy of one set of instructions below (or tell them to turn to their student books, if you're using those, to find the exercise).

Exercise #1: The Lord's Call to Repentance. With your partner, reread Zechariah 1:1-6. Then answer the following questions: *1.* Why had God been displeased with their ancestors? *2.* What positive offer did God make to the Judeans of Zechariah's day, and how had the people responded to previous offers (see Ezekiel 18:21-23)? *3.* What two reasons did God give the Judeans for not imitating their ancestors but for obeying Him?

Exercise #2: The Lord's Call to Action. With your partner, reread Zechariah 7:8-14. Then answer the following questions: *1.* What three things were the Judeans to do to demonstrate the sincerity of their repentance? *2.* What acts and attitudes were the Judeans to eliminate from their lives, and how were these related to the positive actions God commanded them to do? *3.* What was the reaction of the people to this call for repentance in times past, and what is significant about their rejection of both the law and the prophets? *4.* How did God respond to their hard hearts, and what lesson should the Judeans in Zechariah's day have learned from their history? *5.* What lesson should we learn from these events?

When your pairs complete their exercises, discuss their findings. Emphasize that God's call to repentance involves a call to action as well.

Into Life

Join your pairs together to make groups of four. Instruct each group to read Ephesians 5 and brainstorm some common negative attitudes and behaviors that hinder people from experiencing the full joy of being a Christian. Give each group pencil and paper to record their results (or refer them to this activity in the student books, if you're using those). When groups have had sufficient time to develop lists of negatives, ask volunteers to share their lists. Write examples on the board.

Next, ask your groups to brainstorm some scriptural attitudes and behaviors that are antidotes to these negatives, again referring to Ephesians 5 for ideas. When they have assembled lists, call for volunteers once more. List their solutions on the board, parallel to the negatives.

Challenge each student to find one (or more) negative attitude or behavior from the list that is a particular problem to him or her. Pray for your students to seek to eliminate those negatives by practicing the biblical positives you have discussed today.

Let's Talk It Over

The questions on this page are designed to promote discussion of the lesson by the class and to encourage application of the lesson Scriptures. The answers provided are only discussion starters. Let your class talk it over from there.

1. Is there a danger today of Christians returning to "the land of God" physically without really returning to God spiritually? If so, how do we avoid this danger?

Some hold the perception that the church building is the place of God. After a time away from involvement in church, people may feel a need to return to church to fulfill some type of religious ritual and feel better about themselves. Don't we find it easier to perform outward acts that appear to evidence faith when our hearts actually are shallow toward God? See Matthew 15:8.

There is no physical, earthly "promised land" for the church of the New Testament as there was for Israel of the Old Testament. This fact should make it easier for us to avoid Israel's mistake of equating any kind of physical return with a spiritual return. But the physical should not be separated from the spiritual too much. Developing a deep faith is quite difficult when Christians neglect to be physically present with one another (Hebrews 10:25).

2. What are some specific things you need to do to conform your thoughts and actions to God's standards?

This can lead to a wide-open discussion, even to a time of repentance. Expect answers that deal with prayer, Bible study, acts of benevolence, and a greater emphasis on evangelism.

One problem that can distract from the need to conform thoughts and actions to God's standards is the danger being devoted more to a certain messenger than to the message itself. Paul spoke of those who were more interested in lining up behind certain church leaders rather than behind Christ (1 Corinthians 1:12). Some may quit going to a particular church when the preacher leaves. A church may fail to take action against a leader who has fallen morally, excusing or even rationalizing the sin. Such undue loyalty to the *messenger* of God demonstrates a disloyalty to the *person* of God by violating His Word.

3. The heart is considered the seat of the emotions. What steps have you taken to develop a proper heart for God and His kingdom? What steps do you yet need to take?

A good starting point is to examine how Bible characters developed a heart for God. David, as he cried for mercy from God because of his sin, said, "Create in me a clean heart, O God; and renew a right spirit within me" (Psalm 51:10). The first step is humility.

Forsaking the lure of this world is also necessary in developing a heart for God. Paul says, "And be not conformed to this world: but be ye transformed" (Romans 12:2). Keeping God's Word leads to a renewed heart. Jesus said, "But that [seed] on the good ground are they, which in an honest and good heart, having heard the word, keep it, and bring forth fruit with patience" (Luke 8:15). These biblical examples and precepts should shape our individual practices.

4. What modern applications can we see in Zechariah 7:12?

We remind ourselves that people have free will—they can choose to close their ears and refuse to hear. Instead of their rejection causing us to be reluctant to share the message in the future, God expects us to continue to do our part by faithfully proclaiming His message. Jesus did! Even a cursory reading of Scripture reveals that the majority of people will reject the message (Matthew 7:13, 14). This fact should not dissuade us from being teachers of God's Word, sharing the message of eternal hope.

5. What are some modern examples of crying out to God as a last resort? Do you think God ever honors those cries? Why, or why not?

A deathbed confession of faith is an example of a last-resort cry. Deathbed confessions comfort some people when they coax an acknowledgment of God from the lips of the one who is dying. Such confessions may or may not demonstrate true repentance. Only God knows the heart.

After the person dies following such a confession, there are no actions possible by which that person can demonstrate true repentance. This is not true in other situations. A person who cries to God for deliverance from an approaching tornado may live through the experience to demonstrate true repentance. God always honors true repentance!

Committed to Doing Right

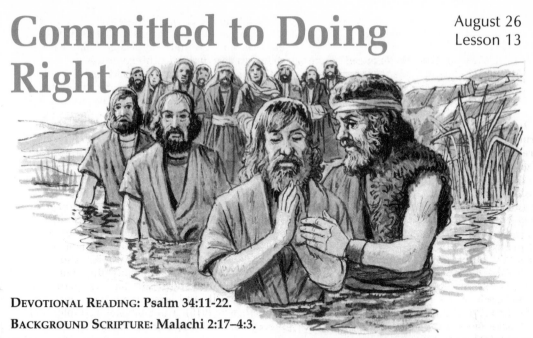

DEVOTIONAL READING: Psalm 34:11-22.

BACKGROUND SCRIPTURE: Malachi 2:17–4:3.

PRINTED TEXT: Malachi 2:17–3:5; 4:1.

Malachi 2:17

17 Ye have wearied the LORD with your words. Yet ye say, Wherein have we wearied him? When ye say, Every one that doeth evil is good in the sight of the LORD, and he delighteth in them; or, Where is the God of judgment?

Malachi 3:1-5

1 Behold, I will send my messenger, and he shall prepare the way before me: and the Lord, whom ye seek, shall suddenly come to his temple, even the messenger of the covenant, whom ye delight in: behold, he shall come, saith the LORD of hosts.

2 But who may abide the day of his coming? and who shall stand when he appeareth? for he is like a refiner's fire, and like fullers' soap:

3 And he shall sit as a refiner and purifier of silver: and he shall purify the sons of Levi, and purge them as gold and silver, that they may offer unto the LORD an offering in righteousness.

4 Then shall the offering of Judah and Jerusalem be pleasant unto the LORD, as in the days of old, and as in former years.

5 And I will come near to you to judgment; and I will be a swift witness against the sorcerers, and against the adulterers, and against false swearers, and against those that oppress the hireling in his wages, the widow, and the fatherless, and that turn aside the stranger from his right, and fear not me, saith the LORD of hosts.

Malachi 4:1

1 For, behold, the day cometh, that shall burn as an oven; and all the proud, yea, and all that do wickedly, shall be stubble: and the day that cometh shall burn them up, saith the LORD of hosts, that it shall leave them neither root nor branch.

GOLDEN TEXT: Behold, I will send my messenger, and he shall prepare the way before me. . . . But who may abide the day of his coming? and who shall stand when he appeareth?—Malachi 3:1, 2.

Committed to Doing Right
Unit 3: How Shall We Respond?
(Lessons 10-13)

Lesson Aims

After participating in this lesson, each student will be able to:

1. Summarize what Malachi said in response to questions about God's justice.

2. List some ways that a lack of commitment to doing right wearies the Lord today.

3. Make a plan to resist one cultural trend that opposes God's expectations for justice.

Lesson Outline

INTRODUCTION
  A. "Now Go Do the Right Thing"
  B. Lesson Background
I. PEOPLE'S COMPLAINT (Malachi 2:17)
  A. Malachi Alleges (v. 17a)
  B. People Ask (v. 17b)
  C. Malachi Answers (v. 17c)
II. LORD'S COMING (Malachi 3:1-5; 4:1)
  A. Preparation (v. 1a)
    The Advance Team
  B. Place (v. 1b)
  C. Program (v. 1c)
  D. Purpose (vv. 2, 3a)
  E. Product (vv. 3b, 4)
  F. Punishment (3:5; 4:1)
    Mistaken Identity
CONCLUSION
  A. Right Makes Might
  B. Prayer
  C. Thought to Remember

Introduction

A. "Now Go Do the Right Thing"

Laura Schlesinger's radio program has become one of the most well known and most listened to in the highly competitive world of talk radio. Her no-nonsense approach, characterized by a strong emphasis on Judeo-Christian values, has gained her a significant following. At the end of each hour of her broadcast, "Dr. Laura" concludes with this brief but compelling advice: "Now go do the right thing."

Such counsel seems simple. Yet there is no question that if listeners really took it to heart and applied it to their circumstances, they would avoid numerous heartaches and tensions. Perhaps Dr. Laura would find herself with far fewer callers to deal with!

Today's lesson comes from Malachi, the last book in the Old Testament. Malachi, the last Old Testament prophet chronologically, is the final messenger of God to address God's people before the gap of 400 years until the New Testament era begins. As we will see today, the book of Malachi closes the Old Testament with an appeal from God that is appropriate for His people to hear, whether in an Old Testament or a New Testament setting. It may be summarized as, "Now go do the right thing."

B. Lesson Background

Malachi's circumstances were somewhat different from those of the other prophets we have studied this quarter. Yet the basic thrust of what all these men of God had to say is the same: being part of God's covenant people means much more than basking in a special status. God expects a certain lifestyle of those who lay claim to that status. One of the primary tasks of God's prophets throughout the Old Testament was to call His people to account when they failed to carry out their sacred responsibility.

Not much is known about Malachi himself. One bit of information is his name. In Hebrew it means "my messenger"—a theme that will become crucial in today's text. We must examine information within the book itself to learn the time in the history of God's people when Malachi likely prophesied.

Such an investigation points to the time of Nehemiah as perhaps the best fit for Malachi's ministry. This is because many of the sins highlighted in the book of Malachi are the same sins that Nehemiah had to confront. These included indifference toward the kind of sacrifices required by the Lord (Nehemiah 10:37-39; Malachi 1:6-14), disregard for the Lord's teaching concerning marriage (Nehemiah 13:23-27; Malachi 2:14-16), and the bringing of tithes and offerings to support the Lord's work (Nehemiah 10:37-39; 13:10-13; Malachi 3:8-10). Furthermore, the mention of a governor in Malachi 1:8 fits well with Nehemiah's time, since he was recognized by that title (Nehemiah 5:14).

Nehemiah had traveled to Jerusalem in the twentieth year of Artaxerxes, king of Persia (445 BC). He went there primarily to spearhead efforts to rebuild the wall of the city (Nehemiah 2:1-11). This was approximately 100 years after the Jews had first returned from captivity in Babylon, and

[handwritten margin notes: "worship is acute..." "Psalm 73" "The closer we get to the cows the more we see how unpure we are"]

about 70 years after the second temple had been completed through the encouragement of the prophets Haggai and Zechariah. Today's Scripture from Malachi focuses on his challenges to God's people in his own day. But it also highlights a portion of his glimpse into the future and of what God planned to accomplish through a messenger far greater than Malachi—the Lord Jesus Christ.

I. People's Complaint
(Malachi 2:17)

A. Malachi Alleges (v. 17a)

17a. Ye have wearied the LORD with your words.

Much of Malachi is written as if the Lord is engaging His people in a dialogue. Malachi pictures the Lord as making a statement, then he pictures the people as challenging the statement. The Lord then responds to the challenge. In so doing He calls attention to an area of His people's relationship with Him that they have neglected. Examples of these dialogues are found in Malachi 1:2, 6, 7; 2:13, 14; 3:7, 8, 13-15, as well as in the verses before us.

Here Malachi claims *ye have wearied the Lord with your words*. One may ask how this can be true in light of Isaiah 40:28, which declares, "Hast thou not known? hast thou not heard, that the everlasting God, the Lord, . . . fainteth not, neither is weary? there is no searching of his understanding."

But there is no contradiction. The Lord does not grow weary in the sense of losing His power, strength, or majesty; He can become weary (meaning frustrated and disappointed) with the behavior of His people and their refusal to heed His call to change. [See question #1, page 446.]

How to Say It

ARTAXERXES. Are-tuh-*zerk*-seez.
BABYLON. *Bab*-uh-lun.
ELIJAH. Ee-*lye*-juh.
EZEKIEL. Ee-*zeek*-ee-ul or Ee-*zeek*-yul.
HAGGAI. *Hag*-eye or *Hag*-ay-eye.
HEZEKIAH. Hez-ih-*kye*-uh.
MALACHI. *Mal*-uh-kye.
NEHEMIAH. *Nee*-huh-*my*-uh (strong accent on *my*).
PERSIA. *Per*-zhuh.
SINAI. *Sigh*-nye or *Sigh*-nay-eye.
ZECHARIAH. *Zek*-uh-*rye*-uh (strong accent on *rye*).

B. People Ask (v. 17b)

17b. Yet ye say, Wherein have we wearied him?

One can understand why the people would want to know how they have *wearied* the Lord. Have they spoken blasphemous, angry, or lying words? Have they been practicing what Jesus would later call "vain repetitions" (Matthew 6:7)? Is God concerned because their lives are not consistent with their words? What's the deal?

C. Malachi Answers (v. 17c)

17c. When ye say, Every one that doeth evil is good in the sight of the LORD, and he delighteth in them; or, Where is the God of judgment?

Here is the answer to the people's inquiry. The words that have wearied the Lord are words that have questioned His *judgment* (meaning "justice"). It appears to the people that the Lord no longer cares whether *evil* is punished or *good* is rewarded. Earlier, the prophet Isaiah declared, "Woe unto them that call evil good, and good evil" (Isaiah 5:20). Has the Lord done the same? It seems so in the eyes of Malachi's audience. [See question #2, page 446.]

Why would God's people speak so critically of the Lord? At this point in Old Testament history, God's people have been back in the promised land for nearly 100 years. They know the words of the prophets who had spoken of a glorious new day for God's people. That day is to be ushered in by the coming of the Branch (Isaiah 4:2-6; 11:1-3; Jeremiah 23:5-8; 33:15, 16). They know of God's promise to "set up one shepherd over them, and he shall feed them, even my servant David" (Ezekiel 34:23).

But where is this special person? When will He come and do all that the prophets had said He would do? God's people had finished the temple many decades previously. Hadn't a prophet declared that at that time the Lord would "fill this house with glory" and that "the glory of this latter house shall be greater than of the former" (Haggai 2:7, 9)? The people have done their part—why hasn't the Lord done His? Where is His glory?

II. Lord's Coming
(Malachi 3:1-5; 4:1)

A. Preparation (v. 1a)

1a. Behold, I will send my messenger, and he shall prepare the way before me.

The Lord proceeds to answer the challenge. He has not forgotten His promises. "Where is the God of judgment?" He is coming, but He will not

"I will send my messenger."
—Malachi 3:1

Visual for
Lesson 13

Point to this depiction of John the Baptist as you ask, "How will you be the Lord's messenger today?"

come without a *messenger* to *prepare the way before* Him.

Earlier we noted that the name *Malachi* means "my messenger." Here the Lord promises another messenger. Malachi 4:5 describes him as "Elijah the prophet." The New Testament is clear that John the Baptist is the one who fulfills Malachi's prophecy in his role as the forerunner of Jesus Christ (Mark 1:1-4). Jesus equated John the Baptist's ministry with the promised coming of Elijah (Matthew 17:10-13).

THE ADVANCE TEAM

My wife and I were in Cincinnati, Ohio, in the 1980s when then-President Ronald Reagan was to visit the city for a speech. As we drove down the highway on which the presidential motorcade was to pass, we noticed police officers guarding the route. We drove downtown that evening to see if we would get a glimpse of the president. The streets were cleared of traffic and there were no parked cars along the path the motorcade was to follow. Barricades were up.

Arriving that evening at our friends' house, we greeted our hostess. She worked as a nurse at a hospital between the airport and downtown. She said she would not be coming home until the president's plane had cleared Cincinnati airspace later that evening.

All of these details were accomplished by an *advance team*. This team took great care and precaution to ensure that every eventuality was covered and that the president was kept safe for his entire visit. The team wanted nothing to impede the safe progress of the president in accomplishing his mission.

John the Baptist came as a kind of one-man advance team for the Messiah. He did all he could to prepare the way for Jesus. The church today plays the role of the advance team for the second coming of Christ. How are you preparing yourself and the world for His return? —A. E. A.

B. Place (v. 1b)

1b. And the Lord, whom ye seek, shall suddenly come to his temple.

As noted previously, part of the reason why God's people question His whereabouts and His justice is the fact that the temple had been finished many decades previously. Perhaps they are expecting a display of glory similar to what occurred when the first temple was dedicated (1 Kings 8:10, 11). Thus far nothing at all like that has been witnessed with the second temple.

However, the glory of *the Lord* will, in time, fill this second temple. That is exactly what takes place when the Lord Jesus Christ enters there during His earthly ministry.

The word *suddenly* depicts how most people are caught off guard when He arrives because He comes in a manner that is unexpected. God's glory will enter the temple but not in the dramatic way it had filled the tabernacle (Exodus 40:34, 35) or the first temple. Rather it will come about because "the Word was made flesh, and dwelt among us, (and we beheld his glory, the glory as of the only begotten of the Father,) full of grace and truth" (John 1:14). [See question #3, page 446.]

C. Program (v. 1c)

1c. Even the messenger of the covenant, whom ye delight in: behold, he shall come, saith the LORD of hosts.

Malachi now declares the Lord to be another type of messenger—*the messenger of the covenant.* Thus one messenger (John the Baptist) will prepare the way for another messenger (Jesus), who will establish a new covenant.

Earlier, Malachi referred to two other covenants. One was "the covenant of Levi," involving the priests; in Malachi's day they have "departed out of the way" (Malachi 2:8) and neglected their sacred duties. The other is "the covenant of our fathers" (2:10), which probably refers to the covenant God had established at Sinai. That covenant had been profaned (again, 2:10). Clearly there was a need for a new and better covenant. That is exactly what Jesus comes to establish (Jeremiah 31:31-34; compare Hebrews 8:8-12; 10:16, 17).

It may be with a tinge of sarcasm that Malachi describes the messenger of the covenant as one *whom ye delight in.* The people of Malachi's day act as if they desire the Lord to come and vindicate himself. But will they be ready to welcome Him when he does? Sadly, most in Jesus' day were not (John 1:11).

D. Purpose (vv. 2, 3a)

2, 3a. But who may abide the day of his coming? and who shall stand when he appeareth? For he is like a refiner's fire, and like fullers' soap: and he shall sit as a refiner and purifier of silver.

The two questions in this portion of our text are to be considered rhetorical; that is, they are asked not in order to produce an answer but to challenge people to think. Lest people become too complacent about the Lord's promised coming, they should realize that when He comes He will make some serious changes!

A *refiner's fire* is used to burn away impurities from precious metals such as *silver* (compare Isaiah 48:10; Zechariah 13:9). *Fullers' soap* (an alkaline lye) is used to cleanse, bleach, and sometimes dye cloth. Most likely the cleansing represented by these processes refers to a spiritual cleansing.

Thus it is easy to see why the question is raised as to who can *abide* or *stand* such treatment. The sins from which people need to be cleansed are too numerous to count. This messenger of the covenant comes to perform what in today's terms would be considered an extreme makeover—on the inside! [See question #4, page 446.]

E. Product (vv. 3b, 4)

3b, 4. And he shall purify the sons of Levi, and purge them as gold and silver, that they may offer unto the LORD an offering in righteousness. Then shall the offering of Judah and Jerusalem be pleasant unto the LORD, as in the days of old, and as in former years.

The sons of Levi include the priests, who have already been called to account for having "corrupted the covenant of Levi" (Malachi 2:8). The priests have also been charged with offering blemished, unacceptable offerings to the Lord (1:6-10). All of this will change when the Lord's purifying work has been accomplished.

These verses describe another dimension of the consequences of Jesus' work as the "messenger of the [new] covenant" (Malachi 3:1). One of the most significant characteristics of the new covenant is that every Christian serves the Lord as a priest (1 Peter 2:9; Revelation 1:6). Priests offer sacrifices and good works. Similarly, every Christian is called to offer the sacrifice of praise and good works to God (Hebrews 13:15, 16).

The period described as *the days of old* and *former years* may refer to any period in the history of God's people when there was a greater consistency between the sacrifices they offered and the lives they lived. This would have been true during the reigns of godly kings such as David, Hezekiah, and Josiah.

F. Punishment (3:5; 4:1)

5. And I will come near to you to judgment; and I will be a swift witness against the sorcerers, and against the adulterers, and against false swearers, and against those that oppress the hireling in his wages, the widow, and the fatherless, and that turn aside the stranger from his right, and fear not me, saith the LORD of hosts.

While some will choose to accept the refiner's cleansing fire, others will refuse to undergo the purifying process. Those who refuse will one day learn, to their ruination, that the fire of refinement can also become a fire of *judgment*.

Several of the sins mentioned in this verse bring to mind some of the Ten Commandments as listed in Deuteronomy 5. These include the actions of *adulterers* (Seventh Commandment), *false swearers* (Ninth Commandment), and *those that oppress the hireling*, or worker, in his wages (this amounts to stealing, a violation of the Eighth Commandment).

To engage in the practices of *sorcerers* could violate the First Commandment, which prohibits the worship of other gods. The neglect of *the widow, the fatherless*, and *the stranger* is forbidden in Exodus 22:21, 22; Deuteronomy 24:17-22. All of these sins (indeed, any sin) can be traced to one root cause: they are the consequence of failing to *fear* the Lord. [See question #5, page 446.]

Recall how our printed text began with Malachi alluding to the people's inquiry: "Where is the God of judgment?" (Malachi 2:17). The verse before us gives the answer: He will come, and His judgment will be *swift* when He does come. Malachi's words are reminiscent of what Peter writes concerning Jesus' return in 2 Peter 3:9, 10.

MISTAKEN IDENTIFY

I was visiting a church one Sunday for the first time. In talking with the minister, he learned that I too was a preacher. But somewhere along the line he got my first name (Gene) confused with another man he knew (Gus). Gus and I have the same last name, although we are not related and have never met.

At the close of the service, the preacher called on me for the prayer. Before I prayed, he told the congregation about the family of Gus and how they had meant so much to his family through the years back in West Virginia. Many came to me after the service just thrilled at the great story the preacher had told about "my family."

This case of mistaken identity was hard to deal with given the situation. But there is another case of mistaken identity that is even worse. We see the fatherless and the widow, and we mistake them for the lazy who shouldn't eat (2 Thessalonians 3:10). Though we may smugly rejoice at the thought that swift judgment will be meted out on the sorcerers and the adulterers, we fail to see that the same judgment will be made against those who ignore innocent people who are in genuine need. —A. E. A.

4:1. For, behold, the day cometh, that shall burn as an oven; and all the proud, yea, and all that do wickedly, shall be stubble: and the day that cometh shall burn them up, saith the LORD of hosts, that it shall leave them neither root nor branch.

This verse also emphasizes the certainty of coming judgment. Both the attitudes of *the proud* and the actions of *all that do wickedly* are highlighted. Earlier prophets had used the terms *root* and *branch* as the basis for prophecies concerning the coming Messiah (Isaiah 4:2; 11:1; Jeremiah 23:5; 33:15). Now we see that this judgment pronounced by Malachi will be so complete as to leave *neither root nor branch*.

Thus we have seen today's text describe the impact of both the first and second comings of the messenger of the covenant—Jesus. With His first coming, He initiates a ministry of cleansing and purifying through His sacrificial death on the cross and His resurrection. That ministry continues through the testimony of faithful Christians who bear witness to what Jesus can do for others through the gospel message.

At His second coming, however, the refining ministry of Jesus will mean judgment upon those who have not accepted for themselves His cleansing power. It is similar to saying that those who do not acknowledge Jesus as the "chief corner stone" (1 Peter 2:6) will find Him to be "a stone of stumbling" and "a rock of offense" (1 Peter 2:8). The kind of rock and the kind of refiner that Jesus will be for us is up to us. Our choice!

Conclusion

A. Right Makes Might

The phrase "might makes right" is familiar. This reflects a belief that the strong or those in positions of authority generally gain the upper hand because of their ability to exercise sheer force. The supremacy they possess due to these factors gives them the power to determine what is "right" and to enforce their will on others.

The more biblical view (and the theme of today's study) is that "right makes might." When an individual is committed to doing right in the sight of the Lord, he or she gains a sense of accomplishment and purpose that not even the mightiest "might makes right" advocate can possess.

We began with a reference to Dr. Laura's oft-heard counsel, "Now go do the right thing." Consider how often Jesus gave essentially the same challenge. After telling the parable of the Good Samaritan, Jesus said, "Go, and do thou likewise" (Luke 10:37). He told the disciples after washing their feet, "I have given you an example, that ye should do as I have done to you" (John 13:15).

Have you learned some important lessons from your studies this quarter? Sit down and make a list of the top ten lessons you have gleaned. With each one, list an action step that you can take in order to apply that particular insight. And then—"Go, and do *thou* likewise."

B. Prayer

Father, forgive us when we fail to do right. Forgive us for those times when a Christian's influence was needed—yet we remained silent and inactive. May we follow the example of Jesus, "who went about doing good" (Acts 10:38). May our light shine in this sinful world. In Jesus' name, amen.

C. Thought to Remember

Right makes might—
not just believing it, but doing it.

Home Daily Bible Readings

Monday, Aug. 20—God's Concern for the People (Psalm 34:11-22)

Tuesday, Aug. 21—Our Works Are Tested (1 Corinthians 3:10-15)

Wednesday, Aug. 22—God Judges Our Hearts (1 Corinthians 4:1-5)

Thursday, Aug. 23—God Will Judge (Malachi 2:17–3:7)

Friday, Aug. 24—Will Anyone Rob God? (Malachi 3:8-12)

Saturday, Aug. 25—Choosing Between Good and Evil (Malachi 3:13-18)

Sunday, Aug. 26—The Day of the Lord (Malachi 4:1-6)

Learning by Doing

This page contains an alternative lesson plan emphasizing learning activities.
Classes desiring such student involvement will find these suggestions helpful.

Learning Goals

After participating in this lesson, each student will be able to:

1. Summarize what Malachi said in response to questions about God's justice.

2. List some ways that a lack of commitment to doing right wearies the Lord today.

3. Make a plan to resist one cultural trend that opposes God's expectations for justice.

Into the Lesson

To open today's lesson, say, "In 1989, a researcher developed a model for robotic behavior. The author, Pattie Maes, says that for a robot the act of 'doing the right thing' should have the following characteristics:

1. It favors actions that are goal-oriented;

2. It favors actions that are relevant to the current situation;

3. It favors actions that contribute to the ongoing goal/plan;

4. It looks ahead to avoid hazardous situations;

5. It never completely breaks down, even when certain parts fail;

6. It is reactive and fast."

Ask your students to imagine they are writing a manual for humans "to do the right thing." What characteristics would they specify for humans in this regard? Write ideas on the board. When you finish discussing this exercise, tell your students that today's lesson deals with God's explanation of how to do the right thing.

As an alternative, obtain a recording of Handel's *Messiah* and play one or two tracks based on today's text (Malachi 3:2, 3): "But Who May Abide the Day of His Coming?" and "And He Shall Purify." Then tell your class that today's lesson explains these words from Malachi.

Into the Word

Use the Lesson Background and commentary on Malachi 2:17 to discuss the situation in Judah leading up to Malachi 3. Focus on the final question in verse 17: "Where is the God of judgment?" Ask why students think that God would be weary of Judah's whining and how Malachi 3:1–4:1 is God's answer to the above question.

Next, divide your class into groups of three or four. Direct attention to the activity The Lord Has Come! in the student book. If you don't use the student book, provide paper and pencils; assign each team the following passages: Malachi 3:1-5; 4:1; Mark 1:1-4; Luke 2:21-32, 41-47; John 1:14; 7:14, 33-41; Hebrews 8:8-10; 13:15, 16; 2 Peter 3:8-13; Revelation 20:7-15.

Instruct each group to paraphrase the Malachi passages, indicating how each verse is fulfilled in the New Testament. For example, Malachi 3:1a could be paraphrased, "See, I'm going to send John the Baptist to prepare the way for Jesus."

Tell your students that their paraphrases should answer the following questions: *1.* Who prepared the way for the promised Messiah? *2.* On what occasions did Jesus come to His temple? *3.* What new covenant was brought by the Messiah? Why? *4.* How were the people to be refined? *5.* What will judgment be like for the wicked?

When your teams finish their studies, use the lesson commentary to evaluate the results.

Into Life

Remind your students of their answers to the first exercise in today's lesson, then read the following hypothetical situations. Ask volunteers to suggest responses to each that reflect God's concern for doing the right thing.

Situation #1. A pro-abortion organization has opened a clinic in your area "to ensure the availability of safe, legal abortions to women who desire to make that choice." What can your congregation do to offer women an alternative consistent with God's Word? How will your response promote justice for pre-born children?

Situation #2. A local atheist has sued your school district to stop the daily recital of the Pledge of Allegiance on the ground that the phrase *under God* violates the U.S. Constitution's First Amendment's separation of church and state. What can you do in response?

Situation #3. Your community newspaper has printed an editorial accusing a political candidate of being "too religious" because he has admitted that he consults the Bible when he is forming his position on moral and political issues. What would you say in a letter to the editor?

After discussing their thoughts, encourage your students to act accordingly this coming week in response to other challenges to their faith.

Let's Talk It Over

The questions on this page are designed to promote discussion of the lesson by the class and to encourage application of the lesson Scriptures. The answers provided are only discussion starters. Let your class talk it over from there.

1. What was a situation in which you think you may have wearied the Lord with your words? How do you guard against doing so again?

We are suspicious of someone who says kind things to a person's face and evil things behind that same person's back. But we can be guilty of treating God the same way. We can say good things about God and tell others we believe in Him, yet fail to honor Him in our lives.

Psalm 78:35, 36 says concerning God's people, "They remembered that God was their rock, and the high God their redeemer. Nevertheless they did flatter him with their mouth, and they lied unto him with their tongues." Calling Jesus "Lord" while failing to do the will of the Father is one way we can weary God with our words (Matthew 7:21). Titus 1:16 says that we may profess that we know God, but our actions may deny that very profession.

2. We hope that there would be very few who would openly state that those who do evil are good in the sight of God! Yet may we unknowingly convey this false message in other ways? How do you guard yourself in this respect?

When we fail to call sin what it really is, we are, in effect, leaving the impression that what is happening is OK. Though divorce and homosexuality are both called sin in the New Testament, we can be guilty of rationalizing and accepting one of those two while standing in strong denouncement of the other.

When we tolerate sin, we are saying that it is not that bad. Some in the church have been so lenient in trying to be "open" to others that they begin to adopt a pluralistic worldview that says all beliefs are of equal value and one religion is just as good as another. Coming to grips with the holiness of God is an important safeguard.

3. How will you use Malachi 3:1b to influence your behavior as you wait for the return of Christ?

Majoring in the minors and *minoring in the majors* is a trap! There are some who try to predict when Christ is coming again. Much time is spent in studying Scripture to uncover some se-

cret that will reveal the date of His coming. This is not useful.

Jesus can return at any time, and we must be ready. We should be motivated to prepare ourselves and others for the return of Christ, but not spend time trying to determine the exact date. The major thing is to be prepared; it is a minor detail for us as to when this event takes place. What Malachi 3:1b implies about Jesus' first coming is thus very useful when we ponder His second.

4. In what areas of your life has God had to apply His refining fire and purifying soap? How is your life better as a result? In what areas do you still need God's purification?

When we surrender our lives to Christ according to the biblical plan of salvation, we are cleansed from our sin guilt. Yet even after that cleansing, we carry with us some residual effects. The Holy Spirit has to continue to work in our lives, refining and cleansing. Paul spoke of his continual struggle with sin even after becoming a follower of Christ (see Romans 7:19).

God promises, "If we confess our sins, he is faithful and just to forgive us our sins" (1 John 1:9). There are areas for each of us to recognize our sin, confess it to God, and allow Him to do His cleansing work. It may be the sin of gossip, lust, greed, or pride. We are not able to conquer these sins on our own; we need the refining power of God.

5. Why do you think that many today do not fear the Lord? In what ways would your life change for the better if you had a greater fear of the Lord?

A lack of fear of God often may be traced to a conscious or unconscious belief that a person is ultimately accountable to self. An emphasis on God's love to the exclusion of His holiness may also be the problem.

Parents who truly love their children and want the best for them also desire that their children respect them and honor them. They want their children to have a healthy fear of them and not think they can get away with just anything. It is similar with God.

Comm_tment:

What Is Missing?

by Ronald G. Davis

OMMITMENT IS ONE CHARACTERISTIC for which church leaders search high and low, often without finding it. Few today choose to make a commitment to church ministries that demand persistent presence and active participation. Just ask your minister if there is a surplus of Bible teachers in the congregation!

Church leaders sometimes question why few have a commitment to the church's programs and ministries. The answer is simple: few are truly committed to God. Thus, few are committed to God's demands for a life of doing right. This quarter's lessons offer an opportunity to challenge commitment in the learners. Some simple learning activities that run through the quarter of study may be a step in the right direction to "getting an *I* back into commitment."

How Am I Doing?

God's prophets had a primary task: to call God's wayward people back to His ways. Consider having your class members maintain a notebook (journal) during this series, a record of their own responses to the truths studied.

Make multiple copies of the following form so you can provide one to each student each week. At the end of the first week's study, introduce the concept by saying, "At the end of the week ahead, sit down and ponder how well you are doing in relationship to the commitment we have studied today. Fill in the word *Justice* (the key word in the first week's lesson title) on the lines marked with an asterisk (*); then write your thoughtful responses in the other spaces."

When it comes to being committed to
*_____, I rate myself a ____. [Use a scale of 1 for "barely noticeable" to 5 for "giving daily evidence."]

One occasion this week when I gave evidence I am committed to *_____ was when I _____. This event or behavior best exemplified such a commitment because it _____.

One occasion this week when my behavior or words demonstrated a lack of commitment to *_____ was when I _____.

The verse from this week's text that has the greatest impact on me is _____. The reason for this impact is _____.

Have students use the same form each week. The key words or themes for the 13 weeks from the lesson titles are (1) justice, (2) God's ways, (3) true worship, (4) seeking God, (5) God's requirements, (6) righteousness, (7) hope, (8) accountability, (9) trusting God, (10) hope even in pain, (11) taking responsibility, (12) returning to God, and (13) doing right.

What Is Lacking?

This weekly journalizing will allow students to confront their own levels of commitment. Ask for volunteers to give candid self-assessments to the class as a whole.

The problems that your students reveal actually may be symptoms of a deeper problem: a lack of knowledge. God's lament, through the pen of Hosea, was, "My people are destroyed for lack of knowledge" (Hosea 4:6). When disciples thoroughly know the person and will of God, commitment should be a by-product. In Simon Peter's words, "Lord, to whom shall we go? thou hast the words of eternal life" (John 6:68).

Consider how you can facilitate greater knowledge through memorization of pivotal verses. In the first week of the study, for example, tell your students, "I have found some significant thoughts of God in my preparation for this series of studies in the theme of commitment from God's prophets. So I have committed to learning some of those great ideas by heart." Then quote, for example, part of Amos 5:15: "Hate the evil, and love the good, and establish judgment."

Offer your class an opportunity to join you in your quest to increase their own knowledge of God as found in the prophets. To this end, you can distribute commitment cards like this:

Dear God, thank You for revealing Your will through your prophets. I hereby commit to learning at least ___ verses of beauty and challenge during our class's study this quarter. My prayer is that Your Word will cure my lack of knowledge. Signed _____; date ____.

Indicate that this commitment activity is strictly a personal matter and that the cards can be carried in one's Bible. Make suggestions for good verses to memorize. Regularly talking about your own progress will encourage participation.